THE WHITE GODDESS

D0761177

The WHITE GODDESS

GODDESS

A historical grammar of poetic myth

by
Robert Graves

Amended and enlarged edition

FARRAR, STRAUS AND GIROUX

NEW YORK

IN DEDICATION

All saints revile her, and all sober men
Ruled by the God Apollo's golden mean—
In scorn of which I sailed to find her
In distant regions likeliest to hold her
Whom I desired above all things to know,
Sister of the mirage and echo.

It was a virtue not to stay,
To go my headstrong and heroic way
Seeking her out at the volcano's head,
Among pack ice, or where the track had faded
Beyond the cavern of the seven sleepers:
Whose broad high brow was white as any leper's,
Whose eyes were blue, with rowan-berry lips,
With hair curled honey-coloured to white hips.

Green sap of Spring in the young wood a-stir
Will celebrate the Mountain Mother,
And every song-bird shout awhile for her;
But I am gifted, even in November
Rawest of seasons, with so huge a sense
Of her nakedly worn magnificence
I forget cruelty and past betrayal,
Careless of where the next bright bolt may fall.

CONTENTS

CONTENTS

FOREWORD

I am grateful to Philip and Sally Graves, Christopher Hawkes, John Knittel, Valentin Iremonger, Max Mallowan, E. M. Parr, Joshua Podro, Lynette Roberts, Martin Seymour-Smith, John Heath-Stubbs and numerous correspondents, who have supplied me with source-material for this book: and to Kenneth Gay who has helped me to arrange it. Yet since the first edition appeared in 1946, no expert in ancient Irish or Welsh has offered me the least help in refining my argument, or pointed out any of the errors which are bound to have crept into the text, or even acknowledged my letters. I am disappointed, though not really surprised. The book does read very queerly: but then of course a historical grammar of the language of poetic myth has never previously been attempted, and to write it conscientiously I have had to face such 'puzzling questions, though not beyond all conjecture', as Sir Thomas Browne instances in his *Hydriotaphia:* 'what song the Sirens sang, or what name Achilles assumed when he hid himself among the women.' I found practical and unevasive answers to these and many other questions of the same sort, such as:

Who cleft the Devil's foot?
When did the Fifty Danaids come with their sieves to Britain?
What secret was woven into the Gordian Knot?
Why did Jehovah create trees and grass before he created the Sun, Moon and stars?
Where shall Wisdom be found?

But it is only fair to warn readers that this remains a very difficult book, as well as a very queer one, to be avoided by anyone with a distracted, tired or rigidly scientific mind. I have not cared to leave out any step in the laborious argument, if only because readers of my recent historical novels have grown a little suspicious of unorthodox conclusions for which the authorities are not always quoted. Perhaps they will now be satisfied, for example, that the mystical Bull-calf formula and the two Tree-alphabets which I introduced into *King Jesus* are not 'wanton figments' of my imagination but logically deduced from reputable ancient documents.

My thesis is that the language of poetic myth anciently current in the Mediterranean and Northern Europe was a magical language bound up with popular religious ceremonies in honour of the Moon-goddess, or

Muse, some of them dating from the Old Stone Age, and that this remains the language of true poetry—'true' in the nostalgic modern sense of 'the unimprovable original, not a synthetic substitute'. The language was tampered with in late Minoan times when invaders from Central Asia began to substitute patrilinear for matrilinear institutions and remodel or falsify the myths to justify the social changes. Then came the early Greek philosophers who were strongly opposed to magical poetry as threatening their new religion of logic, and under their influence a rational poetic language (now called the Classical) was elaborated in honour of their patron Apollo and imposed on the world as the last word in spiritual illumination: a view that has prevailed practically ever since in European schools and universities, where myths are now studied only as quaint relics of the nursery age of mankind.

One of the most uncompromising rejections of early Greek mythology was made by Socrates. Myths frightened or offended him; he preferred to turn his back on them and discipline his mind to think scientifically: 'to investigate the reason of the being of everything—of everything as it is, not as it appears, and to reject all opinions of which no account can be given.'

Here is a typical passage from Plato's *Phaedrus*, (Cary's translation):

Phae. Tell me, Socrates, is not Boreas reported to have carried off Orithya from somewhere about this part of the Ilissus?

Socr. So it is said.

Phae. Must it not have been from this spot? for the water hereabouts appears beautiful, clear and transparent, and well suited for damsels to sport about.

Socr. No, but lower down, as much as two or three stadia, where we cross over to the temple of the Huntress, and where there is, on the very spot, a kind of altar sacred to Boreas.

Phae. I never noticed it. But tell me, by Jupiter, Socrates, do you believe that this fabulous account is true?

Socr. If I disbelieved it, as the wise do, I should not be guilty of any absurdity: then having recourse to subtleties, I should say that a blast of Boreas threw her down from the neighbouring cliffs, as she was sporting with Pharmacea, and that having thus met her death she was said to have been carried off by Boreas, or from Mars' hill; for there is also another report that she was carried off from thence and not from this spot. But I, for my part, Phaedrus, consider such things as pretty enough, but as the province of a very curious, painstaking, and not very happy man, and for no other reason than that after this he must set us right as to the form of the Hippocentaurs, and then as to that of the Chimaera; besides, there pours in upon him a crowd of similar monsters, Gorgons and Pegasuses, and other monstrous creatures, incredible in number and absurdity, which if anyone were to disbelieve and endeavour to reconcile each with probability, employing for this purpose a kind of vulgar cleverness, he will stand in need of abundant leisure. But I have no leisure at all for such matters; and the cause of it, my friend, is this: I am not yet able, according to the Delphic precept, to know myself. But it appears to me to be ridiculous, while I am still ignorant of this, to busy myself about matters that do not concern me.

The fact was, that by Socrates' time the sense of most myths belonging to the previous epoch was either forgotten or kept a close religious secret, though they were still preserved pictorially in religious art and still current as fairy-tales from which the poets quoted. When invited to believe in the Chimaera, the horse-centaurs, or the winged horse Pegasus, all of them straight-forward Pelasgian cult-symbols, a philosopher felt bound to reject them as a-zoölogical improbabilities; and because he had no notion of the true identity of 'the nymph Orithya' or of the history of the ancient Athenian cult of Boreas, he could give only an inept naturalistic explanation of her rape at Mount Ilissus: 'doubtless she was blown off one of the cliffs hereabouts and met her death at the foot.'

All the problems that Socrates mentions have been faced in this book and solved to my own satisfaction at least; but though 'a very curious and painstaking person' I cannot agree that I am any less happy than Socrates was, or that I have more leisure than he had, or that an understanding of the language of myth is irrelevant to self-knowledge. I deduce from the petulant tone of his phrase 'vulgar cleverness' that he had spent a long time worrying about the Chimaera, the horse-centaurs and the rest, but that the 'reasons of their being' had eluded him because he was no poet and mistrusted poets, and because, as he admitted to Phaedrus, he was a confirmed townsman who seldom visited the countryside: 'fields and trees will not teach me anything, but men do.' The study of mythology, as I shall show, is based squarely on tree-lore and seasonal observation of life in the fields.

Socrates, in turning his back on poetic myths, was really turning his back on the Moon-goddess who inspired them and who demanded that man should pay woman spiritual and sexual homage: what is called Platonic love, the philosopher's escape from the power of the Goddess into intellectual homosexuality, was really Socratic love. He could not plead ignorance: Diotima Mantinice, the Arcadian prophetess who magically arrested the plague at Athens, had reminded him once that man's love was properly directed towards women and that Moira, Ilithyia and Callone—Death, Birth and Beauty—formed a triad of

Goddesses who presided over all acts of generation whatsoever: physical, spiritual or intellectual. In the passage of the *Symposium* where Plato reports Socrates' account of Diotima's wise words, the banquet is interrupted by Alcibiades, who comes in very drunk in search of a beautiful boy called Agathon and finds him reclining next to Socrates. Presently he tells everyone that he himself once encouraged Socrates, who was in love with him, to an act of sodomy from which, however, he philosophically abstained, remaining perfectly satisfied with night-long chaste embraces of his beloved's beautiful body. Had Diotima been present to hear this she would have made a wry face and spat three times into her bosom: for though the Goddess as Cybele and Ishtar tolerated sodomy even in her own temple-courts, ideal homosexuality was a far more serious moral aberrancy—it was the male intellect trying to make itself spiritually self-sufficient. Her revenge on Socrates—if I may put it this way—for trying to know himself in the Apollonian style instead of leaving the task to a wife or mistress, was characteristic: she found him a shrew for a wife and made him fix his idealistic affections on this same Alcibiades, who disgraced him by growing up vicious, godless, treacherous and selfish— the ruin of Athens. She ended his life with a draught of the white-flowered, mousey-smelling hemlock, a plant sacred to herself as Hecate,[1] prescribed him by his fellow-citizens in punishment for his corruption of youth. After his death his disciples made a martyr of him and under their influence myths fell into still greater disrepute, becoming at last the subject of street-corner witticisms or being 'explained away' by Euhemerus of Messenia and his successors as corruptions of history. The Euhemerist account of the Actaeon myth, for instance, is that he was an Arcadian gentleman who was so addicted to hunting that the expense of keeping a pack of hounds ate him up.

But even after Alexander the Great had cut the Gordian Knot—an act of far greater moral significance than is generally realized—the ancient language survived purely enough in the secret Mystery-cults of Eleusis, Corinth, Samothrace and elsewhere; and when these were suppressed by the early Christian Emperors it was still taught in the poetic colleges of Ireland and Wales, and in the witch-covens of Western Europe. As a popular religious tradition it all but flickered out at the close of the seventeenth century: and though poetry of a magical quality is still occasionally written, even in industrialized Europe, this always results from an inspired, almost pathological, reversion to the original language—a wild Pentecostal 'speaking with tongues'—rather than from a conscientious study of its grammar and vocabulary.

English poetic education should, really, begin not with the *Canterbury Tales*, not with the *Odyssey*, not even with *Genesis*, but with the *Song of*

[1] As Shakespeare knew. See *Macbeth*, *IV*, *1*, *25*.

Amergin, an ancient Celtic calendar-alphabet, found in several purposely garbled Irish and Welsh variants, which briefly summarizes the prime poetic myth. I have tentatively restored the text as follows:

> I am a stag: *of seven tines,*
> I am a flood: *across a plain,*
> I am a wind: *on a deep lake,*
> I am a tear: *the Sun lets fall,*
> I am a hawk: *above the cliff,*
> I am a thorn: *beneath the nail,*
> I am a wonder: *among flowers,*
> I am a wizard: *who but I*
> *Sets the cool head aflame with smoke?*
>
> I am a spear: *that roars for blood,*
> I am a salmon: *in a pool,*
> I am a lure: *from paradise,*
> I am a hill: *where poets walk,*
> I am a boar: *ruthless and red,*
> I am a breaker: *threatening doom,*
> I am a tide: *that drags to death,*
> I am an infant: *who but I*
> *Peeps from the unhewn dolmen arch?*
>
> I am the womb: *of every holt,*
> I am the blaze: *on every hill,*
> I am the queen: *of every hive,*
> I am the shield: *for every head,*
> I am the tomb: *of every hope.*

It is unfortunate that, despite the strong mythical element in Christianity, 'mythical' has come to mean 'fanciful, absurd, unhistorical'; for fancy played a negligible part in the development of the Greek, Latin and Palestinian myths, or of the Celtic myths until the Norman-French *trovères* worked them up into irresponsible romances of chivalry. They are all grave records of ancient religious customs or events, and reliable enough as history once their language is understood and allowance has been made for errors in transcription, misunderstandings of obsolete ritual, and deliberate changes introduced for moral or political reasons. Some myths of course have survived in a far purer form than others; for example, the *Fables* of Hyginus, the *Library* of Apollodorus and the earlier tales of the Welsh *Mabinogion* make easy reading compared with the deceptively simple chronicles of *Genesis, Exodus, Judges* and *Samuel.* Perhaps the greatest difficulty in solving complex mythological problems is that:

> Conquering gods their titles take
> From the foes they captive make,

and that to know the name of a deity at any given place or period, is far less important than to know the nature of the sacrifices that he or she was then offered. The powers of the gods were continuously being redefined. The Greek god Apollo, for instance, seems to have begun as the Demon of a Mouse-fraternity in pre-Aryan totemistic Europe: he gradually rose in divine rank by force of arms, blackmail and fraud until he became the patron of Music, Poetry and the Arts and finally, in some regions at least, ousted his 'father' Zeus from the Sovereignty of the Universe by identifying himself with Belinus the intellectual God of Light. Jehovah, the God of the Jews, has a still more complex history.

'What is the use or function of poetry nowadays?' is a question not the less poignant for being defiantly asked by so many stupid people or apologetically answered by so many silly people. The function of poetry is religious invocation of the Muse; its use is the experience of mixed exaltation and horror that her presence excites. But 'nowadays'? Function and use remain the same; only the application has changed. This was once a warning to man that he must keep in harmony with the family of living creatures among which he was born, by obedience to the wishes of the lady of the house; it is now a reminder that he has disregarded the warning, turned the house upside down by capricious experiments in philosophy, science and industry, and brought ruin on himself and his family. 'Nowadays' is a civilization in which the prime emblems of poetry are dishonoured. In which serpent, lion and eagle belong to the circus-tent; ox, salmon and boar to the cannery; racehorse and greyhound to the betting ring; and the sacred grove to the saw-mill. In which the Moon is despised as a burned-out satellite of the Earth and woman reckoned as 'auxiliary State personnel'. In which money will buy almost anything but truth, and almost anyone but the truth-possessed poet.

Call me, if you like, the fox who has lost his brush; I am nobody's servant and have chosen to live on the outskirts of a Majorcan mountain-village, Catholic but anti-ecclesiastical, where life is still ruled by the old agricultural cycle. Without my brush, namely my contact with urban civilization, all that I write must read perversely and irrelevantly to such of you as are still geared to the industrial machine, whether directly as workers, managers, traders or advertisers or indirectly as civil servants, publishers, journalists, schoolmasters or employees of a radio corporation. If you are poets, you will realize that acceptance of my historical thesis commits you to a confession of disloyalty which you will be loth to make; you chose your jobs because they promised to provide you with a steady income and leisure to render the Goddess whom you adore valuable part-time service. Who am I, you will ask, to warn you that she demands either whole-time service or none at all? And do I suggest that you should resign your jobs and for want of sufficient capital to set up as small-holders, turn romantic shepherds—as Don Quixote did after his failure to come to terms with the modern world—in remote unmechanized farms? No, my brushlessness debars me from offering any practical suggestion. I dare attempt only a historical statement of the problem; how you come to terms with the Goddess is no concern of mine. I do not even know that you are serious in your poetic profession.

R. G.

Deyà,
  Mallorca,
    Spain.

Chapter One

POETS AND GLEEMEN

Since the age of fifteen poetry has been my ruling passion and I have never intentionally undertaken any task or formed any relationship that seemed inconsistent with poetic principles; which has sometimes won me the reputation of an eccentric. Prose has been my livelihood, but I have used it as a means of sharpening my sense of the altogether different nature of poetry, and the themes that I choose are always linked in my mind with outstanding poetic problems. At the age of sixty-five I am still amused at the paradox of poetry's obstinate continuance in the present phase of civilization. Though recognized as a learned profession it is the only one for the study of which no academies are open and in which there is no yard-stick, however crude, by which technical proficiency is considered measurable. 'Poets are born, not made.' The deduction that one is expected to draw from this is that the nature of poetry is too mysterious to bear examination: is, indeed, a greater mystery even than royalty, since kings can be made as well as born and the quoted utterances of a dead king carry little weight either in the pulpit or the public bar.

The paradox can be explained by the great official prestige that still somehow clings to the name of poet, as it does to the name of king, and by the feeling that poetry, since it defies scientific analysis, must be rooted in some sort of magic, and that magic is disreputable. European poetic lore is, indeed, ultimately based on magical principles, the rudiments of which formed a close religious secret for centuries but which were at last garbled, discredited and forgotten. Now it is only by rare accidents of spiritual regression that poets make their lines magically potent in the ancient sense. Otherwise, the contemporary practice of poem-writing recalls the mediaeval alchemist's fantastic and foredoomed experiments in transmuting base metal into gold; except that the alchemist did at least recognize pure gold when he saw and handled it. The truth is that only gold ore can be turned into gold; only poetry into poems. This book is about the rediscovery of the lost rudiments, and about the active principles of poetic magic that govern them.

My argument will be based on a detailed examination of two extraordinary Welsh minstrel poems of the thirteenth century, in which the clues to this ancient secret are ingeniously concealed.

By way of historical introduction, a clear distinction must first be drawn between the court-bards and the wandering minstrels of ancient Wales. The Welsh bards, or master-poets, like the Irish, had a professional tradition, embodied in a corpus of poems which, literally memorized and carefully weighed, they passed on to the pupils who came to study under them. The English poets of to-day, whose language began as a despised late-mediaeval vernacular when Welsh poetry was already a hoary institution, may envy them in retrospect: the young poet was spared the curse of having doubtfully to build up his poetic lore for himself by haphazard reading, consultation with equally doubtful friends, and experimental writing. Latterly, however, it was only in Ireland that a master-poet was expected, or even permitted, to write in an original style. When the Welsh poets were converted to orthodox Christianity and subjected to ecclesiastical discipline—a process completed by the tenth century, as the contemporary Welsh Laws show—their tradition gradually ossified. Though a high degree of technical skill was still required of master-poets and the Chair of Poetry was hotly contested in the various Courts, they were pledged to avoid what the Church called 'untruth', meaning the dangerous exercise of poetic imagination in myth or allegory. Only certain epithets and metaphors were authorized; themes were similarly restricted, metres fixed, and *Cynghanedd*, the repetitive use of consonantal sequences with variation of vowels[1], became a burdensome obsession. The master-poets had become court-officials, their first obligation being to praise God, their second to praise the king or prince who had provided a Chair for them at his royal table. Even after the fall of the Welsh princes in the late thirteenth century this barren poetic code was maintained by the family bards in noble houses.

T. Gwynn Jones writes in *The Transactions of the Honourable Society of Cymmrodorion* (1913–1914):

> The few indications which may be gathered from the works of the bards, down to the fall of the Welsh princes, imply that the system detailed in the Laws was preserved, but probably with progressive modification. The *Llyfr Coch Hergest* metrical Code shows a still further development, which in the fifteenth century resulted in the Carmarthen Eisteddfod.... The subject tradition recorded in this Code,

---

[1] *Cynghanedd* may be illustrated in English thus:

> Billet spied,
> Bolt sped.
> Across field
> Crows fled,
> Aloft, wounded,
> Left one dead.

But the correspondence of the *ss* in 'across' and the *s* of 'crows', which has a 'z' sound would offend the purist.

practically restricting the bards to the writing of eulogies and elegies, and excluding the narrative, is proved to have been observed by the Gogynfeirdd [court-bards]. Their adherence to what they conceived to be historical truth was probably due to the early capture of their organization by ecclesiastics. They made practically no use of the traditional material contained in the popular Romances, and their knowledge of the names of mythical and quasi-historical characters was principally derived from the *Triads*. . . . Nature poetry and love poetry are only incidental in their works, and they show practically no development during the period. . . . References to nature in the poems of the court-bards are brief and casual, and mostly limited to its more rugged aspects—the conflict of sea and strand, the violence of winter storms, the burning of spring growths on the mountains. The characters of their heroes are only indicated in epithets; no incident is completely described; battles are dismissed in a line or two at most. Their theory of poetry, particularly in the eulogy, seems to have been that it should consist of epithets and allusions, resuming the bare facts of history, presumably known to their hearers. They never tell a story; they rarely even give anything approaching a coherent description of a single episode. Such, indeed, has been the character of most Welsh verse, outside the popular ballads, practically down to the present day.

The tales and Romances, on the other hand, are full of colour and incident; even characterization is not absent from them. In them, fancy, not affected by restrictions applying both to subject and form, develops into imagination.

These tales were told by a guild of Welsh minstrels whose status was not regularized by the Laws, who counted no bishops or ministers of State among their associates, and who were at liberty to use whatever diction, themes and metres they pleased. Very little is known about their organization or history, but since they were popularly credited with divinatory and prophetic gifts and the power of injurious satire it is likely that they were descended from the original Welsh master-poets who either refused or were refused court-patronage after the Cymric conquest of Wales. The Cymry, whom we think of as the real Welsh, and from whom the proud court-bards were recruited, were a tribal aristocracy of Brythonic origin holding down a serf-class that was a mixture of Goidels, Brythons, Bronze Age and New Stone Age peoples and Aboriginals; they had invaded Wales from the North of England in the fifth century A.D. The non-Cymric minstrels went from village to village, or farm-house to farm-house, entertaining under the trees or in the chimney corner according to the season. It was they who kept alive an astonishingly ancient literary tradition, mainly in the form of popular tales which preserved fragments not only of pre-Cymric, but of pre-Goidelic myth, some of which goes back as far as the Stone Age. Their poetic principles are summed up in a Triad in the *Llyfr Coch Hergest* ('The Red Book of Hergest'):

> *Three things that enrich the poet:*
> *Myths, poetic power, a store of ancient verse.*

The two poetic schools did not at first come in contact, the 'big-bellied' well-dressed court-bards being forbidden to compose in the minstrel style and penalized if they visited any but the houses of princes or nobles; the lean and ragged minstrels not being privileged to perform at any court, nor trained to use the complicated verse-forms required of the court-bards. However, in the thirteenth century the minstrels were taken up by the Norman-French invaders, apparently through the influence of Breton knights who could understand Welsh and who recognized some of the tales as better versions of those which they had heard at home. The *trovères*, or finders, translated them into contemporary French and adapted them to the Provençal code of chivalry, and in their new dress they conquered Europe.

Welsh and Norman families now intermarried and it was no longer easy to keep the minstrel out of the courts. In an early thirteenth-century poem one Phylip Brydydd records a contention between himself and certain 'vulgar rhymesters' as to who should first present a song on Christmas Day to his patron, Prince Rhys Ieuanc at Llanbadarn Fawr in South Wales. Prince Rhys was a close ally of the Normans. The two thirteenth-century poems which will be here examined are the work of a 'vulgar rhymester'—vulgar at least by Phylip's aristocratic canon of what a poet should be. They are called the *Câd Goddeu* and the *Hanes Taliesin*.

By the fourteenth century the literary influence of the minstrels began to show even in court poetry, and according to fourteenth-century versions of the bardic statute, *Trioedd Kerdd*, the *Prydydd*, or court-bard, might write love-poems, though debarred from satires, lampoons, charms, divination, or lays of magic. It was not until the fifteenth century that the poet Davydd ap Gwilym won approval for a new form, the *Kywydd*, in which court poetry and minstrel poetry are united. For the most part the court-poets would not modify their obsolescent practice; remaining scornful and jealous of the favour shown to 'tellers of untruth'. Their position declined with that of their patrons and their authority finally collapsed as a result of the Civil Wars, in which Wales favoured the losing side, shortly before the Cromwellian conquest of Ireland also broke the power of the *ollaves*, or master-poets, there. Its revival in the bardic Gorsedd of the National Eisteddfod is somewhat of a mock-antique, coloured by early nineteenth-century misconceptions of

Druidic practice; yet the Eisteddfod has served to keep alive a public sense of the honour due to poets, and contests for the bardic Chair are as keen as ever.

English poetry has had only a short experience of similar bardic discipline: the Classicism of the eighteenth century, when highly stylized diction and metre and 'decorum' of theme were insisted upon by the admirers and imitators of Alexander Pope. A violent reaction followed, the 'Romantic Revival'; then another partial return to discipline, Victorian Classicism; then a still more violent reaction, the 'modernistic' anarchy of the 1920's and 1930's. English poets now appear to be considering a voluntary return to discipline: not to the eighteenth-century strait-jacket, nor to the Victorian frock-coat, but to that logic of poetic thought which gives a poem strength and grace. But where can they study metre, diction, and theme? Where can they find any poetic government to which they may yield a willing loyalty? Metre, they would all probably agree, is the norm to which a poet relates his personal rhythm, the original copybook copper-plate from which he gradually develops a unique personal handwriting; unless such a norm is assumed, his rhythmic idiosyncrasies are meaningless. They would also probably agree about diction, that it should be neither over-stylized nor vulgar. But what of theme? Who has ever been able to explain what theme is poetic and what is unpoetic, except by the effect that it has on the reader?

The rediscovery of the lost rudiments of poetry may help to solve the question of theme: if they still have validity they confirm the intuition of the Welsh poet Alun Lewis who wrote just before his death in Burma, in March 1944, of 'the *single* poetic theme of Life and Death ... the question of what survives of the beloved.' Granted that there are many themes for the journalist of verse, yet for the poet, as Alun Lewis understood the word, there is no choice. The elements of the single infinitely variable Theme are to be found in certain ancient poetic myths which though manipulated to conform with each epoch of religious change—I use the word 'myth' in its strict sense of 'verbal iconograph' without the derogatory sense of 'absurd fiction' that it has acquired—yet remain constant in general outline. Perfect faithfulness to the Theme affects the reader of a poem with a strange feeling, between delight and horror, of which the purely physical effect is that the hair literally stands on end. A. E. Housman's test of a true poem was simple and practical: does it make the hairs of one's chin bristle if one repeats it silently while shaving? But he did not explain *why* the hairs should bristle.

The ancient Celts carefully distinguished the poet, who was originally a priest and judge as well and whose person was sacrosanct, from the mere gleeman. He was in Irish called *fili*, a seer; in Welsh *derwydd*, or oak-seer, which is the probable derivation of 'Druid'. Even kings came under his moral tutelage. When two armies engaged in battle, the poets of both sides would withdraw together to a hill and there judiciously discuss the fighting. In a sixth-century Welsh poem, the *Gododin*, it is remarked that 'the poets of the world assess the men of valour'; and the combatants—whom they often parted by a sudden intervention—would afterwards accept their version of the fight, f worth commemorating in a poem, with reverence as well as pleasure. The gleeman, on the other hand, was a *joculator*, or entertainer, not a priest: a mere client of the military oligarchs and without the poet's arduous professional training. He would often make a variety turn of his performance, with mime and tumbling. In Wales he was styled an *eirchiad*, or suppliant, one who does not belong to an endowed profession but is dependent for his living on the occasional generosity of chieftains. As early as the first century B.C. we hear from Poseidonius the Stoic of a bag of gold flung to a Celtic gleeman in Gaul, and this at a time when the Druidic system was at its strongest there. If the gleeman's flattery of his patrons were handsome enough and his song sweetly enough attuned to their mead-sodden minds, they would load him with gold torques and honey cakes; if not, they would pelt him with beef bones. But let a man offer the least indignity to an Irish poet, even centuries after he had forfeited his priestly functions to the Christian cleric, and he would compose a satire on his assailant which would bring out black blotches on his face and turn his bowels to water, or throw a 'madman's wisp' in his face and drive him insane; and surviving examples of the cursing poems of the Welsh minstrels show that they were also to be reckoned with. The court-poets of Wales, on the other hand, were forbidden to use curses or satires, and had to depend on legal redress for any insult to their dignity: according to a tenth-century digest of laws affecting the Welsh 'household bard' they could demand an *eric* of 'nine cows, and nine-score pence of money besides'. The figure nine recalls the nine-fold Muse, their former patroness.

In ancient Ireland the *ollave*, or master-poet, sat next to the king at table and was privileged, as none else but the queen was, to wear six different colours in his clothes. The word 'bard', which in mediaeval Wales stood for a master-poet, had a different sense in Ireland, where it meant an inferior poet who had not passed through the 'seven degrees of wisdom' which made him an ollave after a very difficult twelve-year course. The position of the Irish bard is defined in the seventh-century *Sequel to the Crith Gabhlach Law*: 'A bard is one without lawful learning but his own intellect'; but in the later *Book of Ollaves* (bound up in the fourteenth-century *Book of Ballymote*) it is made clear that to have got as far as the seventh year of his poetic education entitled a student to the 'failed B.A.' dignity of bardism. He had memorized only half the pre-scribed tales and poems, had not studied advanced prosody and metrical composition, and was deficient in knowledge of Old Goidelic. However, the seven years' course that he had taken was a great deal more severe than that insisted upon in the poetic schools of Wales, where the bards had a proportionately lower status. According to the Welsh Laws, the *Penkerdd,* or Chief Bard, was only the tenth dignitary at Court and sat on the left of the Heir Apparent, being reckoned equal in honour with the Chief Smith.

The Irish ollave's chief interest was the refinement of complex poetic truth to exact statement. He knew the history and mythic value of every word he used and can have cared nothing for the ordinary man's appreciation of his work; he valued only the judgement of his colleagues, whom he seldom met without a lively exchange of poetic wit in extempore verse. Yet it cannot be pretended that he was always true to the Theme. His education, which was a very general one, including history, music, law, science and divination, encouraged him to versify in all these departments of knowledge; so that often Ogma the God of Eloquence seemed more important than Brigit, the Three-fold Muse. And it is a paradox that in mediaeval Wales the admired court-poet had become a client of the prince to whom he addressed formal begging odes and forgotten the Theme almost entirely; while the despised and unendowed minstrel who seemed to be a mere gleeman showed the greater poetic integrity, even though his verse was not so highly polished.

The Anglo-Saxons had no sacrosanct master-poets, but only gleemen; and English poetic lore is borrowed at third hand, by way of the Norman French romances, from ancient British, Gallic and Irish sources. This explains why there is not the same instinctive reverence for the name of poet in the English countryside as there is in the remotest parts of Wales, Ireland and the Highlands. English poets feel obliged to apologize for their calling except when moving in literary circles; they describe themselves to the registrar, or when giving evidence in a law-court, as civil servants, journalists, schoolmasters, novelists, or whatever else they happen to be besides poets. Even the English poet-laureateship was not instituted until the reign of Charles I. (John Skelton's laurel-crown was a university award for Latin eloquence unconnected with Henry VIII's patronage of him as a poet.) It does not carry with it any authority over national poetic practice or any obligation to preserve the decencies of poetry, and is awarded, without a contest, by the First Lord of the Treasury, not by any learned society. Nevertheless many English poets have written with exquisite technical skill, and since the twelfth century no generation has been entirely faithless to the Theme. The fact is that though the Anglo-Saxons broke the power of the ancient British chieftains and poets they did not exterminate the peasants, so that the continuity of the ancient British festal system remained unaffected even when the

Anglo-Saxons professed Christianity. English social life was based on agriculture, grazing, and hunting, not on industry, and the Theme was still everywhere implicit in the popular celebration of the festivals now known as Candlemas, Lady Day, May Day, Midsummer Day, Lammas, Michaelmas, All-Hallowe'en, and Christmas; it was also secretly preserved as religious doctrine in the covens of the anti-Christian witch-cult. Thus the English, though with no traditional respect for the poet, have a traditional awareness of the Theme.

The Theme, briefly, is the antique story, which falls into thirteen chapters and an epilogue, of the birth, life, death and resurrection of the God of the Waxing Year; the central chapters concern the God's losing battle with the God of the Waning Year for love of the capricious and all-powerful Threefold Goddess, their mother, bride and layer-out. The poet identifies himself with the God of the Waxing Year and his Muse with the Goddess; the rival is his blood-brother, his other self, his weird. All true poetry—true by Housman's practical test—celebrates some incident or scene in this very ancient story, and the three main characters are so much a part of our racial inheritance that they not only assert themselves in poetry but recur on occasions of emotional stress in the form of dreams, paranoiac visions and delusions. The weird, or rival, often appears in nightmare as the tall, lean, dark-faced bed-side spectre, or Prince of the Air, who tries to drag the dreamer out through the window, so that he looks back and sees his body still lying rigid in bed; but he takes countless other malevolent or diabolic or serpent-like forms.

The Goddess is a lovely, slender woman with a hooked nose, deathly pale face, lips red as rowan-berries, startlingly blue eyes and long fair hair; she will suddenly transform herself into sow, mare, bitch, vixen, she-ass, weasel, serpent, owl, she-wolf, tigress, mermaid or loathsome hag. Her names and titles are innumerable. In ghost stories she often figures as 'The White Lady', and in ancient religions, from the British Isles to the Caucasus, as the 'White Goddess'. I cannot think of any true poet from Homer onwards who has not independently recorded his experience of her. The test of a poet's vision, one might say, is the accuracy of his portrayal of the White Goddess and of the island over which she rules. The reason why the hairs stand on end, the eyes water, the throat is constricted, the skin crawls and a shiver runs down the spine when one writes or reads a true poem is that a true poem is necessarily an invocation of the White Goddess, or Muse, the Mother of All Living, the ancient power of fright and lust—the female spider or the queen-bee whose embrace is death. Housman offered a secondary test of true poetry: whether it matches a phrase of Keats's, 'everything that reminds me of her goes through me like a spear'. This is equally pertinent to the Theme. Keats was writing under the shadow of death about his Muse, Fanny

Brawne; and the 'spear that roars for blood' is the traditional weapon of the dark executioner and supplanter.

Sometimes, in reading a poem, the hairs will bristle at an apparently unpeopled and eventless scene described in it, if the elements bespeak her unseen presence clearly enough: for example, when owls hoot, the moon rides like a ship through scudding cloud, trees sway slowly together above a rushing waterfall, and a distant barking of dogs is heard; or when a peal of bells in frosty weather suddenly announces the birth of the New Year.

Despite the deep sensory satisfaction to be derived from Classical poetry, it never makes the hair rise and the heart leap, except where it fails to maintain decorous composure; and this is because of the difference between the attitudes of the Classical poet, and of the true poet, to the White Goddess. This is not to identify the true poet with the Romantic poet. 'Romantic', a useful word while it covered the reintroduction into Western Europe, by the writers of verse-romances, of a mystical reverence for woman, has become tainted by indiscriminate use. The typical Romantic poet of the nineteenth century was physically degenerate, or ailing, addicted to drugs and melancholia, critically unbalanced and a true poet only in his fatalistic regard for the Goddess as the mistress who commanded his destiny. The Classical poet, however gifted and industrious, fails to pass the test because he claims to be the Goddess's master—she is his mistress only in the derogatory sense of one who lives in coquettish ease under his protection. Sometimes, indeed, he is her bawdmaster: he attempts to heighten the appeal of his lines by studding them with 'beauties' borrowed from true poems. In Classical Arabic poetry there is a device known as 'kindling' in which the poet induces the poetic atmosphere with a luscious prologue about groves, streams and nightingales, and then quickly, before it disperses, turns to the real business in hand— a flattering account, say, of the courage, piety and magnanimity of his patron or sage reflexions on the shortness and uncertainty of human life. In Classical English poetry the artificial kindling process is often protracted to the full length of the piece.

The following chapters will rediscover a set of sacred charms of varying antiquity in which successive versions of the Theme are summarized. Literary critics whose function it is to judge all literature by gleeman standards—its entertainment value to the masses—can be counted upon to make merry with what they can only view as my preposterous group of mares' nests. And the scholars can be counted upon to refrain from any comment whatsoever. But, after all, what is a scholar? One who may not break bounds under pain of expulsion from the academy of which he is a member.

And what is a mare's nest? Shakespeare hints at the answer, though he substitutes St. Swithold for Odin, the original hero of the ballad:

> *Swithold footed thrice the wold.*
> *He met the Night-Mare and her nine-fold,*
> *Bid her alight and her troth plight,*
> *And aroynt thee, witch, aroynt thee!*

A fuller account of Odin's feat is given in the North Country *Charm against the Night Mare*, which probably dates from the fourteenth century:

> *Tha mon o' micht, he rade o' nicht*
> *Wi' neider swerd ne ferd ne licht.*
> *He socht tha Mare, he fond tha Mare,*
> *He bond tha Mare wi' her ain hare,*
> *Ond gared her swar by midder-micht*
> *She wolde nae mair rid o' nicht*
> *Whar aince he rade, thot mon o' micht.*

The Night Mare is one of the cruellest aspects of the White Goddess. Her nests, when one comes across them in dreams, lodged in rock-clefts or the branches of enormous hollow yews, are built of carefully chosen twigs, lined with white horse-hair and the plumage of prophetic birds and littered with the jaw-bones and entrails of poets. The prophet Job said of her: 'She dwelleth and abideth upon the rock. Her young ones also suck up blood.'

Chapter Two

THE BATTLE OF THE TREES

It seems that the Welsh minstrels, like the Irish poets, recited their traditional romances in prose, breaking into dramatic verse, with harp accompaniment, only at points of emotional stress. Some of these romances survive complete with the incidental verses; others have lost them; in some cases, such as the romance of Llywarch Hen, only the verses survive. The most famous Welsh collection is the *Mabinogion*, which is usually explained as 'Juvenile Romances', that is to say those that every apprentice to the minstrel profession was expected to know; it is contained in the thirteenth-century *Red Book of Hergest*. Almost all the incidental verses are lost. These romances are the stock-in-trade of a minstrel and some of them have been brought more up-to-date than others in their language and description of manners and morals.

The Red Book of Hergest also contains a jumble of fifty-eight poems, called *The Book of Taliesin*, among which occur the incidental verses of a *Romance of Taliesin* which is not included in the *Mabinogion*. However, the first part of the romance is preserved in a late sixteenth-century manuscript, called the 'Peniardd M.S.', first printed in the early nineteenth-century *Myvyrian Archaiology*, complete with many of the same incidental verses, though with textual variations. Lady Charlotte Guest translated this fragment, completing it with material from two other manuscripts, and included it in her well-known edition of the *Mabinogion* (1848). Unfortunately, one of the two manuscripts came from the library of Iolo Morganwg, a celebrated eighteenth-century 'improver' of Welsh documents, so that her version cannot be read with confidence, though it has not been proved that this particular manuscript was forged.

The gist of the romance is as follows. A nobleman of Penllyn named Tegid Voel had a wife named Caridwen, or Cerridwen, and two children, Creirwy, the most beautiful girl in the world, and Afagddu, the ugliest boy. They lived on an island in the middle of Lake Tegid. To compensate for Afagddu's ugliness, Cerridwen decided to make him highly intelligent. So, according to a recipe contained in the books of Vergil of Toledo the magician (hero of a twelfth-century romance), she boiled up a cauldron of inspiration and knowledge, which had to be kept on the simmer for a year and a day. Season by season, she added to the brew magical herbs gathered in their correct planetary hours. While she gathered the herbs she put little Gwion, the son of Gwreang, of the parish of Llanfair in Caereinion, to stir the cauldron. Towards the end of the year three burning drops flew out and fell on little Gwion's finger. He thrust it into his mouth and at once understood the nature and meaning of all things past, present and future, and thus saw the need of guarding against the wiles of Cerridwen who was determined on killing him as soon as he had completed his work. He fled away, and she pursued him like a black screaming hag. By use of the powers that he had drawn from the cauldron he changed himself into a hare; she changed herself into a greyhound. He plunged into a river and became a fish; she changed herself into an otter. He flew up into the air like a bird; she changed herself into a hawk. He became a grain of winnowed wheat on the floor of a barn; she changed herself into a black hen, scratched the wheat over with her feet, found him and swallowed him. When she returned to her own shape she found herself pregnant of Gwion and nine months later bore him as a child. She could not find it in her heart to kill him, because he was very beautiful, so tied him in a leather bag and threw him into the sea two days before May Day. He was carried into the weir of Gwyddno Garanhair near Dovey and Aberystwyth, in Cardigan Bay, and rescued from it by Prince Elphin, the son of Gwyddno and nephew of King Maelgwyn of Gwynedd (North Wales), who had come there to net fish. Elphin, though he caught no fish, considered himself well rewarded for his labour and renamed Gwion 'Taliesin', meaning either 'fine value', or 'beautiful brow'—a subject for punning by the author of the romance.

When Elphin was imprisoned by his royal uncle at Dyganwy (near Llandudno), the capital of Gwynedd, the child Taliesin went there to rescue him and by a display of wisdom, in which he confounded all the twenty-four court-bards of Maelgwyn—the eighth-century British historian Nennius mentions Maelgwyn's sycophantic bards—and their leader the chief bard Heinin, secured the prince's release. First he put a magic spell on the bards so that they could only play *blerwm blerwm* with their fingers on their lips like children, and then he recited a long riddling poem, the *Hanes Taliesin*, which they were unable to understand, and which will be found in Chapter V. Since the Peniardd version of the romance is not complete, it is just possible that the solution of the riddle was eventually given, as in the similar romances of Rumpelstiltskin, Tom Tit Tot, Oedipus, and Samson. But the other incidental poems suggest that Taliesin continued to ridicule the ignorance and stupidity of Heinin and the other bards to the end and never revealed his secret.

The climax of the story in Lady Charlotte's version comes with another riddle, proposed by the child Taliesin, beginning:

Discover what it is:
The strong creature from before the Flood
Without flesh, without bone,
Without vein, without blood,
Without head, without feet . . .
In field, in forest . . .
Without hand, without foot.
It is also as wide
As the surface of the earth,
And it was not born,
Nor was it seen . . .

The solution, namely 'The Wind', is given practically with a violent
storm of wind which frightens the King into fetching Elphin from the
dungeon, whereupon Taliesin unchains him with an incantation. Probably
in an earlier version the wind was released from the mantle of his comrade
Afagddu or Morvran, as it was by Morvran's Irish counterpart Marvan in
the early mediaeval *Proceedings of the Grand Bardic Academy*, with
which *The Romance of Taliesin* has much in common. 'A part of it blew
into the bosom of every bard present, so that they all rose to their feet.' A
condensed form of this riddle appears in the *Flores* of Bede, an author
commended in one of the *Book of Taliesin* poems:

Dic mihi quae est illa res quae caelum, totamque terram replevit, silvas
et sirculos confringit . . . *omnia-que fundamenta concutit, sed nec oculis*
videri aut [sic] *manibus tangi potest.*

[Answer] *Ventus.*

There can be no mistake here. But since the *Hanes Taliesin* is not preceded
by any formal *Dychymig Dychymig* ('riddle me this riddle') or *Dechymic
pwy yw* ('Discover what it is')[1] commentators excuse themselves from
reading it as a riddle at all. Some consider it to be solemn-sounding nonsense, an early anticipation of Edward Lear and Lewis Carroll, intended
to raise a laugh; others consider that it has some sort of mystical sense
connected with the Druidical doctrine of the transmigration of souls, but
do not claim to be able to elucidate this.

Here I must apologize for my temerity in writing on a subject which is
not really my own. I am not a Welshman, except an honorary one through
eating the leek on St. David's Day while serving with the Royal Welch
Fusiliers and, though I have lived in Wales for some years, off and on,

---

[1] Another form is *dychymig dameg* ('a riddle, a riddle'), which seems to explain the mysterious *ducdame ducdame* in *As You Like It*, which Jaques describes as 'a Greek invocation to call
fools into a circle'—perhaps a favourite joke of Shakespeare's Welsh schoolmaster, remembered for its oddity.

have no command even of modern Welsh; and I am not a mediaeval historian. But my profession is poetry, and I agree with the Welsh minstrels that the poet's first enrichment is a knowledge and understanding of myths. One day while I was puzzling out the meaning of the ancient Welsh myth of *Câd Goddeu* ('The Battle of the Trees'), fought between Arawn King of Annwm ('The Bottomless Place'), and the two sons of Dôn, Gwydion and Amathaon, I had much the same experience as Gwion of Llanfair. A drop or two of the brew of Inspiration flew out of the cauldron and I suddenly felt confident that if I turned again to Gwion's riddle, which I had not read since I was a schoolboy, I could make sense of it.

This Battle of the Trees was 'occasioned by a Lapwing, a White Roebuck and a Whelp from Annwm.' In the ancient Welsh *Triads*, which are a collection of sententious or historical observations arranged epigrammatically in threes, it is reckoned as one of the 'Three Frivolous Battles of Britain'. And the *Romance of Taliesin* contains a long poem, or group of poems run together, called *Câd Goddeu*, the verses of which seem as nonsensical as the *Hanes Taliesin* because they have been deliberately 'pied'. Here is the poem in D. W. Nash's mid-Victorian translation, said to be unreliable but the best at present available. The original is written in short rhyming lines, the same rhyme often being sustained for ten or fifteen lines. Less than half of them belong to the poem which gives its name to the whole medley, and these must be laboriously sorted before their relevance to Gwion's riddle can be explained. Patience!

CÂD GODDEU

(The Battle of the Trees)

I have been in many shapes,
Before I attained a congenial form.
I have been a narrow blade of a sword.
(I will believe it when it appears.)
5 *I have been a drop in the air.*
I have been a shining star.
I have been a word in a book.
I have been a book originally.
I have been a light in a lantern.
10 *A year and a half.*
I have been a bridge for passing over
Three-score rivers.
I have journeyed as an eagle.
I have been a boat on the sea.
15 *I have been a director in battle.*

I have been the string of a child's swaddling clout.
I have been a sword in the hand.
I have been a shield in the fight.
I have been the string of a harp,
20 *Enchanted for a year*
In the foam of water.
I have been a poker in the fire.
I have been a tree in a covert.
There is nothing in which I have not been.
25 *I have fought, though small,*
In the Battle of Goddeu Brig,
Before the Ruler of Britain,
Abounding in fleets.
Indifferent bards pretend,
30 *They pretend a monstrous beast,*
With a hundred heads,
And a grievous combat
At the root of the tongue.
And another fight there is
35 *At the back of the head.*
A toad having on his thighs
A hundred claws,
A spotted crested snake,
For punishing in their flesh
40 *A hundred souls on account of their sins.*
I was in Caer Fefynedd,
Thither were hastening grasses and trees.
Wayfarers perceive them,
Warriors are astonished
45 *At a renewal of the conflicts*
Such as Gwydion made.
There is calling on Heaven,
And on Christ that he would effect
Their deliverance,
50 *The all-powerful Lord.*
If the Lord had answered,
Through charms and magic skill,
Assume the forms of the principal trees,
With you in array
55 *Restrain the people*
Inexperienced in battle.
When the trees were enchanted
There was hope for the trees,

That they should frustrate the intention
60 *Of the surrounding fires.* ....
Better are three in unison,
And enjoying themselves in a circle,
And one of them relating
The story of the deluge,
65 *And of the cross of Christ,*
And of the Day of Judgement near at hand.
The alder-trees in the first line,
They made the commencement.
Willow and quicken tree,
70 *They were slow in their array.*
The plum is a tree
Not beloved of men;
The medlar of a like nature,
Overcoming severe toil.
75 *The bean bearing in its shade*
An army of phantoms.
The raspberry makes
Not the best of food.
In shelter live,
80 *The privet and the woodbine,*
And the ivy in its season.
Great is the gorse in battle.
The cherry-tree had been reproached.
The birch, though very magnanimous,
85 *Was late in arraying himself;*
It was not through cowardice,
But on account of his great size.
The appearance of the ...
Is that of a foreigner and a savage.
90 *The pine-tree in the court,*
Strong in battle,
By me greatly exalted
In the presence of kings,
The elm-trees are his subjects.
95 *He turns not aside the measure of a foot,*
But strikes right in the middle,
And at the farthest end.
The hazel is the judge,
His berries are thy dowry.
100 *The privet is blessed.*
Strong chiefs in war

Are the . . . and the mulberry.
Prosperous the beech-tree.
The holly dark green,
105 He was very courageous:
Defended with spikes on every side,
Wounding the hands.
The long-enduring poplars
Very much broken in fight.
110 The plundered fern;
The brooms with their offspring:
The furze was not well behaved
Until he was tamed.
The heath was giving consolation,
115 Comforting the people.
The black cherry-tree was pursuing.
The oak-tree swiftly moving,
Before him tremble heaven and earth,
Stout doorkeeper against the foe
120 Is his name in all lands.
The corn-cockle bound together,
Was given to be burnt.
Others were rejected
On account of the holes made
125 By great violence
In the field of battle.
Very wrathful the . . .
Cruel the gloomy ash.
Bashful the chestnut-tree,
130 Retreating from happiness.
There shall be a black darkness,
There shall be a shaking of the mountain,
There shall be a purifying furnace,
There shall first be a great wave,
135 And when the shout shall be heard—
Putting forth new leaves are the tops of the beech,
Changing form and being renewed from a withered state;
Entangled are the tops of the oak.
From the Gorchan of Maelderw.
140 Smiling at the side of the rock
(Was) the pear-tree not of an ardent nature.
Neither of mother or father,
When I was made,
Was my blood or body;

33

145 *Of nine kinds of faculties,*
Of fruit of fruits,
Of fruit God made me,
Of the blossom of the mountain primrose,
Of the buds of trees and shrubs,
150 *Of earth of earthly kind.*
When I was made
Of the blossoms of the nettle,
Of the water of the ninth wave,
I was spell-bound by Math
155 *Before I became immortal.*
I was spell-bound by Gwydion,
Great enchanter of the Britons,
Of Eurys, of Eurwn,
Of Euron, of Medron,
160 *In myriads of secrets,*
I am as learned as Math....
I know about the Emperor
When he was half burnt.
I know the star-knowledge
165 *Of stars before the earth (was made),*
Whence I was born,
How many worlds there are.
It is the custom of accomplished bards
To recite the praise of their country.
170 *I have played in Lloughor,*
I have slept in purple.
Was I not in the enclosure
With Dylan Ail Mor,
On a couch in the centre
175 *Between the two knees of the prince*
Upon two blunt spears?
When from heaven came
The torrents into the deep,
Rushing with violent impulse.
180 *(I know) four-score songs,*
For administering to their pleasure.
There is neither old nor young,
Except me as to their poems,
Any other singer who knows the whole of the nine hundred
185 *Which are known to me,*
Concerning the blood-spotted sword.
Honour is my guide.

Profitable learning is from the Lord.
(I know) of the slaying of the boar,
190 Its appearing, its disappearing,
Its knowledge of languages.
(I know) the light whose name is Splendour,
And the number of the ruling lights
That scatter rays of fire
195 High above the deep.
I have been a spotted snake upon a hill;
I have been a viper in a lake;
I have been an evil star formerly.
I have been a weight in a mill. (?)
200 My cassock is red all over.
I prophesy no evil.
Four score puffs of smoke
To every one who will carry them away:
And a million of angels,
205 On the point of my knife.
Handsome is the yellow horse,
But a hundred times better
Is my cream-coloured one,
Swift as the sea-mew,
210 Which cannot pass me
Between the sea and the shore.
Am I not pre-eminent in the field of blood?
I have a hundred shares of the spoil.
My wreath is of red jewels,
215 Of gold is the border of my shield.
There has not been born one so good as I,
Or ever known,
Except Goronwy,
From the dales of Edrywy.
220 Long and white are my fingers,
It is long since I was a herdsman.
I travelled over the earth
Before I became a learned person.
I have travelled, I have made a circuit,
225 I have slept in a hundred islands;
I have dwelt in a hundred cities.
Learned Druids,
Prophesy ye of Arthur?
Or is it me they celebrate,
230 And the Crucifixion of Christ,

And the Day of Judgement near at hand,
And one relating
The history of the Deluge?
With a golden jewel set in gold
235 I am enriched;
And I am indulging in pleasure
Out of the oppressive toil of the goldsmith.

With a little patience most of the lines that belong to the poem about the Battle of the Trees can be separated from the four or five other poems with which they are mixed. Here is a tentative restoration of the easier parts, with gaps left for the more difficult. The reasons that have led me to this solution will appear in due course as I discuss the meaning of the allusions contained in the poem. I use the ballad metre as the most suitable English equivalent of the original.

THE BATTLE OF THE TREES

From my seat at Fefynedd,   (lines 41–42)
    A city that is strong,
I watched the trees and green things
    Hastening along.

Wayfarers wondered,   (lines 43–46)
    Warriors were dismayed
At renewal of conflicts
    Such as Gwydion made,

Under the tongue-root   (lines 32–35)
    A fight most dread,
And another raging
    Behind, in the head.

The alders in the front line   (lines 67–70)
    Began the affray.
Willow and rowan-tree
    Were tardy in array.

The holly, dark green,   (lines 104–107)
    Made a resolute stand;
He is armed with many spear-points
    Wounding the hand.

36

With foot-beat of the swift oak   (lines 117–120)
  Heaven and earth rung;
'Stout Guardian of the Door'
  His name in every tongue.

Great was the gorse in battle,   (lines 82, 81, 98, 57)
  And the ivy at his prime;
The hazel was arbiter
  At this charmed time.

Uncouth and savage was the [fir?]   (lines 88, 89, 128, 95, 96)
  Cruel the ash-tree—
Turns not aside a foot-breadth,
  Straight at the heart runs he.

The birch, though very noble,   (lines 84–87)
  Armed himself but late:
A sign not of cowardice
  But of high estate.

The heath gave consolation   (lines 114, 115, 108, 109)
  To the toil-spent folk,
The long-enduring poplars
  In battle much broke.

Some of them were cast away   (lines 123–126)
  On the field of fight
Because of holes torn in them
  By the enemy's might.

Very wrathful was the [vine?]   (lines 127, 94, 92, 93)
  Whose henchmen are the elms;
I exalt him mightily
  To rulers of realms.

In shelter linger   (lines 79, 80, 56, 90)
  Privet and woodbine
Inexperienced in warfare;
  And the courtly pine.

Little Gwion has made it clear that he does not offer this encounter as
the original *Câd Goddeu* but as:

A renewal of conflicts
Such as Gwydion made.

Commentators, confused by the pied verses, have for the most part been content to remark that in Celtic tradition the Druids were credited with the magical power of transforming trees into warriors and sending them into battle. But, as the Rev. Edward Davies, a brilliant but hopelessly erratic Welsh scholar of the early nineteenth century, first noted in his *Celtic Researches* (1809), the battle described by Gwion is not a frivolous battle, or a battle physically fought, but a battle fought intellectually in the heads and with the tongues of the learned. Davies also noted that in all Celtic languages *trees* means *letters*; that the Druidic colleges were founded in woods or groves; that a great part of the Druidic mysteries was concerned with twigs of different sorts; and that the most ancient Irish alphabet, the Beth-Luis-Nion ('Birch-Rowan-Ash') takes its name from the first three of a series of trees whose initials form the sequence of its letters. Davies was on the right track and though he soon went astray because, not realizing that the poems were pied, he mistranslated them into what he thought was good sense, his observations help us to restore the text of the passage referring to the hastening green things and trees:

> *Retreating from happiness,*   (lines 130 and 53)
> *They would fain be set*
> *In forms of the chief letters*
> *Of the alphabet.*

The following lines seem to form an introduction to his account of the battle:

> *The tops of the beech-tree*   (lines 136–137)
> *Have sprouted of late,*
> *Are changed and renewed*
> *From their withered state.*

> *When the beech prospers,*   (lines 103, 52, 138, 58)
> *Though spells and litanies*
> *The oak-tops entangle,*
> *There is hope for trees.*

This means, if anything, that there had been a recent revival of letters in Wales. 'Beech' is a common synonym for 'literature'. The English word 'book', for example, comes from a Gothic word meaning letters and, like the German *buchstabe*, is etymologically connected with the word 'beech'—the reason being that writing tablets were made of beech. As Venantius Fortunatus, the sixth-century bishop-poet, wrote: *Barbara fraxineis pingatur runa tabellis*—'Let the barbarian rune be marked on beechwood tablets.' The 'tangled oak-tops' must refer to the ancient poetic mysteries: as has already been mentioned, the *derwydd*, or Druid, or poet, was an 'oak-seer'. An early Cornish poem describes how the Druid Merddin, or Merlin, went early in the morning with his black dog to seek the *glain*, or magical snake's-egg (probably a fossiled sea-urchin of the sort found in Iron Age burials), cull cresses and *samolus* (*herbe d'or*), and cut the highest twig from the top of the oak. Gwion, who in line 225 addresses his fellow-poets as Druids, is saying here: 'The ancient poetic mysteries have been reduced to a tangle by the Church's prolonged hostility, but they have a hopeful future, now that literature is prospering outside the monasteries.'

He mentions other participants in the battle:

> *Strong chiefs in war*
> > *Are the* [?] *and mulberry. . . .*
>
> *The cherry had been slighted. . . .*
>
> *The black cherry was pursuing . . . .*
>
> *The pear that is not ardent. . . .*
>
> *The raspberry that makes*
> > *Not the best of foods. . . .*
>
> *The plum is a tree*
> > *Unbeloved of men. . . .*
>
> *The medlar of like nature. . . .*

None of these mentions makes good poetic sense. Raspberry is excellent food; the plum is a popular tree; pear-wood is so ardent that in the Balkans it is often used as a substitute for cornel to kindle the ritual need-fire; the mulberry is not used as a weapon-tree; the cherry was never slighted and in Gwion's day was connected with the Nativity story in a popular version of the Gospel of Pseudo-Matthew; and the black cherry does not 'pursue'. It is pretty clear that these eight names of orchard fruits, and another which occupied the place that I have filled with 'fir', have been mischievously robbed from the next riddling passage in the poem:

> *Of nine kinds of faculty,*
> > *Of fruits of fruit,*
> > *Of fruit God made me. . . .*

and have been substituted for the names of nine forest trees that did engage in the fight.

It is hard to decide whether the story of the fruit man belongs to the *Battle of the Trees* poem, or whether it is a 'Here come I' speech like the four others muddled up in the *Câd Goddeu*, of whom the speakers are evidently Taliesin, the Flower-goddess Blodeuwedd, Hu Gadarn the ancestor of the Cymry, and the God Apollo. On the whole, I think it does belong to the *Battle of the Trees*:

> *With nine sorts of faculty*   (lines 145–147)
> *God has gifted me:*
> *I am fruit of fruits gathered*
> *From nine sorts of tree—*

> *Plum, quince, whortle, mulberry,*   (lines 71, 73, 77, 83,
> *Raspberry, pear,*   102, 116, 141)
> *Black cherry and white*
> *With the sorb in me share.*

By a study of the trees of the Irish Beth-Luis-Nion tree-alphabet, with which the author of the poem was clearly familiar, it is easy to restore the original nine trees which have been replaced with the fruit names. We can be sure that it is the sloe that 'makes not the best of foods'; the elder, a notoriously bad wood for fuel and a famous country remedy for fevers, scalds and burns, that is 'not ardent'; the unlucky whitethorn, and the blackthorn 'of like nature', that are 'unbeloved of men' and, with the archer's yew, are the 'strong chiefs in war'. And on the analogy of the oak from which reverberating clubs were made, the yew from which deadly bows and dagger-handles were made, the ash from which sure-thrusting spears were made, and the poplar from which long-enduring shields were made, I suggest that the original of 'the black cherry was pursuing' was the restless reed from which swift-flying arrow-shafts were made. The reed was reckoned a 'tree' by the Irish poets.

The 'I' who was slighted because he was not big is Gwion himself, whom Heinin and his fellow-bards scoffed at for his childish appearance; but he is perhaps speaking in the character of still another tree—the mistletoe, which in the Norse legend killed Balder the Sun-god after having been slighted as too young to take the oath not to harm him. Although in ancient Irish religion there is no trace of a mistletoe cult, and the mistletoe does not figure in the Beth-Luis-Nion, to the Gallic Druids who relied on Britain for their doctrine it was the most important of all trees, and remains of mistletoe have been found in conjunction with oak-branches in a Bronze Age tree-coffin burial at Gristhorpe near Scarborough in Yorkshire. Gwion may therefore be relying here on a British tradition of the original *Câd Goddeu* rather than on his Irish learning.

The remaining tree-references in the poem are these:

> *The broom with its children. . . .*

> *The furze not well behaved*
> *Until he was tamed....*
>
> *Bashful the chestnut-tree....*

The furze is tamed by the Spring-fires which make its young shoots edible for sheep.

The bashful chestnut does not belong to the same category of letter trees as those that took part in the battle; probably the line in which it occurs is part of another of the poems included in *Câd Goddeu*, which describes how the lovely Blodeuwedd ('Flower-aspect') was conjured by the wizard Gwydion, from buds and blossoms. This poem is not difficult to separate from the rest of *Câd Goddeu*, though one or two lines seem to be missing. They can be supplied from the parallel lines:

> *Of nine kinds of faculties,*   (lines 145–147)
> *Of fruits of fruit,*
> *Of fruit God made me.*

The fruit man is created from nine kinds of fruit; the flower woman must have been created from nine kinds of flower. Five are given in *Câd Goddeu*; three more—broom, meadow-sweet and oak-blossom—in the account of the same event in the *Romance of Math the Son of Mathonwy*; and the ninth is likely to have been the hawthorn, because Blodeuwedd is another name for Olwen, the May-queen, daughter (according to the *Romance of Kilhwych and Olwen*) of the Hawthorn, or Whitethorn, or May Tree; but it may have been the white-flowering trefoil.

HANES BLODEUWEDD

Not of father nor of mother	line 142
Was my blood, was my body.	144
I was spellbound by Gwydion,	156
Prime enchanter of the Britons,	157
When he forı ɗ me from nine blossoms,	143
Nine buɑ. of various kind:	149
From primrose of the mountain,	148
Broom, meadow-sweet and cockle,	121
Together intertwined,	
From the bean in its shade bearing	75
A white spectral army	76
Of earth, of earthly kind,	150
From blossoms of the nettle,	152
Oak, thorn and bashful chestnut—	129
Nine powers of nine flowers,	[146
Nine powers in me combined,	145]

> *Nine buds of plant and tree.*
> *Long and white are my fingers*
> *As the ninth wave of the sea.*

In Wales and Ireland primroses are reckoned fairy flowers and in English folk tradition represent wantonness (cf. 'the primrose path of dalliance' —*Hamlet*; the 'primrose of her wantonness'—Brathwait's *Golden Fleece*). So Milton's 'yellow-skirted fayes' wore primrose. 'Cockles' are the 'tares' of the Parable that the Devil sowed in the wheat; and the bean is traditionally associated with ghosts—the Greek and Roman homoeopathic remedy against ghosts was to spit beans at them—and Pliny in his *Natural History* records the belief that the souls of the dead reside in beans. According to the Scottish poet Montgomerie (1605), witches rode on bean-stalks to their sabbaths.

To return to the Battle of the Trees. Though the fern was reckoned a 'tree' by the Irish poets, the 'plundered fern' is probably a reference to fern-seed which makes invisible and confers other magical powers. The twice-repeated 'privet' is suspicious. The privet figures unimportantly in Irish poetic tree-lore; it is never regarded as 'blessed'. Probably its second occurrence in line 100 is a disguise of the wild-apple, which is the tree most likely to smile from beside the rock, emblem of security: for Olwen, the laughing Aphrodite of Welsh legend, is always connected with the wild-apple. In line 99 'his berries are thy dowry' is absurdly juxtaposed to the hazel. Only two fruit-trees could be said to dower a bride in Gwion's day: the churchyard yew whose berries fell at the church porch where marriages were always celebrated, and the churchyard rowan, often substituted for the yew in Wales. I think the yew is here intended; yew-berries were prized for their sticky sweetness. In the tenth-century Irish poem, *King and Hermit*, Marvan the brother of King Guare of Connaught commends them highly as food.

The remaining stanzas of the poem may now be tentatively restored:

> *I have plundered the fern,*   (lines 110, 160, and 161)
> *Through all secrets I spy,*
> *Old Math ap Mathonwy*
> *Knew no more than I.*

> *Strong chieftains were the blackthorn*   (lines 101, 71–73, 77
> *With his ill fruit,*   and 78)
> *The unbeloved whitethorn*
> *Who wears the same suit.*

> *The swift-pursuing reed,*   (lines 116, 111–113)
> *The broom with his brood,*

And the furze but ill-behaved
Until he is subdued.

The dower-scattering yew   (lines 97, 99, 128, 141, 60)
   Stood glum at the fight's fringe,
With the elder slow to burn
   Amid fires that singe,

And the blessed wild apple   (lines 100, 139, and 140)
   Laughing for pride
From the Gorchan *of Maelderw,*
   By the rock side.

But I, although slighted   (lines 83, 54, 25, 26)
   Because I was not big,
Fought, trees, in your array
   On the field of Goddeu Brig.

The broom may not seem a warlike tree, but in Gratius's *Genistae Altinates* the tall white broom is said to have been much used in ancient times for the staves of spears and darts: these are probably the 'brood'. *Goddeu Brig* means Tree-tops, which has puzzled critics who hold that the *Câd Goddeu* was a battle fought in Goddeu, 'Trees', the Welsh name for Shropshire. The *Gorchan* of Maelderw ('the incantation of Maelderw') was a long poem attributed to the sixth-century poet Taliesin, who is said to have particularly prescribed it as a classic to his bardic colleagues. The apple-tree was a symbol of poetic immortality, which is why it is here presented as growing out of this incantation of Taliesin's.

Here, to anticipate my argument by several chapters, is the Order of Battle in the *Câd Goddeu*:

Birch	Rowan	Alder	Willow	Ash
Whitethorn	Oak	Holly	Hazel	Wild-apple
Vine	Ivy	{Reed	Blackthorn	Elder
		{Broom		
Palm	Fir	{Gorse	Heath	Poplar	Yew	Mistletoe
		{Furze		
		Privet	Woodbine	Pine

It should be added that in the original, between the lines numbered 60 and 61, occur eight lines unintelligible to D. W. Nash: beginning with 'the chieftains are falling' and ending with 'blood of men up to the buttocks'. They may or may not belong to the *Battle of the Trees*.

I leave the other pieces included in this medley to be sorted out by someone else. Besides the monologues of Blodeuwedd, Hu Gadarn and

Apollo, there is a satire on monkish theologians, who sit in a circle gloomily enjoying themselves with prophecies of the imminent Day of Judgement (lines 62–66), the black darkness, the shaking of the mountain, the purifying furnace (lines 131–134), damning men's souls by the hundred (lines 39–40) and pondering the absurd problems of the Schoolmen:

> *Room for a million angels*   (lines 204, 205)
>   *On my knife-point, it appears.*
> *Then room for how many worlds*   (lines 167 and 176)
>   *A-top of two blunt spears?*

This introduces a boast of Gwion's own learning:

> *But* I *prophesy no evil,*   (lines 201, 200)
>   *My cassock is wholly red.*
> *'He knows the Nine Hundred Tales'*—   (line 184)
>   *Of whom but me is it said?*

Red was the most honourable colour for dress among the ancient Welsh, according to the twelfth-century poet Cynddelw; Gwion is contrasting it with the dismal dress of the monks. Of the Nine Hundred Tales he mentions only two, both of which are included in the *Red Book of Hergest*: the *Hunting of the Twrch Trwyth* (line 189) and the *Dream of Maxen Wledig* (lines 162–3).

Lines 206 to 211 belong, it seems, to *Can y Meirch*, 'The Song of the Horses', another of the Gwion poems, which refers to a race between the horses of Elphin and Maelgwyn which is an incident in the Romance.

One most interesting sequence can be built up from lines 29–32, 36–37 and 234–237:

> *Indifferent bards pretend,*
> *They pretend a monstrous beast,*
> *With a hundred heads,*
> *A spotted crested snake,*
>
> *A toad having on his thighs*
> *A hundred claws,*
>
> *With a golden jewel set in gold*
> *I am enriched;*
> *And indulged in pleasure*
> *By the oppressive toil of the goldsmith.*

Since Gwion identifies himself with these bards, they are, I think, described as 'indifferent' by way of irony. The hundred-headed serpent watching over the jewelled Garden of the Hesperides, and the hundred-clawed toad wearing a precious jewel in his head (mentioned by Shakespeare's Duke Senior) both belonged to the ancient toadstool mysteries, of which Gwion seems to have been an adept. The European mysteries are less fully explored than their Mexican counterpart; but Mr. and Mrs. Gordon Wasson and Professor Heim show that the pre-Columbian Toadstool-god Tlalóc, represented as a toad with a serpent head-dress, has for thousands of years presided at the communal eating of the hallucigenic toadstool *psilocybe*: a feast that gives visions of transcendental beauty. Tlalóc's European counterpart, Dionysus, shares too many of his mythical attributes for coincidence: they must be versions of the same deity; though at what period cultural contact took place between the Old World and the New is debatable.

In my foreword to a revised edition of *The Greek Myths*, I suggest that a secret Dionysiac mushroom cult was borrowed from the native Pelasgians by the Achaeans of Argos. Dionysus's Centaurs, Satyrs and Maenads, it seems, ritually ate a spotted toadstool called 'flycap' (*amanita muscaria*), which gave them enormous muscular strength, erotic power, delirious visions, and the gift of prophecy. Partakers in the Eleusinian, Orphic and other mysteries may also have known the *panaeolus papilionaceus*, a small dung-mushroom still used by Portuguese witches, and similar in effect to mescalin. In lines 234–237, Gwion implies that a single gem can enlarge itself under the influence of 'the toad' or 'the serpent' into a whole treasury of jewels. His claim to be as learned as Math and to know myriads of secrets may also belong to the toad-serpent sequence; at any rate, *psilocybe* gives a sense of universal illumination, as I can attest from my own experience of it. 'The light whose name is Splendour' may refer to this brilliance of vision, rather than to the Sun.

The *Book of Taliesin* contains several similar medleys or poems awaiting resurrection: a most interesting task, but one that must wait until the texts are established and properly translated. The work that I have done here is not offered as in any sense final.

Câd Goddeu

'The Battle of the Trees'.

The tops of the beech tree
	Have sprouted of late,
Are changed and renewed
	From their withered state.

When the beech prospers,
	Though spells and litanies
The oak tops entangle,
	There is hope for trees.

I have plundered the fern,
        Through all secrets I spy,
Old Math ap Mathonwy
        Knew no more than I.

For with nine sorts of faculty
        God has gifted me:
I am fruit of fruits gathered
        From nine sorts of tree—

Plum, quince, whortle, mulberry,
        Raspberry, pear,
Black cherry and white
        With the sorb in me share.

From my seat at Fefynedd,
        A city that is strong,
I watched the trees and green things
        Hastening along.

Retreating from happiness
        They would fain be set
In forms of the chief letters
        Of the alphabet.

Wayfarers wondered,
        Warriors were dismayed
At renewal of conflicts
        Such as Gwydion made;

Under the tongue root
        A fight most dread,
And another raging
        Behind, in the head.

The alders in the front line
        Began the affray.
Willow and rowan-tree
        Were tardy in array.

The holly, dark green,
        Made a resolute stand;
He is armed with many spear points
        Wounding the hand.

46

With foot-beat of the swift oak
    Heaven and earth rung;
'Stout Guardian of the Door',
    His name in every tongue.

Great was the gorse in battle,
    And the ivy at his prime;
The hazel was arbiter
    At this charmed time.

Uncouth and savage was the fir,
    Cruel the ash tree—
Turns not aside a foot-breadth,
    Straight at the heart runs he.

The birch, though very noble,
    Armed himself but late:
A sign not of cowardice
    But of high estate.

The heath gave consolation
    To the toil-spent folk,
The long-enduring poplars
    In battle much broke.

Some of them were cast away
    On the field of fight
Because of holes torn in them
    By the enemy's might.

Very wrathful was the vine
    Whose henchmen are the elms;
I exalt him mightily
    To rulers of realms.

Strong chieftains were the blackthorn
    With his ill fruit,
The unbeloved whitethorn
    Who wears the same suit,

The swift-pursuing reed,
    The broom with his brood,
And the furze but ill-behaved
    Until he is subdued.

The dower-scattering yew
  Stood glum at the fight's fringe,
With the elder slow to burn
  Amid fires that singe,

And the blessed wild apple
  Laughing in pride
From the Gorchan of Maeldrew,
  By the rock side.

In shelter linger
  Privet and woodbine,
Inexperienced in warfare,
  And the courtly pine.

But I, although slighted
  Because I was not big,
Fought, trees, in your array
  On the field of Goddeu Brig.

Chapter Three

DOG, ROEBUCK AND LAPWING

The fullest account of the original Battle of the Trees, though the Lapwing is not mentioned in it, is published in the *Myvyrian Archaiology*. This is a perfect example of mythographic short-hand and records what seems to have been the most important religious event in pre-Christian Britain:

'These are the Englyns [epigrammatic verses] that were sung at the *Câd Goddeu*, or, as others call it, the Battle of Achren, which was on account of a white roebuck, and a whelp; and they came from Annwm [the Underworld], and Amathaon ap Don brought them. And therefore Amathaon ap Don, and Arawn, King of Annwm, fought. And there was a man in that battle, who unless his name were known could not be overcome and there was on the other side a woman called Achren ['Trees'], and unless her name were known her party could not be overcome. And Gwydion ap Don guessed the name of the man, and sang the two Englyns following:

> *Sure-hoofed is my steed impelled by the spur;*
> *The high sprigs of alder are on thy shield;*
> *Bran art thou called, of the glittering branches.*
>
> *Sure-hoofed is my steed in the day of battle:*
> *The high sprigs of alder are in thy hand:*
> *Bran thou art, by the branch thou bearest—*
> *Amathaon the Good has prevailed.'*

The story of the guessing of Bran's name is a familiar one to anthro-pologists. In ancient times, once a god's secret name had been discovered, the enemies of his people could do destructive magic against them with it. The Romans made a regular practice of discovering the secret names of enemy gods and summoning them to Rome with seductive promises, a process technically known as *elicio*. Josephus in his *Contra Apionem* quotes an account of a magic ceremony of this sort carried out at Jerusalem in the second century B.C. at the instance of King Alexander Jannaeus the Maccabee; the god summoned was the Edomite Ass-god of Dora, near

Hebron. Livy (v. 21) gives the formula used to summon the Juno of Veii to Rome, and Diodorus Siculus (xvii, 41) writes that the Tyrians used to chain up their statues as a precaution. Naturally the Romans, like the Jews, hid the secret name of their own guardian-deity with extra-ordinary care; nevertheless one Quintus Valerius Soranus, a Sabine, was put to death in late Republican times for divulging it irresponsibly. The tribes of Amathaon and Gwydion in the *Câd Goddeu* encounter were as intent on keeping the secret of Achren—presumably the trees, or letters, that spelt out the secret name of their own deity—as on discovering that of their opponents. The subject of this myth, then, is a battle for religious mastery between the armies of Dôn, the people who appear in Irish legend as the Tuatha dé Danaan, 'the folk of the God whose mother is Danu', and the armies of Arawn ('Eloquence'), the King of Annwfn, or Annwm, which was the British Underworld or national necropolis. In the *Romance of Pwyll, Prince of Dyved* Arawn appears as a huntsman on a large pale horse, pursuing a stag with the help of a pack of white dogs with red ears—the Hounds of Hell familiar in Irish, Welsh, Highland and British folklore.

The Tuatha dé Danaan were a confederacy of tribes in which the king-ship went by matrilinear succession, some of whom invaded Ireland from Britain in the middle Bronze Age. The Goddess Danu was eventually masculinized into Dôn, or Donnus, and regarded as the eponymous ancestor of the confederacy. But in the primitive *Romance of Math the Son of Mathonwy* she appears as sister to King Math of Gwynedd, and Gwydion and Amathaon are reckoned as her sons—that is to say, as tribal gods of the Danaan confederacy. According to an archaeologically plausible Irish tradition in the *Book of Invasions,* the Tuatha dé Danaan had been driven northward from Greece as a result of an invasion from Syria and eventually reached Ireland by way of Denmark, to which they gave their own name ('The Kingdom of the Danaans'), and North Britain. The date of their arrival in Britain is recorded as 1472 B.C.—for what that is worth. The Syrian invasion of Greece which set them moving north is perhaps the one hinted at by Herodotus in the first paragraph of his *History*: the capture by 'Phoenicians' of the Danaan shrine of the White Goddess Io at Argos, then the religious capital of the Peloponnese; the Cretans had colonized it about the year 1750 B.C. Herodotus does not date the event except by making it happen before the *Argo* expedition to Colchis, which the Greeks dated 1225 B.C. and before 'Europa' went from Phoenicia to Crete, a tribal emigration which probably took place some centuries earlier, prior to the sack of Cnossos in 1400 B.C. In the *Book of Invasions* there is a record, confirmed in Bede's *Ecclesiastical History,* of another invasion of Ireland, which took place two hundred years after the arrival of the Tuatha dé Danaan. These people, sailing westwards from Thrace through the Mediterranean and out into the Atlantic, landed in Wexford Bay where they came in conflict with the Danaans; but were persuaded to pass on into Northern Britain, then called Albany. They were known as the Picts, or tattooed men, and had the same odd social habits—exogamy, totemism, public coition, cannibalism, tattooing, the participation of women in battle—that obtained in Thessaly before the coming of the Achaeans, and in Classical times among the primitive tribes of the Southern Black Sea coast, the Gulf of Sirté in Libya, Majorca (populated by Bronze Age Libyans) and North-West Galicia. Their descendants still kept their non-Celtic language in Bede's day.

Amathaon, or Amaethon, is said to take his name from the Welsh word *amaeth*, a ploughman, but it may be the other way about: that ploughmen were under the patronage of the god Amathaon. Perhaps the tribe was originally mothered by Amathaounta, a well-known Aegean Sea-goddess; another tribe of the same name, whose ancestral hero was Hercules, migrated from Crete to Amathus in Cyprus towards the end of the second millennium B.C.. Amathaon is credited with having taught Gwydion the wizardry for which he was afterwards famous; and this suggests that Gwydion was a late-comer to Britain, perhaps a god of the Belgic tribes that invaded Britain about 400 B.C., and was given honorary sonship of Danu some centuries after the first Danaan invasion. Amathaon was maternal nephew to Math Hen ('Old Math'), *alias* Math the son of Mathonwy. 'Math' means 'treasure'; but since Math is also credited with having taught Gwydion his magic, 'Math son of Mathonwy' may be a truncated version of 'Amathus son of Amathaounta'. Part of the tribe seems to have emigrated to Syria where it founded the city of Amathus (Hamath) on the Orontes, and another part to Palestine where it founded Amathus in the angle between the Jordan and the Jabbok. In the Table of Nations in *Genesis X* the Amathites are reckoned late among the Sons of Canaan, along with Hivites, Gergasites and other non-Semitic tribes. According to *II Chronicles, XVII, 30,* some of the Amathites were planted as a colony in Samaria, where they continued to worship their Goddess under the name of Ashima.

Bran's name was guessed by Gwydion from the sprigs of alder in his hand, because though 'Bran' and *Gwern,* the word for 'alder' used in the poem, do not sound similar, Gwydion knew that Bran, which meant 'Crow' or 'Raven', also meant 'alder'—the Irish is *fearn,* with the 'f' pronounced as 'v'—and that the alder was a sacred tree. The third of the four sons of King Partholan the Milesian, a legendary ruler of Ireland in the Bronze Age, had been called Fearn; there had also been young Gwern, King of Ireland, the son of Bran's sister, Branwen ('White Crow'). Various confirmations of Gwydion's guess appear in the *Romance of Branwen,* as will be shown later. But the name spelt out by the trees, for the letters, ranged on the side of Amathaon and Gwydion remained unguessed.

The Bran cult seems also to have been imported from the Aegean. There are remarkable resemblances between him and the Pelasgian hero Aesculapius who, like the chieftain Coronus ('crow') killed by Hercules, was a king of the Thessalian crow-totem tribe of Lapiths. Aesculapius was a Crow on both sides of the family: his mother was Coronis ('crow'), probably a title of the Goddess Athene to whom the crow was sacred. Tatian, the Church Father, in his *Address to the Greeks,* suggests a mother and son relationship between Athene and Aesculapius:

> After the decapitation of the Gorgon ... Athene and Aesculapius divided the blood between them, and while he saved lives by means of them, she by the same blood became a murderess and instigator of wars.

Aesculapius's father was Apollo whose famous shrine of Tempe stood in Lapith territory and to whom the crow was also sacred; and Apollo is described as the father of another Coronus, King of Sicyon in Sicily. The legend of Aesculapius is that after a life devoted to healing, he raised Glaucus, son of Sisyphus the Corinthian, from the dead, and was burned to cinders by Zeus in a fit of jealousy; he had been rescued as a child from a bonfire in which his mother and her paramour Ischys ('Strength') perished. Bran was likewise destroyed by his jealous enemy Evnissyen, a comrade of Matholwch King of Ireland to whom he had given a magical cauldron for raising dead soldiers to life; but in the Welsh legend it is Bran's nephew and namesake, the boy Gwern, who after being crowned King is immediately thrown into a bonfire and burned to death; Bran himself is wounded in the heel by a poisoned dart—like Achilles the Minyan, the Centaur Cheiron's pupil, and Cheiron himself—then beheaded; his head continues to sing and prophesy. (In Irish legend Aesculapius figures as Midach, killed after the Second Battle of Moytura by his father Diancecht, the Apollo of Healing, who was jealous of his cures.) Aesculapius and Bran were both demi-gods with numerous shrines, and both were patrons of healing and resurrection. Another point of resemblance between them is their love-adventures: Aesculapius lay with fifty amorous girls in a night, and Bran had a similar jaunt in the Isle of Women, one of three times fifty that he visited on a famous voyage. Aesculapius is represented in Greek art with a dog beside him and a staff in his hand around which twine oracular snakes.

The theft of the Dog and the Roebuck from the Underworld by Amathaon supports the Irish view that the Children of Danu came from Greece in the middle of the second millennium B.C., since there are several analogous Greek legends of Bronze Age origin. For example, that of Hercules, the oak-hero, who was ordered by his task-master King

Eurystheus of Mycenae to steal the dog Cerberus from the King of the Underworld, and the brass-shod white roebuck from the Grove of the Goddess Artemis at Ceryneia in Arcadia. In another of his adventures Hercules snatched from Herophile—the priestess of Delphi whose father (according to Clement of Alexandria) was Zeus disguised as a lapwing, and whose mother was Lamia, the Serpent-goddess—the oracular tripod on which she was sitting, but was forced to restore it. Among the favourite subjects of Greek and Etruscan art are Hercules carrying off the Dog and his struggles with the guardian of the Lamian oracle at Delphi for the possession of the roebuck and of the tripod. To call this guardian Apollo is misleading because Apollo was not at that time a Sun-god, but an Underworld oracular hero. The sense of these myths seems to be that an attempt to substitute the cult of the oracular oak for that of the oracular laurel at Delphi failed, but that the shrines at Ceryneia in Arcadia and Cape Taenarum in Laconia, where most mythographers place the entrance to the Underworld visited by Hercules, were captured. Other mythographers say that the entrance was at Mariandynian Acherusia (now Heracli in Anatolia) and that where the saliva of Cerberus fell on the ground, up sprang the witch-flower aconite—which is a poison, a paralysant and a febrifuge; but this account refers to another historical event, the capture of a famous Bithynian shrine by the Henetians.

But why Dog? Why Roebuck? Why Lapwing?

The Dog with which Aesculapius is pictured, like the dog Anubis, the companion of Egyptian Thoth, and the dog which always attended Melkarth the Phoenician Hercules, is a symbol of the Underworld; also of the dog-priests, called Enariae, who attended the Great Goddess of the Eastern Mediterranean and indulged in sodomitic frenzies in the Dog days at the rising of the Dog-star, Sirius. But the poetic meaning of the Dog in the *Câd Goddeu* legend, as in all similar legends, is 'Guard the Secret', the prime secret on which the sovereignty of a sacred king depended. Evidently Amathaon had seduced some priest of Bran—whether it was a homosexual priesthood I do not pretend to know—and won from him a secret which enabled Gwydion to guess Bran's name correctly. Hercules overcame the Dog Cerberus by a narcotic cake which relaxed its vigilance; what means Amathaon used is not recorded.

The Lapwing, as Cornelius Agrippa, the early sixteenth-century occult philosopher, reminds us in his *Vanity and Uncertainty of the Arts and Sciences* (translated by James Sanford in 1569): 'seemeth to have some royal thing and weareth a crown.' I do not know whether Agrippa seriously meant to include the lapwing among royal birds, but if he did his best authority was *Leviticus XI, 19*. The lapwing is there mentioned as an unclean, that is to say tabooed, bird in the distinguished company of the eagle, the griffon-vulture, the ibis, the cuckoo, the swan, the kite, the raven, owl and little owl, the solan-goose (here not gannet but barnacle goose[1]), the stork, the heron and the pious pelican. That these taboos were of non-Semitic origin is proved by their geographical distribution: several of the birds do not belong to the heat-belt which is the Semitic homeland, and every one of them was sacred in Greece or Italy, or both, to a major deity. Biblical scholars have been puzzled by the 'uncleanness' of the lapwing—and doubt whether the bird *is* a lapwing and not a hoopoe or a hedgehog—but whenever uncleanness means sanctity the clue must be looked for in natural history. The Greeks called the lapwing *polyplagktos*, 'luring on deceitfully', and had a proverbial phrase 'more beseechful than a lapwing' which they used for artful beggars. In Wales as a boy I learned to respect the lapwing for the wonderful way in which she camouflages and conceals her eggs in an open field from any casual passer-by. At first I was fooled every time by her agonized *peewit, peewit*, screamed from the contrary direction to the one in which her eggs lay, and sometimes when she realized that I was a nest-robber, she would flap about along the ground, pretending to have a broken wing and inviting capture. But as soon as I had found one nest I could find many. The lapwing's poetic meaning is 'Disguise the Secret' and it is her extraordinary discretion which gives her the claim to sanctity. According to the *Koran* she was the repository of King Solomon's secrets and the most intelligent of the flock of prophetic birds that attended him.

As for the White Roebuck, how many kings in how many fairy tales have not chased this beast through enchanted forests and been cheated of their quarry? The Roebuck's poetic meaning is 'Hide the Secret'.

So it seems that in the *Câd Goddeu* story elements of a Hercules myth, which in Greek legend describes how the Achaeans of Mycenae captured the most important tribal shrines in the Peloponnese from some other Greek tribe, probably the Danaans, are used to describe a similar capture in Britain many centuries later. Any attempt to date this event involves a brief summary of British pre-history. The generally accepted scheme of approximate dates derived from archaeological evidence is as follows:

6000–3000 B.C.

Old Stone Age hunters, not numerous, maintained a few settlements in scattered places.

3000–2500 B.C.

Occasional and gradual immigration of New Stone Age hunters who brought polished stone axes with them and the art of making rough pots.

[1] *As barnacles turn Soland-geese,*
I' th' Islands of the Orcades.

(Butler's *Hudibras*)

2500–2000 B.C.

Regular traffic across the English Channel and invasion by New Stone Age long-headed agriculturists, who domesticated animals, practised flint-mining on a large scale and made crude ornamented pottery which has affinities with the ware found in burials in the Baltic islands of Bornholm and Aland. They came from Libya, by way of Spain, Southern and Northern France, or by way of Spain, Portugal and Brittany; some of them went on from France to the Baltic, and then crossed over into Eastern England after trade contact with the Black Sea area. They introduced megalithic burials of the long-barrow style found in the Paris area, with inhumation but with little funeral furniture except the leaf-shaped arrow-head, the manufacture of which goes back to the Old Stone Age; the leaves copied are apparently the crack-willow, or purple osier, and the elder. Sometimes a leaf-shaped 'port-hole' is knocked out between two contiguous slabs of the burial chamber, the leaf copied being apparently the elder.

2000–1500 B.C.

Invasion by a bronze-weaponed, broad-headed, beaker-making, avenue-building people from Spain by way of Southern France and the Rhine. Further immigration of long-heads from the Baltic, and from South-Eastern Europe by way of the Rhine. Cremation and the less ostentatious though better furnished round barrows were introduced. The leaf-shaped arrow-heads persisted, as they did in burials in France until early Imperial times; but the characteristic type was barbed and tanged in the shape of a fir-tree.

1500–600 B.C.

Uninterrupted development of Bronze Age culture. Cross-channel traffic without large-scale invasion, though settlements of iron-weaponed visitors dating from about 800 B.C. are found in the South. Invasion of North Britain by the Picts. Small segmented blue faience beads manufactured in Egypt between 1380 and 1350 B.C. were imported into Wiltshire in large quantities. The language spoken in Britain except by the Picts and Old Stone Age Aboriginals is thought to have been 'proto-Celtic'.

600 B.C.

Invasion by a Goidelic people, identified by their 'frill-comb-smear' pottery, who migrated from the Baltic coast of Germany, entered the Rhineland where they adopted the 'Hallstadt' Iron Age culture, then invaded Britain; but were forced to remain in the South-Eastern counties.

400 B.C.

First Belgic invasion of Britain—'La Tène' Iron Age culture; and of

Ireland between 350 and 300 B.C. These people were a mixture of Teutons and Brythons ('P-Celts') and overran the greater part of the country: they were the ancient British whom the Romans knew. The Druidic culture of Gaul was 'La Tène'.

50 B.C.–45A.D.

Second Belgic invasion. The principal tribesmen were the Atrebates who came from Artois, their settlements being identified by their bead-rimmed bowls. They had their capital at Calleva Atrebatum (Silchester) in North Hampshire, and their area of conquest extended from Western Surrey to the Vale of Trowbridge in Wiltshire, including Salisbury Plain.

If the story of *Câd Goddeu* concerns the capture of the national necropolis on Salisbury Plain from its former holders, this is most likely to have happened during either the first or the second Belgic invasion. Neither the coming of the round-barrow men, nor the Goidelic seizure of South-Eastern Britain, nor the Claudian conquest, which was the last before the coming of the Saxons, corresponds with the story. But according to Geoffrey of Monmouth's mediaeval *History of the Britons* two brothers named Belinus and Brennius fought for the mastery of Britain in the fourth century B.C.; Brennius was beaten and forced north of the Humber. Brennius and Belinus are generally acknowledged to be the gods Bran and Beli; and Beli in the Welsh *Triads* is described as the father of Arianrhod (Silver Wheel'), the sister of Gwydion and Amathaon. Amathaon evidently entered the Battle of the Trees as champion of his father Beli, the Supreme God of Light.

So the *Câd Goddeu* can perhaps be explained as the expulsion of a long-established Bronze Age priesthood from the national necropolis by an alliance of agricultural tribesmen, long settled in Britain and worshippers of the Danaan god Bel, Beli, Belus or Belinus, with an invading Brythonic tribe. The Amathaonians communicated to their Brythonic allies—Professor Sir John Rhys takes Gwydion for a mixed Teuton-Celt deity and equates him with Woden—a religious secret which enabled Amathaon to usurp the place of Bran, the God of Resurrection, a sort of Aesculapius, and Gwydion to usurp that of Arawn King of Annwm, a god of divination and prophecy, and both together to institute a new religious system in the place of the old. That it was Gwydion who usurped Arawn's place is suggested by the cognate myth in the *Romance of Math the Son of Mathonwy* where Gwydion stole the sacred swine from Pryderi, the King of the Pembrokeshire Annwm. Thus the high sprigs of Bran's alder were humbled, and the Dog, Roebuck and Lapwing stolen from Arawn were installed as guardians of the new religious secret. The Amathaonians' motive for betraying their kinsmen to the foreign invaders will be discussed in Chapter Eight.

It appears that Bran's people did not retire, after their spiritual defeat, without offering armed resistance; for the tradition is that 71,000 men fell in battle after the secret was lost.

What sort of a secret? Caesar records that the Gallic Celts claimed descent from 'Dis'—that is to say, from a god of the dead corresponding to Dis in the Latin pantheon—and also worshipped deities corresponding with Minerva, Apollo, Mars, Juppiter and Mercury. Since he also records that the Gallic Druids came to Britain for instruction in religion, the principal seat of the Dis cult was evidently in Britain. The capture of this shrine by a continental tribe was an epoch-making event, for it is clear from Caesar's account that the Druidic 'Dis' was a transcendent god who took precedence of Minerva, Apollo, Mars, Mercury, (to whom we may add Venus and Saturn, the Latin Crow-god, cognate with Aesculapius) and even of Juppiter. And Lucan, a contemporary of Nero's, in his poem *Pharsalia* expressly states that souls, according to the Druids, do not go down to the gloomy Underworld of the Latin Dis, but proceed elsewhere and that death 'is but the mid-point of a long life'.

The British Dis, in fact, was no mere Pluto but a universal god corresponding closely with the Jehovah of the Hebrew prophets. Similarly, it can be argued that since the prime religious ritual of the Druids 'in the service of God Himself', as Pliny records, was bound up with the mistletoe, 'which they call all-heal in their language' and 'which falls from Heaven upon the oak', the name of 'Dis' could not have been Bran, there being no mythic or botanical connexion between the alder and the mistletoe. Thus it is likely that the guessing of Bran's name was merely a clue towards guessing that of the Supreme God: Gwydion did not become Dis, nor did Amathaon; but they together displaced Bran (Saturn) and Arawn (Mercury) in their service of Dis, and redefined his godhead as Beli. But if so, was Dis originally Donnus, in fact Danu?

It happens that we know the Norse name of Gwydion's horse, if Gwydion was indeed Woden, or Odin. It was *Askr Yggr-drasill*, or Ygdrasill, 'the ash-tree that is the horse of Yggr', Yggr being one of Woden's titles. Ygdrasill was the enchanted ash, sacred to Woden, whose roots and branches in Scandinavian mythology extended through the Universe. If Bran had been clever enough at the *Câd Goddeu* he would have pronounced his *englyn* first, with:

> *Sure-hoofed is my steed in the day of battle.*
> *The high sprigs of ash are in thy hand—*
> *Woden thou art, by the branch thou bearest.*

The Battle of the Trees thus ended in a victory of the Ash-god and his ally over the Alder-god and his ally.

The pre-Celtic Annwm from which Gwydion is said to have stolen the sacred swine of King Pryderi, and over which Arawn reigned in the *Romance of Pwyll Prince of Dyred*, was in the Prescelly Mountains of Pembrokeshire. But it is likely that there were at least two Annwms, and that the 'Battle of the Trees' took place at the Annwm in Wiltshire before Gwydion's people invaded South Wales. It would be fallacious to regard Stonehenge as Bran's shrine, because it is an unsuitable site for the worship of an Alder-god. The older, larger, grander Avebury ring thirty miles to the north at the junction of the Kennet and a tributary, is the more likely site; and is proved by the débris removed from the ditch about it to have been in continuous use from the early Bronze Age to Roman times. All the available evidence points to Stonehenge as Beli's seat, not Bran's; it is laid out as a sun-temple in cultured Apollonian style which contrasts strangely with the archaic roughness of Avebury.

Geoffrey records that Bran and Beli (who, he says, gave his name to Billingsgate) were later reconciled, and together fought battles on the Continent. It is possible that troops from Britain served in the successful expedition of the Gauls against Rome in 390 B.C. The Gaulish leader was Brennus—Celtic kings habitually took the name of their tribal gods—and Geoffrey's confused account of subsequent Continental wars undertaken by Bran and Belin evidently refers to the Gaulish invasion of Thrace and Greece in 279 B.C. when Delphi was plundered, the chief commander of the Gauls being another Brennus. At any rate, the alder remained a sacred tree in Britain for long after this *Câd Goddeu*; a King of Kent as late as the fifth century A.D. was named Gwerngen, 'son of the Alder'. The answer to one of the riddles in the 'Taliesin' poem-medley called *Angar Cyvyndawd* ('Hostile Confederacy'), 'Why is the alder of purplish colour?', is doubtless: 'Because Bran wore royal purple.'

The ultimate origin of the god Beli is uncertain, but if we identify the British Belin or Beli with Belus the father of Danäus (as Nennius does), then we can further identify him with Bel, the Babylonian Earth-god, one of a male trinity, who succeeded to the titles of a far more ancient Mesopotamian deity, the mother of Danaë as opposed to the father of Danäus. This was Belili, the Sumerian White Goddess, Ishtar's predecessor, who was a goddess of trees as well as a Moon-goddess, Love-goddess and Underworld-goddess. She was sister and lover to Du'uzu, or Tammuz, the Corn-god and Pomegranate-god. From her name derives the familiar Biblical expression 'Sons of Belial'—the Jews having characteristically altered the non-Semitic name Belili into the Semitic Beliy ya'al ('from which one comes not up again', i.e. the Underworld)—meaning 'Sons of Destruction'. The Slavonic word *beli* meaning 'white' and the Latin *bellus* meaning 'beautiful' are also ultimately connected with her name. Originally every tree was hers, and the Goidelic *bile*, 'sacred tree', the mediaeval Latin *billa* and *billus*, 'branch, trunk of tree', and the English *billet* are all recollections of her name. Above all, she was a Willow-goddess and goddess of wells and springs.

The willow was of great importance in the worship of Jehovah at Jerusalem, and the Great Day of the Feast of Tabernacles, a fire and water ceremony, was called the Day of Willows. Though alder and willow are not differentiated in Hebrew—they are of the same family—Tanaitic tradition, dating from before the destruction of the Temple, prescribed that the red-twigged willow with lanceolate leaves, i.e. the purple osier, should be the sort used in the thyrsus of palm, quince and willow carried during the Feast; if none were obtainable, then the round-leaved willow, i.e. the sallow or 'palm', might be used, but the variety with toothed leaves, i.e. the alder, was forbidden—presumably because it was used in idolatrous rites in honour of Astarte and her son the Fire-god. Although the use of the thyrsus was obligatory, the Israelites having taken it over with the Canaanites' Tabernacle ceremonies and incorporated it in the Mosaic Law, the willow (or osier) was mistrusted by the more intelligent Jews in later days. According to one *Hagadah*, the willow in the thyrsus symbolized the 'inferior and ignorant of Israel who have neither righteousness nor knowledge, as the willow has neither taste nor smell': in fact, even, the indifferent would be provided for by Jehovah.

By his triumphant supersession of Queen Belili, Bel became the Supreme Lord of the Universe, father of the Sun-god and the Moon-god, and claimed to be the Creator: a claim later advanced by the upstart Babylonian god Marduk. Bel and Marduk were finally identified, and since Marduk had been a god of the Spring Sun and of thunder, Bel had similarly become a sort of Solar Zeus before his emigration to Europe from Phoenicia.

It seems then that Beli was originally a Willow-god, a divinatory son of Belili, but became the God of Light, and that in fourth-century B.C. Britain, at the *Câd Goddeu*, his power was invoked by his son Amathaon as a means of supplanting Bran of the alder, whose counterpart had perhaps been similarly supplanted in Palestine. At the same time Gwydion of the ash supplanted Arawn, another divinatory god whose tree is not known. The implications of these peculiar interchanges of divine function will be discussed in a later chapter.

The author of the *Romance of Taliesin* evidently knew Amathaon as 'Llew Llaw', a Brythonic title of Hercules, since he says in the *Cerdd am Veib Llyr* ('Song Concerning the Sons of Llyr'):

> *I was at the* Câd Goddeu *with Llew and Gwydion,*
> *He who transformed timber, earth and plants.*

The case is complicated by occasional bardic references to Beli and the sea which at first sight suggest that he is a Sea-god: the waves are his horses, the brine is his liquor. But this probably honours him as the tutelary deity of Britain, his 'honey isle' as it is called in a *Triad*—no god can rule over an island unless he also commands the adjacent waters—with a hint also that as the Sun-god he 'drinks the waters of the West' every evening at sunset, and that white horses are traditionally sacred to the sun.

The last form in which the famous conflict between Beli and Bran occurs is the story of the brothers Balin and Balan in Malory's *Morte D'Arthur*, who killed each other by mistake. But, as Charles Squire points out in his *Celtic Myth and Legend*, Bran appears in various other disguises in the same jumbled romance. As King Brandegore (Bran of Gower) he brings five thousand men to oppose King Arthur; but as Sir Brandel or Brandiles (Bran of Gwales) he fights valiantly on Arthur's side. As King Ban of Benwyk ('the square enclosure', called 'Caer Pedryvan' in the poem *Preiddeu Annwm* which will be examined in Chapter Six) he is a foreign ally of Arthur's; as Leodegrance—in the Welsh, Ogyr Vran—he is Arthur's father-in-law; and as Uther Ben ('the wonderful head'), which is a reference to the story of the singing head buried on Tower Hill, he is Arthur's father. The Norman-French *trovères* and Malory who collected and collated their Arthurian romances had no knowledge of, or interest in, the historical and religious meaning of the myths that they handled. They felt themselves free to improve the narrative in accordance with their new gospel of chivalry fetched from Provence—breaking up the old mythic patterns and taking liberties of every sort that the Welsh minstrels had never dared to take.

The modern licence claimed by novelists and short-story writers to use their imaginations as freely as they please prevents students of mythology from realizing that in North-Western Europe, where the post-Classical Greek novel was not in circulation, story-tellers did not invent their plots and characters but continually retold the same traditional tales, extemporizing only when their memory was at fault. Unless religious or social change forced a modification of the plot or a modernization of incident, the audience expected to hear the tales told in the accustomed way. Almost all were explanations of ritual or religious theory, overlaid with history: a body of instruction corresponding with the Hebrew Scriptures and having many elements in common with them.

Chapter Four

THE WHITE GODDESS

Since the close connexion here suggested between ancient British, Greek, and Hebrew religion will not be easily accepted, I wish to make it immediately clear that I am not a British Israelite or anything of that sort. My reading of the case is that at different periods in the second millennium B.C. a confederacy of mercantile tribes, called in Egypt 'the People of the Sea', were displaced from the Aegean area by invaders from the north-east and south-east; that some of these wandered north, along already established trade-routes, and eventually reached Britain and Ireland; and that others wandered west, also along established trade-routes, some elements reaching Ireland by way of North Africa and Spain. Still others invaded Syria and Canaan, among them the Philistines, who captured the shrine of Hebron in southern Judaea from the Edomite clan of Caleb; but the Calebites ('Dog-men'), allies of the Israelite tribe of Judah, recovered it about two hundred years later and took over a great part of the Philistine religion at the same time. These borrowings were eventually harmonized in the Pentateuch with a body of Semitic, Indo-European and Asianic myth which composed the religious traditions of the mixed Israelite confederacy. The connexion, then, between the early myths of the Hebrews, the Greeks and the Celts is that all three races were civilized by the same Aegean people whom they conquered and absroved. And this is not of merely antiquarian interest, for the popular appeal of modern Catholicism, is, despite the patriarchal Trinity and the all-male priesthood, based rather on the Aegean Mother-and-Son religious tradition, to which it has slowly reverted, than on its Aramaean or Indo-European 'warrior-god' elements.

To write in greater historical detail about the Danaans. Danu, Danaë, or Dôn, appears in Roman records as Donnus, divine father of Cottius, the sacred king of the Cottians, a Ligurian confederacy that gave its name to the Cottian Alps. Cottys, Cotys, or Cottius is a widely distributed name. Cotys appears as a dynastic title in Thrace between the fourth century B.C. and the first century A.D., and the Cattini and Attacoti of North Britain and many intervening Catt- and Cott- tribes between there and Thrace are held to be of Cottian stock. There was also a Cotys dynasty in

Paphlagonia on the southern shore of the Black Sea. All seem to take their name from the great Goddess Cotytto, or Cotys, who was worshipped orgiastically in Thrace, Corinth and Sicily. Her nocturnal orgies, the Cotyttia, were according to Strabo celebrated in much the same way as those of Demeter, the Barley-goddess of primitive Greece, and of Cybele, the Lion-and-Bee goddess of Phrygia in whose honour young men castrated themselves; in Sicily a feature of the Cotyttia was the carrying of boughs hung with fruit and barley-cakes. In Classical legend Cottys was the hundred-handed brother of the hundred-handed monsters Briareus and Gyes, allies of the God Zeus in his war against the Titans on the borders of Thrace and Thessaly. These monsters were called Hecatontocheiroi ('the hundred-handed ones').

The story of this war against the Titans is intelligible only in the light of early Greek history. The first Greeks to invade Greece were the Achaeans who broke into Thessaly about 1900 B.C.; they were patriarchal herdsmen and worshipped an Indo-European male trinity of gods, originally perhaps Mitra, Varuna and Indra whom the Mitanni of Asia Minor still remembered in 1400 B.C., subsequently called Zeus, Poseidon and Hades. Little by little they conquered the whole of Greece and tried to destroy the semi-matriarchal Bronze Age civilization that they found there, but later compromised with it, accepted matrilinear succession and enrolled themselves as sons of the variously named Great Goddess. They became allies of the very mixed population of the mainland and islands, some of them long-headed, some broad-headed, whom they named 'Pelasgians', or seafarers. The Pelasgians claimed to be born from the teeth of the cosmic snake Ophion whom the Great Goddess in her character of Eurynome ('wide rule') had taken as her lover, thereby initiating the material Creation; but Ophion and Eurynome are Greek renderings of the original names. They may have called themselves Danaans after the same goddess in her character of Danaë, who presided over agriculture. At any rate the Achaeans who had occupied Argolis now also took the name of Danaans, and also became seafarers; while those who remained north of the isthmus of Corinth were known as Ionians, children of the Cow-goddess Io. Of the Pelasgians driven out of Argolis some founded cities in Lesbos, Chios and Cnidos; others escaped to Thrace, the Troad and the North Aegean islands. A few clans remained in Attica, Magn sia and elsewhere.

The most warlike of the remaining Pelasgians were the Centaurs of Magnesia, whose clan totems included the wryneck and mountain lion. They also worshipped the horse, probably not the Asiatic horse brought from the Caspian at the beginning of the second millennium B.C., but an earlier, and inferior, European variety, a sort of Dartmoor pony. The Centaurs under their sacred king Cheiron welcomed Achaean aid against their enemies the Lapiths, of Northern Thessaly. The word 'Cheiron' is apparently connected with the Greek *cheir*, a hand, and 'Centaurs' with *centron*, a goat. In my essay *What Food the Centaurs Ate*, I suggest that they intoxicated themselves by eating 'fly-cap' (*amanita muscaria*), the hundred-clawed toad, an example of which appears, carved on an Etruscan mirror, at the feet of their ancestor Ixion. Were the Hecatontocheiroi the Centaurs of mountainous Magnesia, whose friendship was strategically necessary to the Achaean pastoralists of Thessaly and Boeotia? The Centaurs' mother goddess was called, in Greek, Leucothea, 'the White Goddess', but the Centaurs themselves called her Ino or Plastene, and her rock-cut image is still shown near the ancient pinnacle-town of Tantalus; she had also become the 'mother' of Melicertes, or Hercules Melkarth, the god of earlier semi-Semitic invaders.

The Greeks claimed to remember the date of Zeus's victory in alliance with the Hecatontocheiroi over the Titans of Thessaly: the well-informed Tatian quotes a calculation by the first-century A.D. historian Thallus,[1] that it took place 322 years before the ten-year siege of Troy. Since the fall of Troy was then confidently dated at 1183 B.C., the answer is 1505 B.C. If this date is more or less accurate[2] the legend probably refers to an extension of Achaean power in Thessaly at the expense of Pelasgian tribes, who were driven off to the north. The story of the *Gigantomachia*, the fight of the Olympian gods with the giants, probably refers to a similar but much later occasion, when the Greeks found it necessary to subdue the warlike Magnesians in their fastnesses of Pelion and Ossa—apparently because of trouble caused by their exogamic practices which conflicted with the Olympian patriarchal theory and gave them an undeserved reputation as sexual maniacs; it also records Hercules's charm against the nightmare.

The Achaeans became Cretanized between the seventeenth and fifteenth centuries in the Late Minoan Age, which in Greece is called the Mycenaean, after Mycenae, the capital city of the Atreus dynasty. The Aeolian Greeks invaded Thessaly from the north and were further able to occupy Boeotia and the Western Peloponnese. They settled down amicably with the Achaean Danaans and became known as the Minyans. It is likely that both nations took part in the sack of Cnossos about the year 1400, which ended Cretan sea-power. The reduction of Crete, by now become largely Greek-speaking, resulted in a great expansion of Mycenaean power:

---

[1] Thallus gives the earliest historical record of the Crucifixion.

[2] A. R. Burn in his *Minoans, Philistines and Greeks* suggests that all traditional dates before 500 B.C. should be reduced to five-sixths of their distance from that date, since the Greeks reckoned three generations to a century, when four would be nearer the mark. However, Walter Leaf approves of 1183 B.C. as the date of the Fall of Troy, because the curse of one thousand years that had fallen on the city of Ajax in punishment for his rape of the Trojan priestess Cassandra was lifted about 183 B.C. The date now favoured by most archaeologists is 1230 B.C.

conquests in Asia Minor, Phoenicia, Libya and the Aegean islands. About the year 1250 B.C. a distinction arose between the Achaean Danaans and other less civilized Achaeans from North-western Greece who invaded the Peloponnese, founded a new patriarchal dynasty, repudiated the sovereignty of the Great Goddess, and instituted the familiar Olympian pantheon, ruled over by Zeus, in which gods and goddesses were equally represented. Myths of Zeus's quarrels with his wife Hera (a name of the Great Goddess), with his brother Poseidon, and with Apollo of Delphi, suggest that the religious revolution was at first strongly resisted by the Danaans and Pelasgians. But a united Greece captured Troy, at the entrance to the Dardanelles, a city which had taken toll of their commerce with the Black Sea and the East. A generation after the fall of Troy, another Indo-European horde pressed down into Asia Minor and Europe —among them the Dorians who invaded Greece, killing, sacking and burning—and a great tide of fugitives was let loose in all directions.

Thus we may, without historical qualms, identify Danu of the Tuatha dé Danaan, who were Bronze Age Pelasgians expelled from Greece in the middle of the second millennium, with the pre-Achaean Goddess Danaë of Argos. Her power extended to Thessaly, and she mothered the early Achaean dynasty called the House of Perseus (more correctly *Pterseus*, 'the destroyer'); but by Homer's time Danaë was masculinized into 'Danäus, son of Belus', who was said to have brought his 'daughters' to Greece from Libya by way of Egypt, Syria and Rhodes. The names of the three daughters, Linda, Cameira and Ialysa, are evidently titles of the Goddess, who also figures as 'Lamia, daughter of Belus, a Libyan Queen'. In the well-known legend of the massacre of the sons of Aegyptus on their wedding night the number of these daughters of Danäus, or Danaids, is enlarged from three to fifty, probably because that was the regular number of priestesses in the Argive and Elian colleges of the Mother-goddess cult. The original Danaans may well have come up to the Aegean from Lake Tritonis in Libya (now a salt marsh), by the route given in the legend, though it is unlikely that they were so called until they reached Syria. That the Cottians, who came to Northern Greece from the Black Sea by way of Phrygia and Thrace, were also reckoned as Danaans, proves that they arrived there before the Aeolians, who were not so reckoned. A. B. Cook in his *Zeus* gives strong reasons for believing that the Graeco-Libyans and the Thraco-Phrygians were related, and that both tribal groups had relatives among the early Cretans.

We may further identify Danu with the Mother-goddess of the Aegean 'Danuna', a people who about the year 1200 B.C., according to contemporary Egyptian inscriptions, invaded Northern Syria in company with the Sherdina and Zakkala of Lydia, the Shakalsha of Phrygia, the Pulesati of Lycia, the Akaiwasha of Pamphylia, and other Eastern

Mediterranean peoples. To the Egyptians these were all 'Peoples of the Sea'—the Akaiwasha are Achaeans—forced by the pressure of the new Indo-European horde to emigrate from the coastal parts of Asia Minor as well as from Greece and the Aegean islands. The Pulesati became the Philistines of Southern Phoenicia; they were mixed with Cherethites (Cretans), some of whom served in King David's bodyguard at Jerusalem —possibly Greek-speaking Cretans, Sir Arthur Evans suggests. One emigrant people, the conquerors of the Hittites, known to the Assyrians as the Muski and to the Greeks as the Moschians, established themselves on the Upper Euphrates at Hierapolis. Lucian's account in his *De Dea Syria* of the antique rites still practised in the second century A.D. at their temple of the Great Goddess gives the clearest picture of Aegean Bronze Age religion that has been preserved. Tribes or clans of the same confederacy drifted westward to Sicily, Italy, North Africa, Spain. The Zakkala became the Sicels of Sicily; the Sherdina gave their name to Sardinia; the Tursha are the Tursenians (or Tyrrhenians) of Etruria.

Some Danaans seem to have travelled west, since Silius Italicus, a first-century Latin poet, said to have been a Spaniard, records a tradition that the Balearic islands—a centre of megalithic culture and one of the chief sources of tin in the ancient world—were first made into a kingdom by the Danaans Tleptolemus and Lindus. Lindus is a masculization of the Danaan Linda. At least one part of the people remained in Asia Minor. Recently a Danaan city has been discovered in the foothills of the Taurus Mountains near Alexandretta and the inscriptions (not yet deciphered) are in Hittite hieroglyphs of the ninth century B.C. and in Aramaic script. The language is thought to be Canaanitish and the sculptures are a mixture of Assyrio-Hittite, Egyptian and Aegean styles; which bears out the Greek account of Danaus as a son of Agenor (Canaan) who came up north from Libya by way of Egypt and Syria.

The myth of the emasculation of Uranus by his son Cronos and the vengeance subsequently taken on Cronos by his son Zeus, who banished him to the Western Underworld under charge of the 'hundred-handed ones', is not an easy one to disentangle. In its original sense it records the annual supplanting of the old oak-king by his successor. Zeus was at one time the name of a herdsmen's oracular hero, connected with the oak-tree cult of Dodona in Epirus, which was presided over by the dove-priestesses of Dionë, a woodland Great Goddess, otherwise known as Diana. The theory of Frazer's *Golden Bough* is familiar enough to make this point unnecessary to elaborate at length, though Frazer does not clearly explain that the cutting of the mistletoe from the oak by the Druids typified the emasculation of the old king by his successor—the mistletoe being a prime phallic emblem. The king himself was eucharistically eaten after castration, as several legends of the Pelopian dynasty testify; but in the Peloponnese at least this oak-tree cult had been superimposed on a barley-cult of which Cronos was the hero, and in which human sacrifice was also the rule. In the barley-cult, as in the oak-cult, the successor to the kingship inherited the favours of the priestesses of his Goddess mother. In both cults the victim became an immortal, and his oracular remains were removed for burial to some sacred island—such as Samothrace, Lemnos, Pharos near Alexandria, Ortygia the islet near Delos, the other Ortygia[1] off Sicily, Leuce off the mouth of the Danube, where Achilles had a shrine, Circe's Aeaea (now Lussin in the Adriatic), the Atlantic Elysium where Menelaus went after death, and the distant Ogygia, perhaps Torrey Island off the west coast of Ireland—under the charge of magic-making and orgiastic priestesses.

That Cronos the emasculator was deposed by his son Zeus is an economical statement: the Achaean herdsmen who on their arrival in Northern Greece had identified their Sky-god with the local oak-hero gained ascendancy over the Pelasgian agriculturalists. But there was a compromise between the two cults. Dionë, or Diana, of the woodland was identified with Danaë of the barley; and that an inconvenient golden sickle, not a bill-hook of flint or obsidian, was later used by the Gallic Druids for lopping the mistletoe, proves that the oak-ritual had been combined with that of the barley-king whom the Goddess Danaë, or Alphito, or Demeter, or Ceres, reaped with her moon-shaped sickle. Reaping meant castration; similarly, the Galla warriors of Abyssinia carry a miniature sickle into battle for castrating their enemies. The Latin Cronos was called Saturn and in his statues he was armed with a pruning-knife crooked like a crow's bill: probably a rebus on his name. For though the later Greeks liked to think that the name meant *chronos*, 'time', because any very old man was humorously called 'Cronos', the more likely derivation is from the same root *cron* or *corn* that gives the Greek and Latin words for crow—*corone* and *cornix*. The crow was a bird much consulted by augurs and symbolic, in Italy as in Greece, of long life. Thus it is possible that another name for Cronos, the sleeping Titan, guarded by the hundred-headed Briareus, was Bran, the Crow-god. The Cronos myth, at any rate, is ambivalent: it records the supersession and ritual murder, in both oak and barley cults, of the Sacred King at the close of his term of office; and it records the conquest by the Achaean herdsmen of the pre-Achaean husbandmen of Greece. At the Roman *Saturnalia* in Republican times, a festival corresponding with the

[1] There was a third Ortygia ('quail place'). According to Tacitus, the Ephesians in their plea before the Emperor Tiberius for the right of asylum in the Artemisian precinct, stated that the cult of their Great Goddess Artemis (whom the Romans called Diana) was derived from Ortygia, where her name was then Leto. Dr. D. G. Hogarth places this Ortygia in the Arvalian Valley to the north of Mount Solmissos, but the suggestion is not plausible unless, like the islets of the same name, it was a resting place for quail in the Spring migration from Africa.

old English Yule, all social restraints were temporarily abandoned in memory of the golden reign of Cronos.

I call Bran a Crow-god, but crow, raven, scald-crow and other large black carrion birds are not always differentiated in early times. *Corone* in Greek also included the *corax*, or raven; and the Latin *corvus*, raven, comes from the same root as *cornix*, crow. The crows of Bran, Cronos, Saturn, Aesculapius and Apollo are, equally, ravens.

The fifty Danaids appear in early British history. John Milton in his *Early Britain* scoffs ponderously at the legend preserved by Nennius that Britain derives its earliest name, Albion, by which it was known to Pliny, from Albina ('the White Goddess'), the eldest of the Danaids. The name Albina, a form of which was also given to the River Elbe (*Albis* in Latin); and which accounts for the Germanic words *elven*, an elf-woman, *alb*, elf and *alpdrücken*, the nightmare or incubus, is connected with the Greek words *alphos*, meaning 'dull-white leprosy'[1] (Latin *albus*), *alphiton*, 'pearl-barley', and *Alphito*, 'the White Goddess', who in Classical times had degenerated into a nursery bugbear but who seems originally to have been the Danaan Barley-goddess of Argos. Sir James Frazer regards her as 'either Demeter or her double, Persephone'. The word 'Argos' itself means 'shimmering white', and is the conventional adjective to describe white priestly vestments. It also means 'quick as a flash'. That we are justified in connecting the hundred-armed men with the White Goddess of Argos is proved by the myth of Io, the same goddess, nurse to the infant Dionysus, who was guarded by Argus Panoptes ('all-eyes'), the hundred-eyed monster, probably represented as a white dog; Argo was the name of Odysseus's famous dog. Io was the white cow aspect of the Goddess as Barley-goddess. She was also worshipped as a white mare, Leucippe, and as a white sow, Choere or Phorcis, whose more polite title was Marpessa, 'the snatcher'.

Now, in the *Romance of Taliesin*, Gwion's enemy Caridwen, or Cerri-dwen, was a white Sow-goddess too, according to Dr. MacCulloch who, in his well-documented *Religion of the Ancient Celts*, quotes Geoffrey of Monmouth and the French Celtologist Thomas in evidence and records that she was also described by Welsh bards as a Grain-goddess; he equates her with the Sow Demeter mentioned above. Her name is composed of the words *cerdd* and *wen*. *Wen* means 'white', and *cerdd* in Irish and Welsh

---

[1] The White Hill, or Tower Hill, at London preserves Albina's memory, the Keep built in 1078 by Bishop Gundulf being still called the White Tower. Herman Melville in his *Moby Dick* devotes an eloquent chapter to a consideration of the contradictory emotions aroused by the word 'white'—the grace, splendour and purity of milk-white steeds, white sacrificial bulls, snowy bridal veils and white priestly vestments, as opposed to the nameless horror aroused by albinos, lepers, visitants in white hoods and so forth—and records that the blood of American visitors to Tower Hill is far more readily chilled by 'This is the White Tower', than by 'This is the Bloody Tower.' Moby Dick was an albino whale.

means 'gain' and also 'the inspired arts, especially poetry', like the Greek words *cerdos* and *cerdeia*, from which derives the Latin *cerdo*, a craftsman. In Greek, the weasel, a favourite disguise of Thessalian witches, was called *cedro*, usually translated 'the artful one'; and *cerdo*, an ancient word of uncertain origin, is the Spanish for 'pig'[1]. Pausanias makes Cerdo the wife of the Argive cult-hero Phoroneus, the inventor of fire and brother of both Io and Argus Panoptes, who will be identified in Chapter Ten with Bran. The famous *cerdaña* harvest-dance of the Spanish Pyrenees was perhaps first performed in honour of this Goddess, who has given her name to the best corn-land in the region, the valley of Cerdaña, dominated by the town of Puigcerdá, or Cerdo's Hill. The syllable *Cerd* figures in Iberian royal names, the best known of which is Livy's Cerdubelus, the aged chieftain who intervened in a dispute between the Romans and the Iberian city of Castulo. Cerridwen is clearly the White Sow, the Barley-goddess, the White Lady of Death and Inspiration; is, in fact, Albina, or Alphito, the Barley-goddess who gave her name to Britain. Little Gwion had every reason to fear her; it was a great mistake on his part to try to conceal himself in a heap of grain on her own threshing floor.

The Latins worshipped the White Goddess as Cardea, and Ovid tells a muddled story about her in his *Fasti*, connecting her with the word *cardo*, a hinge. He says that she was the mistress of Janus, the two-headed god of doors and of the first month of the year, and had charge over door-hinges. She also protected infants against witches disguised as formidable night-birds who snatched children from their cradles and sucked their blood. He says that she exercised this power first at Alba ('the white city'), which was colonized by emigrants from the Peloponnese at the time of the great dispersal, and from which Rome was colonized, and that her principal prophylactic instrument was the hawthorn. Ovid's story is inside out: Cardea was Alphito, the White Goddess who destroyed children after disguising herself in bird or beast form, and the hawthorn which was sacred to her might not be introduced into a house lest she destroyed the children inside. It was Janus, 'the stout guardian of the oak door', who kept out Cardea and her witches, for Janus was really the oak-god Dianus who was incarnate in the King of Rome and after-wards in the Flamen Dialis, his spiritual successor; and his wife Jana was Diana (Dione) the goddess of the woods and of the moon. Janus and Jana were in fact a rustic form of Juppiter and Juno. The reduplicated *p* in Juppiter represents an elided *n*: he was Jun-pater—father Dianus. But before Janus, or Dianus, or Juppiter, married Jana or Diana or Juno, and put her under subjection, he was her son, and she was the White Goddess

---

[1] *Cerdo* is said to be derived from *Setula*, 'a little sow', but the violent metathesis of consonants that has to be assumed to make this derivation good cannot be paralleled in the names of other domestic animals.

Cardea. And though he became the Door, the national guardian, she became the hinge which connected him with the door-post; the importance of this relationship will be explained in Chapter Ten. *Cardo*, the hinge, is the same word as *cerdo*, craftsman—in Irish myth the god of craftsmen who specialized in hinges, locks and rivets was called *Credne*—the craftsman who originally claimed the goddess Cerdo or Cardea as his patroness. Thus as Janus's mistress, Cardea was given the task of keeping from the door the nursery bogey who in matriarchal times was her own august self and who was propitiated at Roman weddings with torches of hawthorn. Ovid says of Cardea, apparently quoting a religious formula: 'Her power is to open what is shut; to shut what is open.'

Ovid identifies Cardea with the goddess Carnea who had a feast at Rome on June 1, when pig's flesh and beans were offered to her. This is helpful in so far as it connects the White Goddess with pigs, though the Roman explanation that Carnea was so called *quod carnem offerunt* ('because they offer her flesh') is nonsense. Moreover, as has already been noted in the *Câd Goddeu* context, beans were used in Classical times as a homoeopathic charm against witches and spectres: one put a bean in one's mouth and spat it at the visitant; and at the Roman feast of the *Lemuria* each householder threw black beans behind his back for the *Lemures*, or ghosts, saying: 'With these I redeem myself and my family.' The Pythagorean mystics, who derived their doctrine from Pelasgian sources,[1] were bound by a strong taboo against the eating of beans and quoted a verse attributed to Orpheus, to the effect that to eat beans was to eat one's parents' heads.[2] The flower of the bean is white, and it blooms at the same season as the hawthorn. The bean is the White Goddess's— hence its connexion with the Scottish witch cult; in primitive times only her priestesses might either plant or cook it. The men of Pheneus in Arcadia had a tradition that the Goddess Demeter, coming there in her wanderings, gave them permission to plant all grains and pulses except only beans. It seems, then, that the reason for the Orphic taboo was that the bean grows spirally up its prop, portending resurrection, and that ghosts contrived to be reborn as humans by entering into beans—Pliny mentions this—and being eaten by women; thus, for a man to eat a bean might be an impious frustration of his dead parents' designs. Beans were

[1] Pythagoras is said to have been a Tyrrhenian Pelasgian from Samos in the Northern Aegean. This would account for the close connection of his philosophy with the Orphic and Druidic. He is credited with having refrained not only from beans but from fish, and seems to have developed an inherited Pelasgian cult by travel among other nations. His theory of the transmigration of souls is Indian rather than Pelasgian. At Crotona he was accepted, like his successor Empedocles, as a reincarnation of Apollo.

[2] The Platonists excused their abstention from beans on the rationalistic ground that they caused flatulence; but this came to much the same thing. Life was breath, and to break wind after eating beans was a proof that one had eaten a living soul—in Greek and Latin the same words, *anima* and *pneuma*, stand equally for gust of wind, breath and soul or spirit.

tossed to ghosts by Roman householders at the *Lemuria* to give them a chance of rebirth; and offered to the Goddess Carnea at her festival because she held the keys of the Underworld.

Carnea is generally identified with the Roman goddess Cranaë, who was really Cranaea, 'the harsh or stony one', a Greek surname of the Goddess Artemis whose hostility to children had constantly to be appeased. Cranaea owned a hill-temple near Delphi in which the office of priest was always held by a boy, for a five-year term; and a cypress-grove, the Cranaeum, just outside Corinth, where Bellerophon had a hero-shrine. Cranaë means 'rock' and is etymologically connected with the Gaelic 'cairn' —which has come to mean a pile of stones erected on a mountain-top.

I write of her as the White Goddess because white is her principal colour, the colour of the first member of her moon-trinity, but when Suidas the Byzantine records that Io was a cow that changed her colour from white to rose and then to black he means that the New Moon is the white goddess of birth and growth; the Full Moon, the red goddess of love and battle; the Old Moon, the black goddess of death and divination. Suidas's myth is supported by Hyginus's fable of a heifer-calf born to Minos and Pasiphaë which changed its colours thrice daily in the same way. In response to a challenge from an oracle one Polyidus son of Coeranus correctly compared it to a mulberry—a fruit sacred to the Triple Goddess. The three standing stones thrown down from Moeltre Hill near Dwygyfylchi in Wales in the iconoclastic seventeenth century may well have represented the Io trinity. One was white, one red, one dark blue, and they were known as the three women. The local monkish legend was that three women dressed in those colours were petrified as a punishment for winnowing corn on a Sunday.

The most comprehensive and inspired account of the Goddess in all ancient literature is contained in Apuleius's *Golden Ass,* where Lucius invokes her from the depth of misery and spiritual degradation and she appears in answer to his plea; incidentally it suggests that the Goddess was once worshipped at Moeltre in her triple capacity of white raiser, red reaper and dark winnower of grain. The translation is by William Adlington (1566):

About the first watch of the night when as I had slept my first sleep, I awaked with sudden fear and saw the moon shining bright as when she is at the full and seeming as though she leaped out of the sea. Then I thought with myself that this was the most secret time, when that goddess had most puissance and force, considering that all human things be governed by her providence; and that not only all beasts private and tame, wild and savage, be made strong by the governance of her light and godhead, but also things inanimate and without life; and I considered that all bodies in the heavens, the earth, and the seas be by her increasing motions increased, and by her diminishing motions diminished: then as weary of all my cruel fortune and calamity, I found good hope and sovereign remedy, though it were very late, to be delivered from my misery, by invocation and prayer to the excellent beauty of this powerful goddess. Wherefore, shaking off my drowsy sleep I arose with a joyful face, and moved by a great affection to purify myself, I plunged my head seven times into the water of the sea; which number seven is convenable and agreeable to holy and divine things, as the worthy and sage philosopher Pythagoras hath declared. Then very lively and joyfully, though with a weeping countenance, I made this oration to the puissant goddess.

'O blessed Queen of Heaven, whether thou be the Dame Ceres which art the original and motherly source of all fruitful things on the earth, who after the finding of thy daughter Proserpine, through the great joy which thou didst presently conceive, didst utterly take away and abolish the food of them of old time, the acorn, and madest the barren and unfruitful ground of Eleusis to be ploughed and sown, and now givest men a more better and milder food; or whether thou be the celestial Venus, who, at the beginning of the world, didst couple together male and female with an engendered love, and didst so make an eternal propagation of human kind, being now worshipped within the temples of the Isle Paphos; or whether thou be the sister of the God Phoebus, who hast saved so many people by lightening and lessening with thy medicines the pangs of travail and art now adored at the sacred places of Ephesus; or whether thou be called terrible Proserpine by reason of the deadly howlings which thou yieldest, that hast power with triple face to stop and put away the invasion of hags and ghosts which appear unto men, and to keep them down in the closures of the Earth, which dost wander in sundry groves and art worshipped in divers manners; thou, which dost illuminate all the cities of the earth by thy feminine light; thou, which nourishest all the seeds of the world by thy damp heat, giving thy changing light according to the wanderings, near or far, of the sun: by whatsoever name or fashion or shape it is lawful to call upon thee, I pray thee to end my great travail and misery and raise up my fallen hopes, and deliver me from the wretched fortune which so long time pursued me. Grant peace and rest, if it please thee, to my adversities, for I have endured enough labour and peril. . . .'

When I had ended this oration, discovering my plaints to the goddess, I fortuned to fall again asleep upon that same bed; and by and by (for mine eyes were but newly closed) appeared to me from the midst of the sea a divine and venerable face, worshipped even of the gods themselves. Then, little by little, I seemed to see the whole figure of her body, bright and mounting out of the sea and standing before me: wherefore

I purpose to describe her divine semblance, if the poverty of my human speech will suffer me, or the divine power give me a power of eloquence rich enough to express it. First, she had a great abundance of hair, flowing and curling, dispersed and scattered about her divine neck; on the crown of her head she bare many garlands interlaced with flowers, and in the middle of her forehead was a plain circlet in fashion of a mirror, or rather resembling the moon by the light it gave forth; and this was borne up on either side by serpents that seemed to rise from the furrows of the earth, and above it were blades of corn set out. Her vestment was of finest linen yielding diverse colours, somewhere white and shining, somewhere yellow like the crocus flower, somewhere rosy red, somewhere flaming; and (which troubled my sight and spirit sore) her cloak was utterly dark and obscure covered with shining black, and being wrapped round her from under her left arm to her right shoulder in manner of a shield, part of it fell down, pleated in most subtle fashion, to the skirts of her garment so that the welts appeared comely. Here and there upon the edge thereof and throughout its surface the stars glimpsed, and in the middle of them was placed the moon in midmonth, which shone like a flame of fire; and round about the whole length of the border of that goodly robe was a crown or garland wreathing unbroken, made with all flowers and all fruits. Things quite diverse did she bear: for in her right hand she had a timbrel of brass [*sistrum*], a flat piece of metal carved in manner of a girdle, wherein passed not many rods through the periphery of it; and when with her arm she moved these triple chords, they gave forth a shrill and clear sound. In her left hand she bare a cup of gold like unto a boat, upon the handle whereof, in the upper part which is best seen, an asp lifted up his head with a wide-swelling throat. Her odoriferous feet were covered with shoes interlaced and wrought with victorious palm. Thus the divine shape, breathing out the pleasant spice of fertile Arabia, disdained not with her holy voice to utter these words to me:

'Behold, Lucius, I am come; thy weeping and prayer hath moved me to succour thee. I am she that is the natural mother of all things, mistress and governess of all the elements, the initial progeny of worlds, chief of the powers divine, queen of all that are in Hell, the principal of them that dwell in Heaven, manifested alone and under one form of all the gods and goddesses [*deorum dearum-que facies uniformis*]. At my will the planets of the sky, the wholesome winds of the seas, and the lamentable silences of hell be disposed; my name, my divinity is adored throughout the world, in divers manners, in variable customs, and by many names. For the Phrygians that are the first of all men call me The Mother of the Gods at Pessinus; the Athenians, which are spring from their own soil, Cecropian Minerva; the Cyprians, which are girt about by the sea, Paphian Venus; the Cretans which bear arrows, Dictynnian Diana; the Sicilians, which speak three tongues, Infernal Proserpine; the Eleusinians, their ancient goddess Ceres; some Juno, other Bellona, other Hecate, other Rhamnusia, and principally both sort of the Ethiopians which dwell in the Orient and are enlightened by the morning rays of the sun, and the Egyptians, which are excellent in all kind of ancient doctrine and by their proper ceremonies accustom to worship me, do call me by my true name, Queen Isis. Behold, I am come to take pity of thy fortune and turbulation; behold I am present to favour and aid thee; leave off thy weeping and lamentation, put away all thy sorrow, for behold the healthful day which is ordained by my providence.'

Much the same prayer is found in Latin in a twelfth-century English herbal (*Brit. Mus. MS. Harley*, 1585, *ff* 12*v*–13*r*):

Earth, divine goddess, Mother Nature, who dost generate all things and bringest forth ever anew the sun which thou hast given to the nations; Guardian of sky and sea and of all Gods and powers; through thy influence all nature is hushed and sinks to sleep. . . . Again, when it pleases thee, thou sendest forth the glad daylight and nurturest life with thine eternal surety; and when the spirit of man passes, to thee it returns. Thou indeed art rightly named Great Mother of the Gods; Victory is in thy divine name. Thou art the source of the strength of peoples and gods; without thee nothing can either be born or made perfect; thou art mighty, Queen of the Gods. Goddess, I adore thee as divine, I invoke thy name; vouchsafe to grant that which I ask of thee, so shall I return thanks to thy godhead, with the faith that is thy due. . . .

Now also I make intercession to you, all ye powers and herbs, and to your majesty: I beseech you, whom Earth the universal parent hath borne and given as a medicine of health to all peoples and hath put majesty upon, be now of the most benefit to humankind. This I pray and beseech you: be present here with your virtues, for she who created you hath herself undertaken that I may call you with the good will of him on whom the art of medicine was bestowed; therefore grant for health's sake good medicine by grace of these powers aforesaid. . . .

How the god of medicine was named in twelfth-century pagan England is difficult to determine; but he clearly stood in the same relation to the Goddess invoked in the prayers as Aesculapius originally stood to Athene, Thoth to Isis, Esmun to Ishtar, Diancecht to Brigit, Odin to Freya, and Bran to Danu.

Chapter Five

GWION'S RIDDLE

When with this complicated mythological argument slowly forming in my mind, I turned again to the *Hanes Taliesin* ('The Tale of Taliesin'), the riddling poem with which Taliesin first addresses King Maelgwyn in the Romance, I already suspected that Gwion was using the Dog, the Lapwing and the Roebuck to help him conceal in his riddle the new Gwydionian secret of the Trees, which he had somehow contrived to learn, and which had invested him with poetic power. Reading the poem with care, I soon realized that here again, as in the *Câd Goddeu*, Gwion was no irresponsible rhapsodist, but a true poet; and that whereas Heinin and his fellow-bards, as stated in the Romance, knew only 'Latin, French, Welsh and English', he was well read also in the Irish classics—and in Greek and Hebrew literature too, as he himself claims:

> *Tracthator fyngofeg*
> *Yn Efrai, yn Efroeg,*
> *Yn Efroeg, yn Efrai.*

I realized too, that he was hiding an ancient religious mystery—a blasphemous one from the Church's point of view—under the cloak of buffoonery, but had not made this secret altogether impossible for a well-educated fellow-poet to guess.

I here use the name 'Gwion' for 'Taliesin', to make it quite clear that I am not confusing the miraculous child Taliesin of the *Romance of Taliesin* with the historic Taliesin of the late sixth century, a group of whose authentic poems is contained in the *Red Book of Hergest*, and who is noticed by Nennius, in a quotation from a seventh-century genealogy of the Saxon Kings, as 'renowned in British poetry'. The first Taliesin spent much of his time during the last third of the sixth century as a guest of various chiefs and princes to whom he wrote complimentary poems (Urien ap Cynvarch, Owein ap Urien Gwallag ap Laenaug, Cynan Garwyn ap Brochfael Ysgythrog, King of Powys, and the High King Rhun ap Maelgwn until he was killed by the Coeling in a drunken quarrel). He went with Rhun in the first campaign against the men of the

North, the occasion of which was the killing of Elidir (Heliodorus) Mwynfawr, and the avenging raid of Clydno Eiddin, Rhydderch Hael (or Hen) and others, to which Rhun retaliated with a full-scale invasion. This Taliesin calls the English 'Eingl' or 'Deifyr' (Deirans) as often as he calls them 'Saxons', and the Welsh 'Brython' not 'Cymry'. 'Gwion' wrote about six centuries later, at the close of the Period of the Princes.

In his *Lectures on Early Welsh Poetry*, Dr. Ifor Williams, the greatest living authority on the text of the Taliesin poems, postulates from internal literary evidence that parts of the Romance existed in a ninth-century original. I do not dispute this, or his conclusion that the author was a paganistic cleric with Irish connexions; but must dispute his denial that there is 'any mysticism, semi-mysticism, or demi-semi-mysticism, in the poems and that the whole rigmarole can be easily explained as follows:

> Taliesin is just showing off; like the Kangaroo in Kipling's story— he had to! That was the rôle he had to play.

As a scholar, Dr. Williams naturally feels more at home with the earlier Taliesin, who was a straight-forward court bard of the skaldic sort. But the point of the Romance to me is not that a pseudo-Taliesin humorously boasted himself omniscient, but that someone who styled himself Little Gwion, son of Gwreang of Llanfair in Caereinion, a person of no importance, accidentally lighted on certain ancient mysteries and, becoming an adept, began to despise the professional bards of his time because they did not understand the rudiments of their traditional poetic lore. Proclaiming himself a master-poet, Gwion took the name of Taliesin, as an ambitious Hellenistic Greek poet might have taken the name of Homer. 'Gwion son of Gwreang' is itself probably a pseudonym, not the baptismal name of the author of the Romance. Gwion is the equivalent (*gw* for *f*) of Fionn, or Finn, the Irish hero of a similar tale. Fionn son of Mairne, a Chief Druid's daughter, was instructed by a Druid of the same name as himself to cook for him a salmon fished from a deep pool of the River Boyne, and forbidden to taste it; but as Fionn was turning the fish over in the pan he burned his thumb, which he put into his mouth and so received the gift of inspiration. For the salmon was a salmon of knowledge, that had fed on nuts fallen from the nine hazels of poetic art. The equivalent of Gwreang is Freann, an established variant of Fearn, the alder. Gwion is thus claiming oracular powers as a spiritual son of the Alder-god Bran. His adoption of a pseudonym was justified by tradition. The hero Cuchulain ('hound of Culain') was first named Setanta and was a reincarnation of the god Lugh; and Fionn ('fair') himself was first named Deimne. Bran was a most suitable father for Gwion, for by this time he was known as the Giant Ogyr Vran, Guinevere's father—his name, which means 'Bran the Malign' (*ocur vran*),[1] has apparently given English the word 'ogre' through Perrault's *Fairy Tales*—and was credited by the bards with the invention of their art and with the ownership of the Cauldron of Cerridwen from which they said that the Triple Muse had been born. And Gwion's mother was Cerridwen herself.

It is a pity that one cannot be sure whether the ascription of the romance in an *Iolo* manuscript printed by the *Welsh MSS. Society*, to one 'Thomas ap Einion Offeiriad, a descendant of Gruffydd Gwyr', is to be trusted. This manuscript, called 'Anthony Powel of Llwydarth's MS.', reads authentically enough—unlike the other notices of Taliesin printed by Lady Guest, on Iolo Morganwg's authority, in her notes to the *Romance of Taliesin*:

Taliesin, Chief of the Bards, the son of Saint Henwg of Caerlleon upon Usk, was invited to the court of Urien Rheged, at Aberllychwr. He, with Elffin, the son of Urien, being once fishing at sea in a skin coracle, an Irish pirate ship seized him and his coracle, and bore him away towards Ireland; but while the pirates were at the height of their drunken mirth, Taliesin pushed his coracle to the sea, and got into it himself, with a shield in his hand which he found in the ship, and with which he rowed the coracle until it verged the land; but, the waves breaking then in wild foam, he lost his hold on the shield, so that he had no alternative but to be driven at the mercy of the sea, in which state he continued for a short time, when the coracle stuck to the point of a pole in the weir of Gwyddno, Lord of Ceredigion, in Aberdyvi; and in that position he was found, at the ebb, by Gwyddno's fishermen, by whom he was interrogated; and when it was ascertained that he was a bard, and the tutor of Elffin, the son of Urien Rheged, the son of Cynvarch: 'I, too, have a son named Elffin,' said Gwyddno, 'be thou a bard and teacher to him, also, and I will give thee lands in free tenure.' The terms were accepted, and for several successive years he spent his time between the courts of Urien Rheged and Gwyddno, called Gwyddno Garanhir, Lord of the Lowland Cantred; but after the territory of Gwyddno had become overwhelmed by the sea, Taliesin was invited by the Emperor Arthur to his court at Caerlleon upon Usk, where he became highly celebrated for poetic genius and useful, meritorious sciences. After Arthur's death he retired to the estate given to him by Gwyddno, taking Elffin, the son of that prince, under his protection. It was from this account that Thomas, the son of Einion Offeiriad, descended from Gruffyd Gwyr, formed his romance of

[1] The syllable *ocur*, like the Old Spanish word for a man-eating demon, Huergo or Uergo, is probably cognate with *Orcus*, the Latin God of the Dead, originally a masculinization of Phorcis, the Greek Sow-Demeter.

Taliesin, the son of Cariadwen—Elffin, the son of Goddnou—Rhun, the son of Maelgwn Gwynedd, and the operations of the Cauldron of Ceridwen.

If this is a genuine mediaeval document, not an eighteenth-century forgery, it refers to a muddled tradition about the sixth-century poet Taliesin and accounts for the finding of the Divine Child in the weir near Aberdovey rather than anywhere else. But probably 'Gwion' was more than one person, for the poem *Yr Awdyl Vraith*, which is given in full in Chapter Nine, is ascribed in the *Peniardd MS.* to Jonas Athraw, the 'Doctor' of Menevia (St. David's), who lived in the thirteenth century. A complimentary reference to the See of St. David's concealed in the *Hanes Taliesin* supports this ascription. (Menevia is the Latin form of the original name of the place, *Hen Meneu,* 'the old bush'; which suggests the cult of a Hawthorn-goddess.)

Dr. Williams explains the confused state of the texts of the poems contained in the Romance by suggesting that they are the surviving work of the *Awenyddion* of the twelfth century, described by Giraldus Cambrensis:

There are certain persons in Cambria, whom you will find nowhere else, called *Awenyddion*, or people inspired; when consulted upon any doubtful event, they roar out violently, are rendered beside themselves, and become, as it were, possessed by a spirit. They do not deliver the answer to what is required in a connected manner; but the person who skilfully observes them will find, after many preambles, and many nugatory and incoherent though ornamented speeches, the desired explanation conveyed in some turn of word; they are then roused from their ecstasy, as from a deep sleep, and, as it were, by violence compelled to return to their proper senses. After having answered the question they do not recover until violently shaken by other people; nor can they remember the replies they have given. If consulted a second or third time upon the same point, they will make use of expressions totally different; perhaps they speak by means of fanatic and ignorant spirits. These gifts are usually conferred upon them in dreams; some seem to have sweet milk and honey poured on their lips; others fancy that a written schedule is applied to their mouths, and on awakening they publicly declare that they have received this gift. . . . They invoke, during their prophecies, the true and living God, and the Holy Trinity, and pray that they may not by their sins be prevented from finding the truth. These prophets are found only among those Britons who are descended from the Trojans.

The *Awenyddion,* the popular minstrels, may indeed have disguised their secrets by a pretence of being possessed by spirits, as the Irish poets are recorded to have done by buffoonery, and they may have induced these ecstasies by toadstool eating; but *Câd Goddeu*, *Angar Cyvyndawd* and all the other strange poems of the *Book of Taliesin* medley read like nonsense only because the texts have been deliberately confused, doubtless as a precaution against their being denounced as heretical by some Church officer. This explanation would also account for the presence of simple, dull religious pieces in the medley—plausible guarantees of orthodoxy. Unfortunately a large part of the original material seems to be lost, which makes a confident restoration of the remainder difficult. When an authoritative version of the text and an authoritative English translation has been published—none is so far available, else I should have used it—the problem will be simpler. But that the Awenyddion were descended from the Trojans is an important statement of Gerald's; he means that they inherited their traditions not from the Cymry but from the earlier inhabitants of Wales whom the Cymry dispossessed.

The context of the thirteenth-century version of the Romance can be reconstructed from what Gwynn Jones has written of Phylip Brydydd of Llanbadarn Fawr and the poem in which he mentions his contention with the *beirdd yspyddeid*, vulgar rhymesters, as to who should first present a song to Prince Rhys Ieuanc on Christmas Day.

'The evidence of this poem is extremely valuable, as it shows us conclusively that, by this time, at any rate, the lower order of bards had won for themselves the privilege of appearing at a Welsh court, and of being allowed to compete with the members of the closer corporation. It is exceedingly difficult to make out with certainty the meaning of the poem, but the bard seems to lament the relaxation or abandonment of the ancient custom of the court of the house of Tewdwr [afterwards the English House of Tudor], where formerly, after a battle, none were without recompense, and where frequently he had himself been presented with gifts. If praise were the pledge of bravery, then his desert should have been to receive liquor, rather than to become an 'ermid'. The bard also mentions a certain Bleiddriw, who would not have given him his due, and seems to imply that this person was guilty of versifying untruth, as well as to apply to him the epithet *twyll i gwndid* [sc. perverter of poetic practice]. The suggestion in this poem, therefore, is that the person referred to was the author of a broken or irregular song. We are further told by Phylip that the Chair of Maelgwn Hir was meant for bards, not for the irregular rhymesters, and that if that chair in his day were deserved, it should be contended for by the consent of saints and in accordance with truth and privilege. A Penkerdd [privileged bard] could not be made of a man without art. In a second poem, the poet's patron, probably also of the house of Tewdwr, is asked to pay heed to the contention of the bards and the rhymesters, and the appearance of Elffin in the contentions of Maelgwn is referred to. The bard says that, since then, mere chattering had caused long unpleasantness, and the speech of strangers, the vices of women and many a foolish tale had come to Gwynedd [North Wales], through the songs of false bards whose grammar was bad and who had no honour. Phylip solemnly states that it is not for man to destroy the privilege of the gift of God. He laments the fall of the office of the bards, and describes his own song as "the ancient song of Taliesin" which, he says—and this is significant—"was itself new for nine times seven years". "And", he adds finally, "though I be placed in a foul grave in the earth, before the violent upheaval of judgement, the muse shall not cease from deserving recognition while the sun and moon remain in their circles; and unless untruth shall overcome truth, or the gift of God shall cease in the end, it is they who shall be disgraced in the contention: He will remove from the vulgar bards their vain delight."

'It will be observed that these poems supply a very interesting account of the points of contention. We see that the song of Taliesin and the contentions of Maelgwn Hir are set up as standards; that those standards were believed to have been regulated in agreement with the will of saints and in accordance with truth and privilege; that the contentions were not open to the lower order of bards; and that a man without art could not become a Penkerdd. It is alleged that the speech of strangers, the vices of women, and numerous foolish tales had come to Gwynedd—even to Gwynedd, where the contentions of Maelgwn had been held—by means of the songs of false bards whose grammar was faulty. We see that the song of the official or traditional bards is claimed to be the gift of God; that its essence was truth, compared with the untruth of the newer song; and that Phylip Brydydd was prepared, as it were, to die in the last ditch, fighting for the privilege of the true gift of poesy. We observe that, in spite of all this, the rhymesters were allowed to tender a song on Christmas Day at the court of Rhys Ieuanc.

'It will have been observed that the first poem of Phylip Brydydd mentions a Bleiddriw who refused to acknowledge him, and whose own song, as I interpret the extremely compressed syntax of the poem, Phylip describes as broken and irregular. It is not improbable that we have here a reference to the much discussed Bledri of Giraldus Cambrensis, "that famous dealer in fables, who lived a little before our time". The probability is that, in this Bledri, we have one of the men who recited Welsh stories in French, and so assisted their passage into other languages. Gaston Paris, so long ago as 1879, identified him with the Breri, to whom Thomas, the author of the French poem of Tristan, acknowledges his debt, describing him as having known "*les histoires et*

les contes de tous les rois et comtes qui avaient vécu en Bretagne". Phylip
Brydydd is said to have flourished between 1200 and 1250. As Rhys
Ieuanc, his patron, died about 1220, probably Phylip was born before
1200. Giraldus himself died in 1220. This brings them sufficiently near
to allow of the possibility of their both referring to the same Bledri.
At any rate, this is the only case known to me in Welsh of a contemporary reference to a Bledri corresponding to the person mentioned by
Giraldus. But I would base no argument upon this possible identity.
If the Bleiddri of Phylip's poem be another Bleiddri, the fact still
remains that he was regarded as being of the lower order of bards, and
that Phylip, the traditional bard, charged his class, at any rate, with
debasing the poetic diction of the bards and with making untruth the
subject of poetry.

'What then could be the meaning of untruth as the subject of song?
Considering the word in the light of the Codes, and of the contents of
the poems of the court-bards themselves, I submit that it simply means
tales of imagination. The official bards were prohibited from writing
imaginative narrative and material for representation; they were
enjoined to celebrate the praise of God and of brave or good men.
This they did, as we have seen, in epithetical verse of which the style is
remarkably and intentionally archaic.'

Phylip's complaint that his opponent Bleiddri had no 'honour' means
that he did not belong to the privileged class of Cymric freemen from
which the court-bards were chosen. In the *Romance of Taliesin* we have
the story from the side of the minstrel, but an extraordinarily gifted
minstrel, who had studied abroad among men of greater learning than
were to be found anywhere in Wales and who insisted that the court-
bards had forgotten the meaning of the poetry that they practised.
Throughout the poems the same scornful theme is pressed:

> *Am I not a candidate for fame, to be heard in song? . . .*
> *Avaunt, you boastful bards. . . .*

This unprivileged minstrel boasts that the Chair is rightly his: he, not any
poet of Phylip Brydydd's merely academic attainment, is the true heir of
Taliesin. However, for courtesy's sake, the tale of Gwion and Cerridwen
is told in terms of sixth-century, not thirteenth-century, history. 'The
speech of strangers' which, Phylip complains, has corrupted Gwynedd is
likely to have been Irish: for Prince Gruffudd ap Kynan, a gifted and pro-
gressive prince educated in Ireland, had introduced Irish bards and
minstrels into his principality in the early twelfth century. It may have
been from this Irish literary colony, not from Ireland itself, that Gwion
first derived his superior knowledge. Gruffudd also had Norsemen in his

entourage. His careful regulations for the government of bards and musicians were revived at the Caerwys Eisteddfod in 1523.

Here, finally, is the *Hanes Taliesin* riddle in Lady Charlotte Guest's translation. In it, Little Gwion answers King Maelgwyn's questions as to who he was and whence he came:

> *Primary chief bard am I to Elphin,*
> *And my original country is the region of the summer stars;*
> *Idno and Heinin called me Merddin,*
> *At length every king will call me Taliesin.*
> 5 *I was with my Lord in the highest sphere,*
> *On the fall of Lucifer into the depth of hell;*
> *I have borne a banner before Alexander;*
> *I know the names of the stars from north to south;*
> *I have been on the Galaxy at the throne of the Distributor;*
> 10 *I was in Canaan when Absalom was slain;*
> *I conveyed Awen [the Divine Spirit] to the level of the*
>   *vale of Hebron;*
> *I was in the court of Dôn before the birth of Gwydion.*
> *I was instructor to Eli and Enoch;*
> *I have been winged by the genius of the splendid crozier;*
> 15 *I have been loquacious prior to being gifted with speech;*
> *I was at the place of the crucifixion of the merciful son of God;*
> *I have been three periods in the prison of Arianrhod;*
> *I have been the chief director of the work of the tower of*
>   *Nimrod.*
> *I am a wonder whose origin is not known.*
> 20 *I have been in Asia with Noah in the Ark,*
> *I have witnessed the destruction of Sodom and Gomorrah;*
> *I have been in India when Roma was built;*
> *I am now come here to the remnant of Troia.*
> *I have been with my Lord in the manger of the ass;*
> 25 *I strengthened Moses through the water of Jordan;*
> *I have been in the firmament with Mary Magdalene;*
> *I have obtained the muse from the Cauldron of Caridwen;*
> *I have been bard of the harp to Lleon of Lochlin.*
> *I have been on the White Hill, in the court of Cynvelyn,*
> 30 *For a day and a year in stocks and fetters,*
> *I have suffered hunger for the Son of the Virgin,*
> *I have been fostered in the land of the Deity,*
> *I have been teacher to all intelligences,*
> *I am able to instruct the whole universe.*
> 35 *I shall be until the day of doom on the face of the earth;*

> *And it is not known whether my body is flesh or fish.*
> *Then I was for nine months*
> *In the womb of the hag Caridwen;*
> *I was originally little Gwion,*
> 40 *And at length I am Taliesin.*

The deceitful cry of the Lapwing! Gwion was not so ignorant of sacred history as he pretended: he must have known perfectly well that Moses never crossed the Jordan, that Mary Magdalene was never in the Firmament, that Lucifer's fall had been recorded by the prophet Isaiah centuries before the time of Alexander the Great. Refusing to be lured away from the secret by his apparently nonsensical utterances, I began my unravelling of the puzzle by answering the following questions:

Line 11. Who did convey the Divine Spirit to Hebron?
   „ 13. Who did instruct Enoch?
   „ 16. Who did attend the Crucifixion?
   „ 25. Who did pass through Jordan water when Moses was forbidden to do so?

I felt confident that I would presently catch a gleam of white through the tangled thicket where the Roebuck was harboured.

Now, according to the Pentateuch, Moses died on Pisgah on the other side of Jordan and 'no man knoweth his sepulchre to this day'; and of all the Children of Israel who had come with him into the wilderness out of the house of bondage, only two, Caleb and Joshua, crossed into the Promised Land. As spies they had already been bold enough to cross and recross the river. It was Caleb who seized Hebron from the Anakim on behalf of the God of Israel and was granted it by Joshua as his inheritance. So I realized that the Dog had torn the whole poem into shreds with his teeth and that the witty Lapwing had mixed them up misleadingly, as she did with the torn shreds of the fruit passage in the *Câd Goddeu*. The original statement was: 'I conveyed the Divine Spirit through the water of Jordan to the level of the vale of Hebron.' And the 'I' must be Caleb.

If the same trick had been played with every line of the *Hanes Taliesin*, I could advance a little further into the thicket. I could regard the poem as a sort of acrostic composed of twenty or thirty riddles, each of them requiring separate solution; what the combined answers spelt out promised to be a secret worth discovering. But first I had to sort out and reassemble the individual riddles.

After the misleading 'through the water of Jordan' had been removed from line 25, 'I strengthened Moses' remained. Well, who *did* strengthen Moses? And where was this strengthening done? I remembered that Moses was strengthened at the close of his battle with the Amalekites, by having his hands held up by two companions. Where did this battle take place and who were the strengtheners? It took place at Jehovah-Nissi, close to the Mount of God, and the strengtheners were Aaron and Hur. So I could recompose the riddle as: 'I strengthened Moses in the land of the Deity'. And the answer was: 'Aaron and Hur'. If only one name was needed, it would probably be Hur because this is the only action recorded of him in the Pentateuch.

Similarly, in line 25, 'I have been with Mary Magdalene' had to be separated from the misleading 'in the firmament' and the other part of the riddle looked for in another verse. I had already found it by studying the list of people present at the Crucifixion: St. Simon of Cyrene, St. John the Apostle, St. Veronica, Dysmas the good thief, Gestas the bad thief, the Centurion, the Virgin Mary, Mary Cleopas, Mary Magdalene. . . . But I had not overlooked the woman who (according to the *Proto-evangelium* of St. James) was the first person ever to adore the child Jesus, the prime witness of his parthenogenesis, and his most faithful follower. She is mentioned in *Mark XV*, as standing beside Mary Magdalene. So: 'I was with Mary Magdalene at the place of the Crucifixion of the merciful Son of God.' The answer was: 'Salome'.

Who instructed Enoch? (Eli does not, apparently, belong to this riddle.) I agree with Charles, Burkitt, Oesterley, Box and other Biblical scholars that nobody can hope to understand the Sayings of Jesus who has not read the *Book of Enoch*, omitted from the canon of the *Apocrypha* but closely studied by the primitive Christians. I happened to have been reading the book and knew that the answer was 'Uriel', and that Uriel instructed Enoch 'on the fall of Lucifer into the depth of hell'. A curious historical point is that the verse about Uriel's instruction of Enoch is not included in the fragments of the Greek *Book of Enoch* quoted by the ninth-century Byzantine historian Syncellus, nor in the Vatican MS. (1809), nor in the quotations from the *Book of Enoch* in the *Epistle of St. Jude*. It occurs only in the text dug up at Akhmim in Egypt in 1886, and in the Ethiopian translation of an earlier Greek text, which is the only version which we know to have been extant in the thirteenth century. Where did Gwion find the story? Was a knowledge of Ethiopian among this atainments? Or did he find a complete Greek manuscript in the library of some Irish abbey that had escaped the fury of the Vikings' war against books? The passage in the *First Book of Enoch, XVIII, 11,* and *XIX, 1, 2, 3,* runs:

> And I saw a deep abyss and columns of heavenly fire, and among them I saw columns of fire falling, which were beyond measure alike upwards and downwards. . . . And Uriel said to me: 'Here shall stand the angels who have lain with women and whose spirits, assuming many different forms, defile mankind and lead them astray into

demonolatry and sacrificing to demons: here shall they stand until the Day of Judgement. . . . And the women whom they seduced shall become Sirens.' I, Enoch, alone saw this vision of the end of all things; no other shall see as far as I.

This discovery took me a stage further, to line 7: 'I have borne a banner before Alexander.' Among the poems attributed to Taliesin in the *Red Book of Hergest* is a fragment called *Y Gofeisws Byd* ('A Sketch of the World') which contains a short panegyric of the historical Alexander, and another *Anrhyfeddonau Alexander*, 'The Not-wonders of Alexander'—a joke at the expense of a thirteenth-century Spanish romance ascribing to Alexander adventures properly belonging to the myth of Merlin—which tells mockingly how he went beneath the sea and met 'creatures of distinguished lineage among the fish. . . .' But neither of these poems gave me a clue to the riddle. If it must be taken literally I should perhaps have guessed the answer to be 'Neoptolemus', who was one of Alexander's bodyguard and the first man to scale the walls of Gaza at the assault. But more probably the reference was to Alexander as a re-incarnation of Moses.

According to Josephus, when Alexander came to Jerusalem at the outset of his Eastern conquests, he refrained from sacking the Temple but bowed down and adored the Tetragrammaton on the High Priest's golden frontlet. His astonished companion Parmenio asked why in the world he had behaved in this unkingly way. Alexander answered: 'I did not adore the High Priest himself but the God who has honoured him with office. The case is this: that I saw this very person in a dream, dressed exactly as now, while I was at Dios in Macedonia. In my dream I was debating with myself how I might conquer Asia, and this man exhorted me not to delay. I was to pass boldly with my army across the narrow sea, for his God would march before me and help me to defeat the Persians. So I am now convinced that Jehovah is with me and will lead my armies to victory.' The High Priest then further encouraged Alexander by showing him the prophecy in the *Book of Daniel* which promised him the dominion of the East; and he went up to the Temple, sacrificed to Jehovah and made a generous peace-treaty with the Jewish nation. The prophecy referred to Alexander as the 'two-horned King' and he subsequently pictured himself on his coins with two horns. He appears in the *Koran* as Dhul Karnain, 'the two-horned'. Moses was also 'two-horned', and in Arabian legend 'El Hidr, the ever-young prophet', a former Sun-hero of Sinai, befriended both Moses and Alexander 'at the meeting place of two seas'. To the learned Gwion, therefore, a banner borne before Alexander was equally a banner borne before Moses; and St. Jerome, or his Jewish mentors, had already made a poetic identification of Alexander's horns with those of Moses.

The banner of Moses was 'Nehushtan', the Brazen Serpent, which he raised up to avert the plague in the wilderness. When he did so he became an 'Alexander', i.e. a 'warder-off-of-evil-from-man'. So the answer of this riddle is 'Nehushtan' or, in the Greek Septuagint spelling, in which I imagine Gwion had read the story, 'Ne-Esthan'. It should be remembered that this Brazen Serpent in the *Gospel According to John, III, 14* and the apocryphal *Epistle of Barnabas, XII, 7* is a type of Jesus Christ. Barnabas emphasizes that the Serpent 'hung on a wooden thing', i.e. the Cross, and had the power of making alive. In *Numbers, XXI, 9* it is described as a 'seraph', a name given by Isaiah to the flying serpents that appeared in his vision as the attendants of the Living God and flew to him with a live coal from the altar.

The next riddle I had to solve, a combination of lines 9 and 26, was: 'I have been in the firmament, on the Galaxy.' The Galaxy, or Milky Way, is said to have been formed when the milk of the Great Goddess Rhea of Crete spouted abundantly into the sky after the birth of the infant Zeus. But since the Great Goddess's name varies from mythographer to mythographer—Hyginus, for example, debates whether to call her Juno or Ops (Wealth)—Gwion has considerately given us another clue: 'When Roma was built'. He is correctly identifying a Cretan with a Roman goddess, and what is more surprising, recognizes Romulus as a Latin deity of the same religious system as Cretan Zeus. Romulus's mother was also named Rhea, and if she had trouble with her milk when she was forced to wean her twins in order to conceal their birth, so had Cretan Rhea in the same circumstances. The main difference was that Romulus and Remus had a she-wolf for their foster-mother, whereas Zeus (and some say his foster-brother Goat Pan, too), was suckled by the she-goat Amalthea, whose hide he afterwards wore as a coat; or, as still others say, by a white sow. Both Romulus and Zeus were brought up by shepherds. So: 'I have been in the firmament, on the Galaxy, when Roma was built.' The answer is Rhea, though it was not Rhea herself but the spurt of her milk, *rhea* in Greek, that was on the Galaxy. Gwion had been anticipated by Nennius in giving more importance to Rhea, mother of Romulus, than the Classical mythologists had done: Nennius called her 'the most holy queen'.

This riddle is purposely misleading. The only legend about the Galaxy that Heinin and the other bards at Maelgwyn's court would have known concerns Blodeuwedd, conjured by Gwydion to be the bride of Llew Llaw Gyffes. Llew's other name was Huan and Blodeuwedd was transformed into an owl and called Twyll Huan ('the deceiving of Huan') for having caused Llew's death: the Welsh for owl being *tylluan*. The legend of Blodeuwedd and the Galaxy occurs in the *Peniardd MSS.*:

The wife of Huan ap Dôn was a party to the killing of her husband

and said that he had gone to hunt away from home. His father Gwydion, the King of Gwynedd, traversed all countries in search of him, and at last made Caer Gwydion, that is the Milky Way, as a track by which to seek his soul in the heavens; where he found it. In requital for the injury that she had done he turned the young wife into a bird, and she fled from her father-in-law and s called to this day Twyll Huan. Thus the Britons formerly treated their stories and tales after the manner of the Greeks, in order to keep them in memory.

It should be added that the form 'Caer Gwydion', instead of 'Caer Wydion', proves the myth to be a late one. Blodeuwedd (as shown in Chapter Two) was Olwen, 'She of the White Track', so Gwydion was right to search for her in the Galaxy: Rhea with her white track of stars was the celestial counterpart of Olwen-Blodeuwedd with her white track of trefoil.

Who, in line 21, witnessed the destruction of Sodom and Gomorrah? Lot, or perhaps the unnamed 'wife of Lot'.

Who, in line 18, was 'the chief director of the work of the tower of Nimrod'? I saw that the Lapwing was at her tricks again. The question really ran: 'Of the work on what tower was Nimrod the chief director?' The answer was 'Babel'. Gower's lines on the inconvenience caused to Nimrod and his masons when the confusion of tongues began, had run in my head for years:

> One called for stones, they brought him tyld [tiles]
> And Nimrod, that great Champioun,
> He ragèd like a young Lioun.

Who, in line 24, was 'with my Lord in the manger of the Ass'? Was the answer 'swaddling clothes'? Then someone called my attention to the text of *Luke II, 16*: 'And they came with haste and found Mary and Joseph and the babe lying in a manger.' Gwion was being mischievous: literally, the sentence reads as though Joseph, Mary and the child were all together in the manger. The answer was evidently 'Joseph', since that was St. Joseph's most glorious moment.

Who was it that said, in line 23: 'I am now come here to the remnant of Troia.' According to Nennius, Sigebertus Gemblasensis, Geoffrey of Monmouth and others, Brutus the grandson of Aeneas landed with the remnants of the Trojans at Totnes in Devon in the year 1074 B.C.—109 years after the accepted date of the Fall of Troy. A people who came over the Mor Tawch (the North Sea) some seven centuries later to join them were the Cymry. They cherished the notion that they were descended from Gomer, son of Japhet, and had wandered all the way from Taprobane (Ceylon—see *Triad 54*) by way of Asia Minor before finally settling at Llydaw in North Britain. So: 'I have been in India and Asia (line 20) and am now come here to the remnant of Troia.' The answer was 'Gomer'.

'I know the names of the stars from north to south' in line 8, suggested one of the Three Happy Astronomers of Britain mentioned in the *Triads,* and I judged from the sentence 'my original country is the region of the summer stars' (i.e. the West) which seemed to belong to this riddle, that no Greek, Egyptian, Arabic, or Babylonian astronomer was intended. Idris being the first named of the three astronomers, the answer was probably 'Idris'.

'I have been on the White Hill, in the Court of Cynvelyn (Cymbeline)' in line 29, evidently belonged with 'I was in the Court of Dôn before the birth of Gwydion', in line 12. The answer was 'Vron' or 'Bran', whose head, after his death, was according to the *Romance of Branwen* buried on the White Hill (Tower Hill) at London as a protection against invasion—as the head of King Eurystheus of Mycenae was buried in a pass that commanded the approach to Athens, and the alleged head of Adam was buried at the northern approach to Jerusalem—until King Arthur exhumed it. For Bran was a son of Dôn (Danu) long before the coming of the Belgic Gwydion.[1]

The answer to 'I was in Canaan when Absalom was slain' (line 10), was clearly 'David'. King David had crossed over Jordan to the Canaanite refuge-city of Mahanaim, while Joab fought the Battle of the Wood of Ephraim. There in the gateway he heard the news of Absalom's death. In compliment to the See of St. David's, Gwion has combined this statement with 'I have been winged by the genius of the splendid crozier.' ('*And* St. David!' as we Royal Welch Fusiliers loyally add to all our toasts on March 1st.) One of the chief aims of Prince Llewelyn and the other Welsh patriots of Gwion's day was to free their Church from English domination. Giraldus Cambrensis had spent the best part of his quarrelsome ecclesiastical life (1145–1213) in campaigns to make the See of St. David's independent of Canterbury and to fill it with a Welsh Archbishop. But King Henry II and his two sons saw to it that only politically reliable Norman-French churchmen were appointed to the Welsh sees, and appeals by the Welsh to the Pope were disregarded because the power of the Angevin kings weighed more at the Vatican than the possible gratification of a poor, divided and distant principality.

Who, in line 20, when the misleading 'in Asia' has been removed, was 'with Noah in the Ark'? I guessed 'Hu Gadarn', who according to the *Triads* led the Cymry from the East. With his plough-oxen he also drew

---

[1] Bran's connexion with the White Hill may account for the curious persistence at the Tower of London of tame ravens, which are regarded by the garrison with superstitious reverence. There is even a legend that the security of the Crown depends on their continuance there: a variant of the legend about Bran's head. The raven, or crow, was Bran's oracular bird.

up from the magic lake the monster *avanc* which caused it to overflow in a universal flood. He had been 'fostered between the knees of Dylan in the Deluge'. But the Lapwing, I found later, was deliberately confusing Dylan with Noah; Noah really belongs to the Enoch riddle in line 13. The present riddle must run: 'I have been fostered in the Ark.' But it could be enlarged with the statement in line 33: 'I have been teacher to all intelligences', for Hu Gadarn, 'Hu the Mighty', who has been identified with the ancient Channel Island god Hou, was the Menes, or Palamedes, of the Cymry and taught them ploughing—'in the region where Constantinople now stands'—music and song.

Who, in line 27, 'obtained the Muse from the cauldron of Caridwen'? Gwion himself. However, the cauldron of Caridwen was no mere witch's cauldron. It would not be unreasonable to identify it with the cauldron depicted on Greek vases, the name written above Caridwen being 'Medea', the Corinthian Goddess who killed her children, as the Goddess Thetis also did. In this cauldron she boiled up old Aeson and restored him to youth; it was the cauldron of rebirth and re-illumination. Yet when the other Medea, Jason's wife, played her famous trick (recorded by Diodorus Siculus) on old Pelias of Iolcos, persuading his daughters to cut him up and stew him back to youth and then calmly denouncing them as parricides, she disguised her Corinthian nationality and pretended to be a Hyperborean Goddess. Evidently Pelias had heard of the Hyperborean cauldron and had greater faith in it than in the Corinthian one.

'It is not known whether my body is flesh or fish.' This riddle, in line 36, was not hard to answer. I remembered the long-standing dispute in the mediaeval Church whether or not it was right to eat barnacle goose on Fridays and other fast-days. The barnacle goose does not nest in the British Isles. (I handled the first clutch of its eggs ever brought there; they were found at Spitzbergen in the Arctic.) It was universally believed to be hatched out of the goose barnacle—to quote the *Oxford English Dictionary*, 'a white sea-shell of the pedunculate genus of Cirripedes.' The long feathery *cirri* protruding from the valves suggested plumage. Giraldus Cambrensis once saw more than a thousand embryo barnacle geese hanging from one piece of drift wood on the shore. Campion wrote in his Elizabethan *History of Ireland*: 'Barnacles, thousands at once, are noted along the shoares to hang by the beakes about the edges of putrified timber . . . which in processe taking lively heate of the Sunne, become water-foules.' Barnacle geese were therefore held by some to be fish, not fowl, and legitimate Friday eating for monks. The word 'barnacle', the same dictionary suggests, is formed from the Welsh *brenig*, or Irish *bairneach*, meaning a limpet or barnacle-shell. Moreover, the other name for the barnacle goose, the 'brent' or the 'brant', is apparently formed from the same word. Caius, the Elizabethan naturalist, called it

Anser Brendinus and wrote of it: ' "*Bernded*" *seu* "*Brended*" *id animal dicitur.*' This suggests a connexion between *bren, bairn, brent, brant, bern* and *Bran* who, as the original *Câd Goddeu* makes plain, was an Underworld-god. For the northward migration of wild geese is connected in British legend with the conducting to the icy Northern Hell of the souls of the damned, or of unbaptized infants. In Wales the sound of the geese passing unseen overhead at night is supposed to be made by the *Cwm Annwm* ('Hounds of Hell' with white bodies and red ears), in England by Yell Hounds, Yeth Hounds, Wish Hounds, Gabriel Hounds, or Gabriel Ratchets. The Hunter is called variously *Gwyn* ('the white one')—there was a Gwyn cult in pre-Christian Glastonbury—Herne the Hunter, and Gabriel. In Scotland he is Arthur. 'Arthur' here may stand for *Arddu* ('the dark one')...Satan's name in the Welsh Bible. But his original name in Britain seems to have been Bran, which in Welsh is Vron. The fish-or-flesh riddle must therefore belong with the other two Vron riddles already answered.

The alternative text of the *Hanes Taliesin* published in the *Myvyrian Archaiology* is translated by D. W. Nash as follows:

1   *An impartial Chief Bard*
    Am I to Elphin.
    My accustomed country
    Is the land of the Cherubim.

2   *Johannes the Diviner*
    I was called by Merddin,
    At length every King
    Will call me Taliesin.

3   *I was nine months almost*
    In the belly of the hag Caridwen;
    I was at first little Gwion,
    At length I am Taliesin.

4   *I was with my Lord*
    In the highest sphere,
    When Lucifer fell
    Into the depths of Hell.

5   *I carried the banner*
    Before Alexander.
    I know the names of the stars
    From the North to the South.

6   *I was in Caer Bedion*
    Tetragrammaton;
    I conveyed Heon [*the Divine Spirit*]
    Down to the vale of Ebron.

7 *I was in Canaan*
    When Absalom was slain;
    I was in the Hall of Dôn
    Before Gwydion was born.

8 *I was on the horse's crupper*
    Of Eli and Enoch;
    I was on the high cross
    Of the merciful Son of God.

9 *I was the chief overseer*
    At the building of the tower of Nimrod;
    I have been three times resident
    In the castle of Arianrhod.

10 *I was in the Ark*
    With Noah and Alpha;
    I saw the destruction
    Of Sodom and Gomorrah.

11 *I was in Africa [Asia?]*
    Before the building of Rome;
    I am now come here
    To the remnants of Troia.

12 *I was with my King*
    In the manger of the ass;
    I supported Moses
    Through the waters of Jordan.

13 *I was in the Firmament*
    With Mary Magdalene;
    I obtained my inspiration
    From the cauldron of Caridwen.

14 *I was Bard of the harp*
    To Deon of Llychlyn;
    I have suffered hunger
    With the son of the Virgin.

15 *I was in the White Hill*
    In the Hall of Cynvelyn,
    In stocks and fetters
    A year and a half.

16 *I have been in the buttery*
    In the land of the Trinity;

It is not known what is the nature
Of its meat and its fish.

17 *I have been instructed*
In the whole system of the universe;
I shall be till the day of judgement
On the face of the earth.

18 *I have been in an uneasy chair*
Above Caer Sidin,
And the whirling round without motion
Between three elements.

19 *Is it not the wonder of the world*
That cannot be discovered?

The sequence is different and the Lapwing has been as busy as ever. But I learned a good deal from the variants. In place of 'the land of the Summer Stars', 'the land of the Cherubim' is mentioned. Both mean the same thing. The Eighteenth Psalm (verse 10) makes it clear that the Cherubim are storm-cloud angels; and therefore, for Welshmen, they are resident in the West, from which quarter nine storms out of every ten blow. The Summer Stars are those which lie in the western part of the firmament.

The first two lines in stanza 18, 'I have been in an uneasy chair above Caer Sidin' helped me. There is a stone seat at the top of Cader Idris, 'the Chair of Idris' where, according to the local legend, whoever spends the night is found in the morning either dead, mad, or a poet. The first part of this sentence evidently belongs to the Idris riddle, though Gwion, in his *Kerdd am Veib Llyr* mentions a 'perfect chair' in Caer Sidi ('Revolving Castle'), the Elysian fortress where the Cauldron of Caridwen was housed.

The text of stanza 2, 'Johannes the Diviner I was called by Merddin', seems to be purposely corrupt, since in the *Mabinogion* version the sense is: 'Idno and Heinin called me Merddin.' I thought at first that the original line ran: 'Johannes I was called, and Merddin the Diviner', and I was right so far as I went. Merddin, who in mediaeval romances is styled Merlin, was the most famous ancient prophet in British tradition. The manifest sense of the stanza is that Gwion had been called Merddin, 'dweller in the sea', by Heinin, Maelgwyn's chief bard, because like the original Merddin he was of mysterious birth and, though a child, had confounded the bardic college at Dyganwy exactly as Merddin (according to Nennius and Geoffrey of Monmouth) had confounded Vortigern's sages; that he had also been called 'John the Baptist' ('But thou, child, shalt be called the prophet of the Most Highest'); but that eventually everyone would call him Taliesin ('radiant brow') the chief of poets. Dr. MacCulloch suggests that there was an earlier Taliesin than the sixth-century bard, and that he was a Celtic Apollo; which would account for the 'radiant brow' and for his appearance among other faded gods and heroes at King Arthur's Court in the *Romance of Kilhwch and Olwen.* (Apollo himself had once been a dweller in the sea—the dolphin was sacred to him—and oddly enough John the Baptist seems to have been identified by early Christian syncretists in Egypt with the Chaldean god Oannes who according to Berossus used to appear at long intervals in the Persian Gulf, disguised as the merman Odacon, and renew his original revelation to the faithful. The case is further complicated by the myth of Huan, the Flower-goddess Blodeuwedd's victim, who was really the god Llew Llaw, another 'sea-dweller'.)

It took me a long time to realize that the concealed sense of stanza 2, which made the textual corruption necessary, was a heretical paraphrase of the passage in the three synoptic Gospels (*Matt. XVI, 14, Mark VI, 15, Luke IX, 7, 8*):

> Some say thou art John the Baptist, and some Elias; and some, one of the ancient prophets risen from the dead. . . .' But Peter answered: 'Thou art the Christ.'

The completing phrase 'and Elias' occurs in stanza 8. The Divine Child is speaking as Jesus Christ, as I believe he also is in stanza 14: 'I have suffered hunger with the Son of the Virgin.' Jesus was alone then except for the Devil and the 'wild beasts'. But the Devil did not go hungry; and the 'wild beasts' in the Temptation context, according to the acutest scriptural critics—e.g. Professor A. A. Bevan and Dr. T. K. Cheyne— were also of the Devil's party. The *Mabinogion* version, line 31, is: 'I have suffered hunger *for* the Son of the Virgin,' which comes to the same thing: Jesus suffered hunger on his own account. The answer to this riddle was simply 'Jesus', as 'Taliesin' was the answer to 'Joannes, and Merddin the Diviner, and Elias I was called'.

'I was in the Ark with Noah and Alpha', in stanza 10, and 'I was in Caer Bedion, Tetragrammaton', stanza 6, must together refer to the 'Holy Unspeakable Name of God'. 'Alpha and Omega' was a divine periphrasis which it was permitted to utter publicly; and the 'tetragrammaton' was the cryptogrammic Hebrew way of spelling the secret Name in four letters as JHWH. I thought at first that 'I was in Caer Bedion' belonged to the Lot riddle: because 'Lot' is the Norman-French name for Lludd, the king who built London, and Caer Bedion is Caer Badus, or Bath, which according to Geoffrey of Monmouth was built by Lludd's father Bladud.

But to Gwion the Welshman Lludd was not 'Lot', nor is there any record of Lludd's having lived at Bath.

I let the 'Caer Bedion' riddle stand over for a while, and also the riddle 'I was Alpha Tetragrammaton'—if this conjunction composed the riddle —the answer to which was evidently a four-lettered Divine Name beginning with A. Meanwhile, who was 'bard of the harp to Deon, or Lleon, of Lochlin, or Llychlyn' (line 28; and stanza 14)? 'Deon King of Lochlin and Dublin', is an oddly composite character. Deon is a variant spelling of Dôn, who, as already pointed out, was really Danu the Goddess of the Tuatha dé Danaan, the invaders of Ireland, patriarchized into a King of Lochlin, or Lochlann, and Dublin. Lochlann was the mythical undersea home of the later Fomorian invaders of Ireland, against whom the Tuatha dé Danaan fought a bloody war. The god Tethra ruled it. It seems that legends of the war between these two nations were worked by later poets into ballad cycles celebrating the ninth-century wars between the Irish and the Danish and Norse pirates. Thus the Scandinavians came to be called 'the Lochlannach' and the Danish King of Dublin was also styled 'King of Lochlin'. When the cult of the Scandinavian god Odin, the rune-maker and magician, was brought to Ireland he was identified with his counterpart Gwydion who in the fourth century B.C. had brought a new system of letters with him to Britain, and had been enrolled as a son of Danu or Dôn. Moreover, according to the legend, the Danaans had come to Britain from Greece by way of Denmark to which they had given the name of their goddess, and in mediaeval Ireland Danaan and Dane became confused, the Danes of the ninth century A.D. getting credit for Bronze Age monuments. So 'Deon of Lochlin' must stand for 'the Danes of Dublin'. These pirates with their sea-raven flag were the terror of the Welsh, and the minstrel to the Danes of Dublin was probably the sea-raven, sacred to Odin, who croaked over their victims. If so, the answer to the riddle was 'Morvran' (sea-raven), who was the son of Caridwen and, according to the *Romance of Kilhwch and Olwen*, the ugliest man in the world. In the *Triads* he is said to have escaped alive from the Battle of Camlan—another of the 'Three Frivolous Battles of Britain'—because everyone shrank from him. He must be identified with Afagddu, son of Caridwen, for whom the same supreme ugliness is claimed in the *Romance of Taliesin*, and whom she determined to make as intelligent as he was ugly.

I wondered whether 'Lleon of Lochlin', in the *Myvyrian* version, was a possible reading. Arthur had his Court at Caerlleon-upon-Usk and the word Caerlleon is generally taken to mean 'The Camp of the Legion'; and certainly the two Caerlleons mentioned in the seventh-century Welsh *Catalogue of Cities*, Caerlleon-upon-Usk and Caerlleon-upon-Dee, are both there explained as *Castra Legionis*. If Gwion accepted this derivation of the word the riddle would read: 'I was bard of the harp to the legions of Lochlin', and the answer would be the same. The name Leon occurs in Gwion's *Kadeir Teyrnon* ('The Royal Chair'): 'the lacerated form of the corsleted Leon'. But the context is corrupt and 'Leon' may be a descriptive title of some lion-hearted prince, not a proper name.

Then there was the riddle in stanza 8 to consider: 'I was on the horse's crupper of Eli and Enoch'—an alternative to the misleading *Book of Enoch* riddle in the *Mabinogion* version:

I was instructor to Eli and Enoch

of which the answer is 'Uriel'. In both texts Elias is really a part of the heretical John the Baptist riddle, from which the Lapwing has done her best to distract attention; her false connexion of Elias and Enoch has been most subtly made. For these two prophets are paired in various Apocryphal Gospels—the *History of Joseph the Carpenter*, the *Acts of Pilate*, the *Apocalypse of Peter* and the *Apocalypse of Paul*. In the *Acts of Pilate*, for instance, which was current in Wales in Latin translation, occurs the verse:

I am Enoch who was translated hither by the word of the Lord, and here with me is Elias the Tishbite who was taken up in a chariot of fire.

But the real riddle in the *Mabinogion* version proves to be: 'I was instructor to Enoch and Noah'. In this other version, 'I was on the horse's crupper of Eli and Enoch', the mention of Elias is otiose: for Enoch, like Elias, was caught up alive into Heaven on a chariot drawn by fiery horses. So the answer again is Uriel, since 'Uriel' means 'Flame of God'. Now perhaps I could also answer 'Uriel' to the riddle 'I was in Caer Bedion'. For, according to Geoffrey of Monmouth, a sacred fire was kept continually burning in a temple at Caer Bedion, or Bath, like that which burned in the House of God at Jerusalem.

There is a variation between the texts: 'a day and a year in stocks and fetters' (line 30) and 'a year and a half in stocks and fetters' (stanza 15). 'A year and a half' makes no obvious sense, but 'a day and a year' can be equated with the Thirteen Prison Locks that guarded Elphin, if each lock was a 28-day month and he was released on the extra day of the 365. The ancient common-law month in Britain, according to Blackstone's *Commentaries* (2, *IX*, 142) is 28 days long, unless otherwise stated, and a lunar month is still popularly so reckoned, although a true lunar month, or lunation, from new moon to new moon, is roughly $29\frac{1}{2}$ days long, and though thirteen is supposed to be an unlucky number. The pre-Christian calendar of thirteen four-week months, with one day over, was superseded by the Julian calendar (which had no weeks) based eventually on the year of twelve thirty-day Egyptian months with five days over. The author of the *Book of Enoch* in his treatise on astronomy and the calendar also reckoned a year to be 364 days, though he pronounced a curse on all who did not reckon a month to be 30 days long. Ancient calendar-makers seem to have interposed the day which had no month, and was not therefore counted as part of the year, between the first and last of their artificial 28-day months: so that the farmer's year lasted, from the calendar-maker's point of view, literally a year and a day.

In the Welsh Romances the number thirteen is of constant occurrence: 'Thirteen Precious Things', 'Thirteen Wonders of Britain', 'Thirteen Kingly Jewels'. The Thirteen Prison Locks, then, were thirteen months and on the extra day, the Day of Liberation, the Day of the Divine Child, Elphin was set free. This day will naturally have fallen just after the winter solstice—two days before Christmas, when the Romans had their mid-winter festival. I saw that if the true reading is 'in stocks and fetters a year and a day', then this clause should be attached to 'Primary chief bard am I to Elphin', in line 1: for it was Elphin who was fettered.

Now, Gwynn Jones dissents from the usual view that the word *Mabino-gion* means 'juvenile romances'; he suggests, by analogy with the Irish title Mac-ind-oic, applied to Angus of the Brugh, that it means 'tales of the son of a virgin mother' and shows that it was originally applied only to the four romances in which Pryderi son of Rhiannon appears. This 'son of a virgin mother' is always born at the winter solstice; which gives point to the story of Phylip Brydydd's contention with the minstrels for the privilege of first presenting Prince Rhys Ieuanc with a song on Christmas Day, and also his mention of Maelgwyn and Elphin in that context.

The riddle in stanza 16, 'I have been in the buttery', must refer to Kai, who was in charge of King Arthur's Buttery. The line, cleverly muddled up with the Barnacle riddle, should probably be attached to 'I was with my Lord in the highest sphere' (line 5 and stanza 5), Kai appearing in the *Triads* as 'one of the three diademed chiefs of battle', possessed of magical powers. In the *Romance of Olwen and Kilhwch* there is this description of him:

He could hold his breath under water for nine days and nights, and sleep for the same period. No physician could heal a wound inflicted by his sword. He could make himself at will as tall as the tallest tree in the wood. His natural heat was so great that in a deluge of rain whatever he carried in his hand remained dry a hand's-breadth above and below. On the coldest day he was like a glowing fuel to his comrades.

This is close to the account given of the Sun-hero Cuchulain in his battle rage. But in the later Arthurian legends Kai had degenerated into a buffoon and Chief of the Cooks.

The memory of the thirteen-month year was kept alive in the pagan English countryside until at least the fourteenth century. *The Ballad of Robin Hood and the Curtal Friar* begins:

> *But how many merry monthes be in the yeare?*
> *There are thirteen, I say;*
> *The mid-summer moon is the merryest of all,*
> *Next to the merry month of May.*

This has been altered in manifestly later ballad:

> *There are twelve months in all the year*
> *As I hear many men say.*
> *But the merriest month in all the year*
> *Is the merry month of May.*

Chapter Six

A VISIT TO SPIRAL CASTLE

My suggested answers to the riddles of the *Hanes Taliesin* were as follows:

Babel
Lot or Lota
Vran
Salome
Ne-esthan
Hur
David
Taliesin
Kai
Caleb
Hu Gadarn
Morvran
Gomer
Rhea
Idris
Joseph
Jesus
Uriel

This was as far as I could go without adopting the method of the crossword puzzler, which is to use the answers already secured as clues to the solution of the more difficult riddles that remain, but I made some progress with the riddle: 'I have been three periods in the Castle of Arianrhod.'

Arianrhod ('Silver wheel') appears in the 107th *Triad* as the 'Silver-circled daughter of Dôn', and is a leading character in the *Romance of Math the Son of Mathonwy*. No one familiar with the profuse variants of the same legend in every body of European myth can have doubts about her identity. She is the mother of the usual Divine Fish-Child Dylan who, after killing the usual Wren (as the New Year Robin does on St. Stephen's day) becomes Llew Llaw Gyffes ('the Lion with the Steady Hand'), the usual handsome and accomplished Sun-hero with the usual Heavenly Twin at his side. Arianrhod then adopts the form of Blodeuwedd, the usual Love-goddess, treacherously (as usual) destroys Llew Llaw—the story is at least as old as the Babylonian Gilgamesh epic—and is then transformed first into the usual Owl of Wisdom and then into the usual Old-Sow-who-eats-her-farrow; so feeds on Llew's dead flesh. But Llew, whose soul has taken the form of the usual eagle, is then, as usual, restored to life. The story is given in full in Chapter Seventeen.

In other words Arianrhod is one more aspect of Caridwen, or Cerridwen, the White Goddess of Life-in-Death and Death-in-Life; and to be in the Castle of Arianrhod is to be in a royal purgatory awaiting resurrection. For in primitive European belief it was only kings, chieftains and poets, or magicians, who were privileged to be reborn. Countless other less distinguished souls wandered disconsolately in the icy grounds of the Castle, as yet uncheered by the Christian hope of universal resurrection. Gwion makes this clear in his *Marwnad y Milveib* ('Elegy on the Thousand Children').

> *Incomprehensible numbers there were*
> *Maintained in a chilly hell*
> *Until the Fifth Age of the world,*
> *Until Christ should release the captives.*

Where was this purgatory situated? It must be distinguished from the Celtic Heaven, which was the Sun itself—a blaze of light (as we know from Armorican tradition) caused by the shining together of myriads of pure souls. Well, where should one expect to find it? In a quarter from which the Sun never shines. Where is that? In the cold North. How far to the North? Beyond the source of Boreas, the North Wind; for 'at the back of the North Wind'—a phrase used by Pindar to locate the land of the Hyperboreans—is still a popular Gaelic synonym for the Land of Death. But precisely where beyond the source of the North wind? Only a poet would be persistent enough to ask this last question. The poet is the unsatisfied child who dares to ask the difficult question which arises from the schoolmaster's answer to his simple question, and then the still more difficult question which arises from that. Surprisingly enough there is, on this occasion, a ready answer. Caer Arianrhod (not the submerged twon off the coast of Caernarvon, but the real Caer Arianrhod) is, according to Dr. Owen of the *Welsh Dictionary*, the constellation called 'Corona Borealis'. Not *Corona Septentrionalis*, 'the Northern Crown', but *Corona Borealis*, 'the Crown of the North Wind'. Perhaps we have the answer here to the question which puzzled Herodotus: 'Who are the Hyperboreans?' Were the Hyperboreans, the 'back-of-the-North-Wind-men', members of a North Wind cult, as the Thracians of the Sea of Marmara were? Did they believe that when they died their souls were taken off by Hermes, conductor of souls, to the calm silver-circled castle at the back of the North Wind, of which the bright star Alpheta was the guardian?

I should not venture to make such a fanciful suggestion if it were not for the mention of Oenopion and Tauropolus by the Scholiast on Apollonius Rhodius's *Argonautica*. This *Corona Borealis,* which is also called 'the Cretan Crown', was in ancient times sacred to a Cretan Goddess, wife to the God Dionysus, and according to this Scholiast the mother of—that is, worshipped by—Staphylus, Thoas, Oenopion, Tauropolus and others. These men were the eponymous ancestors of Pelasgo-Thracian clans or tribes settled in the Aegean islands of Chios and Lemnos, on the Thracian Chersonese, and in the Crimea, and culturally connected with North-Western Europe. The Goddess was Ariadne, ('Most Holy',) *alias* Alpheta—*alpha* and *eta* being the first and last letters of her name. She was the daughter, or younger self, of the ancient Cretan Moon-Goddess Pasiphaë, 'She who shines for all', and the Greeks made her a sister of their ancient vine-hero Deucalion, who survived the Great Flood. Ariadne, on whom 'Arianrhod' seems to be modelled, was an orgiastic goddess, and it is evident from the legends of Lemnos, Chios, the Chersonese and the Crimea, that male human sacrifice was an integral part of her worship, as it was among the pre-Roman devotees of the White Goddess of Britain. Orpheus himself, who lived 'among the savage Cauconians' close to Oenopion's home, was a sacred victim of her fury. He was torn in pieces by a pack of delirious women intoxicated by ivy and also, it seems, by the toadstool sacred to Dionysus. Eratosthenes of Alexandria, quoting Aeschylus's *Bassarides,* records that Orpheus refused to conform to local religion but 'believed the sun, whom he named Apollo, to be the greatest of the gods. Rising up in the night he ascended before dawn to the mountain called Pangaeum that he might see the sun first. At which Dionysus, being enraged, sent against him the Bassarids, who tore him in pieces. . . .' That is a dishonest way of telling the story. Proclus in his commentary on Plato is more to the point: 'Orpheus, because he was the leader in the Dionysian rites, is said to have suffered the same fate as the god.' But the head of Orpheus continued to sing and prophesy, like that of the God Bran. Orpheus, according to Pausanias, was worshipped by the Pelasgians, and the termination *eus* is always a proof of antiquity in a Greek name. 'Orpheus', like 'Erebus', the name of the Underworld over which the White Goddess ruled, is derived by grammarians from the root *ereph*, which means 'to cover or conceal'. It was the Moon-goddess, not the Sun-god, who originally inspired Orpheus.

The clearest sign that in Arianrhod we have the old matriarchal

Triple Goddess, or White Goddess, lies in her giving her son Llew Llaw a name and a set of arms. In patriarchal society it is always the father who gives both. Llew Llaw has no father at all, in the Romance, and must remain anonymous until his mother is tricked into making a man of him.

I thought at first that Gwion's riddle about Caer Arianrhod was to be completed with 'and the whirling round without motion between three elements'. The three elements are clearly fire, air and water, and the *Corona Borealis* revolves in a very small space compared with the southern constellations. But Gwion must have been taught that Arianrhod's Castle does not lie within 'the Arctic Circle', which includes the two Bears and the Bear-Warden, and that when the Sun rises in the House of the Crab, it begins to dip over the Northern horizon and does not free itself until the summer is over. To describe it as whirling round without motion would have been inaccurate; only the Little Bear does so, pivoted on the Pole-star. (As I show in Chapter Ten, the whirling-round is part of the riddle to which the answer is Rhea; but I will not anticipate the argument at this point.)

Yet, even if I knew the meaning of 'a period in the Castle of Arianrhod', could I answer the riddle? Who spent three periods there?

The sequences of 'I have been' or 'I am'—the earliest of them indisputably pre-Christian—which occur in so many bardic poems of Wales and Ireland seem to have several different though related senses. The primitive belief is plainly not in individual metempsychosis of the vulgar Indian sort—at one time a bluebottle, at the next a flower, at the next perhaps a Brahmini bull or a woman, according to one's merit. The 'I' is the Apollo-like god on whose behalf the inspired poet sings, not the poet himself. Sometimes the god may be referring mythically to his daily cycle as the Sun from dawn to dawn; sometimes to his yearly cycle from winter solstice to winter solstice with the months as stations of his progress; perhaps sometimes even to his grand cycle of 25,800 years around the Zodiac. All these cycles are types of one another; as we still speak either of the 'evening' or 'autumn' of our lives when we mean old age.

The commonest 'I have been' reference is to the yearly cycle, and to examine these seasonal 'I have been's (though for reasons of discretion the order has always been deliberately confused) is usually to find that they contain a complete series of round-the-year symbols.

> *I am water, I am a wren,*
> *I am a workman, I am a star,*
> *I am a serpent;*
> *I am a cell, I am a chink,*
> *I am a depository of song,*
> *I am a learned person, etc.*

Though the Pythagorean theory of metempsychosis, imported from the Greek colonies in Southern France, has been suspected in the Irish legend of Tuan MacCairill, one of the royal immigrants from Spain, who went through the successive metamorphoses of stag, boar, hawk and salmon before being born as a man, this is unlikely: the four beasts are all seasonal symbols, as will be shown.

The poetic language of myth and symbol used in ancient Europe was not, in principle, a difficult one but became confused, with the passage of time, by frequent modifications due to religious, social and linguistic change, and by the tendency of history to taint the purity of myth—that is to say, the accidental events in the life of a king who bore a divine name were often incorporated in the seasonal myth which gave him the title to royalty. A further complication was that anciently a large part of poetic education, to judge from the Irish *Book of Ballymote,* which contains a manual of cryptography, was concerned with making the language as difficult as possible in order to keep the secret close; in the first three years of his educational course, the Irish student for the Ollaveship had to master one hundred and fifty cypher-alphabets.[1]

What is the relation of Caer Sidi to Caer Arianrhod? Were they the same place? I think not, because Caer Sidi has been identified with Puffin Island off the coast of Anglesey and with Lundy Island in the Severn: both of them island Elysiums of the usual type. A clue to the problem is that though Caer Sidi, or Caer Sidin, means 'Revolving Castle' in Welsh, and though revolving islands are common in Welsh and Irish legend, the word 'Sidi' is apparently a translation of the Goidelic word *Sidhe,* a round barrow fortress belonging to the Aes Sidhe (Sidhe for short), the prime magicians of Ireland. There are several 'Fortresses of the Sidhe' in Ireland, the most remarkable ones being Brugh-na-Boyne (now called 'New Grange'), Knowth and Dowth, on the northern banks of the River Boyne. Their date and religious use must be considered in detail.

New Grange is the largest, and is said to have been originally occupied by The Dagda himself, the Tuatha dé Danaan Father-god who corresponds with the Roman Saturn, but afterwards by his Apollo-like son Angus who won it from him by a legal quibble. The Dagda on his first arrival in Ireland was evidently a son of the Triple Goddess Brigit ('the High One'); but the myth has been tampered with by successive editors. First, he is said to have married the Triple Goddess. Then he is said to have had only one wife with three names, Breg, Meng and Meabel ('Lie, Guile and Disgrace'), who bore him three daughters all called Brigit. Then it is said that not he but three of his descendants, Brian, Iuchar and

[1] 'The Thirteen Precious Things', 'The Thirteen Kingly Jewels', 'The Thirteen Wonders of Britain', etc., mentioned in the *Mabinogion* are likely to represent sets of cypher equivalents for the thirteen consonants of the British Beth-Luis-Nion alphabet.

Iuchurba married three princesses who together owned Ireland—Eire, Fodhla and Banbha. He was the son of 'Eladu' which the Irish glossarists explain as 'Science or Knowledge' but which may be a form of the Greek *Elate* ('fir-tree'); Elatos ('fir-man') was an early Achaean King of Cyllene, a mountain in Arcadia sacred to Demeter and later renowned for its college of learned and sacrosanct heralds. The Dagda and Elatos may thus both be equated with Osiris, or Adonis, or Dionysus, who was born from a fir and mothered by the horned Moon-goddess Isis, or Io, or Hathor.

New Grange is a flat-topped round barrow, about a quarter of a mile in circumference and fifty feet high. But it is built of heaped stones, some 50,000 tons of them, not of earth, and was originally covered with white quartz pebbles: a Bronze Age sepulchral practice in honour of the White Goddess which may account in part for the legends of Kings housed after death in glass castles. Ten enormous stone herms, weighing eight or ten tons apiece stand in a semi-circle around the southern base of the barrow, and one formerly stood at the summit. It is not known how many more have been removed from the semi-circle but the gaps suggest an original set of twelve. A hedge of about a hundred long flat stones, set edge to edge, rings the base around. Deep inside the barrow is a pre-Celtic passage-burial cave built with great slabs of stone, several of them measuring as much as seven feet by four.

The ground plan is the shape of a Celtic cross; one enters by a dolmen door at the base of the shaft. The shaft consists of a narrow passage, sixty feet long, through which one has to crawl on hands and knees. It leads to a small circular chamber, with a bee-hive corbelled vault twenty feet high; and there are three recesses which make the arms of the cross. When this cave was re-discovered in 1699 it contained three large empty boat-shaped stone basins, the sides engraved with stripes; two complete skeletons lying beside a central altar, stags' antlers, bones, and nothing else. Roman gold coins of the fourth century A.D., gold torques and remains of iron weapons were later found on the site of the fort, not in the cave. The fort was sacked by the Danes but there is nothing to show whether they, or earlier invaders, rifled the chamber of its other funerary furniture. Slabs of the doorway and of the interior are decorated with spiral patterns and there is forked lightning carved on one lintel. Since the old poets record that each rath was presided over by an enchantress and since, as will be shown, the Sidhe were such skilful poets that even the Druids were obliged to go to them for the spells that they needed, it seems likely that the original Caer Sidi, where the Cauldron of Inspiration was housed, was a barrow of the New Grange sort. For these barrows were fortresses above and tombs below. The Irish 'Banshee' fairy is a Bean-Sidhe ('Woman of the Hill'); as priestess of the great dead she wails in prophetic anticipation whenever anyone of royal blood is about to die. From an incident in the Irish romance of *Fionn's Boyhood*, it appears that the entrances to these burial caves were left open at *Samhain*, All Souls' Eve, which was also celebrated as a feast of the Dead in Ancient Greece, to allow the spirits of the heroes to come out for an airing; and that the interiors were illuminated until cock-crow the next morning.

On the east side of the mound, diametrically opposite the entrance, a stone was discovered in 1901 which has three suns carved on it, two of them with their rays enclosed in a circle as if in prison, the other free. Above them is a much rougher, unenclosed sun and above that, notched across a straight line, the Ogham letters B and I—which, as will be explained presently, are the first and last letters of the ancient Irish alphabet, dedicated respectively to Inception and Death. The case is pretty plain: the sacred kings of Bronze Age Ireland, who were solar kings of a most primitive type, to judge by the taboos which bound them and by the reputed effect of their behaviour on crops and hunting, were buried beneath these barrows; but their spirits went to 'Caer Sidi', the Castle of Ariadne, namely *Corona Borealis*. Thus the pagan Irish could call New Grange 'Spiral Castle' and, revolving a fore-finger in explanation, could say, 'Our king has gone to Spiral Castle': in other words, 'he is dead'. A revolving wheel before the door of a castle is common in Goidelic legend. According to Keating, the magic fortress of the enchantress Blanaid, in the Isle of Man, was protected by one—nobody could enter until it was still. In front of the doorway of New Grange there is a broad slab carved with spirals, which forms part of the stone hedge. The spirals are double ones: follow the lines with your finger from outside to inside and when you reach the centre, there is the head of another spiral coiled in the reverse direction to take you out of the maze again. So the pattern typifies death and rebirth; though, according to Gwion's poem *Preiddeu Annwm*, 'only seven ever returned from Caer Sidi'. It may well be that oracular serpents were once kept in these sepulchral caves, and that these were the serpents which St. Patrick expelled, though perhaps only metaphorically. Delphi, the home of Apollo, was once an oracular tomb of this same sort, with a spiralled python and a prophetic priestess of the Earth Goddess, and the 'omphalos' or 'navel shrine' where the python was originally housed, was built underground in the same beehive style, which derives originally from the African *masabo*, or ghosthouse. The antlers at New Grange were probably part of the sacred king's head-dress, like the antlers worn by the Gaulish god Cernunnos, and the horns of Moses, and those of Dionysus and King Alexander shown on coins.

The provenience of the bee-hive tomb with a passage entrance and lateral niches is no mystery. It came to Ireland from the Eastern Mediter-

ranean by way of Spain and Portugal at the close of the third millennium
B.C.: the corbelled roof of New Grange occurs also at Tirbradden, Dowth
and Seefin. But the eight double-spirals at the entrance, which are merely
juxtaposed, not cunningly wreathed together in the Cretan style, are
paralleled in Mycenaean Greece; and this suggests that the carvings were
made by the Danaans when they took over the shrine from the previous
occupants, who in Irish history appear as the tribes of Partholan and
Nemed that invaded the country in the years 2048 and 1718 B.C., coming
from Greece by way of Spain. If so, this would account for the legend of
the usurpation of the shrine by the god Angus from his father The Dagda.
The arrival of the Danaans in Ireland, as was mentioned in Chapter III, is
dated in the *Book of Invasions* at the middle of the fifteenth century B.C.
This is plausible: they will have been late-comers of the round-barrow
tribes that first reached Ireland from Britain about 1700 B.C. That they
propitiated the heroes of the previous cult is well established: their food-
vessels are found in passage-grave burials.

Dr. R. S. Macalister in his *Ancient Ireland* (1935) takes an original
view of New Grange. He holds that it was built by the Milesians, whom he
dates about 1000 B.C. and supposes to have come from Britain, not Spain,
on the ground that it incorporates a number of ornamental stones in the
passage and chamber, one of them with its pattern broken, apparently
arranged haphazard, and that on some of these the carving has been
defaced by pick-surfacing like that found on the trilithons of Stonehenge.
This is to suggest that it is a mock-antique in the style of several hundred
years before; a theory to which no other archaeologist of repute seems to
have subscribed. But his observations do suggest that the Milesians took
over the oracular shrine from the Danaans and patched it, where it showed
signs of decay, with ornamental stones borrowed from other burials.
Another suggestion of his carries greater conviction: that Angus' Brugh
('palace') was not New Grange but a huge circular enclosure not far off
in a bend of the Boyne, which may have been an amphitheatre for funerary
games in connexion with all the many burials of the neighbourhood.

Most Irish archaeologists are now, I find, agreed that New Grange was
built by a matriarchal passage-grave-making people that first reached
Ireland about the year 2100 B.C., but not until they had become well-
established some five hundred years later and were able to command the
enormous labour necessary for the task. The spirals, though paralleled
in Mycenean shaft-burials of 1600 B.C., may be far earlier since examples
of unknown date occur also at Malta. On one of the outer stones a symbol
is carved which suggests a Cretan ideogram and apparently represents a
ship with a high prow and stern and a single large sail; beside it are vertical
scratches and a small circle. Christopher Hawkes, my principal informant
on this subject, has written to me that not only are the skeletons and

antlers unlikely to be co-eval with the building but that there may have been many successive despoilments of the burial before they were put there. The original funerary furniture cannot be guessed at, since no virgin passage-grave of this type has been opened in recent years; we must wait until the Cairn of Queen Maeve is opened. This overlooks Sligo Bay; it is built of some 40,000 tons of stone and the entrance is lost. We may have to wait a long time, because the Sligo people are superstitious and would consider a desecration of the tomb unlucky: Maeve is Mab, the Queen of Faery.

What the basins contained may be inferred from *Exodus, XXIV* (verses 4–8). Moses, having set up twelve stone herms, or posts, at the foot of a sacred hill, offered bull-sacrifices and sprinkled half the blood on a thirteenth herm in the middle of the circle, or semi-circle; the rest of the blood he put into basins, which must have been of considerable size. Then he and his colleague Aaron, with seventy-two companions, went up to feast on the roasted flesh. On this occasion, the blood in the basins was sprinkled on the people as a charm of sanctification; but its use in the oracular shrine was always to feed the ghost of the dead hero and to encourage him to return from Caer Sidi or Caer Arianrhod to answer questions of importance.

The visit of Aeneas, mistletoe-bough in hand, to the Underworld to cross-examine his father Anchises must be read in this sense. Aeneas sacrificed a bull and let the blood gush into a trough, and the ghost of Anchises (who had married the Love-goddess Venus Erycina, and been killed by lightning and was, in fact, a sacred king of the usual Herculean type), drank the blood and obligingly prophesied about the glories of Rome. Of course, the ghost did not really lap the blood, but a lapping sound was heard in the dark; what happened was that the Sibyl, who conducted Aeneas below, drank the blood and it produced in her the desired prophetic ecstasy. That Sibyls acted so is known from the case of the Priestess of Mother Earth at Aegira ('Black Poplar', a tree sacred to heroes) in Achaea. The peeping and muttering of ghosts on such occasions is understandable: two or three Biblical texts refer to the queer bat-like voices in which demons, or familiars, speak through the mouths of prophets or prophetesses. Bull's blood was most potent magic and was used, diluted with enormous quantities of water, to fertilize fruit-trees in Crete and Greece. Taken neat it was regarded as a poison deadly to anyone but a Sibyl or a priest of Mother Earth; Jason's father and mother died from a draught of it. So did ass-eared King Midas of Gordium.

That bull's blood was used for divination in ancient Ireland is not mere supposition. A rite called 'The Bull Feast' is mentioned in the *Book of the Dun Cow*:

A white bull was killed and a man ate his fill of the flesh and drank of the broth; and a spell of truth was chanted over him as he slept off the meal. He would see in a dream the shape and appearance of the man who should be made king, and the sort of work in which he was at that time engaged.

The white bull recalls the sacred white bulls of the Gaulish mistletoe rite; the white bull on which the Thracian Dionysus rode; the white bulls sacrificed on the Alban Mount and at the Roman Capitol; and the white bull representing the true seed of Israel in the apocalyptic *Book of Enoch*.

Now we begin to understand the mysterious *Preiddeu Annwm* ('the Spoils of Annwm') in which—between Gwion's interpolative taunts at the ignorance of Heinin and the other court-bards—one Gwair ap Geirion laments that he cannot escape from Caer Sidi. The refrain is: 'Except seven none returned from Caer Sidi.' We know at least two who did return: Theseus and Daedalus, both Attic Sun-heroes. The stories of Theseus's expedition to the Underworld and of his adventure in the Cretan labyrinth of Cnossos are really two parts of a single confused myth. Theseus ('he who disposes') goes naked, except for his lion-skin, to the centre of the maze, there kills the bull-headed monster of the double-axe—the *labris* from which the word 'labyrinth' is derived—and returns safely: and the goddess who enables him to do so is the Goddess Ariadne whom the Welsh called Arianrhod. In the second part of the myth he fails in his Underworld expedition: he has to be rescued by Hercules, and his companion Peirithoüs remains behind like Gwair, perpetually sighing for deliverance. The myth of the hero who defeats Death was combined by the Greek mythographers with a historical event: the sack of the labyrinthine palace of Cnossos by Danaan raiders from Greece about 1400 B.C. and the defeat of King Minos, the Bull-king. Daedalus ('the bright one') similarly escapes from the Cretan labyrinth, guided by the Moon-goddess Pasiphaë, but without using violence; he was a Sun-hero of the Aegean colonists of Cumae, and of the Sardinians, as well as of the Athenians.

Caer Sidi in the *Preiddeu Annwm* is given a new synonym in each of the seven stanzas. It appears as Caer Rigor ('the royal castle') with a pun maybe on the Latin *rigor mortis*; Caer Colur ('the gloomy castle'); Caer Pedryvan ('four-cornered castle'), four times revolving; Caer Vediwid ('the castle of the perfect ones'); Caer Ochren ('the castle of the shelving side'—i.e. entered from the side of a slope); Caer Vandwy ('the castle on high').

I do not know who the canonical seven were, but among those eligible for the honour were Theseus, Hercules, Amathaon, Arthur, Gwydion, Harpocrates, Kay, Owain, Daedalus, Orpheus and Cuchulain. (When

Cuchulain, mentioned by Gwion in a poem, harrowed Hell, he brought back three cows and a magic cauldron.) Aeneas is unlikely to have been one of the seven. He did not die as the others did; he merely visited an oracular cave, just as King Saul had done at Endor, or Caleb at Machpelah. The castle that they entered—revolving, remote, royal, gloomy, lofty, cold, the abode of the Perfect Ones, with four corners, entered by a dark door on the shelving side of a hill—was the castle of death or the Tomb, the Dark Tower to which Childe Roland came in the ballad. This description fits the New Grange burial cave, but 'four-cornered' refers, I think, to the kist-vaen method of burial which was invented by the pre-Greek inhabitants of Northern Greece and the islands about Delos and thence conveyed to Western Europe by Bronze Age immigrants, the round-barrow men: the kist being a small rectangular stone box in which the dead body was laid in a crouched position. Odysseus may be said to have been 'three periods in the castle of Arianrhod' because he entered with twelve companions into the Cyclops' cave, but escaped; was detained by Calypso on Ogygia, but escaped; and by the enchantress Circe on Aeaea —another sepulchral island—but escaped. Yet it is unlikely that Odysseus is intended: I think that Gwion is referring to Jesus Christ, whom the twelfth-century poet Dafydd Benfras makes visit a Celtic Annwm, and who escaped from the gloomy cave in the hillside in which he had been laid by Joseph of Arimathea. But how was Jesus 'three periods in the Castle of Arianrhod'? I take this for a heresy making Jesus, as the Second Adam, a reincarnation of Adam, and, as the Davidic Messiah, a reincarnation also of David. The Age of Adam and the Age of David are particularized in Gwion's *Divregwawd Taliesin*. Jesus is pictured there at still waiting in the heavens for the dawn of the Seventh Age: 'Was it nos to Heaven he went when he departed hence? And at the Day of Judgement he will come to us here. For the fifth age was the blessed one of David the Prophet. The sixth age is the age of Jesus, which shalll last till the Day of Judgement.' In the Seventh Age he would be called Taiesin.

PREIDDEU ANNWM

(The Spoils of Annwm)

Praise to the Lord, Supreme Ruler of the Heavens,
Who hath extended his dominion to the shore of the world.
Complete was the prison of Gwair in Caer Sidi
Through the spite of Pwyll and Pryderi.
No one before him went into it;
A heavy blue chain firmly held the youth,
And for the spoils of Annwm gloomily he sings,
And till doom shall he continue his lay.

Thrice the fullness of Prydwen we went into it;
Except seven, none returned from Caer Sidi.

Am I not a candidate for fame, to be heard in the song?
In Caer Pedryvan four times revolving,
The first word from the cauldron, when was it spoken?
By the breath of nine damsels it is gently warmed.
Is it not the cauldron of the chief of Annwm, in its fashion
With a ridge around its edge of pearls?
It will not boil the food of a coward or one forsworn,
A sword bright flashing to him will be brought,
And left in the hand of Lleminawg,
And before the portals of the cold place the horns of light shall be burning.
And when we went with Arthur in his splendid labours,
Except seven, none returned from Caer Vediwid.

Am I not a candidate for fame, to be heard in the song?
In the four-cornered enclosure, in the island of the strong door,
Where the twilight and the black of night move together,
Bright wine was the beverage of the host.
Three times the fulness of Prydwen, we went on sea,
Except seven, none returned from Caer Rigor.

I will not allow praise to the lords of literature.
Beyond Caer Wydr they behold not the prowess of Arthur.
Three times twenty-hundred men stood on the wall.
It was difficult to converse with their sentinel.
Three times the fulness of Prydwen, we went with Arthur.
Except seven, none returned from Caer Colur.

I will not allow praise to the men with trailing shields.
They know not on what day, or who caused it,
Or at what hour of the splendid day Cwy was born,
Or who prevented him from going to the dales of Devwy.
They know not the brindled ox, with his thick head band,
And seven-score knobs in his collar.
And when we went with Arthur of mournful memory,
Except seven, none returned from Caer Vandwy.

I will not allow praise to men of drooping courage,
They know not on what day the chief arose,
Or at what hour in the splendid day the owner was born;
Or what animal they keep of silver head.
When we went with Arthur of mournful contention,
Except seven, none returned from Caer Ochren.

Pwyll and Pryderi were successive rulers of the 'Africans' of Annwm in Pembroke, the earliest invaders of Wales; at their death, like Minos and Rhadamanthus of Crete, they became Lords of the Dead. It was from Pryderi, son of Rhiannon, that Gwydion stole the sacred swine and Gwair seems to have gone on a similar marauding expedition in the company of Arthur; for his prison called, in *Triad 61*, the Castle of Oeth and Anoeth is also the prison from which, according to *Triad 50*, Arthur was rescued by his page Goreu, son of Custennin; Gwair is thus to Arthur as Peirithoüs was to Theseus, and Goreu is to Arthur as Hercules was to Theseus. Possibly Gwion in the Romance is counting on the court-bards to guess 'Arthur', not 'Jesus', as the answer to 'I was three periods in the Castle of Arianrhod', since in *Triad 50* Arthur is said to have been rescued by this same Goreu from three prisons—the Castle of Oeth and Anoeth; the Castle of Pendragon ('Lord of Serpents'); the Dark Prison under the Stone—all of them death-prisons. Or is he covertly presenting Jesus as an incarnation of Arthur?

Prydwen was King Arthur's magic ship; Llaminawg, in whose hands Arthur left the flashing sword, appears in the *Morte D'Arthur* as 'Sir Bedivere'. Caer Wydr is Glastonbury, or *Inis Gutrin*, thought of as the glass castle[1] in which Arthur's soul was housed after death; Glastonbury is also the Isle of Avalon (Appletrees) to which his dead body was conveyed by Morgan le Faye. The heavy blue chain is the water around the Island of Death. The myth of Cwy, like that of Gwair and Arthur, is no longer extant, but the 'animal with the silver head' is perhaps the White Roebuck of which we are in search, and the name of the Ox's headband is one of the prime bardic secrets which Gwion in his *Cyst Wy'r Beirdd* ('Reproof of the Bards') taunts Heinin with not possessing:

> *The name of the firmament,*
> *The name of the elements,*
> *And the name of the language,*
> *And the name of the Head-band.*
> *Avaunt, ye bards—*

About a hundred years before Gwion wrote this, the Glastonbury monks had dug up an oak coffin, from sixteen feet underground, which they claimed to be Arthur's, and faked a Gothic inscription on a leaden

[1] Caer Wydr (Glass Castle) is a learned pun of Gwion's. The town of Glastonbury is said by William of Malmesbury to have been named after its secular founder Glasteing, who came there from the north with his twelve brothers at some time before 600. The Latin equivalent of *Gutrin* was *vitrinus*; and the Saxon was *glas*. This colour word covered any shade between deep blue and light-green—it could be applied equally to Celtic blue enamel and Roman bottle-glass. The 'glass' castles of Irish, Manx and Welsh legend are thus seen to be either island shrines, surrounded by glassy-green water, or star-prisons islanded in the dark-blue night sky; but in mediaeval legend they were made of glass, and their connexion with death and with the Moon-goddess has been preserved in the popular superstition that it is unlucky to see the Moon through glass.

cross a foot long, said to have been found inside, which Giraldus Cambrensis saw and believed authentic. I think Gwion is here saying: 'You bards think that Arthur's end was in that oak coffin at Glastonbury. I know better.' The inscription ran: 'Here lies buried the renowned King Arthur with Guenevere his second wife in the Isle of Avalon.'

It will be objected that man has as valid a claim to divinity as woman. That is true only in a sense; he is divine not in his single person, but only in his twinhood. As Osiris, the Spirit of the Waxing Year he is always jealous of his wierd, Set, the Spirit of the Waning Year, and vice-versa; he cannot be both of them at once except by an intellectual effort that destroys his humanity, and this is the fundamental defect of the Apollonian or Jehovistic cult. Man is a demi-god: he always has either one foot or the other in the grave; woman is divine because she can keep both her feet always in the same place, whether in the sky, in the underworld, or on this earth. Man envies her and tells himself lies about his own completeness, and thereby makes himself miserable; because if he is divine she is not even a demi-goddess—she is a mere nymph and his love for her turns to scorn and hate.

Woman worships the male infant, not the grown man: it is evidence of her deity, of man's dependence on her for life. She is passionately interested in grown men, however, because the love-hate that Osiris and Set feel for each other on her account is a tribute to her divinity. She tries to satisfy both, but can only do so by alternate murder, and man tries to regard this as evidence of her fundamental falsity, not of his own irreconcilable demands on her.

The joke is that the monks had really, it seems, discovered the body of Arthur, or Gwyn, or whatever the original name of the Avalon hero was. Christopher Hawkes describes in his *Prehistoric Foundations of Europe* this form of burial:

Inhumation (and more rarely burial after cremation in tree-trunk coffins covered by a barrow) was already practised in Schleswig-Holstein in the beginning of its Bronze Age. . . . It is probable that the coffin originally represented a dug-out boat, and that the idea of a voyage by water to the next world, well attested in Scandinavia in the later Bronze Age and again in the Iron Age down to its famous culmination in Viking times, is here to be recognized at its first beginning, inspired, it may well be, ultimately from Egypt through the Baltic connexions with the South now passing along the Amber Route. The same rite of boat- or coffin-burial appears simultaneously in Britain in the middle centuries of the second millennium, when the North Sea trade-route was flourishing, and penetrates the Wessex culture along the south coast where the burial at Hove noted for its Scandinavian affinities [it contained a handled cup of Baltic amber] was of this type, but more prominent on the east coast, especially in Yorkshire where the Irish route over the Pennines [barter of Irish gold against Baltic amber] reached the sea. The classic example is the Gristhorpe coffin-burial near Scarborough [an oak coffin containing the skeleton of an old man, with oak-branches and what appeared to be mistletoe over it], but the recent discovery in the great barrow of Loose Howe on the Cleveland Moors of a primary burial with no less than three boat dug-outs must henceforward stand at the head of the series and serve to show how the same rite took hold among the seafarers on both sides of the North Sea between about 1600 and 1400 B.C.

The nine damsels of the cauldron recall the nine virgins of the Isle of Sein in Western Brittany in the early fifth century A.D., described by Pomponius Mela. They were possessed of magical powers and might be approached by those who sailed to consult them.[1]

The sacred king, then, is a Sun-king and returns at death to the Universal Mother, the White Moon Goddess, who imprisons him in the extreme north. Why the north? Because that is the quarter from which the Sun never shines, from which the wind brings snow; only dead suns are to be found in the cold polar north. The Sun-god is born at mid-winter when the Sun is weakest and has attained his most southerly station; therefore his representative, the Sun-king, is killed at the summer solstice when the Sun attains his most northerly station. The relation between Caer Sidi and Caer Arianrhod seems to be that the burial place of the dead king was a barrow on an island, either in the river or the sea, where his spirit lived under charge of oracular and orgiastic priestesses; but his soul went to the stars and there hopefully awaited rebirth in another king. And the evidence of the oak coffin at the Isle of Avalon points plainly to the derivation of the Arthur cult from the Eastern Mediterranean by way of the Amber Route, the Baltic and Denmark, between 1600 and 1400 B.C.; though the cult of other oracular heroes in Britain and Ireland is likely to be seven or eight centuries older.

In Britain the tradition of Spiral Castle survives in the Easter Maze dance of country villages, the mazes being called 'Troy Town' in England and in Wales 'Caer-droia'. The Romans probably named them after the Troy Game, a labyrinthine dance of Asia Minor, performed by young

[1] The Island of Sein, which is not far from the great religious centre of Carnac and must have had a ritual connexion with it, retained its magical reputation very late. It was the last place in Europe to be Christianized: by seventeenth-century Jesuits. The island women wear the highest head-dresses in Brittany—the nine priestesses must have worn the same—and until recently had a reputation for enticing sailors to destruction on the rocks by witchcraft. There are two megalithic menhirs on the island, which is completely treeless, but no archaeological excavations have yet been made there.

noblemen at Rome under the Early Empire in memory of their Trojan origin; but Pliny records that Latin children performed it too. In Delos it was called the Crane Dance and was said to record the escape of Theseus from the Labyrinth. The maze dance seems to have come to Britain from the Eastern Mediterranean with the New Stone Age invaders of the third millennium B.C., since ancient rough stone mazes of the same pattern as the English are found in Scandinavia and North-eastern Russia. On a rock slab near Bosinney in Cornwall two mazes are carved; and another is carved on a massive granite block from the Wicklow Hills, now in the Dublin National Museum. These mazes have the same pattern, too: the Labyrinth of Daedalus shown on Cretan coins.

Chapter Seven

GWION'S RIDDLE SOLVED

A Goidelic alphabet, called Ogham, was used in Britain and Ireland some centuries before the introduction of the Latin A B C. Its invention is credited in the mediaeval Irish *Book of Ballymote* to 'Ogma Sun-face son of Breas'—one of the early gods of the Goidels. Ogma, according to Lucian, who wrote in the second century A.D., was pictured as a veteran Hercules, with club and lion-skin, drawing crowds of prisoners along with golden chains connected by their ears to the tip of his tongue. The alphabet consisted of twenty letters—fifteen consonants and five vowels—apparently corresponding to a deaf-and-dumb finger-language.

Numerous examples of this alphabet occur in ancient stone inscriptions in Ireland, the Isle of Man, North and South Wales, and Scotland; with one at Silchester in Hampshire, the capital of the Atrebates who took part in the Second Belgic Invasion of Britain between Julius Caesar's raid and the Claudian conquest. Here are two versions: the first quoted from Brynmor-Jones and Rhys's *History of the Welsh People*, and the second from Dr. Macalister's *Secret Languages of Ireland*:

B.	L.	F*.	S.	N.	B.	L.	F.	S.	N.
H.	D.	T.	C.	Q.	H.	D.	T.	C.	Q.
M.	G.	NG.	FF†.	R.	M.	G.	NG.	Z.	R.

[* pronounced V]   [† pronounced F]

It will be seen that both these alphabets are 'Q-Celt', or Goidelic, because they contain a Q but no P; Goidels from the Continent were established in South-Eastern Britain two hundred years before the Belgic (P-Celt) invasions from Gaul in the early fourth century B.C.; and it is thought that the common language of Bronze Age Britain was an early form of Goidelic, as it was in Ireland. The Ogham alphabet quoted in the *Oxford English Dictionary* (as if it were the only one in existence) differs from both the Rhys and Macalister Oghams by having M.G.Y.Z.R. as its last line of consonants: but the Y is doubtless an error for NY, another way of spelling the Gn as in *Catalogne*. In still another version, quoted in Charles Squire's *Mythology of the British Isles*, the fourteenth letter is given as ST and an X sign is offered for P.

Dr. Macalister proves that in Ireland Oghams were not used in public inscriptions until Druidism began to decline: they had been kept a dark secret and when used for written messages between one Druid and another, nicked on wooden billets, were usually cyphered. The four sets, each of five characters, he suggests, represented fingers used in a sign language: to form any one of the letters of the alphabet, one needed only to extend the appropriate amount of fingers of one hand, pointing them in one of four different directions. But this would have been a clumsy method of signalling. A much quicker, less conspicuous and less fatiguing method would have been to regard the left hand as a key-board, like that of a typewriter, with the letters marked by the tips, the two middle joints, and the bases of the fingers and thumb, and to touch the required spots with the forefinger of the right hand. Each letter in the inscriptions consists of nicks, from one to five in number, cut with a chisel along the edge of a squared stone; there are four different varieties of nick, which makes twenty letters. I assume that the number of nicks in a letter indicated the number of the digit, counting from left to right, on which the letter occurred in the finger language, while the variety of nick indicated the position of the letter on the digit. There were other methods of using the alphabet for secret signalling purposes. The *Book of Ballymote* refers to *Cos-ogham* ('leg-ogham') in which the signaller, while seated, used his fingers to imitate inscriptional Ogham with his shin bone serving as the edge against which the nicks were cut. In *Sron-ogham* ('nose-ogham') the nose was used in much the same way. These alternative methods were useful for signalling across a room; the key-board method for closer work. Gwion is evidently referring to *Sron-ogham* when he mentions, among all the other things he knows, 'why the nose is ridged'; the answer is 'to make ogham-signalling easier'.

This is the inscriptional form of the alphabet as given by Macalister:

Besides these twenty letters, five combinations of vowels were used in the deaf-and-dumb language to represent five foreign sounds. These were:

Ea   Oi   Ia   Ui   Ae

which represented respectively:

Kh   Th   P   Ph   X

In inscriptions these letters were given elaborate characters entirely different from the other letters. Kh had a St. Andrew's cross, Th had a lozenge, P a piece of lattice work, Ph a spiral, and X a portcullis.

I take this to have been the finger key-board, with the vowels conveniently grouped in the centre:

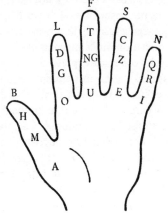

Julius Caesar records in his *Gallic War* that the Druids of Gaul used 'Greek letters' for their public records and private correspondence but did not consign their sacred doctrine to writing 'lest it should become vulgarized and lest, also, the memory of scholars should become impaired.' Dr. Macalister suggests that the Ogham alphabet, when complete with the extra letters, corresponds fairly closely with an early, still somewhat Semitic, form of the Greek alphabet, known as the Formello-Cervetri which is scratched on two vases, one from Caere and the other from Veii in Italy, dated about the fifth century B.C. The letters are written Semitically from right to left and begin with A.B.G.D.E. He assumes that the 'Greek letters' used by the Druids were this alphabet of twenty-six letters, four more than the Classical Greek, though they discarded one as unnecessary; and I think that he has proved his case.

But did the Druids invent their finger-language before they learned this Greek alphabet? Dr. Macalister thinks that they did not, and I should agree with him but for two main considerations. (1) The order of letters in the Ogham is altogether different from the Greek: one would have expected the Druids to follow the original order closely if this was their first experience of alphabetic spelling. (2) If the five foreign letters were an original part of the Ogham alphabet why were they not integrated with the rest in its inscriptional form? It would have been simple to allot them nicks as follows:

⁄	*⁄⁄*	*⁄⁄⁄*	*⁄⁄⁄⁄*	*⁄⁄⁄⁄⁄*
Ea	Oi	Ia	Ui	Ae
[Kh	Th	P	Ph	X]

And why in the finger-alphabet were they not spelt out with the nearest equivalent combinations of consonants—CH for Kh, CS for X, and so on —instead of being expressed allusively in vowel combinations?

That the vowel combinations are allusive is easily understood from the finger diagram above. In order to express the *Kh* sound of the Greek letter *chi*, the Druids used the Latin combination of C and H, but expressed this allusively as Ea, by reference to the fourth finger, the E digit, on which the letter C occurs, and to the thumb, the A digit, on which the letter H occurs. Similarly for X, pronounced 'CS', they used the E digit, on which both C and S occur, but introduced this with the A digit on which H occurs; H being a silent and merely ancillary letter in Celtic languages, and its use here being merely to form a two-vowel combination of A and E. Th is written Oi and Ph is written Ui because Th is a shrill variety of D (as *theos* in Greek corresponds with the Latin *deus* 'god'), and because Ph is a shrill variety of F (as *phegos* in Greek corresponds with the Latin *fagus* 'beech-tree'). D occurs on the O digit and F on the U digit; so to differentiate Th from D and Ph from F, the I is made the combination vowel of O in one case and U in the other—I in Irish being used as an indication of shrillness of sound. Finally P is written Ia, because B which was originally pronounced P in the Celtic languages (the Welsh still habitually confound the two sounds), occurs on the A digit; the I is an indication that P is distinguished from B in foreign languages.

I conclude that the twenty letters of the Ogham alphabet were in existence long before the Formello-Cervetri alphabet was brought to Italy from Greece and that the Gallic Druids added the five foreign letters to them with such disdain as virtually to deny them any part in the system. What complicates the case is that the ancient Irish word for 'alphabet' is 'Beth-Luis-Nion' which suggests that the order of letters in the Ogham alphabet was originally B.L.N., though it had become B.L.F. before the ban on inscriptions was lifted. Besides, the accepted Irish tradition was that the alphabet originated in Greece, not Phoenicia, and was brought to Ireland by way of Spain, not Gaul. Spenser records this in his *View of the Present State of Ireland* (1596): 'it seemeth that they had them [the letters] from the nation that came out of Spaine.'

The names of the letters of the B.L.F. alphabet are given by Roderick O'Flaherty in his seventeenth-century *Ogygia*, on the authority of Duald Mac Firbis, a family bard of the O'Briens who had access to the old records, as follows:

B	BOIBEL	M	MOIRIA
L	LOTH	G	GATH
F[V]	FORANN	Ng	NGOIMAR
N	NEIAGADON	Y	IDRA

S	SALIA	R	RIUBEN
H	UIRIA	A	ACAB
D	DAIBHAITH (DAVID)	O	OSE
T	TEILMON	U	URA
C	CAOI	E	ESU
CC	CAILEP	I	JAICHIM

When recently I wrote on this subject to Dr. Macalister, as the best living authority on Oghams, he replied that I must not take O'Flaherty's alphabets seriously: 'They all seem to me to be late artificialities, or rather pedantries, of little more importance than the affectations of Sir Piercie Shafton and his kind.' I pass on this caution in all fairness, for my argument depends on O'Flaherty's alphabet, and Dr. Macalister's is a very broad back for anyone to shelter behind who thinks that I am writing nonsense. But the argument of this book began with the assumption that Gwion was concealing an alphabetic secret in his riddling poem. And the answers to the riddles if I have not got them wrong—though 'Morvran' and 'Moiria', 'Ne-esthan' and 'Neiagadon', 'Rhea' and 'Riuben' do not seem to match very well—approximate so closely to the 'Boibel Loth' that I feel justified in supposing that O'Flaherty was recording a genuine tradition at least as old as the thirteenth century A.D. and that the answers to the so-far unsolved riddles will be found in the Boibel-Loth letter-names not yet accounted for.

We can begin our secondary process of unravelling Gwion's riddles by putting Idris at place 14 as an equivalent of Idra; and removing the J from Jose (Joseph) and Jesu (Jesus), neither of which names—as Gwion the Hebrew scholar may have known—originally began with J; and transposing Uriel and Hur—for the mediaeval Irish had long lost their aspirated H, so that Hur and Uria easily got confused. Then if the answers to our unsolved riddles are to be found in the unused letters of the Boibel-Loth, this leaves us with ACAB and JAICHIM; and with five unsolved riddles:

I have been at the throne of the Distributor,

I was loquacious before I was gifted with speech;

I am Alpha Tetragrammaton.

I am a wonder whose origin is not known—

I shall be until the day of doom upon the earth.

'Moiria', the Boibel-Loth equivalent of 'Morvran', suggests 'Moreh', or 'Moriah', at both of which places Jehovah, in *Genesis*, makes a covenant with Abraham and allots a dominion to him and to his seed for ever. Another name for Moriah is Mount Zion, and in *Isaiah, XVIII* Mount

Zion is mentioned as the Throne of the Lord of Hosts who 'scatters, distributes and treads underfoot'. 'Moiria' also suggests the Greek word *moira*, a share, lot or distribution. If 'Moriah' is the answer to the first of these five unsolved riddles, it must be linked with 'I have been bard of the harp to Deon of Lochlyn'; and we must credit the scholarly Gwion with interpreting the word as meaning Mor-Iah, or Mor-Jah, 'the god of the sea', the word 'Mor' being the Welsh equivalent of the Hebrew 'Marah' (the salt sea). He is in fact identifying Jah, the Hebrew God, with Bran who was a grain-god as well as a god of the alder. The identification is justified. One of the early gods worshipped at Jerusalem and later included in the synthetic cult of Jehovah was the harvest god Tammuz for whom first-fruits of grain were yearly brought from Bethlehem ('the house of bread'). The natives of Jerusalem were still wailing for him at the Feast of Unleavened Bread in Isaiah's day and according to Jerome he had a sacred grove at Bethlehem. It will be remembered that the Temple was built on the 'threshing floor of Araunah', which sounds uncannily like Arawn. Moreover, Bran's crow was equally sacred to Jehovah. Still more conclusive is Jehovah's claim to the seventh day as sacred to himself. In the contemporary astrological system the week was divided between the sun, moon and seven planets, and the Sabians of Harran in Mesopotamia, who were of Aegean origin, put the days under the rule of seven deities, in the order still current in Europe: Sun, Moon, Nergal (Mars), Nabu (Mercury), Bel (Juppiter), Beltis (Venus), Cronos (Saturn). Thus Jehovah, the god whose holiest day is Saturday, must be identified with Cronos or Saturn, who is Bran. We should credit Gwion with understanding this, and also with knowing that Uriel and Uriah are the same word, El and Jah being interchangeable names of the Hebrew God.

The divine name of Alpha written in four letters turns out to be 'Acab' in O'Flaherty's list of letter-names; which suggests Achab (Ahab) King of Israel, a name borne also by the prophet who appears in the *Acts of the Apostles* as 'Agabus'. It is the name 'Agabus' which explains the secondary riddle 'I have been loquacious before I was gifted with speech', for Agabus (who according to the pseudo-Dorotheus was one of the Seventy Disciples) is mentioned twice in the *Acts of the Apostles*. In the first mention (*Acts XI*) he *signified by the Spirit* that there would be a famine. Gwion pretends to understand from *signified* that Agabus made signs, prophesied in dumb show, on that occasion, whereas in *Acts XXI* he spoke aloud with: 'Thus saith the Holy Ghost.' But Achab is not a divine name: in Hebrew it means merely 'Father's brother'. However, *Acab* is the Hebrew word for 'locust', and the golden locust was among the Greeks of Asia Minor a divine emblem of Apollo, the Sun-god.[1] Gwion in another of

---

[1] Perhaps originally an emblem of destruction borrowed from the Moon-goddess to whom, as we know from the Biblical stories of Rahab and Tamar, the scarlet thread was sacred; for

the poems in the Romance, called *Divregwawd Taliesin,* styles Jesus 'Son of Alpha'. Since *Acab* is the equivalent in this alphabet of *Alpha* in the Greek, this is to make Jesus the son of Acab; and, since Jesus was the Son of God, to make Acab a synonym of God.

As for 'Jaichim', or 'Jachin', that was the name of one of the two mysterious pillars of Solomon's Temple, the other being 'Boaz'. (The rabbis taught that Boaz meant 'In it strength', that Jachim (*yikkon*) meant 'He shall establish', and that they represented respectively the sun and the moon. The Freemasons seem to have borrowed this tradition.) How it happened that Solomon raised two pillars, one on each side of the façade of the Temple, called 'Boaz' (a word which is supposed by Hebrew scholars to have once had an L in the middle of it) and 'Jachin'—is a question that need not concern us yet. All we must notice is that Jaichim is the last letter of this alphabet, and that I in Celtic mythology is the letter of death and associated with the yew tree. Thus Jaichim is a synonym for Death—Euripides in his *Frantic Hercules* used the same word, *iachema,* to mean the deadly hissing of a serpent—and how Death came into the world, and what comes after Death, have always been the grand subjects of religious and philosophical dispute. Death will always remain upon the Earth, according to Christian dogma, until the Day of Doom.

Here, then, is Taliesin's grand conundrum, taken to pieces and re-assembled in orderly form, with the answer attached to each riddle:

I was the tower of the work of which Nimrod was overseer.   *Babel.*

I saw the destruction of Sodom and Gomorrah.   *Lota.*

I was at the Court of Dôn before the birth of Gwydion; my head was at the White Hill in the Hall of Cymbeline; and it is not known whether my body is flesh or fish.   *Vran.*

I stood with Mary Magdalene at the place of Crucifixion of the Merciful Son of God.   *Salome.*

I was the banner carried before Alexander.   *Ne-esthan.*

I strengthened Moses in the land of the Deity.   *Hur.*

I was in Canaan when Absalom was slain; I am winged with the genius of the splendid crozier.   *David.*

A primary chief bard am I to Elphin who was in stocks and fetters for a year and a day. At first I was little Gwion and obtained my inspiration from the cauldron of the hag Cerridwen. Then for nine months almost I was in Cerridwen's belly. At length I became Taliesin. 'Joannes' I was

three locusts and a scarlet thread are mentioned in the Ethiopian *Kebra Nagast* as the magical properties with which the Daughter of Pharoah seduced King Solomon. The myth of Tithonus and Aurora is likely to be derived from a mistaken reading of a sacred picture in which the Moon-goddess is shown hand in hand with Adonis, beside a rising sun as emblem of his youth, and a locust as emblem of the destruction that awaits him.

called, and Merlin the Diviner, and Elias, but at length every King shall call me Taliesin. I am able to instruct the whole Universe.   *Taliesin.*

First I was with my Lord in the Highest Sphere and then I was in his buttery.   *Kai.*

I conveyed the Divine Spirit across Jordan to the level of the Vale of Hebron.   *Caleb.*

I was the Throne of the Distributor; I was minstrel to the Danes of Lochlin.   *Moriah.*

I was fostered in the Ark and have been teacher to all intelligences.   *Hu Gadarn.*

Once I was in India and Asia. I have now come here to the remnant of Troy.   *Gomer.*

I have sat in an uneasy chair; I know the names of the stars from North to South; my original country is the land of the Cherubim, the region of the summer stars.   *Idris.*

I was in the firmament on the Galaxy when Rome was built, and whirled around motionless between three elements.   *Rhea.*

I was loquacious before I was given speech; I am Alpha Tetragrammaton.   *Acab.*

I was with my King in the manger of the Ass.   *Jose.*

On the fall of Lucifer to the lowest depth of Hell, I was instructor to Enoch and Noah; I was on the horse's crupper of Enoch and Elias. I was also at Caer Bedion.   *Uriel.*

I suffered hunger with the Son of the Virgin; I was on the High Cross in the land of the Trinity; I was three periods in the Castle of Arianrhod, above the Castle of the Sidhe.   *Jesus.*

I am a wonder whose origin is not known. I shall remain until the Day of Doom upon the face of the earth.   *Jachin.*

So it seems that the answer to the conundrum is a bardic alphabet, closely resembling O'Flaherty's, but with *Morvran* for *Moiria*, *Ne-esthan* for *Neiagadon*, *Rhea* for *Riuben*, *Salome* for *Salia*,[1] *Gadarn* for *Gath*, *Uriel* for *Uria*, and *Taliesin* for *Teilmon*.

This may seem an anticlimax. Beyond establishing that the *Boibel-Loth* is at any rate as old as the thirteenth-century *Red Book of Hergest* in which the *Hanes Taliesin* occurs, and not a mere pedantry or artificiality of O'Flaherty's, what has been learned?

Well: by the time that O'Flaherty published the alphabet, the secret of its meaning had evidently been lost and there seemed to be no reason for further concealment of the letter-names. It had indeed been published long before in a tenth-century bardic primer. But we may be sure that Gwion with his Dog, Roebuck and Lapwing would never have gone to such

---

[1] I find that the manuscript version of the *Hearings of the Scholars* in the Advocates' Library, Edinburgh, gives Salamon as the name of this letter.

extravagant lengths in confusing the elements of their conundrum unless the answer had been something really secret, something of immensely greater importance than a mere A.B.C. But the only hope of getting any further in the chase lies in discovering what meaning the letters of the alphabet have apart from the proper names which are attached to them in the riddle. Do they perhaps spell out a secret religious formula?

*   *   *

Since solving this grand conundrum I realize that I misread the riddle: 'I was chief overseer of the work of the Tower of Nimrod', though I gave the correct answer. It refers to a passage in *The Hearings of the Scholars*, where' The Work of the Tower of Nimrod' is explained as the linguistic researches carried on there (see Chapter Thirteen) by Feniusa Farsa and his seventy-two assistants. The tower is said to have been built of nine different materials:

> *Clay, water, wool and blood*
> *Wood, lime, and flax-thread a full twist,*
> *Acacia, bitumen with virtue—*
> *The nine materials of Nimrod's Tower.*

and these nine materials are poetically explained as:

> Noun, pronoun, [adjective], verb,
> Adverb, participle, [preposition],
> Conjunction, interjection.

The twenty-five noblest of the seventy-two assistants who worked on the language are said to have given their names to the Ogham letters. The names are as follows:

BABEL	MURIATH
LOTH	GOTLI
FORAIND	GOMERS
SALIATH	STRU
NABGADON	RUBEN
HIRUAD	ACHAB
DABHID	OISE
TALAMON	URITH
CAE	ESSU
KALIAP	IACHIM

ETHROCIUS, UIMELICUS, IUDONIUS, AFFRIM, ORDINES.

It will be noticed that the list is a somewhat degenerate one, with Hiruad (Herod) for Hur, and Nabgadon (Nebuchadnezzar) for Ne-esthan. The five last names represent the 'foreign letters' absent from the original canon. The 'chief overseer' of the riddle is not, as one would suspect, Feniusa Farsa, nor either of his two leading assistants, Gadel and Caoith, but Babel; for it is explained in the same section of the book that Babel is the letter B, that the Birch is its tree and that 'on a switch of Birch was written the first Ogham inscription made in Ireland, namely seven B's, as a warning to Lug son of Ethliu, to wit, "Thy wife will be seven times carried away from thee into fairyland, or elsewhere, unless birch be her overseer."' Lug realized that the seven B's represented birch seven times repeated but, to make sense of the message, he had to convert the seven B's, represented by single nicks, into two other letters of the same flight, namely S and F (four nicks and three nicks) the initials of the operative Irish words *sid* and *ferand*.

This riddle is conclusive proof, if any doubt remains, of Gwion's acquaintance with contemporary Irish bardic lore.

Chapter Eight

HERCULES ON THE LOTUS

To sum up the historical argument.

'Gwion', a North Welsh cleric of the late thirteenth century, whose true name is not known but who championed the popular minstrels against the Court bards, wrote (or rewrote) a romance about a miraculous Child who possessed a secret doctrine that nobody could guess; this doctrine is incorporated in a series of mystical poems which belong to the romance. The romance is based on a more primitive original, of the ninth century A.D., in which Creirwy and Afagddu, the children of Tegid Voel and Caridwen, probably played a more important part than in Gwion's version. (This original has been lost though, strangely enough, the same *dramatis personae* occur in Shakespeare's *Tempest*: Prospero, who like Tegid Voel lived on a magic island; the black screaming hag Sycorax, 'Pig Raven', mother of Caliban the ugliest man alive; Prospero's daughter Miranda the most beautiful woman, whom Caliban tries to rape; Ariel the miraculous Child whom Sycorax imprisons. Perhaps Shakespeare heard the story from his Welsh schoolmaster at Stratford, the original of Sir Hugh Evans in *The Merry Wives of Windsor*.)

The miraculous Child set a riddle, based on a knowledge not only of British and Irish mythology, but of the Greek New Testament and Septuagint, the Hebrew Scriptures and Apocrypha, and Latin and Greek mythology. The answer to the riddle is a list of names which correspond closely with a list that Roderick O'Flaherty, the seventeenth-century confidant of the learned Irish antiquary Duald Mac Firbis, claimed to be the original letter-names of the Ogham alphabet, which is found in numerous inscriptions in Ireland, Scotland, Wales, England and the Isle of Man, some of them pre-Christian. Its invention is ascribed by Irish tradition to the Goidelic god Ogma Sun-Face, who according to the account given by Lucian of Samosata, who wrote in the second century A.D., was represented in Celtic art as a mixture of the gods Cronos, Hercules and Apollo. A connexion between the Ogham found in inscriptions and a fifth-century B.C. Greek alphabet from Etruria, the Formello-Cervetri, has been proved; nevertheless there is evidence that an earlier form of Ogham, with a slightly different order of letters, was current in

Ireland before the Druids of Gaul came into contact with the Formello-Cervetri alphabet. It may also have been current in Britain where, according to Julius Caesar, the Druids of Gaul went for their university training in secret doctrine.

I first suspected that an alphabet was contained in Gwion's conundrum when I began to restore the purposely jumbled text of his *Battle of the Trees*, which refers to a primitive British tradition of the capture of an oracular shrine by the guessing of a god's name. This capture seems to have taken place early in the fourth century B.C. when the Belgic Brythons, worshippers of the Ash-god Gwydion, with the help of an agricultural tribe already settled in Britain, seized the national shrine, perhaps Avebury, from the reigning priesthood, two of whose gods were Arawn and Bran. Bran is the Celtic name for the ancient Crow-god, variously known as Apollo, Saturn, Cronos and Aesculapius, who was also a god of healing and whose worship had been combined with that of a Thunder-god, pictured as a ram or bull, known variously as Zeus, Tantalus, Juppiter, Telamon and Hercules. The letter names of Gwion's alphabet apparently conceal the Name of the transcendent God, whom Caesar calls Dis, worshipped in Britain and Gaul. It may be inferred that the earlier alphabet, containing a pre-Belgic religious secret, had a different series of letter-names from those contained in Gwion's conundrum, that the alphabetical order began with B.L.N., not B.L.F., and that after the capture of the shrine the Divine Name was altered.

It now remains to be discovered:

(1) What the letter-names in Gwion's alphabet, the Boibel-Loth, meant.
(2) What Divine Name was concealed in them.
(3) What were the original names of the letters in the tree-alphabet, the Beth-Luis-Nion.
(4) What they meant.
(5) What Divine Name was concealed in them.

Gwion gives us the first point in our renewed chase of the Roebuck by introducing into his Romance an *Elegy on Hercules,* which I will quote presently; but 'Hercules' is a word of very many meanings. Cicero distinguishes six different legendary figures named Hercules; Varro, forty-four. His name, in Greek *Heracles,* means 'Glory of Hera', and Hera was an early Greek name for the Death-goddess who had charge of the souls of sacred kings and made oracular heroes of them. He is, in fact, a composite deity consisting of a great many oracular heroes of different nations at different stages of religious development; some of whom became real gods while some remained heroes. This makes him the most perplexing character in Classical mythology; for the semi-historical Pelopid prince of the generation before the Trojan War has been confused with various heroes and deities called Hercules, and these with one another.

Hercules first appears in legend as a pastoral sacred king and, perhaps because shepherds welcome the birth of twin lambs, is a twin himself. His characteristics and history can be deduced from a mass of legends, folk-customs and megalithic monuments. He is the rain-maker of his tribe and a sort of human thunder-storm. Legends connect him with Libya and the Atlas Mountains; he may well have originated thereabouts in Palaeolithic times. The priests of Egyptian Thebes, who called him 'Shu', dated his origin as '17,000 years before the reign of King Amasis'. He carries an oak-club, because the oak provides his beasts and his people with mast and because it attracts lightning more than any other tree. His symbols are the acorn; the rock-dove, which nests in oaks as well as in clefts of rock; the mistletoe, or *loranthus*; and the serpent. All these are sexual emblems. The dove was sacred to the Love-goddess of Greece and Syria; the serpent was the most ancient of phallic totem-beasts; the cupped acorn stood for the *glans penis* in both Greek and Latin; the mistletoe was an all-heal and its names *viscus* (Latin) and *ixias* (Greek) are connected with *vis* and *ischus* (strength)—probably because of the spermal viscosity of its berries, sperm being the vehicle of life. This Hercules is male leader of all orgiastic rites and has twelve archer companions, including his spear-armed twin, who is his *tanist* or deputy. He performs an annual green-wood marriage with a queen of the woods, a sort of Maid Marian. He is a mighty hunter and makes rain, when it is needed, by rattling an oak-club thunderously in a hollow oak and stirring a pool with an oak branch—alternatively, by rattling pebbles inside a sacred colocinth-gourd or, later, by rolling black meteoric stones inside a wooden chest—and so attracting thunderstorms by sympathetic magic.

The manner of his death can be reconstructed from a variety of legends, folk customs and other religious survivals. At mid-summer, at the end of a half-year reign, Hercules is made drunk with mead and led into the middle of a circle of twelve stones arranged around an oak, in front of which stands an altar-stone; the oak has been lopped until it is T-shaped. He is bound to it with willow thongs in the 'five-fold bond' which joins wrists, neck and ankles together, beaten by his comrades till he faints, then flayed, blinded, castrated, impaled with a mistletoe stake, and finally hacked into joints on the altar-stone.[1] His blood is caught in a basin and used for sprinkling the whole tribe to make them vigorous and fruitful. The joints are roasted at twin fires of oak-loppings, kindled with sacred fire pre-

---

[1] The five-fold bond was reported from China by the Arab merchant Suleyman in 851 A.D. He writes that 'when the man condemned to death has been trussed up in this fashion, and beaten with a fixed number of blows, his body, still faintly breathing, is given over to those who must devour it'.

served from a lightning-blasted oak or made by twirling an alder- or cornel-wood fire-drill in an oak log. The trunk is then uprooted and split into faggots which are added to the flames. The twelve merry-men rush in a wild figure-of-eight dance around the fires, singing ecstatically and tearing at the flesh with their teeth. The bloody remains are burnt in the fire, all except the genitals and the head. These are put into an alder-wood boat and floated down a river to an islet; though the head is sometimes cured with smoke and preserved for oracular use. His tanist succeeds him and reigns for the remainder of the year, when he is sacrificially killed by a new Hercules.

To this type of Hercules belong such diverse characters as Hercules of Oeta, Orion the Hunter of Crete, Polyphemus the Cyclops, Samson the Danite, Cuchulain of Muirthemne the Irish Sun-hero, Ixion the Lapith—who is always depicted stretched in a 'five-fold bond' around a Sun-wheel—Agag the Amalekite, Romulus of Rome, Zeus, Janus, Anchises, The Dagda and Hermes. This Hercules is the leader of his people in war and hunting and his twelve chieftains are pledged to respect his authority; but his name commemorates his subservience to the Goddess, the Queen of the Woods, whose priestess is the tribal law-giver and disposer of all the amenities of life. The health of the people is bound up with his and he is burdened with numerous royal taboos.

In the Classical myth which authorizes his sovereignty he is a miraculous child born in a shower of gold; strangles a serpent in his cradle, which is also a boat, and is credited (like Zeus) with causing the spurt of milk that made the Milky Way; as a young man he is the undefeated monster-slayer of his age; kills and dismembers a monstrous boar; begets countless sons but no daughters—title is still, in fact, matrilinearly conveyed; willingly undertakes the world-burden of the giant Atlas; does wonderful feats with his oak-club and his arrows; masters the wild horse Arion and brings up the Dog Cerberus from the Underworld; is betrayed by his lovely bride; flays himself by tearing off his poisoned shirt; climbs in agony to the top of Mount Oeta; fells and splits an oak for his own pyre; is consumed; flies up to heaven on the smoke of the pyre in the form of an eagle, and is introduced by the Goddess of Wisdom into the company of the Immortals.

The divine names Bran, Saturn, Cronos must also be referred to this primitive religious system. They are applied to the ghost of Hercules that floats off in the alder-wood boat after his midsummer sacrifice. His tanist, or other self, appearing in Greek legend as Poeas who lighted Hercules' pyre and inherited his arrows, succeeds him for the second half of the year; having acquired royal virtue by marriage with the queen, the representative of the White Goddess, and by eating some royal part of the dead man's body—heart, shoulder or thigh-flesh. He is in turn succeeded by the New Year Hercules, a reincarnation of the murdered man, who beheads him and, apparently, eats his head. This alternate eucharistic sacrifice made royalty continuous, each king being in turn the Sun-god beloved of the reigning Moon-goddess.

But when these cannibalistic rites were abandoned and the system was gradually modified until a single king reigned for a term of years, Saturn-Cronos-Bran became a mere Old Year ghost, permanently overthrown by Juppiter-Zeus-Belin though yearly conjured up for placation at the Saturnalia or Yule feast. Here at last we can guess the political motive behind Amathaon's betrayal of his cousin Bran's name at the Battle of the Trees for the benefit of his friend Gwydion: did the Bronze Age Amathaonians, who worshipped the Immortal Beli in his Stonehenge temple, find that they had less in common with their White-Goddess-worshipping overlords than with the invading Iron Age Belgic tribes whose god Odin (Gwydion) had emancipated himself from the tutelage of the White Goddess Freya? Once the Bran priesthood was banished from Salisbury Plain and driven up North, they would be free to institute a permanent kingship over all Southern Britain under the patronage of Belin; and this is exactly what they seem to have done, after an amicable arrangement with the priesthood of Odin, to whom they gave the control of the national oracle as a reward for their help in the battle.

The next type of Hercules is an agricultural as well as a pastoral king and specializes in the cultivation of barley, so that he is sometimes confused with Eleusinian Triptolemus, Syrian Tammuz or Egyptian Maneros. Early portraits of him, with lion skin, club and grain sprouting from his shoulders, have been found in Mesopotamian cities of the third millennium B.C. In the Eastern Mediterranean he reigns alternatively with his twin, as in the double kingdoms of Argos, Lacedaemon, Corinth, Alba Longa, and Rome. Co-kings of this type are Iphiclus, twin to Tirynthian Hercules; Pollux, twin to Castor; Lynceus, twin to Idas; Calaïs, twin to Zetes; Remus, twin to Romulus; Demophoön, twin to Triptolemus; the Edomite Perez, twin to Zarah; Abel, twin to Cain; and many more. Hercules is now lover to fifty water-priestesses of the Mountain-goddess in whose honour he wears a lion's skin. The twins' joint reign is fixed at eight years, apparently because at every hundredth lunar month occurs a rough approximation of lunar and solar times. Llew Llaw Gyffes ('the Lion with the Steady Hand') is true to type when in the *Romance of Math the Son of Mathonwy* he takes Gwydion as his twin to visit his mother Arianrhod. For each year that the reign of this agricultural Hercules is prolonged he offers a child-victim in his stead; which explains the Greek legends of Hercules killing children by accident or in a fit of madness, and the destruction by fire, after a temporary investiture as king, of various unfortunate young princes, among them Gwern, nephew of Bran; Phaëthon, son of Helios; Icarus, son of Daedalus, who flew too near the sun; Demophoön, son of Celeus of Eleusis, whom Demeter was trying to immortalize; and Dionysus son of Cretan Zeus. It also explains the child-sacrifices of Phoenicia, including those offered to Jehovah Melkarth in the Valley of Hinnom (or Gehenna) the home of the undying serpent, where the sacrificial fire was never quenched.

The custom of burning a child to death as an annual surrogate for the sacred king is well illustrated in the myth of Thetis, Peleus and Achilles. Peleus was an Achaean fratricide in exile from Aegina and became King of Iolcus with a co-king Acastus, in succession to the co-kings Pelias and Neleus. Thetis, a Thessalian Sea goddess is described by the mythographers either as a daughter of Cheiron the Centaur, or as one of the fifty Nereids, from whom she was chosen to be a wife to Zeus. Zeus changed his mind because of an oracle and gave her in marriage to Peleus, to whom she bore seven children, six of whom she burned to death. The seventh, Achilles, was rescued by Peleus in the nick of time—like the infant Aesculapius. The first six had been given immortality by the burning process; with Achilles the process had not yet been completed—his heel was still vulnerable. Thetis fled and Peleus gave Achilles into the custody of Cheiron who tutored him; later Achilles ruled over the Myrmidons of Pthiotis and brought a contingent of them to fight at Troy. When offered the choice of a brief but glorious life or a long and undistinguished one, he chose the brief one.

The myth has kept its main outlines pretty well despite the inability of later editors to understand the system of matrilinear succession. There was a shrine of the Moon-goddess Artemis, alias Nereis, or Thetis, at Iolcus, the chief port of Southern Thessaly, with an attached college of fifty priestesses. This Artemis was a patroness of fishermen and sailors. One of the priestesses was chosen every fiftieth month as representative of the Goddess; perhaps she was the winner of a race. She took a yearly consort who became the Oak-king, or Zeus, of the region and was sacrificed at the close of his term of office. By the time that the Achaeans had established the Olympian religion in Thessaly (it is recorded that all the gods and goddesses attended Peleus's marriage to Thetis) the term had been extended to eight, or perhaps seven, years, and a child sacrificed every winter solstice until the term was complete. (Seven years instead of the Great Year of eight seems to be a blunder of the mythographers; but from the Scottish witch-ballad of *True Thomas* it appears that seven years was the normal term for the Queen of Elphame's consort to reign, and the Scottish witch cult had close affinities with primitive Thessalian religion.)

Achilles, the lucky seventh (or perhaps eighth) child who was saved because Peleus himself had to die, was apparently one of the Centaurs of near-by Pelion with whom the Nereids of Iolcus had ancient exogamic ties and from whom Peleus would naturally choose his child victims—they would not be his own sons by Thetis. When Achilles grew up he became king of the Myrmidons of Pthiotis: presumably by marriage with the tribal representative of the Goddess. He can hardly have inherited the title from Peleus. (Myrmidon means 'ant', so it is likely that the wryneck, which feeds on ants and nests in willow-trees, sacred to the Goddess, was the local totem-bird; Philyra, Cheiron's mother, is traditionally associated with the wryneck.) It is established that there was an Achilles cult in Greece before the Trojan War was fought, so the brief but glorious life was probably that of a stay-at-home king with a sacred heel who won immortality at death by becoming an oracular hero. Thetis was credited with the power to change her appearance; she was, in fact, served by various colleges of priestesses each with a different totem beast or bird—mare, she-bear, crane, fish, wryneck and so on.

The same myth has been twisted in a variety of ways. In some versions the emphasis is on the mock-marriage, which was an integral part of the coronation. The Argive myth of the fifty Danaids who were married to the fifty sons of Aegyptus and killed all but one on their common wedding night, and the Perso-Egypto-Greek myth of Tobit and Raguel's daughter whose seven previous husbands had all been killed by the demon Asmodeus—in Persian, Aēshma Daēva—on their wedding night, are originally identical.

The various contradictory versions of the Danaid myth help us to understand the ritual from which it originated. Pindar in his *Fourth Pythian Ode* says that the brides were pardoned, purified by Hermes and Athene and offered as prizes to the victors of public games. Later authorities, such as Ovid and Horace, say that they were not pardoned but condemned everlastingly to pour water into a vessel full of holes. Herodotus says that they brought the mysteries of Demeter to Argos and taught them to the Pelasgian women. Others say that four of them were worshipped at Argos because they provided the city with water. The real story seems to be that the Danaids were an Argive college of fifty priestesses of the Barley-goddess Danaë, who was interested in giving rain to the crops and was worshipped under four different divine titles; pouring water through a vessel with holes so that it looked like rain was their usual rain-bringing charm. Every four years at the fiftieth lunar month a contest was held as to who should become the Hercules, or Zeus, of the next four years and the lover of these fifty priestesses. This term was afterwards prolonged to eight years, with the usual yearly sacrifice of a child. Danaan Argos was captured by the Sons of Aegyptus who invaded the Peloponnese from Syria, and many of the Danaans who resisted them were driven northward out of Greece; as has already been mentioned.

In the *Book of Tobit*, Tobit is the lucky eighth, the new Zeus bride-groom, who escapes his fate when the reigning Zeus has to die at the end of his term. Asmodeus is the Persian counterpart of Set, the yearly mur-derer of Osiris, but he is charmed away with the fish of immortality and flees to his southern deserts. Tobit's dog is a helpful clue; he always accompanied Hercules Melkarth, or his Persian counterpart Sraosha, or the Greek Aesculapius, wherever he went.

A typical set of taboos binding this Hercules is quoted by Sir James Frazer in his *Golden Bough*: they were applied to the Flamen Dialis, the successor of the Sacred King of Rome whose war-leadership passed to the twin Consuls at the foundation of the Republic.

> The Flamen Dialis might not ride or even touch a horse, nor see an army under arms, nor wear a ring which was not broken, nor have a knot in any part of his garments; no fire except a sacred one might be taken out of his house; he might not touch wheaten flour or leavened bread; he might not touch or even name a goat, a dog, raw meat, beans and ivy; he might not walk under a vine; the feet of his bed had to be daubed with mud; his hair could be cut only by a free man and with a bronze knife; and his hair and nails when cut had to be buried under a lucky tree; he might not touch a dead body nor enter a place where one was buried; he might not see work being done on holy days; he might not be uncovered in the open air; if a man in bonds were taken into his house, the captive had to be unbound and the cords had to be drawn up through a hole in the roof and so let down into the street.

Frazer should have added that the Flamen owed his position to a sacred marriage with the Flaminica: Plutarch records in his *Roman Questions* (50) that he could not divorce her, and had to resign his office if she died.

In Ireland this Hercules was named *Cenn Cruaich*, 'the Lord of the Mound', but after his supersession by a more benignant sacred king was remembered as *Cromm Cruaich* ('the Bowed One of the Mound'). In a Christian poem occurring in the eleventh-century *Book of Leinster* he is thus described:

> *Here once dwelt*
> *A high idol of many fights,*
> *The Cromm Cruaich by name,*
> *And deprived every tribe of peace.*
>
> *Without glory in his honour,*
> *They would sacrifice their wretched children*
> *With much lamentation and danger,*
> *Pouring their blood around Cromm Cruaich.*

Milk and corn
They would urgently desire of him,
In barter for one-third of their healthy offspring—
Their horror of him was great.

To him the noble Goidels
Would prostrate themselves;
From the bloody sacrifices offered him
The plain is called 'The Plain of Adoration'.

They did evilly,
Beat on their palms, thumped their bodies,
Wailing to the monster who enslaved them,
Their tears falling in showers.

In a rank stand
Twelve idols of stone;
Bitterly to enchant the people
The figure of the Cromm was of gold.

From the reign of Heremon,
The noble and graceful,
Such worshipping of stones there was
Until the coming of good Patrick of Macha.

It is likely enough that this cult was introduced into Ireland in the reign of Heremon, the nineteenth King of All Ireland, the date of whose accession is traditionally given as 1267 B.C., though Dr. Joyce, a reliable modern authority, makes it 1015 B.C. Heremon, one of the invading Milesians from Spain, became sole monarch of Ireland by his victory over the armies of the North and put his enemies under heavy tribute.

(The Milesians of Irish legend are said to have originated in Greece early in the second millennium B.C. and to have taken many generations to reach Ireland, after wandering about the Mediterranean. The Milesians of Greek legend claimed descent from Miletus, a son of Apollo, who emigrated from Crete to Caria in very early times, and built the city of Miletus; there was another city of the same name in Crete. The Irish Milesians similarly claimed to have visited Crete and to have gone thence to Syria, and thence by way of Carenia in Asia Minor to Gaetulia in North Africa, Baelduno or Baelo, a port near Cadiz, and Breagdun or Brigantium (now Compostella), in North-western Spain. Among their ancestors were Gadel—perhaps a deity of the river Gadylum on the southern coast of the Black Sea near Trebizond; 'Niulus or Neolus of Argos'; Cecrops of Athens; and 'Scota daughter of the king of Egypt'.

If this account has any sense it refers to a westward migration from the

Aegean to Spain in the late thirteenth century B.C. when, as we have seen, a wave of Indo-Europeans from the north, among them the Dorian Greeks, was slowly displacing the Mycenaean 'Peoples of the Sea' from Greece, the Aegean Islands, and Asia Minor.

Neleus (if this is the 'Niulus or Neolus' of the Irish legend) was a Minyan, an Aeolian Greek, who reigned over Pylos, a Peloponnese kingdom that traded extensively with the western Mediterranean. The Achaeans subdued him in a battle from which only his son Nestor (a garrulous old man at the time of the Trojan War) escaped. Neleus was reckoned a son of the Goddess Tyro, and she was mother also of Aeson the Minyan, who was rejuvenated in the Cauldron, and Amythaon— Amathaon again? Tyro was probably the Goddess of the Tyrrhenians who were expelled from Asia Minor a century or two later and sailed to Italy. These Tyrrhenians, usually known as Etruscans, dated their national existence from 967 B.C. Cecrops appears in Greek legend as the first Greek king of Attica and the reputed originator of barley-cake offerings to Zeus. Scota, who has been confused in Irish legend with the ancestor of the Cottians, is apparently Scotia ('The Dark One'), a well-known Greek title of the Sea-goddess of Cyprus. The Milesians would naturally have brought the cult of the Sea-goddess and of her son Hercules with them to Ireland, and would have found the necessary stone-altars already in position.)

In the Peloponnese the Olympic Games were the occasion of this agricultural Hercules's death and of the election of his successor. The legend is that they were founded in celebration of Zeus's emasculation of Cronos; since the tomb of the early Achaean Oak-king Pelops was at Olympia, this means that the oak-cult was there superimposed on the Pelasgian barley-cult. The most ancient event in the Games was a race between fifty young priestesses of the Goddess Hera for the privilege of becoming the new Chief Priestess. Hercules was cut into pieces and eucharistically eaten as before, until perhaps the later Achaeans put an end to the practice, and for centuries after retained some of his oak-tree characteristics: he was known as the 'green Zeus'. The sacrifice of the agricultural Hercules, or the victim offered in his stead, continued to take place within a stone-circle dedicated to the Barley Mother. At Hermion, near Corinth, the stone-circle was in ritual use until Christian times.

Hercules of Canopus, or Celestial Hercules, is a fusion of the first two types of Hercules with Asclepius, or Aesculapius, the God of Healing, himself a fusion of the Barley-god with a Fire-god. Aesculapius is described by mythographers as a son of Apollo, partly because Apollo in Classical times was identified with the Sun-god Helios; partly because the priesthood of the Aesculapian cult, which was derived from that of Thoth, the Egyptian god of healing and inventor of letters, had been driven from Phoenicia (about the year 1400 B.C.?) and taken refuge in the islands of Cos, Thasos and Delos, where Apollo was by then the ruling deity. When in the fifth century B.C. Herodotus tried to extract information about Canopic Hercules from the Egyptian priests, they referred him to Phoenicia as the land of his origin. We know that the Phoenician Hercules, Melkarth ('King of the City'), died yearly and that the quail was his bird of resurrection; which means that when the migrant quail arrives in Phoenicia early in March from the South, the oak begins to leaf and the new King celebrates his royal marriage. Melkarth was revived when Esmun ('He whom we invoke'), the local Aesculapius, held a quail to his nose. The quail is notorious for its pugnacity and lechery. But at Canopus, in the Nile Delta, the cults of Melkarth and Esmun, or Hercules and Aesculapius, appear to have been fused by Egyptian philosophers: Hercules was worshipped both as the healer and as the healed. Apollo himself had reputedly been born on Ortygia ('Quail Island'), the islet off Delos; so Canopic Hercules is Apollo, too, in a sense—is Apollo, Aesculapius (*alias* Cronos, Saturn or Bran), Thoth, Hermes (whom the Greeks identified with Thoth), Dionysus (who in the early legends is an alias of Hermes), and Melkarth, to whom King Solomon, as son-in-law to King Hiram, was priest, and who immolated himself on a pyre, like Hercules of Oeta. Hercules Melkarth was also worshipped at Corinth under the name of Melicertes, the son of the Pelasgian White Goddess Ino of Pelion.

Hercules becomes more glorious still, as Celestial Hercules. The mythographers record that he borrowed the golden cup of the Sun, shaped like a water lily or lotus, for the homeward journey from one of his Labours. This was the cup in which the Sun, after sinking in the West, nightly floated round again to the East along the world-girdling Ocean stream. The lotus, which grows as the Nile rises, typified fertility, and so attached itself to the Egyptian sun-cult. 'Hercules' in Classical Greece became in fact another name for the Sun. Celestial Hercules was worshipped both as the undying Sun, and as the continually dying and continually renewed Spirit of the Year—that is, both as a god and as a demi-god. This is the type of Hercules whom the Druids worshipped as Ogma Sun-face, the lion-skinned inventor of Letters,[1] god of eloquence, god of healing, god of fertility, god of prophecy; and whom the Greeks worshipped as 'assigner of titles', as ruler of the Zodiac, as president of festivals, as founder of cities, as healer of the sick, as patron of archers and athletes.

Hercules is represented in Greek art as a bull-necked champion, and

---

[1] The ape, the sacred animal which identified this Hercules with Thoth the inventor of Letters, does not seem to have become acclimatized in Western Europe. In Egypt, Thoth was sometimes portrayed as an ape, in Asia Minor he merely led one; the tradition apparently originates in India.

may for all practical purposes be identified with the demi-god Dionysus of Delphi, whose totem was a white bull. Plutarch of Delphi, a priest of Apollo, in his essay *On Isis and Osiris* compares the rites of Osiris with those of Dionysus. He writes:

> The affair about the Titans and the Night of Accomplishment corresponds with what are called 'Tearings to pieces', 'Resurrections' and 'Regenerations' in the rites of Osiris. The same applies to burial rites. There are burial chests of Osiris in many Egyptian cities; similarly we claim at Delphi that the remains of Dionysus are buried near the place of the Oracle. And our consecrated priests perform a secret sacrifice in Apollo's sanctuary at the time of the awakening of the Divine Child by the Thyiades.

Thus 'Hercules' is seen to be also another name for Osiris whose yearly death is still celebrated in Egypt, even after thirteen centuries of Mohammedanism. Rubber is now used for the traditional fertility symbol; prodigiously inflated, it still excites the same cries of laughter and grief as in the days of Joseph the Patriarch and Joseph the Carpenter.

Plutarch carefully distinguishes Apollo (Hercules as god) from Dionysus (Hercules as demi-god). This Apollo never dies, never changes his shape; he is eternally young, strong and beautiful. Dionysus perpetually changes, like Proteus the Pelasgian god, or Periclymenus the Minyan, son of Neleus, or the ancient Irish Uath Mac Immomuin ('Horror son of Terror'), into an infinity of shapes. So Pentheus in the *Bacchae* of Euripides charges him to appear 'as a wild bull, as a many-headed snake, or as a fire-breathing lion'—whichever he pleases: almost exactly in the words of the Welsh bard Cynddelw, a contemporary of Gruffudd ap Kynan's: *Yn rith llew rac llyw goradein, yn rith dreic rac dragon prydein.*

Thus in Britain, Amathaon was Hercules as Dionysus; his father Beli was Hercules as Apollo.

Plutarch writes, in his essay *On the Ei at Delphi,* revealing as much Orphic secret doctrine as he dares:

> In describing the manifold changes of Dionysus into winds, water, earth, stars and growing plants and animals, they use the riddling expressions 'render asunder' and 'tearing limb from limb'. And they call the god 'Dionysus' or 'Zagreus' ('the torn') or 'The Night Sun' or 'The Impartial Giver', and record various Destructions, Disappearances, Resurrections and Rebirths, which are their mythographic account of how those changes came about.

That Gwion knew Hercules to be another name for Ogma Sun-face, the inventor of the Ogham alphabet, is made perfectly clear in his Elegy on 'Ercwlf' where the alphabet figures as the four pillars, of five letters each, that support the whole edifice of literature:

The earth turns,
So night follows day.
When lived the renowned
Ercwlf, chief of baptism?
Ercwlf said
He did not take account of death.
The shield of Mordei
By him was broken.
Ercwlf placed in order,
Impetuous, frantic,
Four columns of equal height,
Red gold upon them,
A work not easily to be believed,
Easily believed it will not be.
The heat of the sun did not vex him;
None went nearer heaven
Than he went.
Ercwlf the wall-breaker,
Thou art beneath the sand;
May the Trinity give thee
A merciful day of judgement.

'The shield of Mordei' is a reference to the famous Battle of Catterick Bridge in the late sixth century A.D.:

Ym Mordei ystyngeo dyledawr.
'In Mordei he laid low the mighty.'

The 'he' is a British hero named Erthgi, presumably a reincarnation of Ercwlf, who 'went to Catterick in the dawn with the aspect of a prince in the shield-guarded battle-field'. The reference to Hercules as 'Chief of Baptism' identifies him with St. John the Baptist, in whose honour Hercules's midsummer fires were lighted in Gwion's day. As Sir James Frazer points out, Midsummer Day was always a water as well as a fire festival. 'May the Trinity give thee a merciful day of judgement' is Gwion's view of Hercules as resident *'in limbo patrum'*—in the abode of the just who had died before Jesus Christ's advent. Baptism was not, of course, invented by the Christians. They had it from St. John, and he had it from the Hemero-baptists, a mysterious Hebrew sect usually regarded as a branch of the Pythagorean Essenes, who worshipped Jehovah in his Sun-god aspect. It should be observed that the devotees of the Thracian goddess Cotytto, the mother of the Cottians, had employed mystagogues called 'Baptists'—whether this was because they baptized the devotee before the orgies, or because they were charged with the ritual dipping (dyeing) of clothes or hair, is disputed—and that both the ancient Irish and ancient British used baptism before the Christians came. This is recorded in the Irish tales of *Conall Derg* and *Conall Kernach*, and the Welsh tale of *Gwri of the Golden Hair*.

Taliesin's name in Welsh means 'radiant brow', a characteristic of Apollo's, but the 'Tal' syllable is often present in the primitive names of Hercules. In Crete he was Talus, the man of bronze, whom Medea killed. In Pelasgia he was the tortured Tan-talus, from whose name the word 'tantalize' derives. The Irish Tailltean Games are probably called after an agricultural Hercules the first syllable of whose name was Tal. In Syria he was Telmen. In Greece he was Atlas Telamon, and 'Atlas', like 'Telamon', was derived from the root *Tla* or *Tal* which contains the senses 'take upon oneself', 'dare', and 'suffer'. Dr. MacCulloch suggests that 'Taliesin' is also a divine name and that the swallowing of the grain of corn by the black hen in the *Romance of Taliesin* proves Taliesin to have been a Barley-god.

The time has now come to draw closely around the thicket where the Roebuck is known to be harboured. And here is a hunting song from Gwion's poem, *Angar Cyvyndawd*:

> Bum Twrch ym Mynydd
> Bum cyff mewn rhaw
> Bum bwall yn llaw.

> *I have been a roebuck on the mountain,*
> *I have been a tree stump in a shovel,*
> *I have been an axe in the hand.*

But we must transpose the lines of the couplet, because logically the axe comes first, then the tree is cut down, and one cannot put the oak-stump into one's shovel unless it has been reduced to ashes—which are afterwards used to fertilize the fields. So:

> *I have been a roebuck on the mountain,*
> *I have been an axe in the hand,*
> *I have been a tree stump in a shovel.*

If one looks carefully again at the names of the fifteen consonants of the Boibel-Loth, or the Babel-Lota, one notices clear correspondences with Greek legend. Not only 'Taliesin' with 'Talus', and 'Teilmon' with 'Telamon', but 'Moiria' with the 'Moirae', the Three Fates; and 'Cailep' with 'Calypso', daughter of Atlas, whose island of Ogygia—placed by Plutarch in the Irish Seas—was protected by the very same enchantment as Morgan le Faye's Avalon, Cerridwen's Caer Sidi, or Niamh of the

Golden Hair's 'Land of Youth'. Put the whole series of letter-names into the nearest Greek words that make any sort of sense, using Latin characters and allowing for the difference between Greek and Irish vowels (the ancillary I in Irish is used as a sign of a long vowel) and for transposition of letters. Retain the digamma (F or V) in words in which it originally occurred, such as ACHAIVA and DAVIZO, and use the Aeolic A for long E, in FORĒMENOS, NE-ĒGATOS, GĒTHEO.

The consonants spell out the familiar story of Hercules in three chapters of five words each:

BOIBEL	B	BOIBALION	I, the Roebuck fawn (or Antelope-bull calf)
LOTH	L	LŌTO-	On the Lotus
FORANN	F	FORĀMENON	Ferried
SALIA	S	SALOÖMAI	Lurch to and fro
NEIAGADON	N	NE-ĀGATON	New-born
UIRIA	H	ŪRIOS	I, the Guardian of Boundaries (or the Benignant One)
DAIBHAITH	D	DAVIZŌ	Cleave wood.
TEILMON	T	TELAMŌN or TLĀMŌN	I, the suffering one
CAOI	C	CAIOMAI	Am consumed by fire,
CAILEP	CC	CALYPTOMAI	Vanish.
MOIRIA	M	MOIRAŌ	I distribute,
GATH	G	GĀTHEŌ	I rejoice,
NGOIMAR	NG	GNŌRIMOS	I, the famous one,
IDRA	Y	IDRYOMAI	Establish,
RHEA	R	RHEŌ	I flow away.[1]

[1] As an alphabetic invocation it goes readily into English rhyme, with *Kn* standing for *Ng* and J for Y:

B ull-calf in
L otus-cup
F erried, or
S waying
N ew-dressed,

H elpful
D ivider, in
T orment,
C onsumed beyond
Q uest,

M ete us out
G aiety,
Kn ightliest
J udge,
R unning west.

137

The vowels do not spell out a story but they characterize the progress of Hercules through the five stations of the year, typified by the five petals of the Lotus-cup—Birth, Initiation, Marriage, Rest from Labour, and Death:

ACHAIVA   The Spinner—a title of Demeter, the White Goddess.
            (Compare also *Acca* in the Roman Hercules myth, and
            Acco the Greek bug-bear who devoured new-born
            children.)

OSSA   Fame. (Also the name of a sacred mountain in Magnesia,
            and a sacred hill at Olympia.)

URANIA   The Queen of Heaven. The word is perhaps derived
            from *ouros*, a mountain, and *ana*, queen. But Ura (oura)
            means the tail of a lion (sacred to Anatha, the Mountain-
            goddess, Queen of Heaven) and since the lion expresses
            anger with its tail the word may mean 'The Queen with
            the Lion Tail'; certainly the Greek name for the Asp-
            Crown of Egypt which the Pharaohs wore by mother-
            right was 'Uraeus', meaning 'of the Lion Tail', the Asp
            being sacred to the same Goddess.

(H)ESUCHIA Repose. The word is probably shortened in honour of
            the Celtic God Esus, who is shown in a Gaulish bas-
            relief plucking festal branches, with a left hand where
            his right should be.

IACHEMA   Shrieking, or Hissing.

The *boibalis* or *boibalus* (also *boubalis* or *boubalus*) is the ferocious Libyan white antelope-ox or *leucoryx*, from which according to Herodotus the Phoenicians made the curved sides of their lyres—with which they celebrated Hercules Melkarth.

Gwion's version of the alphabet, with Rhea for Riuben, is older than O'Flaherty's if O'Flaherty's 'Riuben' stands for *Rymbonao*, 'I swing about again'—a word first used in the second century A.D.; the difference between Gwion's 'Salome', and O'Flaherty's 'Salia' also suggests that Gwion had an older version. That he has altered 'Telamon' to 'Taliesin' suggests that he is offering *Talasinoös*, 'he that dares to suffer', as an alternative to 'Telamon', which has the same meaning. *Ne-esthan*, the Greek Septuagint transliteration of 'Nehushtan' (*2 Kings, XVIII, 4*) as an equivalent of *ne-āgaton* is puzzling. But since Nehushtan was a name of contempt, meaning 'a piece of brass', said to have been given by King Hezekiah to the therapeutic Serpent or Seraph when idolatrously wor-shipped by his subjects, it is possible that Gwion read the original holy name as the Greek *Neo-sthenios*, or *Neo-sthenaros*, 'with new strength', of which 'Nehushtan' was a Hebrew parody. This would imply that a Jew of Hellenistic times, not Hezekiah, invented the parody name; which is historically more plausible than the Biblical account. For it is incredible that Hezekiah took exception to idolatry: the Jews attempted to dispense with idols only in post-Exilic times.

But though we have learned the secret story of the Spirit of the Year, the Name of the transcendent God still remains hidden. The obvious place to look for it is among the vowels, which are separated from the Hercules story told by the consonants; but Dog, Lapwing, and Roebuck must have learned wisdom after the Battle of the Trees and hidden their secret more deeply even than before.

Gwion evidently knew the Name, and it was this knowledge that gave him his authority at Maelgwn's Court. He says in the *Cyst Wy'r Beirdd* ('Reproof of the Bards'):

> *Unless you are acquainted with the powerful Name,*
> *Be silent, Heinin!*
> *As to the lofty Name*
> *And the powerful Name. . . .*

The best hope of guessing it lies in finding out first what the Name was that Gwydion succeeded in discovering with Amathaon's aid, and then what refinement he made on his discovery.

Chapter Nine

GWION'S HERESY

The concentrated essence of Druidic, as of Orphic Greek, philosophy was *Rheo*, 'I flow away', Gwion's letter-name for R:— '*Panta Rhei*', 'all things flow'. The main problem of paganism is contained in *Riuben*, the alternative name for R, if this stands for *Rymbonao*:—'Must all things swing round again for ever? Or how can one escape from the Wheel?' This was the problem of the blinded Sunhero Samson when he was harnessed to the corn-mill of Gaza; and it should be noted that the term 'corn-mill' was applied in Greek philosophy to the revolving heavens. Samson resolved the problem magnificently by pulling down both posts of the temple so that the roof collapsed upon everyone. The Orphics had another, quieter solution and engraved it in cypher on gold tablets tied around the necks of their beloved dead. It was: not to forget, to refuse to drink the water of cypress-shaded Lethe however thirsty one might be, to accept water only from the sacred (hazel-shaded?) pool of Persephone, and thus to become immortal Lords of the Dead, excused further Tearings-to-Pieces, Destructions, Resurrections and Rebirths. The cypress was sacred to Hercules, who had himself planted the famous cypress grove at Daphne, and typified rebirth; and the word 'cypress' is derived from Cyprus, which was called after Cyprian Aphrodite, his mother. The cult of the sacred cypress is Minoan in origin and must have been brought to Cyprus from Crete.

The Hercules-god of the Orphic mystics was Apollo the Hyperborean; and in the first century A.D. Aelian, the Roman historian, records that Hyperborean priests visited Tempe in Northern Greece regularly to worship Apollo. Diodorus Siculus in his quotation from Hecataeus makes it clear that in the sixth century B.C. the 'land of the Hyperboreans', where Apollo's mother Latona was born, and where Apollo was honoured above all other gods, was Britain. This does not contradict Herodotus's account of an altogether different Hyperborean priesthood, probably Albanian, living near the Caspian Sea; or the view that in Aelian's time, Ireland, which lay outside the Roman Empire, may have been 'the Land of the Hyperboreans'; or the view, which I propose later in this book, that the original Hyperboreans were Libyans.

Edward Davies was justified in regarding these British priests as a sort of Orphics: dress, dogma, ritual and diet correspond closely. And since *Câd Goddeu* proves to have been a battle of letters rather than a battle of trees, his suggestion that the fabulous dance of trees to Orpheus's lyre was, rather, a dance of letters, makes good historical and poetic sense.[1] Orpheus is recorded by Diodorus to have used the Pelasgian alphabet. That Gwion identified the Celestial Hercules of the Boibel-Loth with the Orphic Apollo is plain from this perfectly clear passage embedded in the riddling mazes of *Câd Goddeu*:

> *It is long since I was a herdsman.*
> *I travelled over the earth*
> *Before I became a learned person.*
> *I have travelled, I have made a circuit,*
> *I have slept in a hundred islands,*
> *I have dwelt in a hundred cities.*
> *Learned Druids,*
> *Prophesy ye of Arthur?*
> *Or is it me they celebrate?*

Only Apollo can be the 'I' of this passage. He was herdsman to Admetus, the Minyan king of Pherae in Thessaly, several centuries before he set up at Delphi as the Leader of the Muses. And as a pre-Greek oracular hero he had been laid to rest in a hundred sacred islands. Once the Greeks had found it convenient to adopt him as their god of healing and music, hundreds of cities came to honour him and by Classical times he was making his daily and yearly circuit as the visible sun. Gwion is hinting to Heinin and the other court-bards that the true identity of the hero whom they thoughtlessly eulogize as King Arthur is Hercules-Dionysus, *rex quondam, rex-que futurus* ('King once and King again to be'), who at his second coming will be the immortal Hercules-Apollo. But they will not understand. 'It is long since I was a herdsman' will convey nothing to them but a memory of *Triad* 85 where the Three Tribe Herdsmen of Britain are given as Gwydion who kept the herd of the tribe of Gwynedd, Bennren who kept the herd of Caradoc son of Bran consisting

---

[1] But there may also have been a plainer meaning for the dance of trees. According to Apollonius Rhodius, the wild oak trees which Orpheus had led down from the Pierian mountain were still standing in ordered ranks in his day at Zonë in Thrace. If they were arranged as if for dancing that would mean not in a stiff geometrical pattern, such as a square, triangle or avenue, but in a curved one. Zonë ('a woman's girdle') suggests a round dance in honour of the Goddess. Yet a circle of oaks, like a fastened girdle, would not seem to be dancing: the oaks would seem to be standing as sentinels around a dancing floor. The dance at Zonë was probably an orgiastic one of the 'loosened girdle': for *zone* in Greek also means marriage, or the sexual act, the disrobing of a woman. It is likely therefore that a broad girdle of oaks planted in a double rank was coiled in on itself so that they seemed to be dancing spirally to the centre and then out again.

of 21,000 milch kine, and Llawnrodded Varvawc who kept the equally numerous herd of Nudd Hael. Gwion had fetched his learning from Ireland, and perhaps from Egypt, but re-grafted it on a British stock. For though Druidism as an organized religion had been dead in Wales for hundreds of years, reliques of Druidic lore were contained in the traditional corpus of minstrel poetry, and in popular religious ritual. The primitive Druidic cult, which involved ritual cannibalism after omens had been taken from the victim's death struggle, had been suppressed by the Roman general Paulinus in 61 A.D. when he conquered Anglesey and cut down the sacred groves; the continental Druidism already adopted by the rest of Britain south of the Clyde was respectable Belin, or Apollo, worship of Celto-Thracian type.

From the Imperial Roman point of view Belin-worship constituted no political danger once its central authority, the Druidic Synod at Dreux, had been broken by Caesar's defeat of Vercingetorix and animal victims had been substituted for human ones. The British priests were not converted to Roman religion, for the Roman Pantheon was already allied to theirs and the Mithras-worship of the Roman legionaries was merely an Oriental version of their own Hercules cult. That they should honour the Emperor as the temporal incarnation of their variously named Sungod was the only religious obligation put upon them, and they cannot have found it a difficult one. When Christianity became the official Roman religion, no attempt was made to coerce the natives into uniformity of worship and even in the towns the churches were small and poor; most of the large pagan temples remained in operation, it seems. There was no religious problem in Britain, as there was in Judaea, until the Romans withdrew their garrisons and the barbarous Jutes, Angles and Saxons poured in from the East, and the civilized Roman Britons fled before them into Wales or across the Channel. But the presence in England of these barbarians at least protected the Welsh and Irish churches from any effective intervention in their religious affairs by continental Catholicism, and the Archiepiscopal See of St. David's remained wholly independent until the twelfth century, when the Normans pressed the right of the Archbishop of Canterbury to control it; which was the occasion of the Anglo-Welsh wars.

What, for the early Church Councils, seemed the most diabolical and unpardonable heresy of all was the identification of the Hercules-Dionysus-Mithras bull, whose living flesh the Orphic ascetics tore and ate in their initiation ceremony, with Jesus Christ whose living flesh was symbolically torn and eaten in the Holy Communion. With this heresy, which was second-century Egyptian, went another, the identification of the Virgin Mary with the Triple Goddess. The Copts even ventured to combine 'the Three Maries' who were spectators of the Crucifixion into a single character, with Mary Cleopas as a type of 'Blodeuwedd', the Virgin of 'Arianrhod', and Mary Magdalen as the third person of this ancient trinity, who appears in Celtic legend as Morgan le Faye, King Arthur's sister. Morgan in Irish legend is 'the Morrigan', meaning 'Great Queen', a Death-goddess who assumed the form of a raven; and 'le Faye' means 'the Fate'. According to Cormac's *Glossary* the Morrigan was invoked in battle by an imitation on war-horns of a raven's croaking. She was by no means the gentle character familiar to readers of the *Morte D'Arthur* but like the 'black screaming hag Cerridwen' in the *Romance of Taliesin* was 'big-mouthed, swarthy, swift, sooty, lame, with a cast in her left eye'.

Wherever these heresies survived in mediaeval Europe the Church visited them with such terrible penalties that British or Irish poets who played with them must have derived a dangerous joy from wrapping them up, as Gwion has done here, in riddling disguises. One can sympathize with the poets, in so far as their predecessors had accepted Jesus Christ without compulsion and had reserved the right to interpret Christianity in the light of their literary tradition, without interference. They saw Jesus as the latest theophany of the same suffering sacred king whom they had worshipped under various names from time immemorial. As soon as the big stick of Orthodoxy was waved at them from Rome or Canterbury they felt a pardonable resentment. The first Christian missionaries had conducted themselves with scrupulous courtesy towards the devotees of the pagan Sun-cult, with whom they had much mystical doctrine in common. Celtic and pre-Celtic gods and goddesses became Christian saints—for instance, St. Brigit, whose perpetual sacred fire was kept alight in a monastery at Kildare until the time of Henry VIII—and heathen festivals became Christianized with only a slight change of ritual. St. Brigit according to *The Calendar of Oengus* retained her original firefeast, *Feile Brighde*, on the evening of February 1st. She was so important that bishops were her Master-craftsmen; one of these, Connlaed, is said to have disobeyed her and to have been thrown to the wolves at her orders. She was greeted in the *Hymn of Broccan* as 'Mother of my Sovereign', and in the *Hymn of Ultan* as 'Mother of Jesus'. (She had once been mother of The Dagda). In *The Book of Lismore* she is named: 'The Prophetess of Christ, the Queen of the South, the Mary of the Goidels'. Exactly the same thing had happened in Greece and Italy, where the Goddess Venus became St. Venere; the Goddess Artemis, St. Artemidos; the Gods Mercury and Dionysus, SS. Mercourios and Dionysius; the Sun-god Helios, St. Elias. In Ireland, when St. Columcille founded his church at Derry ('Oak-wood') he was 'so loth to fell certain sacred trees that he turned his oratory to face north rather than east'—north, towards Caer Arianrhod. And when he was in Scotland he declared that 'though he feared Death and Hell, the sound of an axe in the grove of Derry frightened him still more'. But the age of toleration did not last long; once Irish princes lost the privilege of appointing bishops from their own sept, and iconoclasts were politically strong enough to begin their righteous work, the axes rose and fell on every sacred hill.

It would be unfair to call the heretical poets 'apostates'. They were interested in poetic values and relations rather than in prose dogma. It must have been irksome for them to be restricted in their poem-making by ecclesiastical conventions. 'Is it reasonable?' they may have exclaimed. 'The Pope, though he permits our typifying Jesus as a Fish, as the Sun, as Bread, as the Vine, as a Lamb, as a Shepherd, as a Rock, as a Conquering Hero, even as a Winged Serpent, yet threatens us with Hell Fire if we ever dare to celebrate him in terms of the venerable gods whom He has superseded and from whose ritual every one of these symbols has been derived. Or if we trip over a simple article of this extraordinarily difficult Athanasian Creed. We need no reminder from Rome or Canterbury that Jesus was the greatest of all Sacred Kings who suffered death on a tree for the good of the people, who harrowed Hell and who rose again from the Dead and that in Him all prophecies are fulfilled. But to pretend that he was the first whom poets have ever celebrated as having performed these wonderful feats is, despite St. Paul, to show oneself either hypocritical or illiterate. So at his prophesied Second Coming we reserve the right to call him Belin or Apollo or even King Arthur.'

The most virtuous and enlightened of the early Roman Emperors, Alexander Severus (222–235 A.D.) had held almost precisely the same view. He considered himself a reincarnation of Alexander the Great and, according to his biographer Lampridius, worshipped among his house-gods Abraham, Orpheus, Alexander and Jesus Christ. This mention of Alexander Severus suggests a reconsideration of the discredited word 'Helio-Arkite', which was used at the beginning of the nineteenth century to describe a hypothetic heathen cult revived by the bards as a Christian heresy, in which the Sun and Noah's Ark were the principal objects of worship. 'Arkite' without the 'Helio-', was first used by the antiquary Jacob Bryant in 1774 in his *Analysis of Ancient Mythology*; but the word is incorrectly formed if it is to mean 'Arcian', or 'Arcensian', 'concerned with the Ark', as Bryant intended, since '-ite' is a termination which denotes tribal or civic origin, not religious opinion. It seems indeed as if Bryant had borrowed the word 'Arkite' from some ancient work on religion and had misunderstood it.

There is only one famous Arkite in religious history—this same Alexander Severus, who was called 'the Arkite' because he was born in the temple of Alexander the Great at Arka in the Lebanon, where his Roman parents were attending a festival. His mother, Mamea, was some sort of Christian. The Arkites who are mentioned in *Genesis, X, 7*, and also in the Tell Amarna tablets of 1400 B.C., were an ancient Canaanite people well-known for their worship of the Moon-goddess Astarte, or Ishtar, to whom the acacia-wood ark was sacred; but Arka, which in the Tell Amarna tablets appears as 'Irkata', was not necessarily connected with the Indo-European root *arc*—meaning 'protection', from which we derive such Latin words as *arceo*, 'I ward off', *arca*, 'an ark', and *arcana*, 'religious secrets'. The Arkites are listed in *Genesis X* with the Amathites, the Lebanon Hivites (probably Achaifites, or Achaeans) and the Gergasites of Lower Galilee, who seem to have originated in Gergithion near Troy and to be the people whom Herodotus names 'the remnants of the ancient Teucrians'. The Arkite cult, later the Arkite heresy, was Alexander Severus's own syncretic religion and in this sense of the word, Gwion may be styled an Arkite. The Sun and the Ark are, indeed, the most important elements of the Hercules myth, and Ishtar in the Gilgamesh Deluge romance of Babylonia, plays the same false part towards Gilgamesh as Blodeuwedd plays to Llew Llaw in the *Mabinogion*, or Delilah to Samson in *Judges*, or Deianeira to Hercules in Classical legend. It is a great pity that Bryant's enthusiastic followers tried to substantiate a sound thesis by irresponsible and even fraudulent arguments.

The complimentary reference to the See of St. David in Gwion's riddle —it is important to notice that St. David himself was a miraculous child, born from a chaste nun—and the anti-English vaticinations of a tenth-century poet, who also called himself Taliesin, which are bound up with the Gwion poems in the *Red Book of Hergest*, suggest that Gwion was hopefully trying to revive the Arkite heresy and elevate it into a popular pan-Celtic religion which should also include the Celticized Danes of the Dublin region and unite the Bretons, Irish, Welsh, and Scots in a political confederacy against the Anglo-Norman-French. If so, nis hopes were disappointed. The Angevins were too strong: by 1282 Wales had become a province of England, the Normans were firmly established at Dublin and the head of Llewellyn Prince of North Wales, the leader of the nation, had been brought to London and exhibited on Tower Hill, crowned with an ivy wreath: in mocking allusion to the Welsh prophecy that he should be crowned there. Nevertheless, Gwion's romance continued to be recited, and Welsh nationalism was revived towards the end of the fourteenth century under Prince Owen Glendower, who had a doubtful claim to descent from this same Prince Llewellyn, the last prince of the royal line that had been ruling Wales since the third century A.D. Glendower, whose cause was supported by a new self-styled 'Taliesin', kept up a desultory war, with French help, until his death in 1416.

It was about that time that Dr. Sion Kent, the parish priest of Kenchurch, complained of what seems to have been the same Arkite heresy, since Hu Gadarn, the hero who led the Cymry into Britain from Taprobane (Ceylon), was invoked in it as an allegorical champion of Welsh liberty:

> *Two kinds of inspiration in good truth*
> *Exist and manifest their course on earth:*
> *Inspiration from sweet-spoken Christ,*
> *Orthodox and gladdening the soul,*
> *And that most unwise other Inspiration,*
> *Concerned with false and filthy prophecy*
> *Received by the devotees of Hu (Gadarn),*
> *The unjustly usurping bards of Wales.*

The 'false and filthy prophecies' probably concerned the expulsion of the English from Wales and the restored independence of the Welsh Church. Dr. Kent, whose name suggests that he was not of Welsh blood, was naturally anxious for the future, especially since nationalism implied an open return of the people of Kenchurch to a great many pagan superstitions which he spent much of his time trying to suppress; and perhaps, as a poet, was also jealous of the influence of the minstrels over his flock.

That the minstrels continued to stir up popular feeling by their anti-English vaticinations even after the fall of Owen Glendower is suggested by the repressive law of Henry IV enacted in 1402: 'To eschew many diseases and mischiefs which have happened before this time in the Land of Wales by many wasters, rhymers, minstrels and other vagabonds. It is ordained and stablished that no waster, rhymer, minstrel nor vagabond be in any wise sustained in the Land of Wales to make commorthies' [i.e. *kymhorthau,* 'neighbourly gatherings'] 'or gatherings upon the common people there.' Pennant in his *Tours* comments that the object of these commorthies was to 'collect a sufficient number of able-bodied men to make an insurrection'.

It is possible that the original Gwion who revived Druidism in Wales, as a pan-Celtic political weapon against the English, lived as early as in the reign of Prince Owain Gwynedd, son of the gifted Prince Grufudd ap Kynan who first brought Irish bards into North Wales; Owain reigned from 1137 to 1169 and resisted the armies of King Henry II with far greater success than either the Scots, Bretons or Irish. Cynddelw, in whose poems the word Druid first occurs, addressed Owain as 'The Door of the Druids', 'door' being mentioned as a synonym for the princely oak in the *Câd Goddeu.* Owain may also be the hero celebrated in the badly garbled *Song of Daronwy,* from the *Book of Taliesin*:

> *In driving back the oppressor across the sea*
> *What tree has been greater than he, Daronwy?*

Daronwy means 'thunderer', another synonym for oak, and Owain had driven off with heavy loss the sea-borne expedition which Henry sent against Anglesey in 1157.

If anyone should doubt that Gwion could have picked up the Greek and Hebrew knowledge necessary to the construction of this riddle in Ireland, here is a passage from C. S. Boswell's edition of the tenth-century Irish *Fis Adamnain*, 'The Vision of St. Adamnain:

While the Christian Church of Teutonic England owed its existence, in the main, to the missionary enterprise of Rome, the much older Celtic Churches, and notably the Church of Ireland, were more closely connected with Gaul and the East. It was to Gaul that Ireland was mainly indebted for its original conversion, and the intercourse between the two countries remained close and unbroken. But the Church in the south of Gaul—and it was the south alone that preserved any considerable culture, or displayed any missionary activity, in the early Middle Ages—had from the very first been closely in touch with the Churches in the East. The great monastery of Lerins, in which St. Patrick is said to have studied, was founded from Egypt, and for many centuries the Egyptian Church continued to manifest a lively interest in Gallic matters. Indeed, not only Lerins, but Marseilles, Lyons, and other parts of Southern Gaul maintained a constant intercourse with both Egypt and Syria, with the natural result that many institutions of the Gallic Church, despite its increasing subjection to Rome, dating from the year 244, bore the impress of Oriental influences. Hence the close relations with Gaul maintained by the Irish churchmen and scholars necessarily brought them into contact with their Egyptian and Syrian brethren, and with the ideas and practices which prevailed in their respective Churches.

Nor was Ireland's connection with the East confined to the intermediary of Gaul. Irish pilgrimages to Egypt continued until the end of the eighth century, and Dicuil records a topographical exploration of that country made by two Irishmen, Fidelis and his companion. Documentary evidence is yet extant, proving that even home-keeping Irishmen were not debarred from all acquaintance with the East. The *Saltair na Rann* contains an Irish version of the *Book of Adam and Eve*, a work written in Egypt in the fifth or sixth century, of which no mention outside of Ireland is known. Adamnain's work, *De Locis Sanctis*, contains an account of the monastery on Mount Tabor, which might stand for the description of an Irish monastic community of his day. Indeed, the whole system both of the anchoretic and coenobitic life in Ireland corresponds closely to that which prevailed in Egypt and Syria; the monastic communities, consisting of groups of detached huts or beehive cells, and of the other earliest examples of Irish ecclesiastical architecture, all suggest Syrian origin; and Dr. G. T. Stokes holds that 'the Irish schools were most probably modelled after the forms and rules of the Egyptian Lauras'.

But it was not only Syrian and Egyptian influences to which Ireland was subjected by its intercourse with South Gaul. The civilization of that country was essentially Greek, and so remained for many centuries after the Christian era; and this circumstance no doubt contributed to the well-known survival of Greek learning in the Irish schools, long after it had almost perished in the rest of Western Europe. It is not to be supposed that this learning was characterized by accuracy of scholarship, or by a wide acquaintance with Classical literature; but neither was it always restricted to a mere smattering of the language or, to passages and quotations picked up at second-hand. Johannes Scotus Erigena translated the works of the pseudo-Areopagite; Dicuil and Firghil (Virgilius, Bishop of Salzburg), studied the Greek books of Science; Homer, Aristotle, and other Classical authors were known to some of the Irish writers; several of the Irish divines were acquainted with the Greek Fathers and other theological works. Nor were the Greeks in person unknown to Ireland. Many Greek clerics had taken refuge there during the Iconoclast persecution, and left traces which were recognizable in Archbishop Ussher's day; and the old poem on the Fair of Carman makes mention of the Greek merchants who resorted thither.

It is thus apparent that the Irish writer possessed ample means of becoming acquainted with the traditions, both oral and written, of the Greek and Eastern Churches. The knowledge thus acquired extended to the Apocalyptic Visions, as is proved by internal evidence furnished by the Irish Visions, both by way of direct reference, and by the nature of their contents. It remains to see how far the predilection which the Irish writers manifested for this class of literature, and the special characteristics which it assumes in their hands, may have been determined by their familiarity with analogous ideas already existing in their national literature.

At the period in question, the traditional literature of Ireland would appear to have entered into the national life to no less a degree than in Greece itself. Indeed, in certain respects, it was still more closely interwoven with the habits of the people and the framework of society than in Greece, for the literary profession was provided for by a public endowment, something like that of an established National Church, and its professors constituted a body organized by law, and occupying a recognized position in the State.

The reiterated 'I have been' and 'I was' of Gwion's *Hanes Taliesin* riddle suggests that the Boibel-Loth alphabet, which is the solution, originally consisted of twenty mystical titles of a single Protean male deity, corresponding with his seasonal changes; and that these titles were kept secret, at first because of their invocatory power, later because they were regarded as heretical by the Christian Church. But why does the Boibel-Loth contain so many approximations to Biblical names, taken from *Genesis* and *Exodus*, which in Christian times had lost their religious importance: Lot, Telmen, Jachin, Hur, Caleb, Ne-esthan—all names concerned with Sinai, Southern Judaea and the Edomite Dead Sea region?

This is the region in which the Essene communities were settled from about 150 B.C. to 132 A.D. The Essenes appear to have been an offshoot of the Therapeutae, or Healers, an ascetic Jewish sect settled by Lake Mareotis in Egypt; Pliny described them as the strangest religious body in the world. Though Jews, and a sort of Pharisees at that, they believed in the Western Paradise—of which precisely the same account is given by Josephus when describing Essene beliefs as by Homer, Hesiod and Pindar—and, like the later Druids, in the return of pure souls to the Sun, whose rising they invoked every day. They also avoided animal sacrifices, wore linen garments, practised divination, meditated within magic circles, were expert in the virtues of plants and precious stones and are therefore generally supposed to have been under the philosophic influence of Pythagoras, the ascetic pupil of Abaris the Hyperborean. They refrained from worshipping at the Jerusalem Temple, perhaps because the custom of bowing to the East at dawn had been discontinued there, and exacted the penalty of death from anyone who blasphemed God or Moses.

Since among the Jerusalem Pharisees, Moses as a man could not be blasphemed, it follows that for the Essenes he had a sort of divinity. The story of Moses in the Pentateuch was the familiar one of Canopic Hercules —the God who was cradled in an ark on the river Nile, performed great feats, died mysteriously on a mountain-top, and afterwards became a hero and judge. But it is plain that the Essenes distinguished the historic Moses, who led the Israelites out of Egypt, from the demi-god Moses; just as the Greeks distinguished the historic Hercules, Prince of Tiryns, from Celestial Hercules. In Chapter Twenty-Five I shall give reasons for supposing that though the Essenes adapted the Greek formula of Celestial Hercules to their cult of Moses as demi-god, and though they seem to have been disciples of Pythagoras, it was from a sixth-century B.C. Jewish source that the Pythagoreans derived the new sacred name of God that the tribes of Amathaon and Gwydion established in Britain about the year 400 B.C.

The Essene initiates, according to Josephus, were sworn to keep secret the names of the Powers who ruled their universe under God. Were these Powers the letters of the Boibel-Loth which, together, composed the life and death story of their demi-god Moses? 'David' may seem to belong to a later context than the others, but it is found as a royal title in a sixteenth-century B.C. inscription; and the Pentateuch was not composed until long after King David's day. Moreover, David for the Essenes was the name of the promised Messiah.

If all the vowel names of the Boibel-Loth, not merely Jaichin, are preceded by a J, they become Jacab, Jose, Jura, Jesu, Jaichin—which are Jacob, Joseph, Jerah, Joshua and Jachin, all names of tribes mentioned in *Genesis*. The Essene series of letter-names, before Gwion in his riddle altered some of them to names taken from the New Testament, the *Book of Enoch,* and Welsh and Latin mythology, may be reconstructed as follows:

Jacob	Babel	Hur	Moriah
Joseph	Lot	David	Gad
Jerah	Ephron	Telmen	Gomer
Joshua	Salem	Kohath	Jethro
Jachin	Ne-esthan	Caleb	Reu

Of these, only four names are not those of clans or tribes, namely: Babel, the home of wisdom; Moriah, Jehovah's holy mountain; Salem, his holy city; Ne-esthan, his sacred serpent. It seems possible, then, that the Essene version of the Boibel-Loth letter-names was brought to Ireland in early Christian times, by Alexandrian Gnostics who were the spiritual heirs of the Essenes after Hadrian had suppressed the Order in 132 A.D. Dr. Joyce in his *Social History of Ancient Ireland* records that in times of persecution Egyptian monks often fled to Ireland; and that one Palladius was sent from Rome to become a bishop of the Irish Christians long before the arrival of St. Patrick.

The alphabet itself was plainly not of Hebrew origin: it was a Canopic Greek calendar-formula taken over by Greek-speaking Jews in Egypt, who disguised it with the names of Scriptural characters and places. As I suggest in my *King Jesus,* it is likely that in Essene usage each letter became a Power attendant on the Son of Man—Moses as Celestial Hercules —who was subservient to the Ancient of Days, Jehovah as the Transcendent God. It is recorded that the Essene novice wore a blue robe, the adept a white one. Was this because the novice was still 'lotus-borne', that is to say, not yet initiated? The Egyptian lotus was blue. I also suggest in *King Jesus* that the two mysterious Orders of the Essenes, Sampsonians and Helicaeans, were adepts in the calendar mysteries and were named after Samson (the second *s* is a *ps* in some Greek texts) the sun-hero and the *Helix*, or cosmic circle. (An Essene who wished to meditate would insulate himself from the world within a circle drawn around him on the sand.) The twenty Powers of the Babel-Lot will have been among those distastefully mentioned by St. Paul in *Galatians IV, 8–10* as 'weak and cringing Elements (*stoicheia*)'. The back-sliding Galatian Jews were now again worshipping such Powers as gods, with careful observation of the calendar. In *I Corinthians, XV, 24–25* he claims that they have been vanquished by Jesus Christ who alone mediates with the Father. Paul's influence was decisive: to the orthodox Church they soon became demons, not agents of the Divine Will.

The Essenes invoked angels in their mysteries. Here is something odd: that the 'Hounds of Herne the Hunter', or the 'Dogs of Annwm', which hunt souls across the sky are, in British folklore, also called 'Gabriel ratches' or 'Gabriel hounds'. Why Gabriel? Was it because Gabriel, whose day was Monday, ran errands for Sheol (the Hebrew Hecate) and was sent to summon souls to Judgement? This was Hermes's task, and Herne, a British oak-god whose memory survived in Windsor Forest until the eighteenth century, is generally identified with Hermes. Gabriel and Herne are equated in the early thirteenth-century carvings around the church door at Stoke Gabriel in South Devon. The angel Gabriel looks down from above, but on the right as one enters are carved the wild hunter, his teeth bared in a grin and a wisp of hair over his face, and a brace of his hounds close by. But Hermes in Egypt, though Thoth in one aspect, in another was the dog-headed god Anubis, son of Nepthys the Egyptian Hecate; so Apuleius pictures him in the pageant at the end of *The Golden Ass* as 'his face sometimes black, sometimes fair, lifting up the head of the Dog Anubis'. This makes the equation Gabriel = Herne = Hermes = Anubis. But was Gabriel ever equated with Anubis in ancient times? By a piece of good luck an Egyptian gem has been found showing Anubis with palm and pouch on the obverse, and on the reverse an archangel described as GABRIER SABAO, which means 'Gabriel Sabaoth', the Egyptians having, as usual, converted the L into an R. (This gem is described in de Haas's *Bilderatlas*.) Then is 'Annwm', which is a contracted form of 'Annwfn', a Celtic version of 'Anubis'? The B of Anubis would naturally turn into an F in Welsh.

So much nonsense has been written about the Essenes by people who have not troubled to find out from Josephus, Pliny the Elder, Philo the Byblian and others, who they were and what they believed, that I should not bring them into this story if it were not for a poem of Gwion's called *Yr Awdil Vraith*, ('Diversified Song'). The text in the *Peniardd MSS* is incomplete, but in some stanzas preferable to that of the *Red Book of Hergest*:

> 1   *The All-Being made,*
>   *Down the Hebron Vale,*
>   *With his plastic hands,*
>   *Adam's fair form:*
>
>   *And five hundred years,*
>   *Void of any help,*

There he lingered and lay
Without a soul.

He again did form,
In calm paradise,
From a left-side rib,
Bliss-throbbing Eve.

Seven hours they were
The orchard keeping,
Till Satan brought strife,
The Lord of Hell.

5 Thence were they driven,
Cold and shivering,
To gain their living,
Into this world.

To bring forth with pain
Their sons and daughters,
To have possession
Of Asia's land.

Twice five, ten and eight,
She was self-bearing,
The mixed burden
Of man-woman.

And once, not hidden,
She brought forth Abel,
And Cain the solitary
Homicide.

To him and his mate
Was given a spade,
To break up the soil,
Thus to get bread.

10 The wheat pure and white,
In tilth to sow,
Every man to feed,
Till great yule feast.

An angelic hand
From the high Father,
Brought seed for growing
That Eve might sow;

But she then did hide
Of the gift a tenth,
And all did not sow
  In what was dug.

Black rye then was found,
And not pure wheat grain,
To show the mischief,
  Thus of thieving.

For this thievish act,
It is requisite,
That all men should pay
  Tithe unto God.

15 Of the ruddy wine,
Planted on sunny days,
And the white wheat planted
  On new-moon nights;

The wheat rich in grain,
And red flowing wine
Christ's pure body make,
  Son of Alpha.

The wafer is flesh,
The wine, spilt blood,
The words of the Trinity
  Consecrate them.

The concealed books
From Emmanuel's hands
Were brought by Raphael
  As Adam's gift.

When in his old age,
To his chin immersed
In Jordan's water,
  He kept a fast.

20 Twelve young men,
Four of them angels,
Sent forth branches
  From the flower Eve.

To give assistance,
In every trouble,

In all oppression,
    While they wandered.

Very great care
Possessed mankind,
Until they obtained
    The tokens of grace.

Moses obtained
In great necessity
The aid of the three
    Dominical rods.

Solomon obtained
In Babel's tower,
All the sciences
    Of Asia's land.

25 So did I obtain
In my bardic books,
Asia's sciences,
    Europe's too.

I know their arts,
Their course and destiny,
Their going and coming
    Until the end.

Oh! what misery,
Through extreme of woe,
Prophecy will show
    On Troia's race!

A chain-wearing serpent,
The pitiless hawk
With wingèd weapons,
    From Germany.

Loegria and Britain
She will overrun,
From Lychlyn sea-shore
    To the Severn.

30 Then will the Britons
As prisoners be
By strangers swayed
    From Saxony.

Their Lord they will praise,
Their speech they will keep,
Their land they will lose,
    Except Wild Wales.

Till some change shall come,
After long penance,
When shall be made equal
    The pride of birth.

Britons then shall have
Their land and their crown,
And the stranger swarm
    Shall vanish away.

All the angel's words,
As to peace and war,
Will thus be fulfilled
    To Britain's race.

The creation of Adam in Hebron rather than in Lower Mesopotamia is startling: for many Biblical scholars now regard the first three chapters of *Genesis* as a Jerahmeelite legend from the Negeb of Judaea, which was taken over by the Israelites and became Babylonianized during the Captivity. Jerahmeel ('beloved of the moon') is yet another name for Canopic Hercules. Dr. Cheyne restores the text of *Genesis, II, 8,* as 'Yahweh planted a garden in Eden of Jerahmeel.' He writes:

> The Jerahmeelites, from whom the Israelites took the story, probably located Paradise on a vastly high mountain, sometimes in a garden, in some part of Jerahmeelite territory. The mountain with a sacred grove on its summit has dropped out of the story in *Genesis, II* but is attested in *Ezekiel*; and in the Ethiopian *Enoch, XXIV* the tree of life is placed in a mountain range to the south. As to the locality, if it be correct that by the Hebrew phrase 'a land flowing with milk and honey' a part of the Negeb was originally meant (*Numbers, XIII, 23, 27*), we might infer that this fruitful land with its vines, pomegrante trees and fig trees (see *Genesis, III, 7*) had once upon a time been the Jerahmeelite Paradise.

The Hebron valley in Southern Judaea is four thousand feet above sea-level and before agriculture started the process of soil-erosion (which, according to Walter Clay Lowdermilk's recent survey of Palestine, has taken an average of three feet of soil from the whole country), must have been wonderfully fertile. Dr. Cheyne was apparently unaware of this poem of Gwion's, the substance of which can have come only from a Hebrew source uncontaminated by the Babylonian epic which the Jews picked up in their Captivity, and it is difficult to see from whom, other than the Essenes; especially as Gwion explains that the books from which he derives his wisdom were originally brought to Adam of Hebron by the angel Raphael. In *Tobit* and *The Book of Enoch* Raphael is described as the angel of healing and must therefore have been the chief patron of the therapeutic Essenes. 'Emmanuel' refers to Isaiah's prophecy of the birth of the Divine Child from a virgin: Jesus as Hercules.

The story of Adam fasting in Jordan with water to his chin is found in the tenth-century Irish *Saltair na Rann,* and in the early mediaeval *Life of Adam and Eve,* on which the *Saltair* is based; when Adam fasted, according to the *Saltair,* God rewarded him with pardon. But no source is known for the dispensation of wisdom to Moses by means of three Dominical rods (i.e. the rods of Sunday). It may be Essene tradition, for Sunday was the Essenes' great day, and recalls a reference to three rowan sods in one of the Iolo manuscripts. Sir John Rhys regards this manuscript as genuine:

> Then Menw ap Teirgwaedd took the three rowan-rods growing out of the mouth of Einigan Gawr, and learned all the kinds of knowledge and science written on them, and taught them all, EXCEPT THE NAME OF GOD WHICH HAS ORIGINATED THE BARDIC SECRET, and blessed is he who possesses it.

The end of the poem, from stanza 27 onwards, is a separate piece, not Gwion's work, dating perhaps from the year 1210 when, in the reign of King Llewelyn ap Iowerth, King John of England invaded North Wales and temporarily conquered it.

Dr. Ifor Williams has expressed surprise that in the middle of Gwion's *Câd Goddeu* occurs the *Triad*:

> *The three greatest tumults of the world—*
> *The Deluge, the Crucifixion, the Day of Judgement.*

This seems to be a variant text of the lines I have printed from Nash's translation, and which occur twice in the poem:

> *One of them relating*
> *The story of the Deluge*
> *And of the Cross of Christ*
> *And of the Day of Judgement near at hand.*

Dr. Williams's version makes perfect sense also in the Boibel-Loth story of Hercules riding on the flood in his golden cup—sacrificed on the mountain—judging and establishing. The Apostles' Creed, indeed, is the same old story—'conceived by the Holy Ghost, born of the Virgin Mary—suffered, was crucified—shall come to judge the quick and the dead.'

It is possible that the Apostles' Creed, the earliest Latin version of which is quoted by the second-century Tertullian, was originally composed by some Gnostic Christian in Egypt and syncretically modelled on the Hercules formula. For 'conceived by the Holy Ghost', when read in the Gnostic light, has a direct reference to the Flood. In Gnostic theory —the Gnostics first appear as a sect in the first century B.C.—Jesus was conceived in the mind of God's Holy Spirit, who was female in Hebrew and, according to *Genesis I, 2*, 'moved on the face of the waters'. The Virgin Mary was the physical vessel in which this concept was incarnate and 'Mary' to the Gnostics meant 'Of the Sea'. The male Holy Ghost is a product of Latin grammar—*spiritus* is masculine—and of early Christian mistrust of female deities or quasi-deities. Conception by a male principle is illogical and this is the only instance of its occurrence in all Latin literature. The masculinization of the Holy Spirit was assisted by a remark in the *First Epistle of St. John*, that Jesus would act as a paraclete or advocate for man with God the Father; in the *Gospel of St. John* the same figure is put in Jesus's own mouth in a promise that God will send them a paraclete (usually translated 'comforter') after he has gone; and this paraclete, a masculine noun, understood as a mystical emanation of Jesus, was wrongly identified with the archaic Spirit that moved on the face of the waters. The Gnostics, whose language was Greek, identified the Holy Spirit with Sophia, Wisdom; and Wisdom was female. In the early Christian Church the Creed was uttered only at baptism, which was a ceremony of initiation into the Christian mystery and at first reserved for adults; baptism was likewise a preliminary to participation in the Greek mysteries on which the Christian were modelled, as in the Druidic mysteries.

The town of Eleusis, where the most famous mysteries of all took place, was said to be named after the Attic King Eleusis. Eleusis means 'Advent' and the word was adopted in the Christian mysteries to signify the arrival of the Divine Child; in English usage it comprises Christmas and the four preceding weeks. The mother of Eleusis was 'Daeira, daughter of Oceanus', 'the Wise One of the Sea', and was identified with Aphrodite, the Minoan Dove-goddess who rose from the sea at Paphos in Cyprus every year with her virginity renewed. King Eleusis was another name for the Corn-Dionysus, whose life-story was celebrated at the Great Mysteries, a Harvest Thanksgiving festival in late September; and his father was sometimes said to be Ogygus, or Ogyges, the Theban king in whose reign the great flood took place which engulfed the corn-lands of Boeotia. At an early stage of the yearly Eleusinian Mysteries the Divine Child, son of the Wise One who came from the Sea, was produced by mystagogues, dressed as shepherds, for the adoration of the celebrants. He was seated in a *liknos*, or osier harvest-basket. To judge from the corresponding myths of Moses, Taliesin, Llew Llaw, and Romulus, the mystagogues declared that they found him on the river bank where he had landed after sailing over the flood in this same harvest-basket, caulked with sedge. It will shortly be mentioned that the *liknos* was used not only as harvest-basket, manger and cradle, but also as winnowing sieve; the method was to shovel up the corn and chaff together while the wind was blowing strong and sieve them through the osiers; the chaff was blown away and the corn fell in a heap. The Mysteries probably originated as a winnowing feast, for they took place some weeks after the wheat-harvest, and at the time of the equinoctial winds.

An interesting survival of these winnowing-feast mysteries is the Majorcan *xiurell*, or white clay whistle, decorated in red and green, and hand-made in the traditional shapes of mermaid, coiled serpent, bull-headed man, full-skirted woman with a round hat rocking a baby in her arms, or with a flower instead of a baby, the same with a moon-disk surmounted by cow's horns, man with a tall peaked hat and arms upraised in adoration, and little man riding on a hornless, prick-eared, long-legged animal with a very short muzzle. It figures, with quince-boughs and boughs of the sorb-apple, in an ecclesiastical festival held at the village of Bonanova near Palma when the villagers perambulate a hill at night on the first Sunday after the 12th of September (the Feast of the Blessed Name of the Virgin Mary) which corresponds with the 23rd of September Old Style. The object of the whistle must originally have been to induce the North-East winnowing winds which, according to the local almanack, begin to blow at this season and which at the end of the month summon rain clouds from the Atlantic Ocean to soak the winter wheat planted earlier in the month. But this is forgotten: winnowing in Majorca is now done at any time after the harvest and not celebrated with any festivities. The mermaid, locally called a 'siren', evidently represents Daeira (Aphrodite) the moon-mother of Eleusis (the Corn-Dionysus who is shown with her in the woman-and-baby *xiurell*); the bull-headed man is Dionysus himself grown to manhood; the man in the hat is a Tutor, or *gran mascara*; the little rider is likely to be Dionysus again but the species of his tall mount is indeterminate. The quince-boughs, sorb-boughs, and the white clay are also in honour of the Goddess—now invoked as the Virgin Mary. The Serpent is the wind itself. Since this is the only time of the year when wind is welcomed by the Majorcans who, being largely arboricultural, fear the sirocco as they fear the Devil—the farmer's purse, as they say, hangs on the bough of a tree—the sound of whistling is not heard in the island except in the *xiurell* season. The ploughman sings as he drives his mule and the schoolboy as he runs home from school; for the rest *furbis, flabis, flebis*—'whistle shrill, weep long'. More about the White Goddess and whistling for wind will be found in Chapter Twenty-Four.

'King Ogygus' is a name invented to explain why Eleusis was called
'Ogygiades'. There was really no such king as Eleusis: Eleusis signified
the Advent of the Divine Child. And the Child was not really a son of
Ogygus: he was the son of the Queen of the Island of Ogygia, namely
Calypso. And Calypso was Daeira, or Aphrodite, again—the Wise One
of the Sea, the spirit who moved upon the face of the waters. The fact was
that, like Taliesin and Merlin and Llew Llaw and probably in the original
version Moses[1] too, Eleusis had no father, only a virgin mother; he originated before the institution of fatherhood. To the patriarchal Greeks this
seemed shameful and they therefore fathered him on either 'Ogygus' or
Hermes—but more generally on Hermes because of the sacred phalluses
displayed at the festival, heaped in the same useful *liknos*. The Vine-
Dionysus once had no father, either. His nativity appears to have been
that of an earlier Dionysus, the Toadstool-god; for the Greeks believed
that mushrooms and toadstools were engendered by lightning—not
sprung from seed like all other plants. When the tyrants of Athens,
Corinth and Sicyon legalized Dionysus-worship in their cities, they
limited the orgies, it seems, by substituting wine for toadstools; thus the
myth of the Toadstool-Dionysus became attached to the Vine-Dionysus,
who now figured as a son of Semele the Theban and Zeus, Lord of
Lightning. Yet Semele was sister of Agave, who tore off her son Pentheus's head in a Dionysiac frenzy. To the learned Gwion the Vine-
Dionysus and the Corn-Dionysus were both recognizably Christ, Son
of Alpha—that is, son of the letter A:

> *The wheat rich in grain,*
> *And red flowing wine*
> *Christ's pure body make,*
> *Son of Alpha.*

According to the Talmudic *Targum Yerushalmi* on *Genesis II, 7*,
Jehovah took dust from the centre of the earth and from all quarters of the
earth and mingled it with waters of all the seas to create Adam. The angel
Michael collected the dust. Since the Jewish rabbis preferred to alter
rather than destroy ancient traditions which seemed damaging to their
new cult of transcendent Jehovah, an original story may be postulated in
which Michal (not Michael) of Hebron, the goddess from whom David
derived his title of King by marriage with her priestess, was Adam's
creatrix. David married Michal at Hebron, and Hebron may be called the
centre of the earth, from its position near the junction of two seas and the
three ancient continents. This identification of Michal with Michael would
seem forced, were it not that the name Michael occurs only in post-exilic

---

[1] Sir Flinders Petrie holds that Moses is an Egyptian word meaning 'unfathered son of a
princess'.

writings, and is not therefore a part of ancient Jewish tradition, and that in *A Discourse on Mary* by Cyril of Jerusalem, printed by Budge in his *Miscellaneous Coptic Texts*, this passage occurs:

> It is written in the *Gospel to the Hebrews* [a lost gospel of the Ebionites, supposedly the original of St. Matthew] that when Christ wished to come upon earth to men, the Good Father called a mighty power in the Heavens which was called Michael and committed Christ to its care And the power descended on earth and was called Mary, and Christ was in her womb seven months, after which she gave birth to him. . . .

The mystical Essene Ebionites of the first century A.D. believed in a female Holy Spirit; and those members of the sect who embraced Christianity and developed into the second-century Clementine Gnostics made the Virgin Mary the vessel of this Holy Spirit—whom they named Michael ('Who is like God?'). According to the Clementines, whose religious theory is popularized in a novel called *The Recognitions*,[1] the identity of true religion in all ages depends on a series of incarnations of the Wisdom of God, of which Adam was the first and Jesus the last. In this poem of Gwion's, Adam has no soul after his creation until Eve animates him.

But Caleb, according to the *Hanes Taliesin* riddle, conveyed the Holy Spirit to Hebron when, in the time of Joshua, he ousted the Anakim from the shrine of Machpelah. Machpelah, an oracular cave cut from the rock, was the sepulchre of Abraham, and Caleb went there to consult his shade. The priestly editor of *Genesis* describes it as the sepulchre also of Sarah and Jacob (*Genesis XXIII, 19; XXV, 9; L, 13*) and in *XXXV, 29* implies that Isaac was buried there too. The statement about Jacob is contradicted in *Genesis L, 11*, where it is said that he was buried in Abel-Mizraim. Moreover, Isaac originally lived at Beer-Lahai-Roi (*Genesis XXIV, 62; XXV, 11*) where he probably had an oracular shrine at one time, for Beer-Lahai-Roi means 'the Well of the Antelope's Jawbone' and if Isaac was a *Boibalos*, or Antelope-king, his prophetic jawbone—jawbones were the rule in oracular shrines, usually stored there, it seems, with the hero's navel-string—would naturally give its name to the well; there was a sacred cave near by, which eventually became a Christian chapel. Thus it is likely that neither Isaac nor Jacob nor their 'wives' were at first associated with the cave. The story of its purchase from Ephron (a 'Power', as I suggest, of the Boibel-Loth) and the Children of Heth, usually regarded as Hittites, is told in *Genesis XXIII*. Though late and much edited, this chapter seems to record a friendly arrangement between

---

[1] Voltaire modelled his *Candide* on it; and it has the distinction of appearing in the select list of books in Milton's *Areopagitica*, along with John Skelton's *Poems*, as deserving of permanent suppression.

the devotees of the Goddess Sarah, the Goddess of the tribe of Isaac, and their allies the devotees of the Goddess Heth (Hathor? Tethys?) who owned the shrine: Sarah was forced out of Beer-Lahai-Roi by another tribe and came to seek an asylum at near-by Hebron. Since Sarah was a Laughing Goddess and her progeny was destined to be 'like the sand of the sea shore' she was evidently a Sea-goddess of the Aphrodite type.

All that is needed to clinch this argument in poetic logic is for Caleb in Jewish tradition to have married someone called Michal who was a representative of the local Sea-goddess. He did even better: he married Miriam.[1] (The Talmudic tradition is that 'she was neither beautiful nor in good health'). The equation that follows is: Miriam I = Holy Spirit = Michal = Michael = Miriam II. Michael, then, was regarded as the instrument chosen for the creation of the First Adam, and used Hebron dust and sea water; and Jesus was the Second Adam; and Michael, or Miriam ('Sea-brine') the Virgin Mary, was similarly the instrument of his creation.

Jesus was also held to have fulfilled the prophecy in the 110th Psalm:

Jehovah has sworn and will not repent: thou art a priest forever after the order of Melchizedek.

This is enlarged upon in St. Paul's *Epistle to the Hebrews*. Melchizedek (*Genesis XIV, 18–20*) the Sacred King of Salem who welcomed 'Abraham' to Canaan ('Abraham' being in this sense the far-travelled tribe that came down into Palestine from Armenia at the close of the third millennium B.C.) 'had neither father nor mother'. 'Salem' is generally taken to mean Jerusalem and it is probable that Salem occurs in the Boibel-Loth as a compliment to Melchizedek, who was priest to the Supreme God. But J. N. Schofield in his *Historical Background to the Bible* notes that to this day the people of Hebron have not forgiven David for moving his capital to Jerusalem ('Holy Salem') which they refer to as 'The New Jerusalem' as though Hebron were the authentic one. There is a record in the Talmud of a heretical sect of Jews, called Melchizedekians, who frequented Hebron to worship the body (consult the spirit?) of Adam which was buried in the cave of Machpelah. If these Melchizedekians worshipped Adam, the only other character in the Bible who had neither

---

[1] A similar marriage was that of Joshua to Rahab the Sea-goddess, who appears in the Bible as Rahab the Harlot. By this union, according to *Sifre*, the oldest Midrash, they had daughters only, from whom descended many prophets including Jeremiah; and Hannah, Samuel's mother, was Rahab's incarnation. The story of Samuel's birth suggests that these 'daughters of Rahab' were a matrilinear college of prophetic priestesses by ritual marriage with whom Joshua secured his title to the Jericho valley. Since Rahab is also said to have married Salmon (and so to have become an ancestress of David and Jesus) it may well be that Salmon was the title that Joshua assumed at his marriage; for a royal marriage involved a ritual death and rebirth with a change of name, as when Jacob married Rachel the Dove-priestess and became Ish-Rachel or Israel—'Rachel's man'.

father nor mother, they were doubtless identifying Melchizedek's king-ship with the autochthonous Adam's. For Adam, 'the red man', seems to have been the original oracular hero of Machpelah; it is likely that Caleb consulted his shade not Abraham's, unless Adam and Abraham are titles of the same hero. Elias Levita, the fifteenth-century Hebrew commentator, records the tradition that the teraphim which Rachel stole from her father Laban were mummified oracular heads and that the head of Adam was among them. If he was right, the *Genesis* narrative refers to a seizure of the oracular shrine of Hebron by Saul's Benjamites from the Calebites.

Caleb was an Edomite clan; which suggests the identification of Edom with Adam: they are the same word, meaning 'red'. But if Adam was really Edom, one would expect to find a tradition that the head of Esau, the ancestor of the Edomites, was also buried at Hebron; and this is, in fact, supplied by the *Talmud*. The artificial explanation given there is that Esau and his sons opposed the burial of Jacob in the Cave of Machpelah on the ground that it was an Edomite possession; that Joseph, declaring that it had ceased to be Edomite when Jacob sold his birthright to Esau, sent to Egypt for the relevant documents; that a fight ensued in which the sons of Jacob were victorious and Esau was beheaded at one stroke by a dumb Danite; that Esau's body was carried off for burial on Mount Seir by his sons; and that his head was buried at Hebron by Joseph.

Melchizedek's lack of a father is intelligible, but why should he have no mother? Perhaps the stories of Moses, Llew Llaw, Romulus and Cretan Zeus explain this. In every case the boy is removed from his mother as soon as born. Thus, in effect, he has no mother; usually a goat, a wolf or a pig suckles him and he passes under the care of tutors. It is the transitional stage from matriarchy to patriarchy. In the Eleusinian Mysteries the Divine Child was carried in by shepherds, not by his mother or by a nurse.

The seventh and eighth stanzas of *Yr Awdil Vraith* are the strangest of all:

> *Twice five, ten and eight,*
> *She was self-bearing,*
> *The mixed burden*
>   *Of man-woman.*
>
> *And once, not hidden,*
> *She brought forth Abel,*
> *And Cain the solitary*
>   *Homicide.*

This means, I suppose, that Eve bore twenty-eight children, acting as her own midwife, then Cain and Abel and then . . . A stanza has been sup-pressed: a stanza evidently containing the Sethian heresy, a well-known development of the Clementine syncretic theory, in which Seth was viewed as an earlier incarnation of Jesus.[1] It will be recalled that Rhea figures in the *Hanes Taliesin* riddle—Rhea as the mother both of Cretan Zeus and Romulus. The legend was that she bore a number of children, all of whom Saturn her lover ate, until finally she bore Zeus who escaped and eventually avenged his brothers on Saturn by castrating him. Gwion is hinting that Eve, whom he identifies with Rhea, brought forth thirty children in all—and then the Divine Child Seth. Thirty doubtless because the 'reign of Saturn' lasted thirty days and culminated with the mid-winter feast which afterwards became Yule, or Christmas. The letter R (*Riuben* or *Rhea* or *Reu* in the Boibel-Loth, and *Ruis* in the Beth-Luis-Nion) is allotted to the last month of the year. The reign of Saturn there-fore corresponds with the Christian period of Advent, preliminary to the Day of the birth of the Divine Child. Sir James Frazer gives details of this thirty-day period in the *Golden Bough*, in his account of the fourth-century martyr St. Dasius. The Clementines rejected the orthodox story of the Fall as derogatory to the dignity of Adam and Eve, and Gwion in his version similarly puts the blame for their expulsion wholly on Satan.

The 'twelve young men, four of them angels' (i.e. evangels), are evidently the twelve tribes of Israel, four of whom—Joseph, Simeon (Simon), Judah (Jude) and Levi (Matthew)—gave their names to books in the early canon of the New Testament; and they perhaps represent the twelve signs of the Zodiac in Clementine syncretism.

The stanza:

> *Solomon obtained,*
> *In Babel's tower,*
> *All the sciences*
> *Of Asia's lana.*

needs careful examination. 'The confusion of languages after the fall of Babel' was taken by Babylonian Jews to refer to the fall of the famous *ziggorath*, 'the hanging gardens', of Babylon. But the *ziggorath*, unlike the Tower of Babel, was completed. It is much more likely that the myth

---

[1] In the Ethiopian *Legends of Our Lady Mary*, translated by Bridge, the Gnostic theory is clearly given. Hannah the 'twenty-pillared tabernacle of Testimony' who was the Virgin Mary's mother, was one of a triad of sisters—of which the other two were another Mary and Sophia. 'The Virgin first came down into the body of Seth, shining like a white pearl.' Then successively entered Enos, Cainan. . . Jared, Enoch, Methuselah, Lamech, Noah. . . Abraham, Isaac, Jacob. . . David, Solomon. . . and Joachim. 'And Joachim said to his wife Hannah: "I saw Heaven open and a white bird came therefrom and hovered over my head." Now, this bird had its being in the days of old. . . It was the Spirit of Life in the form of a white bird and . . . became incarnate in Hannah's womb when the pearl went forth from Joachim's loins and. . . Hannah received it, namely the body of our Lady Mary. The white pearl is mentioned for its purity, and the white bird because Mary's soul existed aforetime with the Ancient of Days. . . Thus bird and pearl are alike and equal.' From the Body of Mary, the pearl, the white bird of the spirit then entered into Jesus at the Baptism.

originates in the linguistic confusion caused by the Indo-Germanic conquest of Byblos, the Egyptianized metropolis of the People of the Sea, at the beginning of the second millennium B.C. Doubtless there was a 'babble of tongues' in Babylon, but it was not caused by any sudden catastrophe, and the babblers could at least communicate with one another in the official Assyrian language. Whether or not the Byblians had begun work on a gigantic Egyptian temple at the time that the city was stormed and were unable to complete it, I do not know; but if they had done so their misfortune would naturally have been ascribed to divine jealousy at the innovation.

Moreover, 'Asia' was the name of the mother by Iapetus, who appears in *Genesis* as Japhet, Noah's son, of the 'Pelasgians' Atlas and Prometheus; thus the 'Land of Asia' in stanzas 6 and 24 is a synonym for the Eastern Mediterranean, though more properly it meant Southern Asia Minor. King Solomon who reigned about a thousand years after the original fall of Byblos—it had fallen and risen several times meanwhile—may well have learned his religious secrets from Byblos, which the Jews knew as Gebal, for the Byblians helped him to build his Temple. This is mentioned in *1 Kings, V, 18,* though in the Authorised Version 'the men of Gebal' is mistranslated 'stone-squarers'.

And Solomon's builders and Hiram's builders did hew the stones, and the men of Gebal; so they prepared timber and stones to build the house.

'Gebal' means 'mountain-height'. The deep wisdom of Byblos—from which the Greek word for 'book' (and the English word Bible) derives—is compared by Ezekiel, the prophet to whom the Essenes seem to have owed most, to that of Hiram's Tyre (*Ezekiel, XXVII, 8–9*); Tyre was an early Cretan trading centre. Solomon certainly built his temple in Aegean style, closely resembling that of the Great Goddess at Hierapolis described by Lucian in his *De Dea Syria*. There was a Danaan colony close to Byblos, dating from the fourteenth century B.C.

It is possible that though the Calebites interpreted 'Adam' as the Semitic word *Edom* ('red') the original hero at Hebron was the Danaan Adamos or Adamas or Adamastos, 'the Unconquerable', or 'the Inexorable', a Homeric epithet of Hades, borrowed from the Death Goddess his mother.

Chapter Ten

THE TREE ALPHABET (1)

I first found the Beth-Luis-Nion tree-alphabet in Roderick O'Flaherty's *Ogygia*; he presents it, with the Boibel-Loth, as a genuine relic of Druidism orally transmitted down the centuries. It is said to have been latterly used for divination only and consists of five vowels and thirteen consonants. Each letter is named after the tree or shrub of which it is the initial:

Beth	B	Birch
Luis	L	Rowan
Nion	N	Ash
Fearn	F	Alder
Saille	S	Willow
Uath	H	Hawthorn
Duir	D	Oak
Tinne	T	Holly
Coll	C	Hazel
Muin	M	Vine
Gort	G	Ivy
Pethboc	P	Dwarf Elder
Ruis	R	Elder
Ailm	A	Silver Fir
Onn	O	Furze
Ur	U	Heather
Eadha	E	White Poplar
Idho	I	Yew

The names of the letters in the modern Irish alphabet are also those of trees, and most of them correspond with O'Flaherty's list, though T has become gorse; O, broom; and A, elm.

I noticed almost at once that the consonants of this alphabet form a calendar of seasonal tree-magic, and that all the trees figure prominently in European folklore.

The first tree of the series is the self-propagating birch. Birch twigs are used throughout Europe in the beating of bounds and the flogging of delinquents—and formerly lunatics—with the object of expelling evil spirits. When Gwion writes in the *Câd Goddeu* that the birch 'armed himself but late' he means that birch twigs do not toughen until late in the year. (He makes the same remark about the willow and the rowan whose twigs were similarly put to ceremonial use.) Birch rods are also used in rustic ritual for driving out the spirit of the old year. The Roman lictors carried birch rods during the installation of the Consuls at this very same season; each Consul had twelve lictors, making a company of thirteen. The birch is the tree of inception. It is indeed the earliest forest tree, with the exception of the mysterious elder, to put out new leaves (April 1st in England, the beginning of the financial year), and in Scandinavia its leafing marks the beginning of the agricultural year, because farmers use it as a directory for sowing their Spring wheat. The first month begins immediately after the winter solstice, when the days after shortening to the extreme limit begin to lengthen again.

Since there are thirteen consonants in the alphabet, it is reasonable to regard the tree month as the British common-law 'lunar' month of twenty-eight days defined by Blackstone. As has already been pointed out, there are thirteen such months in a solar year, with one day left over. Caesar and Pliny both record that the Druidic year was reckoned by lunar months, but neither defines a lunar month, and there is nothing to prove that it was a 'lunation' of roughly twenty-nine and a half days—of which there are twelve in a year with ten and three-quarter days left over. For the first-century B.C. 'Coligny Calendar', which is one of lunations, is no longer regarded as Druidic; it is engraved in Roman letters on a brass tablet and is now thought to be part of the Romanizing of native religion attempted under the early Empire. Moreover, twenty-eight is a true lunar month not only in the astronomical sense of the moon's revolutions in relation to the sun, but in the mystic sense that the Moon, being a woman, has a woman's normal menstrual period ('menstruation' is connected with the word 'moon')[1] of twenty-eight days.[2] The Coligny system was prob-

---

[1] The magical connection of the Moon with menstruation is strong and widespread. The baleful moon-dew used by the witches of Thessaly was apparently a girl's first menstrual blood, taken during an eclipse of the Moon. Pliny devotes a whole chapter of his *Natural History* to the subject and gives a long list of the powers for good and bad that a menstruating woman possesses. Her touch can blast vines, ivy and rue, fade purple cloth, blacken linen in the wash-tub, tarnish copper, make bees desert their hives, and cause abortions in mares; but she can also rid a field of pests by walking around it naked before sunrise, calm a storm at sea by exposing her genitals, and cure boils, erysipelas, hydrophobia and barrenness. In the *Talmud* it is said that if a menstruating woman passes between two men, one of them will die.

[2] Even in healthy women there is greater variation in the length of time elapsing between periods than is generally supposed: it may be anything from twenty-one to thirty-five days.

ably brought into Britain by the Romans of the Claudian conquest and memories of its intercalated days are said by Professor T. Glynn Jones to survive in Welsh folklore. But that in both Irish and Welsh myths of the highest antiquity 'a year and a day' is a term constantly used suggests that the Beth-Luis-Nion Calendar is one of 364 days plus one. We can therefore regard the Birch month as extending from December 24th to January 20th.

L FOR LUIS

The second tree is the quickbeam ('tree of life'), otherwise known as the quicken, rowan or mountain ash. Its round wattles, spread with newly-flayed bull's hides, were used by the Druids as a last extremity for compelling demons to answer difficult questions—hence the Irish proverbial expression 'to go on the wattles of knowledge', meaning to do one's utmost to get information. The quickbeam is also the tree most widely used in the British Isles as a prophylactic against lightning and witches' charms of all sorts: for example, bewitched horses can be controlled only with a rowan whip. In ancient Ireland, fires of rowan were kindled by the Druids of opposing armies and incantations spoken over them, summoning spirits to take part in the fight. The berries of the magical rowan in the Irish romance of Fraoth, guarded by a dragon, had the sustaining virtue of nine meals; they also healed the wounded and added a year to a man's life. In the romance of Diarmuid and Grainne, the rowan berry, with the apple and the red nut, is described as the food of the gods. 'Food of the gods' suggests that the taboo on eating anything red was an extension of the commoners' taboo on eating scarlet toadstools —for toadstools, according to a Greek proverb which Nero quoted, were 'the food of the gods'. In ancient Greece all red foods such as lobster, bacon, red mullet, crayfish and scarlet berries and fruit were tabooed except at feasts in honour of the dead. (Red was the colour of death in Greece and Britain during the Bronze Age—red ochre has been found in megalithic burials both in the Prescelly Mountains and on Salisbury Plain.) The quickbeam is the tree of quickening. Its botanical name *Fraxinus, or Pyrus, Aucuparia,* conveys its divinatory uses. Another of its names is 'the witch'; and the witch-wand, formerly used for metal divining, was made of rowan. Since it was the tree of quickening it could also be used in a contrary sense. In Danaan Ireland a rowan-stake hammered through a corpse immobilized its ghost; and in the Cuchulain saga three hags spitted a dog, Cuchulain's sacred animal, on rowan twigs to procure his death.

The oracular use of the rowan explains the unexpected presence of great rowan thickets in Rügen and the other Baltic amber-islands, formerly used as oracular places, and the frequent occurrence of rowan,

noted by John Lightfoot in his *Flora Scotica*, 1777, in the neighbourhood
of ancient stone circles. The second month extends from January 21st to
February 17th. The important Celtic feast of Candlemas fell in the middle
of it (February 2nd). It was held to mark the quickening of the year, and
was the first of the four 'cross-quarter days' on which British witches
celebrated their Sabbaths, the others being May Eve, Lammas (August
2nd) and All Hallow E'en, when the year died. These days correspond
with the four great Irish fire-feasts mentioned by Cormac the tenth-
century Archbishop of Cashel. In Ireland and the Highlands February 2nd
is, very properly, the day of St. Brigit, formerly the White Goddess, the
quickening Triple Muse. The connexion of rowan with the Candlemas
fire-feast is shown by Morann Mac Main's Ogham in the *Book of Ballymote*: he gives the poetic name for rowan as 'Delight of the Eye, namely
Luisiu, flame.'

N FOR NION

   The third tree is the ash. In Greece the ash was sacred to Poseidon, the
second god of the Achaean trinity, and the Mĕliai, or ash-spirits, were
much cultivated; according to Hesiod, the Mĕliae sprang from the blood
of Uranus when Cronos castrated him. In Ireland the Tree of Tortu,
The Tree of Dathi, and the Branching Tree of Usnech, three of the
Five Magic Trees whose fall in the year A.D. 665 symbolized the triumph
of Christianity over paganism, were ash-trees. A descendant of the Sacred
Tree of Creevna, also an ash, was still standing at Killura in the nineteenth
century; its wood was a charm against drowning, and emigrants to America
after the Potato Famine carried it away with them piecemeal. In British folklore the ash is a tree of re-birth—Gilbert White describes in his *History of
Selborne* how naked children had formerly been passed through cleft
pollard ashes before sunrise as a cure for rupture. The custom survived in
remoter parts of England until 1830. The Druidical wand with a spiral
decoration, part of a recent Anglesey find dating from the early first
century A.D., was of ash. The great ash Yygdrasill, sacred to Woden, or
Wotan or Odin or Gwydion, has already been mentioned in the context
of the Battle of the Trees; he used it as his steed. But he had taken the
tree over from the Triple Goddess who, as the Three Norns of Scandinavian legend, dispensed justice under it. Poseidon retained his patronage
of horses but also became a god of seafarers when the Achaeans took to
the sea; as Woden did when his people took to the sea. In ancient Wales
and Ireland all oars and coracle-slats were made of ash; and so were the
rods used for urging on horses, except where the deadly yew was preferred. The cruelty of the ash mentioned by Gwion lies in the harmful-
ness of its shade to grass or corn; the alder on the contrary is beneficial to
crops grown in its shade. So also in Odin's own Runic alphabet all the

letters are formed from ash-twigs; as ash-roots strangle those of other forest trees. The ash is the tree of sea-power, or of the power resident in water; and the other name of Woden, 'Yggr', from which Ygdrasill is derived, is evidently connected with *hygra*, the Greek for 'sea' (literally, 'the wet element'). The third month is the month of floods and extends from February 18th to March 17th. In these first three months the nights are longer than the days, and the sun is regarded as still under the tutelage of Night. The Tyrrhenians on this account did not reckon them as part of the sacred year.

F for Fearn

The fourth tree is the alder, the tree of Bran. In the Battle of the Trees the alder fought in the front line, which is an allusion to the letter F being one of the first five consonants of the Beth-Luis-Nion and the Boibel-Loth; and in the Irish Ossianic *Song of the Forest Trees*[1] it is described as 'the very battle-witch of all woods, tree that is hottest in the fight'. Though a poor fuel-tree, like the willow, poplar and chestnut, it is prized by charcoal-burners as yielding the best charcoal; its connexion with fire is shown in the *Romance of Branwen* when 'Gwern' (alder), Bran's sister's son, is burned in a bonfire; and in country districts of Ireland the crime of

[1] To be found in Standish O'Grady's translation in E. M. Hull's *Poem Book of the Gael*. A charming, though emasculated version of the same poem is current on Dartmoor. It tells which trees to burn and which not to burn as follows:

> *Oak-logs will warm you well,*
> *That are old and dry;*
> *Logs of pine will sweetly smell*
> *But the sparks will fly.*
>
> *Birch-logs will burn too fast,*
> *Chestnut scarce at all;*
> *Hawthorn-logs are good to last—*
> *Cut them in the fall.*
>
> *Holly-logs will burn like wax,*
> *You may burn them green;*
> *Elm-logs like to smouldering flax,*
> *No flame to be seen.*
>
> *Beech-logs for winter time,*
> *Yew-logs as well;*
> *Green elder-logs it is a crime*
> *For any man to sell.*
>
> *Pear-logs and apple-logs,*
> *They will scent your room,*
> *Cherry-logs across the dogs*
> *Smell like flower of broom.*
>
> *Ash-logs, smooth and grey,*
> *Burn them green or old,*
> *Buy up all that come your way—*
> *Worth their weight in gold.*

felling a sacred alder is held to be visited with the burning down of one's house. The alder is also proof against the corruptive power of water: its slightly gummy leaves resist the winter rains longer than those of any other deciduous tree and its timber resists decay indefinitely when used for water-conduits or piles. The Rialto at Venice is founded on alder piles, and so are several mediaeval cathedrals. The Roman architect Vitruvius mentions that alders were used as causeway piles in the Ravenna marshes.

The connexion of Bran with the alder in this sense is clearly brought out in the *Romance of Branwen* where the swineherds (oracular priests) of King Matholwch of Ireland see a forest in the sea and cannot guess what it is. Branwen tells them that it is the fleet of Bran the Blessed come to avenge her. The ships are anchored off-shore and Bran wades through the shallows and brings his goods and people to land; afterwards he bridges the River Linon, though it has been protected with a magic charm, by lying down across the river and having hurdles laid over him. In other words, first a jetty, then a bridge was built on alder piles. It was said of Bran, 'No house could contain him.' The riddle 'What can no house ever contain?' has a simple answer: 'The piles upon which it is built.' For the earliest European houses were built on alder piles at the edge of lakes. In one sense the 'singing head' of Bran was the mummied, oracular head of a sacred king; in another it was the 'head' of the alder-tree—namely the topmost branch. Green alder-branches make good whistles and, according to my friend Ricardo Sicre y Cerda, the boys of Cerdaña in the Pyrenees have a traditional prayer in Catalan:

> *Berng, Berng, come out of your skin*
> *And I will make you whistle sweetly.*

which is repeated while the bark is tapped with a piece of willow to loosen it from the wood. Berng (or Verng in the allied Majorcan language) is Bran again. The summons to Berng is made on behalf of the Goddess of the Willow. The use of the willow for tapping, instead of another piece of alder, suggests that such whistles were used by witches to conjure up destructive winds—especially from the North. But musical pipes with several stops can be made in the same way as the whistles, and the singing head of Bran in this sense will have been an alder-pipe. At Harlech, where the head sang for seven years, there is a mill-stream running past the Castle rock, a likely place for a sacred alder-grove. It is possible that the legend of Apollo's flaying of Marsyas the piper is reminiscent of the removal of the alder-bark from the wood in pipe-making.

The alder was also used in ancient Ireland for making milk pails and other dairy vessels: hence its poetical name in the *Book of Ballymote*, *Comet lachta*—'guarding of milk'. This connexion of Bran-Cronos, the alder, with Rhea-Io, the white moon-cow is of importance. In Ireland, Io was called *Glas Gabhnach*, 'the green stripper', because though she yielded milk in rivers she never had a calf. She had been stolen out of Spain by Gavida the flying dwarf-smith; made the circuit of all Ireland in one day, guarded by his seven sons (who presumably stood for the days of the week); and gave the name *Bothar-bó-finné*, 'Track of the White Cow', to the Galaxy. According to *The Proceedings of the Grand Bardic Academy*, she was killed by Guaire at the request of Seanchan Torpest's wife, and according to Keating's *History of Ireland*, was avenged in A.D. 528. King Diarmuid of All Ireland was killed by his eldest son for having murdered another sacred cow.

Bran's connexion with the Western Ocean is proved by *Caer Bran*, the name of the most westerly hill in Britain, overlooking Land's End.

Alder is rarely mentioned in Greek or Latin myth, having apparently been superseded as an oracular tree by the Delphic laurel. But the *Odyssey* and the *Aeneid* contain two important references to it. In the *Odyssey*, alder is the first named of the three trees of resurrection—white poplar and cypress are the two others—that formed the wood around the cave of Calypso, daughter of Atlas, in her Elysian island of Ogygia; in the wood nested chattering sea-crows (sacred to Bran in Britain) falcons and owls. This explains Virgil's version of the metamorphosis of the sisters of the sun-hero Phaëthon: in the *Aeneid* he says that while bewailing their brother's death they were converted, not into a poplar grove, as Euripides and Apollonius Rhodius relate, but into an alder thicket on the banks of the river Po—evidently this was another Elysian islet. The Greek word for alder, *clēthra*, is generally derived from *cleio*, 'I close' or 'I confine'. The explanation seems to be that the alder thickets confined the hero in the oracular island by growing around its shores; the oracular islands seem to have been originally river islands, not islands in the sea.

The alder was, and is, celebrated for yielding three fine dyes: red from its bark, green from its flowers, brown from its twigs: typifying fire, water and earth. In Cormac's tenth-century *Glossary* of obsolete terms the alder is called *ro-eim*, which is glossed as 'that which reddens the face'; from which it may be deduced that the 'crimson-stained heroes' of the Welsh *Triads*, who were sacred kings, were connected with Bran's alder cult. One reason for the alder's sanctity is that when it is felled the wood, at first white, seems to bleed crimson, as though it were a man. The green dye is associated in British folklore with fairies' clothes: in so far as the fairies may be regarded as survivals of dispossessed early tribes, forced to take to hills and woods, the green of the clothes is explainable as protective colouring: foresters and outlaws also adopted it in mediaeval times. Its use seems to be very ancient. But principally the alder is the tree of fire, the power of fire to free the earth from water; and the alder-branch by which Bran was recognized at the *Câd Goddeu* is a token of resurrection—its buds are set in a spiral. This spiral symbol is ante-diluvian: the earliest Sumerian shrines are 'ghost-houses', like those used in Uganda, and are flanked by spiral posts.

The fourth month extends from March 18th, when the alder firts blooms, to April 14th, and marks the drying up of the winter floods by the Spring Sun. It includes the Spring Equinox, when the days become longer than the nights and the Sun grows to manhood. As one can say poetically that the ash trees are the oars and coracle-slats that convey the Spirit of the Year through the floods to dry land, so one can say that the alders are the piles that lift his house out of the floods of winter. Fearn (Bran) appears in Greek mythology as King Phoroneus, ruler of the Peloponnese, who was worshipped as a hero at Argos which he is said to have founded. Hellanicus of Lesbos, a learned contemporary of Herodotus, makes him the father of Pelasgus, Iasus and Agenor, who divided his kingdom between them after his death: in other words, his worship at Argos was immemorially ancient. Pausanias, who went to Argos for his information writes that Phoroneus was the husband of Cerdo (the White Goddess as Muse) and that the River-god Inachus fathered him on the nymph Melia (ash-tree). Since alder succeeds ash in the tree-calendar, and since alders grow by the riverside, this is a suitable pedigree. Pausanias clinches the identification of Phoroneus with Fearn by disregarding the Prometheus legend and making Phoroneus the inventor of fire. Hyginus gives his mother's name as Argeia ('dazzling white'), who is the White Goddess again. So Phoroneus, like Bran and all other sacred kings, was borne by, married to, and finally laid out by, the White Goddess: his layer-out was the Death-goddess Hera Argeia to whom he is said to have first offered sacrifices. Phoroneus, then, is Fearineus, the God of Spring to whom annual sacrifices were offered on the Cronian Mount at Olympia at the Spring equinox.[1] His singing head recalls that of Orpheus whose name is perhaps short for *Orphruoeis* 'growing on the river-bank' i.e. 'the alder'.

In parts of the Mediterranean the cornel or dogwood tree seems to have been used as a substitute for the alder. Its Latin name *cornus* comes from *cornix*, the crow sacred to Saturn or Bran which feeds on its red 'cherries'; as according to Homer the swine of Circe also did. Ovid links it with the esculent oak as supplying men with food in the age of Saturn. Like the

---

[1] The Athenians, however, celebrated their Cronos festival early in July in the month of Cronion or Hecatombeion ('a hundred dead') originally also called Nekusion (corpsemonth) by the Cretans, and Hyacinthion by the Sicilians, after Cronos' counterpart Hyacinth. The barley harvest fell in July, and at Athens Cronos was Sabazius, 'John Barleycorn', who first appeared above the soil at the Spring equinox and whose multiple death they celebrated cheerfully at their harvest-home. He had long lost his connexion with the alder, though he still shared a temple at Athens with Rhea, the lion-guarded Queen of the Year, who was his midsummer bride and to whom the oak was sacred in Greece.

alder it yields a red dye, and was held sacred at Rome where the flight of Romulus's cornel-wood javelin determined the spot where the city was to be built. Its appropriateness to this month is that it is in white blossom by the middle of March.

S FOR SAILLE

The fifth tree is the willow, or osier, which in Greece was sacred to Hecate, Circe, Hera and Persephone, all Death aspects of the Triple Moon-goddess, and much worshipped by witches. As Culpeper says succinctly in his *Complete Herbal*: 'The Moon owns it.' Its connexion with witches is so strong in Northern Europe that the words 'witch' and 'wicked' are derived from the same ancient word for willow, which also yields 'wicker'. The 'witch's besom' in the English countryside is still made of ash stake, birch twigs and osier binding: of birch twigs because at the expulsion of evil spirits some remain entangled in the besom; of ash stake as a protection against drowning—witches are made harmless if detached from their besoms and thrown into running water; of osier binding in honour of Hecate. The Druidical human sacrifices were offered at the full of the moon in wicker-baskets, and funerary flints were knapped in willow-leaf shape. The willow (*helice* in Greek, *salix* in Latin) gave its name to Helicon, the abode of the Nine Muses, orgiastic priestesses of the Moon-goddess. It is likely that Poseidon preceded Apollo as the Leader of the Muses, as he did as guardian of the Delphic Oracle; for a Helicean Grove was still sacred to him in Classical times. According to Pliny, a willow tree grew outside the Cretan cave where Zeus was born; and, commenting on a series of coins from Cretan Gortyna, A. B. Cook in his *Zeus* suggests that Europë who is there shown seated in a willow tree, osier-basket in hand, and made love to by an eagle, is not only Eur-ope, 'she of the broad face', i. e. the Full Moon, but Eu-rope, 'she of the flourishing willow-withies'—alias Helice, sister of Amalthea. The wearing of the willow in the hat as a sign of the rejected lover seems to be originally a charm against the Moon-goddess's jealousy. The willow is sacred to her for many reasons: it is the tree that loves water most, and the Moon-goddess is the giver of dew and moisture generally; its leaves and bark, the source of salicylic acid, are sovereign against rheumatic cramps formerly thought to be caused by witchcraft. The Goddess's prime orgiastic bird, the wry-neck[1], or snake bird, or cuckoo's mate—a Spring migrant which hisses

[1] Dionysus was called Iyngies, 'of the wry-neck', because of the use of the wry-neck in an ancient erotic charm. The wry-neck is said by the third-century B.C. poet Callimachus to have been the messenger of Io which attracted Zeus to her arms; and his contemporary Nicander of Colophon records that nine Pierian maidens who vied with the Muses were transformed into birds, of which one was the wry-neck—which means that the wry-neck was sacred to the original Moon-goddess of Mount Pieria in Northern Thessaly (see Chapter Twenty-one) it was also sacred in Egypt and Assyria.

like a snake, lies flat along a bough, erects its crest when angry, writhes its neck about, lays white eggs, eats ants, and has v-markings on its feathers like those on the scales of oracular serpents in Ancient Greece— always nests in willow-trees. Moreover, the *liknos*, or basket-sieve anciently used for winnowing corn, was made from willow; it was in winnowing-sieves of this sort, 'riddles', that the North Berwick witches confessed to King James I that they went to sea on their witches' sabbaths. A famous Greek picture by Polygnotus at Delphi represented Orpheus as receiving the gift of mystic eloquence by touching willow-trees in a grove of Persephone; compare the injunction in *The Song of the Forest Trees*: 'Burn not the willow, a tree sacred to poets.' The willow is the tree of enchantment and is the fifth tree of the year; five (V) was the number sacred to the Roman Moon-goddess Minerva. The month extends from April 15th to May 12th, and May Day, famous for its orgiastic revels and its magic dew, falls in the middle. It is possible that the carrying of sallow-willow branches on Palm Sunday, a variable feast which usually falls early in April, is a custom that properly belongs to the beginning of the willow month.

H FOR UATH

The sixth tree is the whitethorn or hawthorn or may, which takes its name from the month of May. It is, in general, an unlucky tree and the name under which it appears in the Irish Brehon Laws, *sceith*, is apparently connected with the Indo-Germanic root *sceath* or *sceth*, meaning harm; from which derive the English 'scathe' and the Greek *a-scethes*, scatheless. In ancient Greece, as in Britain, this was the month in which people went about in old clothes—a custom referred to in the proverb 'Ne'er cast a clout ere May be out', meaning 'do not put on new clothes until the unlucky month is over', and not necessarily referring to the variability of the English climate; the proverb is, in fact, also current in North-eastern Spain where, in general, settled hot weather has come by Easter. They also abstained from sexual intercourse—a custom which explains May as an unlucky month for marriage. In Greece and Rome, May was the month in which the temples were swept out and the images of gods washed: the month of preparation for the midsummer festival. The Greek Goddess Maia, though she is represented in English poetry as 'ever fair and young' took her name from *maia*, 'grandmother'; she was a malevolent beldame whose son Hermes conducted souls to Hell. She was in fact the White Goddess, who under the name of Cardea, as has been noticed, cast spells with the hawthorn. The Greeks propitiated her at marriages—marriage being considered hateful to the Goddess— with five torches of hawthorn-wood and with hawthorn blossom before the unlucky month began.

Plutarch in his *Roman Questions* asks: 'Why do not the Romans marry in the month of May?' and answers correctly: 'Is not the reason that in this month they perform the greatest of purification ceremonies?' He explains that this was the month in which puppets called *argeioi* ('white men') were thrown into the river as an offering to Saturn. Ovid in his *Fasti* tells of an oracle given him by the Priestess of Juppiter about the marriage of his daughter—'Until the Ides of June' [the middle of the month] 'there is no luck for brides and their husbands. Until the sweepings from the Temple of Vesta have been carried down to the sea by the yellow Tiber I must myself not comb my locks which I have cut in sign of mourning, nor pare my nails, nor cohabit with my husband though he is the Priest of Juppiter. Be not in haste. Your daughter will have better luck in marriage when Vesta's fire burns on a cleansed hearth.' The unlucky days came to an end on June 15. In Greece the unlucky month began and ended a little earlier. According to Sozomen of Gaza, the fifth-century ecclesiastical historian, the Terebinth Fair at Hebron was celebrated at the same time and with the same taboos on new clothes and sexuality, and with the same object—the washing and cleansing of the holy images.

In Welsh mythology the hawthorn appears as the malevolent Chief of the Giants, Yspaddaden Penkawr, the father of Olwen ('She of the White Track'), another name of the White Goddess. In the *Romance of Kilhwych and Olwen*—Kilhwych was so called because he was found in a swine's burrow—Giant Hawthorn puts all possible obstacles in the way of Kilhwych's marriage to Olwen and demands a dowry of thirteen treasures, all apparently impossible to secure. The Giant lived in a castle guarded by nine porters and nine watch-dogs, proof of the strength of the taboo against marriage in the hawthorn month.

The destruction of an ancient hawthorn tree is in Ireland attended with the greatest peril. Two nineteenth-century instances are quoted in E. M. Hull's *Folklore of the British Isles*. The effect is the death of one's cattle and children and loss of all one's money. In his well-documented study, *Historic Thorn Trees in the British Isles*, Mr. Vaughan Cornish writes of the sacred hawthorns growing over wells in Goidelic provinces. He quotes the case of 'St. Patrick's Thorn' at Tin'ahely in County Wicklow: 'Devotees attended on the 4th of May, rounds were duly made about the well, and shreds torn off their garments and hung on the thorn.' He adds: 'This is St. Monica's Day but I do not know of any association.' Plainly, since St. Monica's Day, New Style, corresponds with May 15th, Old Style, this was a ceremony in honour of the Hawthorn month, which had just begun. The rags were torn from the devotees' clothes as a sign of mourning and propitiation.

The hawthorn, then, is the tree of enforced chastity. The month begins on May 13th, when the may is first in flower, and ends on June 9th.

The ascetic use of the thorn, which corresponds with the cult of the Goddess Cardea must, however, be distinguished from its later orgiastic use which corresponds with the cult of the Goddess Flora, and which accounts for the English mediaeval habit of riding out on May Morning to pluck flowering hawthorn boughs and dance around the maypole. Hawthorn blossom has, for many men, a strong scent of female sexuality; which is why the Turks use a flowering branch as an erotic symbol. Mr. Cornish proves that this Flora cult was introduced into the British Isles in the late first-century B.C. by the second Belgic invaders; further, that the Glastonbury Thorn which flowered on Old Christams Day (January 5th, New Style) and was cut down by the Puritans at the Revolution was a sport of the common hawthorn. The monks of Glastonbury perpetuated it and sanctified it with an improving tale about Joseph of Arimathea's staff and the Crown of Thorns as a means of discouraging the orgiastic use of hawthorn blossom, which normally did not appear until May Day (Old Style).

It is likely that the Old Bush which had grown on the site of St. David's Cathedral was an orgiastic hawthorn; for this would account for the legend of David's mysterious birth.

D FOR DUIR

The seventh tree is the oak, the tree of Zeus, Juppiter, Hercules, The Dagda (the chief of the elder Irish gods), Thor, and all the other Thundergods, Jehovah in so far as he was 'El', and Allah. The royalty of the oaktree needs no enlarging upon: most people are familiar with the argument of Sir James Frazer's *Golden Bough*, which concerns the human sacrifice of the oak-king of Nemi on Midsummer Day. The fuel of the midsummer fires is always oak, the fire of Vesta at Rome was fed with oak, and the need-fire is always kindled in an oak-log. When Gwion writes in the *Câd Goddeu*, 'Stout Guardian of the door, His name in every tongue', he is saying that doors are customarily made of oak as the strongest and toughest wood and that 'Duir', the Beth-Luis-Nion name for 'Oak', means 'door' in many European languages including Old Goidelic *dorus*, Latin *foris*, Greek *thura*, and German *tür*, all derived from the Sanskrit *Dwr*, and that *Daleth*, the Hebrew letter D, means 'Door'—the 'l' being originally an 'r'. Midsummer is the flowering season of the oak, which is the tree of endurance and triumph, and like the ash is said to 'court the lightning flash'. Its roots are believed to extend as deep underground as its branches rise in the air—Virgil mentions this—which makes it emblematic of a god whose law runs both in Heaven and in the Underworld. Poseidon the ash-god and Zeus the oak-god were both once armed with thunderbolts; but when the Achaeans humbled the Aeolians, Poseedon's bolt was converted into a trident or fish-spear and Zeus reserved the sole right to wield the bolt. It has been suggested that oak oracles were introduced into Greece by the Achaeans: that they originally consulted the beech, as the Franks did, but finding no beeches in Greece transferred their allegiance to the oak with edible acorns, its nearest equivalent, to which they gave the name *phegos*—which, as has been mentioned, is the same word as *fagus*, the Latin for beech. At any rate, the oracular oak at Dodona was a *phegos*, not a *drus*, and the oracular ship *Argo* was, according to Apollonius Rhodius, largely made of this timber. But it is more likely that the Dodona oracle was in existence centuries before the Achaeans came and that Herodotus was right in stating on the authority of the Egyptian priests that the black dove and oracular oak cults of Zeus at Ammon in the Libyan desert and of Zeus at Dodona were coeval. Professor Flinders Petrie postulates a sacred league between Libya and the Greek mainland well back into the third millennium B.C. The Ammon oak was in the care of the tribe of Garamantes: the Greeks knew of their ancestor Garamas as 'the first of men'. The Zeus of Ammon was a sort of Hercules with a ram's head akin to ram-headed Osiris, and to Amen-Ra the ram-headed Sun-god of Egyptian Thebes from where Herodotus says that the black doves flew to Ammon and Dodona.

The month, which takes its name from Juppiter the oak-god, begins on June 10th and ends on July 7th. Midway comes St. John's Day, June 24th, the day on which the oak-king was sacrificially burned alive. The Celtic year was divided into two halves with the second half beginning in July, apparently after a seven-day wake, or funeral feast, in the oak-king's honour.

Sir James Frazer, like Gwion, has pointed out the similarity of 'door' words in all Indo-European languages and shown Janus to be a 'stout guardian of the door' with his head pointing in both directions. As usual, however, he does not press his argument far enough. Duir as the god of the oak month looks both ways because his post is at the turn of the year; which identifies him with the Oak-god Hercules who became the door-keeper of the Gods after his death. He is probably also to be identified with the British god Llyr or Lludd or Nudd, a god of the sea—i.e. a god of a sea-faring Bronze Age people—who was the 'father' of Creiddylad (Cordelia) an aspect of the White Goddess; for according to Geoffrey of Monmouth the grave of Llyr at Leicester was in a vault built in honour of Janus. Geoffrey writes:

'Cordelia obtaining the government of the Kingdom buried her father in a certain vault which she ordered to be made for him under the river Sore in Leicester (Leircestre) and which had been built originally under the ground in honour of the god Janus. And here all the workmen of the city, upon the anniversary solemnity of that festival, used to begin their yearly labours.'

Since Llyr was a pre-Roman God this amounts to saying that he was two-headed, like Janus, and the patron of the New Year; but the Celtic year began in the summer, not in the winter. Geoffrey does not date the mourning festival but it is likely to have originally taken place at the end of June.

The old 'Wakes', the hiring-fairs of the English countryside came to be held at various dates between March and October according to the date of the local saint's day. ('At Bunbury Wakes rye-grass and clover should be ready to cut. At Wrenbury Wakes early apples are ripe.' *English Dialect Dictionary*.) But originally they must all have taken place at Lammas between the hay harvest and the corn harvest. That the Wakes were mourning for the dead King is confirmed in Chapter Seventeen. The Anglo-Saxon form of *Lughomass*, mass in honour of the God Lugh or Llew, was *hlaf-mass*, 'loaf-mass', with reference to the corn-harvest and the killing of the Corn-king.

What I take for a reference to Llyr as Janus occurs in the closing paragraph of Merlin's prophecy to the heathen King Vortigern and his Druids, recorded by Geoffrey of Monmouth:

> After this Janus shall never have priests again. His door will be shut and remain concealed in Ariadne's crannies.

In other words, the ancient Druidic religion based on the oak-cult will be swept away by Christianity and the door—the god Llyr—will languish forgotten in the Castle of Arianrhod, the *Corona Borealis*.

This helps us to understand the relationship at Rome of Janus and the White Goddess Cardea who is mentioned at the end of Chapter Four as the Goddess of Hinges who came to Rome from Alba Longa. She was the hinge on which the year swung—the ancient Latin, not the Etruscan year—and her importance as such is recorded in the Latin adjective *cardinalis*—as we say in English 'of cardinal importance'—which was also applied to the four main winds; for winds were considered as under the sole direction of the Great Goddess until Classical times. As Cardea she ruled over the Celestial Hinge at the back of the North Wind around which, as Varro explains in his *De Re Rustica*, the mill-stone of the Universe revolves. This conception appears most plainly in the Norse *Edda*, where the giantesses Fenja and Menja, who turn the monstrous mill-stone Grotte in the cold polar night, stand for the White Goddess in her complementary moods of creation and destruction. Elsewhere in Norse mythology the Goddess is nine-fold: the nine giantesses who were joint-mothers of the hero Rig, alias Heimdall, the inventor of the Norse social system, similarly turned the cosmic mill. Janus was perhaps not originally double-headed: he may have borrowed this peculiarity from the Goddess herself who at the Carmentalia, the Carmenta Festival in early January, was addressed by her celebrants as 'Postvorta and Ante-vorta'—'she who looks both back and forward'. However, a Janus with long hair and wings appears on an early stater of Mallos, a Cretan colony in Cilicia. He is identified with the solar hero Talus, and a bull's head appears on the same coin. In similar coins of the late fifth century B.C. he holds an eight-rayed disc in his hand and has a spiral of immortality sprouting from his double head.

Here at last I can complete my argument about Arianrhod's Castle and the 'whirling round without motion between three elements'. The sacred oak-king was killed at midsummer and translated to the Corona Borealis, presided over by the White Goddess, which was then just dipping over the Northern horizon. But from the song ascribed by Apollonius Rhodius to Orpheus, we know that the Queen of the Cirling Universe, Eurynome, *alias* Cardea, was identical with Rhea of Crete; thus Rhea lived at the axle of the mill, whirling around without motion, as well as on the Galaxy. This suggests that in a later mythological tradition the sacred king went to serve her at the Mill, not in the Castle; for Samson after his blinding and enervation turned a mill in Delilah's prison-house.

Another name for the Goddess of the Mill was Artemis Calliste, or Callisto ('Most Beautiful'), to whom the she-bear was sacred in Arcadia; and in Athens at the festival of Artemis Brauronia, a girl of ten years old and a girl of five, dressed in saffron-yellow robes in honour of the moon, played the part of sacred bears. The Great She-bear and Little She-bear are still the names of the two constellations that turn the mill around. In Greek the Great Bear Callisto was also called *Helice*, which means both 'that which turns' and 'willow-branch'—a reminder that the willow was sacred to the same Goddess.

The evidence, given in the Gwyn context at the close of Chapter Six, for supposing that the oak-cult came to Britain from the Baltic between 1600 and 1400 B.C. suggests that the Beth-Luis-Nion sequence, in which Duir is the principal tree, was at any rate not elaborated before 1600 B.C., though the rowan, willow, elder and alder were perhaps already in sacral use. Gwyn, 'the White One', son of Llyr or Lludd was buried in a boat-shaped oak-coffin in his father's honour: he was a sort of Osiris (his rival 'Victor son of Scorcher' being a sort of Set) and came to be identified with King Arthur. His name supplies the prefix *Win* of many ancient towns in Britain.

T for Tinne

The eighth tree is the holly, which flowers in July. The holly appears in the originally Irish *Romance of Gawain and the Green Knight*. The Green Knight is an immortal giant whose club is a holly-bush. He and

Sir Gawain, who appears in the Irish version as Cuchulain, a typical Hercules, make a compact to behead one another at alternate New Years —meaning midsummer and midwinter—but, in effect, the Holly Knight spares the Oak Knight. In *Sir Gawain's Marriage*, a Robin Hood ballad, King Arthur, who there has a seat at Carlisle, says:

> —*as I came over a moor,*
> *I see a lady where she sate*
> *Between an oak and a green hollén.*
> *She was clad in red scarlét.*

This lady, whose name is not mentioned, will have been the goddess Creiddylad for whom, in Welsh myth, the Oak Knight and Holly Knight fought every first of May until Doomsday. Since in mediaeval practice St. John the Baptist, who lost his head on St. John's Day, took over the oak-king's titles and customs, it was natural to let Jesus, as John's merciful successor, take over the holly-king's. The holly was thus glorified beyond the oak. For example, in the *Holly-Tree Carol*:

> *Of all the trees that are in the wood*
> *The Holly bears the crown*

—a sentiment that derives from the *Song of the Forest Trees*: 'Of all trees whatsoever the critically best is holly.' In each stanza of the carol, with its apt chorus about 'the rising of the Sun, the running of the deer', some property of the tree is equated with the birth or passion of Jesus: the whiteness of the flower, the redness of the berry, the sharpness of the prickles, the bitterness of the bark. 'Holly' means 'holy'. Yet the holly which is native to the British Isles is unlikely to be the original tree of the alphabet: it has probably displaced the evergreen scarlet-oak with which it has much in common, including the same botanical name *ilex*, and which was not introduced into the British Isles until the sixteenth century. The scarlet-oak, or kerm-oak, or holly-oak, is the evergreen twin of the ordinary oak and its Classical Greek names *prinos* and *hysge* are also used for holly in modern Greek. It has prickly leaves and nourishes the kerm, a scarlet insect not unlike the holly-berry (and once thought to be a berry), from which the ancients made their royal scarlet dye and an aphrodisiac elixir. In the Authorised Version of the Bible the word 'oak' is sometimes translated 'terebinth' and sometimes 'scarlet-oak', and these trees make a sacred pair in Palestinian religion. Jesus wore kerm-scarlet when attired as King of the Jews (*Matthew* XXVII, 28).

We may regard the letters D and T as twins: 'the lily white boys clothed all in green o!' of the mediaeval *Green Rushes* song. D is the oak which rules the waxing part of the year—the sacred Druidic oak, the oak of the *Golden Bough*. T is the evergreen oak which rules the waning part, the bloody oak: thus an evergreen oak-grove near the Corinthian Asopus was sacred to the Furies. *Dann* or *Tann,* the equivalent of *Tinne,* is a Celtic word for any sacred tree. In Gaul and Brittany it meant 'oak', in Celtic Germany it meant 'fir'; in Cornwall the compound *glas-tann* ('green sacred tree') meant evergreen holm-oak, and the English word 'to tan' comes from the use of its bark in tanning. However, in ancient Italy it was the holly, not the evergreen oak, which the husbandmen used in their midwinter Saturnalia. Tannus was the name of the Gaulish Thunder-god, and Tina that of the Thunder-god, armed with a triple thunder-bolt, whom the Etruscans took over from the Goidelic tribes among whom they settled.

The identification of the pacific Jesus with the holly or holly-oak must be regretted as poetically inept, except in so far as he declared that he had come to bring not peace, but the sword. The tanist was originally his twin's executioner; it was the oak-king, not the holly-king, who was crucified on a T-shaped cross. Lucian in his *Trial in the Court of Vowels* (about 160 A.D.) is explicit:

> Men weep, and bewail their lot, and curse Cadmus with many curses for introducing *Tau* into the family of letters; they say it was his body that tyrants took for a model, his shape that they imitated, when they set up the erections on which men are crucified. *Stauros* the vile engine is called, and it derives its vile name from him. Now, with all these crimes upon him, does he not deserve death, nay, many deaths? For my part I know none bad enough but that supplied by his own shape—that shape which he gave to the gibbet named *Stauros* after him by men.

And in a Gnostic *Gospel of Thomas,* composed at about the same date, the same theme recurs in a dispute between Jesus and his school-master about the letter T. The schoolmaster strikes Jesus on the head and prophesies the crucifixion. In Jesus's time the Hebrew character *Tav,* the last letter of the alphabet, was shaped like the Greek *Tau.*

The holly rules the eighth month, and eight as the number of increase is well suited to the month of the barley harvest, which extends from July 8th to August 4th.

C FOR COLL

The ninth tree is the hazel, in the nutting season. The nut in Celtic legend is always an emblem of concentrated wisdom: something sweet, compact and sustaining enclosed in a small hard shell—as we say: 'this is the matter in a nut-shell.' The Rennes *Dinnshenchas,* an important early Irish topographical treatise, describes a beautiful fountain called Connla's

Well, near Tipperary, over which hung the nine hazels of poetic art which produced flowers and fruit (i.e. beauty and wisdom) simultaneously. As the nuts dropped into the well they fed the salmon swimming in it, and whatever number of nuts any of them swallowed, so many bright spots appeared on its body. All the knowledge of the arts and sciences was bound up with the eating of these nuts, as has already been noted in the story of Fionn, whose name Gwion adopted. In England a forked hazel-stick was used until the seventeenth century for divining not only buried treasure and hidden water, as now, but guilty persons in cases of murder and theft. And in the *Book of St. Albans* (1496 edition) a recipe is given for making oneself as invisible as if one had eaten fern-seed, merely by carrying a hazel-rod, a fathom and a half long with a green hazel-twig inserted in it.

The letter Coll was used as the Bardic numeral nine—because nine is the number sacred to the Muses and because the hazel fruits after nine years. The hazel was the *Bile Ratha,* 'the venerated tree of the rath'—the rath in which the poetic *Aes Sidhe* lived. It gave its name also to a god named Mac Coll or Mac Cool ('son of the Hazel') who according to Keating's *History of Ireland* was one of the three earliest rulers of Ireland, his two brothers being Mac Ceacht ('son of the Plough') and Mac Greine ('son of the Sun'). They celebrated a triple marriage with the Triple Goddess of Ireland, Eire, Fodhla and Banbha. This legend appears at first sight to record the overthrow of the matriarchal system by patriarchal invaders; but since Greine, the Sun, was a Goddess not a God and since both agriculture and wisdom were presided over by the Triple Goddess, the invaders were doubtless Goddess-worshippers themselves and merely transferred their filial allegiance to the Triple Goddess of the land.

In the Fenian legend of the Ancient Dripping Hazel, the hazel appears as a tree of wisdom that can be put to destructive uses. It dripped a poisonous milk, had no leaves and was the abode of vultures and ravens, birds of divination. It split in two when the head of the God Balor was placed in its fork after his death, and when Fionn used its wood as a shield in battle its noxious vapours killed thousands of the enemy. Fionn's hazel shield is an emblem of the satiric poem that carries a curse. It was as the Druidic heralds' tree that the 'hazel was arbiter' in Gwion's *Câd Goddeu*; ancient Irish heralds carried white hazel wands. The hazel is the tree of wisdom and the month extends from August 5th to September 1st.

M FOR MUIN

The tenth tree is the vine in the vintage season. The vine, though not native to Britain, is an important *motif* in British Bronze Age art; so probably the Danaans carried the tree itself northward with them as well as the emblem. It fruited well there on a few sheltered Southern slopes. But since it could not be established as a wild tree, they will have used the bramble as a substitute: the fruiting season, the colour of the berries, and the shape of the leaf correspond, and blackberry wine is a heady drink. (In all Celtic countries there is a taboo against eating the blackberry though it is a wholesome and nourishing fruit; in Brittany the reason given is '*a cause des fées*', 'because of the fairies'. In Majorca the explanation is different: the bramble was the bush chosen for the Crown of Thorns and the berries are Christ's blood. In North Wales as a child I was warned merely that they were poisonous. In Devonshire the taboo is only on eating blackberries after the last day of September, when 'the Devil enters into them'; which substantiates my theory that the blackberry was a popular substitute for Muin in the West Country.) The vine was sacred to the Thracian Dionysus, and to Osiris, and a golden vine was one of the principal ornaments of the Temple of Jerusalem. It is the tree of joy, exhilaration and wrath. The month extends from September 2nd to September 29th and includes the autumn equinox.

G FOR GORT

The eleventh tree is the ivy in its flowering season. October was the season of the Bacchanal revels of Thrace and Thessaly in which the intoxicated Bassarids rushed wildly about on the mountains, waving the fir-branches of Queen of Artemis (or Ariadne) spirally wreathed with ivy —the yellow-berried sort—in honour of Dionysus (the autumnal Dionysus, who must be distinguished from the Dionysus of the Winter Solstice who is really a Hercules), and with a roebuck tattooed on their right arms above the elbow. They tore fawns, kids, children and even men to pieces in their ecstasy. The ivy was sacred to Osiris as well as to Dionysus. Vine and ivy come next to each other at the turn of the year, and are jointly dedicated to resurrection, presumably because they are the only two trees in the Beth-Luis-Nion that grow spirally. The vine also symbolizes resurrection because its strength is preserved in the wine. In England the ivy-bush has always been the sign of the wine-tavern; hence the proverb 'Good wine needs no bush', and ivy-ale, a highly intoxicating mediaeval drink, is still brewed at Trinity College, Oxford, in memory of a Trinity student murdered by Balliol men. It is likely that the Bassarids' tipple was 'spruce-ale', brewed from the sap of silver-fir and laced with ivy; they may also have chewed ivy-leaves for their toxic effect. Yet the main Maenad intoxicant will have been *amanita muscaria*, the spotted toadstool with white spots, that alone could supply the necessary muscular strength. Here we may reconsider Phoroneus, the Spring-Dionysus, inventor of fire. He built the city of Argos, the emblem of which, according to Apollodorus, was a toad; and Mycenae, the main fortress of Argolis, was so called, according to Pausanias, because Perseus, a convert to Dionysus worship, found a toadstool growing on the site. Dionysus had two feasts—the Spring *Anthesterion*, or 'Flower-uprising'; and the autumn *Mysterion*, which probably means 'uprising of toadstools' (*mykosterion*) was known as *Ambrosia* ('food of the gods'). Was Phoroneus also the discoverer of a divine fire resident in the toadstool, and therefore Phryneus ('toad being') as well as Fearinus ('Spring being')? The *amanita muscaria*, though not a tree, grows under a tree: always a birch northward from Thrace and Celtic countries to the Arctic Circle; but under a fir or pine southward from Greece and Palestine to the Equator. In the North it is scarlet; in the South, fox-coloured. And does this explain the precedence given to the silver-fir among the vowels as A, and the birch among the consonants as B? Does it add a further note to 'Christ son of Alpha'?

(The rivalry mentioned in mediaeval English carols between holly and ivy is not, as one might expect, between the tree of murder and the tree of resurrection, between Typhon-Set and Dionysus-Osiris; instead it represents the domestic war of the sexes. The explanation seems to be that in parts of England the last harvest sheaf to be carted in any parish was bound around with Osirian ivy and called the Harvest May, the Harvest Bride, or the Ivy Girl: whichever farmer was latest with his harvesting was given the Ivy Girl as his penalty, an omen of ill luck until the following year. Thus the ivy came to mean a carline, or shrewish wife, a simile confirmed by the strangling of trees by ivy. But ivy and holly were both associated with the Saturnalia, holly being Saturn's club, ivy being the nest of the Gold Crest Wren, his bird; on Yule morning, the last of his merry reign, the first foot over the threshold had to be that of Saturn's representative, a dark man, called the Holly Boy, and elaborate precautions were taken to keep women out of the way. Thus Ivy Girl and Holly Boy became opposed; which gave rise to the Yule custom in which 'holly boys' and 'ivy girls' contended in a game of forfeits for precedence, and sang songs, mainly satirical, against each other.)

The ivy month extends from September 30th to October 27th.

P FOR PEITH, OR NG FOR NGETAL

The twelfth tree given in O'Flaherty's list is Peith, the whitten, or guelder-rose, or water-elder, an appropriate introduction to the last month which is the true elder. But Peith is not the original letter; it is a Brythonic substitute for the original letter NG, which was of no literary use to the Brythons, or (for that matter) to the Goidels, but which formed part of the original series. The NG tree was the *Ngetal*, or reed, which becomes ready for cutting in November. The canna-reed, which grows from a thick root like a tree, was an ancient symbol of royalty in the Eastern Mediterranean. The Pharaohs used reed sceptres (hence Egypt is satirized by the prophet Isaiah as a 'bruised reed') and a royal reed was put into Jesus's hand when he was attired in Scarlet. It is the tree from which arrows were cut, and therefore appropriate to Pharaoh as a living Sun-god who shot off his arrows in every direction as a symbol of sovereignty. The number twelve has the sense of established power, confirmed by the Irish use of reeds in thatching: a house is not an established house until the roof is on. The month extends from October 28th to November 24th.

R for Ruis

The thirteenth tree is the elder, a waterside tree associated with witches, which keeps its fruit well into December. It is an old British superstition that a child laid in an elderwood cradle will pine away or be pinched black and blue by the fairies—the traditional wood for cradles is the birch, the tree of inception, which drives away evil spirits. And in Ireland elder sticks, rather than ashen ones, are used by witches as magic horses. Although the flowers and inner bark of the elder have always been famous for their therapeutic qualities, the scent of an elder plantation was formerly held to cause death and disease. So unlucky is the elder that in Langland's *Piers Plowman*, Judas is made to hang himself on an elder tree. Spencer couples the elder with the funereal cypress, and T. Scot writes in his *Philomythie* (1616):

> *The cursèd elder and the fatal yew*
> *With witch [rowan] and nightshade in their shadows grew.*

King William Rufus was killed by an archer posted under an elder. The elder is also said to have been the Crucifixion tree, and the elder-leaf shape of the funerary flints in megalithic long-barrows suggest that its association with death is long-standing. In English folklore to burn logs of elder 'brings the Devil into the house'. Its white flowers, which are at their best at midsummer, make the elder another aspect of the White Goddess; and the same is true of the rowan. The elder is the tree of doom —hence the continued unluckiness of the number thirteen—and the month extends from November 25th to the winter solstice of December 22nd.

But what of the extra day? It falls outside the thirteenth-month year and is therefore not ruled by any of the Trees. I am assuming that its natural place is between the letter-months of R and B, in the day after the winter solstice when the hours of daylight begin to lengthen again: in fact, about

Christmas Eve, the birthday of the Divine Child. The R.B. radicals recall *robur*, the Latin for 'oak' and 'strength', and also the Celtic word 'robin'. For at this point in the year, in British folklore, the Robin Red Breast as the Spirit of the New Year sets out with a birch-rod to kill his predecessor the Gold Crest Wren, the Spirit of the Old Year, whom he finds hiding in an ivy bush. Sir James Frazer has shown in his *Golden Bough* that the Christmas Eve folk-custom of hunting the wren with birch rods, which still survives in Ireland and the Isle of Man, was at one time also practised in Rome and ancient Greece, where the Gold Crest was known as 'the little king'. That the Gold Crest does frequent ivy bushes at Christmas time is ornithological fact. The robin is said to 'murder its father', which accounts for its red breast. There is a clear reference to the story in Gwion's *Angar Cyvyndawd*: '*Keing ydd ym Eidduw Bum i arweddawd*', ('Concealed in the ivy bush, I have been carried about'). The wren-boys of Ireland sometimes use a holly-bush instead of an ivy-bush; the holly being the tree of the tanist, who killed the oak-king at midsummer. The wren is protected from injury at all other seasons of the year and it is very unlucky to take its eggs. One of the Devonshire names for the wren is 'the cuddy vran'—'Bran's sparrow'—and in Ireland it was linked with Bran's crow, or raven, as a prophetic bird. R. I. Best has edited a collection of wren and raven omens in *Erin VIII* (1916). Bran, it has been shown, was Saturn.

Perhaps the most ancient wren tradition is quoted by Pausanias in his *Description of Greece*: he says that Triptolemus, the Eleusinian counterpart of Egyptian Osiris, was an Argive priest of mysteries named Trochilus who fled from Argos to Attica when Agenor seized the city. Trochilus means 'wren' and it also means 'of the wheel', presumably because the wren is hunted when the wheel of the year has gone full circle. The connexion of the wren with the wheel was retained until recently in Somersetshire. Swainson records in his *Birds* (1885): 'It is customary on Twelfth Day to carry about a wren, termed the King, enclosed in a box with glass windows, surmounted by a wheel from which are appended various coloured ribbands.' A later version makes Triptolemus a son of Picus (the woodpecker, another prophetic bird), and thus identifies him with Pan or Faunus. Pausanias's story seems to refer to the explusion from Argos by Syrian invaders of the priesthood of Cronos (Bran), to whom the wren was sacred.

As soon as one has mastered the elementary grammar and accidence of myth, and built up a small vocabulary, and learned to distinguish seasonal myths from historical and iconotropic myths, one is surprised how close to the surface lie the explanations, lost since pre-Homeric times, of legends that are still religiously conserved as part of our European cultural inheritance. For example, the various legends of the halcyon, or kingfisher which like the wren, is associated in Greek myth with the winter solstice.

There were fourteen 'halcyon days' in every year, seven of which fell before the winter solstice, seven after: peaceful days when the sea was smooth as a pond and the hen-halcyon built a floating nest and hatched out her young. According to Plutarch and Aelian, she had another habit, of carrying her dead mate on her back over the sea and mourning him with a peculiarly plaintive cry.

The number fourteen is a moon-number, the days of the lucky first half of the month; so the legend (which has no foundation in natural history, because the halcyon does not build a nest at all but lays its eggs in holes by the waterside) evidently refers to the birth of the new sacred king, at the winter solstice—after his mother, the Moon-goddess, has conveyed the old king's corpse to a sepulchral island. Naturally, the winter solstice does not always coincide with the same phase of the moon, so 'every year' must be understood as 'every Great Year', at the close of which solar and lunar time were roughly synchronized and the sacred king's term ended.

Homer connects the halcyon with Alcyone, a title of Meleager's wife Cleopatra (*Iliad, IX*, 562) and with an earlier Alcyone who was daughter to Aegeale, 'she who wards off the hurricane', by Aeolus, the eponymous ancestor of the Aeolian Greeks. The word 'halcyon' cannot therefore mean *hal-cyon*, 'sea-hound', as is usually supposed, but must stand for *alcy-one*, 'princess who averts evil'. This derivation is confirmed by the fable told by Apollodorus and Hyginus, and briefly mentioned by Homer, of the earlier Alcyone: how she and her husband Ceyx ('sea-mew') dared call themselves Hera and Zeus, and how the real Zeus punished them by drowning Ceyx, whereupon Alcyone also drowned herself. Ceyx was then metamorphosed into a sea-mew or, according to Alcman, into a razor-bill, and she into a halcyon. The sea-mew part of the legend need not be pressed, though the bird, which has a very plaintive cry, is sacred to the Sea-goddess Aphrodite; the historical basis seems to be that late in the second millennium B.C. the Aeolians, who had agreed to worship the pre-Hellenic Moon-goddess as their divine ancestress and protectress, became tributary to the Achaeans and were forced to accept the Olympian religion.

Pliny, who carefully describes the halcyon's alleged nest—apparently the zoöphyte called *halcyoneum* by Linnaeus—reports that the halcyon is rarely seen and then only at the winter and summer solstices and at the setting of the Pleiads. This proves her to have originally been a manifestation of the Moon-goddess who was worshipped at the two solstices as the Goddess of alternatively Life-in-Death and Death-in-Life—and who early in November, when the Pleiads set, sent the sacred king his summons to death (as will be pointed out in Chapter Twelve). Still another Alcyone, daughter to Pleione, 'Queen of Sailing', by the oak-hero Atlas, was the mystical leader of the seven Pleiads. The heliacal rising of the Pleiads in May marked the beginning of the navigational year; their setting marked its end when (as Pliny notices in a passage about the halcyon) a remarkably cold North wind blows. The circumstances of Ceyx's death show that the Aeolians, who were famous sailors, gave the goddess the title 'Alcyone' because as Sea-goddess she protected them from rocks and rough weather: for Zeus had wrecked him in defiance of Alcyone's powers by hurling lightning at the ship. The halcyon continued for centuries to be credited with the magical power of allaying storms, and its body when dried was used as a talisman against Zeus' lightning—supposedly on the ground that where once it strikes, it will not strike again. I have twice (with an interval of many years) seen a halcyon skimming the surface of the same Mediterranean bay, on both occasions about midsummer when the sea was without a ripple: its startlingly bright blue and white plumage made it an unforgettable symbol of the Goddess of calm seas.

The connexion made by Homer between Meleager's wife Alcyone and the halcyon is that when her mother, Marpessa, was carried off by Apollo from Idas the Argonaut, her beloved husband, she mourned him as bitterly as the earlier Alcyone had mourned Ceyx and therefore gave her new-born daughter Cleopatra the surname 'Alcyone'. This is nonsense. A priestess named Cleopatra whom the original Meleager married may well have borne the divine title 'Alcyone'; but it is likely that Alcyone was called the Daughter of Marpessa ('the snatcher') because Marpessa was the White Goddess as the Old Sow who ruled mid-winter and because the halcyon days fall at mid-winter. This would, incidentally, explain why Pliny recommended dried and pulverized halcyon nests as a 'wonderful cure' for leprosy; sow's milk was held to cause leprosy (the association of the White Goddess with leprosy is given in detail in Chapter Twenty-Four) and Alcyone as Marpessa's benignant daughter would be immune against the infection. Apollo's rape of Marpessa at Messene, like his rape of Daphne ('the bloody one') at Delphi, are events in early Greek tribal history: seizure of oracular shrines by the Achaean partisans of Apollo.

Chapter Eleven
THE TREE ALPHABET (2)

The vowels of the Beth-Luis-Nion make a complementary seasonal sequence, and like the vowels of the Boibel-Loth represent stations in the year. I take them to be the trees particularly sacred to the White Goddess, who presided over the year and to whom the number five was sacred; for Gwion in his poem *Kadeir Taliesin* ('The Chair of Taliesin'), which was the chair that he claimed as Chief Poet of Wales after his confounding of Heinin and the other bards, describes the Cauldron of Inspiration, Cerridwen's cauldron, as:

Sweet cauldron of the Five Trees.[1]

In Crete, Greece and the Eastern Mediterranean in general sacred trees are formalised as pillars; so these five trees may be the same as the five pillars with vertical and spiral flutings which a man is shown adoring in a Mycenaean cylinder seal.[2] In the newly-discovered Gnostic *Gospel of*

---

[1] It is likely that Gwion was also aware of the value given to the number Five by the Pythagoreans and their successors. The Pythagoreans swore their oaths on the 'holy tetractys', a figure consisting of ten dots arranged in a pyramid, thus:

The top dot represented position; the two dots below, extension; the three dots below those, surface; the four dots at the bottom, three-dimensional space. The pyramid, the most ancient emblem of the Triple Goddess, was philosophically interpreted as Beginning, Prime and End; and the central dot of this figure makes a five with each of the four dots of the sides. Five represented the colour and variety which nature gives to three-dimensional space, and which are apprehended by the five senses, technically called 'the wood'—a quincunx of five trees; this coloured various world was held to be formed by five elements—earth, air, fire, water and the quintessence or soul; and these elements in turn corresponded with seasons. Symbolic values were also given to the numerals from 6 to 10, which was the number of perfection. The tetractys could be interpreted in many other ways: for instance, as the three points of the triangle enclosing a hexagon of dots—six being the number of life—with a central dot increasing this to seven, technically known as 'Athene', the number of intelligence, health and light.

[2] To judge from a design on a glass dish of the Seleucid epoch, showing the façade of Solomon's Temple as rebuilt by Zerubbabel on the original Phoenician model, the spirally fluted pillars correspond with Boaz, Solomon's right-hand pillar dedicated to growth and the waxing sun; the vertically fluted with Jachin, his left-hand pillar dedicated to decay and the waning sun. The symbolism became confused when the Jews made their New Year corres-

Thomas, five trees of Paradise are mentioned—but these are emblems of the five deathless Ones, namely Abraham, Isaac, Jacob, Enoch and Elijah.

A FOR AILM

The first tree is the silver fir, a female tree with leaves closely resembling the yew's, sacred in Greece to Artemis the Moon-goddess who presided over childbirth, and the prime birth-tree of Northern Europe, familiar in the Nativity context. In Orkney, according to Rogers's *Social Life in Scotland,* mother and child are 'sained' soon after delivery with a flaming fir-candle whirled three times round the bed. It is remarkable that *ailm,* in Old Irish, also stood for the palm, a tree not native to Ireland (though it grew well on my grandfather's estate in Co. Kerry). The palm, the birth-tree of Egypt, Babylonia, Arabia and Phoenicia, gives its name *phoenix* ('bloody') to Phoenicia, which formerly covered the whole Eastern Mediterranean, and to the Phoenix which is born and reborn in a palm. Its poetic connexion with birth is that the sea is the Universal Mother and that the palm thrives close to the sea in sandy soil heavily charged with salt; without salt at its roots a young palm remains stunted. The palm is the Tree of Life in the Babylonian Garden of Eden story. Its Hebrew name is 'Tamar'—Tamar was the Hebrew equivalent of the Great Goddess Istar or Ashtaroth; and the Arabians adored the palm of Nejran as a goddess, annually draping it with women's clothes and ornaments. Both Delian Apollo and Nabataean Dusares were born under a palm-tree. In modern Irish 'ailm' has come to mean elm, under the influence of the Latin Classics, for in Italy the elm, *ulmus,* which is not native to the British Isles, was used for supporting the young vine and so became the *alma mater* of the Wine-god. This interdependence of vine and elm was sanctified by a reference in the early Christian book of revelation, *The Shepherd of Hermas.*

But the silver fir, which also likes sandy soil and sea breezes, is as old a birth-tree as the palm, being the tree under which the God of Byblos was born: the prototype of the pre-dynastic Osiris of Egypt. The Greek for fir is *elate,* and Pausanias's account of Elatos the Arcadian is interesting. He was 'father of Ischys, the lover of Aesculapius's mother' and of Cyllen who

pond with the autumn vintage festival, for the pillars were then referred to as Jachin and Boaz, not Boaz and Jachin, but the tradition remained 'Boaz is to Jachin as Gerizim is to Ebal —as blessing is to cursing'. Gerizim and Ebal were the twin peaks covering the Ephraimite shrine of Shechem. Gerizim was on the right-hand as one faced east from Shechem, Ebal on the left, and Shechem was a home of the terebinth cult. In *Deuteronomy XI,* 29 there is a prophecy attributed to Moses. 'You shall put the blessing upon Gerizim and the curse upon Ebal . . . towards the entrance into Shechem where dwell the Canaanites in the towered house beside the sacred terebinth of Moreh.'

This was as it should have been. The terebinth, the hard-wooded Canaanite equivalent of Duir the oak, was naturally placed in the middle with Ebal on the unlucky left, Gerizim on the lucky right.

gave his name to Mount Cyllene 'until then nameless', which became the birth-place of Hermes. Other mythographers convert Cyllen into 'the Nymph Cyllene', wife of Pelasgus who founded the Pelasgian race. It seems that originally Elatos was Elate 'the lofty one', a name transferred from Artemis to her sacred tree—an ivy-twined, fir-cone-tipped branch of which was waved in her honour at the Dionysian revels—and that Cyllene (*Cylle Ana*) 'the curved queen' was another of her titles. The fir-tree of the Birth-goddess is similarly transferred to her son in the myth of Attis, son of Nana, the Phrygian Adonis. He is said to have been metamorphosed into a fir by the Goddess Cybele who loved him, when he lay dying from a wound dealt him by a boar sent by Zeus—or else dealt him by a Phrygian king whom he had emasculated and who emasculated him in return.

The Trojan horse, a peace-offering to the Goddess Athene, originally the same White Goddess, was made of silver-fir: a horse, because sacred to the moon.

In the Museum of Newcastle-on-Tyne is a Roman-British altar dedicated to 'the Mothers'[1] by one Julius Victor. It shows a triangle standing on its base with a fir-cone enclosed. Though Druantia, the name of the Gallic Fir-goddess, contains no reference to her own tree, it makes her 'Queen of the Druids' and therefore mother of the whole tree-calendar.

The silver fir has its station on the first day of the year, the birthday of

---

[1] At Arles, in Provence, the cult of the Goddess as a Triad or Pentad of Mothers has survived under Christian disguise until today, when her festival is celebrated from May 24th to May 28th, the middle of the Hawthorn, or Chastity, month, but now her devotees are largely gipsies. As a Triad she has become known as 'The Three Maries of Provence' or 'The Three Maries of the Sea'; as a Pentad she has had Martha added to her company, and an apocryphal serving-girl called Sara. It seems that these were Christianizations of pre-Christian reliefs on the tombstones of the cemetery of Alyscamps at Arles, in which the Triad, or Pentad, was shown on one panel; and below, on another, the soul in resurrection. The scene was explained as the Raising of Lazarus. As late as the time of Dante the cemetery was used in the ancient style. The corpse was laid in a boat, with money in it, called *drue de mourtilage* and floated down the Rhône to the Alyscamps. The name Alyscamps has been explained as *Campi Elysiani*, 'the Elysian Fields', but it is as likely that Alys was the ancient name of the Goddess; it may even be that the Homeric adjective Elysian (the *e* is a long one) is derived from her name. Alys also appears as *alise* or *alis* in many French place-names. Dauzat's *Dictionnaire Etymologique*, under *alis, alise*, meaning a 'sheltered creek', derives it from `the Gaulish word *alisia*, perhaps pre-Celtic, which is represented by numerous place-names, and which must also have provided the Spanish word for alder, *aliso*.' This makes good mythical sense, because Calypso's sepulchral island of Ogygia was screened by alder thickets. Alys or Alis or Halys is the name of the biggest river of Asia Minor, and that it is pre-Hellenic is shown by the town of Aliassus (-*assus* is a Cretan termination) built on its banks just before it turns north to empty into the Southern Black Sea. There are also two Hales rivers, one in Ionia, the other in Lucania, which may be named after the same goddess. One name for the alder in German is *else*, corresponding with the Scandinavian word *elle*. The Danish *Ellerkonge* is the alder-king, Bran, who carries off children to the other world; but *elle* also means 'elf' which should be regarded as a *clēthrad*, or alder-fairy. Thus in Goethe's well-known ballad, based on this predecessor Herder's *Stimmen der Völker*, Ellerkonge is correctly translated 'Erlkönig', the commoner German word for alder being *erle*.

the Divine Child, the extra day of the winter solstice. Thirteen weeks separate these stations and the last of each was a death week and demanded a blood-sacrifice.

O FOR ONN

The second tree is the furze, which with its golden flowers and prickles typifies the young Sun at the Spring equinox; the time when furze fires are lighted on the hills. The effect of burning away the old prickles is to make tender new ones sprout on the stock, which sheep eat greedily; and to encourage the growth of grass—'The furze but ill-behaved, Until he is subdued.' The religious importance of furze, or gorse, which in Welsh folk-lore is 'good against witches', is enhanced by its flowers being frequented by the first bees of the year, as the ivy's are by the last. The name On-niona, a Goddess worshipped by the Gauls in ash-groves, is a compound of Onn and Nion, which supplies the date of her festival, namely the Spring equinox at the close of the Ash-month.

U FOR URA

The third tree is the heather, sacred to the Roman and Sicilian love-goddess Venus Erycina; and in Egypt and Phoenicia to Isis whose brother Osiris was immured in a heather-tree at Byblos, where she went to seek him. The Isis legend quoted by Plutarch is late and artificial but hints at child-sacrifice in honour of Osiris.

The eighteenth-century antiquary Winslow took Dean Swift to Lough Crew to collect local legends of the Irish Triple Goddess. Among those collected was one of the death of the *Garbh Ogh*, an ancient ageless giantess, whose car was drawn by elks, whose diet was venison milk and eagles' breasts and who hunted the mountain deer with a pack of seventy hounds with bird names. She gathered stones to heap herself a triple cairn and 'set up her chair in a womb of the hills at the season of heather-bloom'; and then expired.

The Gallic Heather-goddess Uroica is attested by inscriptions in Roman Switzerland; her name is half-way between *Ura*, and the Greek word for heather, *ereice*.

The heather is the midsummer tree, red and passionate, and is associated with mountains and bees. The Goddess is herself a queen bee about whom male drones swarm in midsummer, and as Cybele is often so pictured; the ecstatic self-castration of her priests was a type of the emasculation of the drone by the queen bee in the nuptial act. Venus fatally courted Anchises on a mountain to the hum of bees. But white heather is lucky, being a protection against acts of passion. The Sicilian Mount Eryx is famous for the visit of Butes the bee-master, son of the North Wind, who was given a hero-shrine there by the nymphs of the Goddess Erycina.

The reference in Gwion's *Câd Goddeu* to the heather comforting the battered poplars is to 'heather-ale', a favourite restorative in Wales.

The ancient popularity of lindens or lime-trees among love-poets of Germany and Northern France, suggests that they became a substitute, in flat regions, for mountain-heather. Lindens flower from mid-May to mid-August. They do not rank as sacred trees in Britain, where only the small-leaved variety seems to be indigenous. However, in Thessaly, Cheiron the Centaur's goddess-mother associated with the erotic wryneck, was called Philyra ('linden').

E FOR EADHA

The fourth tree, the tree of the autumn equinox and of old age, is the shifting-leaved white poplar, or aspen, the shield-maker's tree. According to Pausanias it was first introduced into Greece from Epirus by Hercules (but which?); and the Latin legend is that he bound his head in triumph with poplar after killing the giant Cacus ('the evil one') in his den on the Aventine Hill at Rome. The side of the leaves next to his brow were whitened by the radiant heat he gave out. Presumably the myth accounts for the difference in leaf and ritual use between the aspen and the black poplar which was a funereal tree sacred to Mother Earth in pre-Hellenic Greece. There is a reference in the *Casina* of Plautus to the divinatory use of black poplar and silver fir, the fir apparently standing for hope, the poplar for loss of hope[1]—somewhat as in Pembrokeshire a girl gives a lover either a piece of birch as a sign of encouragement, 'You may begin', or a piece of hazel, called a *collen*, 'Be wise and desist'. Hercules conquered death, and in ancient Ireland the *fé* or measuring-rod used by coffin-makers on corpses was of aspen, presumably as a reminder to the souls of the dead that this was not the end. Golden head-dresses of aspen leaves are found in Mesopotamian burials of 3000 B.C.

I FOR IDHO

The fifth tree is the yew, the death-tree in all European countries, sacred to Hecate in Greece and Italy. At Rome, when black bulls were sacrificed to Hecate, so that the ghosts should lap their gushing blood, they were wreathed with yew. The yew is mentioned by Pausanias as the tree beside which Epaminondas found the bronze urn on Mount Ithome, containing on a tin scroll the secret mysteries of the Great Goddess. On the other side of the urn, appropriately, grew a myrtle, which (as will appear in Chapter Thirteen) was the Greek equivalent of the elder, the death-consonant R. That the scroll was made of tin is interesting; for the ancient Greeks imported their tin from Spain and Britain. In Ireland the yew was 'the coffin of the vine': wine barrels were made of yew staves. In the Irish

[1] *Sed manendum, tum ista aut populina fors aut abiegina est tua.* (Act II.)

romance of *Naoise and Deirdre*, yew stakes were driven through the corpses of these lovers to keep them apart; but the stakes sprouted and became trees whose tops eventually embraced over Armagh Cathedral. In Brittany it is said that church-yard yews will spread a root to the mouth of each corpse. Yew makes the best bows—as the Romans learned from the Greeks—and the deadliness of the tree was thereby enhanced; it is likely that the Latin *taxus*, yew, is connected with *toxon*, Greek for bow, and with *toxicon*, Greek for the poison with which arrows were smeared. The ancient Irish are said to have used a compound of yew-berry, helle-bore and devil's bit for poisoning their weapons. John Evelyn in his *Silva* (1662) points out that the yew does not deserve its reputation for poisonousness—'whatever Pliny reports concerning its shade, or the story of the air about Thasius, the fate of Cativulcus mentioned by Caesar, and the ill report which the fruit has vulgarly obtained in France, Spain and Arcadia.' Cattle and horses nibble the leaves without ill-effect, he says; but later he suggests that the 'true *taxus*' is indeed 'mortiferous'. Its use in the English witch-cult is recalled in *Macbeth* where Hecate's cauldron contained:

> *... slips of yew*
> *Sliver'd in the Moon's eclipse.*

Shakespeare elsewhere calls it the 'double fatal yew' and makes Hamlet's uncle poison the King by pouring its juice ('hebenon') into his ear. It shares with the oak the reputation of taking longer than any other tree to come to maturity, but is longer lived even than the oak. When seasoned and polished its wood has an extraordinary power of resisting corruption.

One of the 'Five Magical Trees of Ireland' was a yew. This was the Tree of Ross, described as 'a firm straight deity' (the Irish yew differed from the British in being cone-shaped, with branches growing straight up, not horizontally), 'the renown of Banbha' (Banbha was the death aspect of the Irish Triple Goddess), 'the Spell of Knowledge, and the King's Wheel'—that is to say the death-letter that makes the wheel of existence come full circle; as a reminder of his destiny, every Irish king wore a brooch in the form of a wheel, which was entailed on his successor. I place the station of the yew on the last day of the year, the eve of the Winter Solstice. Ailm the Silver-fir of Birth and Idho the Yew of Death are sisters: they stand next to each other in the circle of the year and their foliage is almost identical. Fir is to yew as silver is to lead. The mediaeval alchemists, following ancient tradition, reckoned silver to the Moon as presiding over birth, and lead to Saturn as presiding over death; and extracted both metals from the same mixed ore.

> *Fir, womb of silver pain,*
> *Yew, tomb of leaden grief—*

Viragoes of one vein,
Alike in leaf—
With arms up-flung
Taunt us in the same tongue:
'Here Jove's own coffin-cradle swung'.

An Assyrian sculpture published by Felix Lajard in his *Sur la Culte de Mithra* (1847), shows the year as a thirteen-branched tree. The tree has five bands around the trunk and the sceptre-like branches are arranged six on each side, one at the summit. Here evidently the Eastern Mediterranean agricultural year, beginning in the autumn, has been related to the solar year beginning at the Winter solstice. For there is a small ball, representing a new solar year, suspended above the last three branches; and of the two rampant goats which act as supporters to the tree device, the one on the right, which has turned his head so that his single horn forms a crescent moon, rests a forefoot on the uppermost of these last three branches; while the other goat, a she-goat turning her head in the opposite direction so that her horn forms a decrescent moon, is claiming the first three branches. She has a full udder, appropriate to this season, because the first kids are dropped about the winter solstice. A boat-like new moon swims above the tree, and a group of seven stars, the seventh very much brighter than the others, is placed beside the she-goat; which proves her to be Amalthea, mother of the horned Dionysus. The he-goat is an Assyrian counterpart of Azazel, the scape-goat sacrificed by the Hebrews at the beginning of the agricultural year. The five bands on the tree, of which one is at the base of the trunk, another at the top, are the five stations of

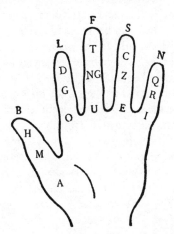

the year; in a Babylonian tree of the year, published in the same book, they are symbolized by five fronds.

In the light of this knowledge we can re-examine the diagram of the hand used as a signalling keyboard by the Druids and understand the puzzling traditional names of the four fingers—'fore-finger', 'fool's-finger', 'leech, or physic-finger' and 'auricular or ear-finger'—in terms of the mythic value of the letters contained on them.

The slight difference in order of letters between the Beth-Luis-Nion and the Boibel-Loth does not affect the argument; though I believe that the system was based on the tree meanings of the Beth-Luis-Nion, because in one of the ancient tales a really dark night is described by a poet as one in which a man could not distinguish oak-leaf from hazel, nor study the five fingers of his own stretched-out hand'. The fore-finger has Duir on 'it, the oak-god who is the foremost of the trees, surmounted by Luis, the rowan, a charm against lightning; the fool's-finger has Tinne on it, the holly-king, or green knight, who appears in the old English 'Christmas Play', a survival of the Saturnalia, as the Fool who is beheaded but rises up again unhurt; the leech-finger has Coll on it, the sage hazel, who is the master-physician; the ear-finger—in French *doigt auriculaire*—is based on the two death-letters Ruis and Idho and therefore has oracular power; as they still say in France of a person who gets information from a mysterious source: '*Son petit doigt le lui dit.*' 'Auricular finger' is usually explained as 'the finger most easily put into one's ear-hole', but the earliest sense of 'auricular' is 'secretly whispered in the ear'. The auricular finger was probably used by the Gallic and British Druids for stopping the ear as an aid to inspiration. Its divinatory character was established early enough in Western Europe for it to appear in a number of folk tales concerning the loss of a little finger, or a little toe, by an ogre's daughter; the hero of the story finds it and it enables him to win the ogre's permission to marry the daughter. These stories occur in Brittany, Lorraine, the West Highlands, Viscaya in Spain, and Denmark. In the *Romance of Taliesin* it is the little finger of Elphin's wife that is said to have been magically cut off.

The 'ring-finger' is another name for the leech-finger. The Romans and Greeks used the thumb, sacred to Venus, for their seal-rings which were usually made of iron; these were prophylactic charms to maintain their virility, the thumb being a synonym for the phallus and iron a compliment to Venus's husband, the Smith-god Vulcan. But for their wedding rings they used the fourth finger of the left hand. This custom was explained by Macrobius, who wrote in the fifth century A.D., on two grounds: that this was the finger in least use of the ten and the least capable of individual movement, therefore the safest to wear precious jewels upon; and (here quoting the authority of the first-century writer Appian) that in this finger an artery runs direct to the heart. The artery to the heart is an astrological, rather than an anatomical, observation—though a small vein, which the ancients could not distinguish from an artery, does show at the bottom joint—because in the late Classical apportionment of the human body to planetary influences it is Apollo, Sun-god and healer, who rules the heart, as Venus rules the kidneys; Mercury, the lungs; Diana (Moon), the head—and so on. The fourth finger is thus used as the ring-finger because the prophylactic wedding-ring, made of gold in honour of Apollo, controls the heart which is the seat of enduring love. The artery legend is also quoted in a medical context by the sixteenth-century German humanist Levinus Lemnius who records that 'the ancient physicians from whom this finger derives its name of "physic-finger" used to mix their medicaments and potions with it, on the theory that no poison can adhere even to its extreme tip without communicating itself directly to the heart.'

Precisely the same system survives in popular cheiromancy, which is late Classical in origin. Palmists give the fore-finger to Juppiter the oak-god; the middle finger to Saturn the Christmas Fool; the fourth finger (in German also called the 'gold finger') to the Sun—Apollo the Sun-god having latterly become the patron of physicians and god of wisdom generally; and the little finger to Mercury in his aspect of Conductor of Dead Souls. The Moon has the heel of the palm, being the Underworld-goddess from whom Mercury derives his inspiration; Venus the thumb (as a phallic emblem); and Mars the centre of the hand, in which the weapon is gripped—his initial M is formed by the principal lines of the hand. A bronze votive hand from Phrygia dedicated to Zeus Sabazius—a rustic Juppiter—contains a little figure in Phrygian cap and breeches, with his feet resting on a ram's head holding up thumb, fore-finger and middle finger in what is called the Latin Blessing—Venus's thumb for increase, Juppiter's fore-finger for fortunate guidance, Saturn's middle finger for rain. He is imitating the posture of the hand in which he is held, and on the fore-finger is perched Juppiter's eagle. It was not so much a blessing as a propitiatory gesture used before embarking on a speech or recital; Greek and Latin orators never omitted it. The Devil's blessing, still used by the Frisian Islanders, consists in raising the fore-finger and ear-finger of the right hand, with the other fingers and the thumb folded against the palm. This is an invocation to the Horned God of the witches, with his lucky right horn and his unlucky left expressing his powers for good and evil.

The Apollo-finger is connected with the poplar in the story of the sun-god Phaëthon whose sisters wept for him when he died: they were metamorphosed into poplars and their tears into amber, sacred to Apollo.

The Saturn-finger is connected with the heather in the story of Osiris, the Egyptian Saturn. Osiris was enclosed in a heather tree, and the lowest consonant on the finger, the reed, was sacred to Osiris as King of Egypt. According to the well-informed fourteenth-century antiquarian Richard of Cirencester, rich Southern Britons of the third century A.D. wore gold rings on the fool's finger; in the B.L.F. alphabet this finger belonged to Bran, whom they must by then have learned from the Romans to identify with Osiris. To wear a ring on the fool's finger naturally expressed a hope of resurrection.

The thumb of Venus is connected with the palm-tree by its sacredness to the orgiastic goddess Isis, Latona or Lat. Lat was the mother of Nabatean Dusares the vine-god, worshipped in Egypt, and the lowest consonant on the thumb was the vine.

The Juppiter-finger is connected with the furze, or gorse, by the Spring gorse-fires burned in his honour as god of shepherds.

The connexion of the Mercury-finger with the yew is made by Mercury's conducting of souls to the place presided over by the death-goddess Hecate, *alias* his mother Maia, to whom the yew was sacred.

It is fitting that the most sensitive part of the hand, the tip of the fore-finger, should belong to Luis as the diviner. But all the finger-tip trees— Luis the rowan, Nion the ash, Fearn the alder and Saille the willow— were used in divination. This perhaps throws light on an Irish poetic rite called the *Dichetal do Chennaib* ('recital from the finger-ends'), of which the ollave was required to be a master, and which Dr. Joyce describes as 'the utterance of an extempore prophecy or poem that seems to have been accomplished with the aid of a mnemonic contrivance of some sort in which the fingers played a principal part'. St. Patrick, while abolishing two other prophetic rites, the *Imbas Forasnai,* 'palm-knowledge of enlighten-ment', and another like it, because they involved preliminary sacrifice to demons, permitted the 'recital from the finger ends' because it did not. In Cormac's *Glossary* the *Dichetal do Chennaib* is explained:

In my day it is by the ends of his finger-bones that the poet accom-plishes the rite in this manner: 'When he sees the person or thing before him he makes a verse at once with his finger ends, or in his mind with-out studying, and composes and repeats at the same time.'

It is less likely that a mnemonic trick involving the use of the finger alphabet was used than that the poets induced a poetic trance by treating their finger-tips as oracular agents; since the *Dichetal do Chennaib* is always mentioned with the other two divinatory rites as of the same general nature.

[At this point my own finger-tips began to itch and when I gave them a pen to hold they reconstructed the original incantation as follows:

> *Tree powers, finger tips,*
> *First pentad of the four,*
> *Discover all your poet asks*
> *Drumming on his brow.*

Birch peg, throbbing thumb,
By power of divination,
Birch, bring him news of love;
Loud the heart knocks.

Rowan rod, forefinger,
By power of divination
Unriddle him a riddle;
The key's cast away.

Ash, middle finger,
By power of divination
Weatherwise, fool otherwise,
Mete him out the winds.

Alder, physic finger,
By power of divination
Diagnose all maladies
Of a doubtful mind.

Willow wand, ear finger,
By power of divination
Force confessions from the mouth
Of a mouldering corpse.

Finger-ends, five twigs,
Trees, true-divining trees,
Discover all your poet asks
Drumming on his brow.]

The finger alphabet was evidently used in the witch cult of mediaeval Britain, to judge from the Devil marks tattooed on the hands of witches. In Joseph Glanvil's *Sadducismus Triumphatus* (1681) a detailed account is given of two covens of Somersetshire witches, one of thirteen formed at Brewham, another at Wincanton, both places being about fourteen miles from Glastonbury. The British racial element, as opposed to the Saxon, predominated in Somerset and popular reverence for Glastonbury as a principal seat of the Old Religion was still strong in the seventeenth century. From the confessions of the members of these covens at their trial in 1664, it appears that the chief, or god, of these witches was known as Robin and that he sealed initiates with a prick from a needle made between the upper and middle joints of the physic-finger. This is precisely the spot at which one would expect the prick, since the covens' activities included both black and white magic: the upper joint belongs to Coll, the hazel, the tree of white magic and healing, the lower to Straif, the blackthorn which, as will be shown in Chapter Fourteen, was the tree of black magic and blasting. These witches used thorns for sticking into the wax images of their enemies under Robin's direction.

In Scotland the fool's-finger was used for the Devil's mark, and though the precise location of the mark is not recorded, it was evidently low down, since Margaret McLevine of Bute complained that the Devil nearly cut this finger off her. The bottom joint of the fool's-finger is Ura, the heather—a suitable tree for the initiation of Scottish witches who, according to Shakespeare, met on blasted heaths.

Two Northampton witches, Elinor Shaw and Mary Phillips, who were condemned to death in 1705, had been pricked at their fingers' ends: unfortunately the finger is not specified, but perhaps it was the finger with Saille as its tip, the willow sacred to Hecate, mother of witches.[1]

Dr. Macalister gives little more importance to the Irish Tree-Ogham than to such other cypher systems recorded in the *Book of Ballymote* as Pig-Ogham, Castle-Ogham and Fruit-Ogham. But that the name for the B.L.N. alphabet, which is admittedly earlier than the B.L.F. alphabet, begins with three trees proves that the original Ogham was a Tree-Ogham; and the mythological associations of the trees that comprise O'Flaherty's list are so ancient, various and coherent, that it seems impossible to regard it as a late mediaeval invention, 'pedantic and artificial'. It seems to be the original alphabet invented by Ogma Sun-Face. Dr. Macalister disparages the invention of Ogham as childish and unworthy of a god; but this is because he regards the Boibel-Loth as the only genuine Ogham alphabet and the Beth-Luis-Nion as an experimental approach to it and considers that both are cribbed from the Greek alphabet. He is not to be convinced that either has any virtue besides the obvious alphabetic one.

An objection against regarding the Beth-Luis-Nion as a complete alphabet is that it has only thirteen consonants, of which one, NG, is useless, while two ancient letters, Q and Z, contained in the Boibel-Loth and known in Ogham as Quert and Straif, are omitted. Straif is the blackthorn and Quert is the wild apple tree: both mythologically important trees. If Ogma Sun-Face raised four pillars of equal length, the original system must have contained five vowels and three sets of five consonants. This objection will be fully met in Chapter Thirteen. It is enough to note meanwhile that O'Flaherty was not alone in recording a B.L.N. alphabet with only thirteen consonants. O'Sullivan's Ogham, quoted in Ledwich's

[1] British sailors used always to be tattooed with a star in the hollow of the hand between the thumb and fore-finger, and the custom survives in some ports. This is originally a plea to Venus as Goddess of the Sea and Juppiter as God of the Air to bring the sailor safe ashore, the star being the symbol of hope and guidance.

Antiquities of Ireland, has the same number, and with a similar omission of Q and Z, though with NG for P; O'Sullivan adds some diphthongs and other mysterious symbols such as *eg, feo* and *oai*, but the canon of the alphabet is the one discussed here.

Edward Davies considered that the Beth-Luis-Nion alphabet was so called because B.L.N. are the radical consonants of Belin the Celtic god of the solar year. This makes sense, since it suggests an identification of the thirteen consonants, months of the year, with various mythological companies of thirteen—for example with Arthur and his Twelve Knights of the Round Table; Balder and his twelve judges; Odysseus and his Twelve Companions; Romulus and his Twelve Shepherds; Roland and the Twelve Peers of France; Jacob and his Twelve Sons; Danish Hrolf and his twelve Berserks. Also, with the head and the twelve other parts of Osiris's torn body which Isis in her boat recovered from the Nile—Osiris having originally been a tree-god. And we may also identify the five seasonal vowels with the mysterious pentads of British Goddesses, the *deae matronae*, (*y Mamau*), which occur in inscriptions of Roman times; and with the various five-pointed leaves sacred to the White Goddess, especially the ivy, vine, bramble, fig and plane;[1] and with the various five petalled flowers sacred to her—the erotic briar-rose and primrose and the baleful blue *vincapervinca*, or periwinkle, which the Italians call the 'flower of death' and with which, in mediaeval England, condemned men were garlanded on their way to the gallows.

But where did the Beth-Luis-Nion series originate? It will have been observed that all its trees are forest trees native to the British Isles, except the vine. That no orchard trees occur in the series suggests to me that it was brought in very early times from a thickly wooded northern region where the vine grew wild. The only region answering this condition, so far as I know, was the Paphlagonia-Pontus stretch of the Southern Black Sea coast. A Cretan origin is out of the question: the principal trees that appear in the very numerous sacred pictures and engravings recently exca-

---

[1] Another five-pointed leaf in sacral use was the cinquefoil, a chief ingredient in the flying ointment used by mediaeval French witches. An alternative in one formula is the poplar leaf, doubtless the five-pointed sort. Like the fleur-de-luce used in the same ointment—apparently because of its three-petalled flower and its red seeds contained in a triangular seed-box—it has no toxic effect, but seems to have been introduced in the Goddess's honour (with a thickening of soot and oil, or infant's fat) to enhance the effect of the other ingredients: namely, the abortificent parsley, bat's blood to assist nocturnal flight, and the highly toxic aconite, belladonna, hemlock and cowbane. The formulas are quoted in Miss M. Murray's *The Witch Cult in Western Europe*. Mr. Trevor Furze has supplied me with two further formulas of English origin: (1) The fat of a newly-born infant; *eleoselinum* (wild celery, also called 'smallage', or 'water-parsley', a mediaeval remedy against cramps); skiwet (wild parsnip, the leaves of which were regarded as poisonous but used in poulticing); soot. (2) Bat's blood, to be obtained at the wake of the new moon; pentaphyllon (cinque foil); poplar leaves; soot. Perhaps the 'parsley' in the French formula is really water-parsley, introduced to protect the witches against cramps when flying.

vated in Crete are the fig, olive, plane-tree, cypress, vine, pine and palm.

Dr. Macalister cannot be blamed for doubting the ancientness of O'Flaherty's Beth-Luis-Nion, since several different systems of classifying trees were current in mediaeval Ireland. For example, under Brehon Law (IV, 147) trees were divided into four categories with a scale of fines for their unlawful felling that diminished in severity according to the category:

(1) Seven Chieftain Trees

Oak	*dair*
Hazel	*coll*
Holly	*cuileann*
Yew	*ibur*
Ash	*iundius*
Pine	*ochtach*
Apple	*aball*

(2) Seven Peasant Trees

Alder	*fernn*
Willow	*sail*
Hawthorn	*sceith*
Rowan	*caerthann*
Birch	*beithe*
Elm	*leam*
?	*idha*

(3) Seven Shrub Trees

Blackthorn	*draidean*
Elder	*trom*
White hazel	*fincoll*
White poplar	*crithach*
Arbutus	*caithne*
?	*feorus*
?	*crann-fir*

(4) Eight Bramble Trees

Fern	*raith*
Bog-myrtle	*rait*
Furze	*aiteand*
Briar	*dris*
Heath	*fraech*
Ivy	*eideand*
Broom	*gilcoch*
Gooseberry	*spin*

This Law is much later than that commemorated in the *Triads of Ireland* under which the death penalty is apparently demanded for the unlawful felling of two of the chieftain trees, the hazel and the apple:

> *Three unbreathing things paid for only with breathing things:*
> *An apple tree, a hazel bush, a sacred grove.*[1]

This may be explained by the seventh-century poem at the end of the *Crib Gablach* in which the seven Chieftain trees are listed, but with alder, willow and birch instead of ash, yew and pine, the fine for the unlawful felling of them being one cow, or three for the whole grove. But I assume that the poem is later than the *Triads*, though earlier than the Brehon Law, and that the death sentence for the felling of hazel and apple has here been commuted to a one-cow fine, as in the case of other trees. According to mediaeval glossarists, *Neimhead*, meaning 'nobility', or sacrosanctity, was applied to kings or chieftains, poets and groves; in its secondary sense of 'worthiness', to musicians, smiths, carpenters, cows and Church dignitaries.

The Commentator on the Brehon Law explains the 'nobility' of its seven Chieftain Trees in the following glosses:

Oak: *its size, handsomeness, and its pig-fattening acorns.*
Hazel: *its nuts and wattles.*
Apple: *its fruit, and bark suitable for tanning.*
Yew: *its timber, used for household vessels, breast-plates, etc.*
Holly: *its timber, used for chariot shafts.*
Ash: *its timber, used for supporting the King's thigh* (i.e. for making regal thrones) *and for the shafts of weapons.*
Pine: *its timber, used for making puncheons.*

The triumph of Gwydion's ash over Bran's alder at the *Câd Goddeu* is incidentally demonstrated here: the ash, which was originally excluded from the sacred grove, is now the only tree mentioned in connection with royalty, and the alder has been degraded to the status of peasant. The utilitarian assessment of nobility made by the glossarist denotes a profound religious change, and when the relative values of the trees can be expressed in terms of cash-compensation for their illegal felling, the sanctity of the grove is annulled and poetry itself declines. However, while this Law was in force the student for the Ollaveship of poetry had to memorize the following ancient catechism, recorded in Calder's *Hearings of the Scholars*, which contains still another classification of trees:

---

[1] At Rome in the second century B.C. a sacred grove could be felled at an even cheaper rate: the sacrifice of a single pig. Cato the Censor in his *De Re Rustica* quotes the prayer of placation that the timber-hungry farmer must offer to the deity concerned.

{	*Cis lir aicme Ogaim?*	*A iii .i. viii n-airigh*
	How many groups of Ogham?	Answer three, namely: 8 chieftain
{	*fedha & viii n-athaigh & viii fidlosa. Ocht n-airigh*
	trees and 8 peasant-trees and 8 shrub trees. 8 chieftain trees
{	*cetus fernn, dur, coll, muin, gort, straif, onn, or.*
	first alder, oak, hazel, vine, ivy, blackthorn, furze, heath.
{	*Ocht n-athaig .i. bethi, luis, sail, nin, huath,*
	8 peasant trees, namely: birch, rowan, willow, ash, whitehorn,
{	*tinne, quert. Ar chuit a feda is athaig*
	whin,[1] appletree. As to their letters, all other shrubs
{	*feda fidlosa olchema.*
	are shrub trees.

Here the trees are those of O'Flaherty's Beth-Luis-Nion, without the intrusion of arbutus, elm, white-hazel and the rest. The unnamed 'shrub trees' evidently include the elder, reed or water-elder, broom and wood-bine. This arrangement according to nobility is eccentric—the apple-tree and holly being excluded from chieftainship—and is possibly connected with the Greek 24-letter alphabet rather than with the Ogham 20-letter one or its 25-letter expansion.

The subject is very difficult, and the Irish ollaves had no interest in making it plain to outsiders.

---

[1] Evidently a mistake for holly.

Chapter Twelve

THE SONG OF AMERGIN

I suggest in the first part of this argument that the 'I am' and 'I have been' sequences frequent in ancient Welsh and Irish poetry are all variants of the same calendar theme. Here, for instance, is the 'Song of Amergin' (or Amorgen) said to have been chanted by the chief bard of the Milesian invaders, as he set his foot on the soil of Ireland, in the year of the world 2736 (1268 B.C.). Unfortunately the version which survives is only a translation into colloquial Irish from the Old Goidelic. Dr. Macalister pronounces it 'a pantheistic conception of a Universe where godhead is everywhere and omnipotent' and suggests that it was a liturgical hymn of as wide a currency as, say, the opening chapters of the *Koran*, or the Apostles' Creed. He writes: 'Was it of this hymn, or of what he had been told of the contents of this hymn, that Caesar was thinking when he wrote: "The Druids teach of the stars and their motions, the world, the size of lands, natural philosophy and the nature of the gods"?' He notes that the same piece 'in a garbled form' is put into the mouth of the Childbard Taliesin when narrating his transformations in previous existences. Sir John Rhys pointed out in his *Hibbert Lectures* that many of Gwion's 'I have been's' imply 'not actual transformation but mere likeness, through a primitive formation of a predicate without the aid of a particle corresponding to such a word as "like".'

The Song of Amergin begins with thirteen statements, provided with mediaeval glosses. The thirteen statements are followed by six questions, also provided with glosses. These are followed in Professor John MacNeill's version by an *envoie* in which the Druid advises the People of the Sea to invoke the poet of the sacred rath to give them a poem. He himself will supply the poet with the necessary material, and together they will compose an incantation.

THE SONG OF AMERGIN

God speaks and says:	*Glosses*
I am a wind of the sea,	*for depth*
I am a wave of the sea,	*for weight*

I am a sound of the sea,   *for horror*
I am an ox of seven fights,   *for strength*
  or   I am a stag of seven tines,
I am a griffon on a cliff,   *for deftness*
  or   I am a hawk on a cliff,
I am a tear of the sun,   *'a dewdrop'—for clearness*
I am fair among flowers,
I am a boar,   *for valour*
I am a salmon in a pool,   *'the pools of knowledge'*
I am a lake on a plain,   *for extent*
I am a hill of poetry,   *'and knowledge'*
I am a battle-waging spear,
I am a god who forms fire for a head.   [*i.e. 'gives inspiration':*
                                                  Macalister]
  or   I am a god who forms smoke from   *'to slay therewith'*
sacred fire for a head.

       *   *   *

1. Who makes clear the ruggedness of the   *'Who but myself will re-*
   mountains?   *solve every question?'*
   or   Who but myself knows the assemb-
   lies of the dolmen-house on the mountain of Slieve Mis?
2. Who but myself knows where the sun
   shall set?
3. Who foretells the ages of the moon?
4. Who brings the cattle from the House of   [*i.e. 'the fish',* Macalister,
   Tethra and segregates them?   *i.e. 'the stars',* MacNeill]
5. On whom do the cattle of Tethra smile?
   or   For whom but me will the fish of
   the laughing ocean be making welcome?
6. Who shapes weapons from hill to hill?   *'wave to wave, letter to*
                                                  letter, point to point'

       *   *   *

Invoke, People of the Sea, invoke the poet, that he may compose a
     spell for you.
For I, the Druid, who set out letters in Ogham,
I, who part combatants,
I will approach the rath of the Sidhe to seek a cunning poet that
     together we may concoct incantations.
I am a wind of the sea.

Tethra was the king of the Undersea-land from which the People of the
Sea were later supposed to have originated. He is perhaps a masculiniza-

tion of Tethys, the Pelasgian Sea-goddess, also known as Thetis, whom, Doge-like, Peleus the Achaean married at Iolcus in Thessaly. The Sidhe are now popularly regarded as fairies: but in early Irish poetry they appear as a real people—a highly cultured and dwindling nation of warriors and poets living in the raths, or round stockaded forts, of which New Grange on the Boyne is the most celebrated. All had blue eyes, pale faces and long curly yellow hair. The men carried white shields, and were organized in military companies of fifty. They were ruled over by two virgin-born kings and were sexually promiscuous but 'without blame or shame'. They were, in fact, Picts (tattooed men) and all that can be learned about them corresponds with Xenophon's observations in his *Anabasis* on the primitive Mosynoechians ('wooden-castle dwellers') of the Black Sea coast. The Mosynoechians were skilfully tattooed, carried long spears and ivy-leaf shields made from white ox-hide, were forest dwellers, and performed the sexual act in public. They lived in the stockaded forts from which they took their name, and in Xenophon's time occupied the territory assigned in early Greek legend to the matriarchal Amazons. The 'blue eyes' of the Sidhe I take to be blue interlocking rings tattooed around the eyes, for which the Thracians were known in Classical times. Their pallor was also perhaps artificial—white 'war-paint' of chalk or powdered gypsum, in honour of the White Goddess, such as we know, from a scene in Aristophanes's *Clouds* where Socrates whitens Strepsiades, was used in Orphic rites of initiation.

Slieve Mis is a mountain in Kerry.

'Of seven tines' probably means of seven points on each horn, fourteen in all: which make a 'royal stag'. But royalty is also conceded to a stag of twelve points, and since a stag must be seven years old before it can have twelve points, 'seven fights' may refer to the years.

It is most unlikely that this poem was allowed to reveal its esoteric meaning to all and sundry; it would have been 'pied', as Gwion pied his poems, for reasons of security. So let us rearrange the order of statements in a thirteen-month calendar form, on the lines of the Beth-Luis-Nion, profiting from what we have learned about the mythic meaning of each letter-month:

		God speaks and says:	*Trees of the month*	
Dec. 24–Jan. 20	B	I am a stag of seven tines, or an ox of seven fights,	Birch	Beth
Jan. 21–Feb. 17	L	I am a wide flood on a plain,	Quick-beam (Rowan)	Luis
Feb. 18–Mar. 17	N	I am a wind on the deep waters,	Ash	Nion

Mar. 18–Apr. 14	F	I am a shining tear of the sun,	Alder	Fearn
Apr. 15–May 12	S	I am a hawk on a cliff,	Willow	Saille
May 13–Jun. 9	H	I am fair among flowers,	Hawthorn	Uath
Jun. 10–July 7	D	I am a god who sets the head afire with smoke,	Oak	Duir
July 8–Aug. 4	T	I am a battle-waging spear,	Holly	Tinne
Aug. 5–Sept. 1	C	I am a salmon in the pool,	Hazel	Coll
Sept. 2–Sept. 29	M	I am a hill of poetry,	Vine	Muin
Sept. 30–Oct. 27	G	I am a ruthless boar,	Ivy	Gort
Oct. 28–Nov. 24	NG	I am a threatening noise of the sea,	Reed	Ngetal
Nov. 25–Dec. 22	R	I am a wave of the sea,	Elder	Ruis
Dec. 23		Who but I knows the secrets of the unhewn dolmen?		

There can be little doubt as to the appropriateness of this arrangement. B is the Hercules stag (or wild bull) which begins the year. The seven fights, or seven tines of his antlers, are months in prospect and in retrospect: for Beth is the seventh month after Duir the oak-month, and the seventh month from Beth is Duir again. The 'Boibalos' of the Hercules charm contained in the Boibel-Loth was an antelope-bull. The Orphic 'ox of seven fights' is hinted at in Plutarch's *Isis and Osiris,* where he describes how at the Winter solstice they carry the golden cow of Isis, enveloped in black cloth, seven times around the shrine of Osiris, whom he identifies with Dionysus. 'The circuit is called "The Seeking for Osiris", for in winter the Goddess longs for the water of the Sun. And she goes around seven times because he completes his passing from the winter to the summer solstice in the seventh month.' Plutarch must be reckoning in months of 28 days, not 30, else the passage would be completed in the sixth of them.

L is February Fill-Dyke, season of floods.

N is centred in early March, which 'comes in like a lion' with winds that dry the floods.

F is explained by the sentiment of the well-known mediaeval carol:

> He came all so still
>   Where his mother was,
> Like dew in April
>   That falleth on grass.

For this is the true beginning of the sacred year, when the deer and wild cow drop their young, and when the Child Hercules is born who was begotten at the mid-summer orgies. Hitherto he has been sailing in his coracle over the floods; now he lies glistening on the grass.

S is the month when birds nest. In Gwion's *Can y Meirch* ('Song of the Horses'), a partial series of 'I have been's' occurs as an interpolation. One of them is: 'I have been a crane on a wall, a wondrous sight.' The crane was sacred to Delian Apollo and, before Apollo, to the Sun-hero Theseus. It also appears, in triad, in a Gaulish bas-relief at Paris, and in another at Trèves, in association with the god Esus and a bull. Crane, hawk, or vulture? That is an important question because the provenience of the poem depends on the answer. The hawk, if not the royal hawk of Egyptian Horus, will have been the kite sacred to Boreas the North Wind; in Greek legend his Thracian sons Calaïs and Zetes wore kite-feathers in his honour and had the power of transforming themselves into kites. These two birds are mythologically linked in the Egyptian hieroglyph for the North Wind, which is a hawk. In Welsh the word is *barcut*, and in Iranian the word is *barqut*, which supports Pliny's suggestion (*Natural History XXX*, 13) of a strong connexion between the Persian and British sun-cults. Another mark of close similarity is that Mithras, the Persian Sun-god whose birthday was celebrated at the winter-solstice, was worshipped as a bull of seven fights: his initiates having to go through seven grades before they were sealed on the brow as 'tried soldiers of Mithras'. Mithraism was a favourite cult of the Roman legionaries in Imperial times, but they never reached Ireland, and the *Song of Amergin* is evidently far older than the Claudian invasion of Britain. The vulture will have been the griffon-vulture sacred to Osiris, a bird also of great importance to the Etruscan augurs and with a wider wing-span than the golden eagle. In the *Song of Moses* (*Deuteronomy XXXII, 11*) Jehovah is identified with this bird, which is a proof that its 'uncleanness' in the Levitical list means sanctity, not foulness. The heraldic griffin is a lion with griffon-vultures' wings and claws and represents the Sun-god as King of the earth and air. The ordinary Welsh word for hawk is *Gwalch*, akin to the Latin *falco*, falcon, and the court-bards always likened their royal patrons to it. The mystical names Gwalchmai ('hawk of May'); Gwalchaved ('hawk of summer') better known as Sir Galahad; and Gwalchgwyn ('white hawk') better known as Sir Gawain, are best understood in terms of this calendar formula.

H, which starts in the second half of May, is the season of flowers, and the hawthorn, or may-tree, rules it. Olwen, the daughter of 'Giant Hawthorn', has already been mentioned. Her hair was yellow as the broom, her fingers pale as wood-anemones, her cheeks the colour of roses and from her footprints white trefoil sprang up—trefoil to show that she was the summer aspect of the old Triple Goddess. This peculiarity gave her the name of

Olwen—'She of the White Track'. Trefoil, by the way, was celebrated by the Welsh bards with praise out of all proportion to its beauty. Homer called it 'the lotus' and mentioned it as a rich fodder for horses.

D is ruled by the midsummer oak. The meaning is, I think, that the painful smoke of green oak gives inspiration to those who dance between the twin sacrificial fires lighted on Midsummer Eve. Compare the *Song of the Forest Trees:*

> *Fiercest heat-giver of all timber is green oak;*
> *From him none may escape unhurt.*
> *By love of him the head is set an-aching,*
> *By his acrid embers the eye is made sore.*

T is the spear month, the month of the tanist; the bardic letter T was shaped like a barbed spear.

C is the nut month. The salmon was, and still is, the King of the river-fish, and the difficulty of capturing him, once he is lodged in a pool, makes him a useful emblem of philosophical retirement. Thus Loki, the Norse God of cunning, disguised himself from his fellow-gods as a salmon and was drawn from his pool only with a special net of his own design. The connexion of salmon with nuts and with wisdom has already been explained.

M is the initial of Minerva, Latin goddess of wisdom and inventor of numbers; of Mnemosyne, the Mother of the Greek Muses; and of the Muses themselves; and of the Moirae, or Fates, who are credited by some mythographers with the first invention of the alphabet. The vine, the prime tree of Dionysus, is everywhere associated with poetic inspiration. Wine is the poets' proper drink, as Ben Jonson knew well when he asked for his fee as Poet Laureate to be paid in sack. The base Colley Cibber asked for a cash payment in lieu of wine, and no Poet Laureate since has been poet enough to demand a return to the old system of payment.

G, the ivy month, is also the month of the boar. Set, the Egyptian Sun-god, disguised as a boar, kills Osiris of the ivy, the lover of the Goddess Isis. Apollo the Greek Sun-god, disguised as a boar, kills Adonis, or Tammuz, the Syrian, the lover of the Goddess Aphrodite. Finn Mac Cool, disguised as a boar, kills Diarmuid, the lover of the Irish Goddess Grainne (Greine). An unknown god disguised as a boar kills Ancaeus the Arcadian King, a devotee of Artemis, in his vineyard at Tegea and, according to the Nestorian *Gannat Busamé* ('Garden of Delights'), Cretan Zeus was similarly killed. October was the boar-hunting season, as it was also the revelry season of the ivy-wreathed Bassarids. The boar is the beast of death and the 'fall' of the year begins in the month of the boar.

NG is the month when the terrible roar of breakers and the snarling noise of pebbles on the Atlantic seaboard fill the heart with terror, and when the wind whistles dismally through the reed-beds of the rivers. In Ireland the roaring of the sea was held to be prophetic of a king's death. The warning also came with the harsh cry of the scritch-owl. Owls are most vocal on moonlight nights in November and then remain silent until February. It is this habit, with their silent flight, the carrion-smell of their nests, their diet of mice, and the shining of their eyes in the dark, which makes owls messengers of the Death-goddess Hecate, or Athene, or Persephone: from whom, as the supreme source of prophecy, they derive their reputation for wisdom.

R is the month when the wave returns to the sea, and the end of the year to its watery beginning. A wave of the sea in Irish and Welsh poetry is a 'sea-stag': so that the year begins and ends with the white roebuck. In Irish legend such gods of the year as Cuchulain and Fionn fight the waves with sword and spear.

The corresponding text in the *Romance of Taliesin* is scattered rather than garbled.

B	I have been a fierce bull and a yellow buck.
L	I have been a boat on the sea.
N	I fled vehemently ... on the foam of water.
F	I have been a drop in the air.
S	I journeyed as an eagle.
H	God made me of blossom.
D	I have been a tree-stump in a shovel.
T	I fled as a spear-head of woe to such as wish for woe.
C	I have been a blue salmon.
M	I have been a spotted snake on a hill.
G	I fled as a bristly boar seen in a ravine.
NG	I have been a wave breaking on the beach.
R	On a boundless sea I was set adrift.

The clue to the arrangement of this alphabet is found in Amergin's reference to the dolmen; it is an alphabet that best explains itself when built up as a dolmen of consonants with a threshold of vowels. Dolmens are closely connected with the calendar in the legend of the flight of Grainne and Diarmuid from Finn Mac Cool. The flight lasted for a year and a day, and the lovers bedded together beside a fresh dolmen every night. Numerous 'Beds of Diarmuid and Grainne' are shown in Cork, Kerry, Limerick, Tipperary and the West, each of them marked by a dolmen. So this alphabet dolmen will also serve as a calendar, with one post for Spring, the other for Autumn, the lintel for Summer, the threshold for New Year's Day. Thus:

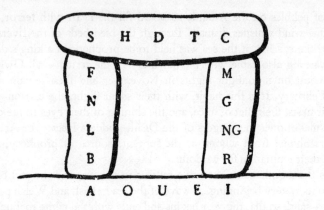

At once one sees the reference to S as a hawk, or griffon, on the cliff; and to M as the hill of poetry or inspiration—a hill rooted in the death letters R and I and surmounted by the C of wisdom. So the text of the first part of Amergin's song may be expanded as follows:

> *God speaks and says:*
> > *I am the stag of seven tines.*
> > *Over the flooded world*
> > *I am borne by the wind.*
> > *I descend in tears like dew, I lie glittering,*
> > *I fly aloft like a griffon to my nest on the cliff,*
> > *I bloom among the loveliest flowers,*
> > *I am both the oak and the lightning that blasts it.*
>
> > *I embolden the spearman,*
> > *I teach the councillors their wisdom,*
> > *I inspire the poets,*
> > *I rove the hills like a ravening boar,*
> > *I roar like the winter sea,*
> > *I return again like the receding wave.*
> > *Who but I can unfold the secrets of the unhewn dolmen?*

For if the poem really consists of two stanzas, each of two triads, ending with a single authoritative statement, then the first 'Who but I' (which does not match the other five) is the conclusion of the second stanza, and is uttered by the New Year God. This Child is represented by the sacred threshold of the dolmen, the central triad of vowels, namely O.U.E. But one must read O.U.E. backwards, the way of the sun, to make sense of it. It is the sacred name of Dionysus, EUO, which in English is usually written 'EVOE'.

It is clear that 'God' is Celestial Hercules again, and that the child-poet

Taliesin is a more appropriate person to utter the song than Amergin, the leader of the Milesians, unles Amergin is speaking as a mouth-piece of Hercules.

There is a mystery connected with the line 'I am a shining tear of the sun', because Deorgreine, 'tear of the Sun', is the name of Niamh of the Golden Hair, the lovely goddess mentioned in the myth of Laegaire mac Crimthainne. Celestial Hercules when he passes into the month F, the month of Bran's alder, becomes a maiden. This recalls the stories of such sun-heroes as Achilles[1], Hercules and Dionysus who lived for a time disguised as girls in the women's quarters of a palace and plied the distaff. It also explains the 'I have been a maiden', in a series corresponding with the Amergin cycle, ascribed to Empedocles, the fifth-century B.C. mystical philosopher. The sense is that the Sun is still under female tutelage for half of this month—Cretan boys not yet old enough to bear arms were called *Scotioi*, members of the women's quarters—then, like Achilles, he is given arms and flies off royally like a griffon or hawk to its nest.

But why a dolmen? A dolmen is a burial chamber, a 'womb of Earth', consisting of a cap-stone supported on two or more uprights, in which a dead hero is buried in a crouched position like a foetus in the womb, awaiting rebirth. In spiral Castle (passage-burial), the entrance to the inner chamber is always narrow and low in representation of the entrance to the womb. But dolmens are used in Melanesia (according to Prof. W. H. R. Rivers) as sacred doors through which the totem-clan initiate crawls in a ceremony of rebirth; if, as seems likely, they were used for the same purpose in ancient Britain, Gwion is both recounting the phases of his past existence and announcing the phases of his future existence. There is a regular row of dolmens on Slieve Mis. They stand between two baetyls with Ogham markings, traditionally sacred to the Milesian Goddess Scota who is said to be buried there; alternatively, in the account preserved by Borlase in his *Dolmens of Ireland*, to 'Bera a queen who came from Spain'. But Bera and Scota seem to be the same person, since the Milesians came from Spain. Bera is otherwise known as the Hag of Beara.

[1] Sir Thomas Browne generously remarked in his *Urn Burial* that 'what song the Sirens sang, or what name Achilles assumed when he hid himself among women, though puzzling questions are not beyond all conjecture'. According to Suetonius the guesses made by various scholars whom the Emperor Tiberius consulted on this point were 'Cercysera' on account of the distaff (*kerkis*) that Achilles wielded; 'Issa', on account of his swiftness (*aisso*, I dart); 'Pyrrha', on account of his red hair. Hyginus gives his vote for Pyrrha. My conjecture is that Achilles called himself Dacryoessa ('the tearful one') or, better, Drosoessa ('the dewy one'), *drosos* being a poetic synonym for tears. According to Apollonius, his original name Liguron ('wailing') was changed to Achilles by his tutor Cheiron. This is to suggest that the Achilles-cult came to Thessaly from Liguria. Homer punningly derives Achilles from *achos* ('distress'), but Apollodorus from *a* 'not' and *cheile* 'lips', a derivation which Sir James Frazer calls absurd; though 'Lipless' is quite a likely name for an oracular hero.

The five remaining questions correspond with the five vowels, yet they are not uttered by the Five-fold Goddess of the white ivy-leaf, as one would expect. They must have been substituted for an original text telling of Birth, Initiation, Love, Repose, Death, and can be assigned to a later bardic period. In fact, they correspond closely with the *envoi* to the first section of the tenth-century Irish *Saltair Na Rann*, which seems to be a Christianized version of a pagan epigram.

> *For each day five items of knowledge*
> *Are required of every understanding person—*
> *From everyone, without appearance of boasting,*
> *Who is in holy orders.*

> *The day of the solar month; the age of the moon;*
> *The state of the sea-tide, without error;*
> *The day of the week; the calendar of the feasts of the perfect saints*
> *In just clarity with their variations.*

For 'perfect saints' read 'blessed deities' and no further alteration is needed. Compare this with Amergin's:

> *Who but myself knows where the sun shall set?*
> *Who foretells the ages of the moon?*
> *Who brings the cattle from the house of Tethra and*
> *   segregates them?*
> *On whom do the cattle of Tethra smile?*
> *Who shapes weapons from hill to hill, wave to wave,*
> *   letter to letter, point to point?*

The first two questions in the *Song of Amergin*, about the day of the solar month and the ages of the moon, coincide with the first two items of knowledge in the *Saltair*: 'Who knows when the Sun shall set?' means both 'who knows the length of the hours of daylight at any given day of the year?'—a problem worked out in exhaustive detail by the author of the *Book of Enoch*—and 'Who knows on any given day how long the particular solar month in which it occurs will last?'

The third question is: 'Who brings the cattle of Tethra (the heavenly bodies) out of the ocean and puts each in his due place?' This assumes a knowledge: of the five planets, Mars, Mercury, Juppiter, Venus, Saturn, which, with the Sun and Moon, had days of the week allotted to them in Babylonian astronomy, and still keep them in all European languages. Thus it corresponds with 'the day of the week'.

The fourth question, as the glossarist explains, amounts to 'Who is lucky in fishing?' This corresponds with 'the state of the sea tide'; for a fisherman who does not know what tide to expect will have no fishing luck.

The fifth question, read in the light of its gloss, amounts to: 'Who orders the calendar from the advancing wave B to the receding wave R; from one calendar month to the next; from one season of the year to the next?' (The three seasons of Spring, Summer and Autumn are separated by points, or angles, of the dolmen.) So it corresponds with 'the calendar of the feasts of the perfect saints'.

Another version of the poem found in *The Book of Leacan* and *The Book of the O'Clerys*, runs as follows when restored to its proper order. The glosses are similar in both books, though the O'Clerys' are the more verbose.

B   I am seven battalions *or* I am an ox in strength—*for strength*
L   I am a flood on a plain—*for extent*
N   I am a wind on the sea—*for depth*
F   I am a ray of the sun—*for purity*
S   I am a bird of prey on a cliff—*for cunning*
H   I am a shrewd navigator—
D   I am gods in the power of transformation—*I am a god, a druid, and a man who creates fire from magical smoke for the destruction of all, and makes magic on the tops of hills*
T   I am a giant with a sharp sword, hewing down an army—*in taking vengeance*
C   I am a salmon in a river *or* pool—*for swiftness*
M   I am a skilled artist—*for power*
G   I am a fierce boar—*for powers of chieftain-like valour*
NG   I am the roaring of the sea—*for terror*
R   I am a wave of the sea—*for might*

This seems a later version, since the T-month is awarded a sword, not the traditional spear; and the original wording of the D-line is recallled in a gloss; and 'Who but I knows the secrets of the unhewn dolmen?' is omitted. Another change of importance is that the H-month is described in terms of navigation, not flowers. May 14th marked the beginning of the deep-sea fishing in ancient Ireland when the equinoctial gales had subsided and it was safe to put to sea in an ox-hide curragh; but the ascetic meaning of Hawthorn is a reminder of the ban against taking women on a fishing trip. The additions to the poem show, even more clearly than Macalister's text, that it was preserved as a charm for successful fishing both in river and sea; the Druid being paid by the fishermen for repeating it and threatening the water with javelin-vengeance if a curragh were to be lost:—

Whither shall we go? Shall we debate in valley or on peak?
Where shall we dwell? In what nobler land than the isle of Sunset?

Where else shall we walk in peace, to and fro, on fertile ground?
Who but I can take you to where the stream runs, or falls, clearest?

Or who but I tell you the age of the moon?
Who but I can bring you Tethra's cattle from the recesses of the sea?
Who but I can draw Tethra's cattle shoreward?
Who can change the hills, mountains or promontories as I can?

I am a cunning poet who invokes prophecy at the entreaty of seafarers.
Javelins shall be wielded to revenge the loss of our ships.
I sing praises, I prophesy victory.
In closing my poem I desire other preferments, and shall obtain them.

The original five-lined pendant to the poem may have run something like this:

A   *I am the womb of every holt,*
O   *I am the blaze on every hill,*
U   *I am the queen of every hive,*
E   *I am the shield to every head,*
I   *I am the tomb to every hope.*

How or why this alphabet of thirteen consonants gave place to the alphabet of fifteen consonants is another question, the solution of which will be helped by a study of Latin and Greek alphabet legends.

That the first line of the *Song of Amergin* has the variant readings 'stag of seven tines' and 'ox of seven fights' suggests that in Ireland during the Bronze Age, as in Crete and Greece, both stag and bull were sacred to the Great Goddess. In Minoan Crete the bull became dominant as the Minotaur, 'Bull-Minos', but there was also a *Minelaphos*, 'Stag-Minos', who figured in the cult of the Moon-goddess Britomart, and a *Minotragos*, 'Goat-Minos' cult. The antlers found in the burial at New Grange suggest that the stag was the royal beast of the Irish Danaans, and the stag figures prominently in Irish myth: an incident in *The Cattle Raid of Cuailgne*, part of the Cuchulain saga, shows that a guild of deer-priests called 'The Fair Lucky Harps' had their headquarters at Assaroe in Donegal. Oisin was born of the deer-goddess Sadb and at the end of his life, when mounted on the fairy-steed of Niamh of the Golden Hair and sped by the wailing of the Fenians to her island paradise, he was shown a vision: a hornless fawn pursued over the waters of the sea by the red-eared white hounds of Hell. The fawn was himself. There is a parallel to this in the *Romance of Pwyll Prince of Dyfed*: Pwyll goes out hunting and meets Arawn King of Annwn mounted on a pale horse hunting a stag with his white, red-eared hounds. In recognition of Pwyll's courtesy, Arawn, though sending him down to Annwm—for the stag is Pwyll's soul—

permits him to reign there in his stead. Another parallel is in the *Romance of Math the Son of Mathonwy:* Llew Llaw in the company of the faithless Blodeuwedd sees a stag being baited to death: it is his soul, and almost immediately afterwards he is put to death by her lover Gronw.

The fate of the antlered king—of whom Cernunnos, 'the horned one' of Gaul, is a familiar example—is expressed in the early Greek myth of Actaeon whom Artemis metamorphosed into a stag and hunted to death with her dogs. She did this at her *anodos*, or yearly reappearance, when she refreshed her virginity by bathing naked in a sacred fountain; after which she took another lover. The Irish *Garbh Ogh* with her pack of hounds was the same goddess: her diet was venison and eagles' breasts. This ancient myth of the betrayed stag-king survives curiously in the convention, which is British as well as Continental, that gives the cuckold a branching pair of antlers. The May-day stag-mummers of Abbot's Bromley in Staffordshire are akin to the stag-mummers of Syracuse in ancient Sicily, and to judge from an epic fragment concerned with Dionysus, one of the mummers disguised as an Actaeon stag was originally chased and eaten. In the Lycaean precinct of Arcadia the same tradition of the man dressed in deer skins who is chased and eaten survived in Pausanias's day, though the chase was explained as a punishment for trespassing. From Sardinia comes a Bronze Age figurine of a man-stag with horns resembling the foliage of an oak, a short tail, an arrow in one hand and in the other a bow that has turned into a wriggling serpent. His mouth and eyes express an excusable terror at the sight; for the serpent is death. That the stag was part of the Elysian oracular cult is shown in the story of Brut the Trojan's visit to the Island of Leogrecia, where the moon-oracle was given him while sleeping in the newly-flayed hide of a white hart whose blood had been poured on the sacrificial fire.

The stag-cult is far older than the Cretan *Minelaphos*: he is shown in palaeolithic paintings in the Spanish caves of Altamira and in the *Caverne des Trois Frères* at Ariège in the French Pyrenees, dating from at least 20,000 B.C. The Altamiran paintings are the work of the Aurignacian people, who have also left records of their ritual in the caves of Domboshawa, and elsewhere in Southern Rhodesia. At Domboshawa a 'Bushman' painting, containing scores of figures, shows the death of a king who wears an antelope mask and is tightly corseted; as he dies, with arms outflung and one knee upraised, he ejaculates and his seed seems to form a heap of corn. An old priestess lying naked beside a cauldron is either mimicking his agony, or perhaps inducing it by sympathetic magic. Close by, young priestesses dance beside a stream, surrounded by clouds of fruit and heaped baskets; beasts are led off laden with fruit; and a huge bison bull is pacified by a priestess accompanied by an erect python. The cults of stag and bull were evidently combined at Domboshawa; but the stag is likely to have been the more royal beast, since the dying king is given the greater prominence. The cults were also combined by the Aurignacians. In a Dordogne cave painting a bull-man is shown dancing and playing a musical instrument shaped like a bow.

The Minotragos goat-cult in Crete seems to have been intermediate between the cults of Minelaphos and Minotaur. Amalthea, the nurse of Cretan Zeus, was a goat. The Goddess Athene carried an *aegis* ('goat-skin') shield, made it was said from Amalthea's hide which had been previously used by her father Zeus as a prophylactic coat. The Goddess Libya appeared in triad to Jason on the shores of Lake Triton, Athene's birth-place, when the *Argo* was landlocked there, and was clad in goat-skins; she thereby identified herself with Aega, sister of Helice ('willow branch') and daughter of a king of Crete—Aega who was the human double of the goat Amalthea; and with Athene herself. The tradition of the Libyan origin of Athene is supported by a comparison of Greek and Roman methods of augury. In Libya the year begins in the autumn with the winter rains and the arrival of birds from the North; but in Northern Europe and the Black Sea area it begins in Spring with the arrival of birds from the South. In most Greek states the year began in the autumn and the Greek augurs faced north when observing birds, presumably because they derived their tradition from the birth-place of Athene, patroness of augury. On the other hand, the Roman augurs faced south, presumably because the Dardanians (whose patrician descendants in the early Roman Republic were alone permitted to take auguries) had migrated from the Black Sea area where birds arrive from Palestine and Syria in the Spring. The Roman year began in the Spring.

The goat-Dionysus, or Pan, was a powerful deity in Palestine. He may have come there from Libya by way of Egypt or taken a roundabout northern route by way of Crete, Thrace, Asia Minor and Syria. The Day of Atonement scape-goat was a left-handed sacrifice to him under the name of Azazel, and the source of the Jordan was a grotto sacred to him as Baal Gad, the goat king, eponymous ancestor of the tribe of Gad. The prohibition in *Deuteronomy XIV* against seething a kid in its mother's milk is puzzling only if sentimentally read; it is clearly written in the severe style of the remainder of the chapter, which begins with a prohibition against self-disfigurement at funerals, and directed against a eucharistical rite no longer tolerated by the priesthood of Jehovah. The clue is to be found in the well-known Orphic formula:

Like a kid I have fallen into milk

which was a password for initiates when they reached Hades and were challenged by the guardians of the dead. They had become one with The Kid, that is to say the immortal Dionysus, originally Cretan Zagreus or Zeus, by partaking of his flesh, and with the Goat-goddess, his mother, in whose cauldron and milk he had been seethed.[1] A song about the birth of the gods on one of the recently discovered Ras Shamra tablets contains an express injunction to seethe a kid in its mother's milk.

The prohibition in *Deuteronomy* explains the glib and obviously artificial myth of Esau, Jacob, Rebeccah and the blessing of Isaac, which is introduced into *Genesis XXVII* to justify the usurpation by the Jacob tribe of priestly and royal prerogatives belonging to the Edomites. The religious picture iconotropically[2] advanced in support of the myth seems to have illustrated the kid-eating ceremony in Azazel's honour. Two celebrants wearing goatskin disguises are shown at a seething cauldron presided over by the priestess (Rebeccah), one of them with bow and quiver (Esau) the other (Jacob) being initiated into the mysteries by the old leader of the fraternity (Isaac) who whispers the secret formula into his ear, blesses him and hands him—rather than is handed by him—a piece of the kid to eat. The ceremony probably included a mock-slaughter and resurrection of the initiate, and this would account for the passage at the close of the chapter where Esau murderously pursues Jacob, Rebeccah directs affairs and the orgiastic 'daughters of Heth' in Cretan costume stand by. The two kids are probably an error: the same kid is shown twice, first being taken from its mother, and then being plunged into the cauldron of milk.

Nonnus, the Orphic writer, explains the shift in Crete from the goat to the bull-sacrifice by saying that Zagreus, or Dionysus, was a horned infant who occupied the throne of Zeus for a day. The Titans tore him in pieces and ate him after he had raced through his changes of shape: Zeus with the goat-skin coat, Cronos making rain, an inspired youth, a lion, a horse, a horned snake, a tiger, a bull. It was as a bull that the Titans ate him. The Persian Mithras was also eaten in bull form.

There seems to have been a goat-cult in Ireland before the arrival of the Danaans and Milesians, for in a passage in the *Book of the Dun Cow* 'goat-heads' are a sort of demon associated with *leprechauns,* pigmies, and the Fomorians, or African aborigines.[3] But by the time of the Ulster hero

---

[1] I find that I have been anticipated in this explanation by Maimonides ('Rambam'), the twelfth-century Spanish Jew who reformed the Judaic religion and was, incidentally, Saladin's physician-royal. In his *Guide to the Erring* he reads the text as an injunction against taking part in Ashtaroth worship.

[2] In the preface to my *King Jesus* I define iconotropy as a technique of deliberate mis-representation by which ancient ritual icons are twisted in meaning in order to confirm a profound change of the existent religious system—usually a change from matriarchal to patriarchal—and the new meanings are embodied in myth. I adduce examples from the myths of Pasiphaë, Oedipus, and Lot.

[3] Demons and bogeys are invariably the reduced gods or priests of a superseded religion: for example the *Empusae* and *Lamiae* of Greece who in Aristophanes's day were regarded as emissaries of the Triple Goddess Hecate. The Lamiae, beautiful women who used to seduce,

Cuchulain, the traditional date of whose death is 2 A.D., the royal bull-cult was well established. His destiny was bound up with that of a brown bull-calf, son of Queen Maeve's famous Brown Bull. The Morrigan, the Fate-goddess, when she first met Cuchulain, warned him that only while the calf was still a yearling would he continue to live. The central episode in the Cuchulain saga is the *War of the Bulls,* fought between the armies of Maeve and her husband King Ailell as the result of an idle quarrel about two bulls. At the close of it, the Brown Bull, Cuchulain's other self, kills his rival, the White-horned, which considering itself too noble to serve a woman, has deserted Maeve's herd for the herd of Ailell; it then goes mad with pride, charges a rock and dashes out its brains. It is succeeded by its calf, and Cuchulain dies.

The bull-cult was also established in Wales at an early date. In a Welsh poetic dialogue contained in the *Black Book of Carmarthen,* Gwyddno Garanhir, Elphin's father, describes the hero Gwyn as: 'A bull of conflict, quick to disperse an embattled host', and 'bull of conflict' here and in later poems seems to have been a sacred title rather than a complimentary metaphor; as 'hawk' and 'eagle' also were.

The War of the Bulls contains an instance of the intricate language of myth: the Brown Bull and the White-horned were really royal swine-herds who had the power of changing their shapes. It seems that in ancient times swine-herds had an altogether different standing from that conveyed in the parable of the Prodigal Son: to be a swine-herd was originally to be a priest in the service of the Death-goddess whose sacred beast was a pig.[1] *The War of the Bulls* is introduced by the *Proceedings of the Grand Bardic Academy,* a seventh-century satire against the greed and arrogance of the ruling caste of bards, apparently composed by some member of an earlier oracular fraternity which had been dispossessed with the advent of Christianity. The leading character here is Marvan, royal swineherd to

enervate and suck the blood of travellers, had been the orgiastic priestesses of the Libyan Snake-goddess Lamia; and the Empusae, demons with one leg of brass and one ass's leg were relics of the Set cult—the Lilim, or Children of Lilith, the devotees of the Hebrew Owl-goddess, who was Adam's first wife, were ass-haunched.

[1] Evidence of a similar function in early Greece is the conventional epithet *dīos,* 'divine' applied in the *Odyssey* to the swine-herd Eumaeus. Because of the horror in which swine-herds were held by the Jews and Egyptians and the contempt in which, thanks to the Prodigal Son, they have long been held in Europe, the word is usually mistranslated 'honest or worthy' though admitted to be an *hapax legomenon.* It is true that except on one night of the year—the full moon that fell nearest to the winter solstice, when the pig was sacrificed to Isis and Osiris and its flesh eaten by every Egyptian—the taboo on any contact with pigs was so strong that swine-herds though full-blooded Egyptians (according to Herodotus) were avoided like the plague and forced to marry within their own caste; but this was a tribute to their sanctity rather than anything else. The public hangman is similarly avoided in France and England because he has courageously undertaken, in the interests of public morality, a peculiarly horrible and thankless trade.

King Guaire of Connaught; he may be identified with Morvran ('black raven') son of the White Sow-goddess Cerridwen, who appears as Afagddu in the similar Welsh satire *The Romance of Taliesin*. In revenge for the loss of a magical white boar, at once his physician, music-maker and messenger, which the ruling bards have persuaded Guaire to slaughter, he routs them in a combat of wit and reduces them to silence and ignominy; Seanchan Torpest, the President of the Academy, addresses him as 'Chief Prophet of Heaven and Earth'. There is a hint in the *Romance of Branwen* that the swine-herds of Matholwch King of Ireland were magicians, with a power of foreseeing the future. And this hint is expanded in *Triad* 56 which attributes to Coll ap Collfrewr, the magician, one of 'the Three Powerful Swine-herds of the Isle of Britain', the introduction into Britain of wheat and barley. But the credit was not really his. The name of the White Sow whom he tended at Dallwr in Cornwall and who went about Wales with gifts of grain, bees and her own young, was Hen Wen, 'the Old White One'. Her gift to Maes Gwenith ('Wheatfield') in Gwent was three grains of wheat and three bees. She was, of course, the Goddess Cerridwen in beast disguise. (The story is contained in three series of Triads printed in the *Myvyrian Archaiology*.)

The unpleasant side of her nature was shown by her gift to the people of Arvon of a savage kitten, which grew up to be one of the Three Plagues of Anglesey, 'the Palug Cat'. Cerridwen then is a Cat-goddess as well as a Sow-goddess. This links her with the Cat-as-corn-spirit mentioned by Sir James Frazer as surviving in harvest festivals in north and north-eastern Germany, and in most parts of France and with the monster Chapalu of French Arthurian legend.

There was also a Cat-cult in Ireland. A 'Slender Black Cat reclining upon a chair of old silver' had an oracular cave-shrine in Connaught at Clogh-magh-righ-cat, now Clough, before the coming of St. Patrick. This cat gave very vituperative answers to inquirers who tried to deceive her and was apparently an Irish equivalent of the Egyptian Cat-goddess Pasht. Egyptian cats were slender, black, long-legged and small-headed. Another seat of the Irish cat-cult was Knowth, a burial in Co. Meath of about the same date as New Grange. In *The Proceedings of the Grand Bardic Academy* the Knowth burial chamber is said to have been the home of the King-cat Irusan, who was as large as a plough-ox and once bore Seanchan Torpest, the chief-ollave of Ireland, away on its back in revenge for a satire. In his *Poetic Astronomy*, Hyginus identifies Pasht with the White Goddess by recording that when Typhon suddenly appeared in Greece—but whether he is referring to an invasion or to a volanic eruption, such as destroyed most of the island of Thera is not clear—the gods fled, disguised in bestial forms: 'Mercury into an ibis, Apollo into a crane, a Thracian bird, Diana into a cat.'

The Old White Sow's gift to the people of Rhiwgyverthwch was a wolf cub which also became famous. The Wolf-as-corn-spirit survives in roughly the same area as the Cat-as-corn-spirit; and in the island of Rügen the woman who binds the last sheaf is called 'The Wolf' and must bite the lady of the house and the stewardess, who placate her with a large piece of meat. So Cerridwen was a Wolf-goddess too, like Artemis. It looks as if she came to Britain between 2500–2000 B.C. with the New Stone Age long-headed agriculturists from North Africa.

Why the cat, pig, and wolf were considered particularly sacred to the Moon-goddess is not hard to discover. Wolves howl to the moon and feed on corpse-flesh, their eyes shine in the dark, and they haunt wooded mountains. Cats' eyes similarly shine in the dark, they feed on mice (symbol of pestilence), mate openly and walk inaudibly, they are prolific but eat their own young, and their colours vary, like the moon, between white, reddish and black. Pigs also vary between white, reddish and black, feed on corpse-flesh, are prolific but eat their own young, and their tusks are crescent-shaped.

Chapter Thirteen

PALAMEDES AND THE CRANES

What interests me most in conducting this argument is the difference that is constantly appearing between the poetic and prosaic methods of thought. The prosaic method was invented by the Greeks of the Classical age as an insurance against the swamping of reason by mythographic fancy. It has now become the only legitimate means of transmitting useful knowledge. And in England, as in most other mercantile countries, the current popular view is that 'music' and old-fashioned diction are the only characteristics of poetry which distinguish it from prose: that every poem has, or should have, a precise single-strand prose equivalent. As a result, the poetic faculty is atrophied in every educated person who does not privately struggle to cultivate it: very much as the faculty of understanding pictures is atrophied in the Bedouin Arab. (T. E. Lawrence once showed a coloured crayon sketch of an Arab Sheikh to the Sheikh's own clansmen. They passed it from hand to hand, but the nearest guess as to what it represented came from a man who took the sheikh's foot to be the horn of a buffalo.) And from the inability to think poetically—to resolve speech into its original images and rhythms and re-combine these on several simultaneous levels of thought into a multiple sense—derives the failure to think clearly in prose. In prose one thinks on only one level at a time, and no combination of words needs to contain more than a single sense; nevertheless the images resident in words must be securely related if the passage is to have any bite. This simple need is forgotten, what passes for simple prose nowadays is a mechanical stringing together of stereotyped word-groups, without regard for the images contained in them. The mechanical style, which began in the counting-house, has now infiltrated into the university, some of its most zombiesque instances occurring in the works of eminent scholars and divines.

Mythographic statements which are perfectly reasonable to the few poets who can still think and talk in poetic shorthand seem either non-sensical or childish to nearly all literary scholars. Such statements, I mean, as: 'Mercury invented the alphabet after watching the flight of cranes', or 'Menw ab Teirgwaedd saw three rowan-rods growing out of the mouth of

Einigan Fawr with every kind of knowledge and science written on them'. The best that the scholars have yet done for the poems of Gwion is 'wild and sublime'; and they never question the assumption that he, his colleagues and his public were people of either stunted or undisciplined intelligence.

The joke is that the more prose-minded the scholar the more capable he is supposed to be of interpreting ancient poetic meaning, and that no scholar dares to set himself up as an authority on more than one narrow subject for fear of incurring the dislike and suspicion of his colleagues. To know only one thing well is to have a barbaric mind: civilization implies the graceful relation of all varieties of experience to a central humane system of thought. The present age is peculiarly barbaric: introduce, say, a Hebrew scholar to an ichthyologist or an authority on Danish place names and the pair of them would have no single topic in common but the weather or the war (if there happened to be a war in progress, which is usual in this barbaric age). But that so many scholars are barbarians does not much matter so long as a few of them are ready to help with their specialized knowledge the few independent thinkers, that is to say the poets, who try to keep civilization alive. The scholar is a quarry-man, not a builder, and all that is required of him is that he should quarry cleanly. He is the poet's insurance against factual error. It is easy enough for the poet in this hopelessly muddled and inaccurate modern world to be misled into false etymology, anachronism and mathematical absurdity by trying to be what he is not. His function is truth, whereas the scholar's is fact. Fact is not to be gainsaid; one may put it in this way, that fact is a Tribune of the People with no legislative right, but only the right of veto. Fact is not truth, but a poet who wilfully defies fact cannot achieve truth.

The story about Mercury and the cranes occurs in the *Fables* of Caius Julius Hyginus who, according to the well-informed Suetonius, was a native of Spain, a freedman of the Emperor Augustus, the Curator of the Palatine Library, and a friend of the poet Ovid. Like Ovid, Hyginus ended his life in Imperial disfavour. If he is the learned author of the *Fables* attributed to him, they have since been abbreviated and botched by unlearned editors; yet they are admitted to contain ancient mythological matter of great importance, not found elsewhere.

In his last Fable (277) Hyginus records:

1. that the Fates invented the seven letters: *Alpha, [Omicron], Upsilon, Eta, Iota, Beta,* and *Tau*.
   Or, alternatively, that Mercury invented them after watching the flight of cranes 'which make letters as they fly'.
2. that Palamedes, son of Nauplius, invented eleven others.

3. that Epicharmus of Sicily added *Theta* and *Chi*
    (*or Psi* and *Pi*).
4. that Simonides added *Omega, Epsilon, Zeta and Psi*
    (*or Omega, Epsilon, Zeta and Phi*).

There is no word here about Cadmus the Phoenician, who is usually credited with the invention of the Greek alphabet, the *characters* of which are indisputably borrowed from the Phoenician alphabet. The statement about Epicharmus reads nonsensically, unless 'of Sicily' is a stupid editorial gloss that has intruded into the text. Simonides was a well-known sixth-century B.C. Greek poet who used the Cadmean Greek alphabet and did introduce certain new characters into his manuscripts, later adopted throughout Greece; and Epicharmus of Sicily, the well-known writer of comedies who lived not long afterwards and was a member of the family of Asclepiads at Cos, evidently seemed to the editor of the *Fables* a likely co-worker with Simonides. The original legend, however, probably refers to another, far earlier, Epicharmus, an ancestor of the writer of comedies. The Asclepiads traced their descent to Apollo's son Asclepius, or Aesculapius, the physician god of Delphi and Cos, and claimed to inherit valuable therapeutic secrets from him. Two Asclepiads are mentioned in the *Iliad* as having been physicians to the Greeks in the siege of Troy.

As for Palamedes, son of Nauplius, he is credited by Philostratus the Lemnian, and by the scholiast on Euripides's *Orestes,* with the invention not only of the alphabet, but also of lighthouses, measures, scales, the disc, and the 'art of posting sentinels'. He took part in the Trojan War as an ally of the Greeks and at his death was granted a hero-shrine on the Mysian coast of Asia Minor opposite Lesbos.

The Three Fates are a divided form of the Triple Goddess, and in Greek legend appear also as the Three Grey Ones and the Three Muses.

Thus, the first two statements made by Hyginus account for the 'thirteen letters' which, according to some authorities (Diodorus Siculus says) formed the 'Pelasgian alphabet' before Cadmus increased them to sixteen. Diodorus evidently means thirteen consonants, not thirteen letters in all which would not have been sufficient. Other authorities held that there had been only twelve of them. Aristotle, at any rate gives the numbers of letters in the first Greek alphabet as thirteen consonants and five vowels and his list of letters corresponds exactly with the *Beth-Luis-Nion,* except that he gives *Zeta* for H-aspirate and *Phi* for F—but, in the case of *Phi,* at least, early epigraphic evidence is against him. This is not the only reference to the Pelasgian alphabet. Eustathius, the Byzantine grammarian, quotes an ancient scholiast on *Iliad, II,* 841 to the effect that the Pelasgians were called *Dioi* ('divine') because they alone of all the Greeks preserved the use of letters after the Deluge—the Deluge meaning to the Greeks the one survived by Deucalion and Pyrrha. Pyrrha, 'the red one', is perhaps the Goddess-mother of the Puresati, or Pulesati, the Philistines.

The Lycians of Asia Minor are described by Herodotus as having come from Crete; so are their neighbours the Carians, who claimed to be kin to the Lydians and Mysians and spoke much the same barbaric, that is to say, non-Greek language. The Carians, formerly members of the Minoan Empire, had dominated the Aegean between the fall of Cnossos in 1400 B.C. and the Dorian invasion of 1050 B.C. Herodotus found the Lycians the least Grecianized of these four nations and recorded that they reckoned descent through the mother, not the father. Female independence of male tutelage and matrilinear descent were characteristic of all peoples of Cretan stock; and the same system survived in parts of Crete long after its conquest by the Greeks. Firmicus Maternus reported it in the fourth century A.D.[1] The Lydians retained another vestige of the system—girls habitually prostituted themselves before marriage, and then disposed of their earnings and their persons as they thought fit.

Palamedes, then, ruled over the Mysians, who were of Cretan stock, but he had a Greek father; his name means perhaps 'Mindful of the Ancient One', and he assisted the Three Fates (the Three Muses) in the composition of the Greek alphabet. But it was well known to the ancients, as it is to us, that all the inventions credited to Palamedes originated in Crete. It follows that a Greek alphabet, based on a Cretan not a Phoenician model, was raised from five vowels and thirteen consonants to five vowels and fifteen consonants, by Epicharmus, an early Asclepiad.

But why did Hyginus not specify the eleven consonants of Palamedes, as he specified the original seven letters and the additions by Epicharmus and Simonides? We must first find out why he quotes *Beta* and *Tau* as the two consonants invented by the Three Fates at the same time as the five vowels.

Simonides, a native of Ceos, introduced into Athens, where he was domiciled, the double-consonants *Psi* and *Xi*, the distinction between the vowels *Omicron* and *Omega* (short and long O), and the distinction between the vowels *Eta* and *Epsilon* (long and short E). These changes were not, however, publicly adopted there until the archonship of Euclides (403 B.C.). To *Eta*, when thus distinguished from *Epsilon*, was allotted the character H, which had hitherto belonged to the aspirate H; and the aspirate H became merely a 'rough breathing', a miniature decrescent moon, while its absence in a word beginning with a vowel was denoted by

---

[1] In Crete today a pre-marital love-affair has only two possible results: a knife between the lover's shoulders, or immediate marriage. The German Panzer Grenadiers stationed in Crete during World War II had to go on leave to Mount Athos if they wanted sexual diversion.

a 'smooth breathing', a crescent moon. The *Digamma* F (which had a V sound) had disappeared as an Attic character long before the time of Simonides; and in many words was supplanted by the letter *Phi*, invented to represent the FF sound which had hitherto been spelt PH. But the *Digamma* was retained for some generations longer by the Aeolian Greeks and disappeared among the Dorians (the last to use it) during this same archonship of Euclides—at about the same time, in fact, as Gwydion and Amathaon won the Battle of the Trees in Britain.

This is a queer business. Though it is possible that the V sound had altogether dropped out of ordinary Greek speech and that therefore the *Digamma* F was an unnecessary letter, this is by no means certain; and the aspirate H was certainly still an integral part of the language. Why then was the aspirate supplanted by *Eta?* Why was a new character not found for the *Eta* sound? Why were the unnecessary double-consonants *Psi,* previously written *Pi-Sigma,* and *Xi,* previously written *Kappa-Sigma,* introduced at the same time? Only religious doctrine can have accounted for this awkward change.

One of the reasons is given in the same fable. Hyginus connects the four additional letters of Simonides with Apollo's zither—*Apollo in cithaera ceteras literas adjecit.* This means, I think, that each of the seven strings of the zither, originally Cretan but brought from Asia Minor to Greece about 676 B.C. by Terpander of Lesbos, now had a letter allotted to it, and that twenty-four, the new number of letters in the alphabet, had a sacred significance in the therapeutic music with which Apollo and his son Aesculapius were honoured in their island shrines. Simonides, it must be noted, belonged to a Cean bardic guild in the service of Dionysus who, according to Plutarch, a priest of Delphian Apollo, was 'also at home in Delphi'. Both Apollo and Dionysus, as we have seen, were gods of the solar year. So were Aesculapius and Hercules; and this was an age of religious amalgamation.

Hyginus says that the original thirteen-consonant alphabet was taken by Mercury into Egypt, brought back by Cadmus into Greece, and thence taken by Evander the Arcadian into Italy, where his mother Carmenta (the Muse) adapted them to the Latin alphabet of fifteen letters. He describes this Mercury as the same one who invented athletic games: in other words, he was a Cretan, or of Cretan stock. And Mercury in Egypt was Thoth, the God whose symbol was a crane-like white ibis, who invented writing and who also reformed the calendar. The story begins to make good historical sense. Hyginus has perhaps drawn it from an Etruscan source: for the Etruscans, or Tyrrhenians, were of Cretan stock, and held the crane in reverence. Cranes fly in V-formation and the characters of all early alphabets, nicked with a knife on the rind of boughs—as Hesiod wrote his poems—or on clay tablets, were naturally angular.

So Hyginus knew that the five vowels of the Arcadian alphabet belonged to an earlier religious system than the seven vowels of the Classical Greek alphabet, and that in Italy these five vowels were sacred to the Goddess Carmenta; also that in Italy a fifteen-consonant sacred alphabet was used some six centuries before the Greek twenty-four-letter 'Dorian' alphabet from which all Italian alphabets—Etruscan, Umbrian, Oscan, Faliscan and Latin—are known to derive. In this, Hyginus is supported by Pliny who states positively in his *Natural History* that the first Latin alphabet was a Pelasgian one. He does not mention his authority but it was probably Gnaeus Gellius, the well-informed second-century B.C. historian, whom he quotes in the same passage as holding that Mercury first invented letters in Egypt and that Palamedes invented weights and measures. One must assume from the lack of inscriptional evidence in support of Hyginus's record that this alphabet was confined, as the Beth-Luis-Nion originally was, to use in deaf-and-dumb signalling. About Carmenta we know from the historian Dionysus Periergetes that she gave oracles to Hercules and lived to the age of 110 years. 110 was a canonical number, the ideal age which every Egyptian wished to reach and the age at which, for example, the patriarch Joseph died. The 110 years were made up of twenty-two Etruscan *lustra* of five years each; and 110 years composed the 'cycle' taken over from the Etruscans by the Romans. At the end of each cycle they corrected irregularities in the solar calendar by intercalation and held Saecular Games. The secret sense of 22—sacred numbers were never chosen haphazardly— is that it is the measure of the circumference of the circle when the diameter is 7. This proportion, now known as *pi*, is no longer a religious secret; and is used today only as a rule-of-thumb formula, the real mathematical value of *pi* being a decimal figure which nobody has yet been able to work out because it goes on without ever ending, as $\frac{22}{7}$ does, in a neat recurrent sequence. Seven lustra add up to thirty-five years, and thirty-five at Rome was the age at which a man was held to reach his prime and might be elected Consul. (The same age was fixed upon by a Classically-minded Convention as the earliest at which an American might be elected President of the United States.) The nymph Egeria, the oak-queen who instructed King Numa of Rome, was 'the fourth Carmenta'. If the age of each Carmenta—or course of Sibylline priestesses—was 110 years, Numa reigned not earlier than 330 years after Evander's arrival in Italy, the traditional date of which is some sixty years before the Fall of Troy, i.e., 1243 B.C.

Evander was banished from Arcadia because he had killed his father; and this implies the supersession of the Triple Goddess, Carmenta or Thetis, by Olympian Zeus. Thetis was the Aeolian Greek name for Carmenta, at whose prompting Evander had struck the blow; and for a king to kill his father (or kingly predecessor) at the prompting of his Goddess mother was common in Italy and Greece at that period. The traditional reason for Partholan's Danaan invasion of Ireland and Brutus's Dardanian invasion of Britain is the same: both were banished for parricide. The date, 1243 B.C., corresponds with that given by the later Greeks for the Achaean invasion, namely 1250 B.C. This was not the original invasion but, apparently, a southward movement, under Dorian pressure, of Achaeans settled in North-western Greece. The story of Pelias and Neleus, sons of Poseidon who dispossessed the Minyans of Iolcos in Thessaly and Pylos in the Western Peloponnese, refers to this invasion which resulted in the institution of Olympianism.

But has not the story of the invention of the pre-Cadmean alphabet of Palamedes, which was taken to Italy by Evander the Arcadian before the Dorian invasion of Greece, been lying concealed all this time in the confusingly iconotropic myth of Perseus and the Gorgon Medusa? Cannot the Palamedes story be recovered intact by the simple method of restoring the Perseus myth to iconographic form, and then re-interpreting the iconographs which compose it?

The myth is that Perseus was sent to cut off the head of the snaky-locked Gorgon Medusa, a rival of the Goddess Athene, whose baleful look turned men into stone; and that he could not accomplish the task until he had gone to the three Graeae, 'Grey Ones', the three old sisters of the Gorgons who had only one eye and one tooth between them, and by stealing eye and tooth had blackmailed them into telling him where the grove of the Three Nymphs was to be found. From the Three Nymphs he then obtained winged sandals like those of Hermes, a bag to put the Gorgon's head into, and a helmet of invisibility. Hermes also kindly gave him a sickle; and Athene gave him a mirror and showed him a picture of Medusa so that he would recognize her. He threw the tooth of the Three Grey Ones, and some say the eye also, into Lake Triton, to break their power, and flew on to Tartessus where the Gorgons lived in a grove on the borders of the ocean; there he cut off the sleeping Medusa's head with the sickle, first looking into the mirror so that the petrifying charm should be broken, thrust the head into his bag, and flew home pursued by other Gorgons.

The Three Nymphs must be understood as the Three Graces, that is to say, the Triple Love-goddess. The Graeae were also known as the Phorcides, which means the daughters of Phorcus, or Orcus, and according to the Scholiast on Aeschylus had the form of swans—which is probably an error for cranes, due to a misreading of a sacred picture, since cranes and swans, equally sacred birds, are alike in flying in V-formation. They were, in fact, the Three Fates. Phorcus, or Orcus, became a synonym for the Underworld; it is the same word as *porcus*, a pig, the beast sacred to the Death-goddess, and perhaps as *Parcae*, a title of the Three Fates, usually called Moirae, 'the distributors'. *Orc* is 'pig' in Irish; hence the *Orcades*, or *Orkneys*, abodes of the Death-goddess. Phorcus was also reputedly the father of the Gorgon Medusa, whom the Argives in Pasesanias's day described as a beautiful Libyan queen decapitated by their ancestor Perseus after a battle with her armies, and who may therefore be identified with the Libyan snake-goddess Lamia (Neith) whom Zeus betrayed and who afterwards killed children.

Imagine the pictures on a vase. First, a naked young man cautiously approaching three shrouded women of whom the central one presents him with an eye and a tooth; the other two point upwards to three cranes flying in a V-formation from right to left. Next, the same young man, wearing winged sandals and holding a sickle, stands pensively under a willow tree. (Willows are sacred to the Goddess, and cranes breed in willow groves.) Next, another group of three beautiful young women sit side by side in a grove with the same young man standing before them. Above them three cranes fly in the reverse direction. One presents him with winged sandals, another with a bag, the third with a winged helmet. Next, various sea-monsters are shown and a helmeted Sea-goddess, with a trident, holding a mirror in which a Gorgon's face is reflected; and the young man is seen flying, bag and sickle in hand, towards a grove with his head turned to look at the mirror. From the bag peeps out the Gorgon's head. The tooth and eye are painted, enlarged, on either side of him, so that he seems to have thrown them away. He is followed by three menacing winged women with Gorgon faces.

This completes the pictures on the vase and one comes again to the first group.

The myth in its familiar form, like that of Zeus's betrayal of Lamia, is descriptive of the breaking of the Argive Triple Goddess's power by the first wave of Achaeans, figured as Perseus, 'the destroyer'. But the original meaning of the iconographs seems to be this: Mercury, or Hermes, or Car, or Palamedes, or Thoth, or whatever his original name was, is given poetic sight by the Shrouded Ones (his mother Carmenta, or Maia, or Danaë, or Phorcis, or Medusa, or whatever her original name was, in her prophetic aspect of the Three Fates) and the power to take omens from the flight of birds; also the power to understand the alphabetic secret represented by the cranes. The tooth was a divinatory instrument, like the one under which Fionn used to put his thumb—after eating the salmon of knowledge—whenever he needed magical counsel. Carmenta has invented the alphabet, but is assigning the thirteen consonants to her son, while keeping the five vowels sacred to herself. He goes off with his sickle, which is moon-shaped in her honour, like the sickle which the Gallic Arch-Druid subsequently used for cutting mistletoe; and will presently cut the first alphabet twig from the grove; in front of which the Goddess, unshrouded now, and playing the nymph not the crone, is discovered sitting in gracious trinity. She gives him as his regalia a winged helmet and winged sandals, symbolizing the swiftness of poetic thought, and a bag in which to keep his letters well hidden.

Next, she is revealed as Athene, the Goddess of Wisdom, who was born on the shores of Lake Triton in Libya and seems to have been originally, before her monstrous rebirth from Father Zeus's head, the Libyan Triple Goddess Neith, whom the Greeks called Lamia, or Libya. Peeping from his bag there is now a Gorgon's head, which is merely an ugly mask assumed by priestesses on ceremonial occasions to frighten away trespassers; at the same time they made hissing noises, which accountf for Medusa's snake locks. There never was a real Gorgon (as J. E. Harrisos was the first to point out); there was only a prophylactic ugly face forn malized into a mask. The ugly face at the mouth of the bag symbolize- that the secrets of the alphabet, which are the real contents, are not to bs divulged or misused. A Gorgon's mask was similarly put on the doors oe all ovens and kilns in ancient Greece to frighten away the bogeys (and inquisitive children) who might spoil the baking. The winged 'Gorgons' in this picture are escorting, not pursuing, Mercury: they are the Triple Goddess again who, by wearing these ritual masks, is protecting him from profane eyes. She is also shown on the earth holding out her mirror with a Gorgon's face reflected in it, to protect him in his poetic flight. He is taking the bag to Tartessus, the Aegean colony on the Guadalquivir; whence presumably the Milesians would carry it to Ireland. Gades, now Cadiz, the principal city of Tartessus, is said by the Augustan historian Velleius Paterculus to have been founded in 1100 B.C., thirteen years before the foundation of Utica in North Africa. Perseus' flight was displayed in gold and silver inlay on the Shield of Hercules, as extravagantly described by Hesiod; who places it between a scene of the Muses singing to a lyre near a dolphin-haunted sea, and one of the Three Fates standing outside a populous seven-gated city. If this city is his own seven-gated Thebes, then the icon which Hesiod has misread is a Boeotian variant of the Mercury myth, and the hero with the tasselled alphabet-bag and the attendant Gorgons is Cadmus the Theban.

Mercury arrived safely at Tartessus, to judge from a cryptic remark by Pausanias (I, 35, 8) that 'there is a tree at Gades that takes diverse forms', which seems to refer to the tree-alphabet. Gades (Cadiz) is built on Leon, an island of Tartessus; the older city was on the western shore and included a famous temple of Cronos mentioned by Strabo. It is likely that the island was once, like Pharos, both a sepulchral island and a trading depôt. Pherecydes guessed that it was the original 'Red Island', Erytheia, over which three-bodied Geryon ruled, but on the insufficient ground that the pasture there was very rich and that Hercules had an ancient shrine on the eastern shore. Pausanias (*X*, 4, 6) records the more plausible legend that Leon was originally owned by the Giant Tityus who, as will be shown in Chapter Sixteen, was really Cronos—the god of the middle, or fool's finger, consigned to Tartarus by Zeus. (Titias whom Hercules killed and Tityus whom Zeus killed are doublets.)

The shrine of Hercules seems to have been set up by the colonists of 1100 B.C., some four hundred years before Phoenician colonists came there from Tyre, having been ordered by an oracle to settle near the Pillars of Hercules. The Phoenicians subsequently worshipped Cronos as Moloch and Hercules as Melkarth. Strabo quotes Poseidonius for holding that the Pillars of Hercules were not, as was vulgarly supposed, the two heights of Gibraltar and Ceuta, but two pillars set up before his shrine; and I have suggested in my *King Jesus* (Chapter XVI) that such columns were connected with the secret of the Pelasgian alphabet. So it is likely that the pre-Phoenician Hercules of Tartessus was Palamedes, or the lion-skinned God Ogmios: whom the Irish credited with the invention of the alphabet that they 'had out of Spain' and whom Gwion, in his Elegy on 'Ercwlf', celebrates as a planter of alphabetic pillars. The people of Tartessus were famous in Classical times for the respect they paid to old men, and Ogmios according to Lucian was represented as an aged Hercules. That the Gorgons lived in a grove at Tartessus can mean only that they had an alphabetic secret to guard. This Ogmian Hercules was also worshipped by the early Latins. King Juba II of Mauretania, who was also an honorary *duumvir* of Gades, is quoted by Plutarch (*Roman Questions* 59) as his authority for saying that Hercules and the Muses once shared an altar because he had taught Evander's people the alphabet. This tallies with Hyginus's account of how Carmenta, the Triple Muse, taught Evander, and Dionysus Periergetes' account of how she 'gave oracles to Hercules'.

Isidore, Archbishop of Seville, who died in 636 A.D. , wrote an encyclopaedic work called *Twenty Books Concerning Origins or Etymologies*, based on a wide, if uncritical, study of Christian and pagan literature, which is the most valuable repository of Iberian tradition extant. In it he treats of the invention of the alphabet. He does not present Palamedes or Hercules or Ogma or Mercury or Cadmus as the original benefactor, but the Goddess herself and names Greece as the land of origin:

Aegyptiorum litteras Isis regina, Inachis [sic] regis filia, de Graecia veniens in Aegyptum repperit et Aegyptis tradidit.

As for the Egyptian alphabet, Queen Isis, daughter of King Inachus, coming from Greece to Egypt brought them with her and gave them to the Egyptians.

Originum I, iii (4–10).

Inachus, a river-god and legendary king of Argos, was the father both of the Goddess Io, who became Isis when she reached Egypt, and of the hero Phoroneus, founder of the Pelasgian race, who has been already identified with the God Bran, *alias* Cronos. Isidore was a compatriot of Hyginus (who reported the legend of Mercury's return to Greece from Egypt with the Pelasgian alphabet); he distinguishes the Egyptian alphabet both from the hieroglyphic and demotic scripts, and ascribes the invention of the ordinary Greek alphabet to the Phoenicians.

What material Mercury's bag was made of, can be discovered in the parallel myth of Manannan, son of Lyr, a Goidelic Sun-hero, predecessor of Fionn and Cuchulain, who carried the Treasures of the Sea (i.e., the alphabet secret of the Peoples of the Sea) in a bag made of the skin of a crane; and in the myth of Mider, a Goidelic Underworld-god, corresponding with the British Arawn ('Eloquence') King of Annwm, who lived in a castle in Manannan's Isle of Man with three cranes at his gate whose duty was to warn off travellers, croaking out: 'Do not enter—keep away—pass by!' Perseus's bag must have been a crane-bag, for the crane was sacred to Athene and to Artemis, her counterpart at Ephesus, as well as being the inspiration for Hermes's invention of letters. The flying Gorgons, then, are cranes with Gorgon-faces,[1] and watch over the secrets of the crane-bag, itself protected by a Gorgon head. It is not known what sort of a dance the Crane Dance was that, according to Plutarch, Theseus introduced into Delos except that it was performed around a horned altar and represented the circles that coiled and uncoiled in the Labyrinth. My guess is that it imitated the fluttering love-dance of courting cranes, and that each movement consisted of nine steps and a leap. As Polwart says in his *Flyting with Montgomery* (1605):

> *The crane must aye*
> *Take nine steps ere shee flie.*

The nine steps prove her sacred to the Triple Goddess; and so does her neck, feathered white and black with reddish skin showing through, or (in the case of the Numidian, or Balearic, crane) with red wattles. Cranes make their spectacular migrations from the Tropic of Cancer to the Arctic Circle and back twice yearly, flying in chevron formation with loud trumpetings at an enormous height; and this must have attached them to the Hyperborean cult as messengers flying to the other world which lies at the back of the North Wind. But Thoth who invented hieroglyphs, was symbolized by the ibis, another wader also sacred to the moon; and the Greeks identified Thoth with Hermes, conductor of souls and messenger of the gods, whom Pherecydes addressed as 'ibis-shaped'.

---

[1] And probably with female breasts, as in a Middle Minoan seal-type from Zakro, published in Sir Arthur Evans' *Palace of Minos*.

So Hermes is credited with having invented the alphabet after watching the flight of cranes, and the crane takes on the scholarly attributes of the ibis, which did not visit Greece.

A peculiarity of wading birds such as the crane and heron is that, when they have speared a quantity of small fish in a river ready to take home to their young, they arrange them on the bank with the tails set together in the form of a wheel, which was formerly the symbol of the sun, and of the king's life. This must have astonished the ancients as it astonished me as a boy when I saw a heron doing it in the Nantcoll River in North Wales: but naturalists explain the arrangement as merely intended to make the fish more easily picked up and carried home. In ancient Ireland the association of the crane with literary secrets is suggested by the augury given by its sudden appearance: a cessation of war; for one of the poet's main functions was to part combatants, and he himself took no part in battle. In Greece the crane was associated with poets not only in the story of Apollo's metamorphosis into 'a crane, a Thracian bird'—meaning the red-wattled Numidian crane which visited the Northern Aegean—but in the story of Ibycus, the sixth-century B.C. Greek erotic poet who, having spent the best part of his life in the island of Samos, was one day set upon by bandits in a lonely place near Corinth and mortally wounded. He called upon a passing flock of cranes to avenge his death and soon afterwards the cranes hovered over the heads of the audience in the Corinthian open-air theatre; whereupon one of the murderers, who was present, cried out: 'Look, the avengers of Ibycus!' He was arrested and made a full confession.

To sum up the historical argument. A Greek alphabet which consisted of thirteen, and later fifteen, consonants and five vowels sacred to the Goddess, and which was ultimately derived from Crete, was current in the Peloponnese before the Trojan War. It was taken to Egypt—though perhaps only to the port of Pharos—and there adapted to Semitic use by Phoenician traders who brought it back into Greece some centuries later when the Dorians had all but destroyed the Mycenaean culture. The characters with their Semitic names were then adapted to the existing Epicharmian system contained in the so-called Pelasgian characters and usually called Cadmean, perhaps because they were current in Boeotian Cadmea. Later, Simonides, a devotee of Dionysus, modified the Cadmean alphabet in conformity with some obscure religious theory.

This is a plausible account. The history of the Greek alphabet has come to light in the last few years. It is now known to have originated in Cretan hieroglyphs, which by late Minoan times had been reduced to something between an alphabet and a syllabary of fifty-four signs: only four more than the Sanskrit system allegedly invented by the Goddess Kali, each letter of which was one of the skulls in her necklace. The Mycenaeans borrowed this Cretan system and did their best to adapt it to the needs of Greek. Messrs Ventris and Chadwick, in 1953, together deciphered the Mycenaean Linear Script B (1450–1400 B.C.), which contains eighty-eight different phonetic signs. It had also been introduced in earlier, more cumbrous, forms into Cyprus, Caria and Lycia. (In the *Iliad, VI, 168 ff.* occurs the story of how Bellerophon left Argos and handed the King of the Lycians a tablet covered with signs.) From the sixteenth century B.C. onward three or four attempts were made to simplify the various syllabaries then current in the near East into pure alphabets. The most successful of these was the Phoenician, from which the 'Cadmean' Greek characters derive. The Semitic princes of Syria wrote Assyrian cuneiform in their correspondence with the Pharaohs of Egypt until the twelfth century B.C., but their merchants had long before been using the Phoenician alphabet, in which one third of the characters was borrowed from the Cretan system—though whether directly from Crete or indirectly through Greece or Asia Minor is not known—the remainder from Egyptian hieroglyphs.

There is nothing to show that the Phoenicians invented the principle of reducing a syllabary to letters; and according to Professor Eustace Glotz's *Aegean Civilization* the names of such Phoenician characters as are not Semitic names for the objects represented in the corresponding Egyptian hieroglyphs cannot be explained in terms of any Semitic language, while their forms are clearly derived from the Cretan lineal script. The Semites, though good business men, were not an inventive people, and the unexplained names of the letters are therefore likely to be Greek. The Danaan Greeks probably simplified the Cretan syllabary into a sacred alphabet and passed it on to the Phoenicians—though confiding only the abbreviations of the letter-names to them and altering the order of letters so as not to give away the secret religious formula that they spelt out. The earliest Phoenician inscription is on a potsherd found at Beth-shemeth in Palestine dating from the sixteenth century B.C. The Palaio-Sinaitic and Ras Shamra alphabets may have been composed in emulation of the Phoenician; they were based on cuneiform, not on Cretan or Egyptian hieroglyphs. The Egyptians had been working towards an alphabet concurrently with the Cretans and it is difficult to say who first achieved the task it was probably the Egyptians.

Now it is remarkable that the names of several letters in the Irish Beth-Luis-Nion correspond more exactly with their counterparts in the Hebrew alphabet, which is Phoenician, than with their Classical Greek counterparts.

Greek	Hebrew	Irish
alpha	aleph	ailm (pronounced 'alev')

Greek	Hebrew	Irish
iota	jod	idho (originally 'ioda')
rho	resh	ruis
beta	beth	beith
nu	nun	nion or nin
eta	heth	eadha ('dh' pronounced 'th')
mu	mim	muin
o (micron)	ain	onn

On the other hand the remaining Greek letters correspond closely enough with their Hebrew counterparts, while the Irish letters are wholly different.

Greek	Hebrew	Irish
lambda	lamed	luis
delta	daleth	duir
gamma	gimmel	gort
tau	tav	tinne
sigma	samech	saille
zeta	tzaddi	straif
kappa	koph	quert

It looks as if the Irish alphabet was formed before the Classical Greek, and that its letter-names correspond with those of the Epicharmian alphabet which Evander brought to Italy from Danaan Greece. It may even have kept the original order of letters.

An ancient Irish tradition supplementing that of Ogma Sunface's invention of the Ogham alphabet is recorded in Keating's *History of Ireland*:

> Feniusa Farsa, a grandson of Magog and King of Scythia, desirous of mastering the seventy-two languages created at the confusion of Babel sent seventy-two persons to learn them. He established a University a Magh Seanair near Athens, over which he and Gadel and Caoith presided. These formed the Greek, Latin and Hebrew letters. Gade, digested the Irish (Goidelic) into five dialects: the Fenian for the soldiers; the poetic and historic for the senachies and bards respectively; the medical for physicians; and the common idiom for the vulgar.

Though at first sight this is a nonsense story, cooked up from scraps to monkish tradition (such as the miraculous translation of the Hebrew Scriptures by seventy-two scholars, each working separately for seventy-two days on the Isle of Pharos and all producing identically the same version) the closer one looks at it the more interestingly it reads. 'Magh Seanair near Athens' suggests that the mention of Babel has led some monk to amend an obscure text by making the event take place on the Magh Seanair, 'Plain of Shinar', in Mesopotamia and assuming that another Athens lay near. That the alphabet was invented in Greece (Achaea) is insisted upon in *The Hearings of the Scholars*, though Achaea has been corrupted to 'Accad' in some manuscripts and to 'Dacia' in others, and the whole account is given a very monkish twist. The original, I think, was 'Magnesia near Athens' meaning Magnesia in Southern Thessaly. It was described as 'near Athens' presumably to distinguish it from other Pelasgian Magnesias—the Carian one on the Meander River, and the Lydian one on the Hermus, connected with the myth of the Titan Tityos, from which in ancient times Hercules sent a colony to Gades in Spain. The three persons in the story, Gadel, Caoith and Feniusa Farsa are perhaps recognizable in Greek translation. Caoith as Coieus the Hyperborean grandfather of Delphic Apollo; Gadel as a tribe from the river Gadilum, or Gazelle, in Paphlagonia from which Pelops the Achaean began his travels; Feniusa Farsa as *Foeneus ho Farsas* ('the vine-man who joins together') or Foeneus father of Atalanta, the first man to plant a vineyard in Greece. According to Greek legend, this Foeneus, or 'Oeneus' when he lost his initial *digamma*, was a son of Aegyptus and came from Arabia, which perhaps means Southern Judaea; exactly the same account is given by the Irish bards of Feniusa Farsa, who was turned out of Egypt 'for refusing to persecute the Children of Israel', wandered in the wilderness for forty-two years and then passed northward to the 'Altars of the Philistines by the Lake of Willows'—presumably Hebron in Southern Judaea, celebrated for its fish-pools and stone altars—thence into Syria, after which he appears in Greece. Foeneus's queen was Althaea, the Birth-goddess associated with Dionysus; and it is known that *foinos*, wine, is a word of Cretan origin.

Why is Feniusa Farsa—who was an ancestor of the Irish Milesians—described as a Scythian, a grandson of Magog, and founder of the Milesian race? Gog and Magog are closely connected names. 'Gogmagog', Gog the Son of Gog—was the name of the giant whom 'Brut the Trojan' is said to have defeated at Totnes in Devonshire in his invasion of Britain at the close of the second millennium. But from where did Gog mac Gog originate? The answer is to be found in *Genesis, X, 2* where Magog is described as a son of Japhet (who figures in Greek myth as Iapetus the Titan, the father by the goddess Asia of Atlas, Prometheus and Epimetheus) and as a brother of Gomer, Madai, Javan, Tubal, Meshech and Tiras—who are generally agreed to have been the Cimmerians, the Medians, the Ionians, the Tibarenians, the Moschians and the Tyrrhenians. The Moschians and the iron-working Tibarenians were tribes of the south-eastern Black Sea region; the wandering Black Sea tribe of Cimmerians eventually became the Cymry; the Ionians ranked as Greeks in historical times but were perhaps Aegean immigrants into Greece from Phoenicia; the Tyrrhenians were an Aegean tribe some of whom emigrated from Lydia to

Etruria, others to Tarsus (St. Paul's city) and Tartessus in Spain; the Medians claimed descent from the Pelasgian goddess Medea. Gog is identified with the northern tribe of Gagi mentioned in an inscription of Amenhotep III, and 'Gogarene', in Strabo's day, was the name of a part of Armenia lying to the east of the territory of the Moschians and Tibarenians. Magog's grandfather was Noah, and Noah's Ararat was in Armenia, so that Magog is usually held to stand for Armenia; though Josephus interprets the word as meaning 'the Scythians', which was an inclusive name for all the Black Sea tribes of his day. The 'King Gog of Meshech and Tubal' mentioned in *Ezekiel, XXXVIII, 17* is now generally identified with Mithradates VI of Pontus, whose kingdom included the country of the Moschians and Tibarenians.

The history of Foeneus is concerned with certain mass emigrations from Canaan. Canaanites are referred to in the Greek myth of 'Agenor, or Chnas, King of Phoenicia', brother of Pelasgus, Iasus and Belus, and father of Aegyptus and Danäus; Agenor invaded Greece and became King of Argos. His was probably the invasion that drove the Tuatha dé Danaan out of Greece. Agenor had other sons, or affiliated tribes, besides Foeneus, Aegyptus and Danäus. These were Cadmus (a Semitic word meaning 'of the East'), who seized part of what afterwards became Boeotia; Cylix, who gave his name to Cilicia; Phoenix, who remained in Phoenicia and became completely Semitized; Thasus, who emigrated to the island of Thasos, near Samothrace; and Phineus, who emigrated to Thynia, near Constantinople, where the Argonauts are said to have found him preyed on by Harpies. The Amorites, a part of whom lived in Judaea, were also Canaanites, according to *Genesis, X,* and in the time of the Hebrew Prophets kept up the old Aegean customs of mouse-feasts, king-crucifixion, snake-oracles, the baking of barley-cakes in honour of the Queen of Heaven, and pre-marital prostitution; but they had early become Semitized in language. In *Genesis* the original Canaanite empire is described as extending as far south as Sodom and Gomorrah at the extreme end of the Dead Sea. This must be a very early legend, for according to *Genesis, XIV* the Canaanites were expelled from their southern territory by the Elamites—an invasion that can be dated to about 2300 B.C.

The historical sense of the Agenor myth is that towards the end of the third millennium B.C., an Indo-European tribal confederacy—part of a huge horde from central Asia that overran the whole of Asia Minor, Greece, Italy and Northern Mesopotamia—marched down from Armenia into Syria, thence into Syria and Canaan, gathering allies as it went. Some tribes under rulers known to the Egyptians as the Hyksos broke into Egypt about 1800 B.C. and were expelled with difficulty two centuries later. The flow and ebb of this mass-movement of tribes, which was complicated by Semitic invasions from across the Jordan, dislodged from Syria, Canaan and the Nile Delta numerous peoples that worshipped the Great Goddess under such titles as Belili, or Baalith, and Danaë, and the Bloody One (Phoenissa). One body whose chief religious emblem was the vine marched, or sailed, along the South Coast of Asia Minor, halted awhile in Milyas, the old name for Lycia, invaded Greece a little before the arrival there of the Indo-European Achaeans from the north, and occupied Argos in the Peloponnese, the chief shrine of the Horned Moon-goddess Io. The Cadmean invasion came later: it seems that a Canaanite tribe originally known as the Cadmeans, or Easterners, had occupied the mountainous district on the frontier of Ionia and Caria, which they called Cadmea; whence they crossed the Aegean and seized the coastal strip facing Euboea, excellent as a naval base, which was thereafter also called Cadmea.

In the Irish myth Caoith is described as a Hebrew. This must be a mistake: he was not one of the Habiru, as the Egyptians called the Hebrews, but probably a Pelasgian, a representative of the well-known priesthood of Samothrace, the Cabeiroi. The myth thus seems to refer to an agreement about a common use of letters reached at Magnesia in Mycenaean times by the Achaeans, typified by Gadel, the invaders of Greece; Canaanite invaders, typified by Feniusa Farsa; and the Pelasgian natives of Greece, typified by Caoith—all of whom were joined in a common reverence for the vine. The figure seventy-two suggests a religious mystery bound up with the alphabet; it is a number closely connected both with the Beth-Luis-Nion and the Boibel-Loth and associated in both cases with the number five (the number of the dialects).

Now, the most famous school of Greek antiquity was kept by Cheiron the Centaur, on the slopes of Mount Pelion in Magnesia. Among his puplis were Achilles the Myrmidon, son of Thetis the Sea-goddess, Jason the Argonaut, Hercules, and all the other most distinguished heroes of the generation before the Trojan War. He was renowned for his skill in hunting, medicine, music, gymnastics and divination, his instructors being Apollo and Artemis, and was accidentally killed by Hercules; after which he became the Bowman of the Greek Zodiac. He was evidently the heir to the Cretan culture which had reached Thessaly by the sheltered port of Iolcos, and to the independent Helladic culture. He is called 'the son of Cronos'.

Perhaps we can make another identification here: of Feniusa Farsa with 'Amphictyon' the founder of the Amphictyonic League, or the League of Neighbours. Magnesia was a member of this ancient federation of twelve tribes—Athens was the most powerful—representatives of which met every autumn at Anthela near the pass of Thermopylae and every Spring at Delphi. 'Amphictyon' was a son of Deucalion ('sweet wine'), whose mother was Pasiphaë the Cretan Moon-goddess, and of Pyrrha ('the red one'), the Noah and Noah's wife of Greece. He was himself 'the first man ever to mix wine with water'. In characteristic style he married the heiress of Attica, Cranë—already mentioned as an aspect of the White Goddess—expelled his predecessor, and set up altars to Phallic Dionysus and the Nymphs. We know that Amphictyon was not his real name, for the League was really founded in honour of the Barley-goddess Demeter, or Danaë, in her character of President of Neighbours ('Amphictyonis') and the sacrifice at the autumn meetings was made to her: but it was the usual habit in Classical Greece, as it was in Classical Britain and Ireland, to deny women the credit of inventing or initiating anything important. So 'Amphictyon' was the male surrogate of Amphictyonis, just as 'Don King of Dublin and Lochlin' was of the Irish Goddess Danu; and as, I believe, the Giant Samothes, after whom Britain had its earliest name 'Samothea', was of the White Goddess, *Samothea*—for Samothes is credited by early British historians, quoting from the Babylonian Berossus, with the invention of letters, astronomy and other sciences usually attributed to the White goddess. And since Amphictyon 'joined together' the various states and was a vine man, we may call him 'Foeneus'—or 'Dionysus'.

The most ancient Greek account of the creation of the vine that has been preserved is that given by Pausanias (X, 38): how in the time of Orestheus son of Deucalion a white bitch littered a stick which he planted and which grew into a vine. The white bitch is obviously the Triple Goddess again: Amphictyonis. Of the Amphictyonic League eight tribes were Pelasgian and, according to Strabo, Callimachus and the Scholiast on Euripides's *Orestes*, it was originally regularized by Acrisius the grandfather of Perseus. But the composition of the League in Classical times was claimed to date from about 1103 B.C., and it included the Achaeans of Phthiotis, who were not there in Acrisius's day. The inference is that four Pelasgian tribes were extruded in successive Greek invasions.

St. Paul quoted a Greek proverb: 'All Cretans are liars'. They were called liars for the same reason that poets are: because they had a different way of looking at things. Particularly because they remained unmoved by Olympian propaganda, which for the previous thousand years or so had insisted on an Eternal, Almighty, Just Father Zeus—Zeus who had swept away with his thunderbolt all the wicked old gods and established his shining throne for ever on Mount Olympus. The True Cretans said: 'Zeus is dead. His tomb is to be seen on one of our mountains.' This was not spoken with bitterness. All that they meant was that ages before Zeus became an Eternal Almighty God in Greece, he had been a simple old-fashioned Sun-king, annually sacrificed, a servant of the Great Goddess, and that his remains were customarily buried in a tomb on Mount Juktas.

They were not liars. There was no Father God in Minoan Crete and their account squares with the archaeological finds recently made on that very mountain. The Pelasgians of Leros had much the same reputation as the Cretans, but seem to have been even more obdurate in their attachment to ancient tradition, to judge from the Greek epigram: 'The Lerians are all bad, not merely some Lerians, but every one of them—all except Procles, and of course he is a Lerian too.'

The early Welsh and Irish historians are also generally regarded as liars because their ancient records are dated to uncomfortably early times and do not square either with conventional Biblical dates or with the obstinate theory that until Roman times the inhabitants of all the British Isles were howling savages who had no native art or literature at all and painted themselves blue. The Picts and Britons certainly tattooed themselves, as the Dacians, Thracians and Mosynoechians did, with pictorial devices. That they used woad for the purpose is a proof of advanced culture, for the extraction of blue dye from the woad-plant, which the ancient Irish also practised, is an extremely complicated chemical process; the blue colour perhaps sanctified them to the Goddess Anu.[1] I do not mean that these records have not undergone a great deal of careless, pious, or dishonest editing at every stage of religious development; but at least they seem to be as trustworthy as the corresponding Greek records, and rather more trustworthy than the Hebrew—if only because ancient Ireland suffered less from wars than Greece or Palestine. To dismiss the Irish and Welsh as incoherent children has one great advantage: it frees the historian of any obligation to add Old Goidelic and Old Welsh to his multifarious other studies.

In modern civilization almost the only place where a scholar can study at ease is a University. But at a University one has to be very careful indeed not to get out of step with one's colleagues and especially not to publish any heterodox theories. Orthodox opinions are in general based on a theory of political and moral expediency, originally refined under Olympianism, which is the largest single gift of paganism to Christianity. Not only to Christianity. Twenty-five years ago, when I was Professor of English Literature at the Royal Egyptian University of Cairo, my colleague the blind Professor of Arabic Literature was imprudent enough to suggest in one of his lectures that the Koran contained certain pre-

[1] It seems to have been in her honour, as Goddess of the dark-blue night sky and the dark blue sea, that the matrons and girls of Britain, according to Pliny, stained themselves all over with woad, for 'certain rites', until they were as swarthy as Ethiopians, then went about naked. An incident in the mediaeval *Life of St. Ciaran* proves that in Ireland woad-dyeing was a female mystery which no male was allowed to witness. If this was also the rule in Thrace and the Northern Aegean, it would account for the nasty stench which, according to Apollodorus, clung to the Lemnian women, and made the men quit their company; for the extraction and use of the dye is such a smelly business that the woad-dyeing families of Lincolnshire have always been obliged to inter-marry.

Mohammedan metrical compositions. This was blasphemy and a good excuse for his examination-funking students to go on strike. So the Rector called him to task and he was faced with the alternatives of losing his job and recantation. He recanted. In American Universities of the Bible Belt the same sort of thing often happens: some incautious junior professor suggests that perhaps the Whale did not really swallow Jonah and supports his view by quoting the opinions of eminent natural historians. He leaves at the end of the University year, if not before. In England the case is not quite so bad, but bad enough. Sir James Frazer was able to keep his beautiful rooms at Trinity College, Cambridge, until his death by carefully and methodically sailing all round his dangerous subject, as if charting the coastline of a forbidden island without actually committing himself to a declaration that it existed. What he was saying-not-saying was that Christian legend, dogma and ritual are the refinement of a great body of primitive and even barbarous beliefs, and that almost the only original element in Christianity is the personality of Jesus. Recent researches that I have made into Christian origins, the history of the American Revolution, and the private life of Milton, three dangerous topics, have astonished me. How calculatedly misleading the textbooks are! Dog, Lapwing and Roebuck have long ago entered the service of the new Olympians.

To return to Dr. Macalister, who does not account for the thirteen-consonant Irish alphabets and assumes that the Druids possessed no alphabet before they formed the BLFSN alphabet from the Formello-Cervetri one. He does not brush aside the question, why the common name for all Irish alphabets was 'Beth-Luis-Nion'—which means that the original sequence began with BLN, not BLF—but makes a complicated postulate for which he has no epigraphic evidence. He suggests that the Druids of Southern Gaul chose out from the Formello-Cervetri list the letters:

B.L.N.F.S., M.Z.R.G.NG., H.C.Q.D.T., A.E.I.O.U.

and that this, their first alphabet of any sort lasted just long enough to give the Irish alphabet its name. He also suggests (without epigraphic evidence) that an intermediate alphabet was devised by a clever phonetician as follows:

B.F.S.L.N., M.G.NG.Z.R., H.D.T.C.Q., A.O.U.E.I.

before the order was finally settled (in Ireland at least) as:

B.L.F.S.N., H.D.T.C.Q., M.G.NG.Z.R., A.O.U.E.I.

plus five 'diphthongs', as he rather misleadingly calls the allusive vowel-combinations referring to the foreign letters, for which characters were found in five of the six supernumerary letters of the Formello-Cervetri alphabet. He does not deny that Beth, Luis and Nion are tree-names, but holds that as cipher equivalents of the Formello-Cervetri letter names, which he says must have retained their original Semitic forms as late as the fifth century B.C., they were chosen merely as having the correct initial, and suggests that L, *Luis* the rowan, might just as well have been the larch.

This argument might pass muster were it not that the Druids were famous for their sacred groves and their tree-cult, and that the old sequence of tree-letters was evidently of such religious importance that the later B.L.F.S.N. alphabet, with its misplacement of N, could never wipe out its memory. Dr. Macalister may regard the Beth-Luis-Nion Tree-Ogham as an 'artificiality'; but the trees in it are placed in a seasonal arrangement which has strong mythological backing, whereas the original sequence which he postulates makes no sense at all after the first five letters, which are in the accepted order. For my part I cannot believe in his postulate; oak and elder cannot change places; it is not easy to overlook the Latin proverb that 'it is not from *every* tree that a statue of Mercury can be carved'; and only in joke does anyone gather nuts, *Coll*, and may, *Uath*, on a cold and frosty morning.

At some time, it seems, in the fifth century B.C. the *characters* of the Formello-Cervetri alphabet were borrowed by the Druids in Southern Gaul for the purpose of recording whatever was not protected by a taboo, and passed on by them into Britain and Ireland. The foreign letters which occur in it were added to an already existing secret alphabet, the Boibel-Loth, the letter names of which formed a charm in honour of Canopic Hercules. But this does not prove that the Druids did not possess an earlier alphabet beginning with B.L.N., with entirely different letter names bound up with the more barbaric religious cult commemorated in Amergin's song and enshrined in a traditional tree-sequence of birch, rowan, ash, alder, willow, etc. Or that the historical tradition, at which Dr. Macalister indulgently smiles, that letters were known in Ireland many centuries before the Formello-Cervetri alphabet reached Italy, is a late fiction. If we can show that the BLFSN alphabet was a logical development from the BLNFS tree-alphabet and can connect it with a new religious dispensation, without having to invent intermediate forms for which there is no literary evidence, then everything will make poetic as well as prose sense. Religious necessity is always a far likelier explanation of changes in an alphabet than phonetic theory, to which alone Dr. Macalister attributes his hypothetic changes in the sequence of the Beth-Luis-Nion: for all right-minded people everywhere naturally oppose the attempts of scholarly phoneticians to improve their familiar ABC, the foundation of all learning and the first thing that they ever learned at school.

But is not the answer to our question to be found in *The Battle of the Trees?* What distinguishes the BLFSN from the BLNFS is that the letter N, *Nion* the ash, the sacred tree of the God Gwydion, has been taken out of the dead period of the year, where it is still in black bud, and put two months ahead to where it is in leaf, while *Fearn* the alder, the sacred tree of the God Bran, which marks the emergence of the solar year from the tutelage of Night, has been thrust back into *Nion's* place. The BLNFS is the trophy raised by Gwydion over Bran. And is it not strange that a few years before the Battle of the Trees was fought in Britain and the letter F humbled, the Greeks had made a dead set against their F, only retaining it as a numerical sign for 6? More than this happened when the order of letters changed; Gwydion's ash, N, took the place of the fifth consonant, *Saille* the willow, S, which was naturally sacred to Mercury, or Arawn; and Gwydion thereupon became an oracular god. Also, Amathaon who had evidently been a willow-god, S, took Bran's place at F and became a fire-god in the service of his father Beli, God of Light. It only remained in this General Post for Bran to take over the maritime ash that Gwydion had relinquished and sail away on his famous voyage to one hundred and fifty islands; yet sailing was no novelty to him, the tradition preserved by Virgil being that the first boats that ever took to the water were alder-trunks.

Chapter Fourteen
THE ROEBUCK IN THE THICKET

The omission from O'Flaherty's and O'Sullivan's Beth-Luis-Nion of the mythically important trees, *Quert*, apple, and *Straif*, blackthorn, must be accounted for. The explanation seems to be that though the Beth-Luis-Nion calendar is a solar one, in so far as it expresses a year's course of the sun, it is ruled by the White Moon-goddess whose sacred number is thirteen in so far as her courses coincide with the solar year, but fifteen in so far as the full moon falls on the fifteenth day of each lunation. Fifteen is also the multiple of three and five: three expressing the three phases of the moon and the Goddess's three aspects of maiden, nymph and hag, and five expressing the five stations of her year: Birth, Initiation, Consummation, Repose and Death. Thus because fifteen letters are needed to present the Goddess as both a triad and a pentad, and to express the days in a month up to full moon, and since only thirteen 28-day months can be fitted into a year, two of the months must be shared between pairs of trees.

Since Q was sometimes written CC by the Irish ollaves—as in O'Flaherty's alphabet—we may conclude that Z was similarly written SS, as it was in Latin during the greater part of the Republic. This is to say that *Quert* the wild apple shared a month with *Coll* the hazel, because the apple and nut harvest coincide, and that *Straif* the blackthorn shared a month with *Saille* the willow, because the White Goddess has to make an appearance in tree form in the Spring—in France the blackthorn is called *La Mère du Bois* ('the Mother of the Wood').

The blackthorn (*bellicum* in Latin) is an unlucky tree; villagers in Galmpton and Dittisham, South Devon, still fear 'the black rod' carried as a walking stick by local witches, which has the effect of causing miscarriages. When Major Weir, the Covenanter and self-confessed witch, was burned at Edinburgh in April 1670, a blackthorn staff was burned with him as the chief instrument of his sorceries. Blackthorn is also the traditional timber with which bellicose Irish tinkers fight at fairs (though the *shillelagh*, contrary to popular belief, is an oak club), and the words 'strife' and 'strive', modelled on the old Northern French *estrif* and *estriver*, may be the same word *Straif*, derived from the Breton; at least, no other plausible derivation has been suggested. Gilbert White remarks in his *Selborne*: 'Blackthorn usually blossoms when cold N.E. winds blow; so that the harsh rugged weather obtaining at this season is called by the country people "blackthorn winter".' The blackthorn is also called the sloe, after its fruit: and the words 'sloe' and 'slay' are closely connected in early English. Since Good Friday falls in this month, the Crown of Thorns was sometimes said to have been made of blackthorn; and this was the explanation that the monks gave for the unluckiness of the tree. It is said that whitethorn, tree of chastity, will destroy any blackthorn growing near by.

That *Coll* and *Quert* share a month between them is appropriate. The hazel is the poet's tree, and the apple's power as the salvation of poets is brought out in the Welsh legend of Sion Kent (a verse of whose I quote in Chapter Nine) whom the Prince of the Air tried to carry off: Kent won permission to 'sip an apple' first, then caught hold of the apple tree, a sanctuary from which he could not be removed. Therefore 'being too sinful for Heaven yet safe from Hell he haunts the earth like a will o' the wisp'. In other words, he secured poetic immortality. *Quert* and *Coll* are also associated in the *Dinnschencas* with the oak, the King of Trees: the Great Tree of Mugna contained in itself the virtues of apple, hazel and oak, 'bearing every year one crop each of goodly apples, blood-red nuts and ridgy acorns: its crown was as broad as the whole plain, its girth thirty cubits, its height three hundred cubits.' It fell with the advent of Christianity.

	SS	H	D	T	C	
S	S	H	D	T	C	CC
F	F				M	M
N	N				G	G
L	L				NG	NG
B	B				R	R

There is a reference in Amergin's song to the 'secrets of the unhewn dolmen'. It will be seen that there is room for an extra letter at each corner of the dolmen arch which I constructed to elucidate the reference: the Oghams being nicked on the edges, not painted on the face, of the stones.

It will be observed that the seventh to eleventh letters of this alphabet, which follow the same sequence in the Boibel-Loth, are the letters H.D.T.C.Q. These letters, as Sir John Rhys has pointed out, form the initials of the Old Goidelic numerals, from one to five: *a hoina, a duou, a ttri, a ccetuor, a qquenque,* which correspond very nearly to the Latin numerals *unum, duo, tres, quattuor, quinque.* This may explain why the inventors of the Boibel-Loth made H.D.T.C.Q. the central five letters of the alphabet and transferred Z to a position between NG and R. Yet the ancientness of the Old Goidelic numerals suggests that in the original Beth-Luis-Nion finger alphabet the first flight of consonants—the Spring months—numbered only five, not six, to allow H.D.T.C.Q. to form the second or Summer series, and that Z was therefore reckoned to the last series, the Winter series, as a premonitory 'blackthorn winter'. Thus:

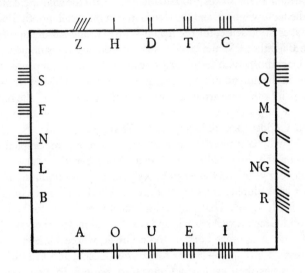

Each series thus has its full five letters, the aggregate number of strokes in each case being fifteen.

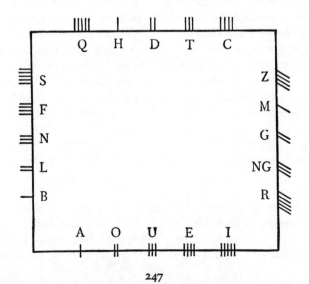

But though this is a logical arrangement, necessitated by the initials of the first five numerals in Latin and Old Goidelic, a sense of mathematical proportion demands that each side of the dolmen should have a single series cut upon it. This would involve a change of places between Z and Q, to make Apple and Willow, Hazel and Blackthorn, share months. (*as above*).

This arrangement makes good seasonal sense, for the wild apple blossoms during the willow month and the sloe is ripe in the hazel month. Poetically it also makes good sense, for the Apple White Goddess is of happier omen than the Blackthorn White Goddess as introducing the summer; and the hostile blackthorn with its mouth-puckering sloe is complementary to the apple, in the nut-month, as representing the poet in his satiric capacity. I believe that both these arrangements were used in Ogham, the necessary ambivalence of poetic meaning being thus maintained: it is an axiom that the White Goddess is both lovely and cruel, ugly and kind.

Now it will be noticed that there are two more unoccupied corner positions on the threshold of the dolmen which represents the extra day of the calendar year; and these can be assigned to J (pronounced Y) and to long O: Y as a reduplication of I, the death-vowel; long O as a reduplication of A, the birth-vowel. That only a single character served for both J and I in Latin and Greek is well known; and the close connexion between long O (Omega) and A appears both in Ionic Greek, where Omega was often written instead of Alpha—*ōristos* for *aristos* ('best'); and in Doric Greek where Alpha was often written for Omega—as *prātistos* for *prōtistos* ('first').

Omega ('Great O') seems to signify the world-egg of the Orphic mysteries which was split open by the Demiurge to make the universe: for the majuscular Greek character for Omega represents the world-egg laid on the anvil and the minuscular character shows it already split in halves. The majuscular Omicron ('little O') and the minuscular Omicron both show the egg of the year waiting to hatch out. The *glain*, or 'red egg of the sea serpent', which figured in the Druidical mysteries may be identified with the Orphic world-egg: for the creation of the world, according to the Orphics, resulted from the sexual act performed between the Great Goddess and the World-Snake Ophion. The Great Goddess herself took the form of a snake and coupled with Ophion; and the coupling of snakes in archaic Greece was consequently a forbidden sight —the man who witnessed it was struck with the 'female disease': he had to live like a woman for seven years, which was the same punishment as was permanently inflicted on the Scythians who sacked the Temple of the Great Goddess of Askalon. The *caduceus* of Hermes, his wand of office while conducting souls to Hell, was in the form of coupling snakes. The Goddess then laid the world-egg, which contained infinite potentiality but which was nothing in itself until it was split open by the Demiurge.

The Demiurge was Helios, the Sun, with whom the Orphics identified their God Apollo—which was natural, because the Sun does hatch snakes' eggs—and the hatching-out of the world was celebrated each year at the Spring festival of the Sun, to which the vowel Omicron is assigned in the alphabet. Since the cock was the Orphic bird of resurrection, sacred to Apollo's son Aesculapius the healer, hens' eggs took the place of snakes' in the later Druidic mysteries and were coloured scarlet in the Sun's honour; and became Easter eggs.

But Little O is not Great O. Great O, Omega, must be regarded as an intensification of Alpha, and as symbolizing the birth of birth. Here then is the new dolmen figure:

```
        SS    H    D    T    C
   ┌─────────────────────────────┐
 S │ S    H    D    T    C │ CC
   │          ┌────────────┐
 F │ F        │         M  │ M
   │          │            │
 N │ N        │         G  │ G
   │          │            │
 L │ L        │        NG  │ NG
   │          │            │
 B │ B        │         R  │ R
   │          │            │
───┼──────────┴────────────┤───
AA │ A    O    U    E    I │ II
   └─────────────────────────────┘
     A    O    U    E    I
```

And at last we can complete our Beth-Luis-Nion calendar, with the proper tree accredited to each letter—for the doubled I, or J, letter-tree, the tree belonging to the Day of Liberation which stands apart from the 364 days of the thirteen months, is soon found. Put the requirements of the tree into a bardic riddle and there can be only one answer:

The day that is no day calls for a tree
That is no tree, of low yet lofty growth.
When the pale queen of Autumn casts her leaves
My leaves are freshly tufted on her boughs.
When the wild apple drops her goodly fruit
My all-heal fruit hangs ripening on her boughs.
Look, the twin temple-posts of green and gold,
The overshadowing lintel stone of white.
For here with white and green and gold I shine—
Graft me upon the King when his sap rises

That I may bloom with him at the year's prime,
That I may blind him in his hour of joy.

For the mistletoe, the berries of which were formerly prized both as an all-heal and as an aphrodisiac, is not a tree in the sense that it grows in the earth; it subsists on other trees. There are two sorts of mistletoe, the mistletoe proper and the loranthus. The Greeks distinguished them as, respectively, *hypear* and *ixos* or *ixias*. The loranthus is found in Eastern Europe, but not in Western and, unlike mistletoe proper, grows on oaks. It also grows on tamarisks, and its flame-coloured leaves may have been the original 'burning bush' from which Jehovah appeared to Moses. Whether the loranthus was once native to Western Europe, or whether the Celtic Druids brought it with them from the Danube area where their religion was first formulated, or whether they grafted mistletoe proper from-poplar, apple, or other host-trees, on their oaks, cannot be determined. It is most likely that they grafted it, to judge from the insistence in Norse myth on oak-mistletoe. Virgil notes that the mistletoe is the only tree that leafs freshly in wintry weather. Its colours are white, green and gold like the pillars and lintel shown to Herodotus in the ancient temple of Hercules at Tyre. On midsummer day, in ancient Europe, the Eye of the year was blinded with a mistletoe stake, all the other trees (according to the Norse legend) having refused to do so. The Church now admits holly and ivy as reputable church decorations at Christmas, but forbids the mistletoe as pagan. However, mistletoe cannot be ousted from its sovereignty of Midwinter, and the exchange of kisses forbidden at all other seasons is still permitted under its bough, if it has berries on it. Chemists have tried to learn how mistletoe won the name 'all-heal', by analyzing its alkaloids. They can find none of any curative virtue, though this is not final proof of the mistletoe's medicinal valuelessness. Camomile, for example, had medicinal properties, but no extractable alkaloid. A plant is rarely awarded mystic virtue unless it has some property beneficial to man. Yet the spectacle of green leaves and white berries on an otherwise bare tree may have been sufficiently odd to invest them with supernatural powers. The wood, by the way, is extremely hard and tough, mistletoe being slow-growing; Haedury's mistletoe spear which pierced Balder's gentle breast in the legend was no poetic fancy—I once cut one for myself in Brittany.

This calendar explains the reference in Gwion's *Preiddeu Annwm* to the 'ox with seven-score knobs on his collar': the ox is the first flight of five months, consisting of 140 days; it is presumably followed by a lion of one hundred and twelve days, and a serpent of the same length, to justify the two texts already quoted (in Chapter Eight) from Euripides and the Welsh poet Cynddelw—both appealing to the God of the year to appear as a wild bull, a fire-breathing lion and a many-headed snake. The griffon-eagle must be the creature of the extra day, since the god becomes immortal in this form. The year of Bull, Lion, Serpent and Eagle is Babylonian: a calendar beast, called *Sir-rush*, on the Dragon Gate at Babylon having the body and horns of a bull; forelegs and mane of a lion; head, scales and tail of a serpent; hindlegs and feet of an eagle. The calendar has several secret qualities. One is that the number of vowels is increased to seven, the Roebuck's own number. Another is that II in Ogham makes a ten-stroke letter, and AA makes a two-stroke letter: thus the aggregate number of letter-strokes for the complete twenty-two letter alphabet is 72, a number constantly recurring in early myth and ritual; for 72 is the multiple of the nine, the number of lunar wisdom, and eight the number of solar increase.[1] 72, Mr. Clyde Stacey suggests, is also linked to the Goddess, astronomically, by the seventy-two-day season during which her planet Venus moves successively from maximum eastern elongation to inferior conjunction (closest approach to earth) and thence to maximum west elongation. A third quality is that the proportion of all the letters in the alphabet to the vowels is 22 to 7, which, as has already been mentioned, is the mathematical formula, once secret, for the relation of the circumference of the circle to the diameter.

Before examining the fourth and, for our purpose, the most important quality of this calendar, the poetic relation between Hazel and Apple must be considered. It has now been established that the Roebuck, originally a White Hind, hides in the thicket, and that the thicket is composed of twenty-two sacred trees. The poet naturally asks a further question: 'But where exactly is the beast lodged in the grove?'

'Where?' is the question that should always weigh most heavily with poets who are burdened with the single poetic Theme of life and death. As Professor Ifor Williams has pointed out, it is because the cuckoo utters its 'Where?' so constantly that it is represented in early Welsh poetry as a kill-joy: for 'cw-cw', pronounced 'ku-ku' means 'where? where?'. It cries: 'Where is my love gone? Where are my lost companions?' Curiously enough, the same sentiment occurs in Omar Khayyam's elegy where the 'solitary ring-dove' broods in the ruined palace crying: 'Ku? Ku? Ku? Ku?'—the Iranian for 'where' being the same as Welsh; and in Greek myth Tereus the hoopoe cries 'Pou? Pou?' for his lost brides. 'Where' in

---

[1] The obsession of the Orphic mystics, from whom the Pythagoreans derived their main doctrines, with sacred numbers is remarked upon by Iamblichus in his life of Pythagoras: 'Orpheus said that the eternal essence of number is the most providential principle of the universe, of heaven, of earth, and of the nature intermediate to these; and, more, that it is the basis of the permanency of divine natures, gods and demons.' The Pythagoreans had a proverb 'all things are assimilated to number', and Pythagoras is quoted by Iamblichus as having laid down in his *Sacred Discourse* that 'number is the ruler of forms and ideas, and the cause of gods and demons'. The numbers 8 and 9 were favourite objects of Pythagorean adoration.

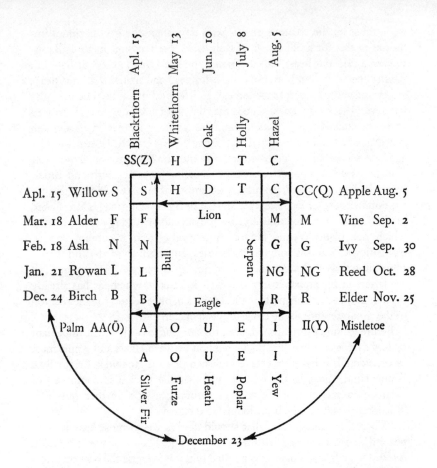

Valentin Iremonger, the poet, has confirmed this for me in the *Hearings of the Scholars*:

English is derived, according to the *Oxford English Dictionary*, 'from the interrogative stem *qua*'. Nearly all interrogatives in Indo-European languages begin with Q (except where Q has been, as in Greek, changed into a P or, as in German, into a W), and in Old Scots 'where' is spelt 'Quhair'. Q, in fact, is the letter of perpetual question. Latin has a fine range of Q's:

Quare? Quis? Quă? Quid? Qualis? Qui? Quo? Quomodo? Quando? Quorsum? Quoties? Quantum? Quot?

And the Serpent's dangerous question *Quidni?* 'Why not?' 'Where?' is *Quā?*

But the Muse's promise to the poet is 'Seek patiently, and you shall find', so where else should the Wild Hind be hiding except under the Q tree, which is the Wild Apple?

252

Queirt dano is o chrand regainmnighead .i. abull ut dicitur clithar
boaiscille .i. elit gelt quert .i. aball.

'The letter Q is from a tree named *Quert,* that is to say, an apple tree.
As the saying is: *"Quert* is the shelter of the wild hind"—meaning that
the apple tree is so.' An interesting poetic gloss on 'shelter of the wild
hind' occurs in the same book:

.i. boscell .i. gelt . basceall .i. is and tic a ciall do in tan degas a bas

'that is to say, of the *boscell,* lunatic, the word being derived from *basceall,* "death-sense", for a lunatic's wits come to him when he goes to his
death.'

The comment means that love of the Goddess makes the poet mad: he
goes to his death and in death is made wise.

Quert is not only one of the 'seven noble sacred trees of the grove' but
is recorded in the *Triads of Ireland* as being, with *Coll,* the Hazel, one of
the only two sacred trees for the wanton felling of which death is exacted.
The apple in European literature and folklore is the symbol of consummation, as the egg is of initiation. The 112 days of the Lion flight of months
in the Beth-Luis-Nion run *ab ovo usque ad malum,* from egg to apple,
from the end of *Saille,* the nesting month, to the end of *Quert,* the apple
month. Thus when the Biblical legend of Adam and Eve reached North-
Western Europe, the fruit of the Tree of Knowledge of Good and Evil
was understood as an apple—not as a fig, despite the fig-leaf context.
Adam had eaten from the forbidden tree of intelligence given him by Eve,
'the Mother of All Living', and the bards therefore translated 'fruit' as
'apple'.

The seven noble sacred trees of the grove particularized in a seventh-
century poem appended to the ancient Irish Law *Crith Gablach* were:
birch, alder, willow, oak, holly, hazel, apple. Except that *Beth,* the birch,
the lucky tree of the birth-month, takes the place of *Huath,* the unlucky
whitethorn, the trees run in a clear sequence from the Spring equinox to
the end of the apple harvest. The Birch is mentioned as 'very noble' in
Gwion's *Câd Goddeu,* but the apple-tree was the noblest tree of all, being
the tree of immortality. The poets of Wales have always been aware of its
spiritual pre-eminence, and the lovely mediaeval *Afallenau:*

> *Sweet apple-tree crimson in hue*
> *Which grows concealed in Forest Celyddon. . . .*

is not a poem about the orchard apple-tree but about the apple-tree of the
sacred thicket, the tree that is the harbourage of the hind. As Gwion writes:
'I fled as a roe to the entangled thicket.'

Where did King Arthur go to be healed of his grievous wounds? To the Isle of Avalon, the secret 'island of apple-trees'. With what talisman was Bran summoned by the White Goddess to enter the Land of Youth? With 'a silver white-blossomed apple branch from Emain in which the bloom and branch were one'. The island of Emain, the Goidelic Elysium, is described thus in a poem by Ragnall, son of Godfrey, King of the Isles:

> *An amaranthine place is faery Emain:*
> *Beauteous is the land where it is found,*
> *Lovely its rath above all other raths.*
> *Plentiful apple-trees grow from that ground.*

Oisin, when taken to the same Land of Youth by Niamh of the Golden Hair, sees his weird first as a hornless fawn pursued by a red-eared white hound, but then in his own shape royally dressed and mounted on a white horse in pursuit of a beautiful girl on a dark horse; in her hand is a golden apple. Both apparitions are skimming over the calm sea; he does not recognize their meaning and Niamh gently evades his questions about them. It has been suggested in a footnote to Chapter Twelve that the Goddess of the sepulchral island of Alyscamps, in the Rhône, was named Alys and that the alder, *aliso* in Spanish, was named after her. Dauzat in his *Dictionnaire Étymologique* connects *alisier*, the service-tree, with *aliso*, the alder which screened these sepulchral islands. The same resemblance is found between the Scandinavian and North-German *els* or *elże* (service-tree) and *else* (alder); and the name Alys seems to be recorded in the Ilse, the stream that runs from the Brocken to the Oker, where a princess Ilse was once drowned. Since the fruit of the service tree (both the Mediterranean and Northern varieties) is a sort of sorb-apple, it is likely that this was the apple of immortality in pre-Christian France, Spain and Scandinavia. If so, the Elysian Fields, or Alyscamps, would have the same meaning as Avalon: apple-orchards. The sorb emblemizes 'from corruption, sweetness': it cannot be eaten until it has rotten to a corpse-like purple-brown. Perhaps this is why the tree is mentioned in *The Hearings of the Scholars* as a euphemism for yew, the death-tree; though the explanation there given is that both bore the name 'oldest of woods'; 'oldest', as applied to the service-tree, could mean only 'of most ancient fame', because it is not particularly long-lived.

Mr. Kenneth Dutfield in a recent letter to the *Times Literary Supplement* plausibly suggests that *Avernus*, the abode of the dead, which the Latins incorrectly derived from the Greek *a-ornis*, 'birdless', is the same word as *Avalon*; which would identify the Elysian Fields with Avernus. Lake Avernus near Cumae apparently won its nickname from the unhealthy airs of the surrounding marshes and from the near-by shrine of the Cumaean Sibyl who conjured up the spirits of the dead.

On August 13th, the pre-Christian feast of the Mother Goddess Diana, or Vesta, was once celebrated with cyder, a roasted kid spitted on hazel-twigs and apples hanging in clusters from a bough. Another name of this Goddess was Nemesis (from the Greek *nemos*, 'grove') which in Classical Greek connotes divine vengeance for breaches of taboo. In her statues she carries an apple-bough in one hand, and the fifth-century Christian poet Commodianus identifies her with Diana Nemorensis ('of the grove') whose followers 'worship a cut branch and call a log Diana'. But both Nemesis and Diana Nemorensis are associated with the deer, not the goat, cult. Nemesis carries a wheel in her other hand to show that she is the goddess of the turning year, like Egyptian Isis and Latin Fortuna, but this has been generally understood as meaning that the wheel will one day come full circle and vengeance be exacted on the sinner.[1] In Gaul she was Diana Nemetona, *nemeton* being a sacred grove; and was represented with an apple-bough, a cyder-bowl with Aethiopians on it, and a lion-eagle griffin to denote the season of her feast. This feast was converted in the Middle Ages into that of the Assumption of the Blessed Virgin (August 15th) which, because of the seventeenth-century calendar changes (referred to in the hawthorn context), means August 6th, the beginning of *Quert*. The Virgin is believed to have died on August 13th, to have risen again and ascended to Heaven on the third day. Since the Virgin was closely associated by the early Church with Wisdom—with the Saint 'Sophia', or Holy Wisdom, of the Cathedral Church at Constantinople—the choice of this feast for the passing of Wisdom into Immortality was a happy one.

The *Litany of the Blessed Virgin* contains the prayer *Sedes sapientiae, ora pro nobis*, 'Seat of Wisdom, pray for us!' For St. Peter Chrysologos in his *Sermon on the Annunciation* had represented the Virgin as the seven-pillared temple which Wisdom (according to *Proverbs, IX, 10*) had built for herself. So the meaning of the mediaeval allegory about the milk-white unicorn which could be captured only with the assistance of a pure virgin is now easily read. The Unicorn is the Roe in the Thicket. It lodges under an apple-tree, the tree of immortality-through-wisdom. It can be captured only by a pure virgin—Wisdom herself. The purity of the virgin stands for spiritual integrity. The unicorn lays its head on her lap and

---

[1] The oracular Wheels of Fortune, worked by a rope, still found in a few early Continental churches, derive from the golden *iynges* (literally 'wrynecks') which were oracular wheels, originally sacred to the White Goddess, that decorated, among others, the temple of Apollo at Delphi. Philostratus in his *Life of Apollonius* connects them with similar wheels used by the Mages of Babylon, and they also occurred in Egyptian temples of the 3rd century B.C. The celebrated Irish Druid Mogh Ruith of Kerry (according to the *Cóir Anmann*) 'derived his name, which signifies *Magus Rotarum*, "the wizard of the wheels", from the wheels by which he used to make his magic observations'. In O'Grady's *Silva Gadelica* there is an account of Mogh Ruith's daughter who went with him to the East to learn magic, and there made a 'rowing wheel'.

weeps for joy. But the Provençal version of the story is that the beast nuzzles to her breasts and attempts other familiarities, whereupon the virgin gently grasps him by the horn and leads him away to the hunters: here he is, in fact, a type of profane love rejected by spiritual love.

The unicorn's wildness and untameability had become proverbial in early Christian times because of the text in *Job, XXXIX, 9*:

Will the unicorn be able to serve thee or abide by thy crib?

and this Biblical unicorn, (a mistranslation by the Septuagint[1] of *rem*, the Judaean aurochs or wild ox) became identified with the goat-stag, the *hirco-cervus* of Dionysian mysteries, which was another wild untameable animal. Charles Doughty in his *Arabia Deserta* suggests that the *rem* is not the aurochs but a large, very dangerous antelope called *wothyhi* or 'wild ox' by the Arabs. He is likely to be right; and I take the *wothyh:* to be the *boubalis* or *boibalis*, 'an oryx the size of an ox', mentioned by Herodotus (*Melpomene, 192*), and also by Martial, as a fierce beast used in the Roman amphitheatre. Doughty writes: 'Her horns are such slender rods as from our childhood we have seen pictured "the horns of the unicorn". We read in Balaam's parable: "El brought them out of Egypt; He hath as it were the strength of the *reem*"; and in Moses's blessing of the tribes Joseph's horns are the two horns of reems.' Doughty illustrates this with a sketch of a *wothyhi's* horn, nearly two feet long and somewhat curved, with raised rings at the base. He adds: 'It was a monkish darkness in natural knowledge to ascribe a single horn to a double forehead.' This is unfair on the monks: it was the pre-Christian Septuagint who had first given the *rem* a single horn. And it is possible that they translated *rem* as 'unicorn' from a misunderstanding of an icon in the margin of an illustrated Hebrew Pentateuch—such there were. In the context of Moses's blessing, Joseph 'with the horns of a *rem*' would naturally have been depicted in the persons of his two sons, Ephraim and Manasseh, jointly called 'Joseph', as twin *rems* with only one horn apiece. The single horn, emphasized by its double occurrence, would suggest to the translators the beast described by Ctesias in his *Indica*. The horn was a cure-all and especially good against poison.

The connexion of the apple-tree with immortality is ancient and widespread in Europe. What does 'apple' mean? According to the *Oxford English Dictionary* its etymology is unknown, but the word runs Northwestward across Europe all the way from the Balkans to Ireland in a form approximating in most languages to *Apol*.

It is clear that the ancient icon of the Three Goddesses, the apple and the young shepherd of Ida, which has been iconotropically interpreted by some early enemy of women in the story of the 'Apple of Discord' (how

Paris adjudicated the apple to the Love-goddess) had an entirely different meaning. To award an apple to the Love-goddess would have been an impertinence on the Shepherd's part. All apples were hers. Did Merddin present Olwen with the apple orchard? Did Adam give the Mother of All Living an apple?[1] Obviously the three Goddesses are, as usual, the three persons of the ancient Triple Goddess, not jealous rivals, and obviously the Love-goddess is giving the apple to the Shepherd (or goatherd), not receiving it from him. It is the apple of immortality and he is the young Dionysus—the god commemorated by the kid stuffed with apples; for according to Hesychius and Stephanus of Byzantium one of Dionysus's titles was Eriphos, 'the Kid'. Virgil has expressed the wrong notion in his *Georgics*: he says that the kid spitted on hazel is sacrificed to Dionysus because the goat and the hazel-tree are both inimical to the vine. Whether the word *Apol* is a chance approximation to Apollo, who is the immortal part of Dionysus, or whether the apple is named after him, is a doubtful point. But it is remarkable that in Greece the words for 'goat' (or sheep) and 'apple' are identical (*mĕlŏn*)—the Latin is *mālum*. Hercules, who combined Dionysus and Apollo in a single person, was called Mēlon because apples were offered to him by his worshippers; and because he was given the bough with the golden apples by the Three Daughters of the West—the Triple Goddess again; it was these apples that made him immortal. The conclusion of the story of the Apple of Discord, that the Shepherd won Helen as a reward for his judgement, evidently derives from a companion icon to the 'Judgement', showing a young Shepherd hand in hand with Helen. But Helen was not a mortal woman; she was Helle, or Persephone, a Goddess of Death and Resurrection. Hercules, Theseus, Castor and Pollux, were all depicted in her company in archaic works of art.

Though the apple was the most palatable of wild fruits growing on

---

[1] In the *Genesis* story of Adam and Eve the iconotropic distortion is, nevertheless, very thorough. Clearly, Jehovah did not figure in the original myth. It is the Mother of all Living, conversing in triad, who casts Adam out of her fertile riverine dominions because he has usurped some prerogative of hers—whether caprifying fig-trees or planting grain is not clear —lest he should also usurp her prerogative of dispensing justice and uttering oracles. He is sent off to till the soil in some less bountiful region. This recalls what seems to be an intermediate version of the same myth: Triptolemus, a favourite of the Barley-goddess Demeter, is sent off from Eleusis in Attica with a bag of seed, to teach the whole world agriculture, and departs in a car drawn by serpents. The curse in *Genesis* on the woman, that she should be at enmity with the serpent, is obviously misplaced: it must refer to the ancient rivalry decreed between the sacred king Adam and the Serpent for the favours of the Goddess; Adam is fated to bruise the Serpent's head, but the Serpent will sting Adam's sacred heel, each in turn bringing the other to his annual death. That Eve, 'the Mother of All Living' was formed by God from Adam's rib seems an anecdote based on a picture of the naked goddess Anatha of Ugarit watching while Aleyn, *alias* Baal, drives a curved knife under the fifth rib of his twin Mot: this murder has been iconotropically misread as Jehovah's removal of a sixth rib, which turns into Eve. The twins, who fought for her favours, were gods of the Waxing and the Waning Year.

trees, why should it have been given such immense mythic importance? The clue is to be found in the legend of Curoi's soul that was hidden in an apple; when the apple was cut across by Cuchulain's sword 'night fell upon Curoi'. For if an apple is halved cross-wise each half shows a five-pointed star in the centre, emblem of immortality, which represents the Goddess in her five stations from birth to death and back to birth again. It also represents the planet of Venus—Venus to whom the apple was sacred—adored as Hesper the evening star on one half of the apple, and as Lucifer Son of the Morning on the other.

The apple of the Thracian Orphic cult seems to have been the sorb rather than the quince, the crab, or the true apple, because Orpheus, whose name and singing head identify him with Bran the alder-god, is called the son of Oeagrius; *Oea Agria* means the wild service-tree'.

Chapter Fifteen

THE SEVEN PILLARS

S ince the seven pillars of Wisdom are identified by Hebrew mystics with the seven days of Creation and with the seven days of the week, one suspects that the astrological system which links each day of the week to one of the heavenly bodies has an arboreal counterpart. The astrological system is so ancient, widespread and consistent in its values that it is worth noting in its various forms. Its origin is probably, but not necessarily, Babylonian. The second list shown here is that of the Sabians of Harran, who took part in the Sea-people's invasion of Northern Syria about 1200 B.C.; it makes the connexion between the Babylonian and the Western lists.

Planet	*Baby-lonian*	*Sabian*	*Latin*	*French*	*German*	*English*
Sun	Samas	Samas	Sol	Dominus	Sun	Sun
Moon	Sin	Sin	Luna	Luna	Moon	Moon
Mars	Nergal	Nergal	Mars	Mars	Zivis	Zio
Mercury	Nabu	Nabu	Mercurius	Mercurius	Wotan	Woden
Juppiter	Marduk	Bel	Juppiter	Juppiter	Thor	Thor
Venus	Ishtar	Beltis	Venus	Venus	Freia	Frigg
Saturn	Ninib	Cronos	Saturnus	Saturn	Saturn	Saturn

In Aristotle's list, Wednesday's planet is ascribed alternatively to Hermes or Apollo, Apollo having by that time exceeded Hermes in his reputation for wisdom; Tuesday's alternatively to Hercules or Ares (Mars), Hercules being a deity of better omen than Ares; Friday's alternatively to Aphrodite or Hera, Hera corresponding more closely than Aphrodite with the Babylonian Queen of Heaven, Ishtar.

The seven sacred trees of the Irish grove were, as has already been mentioned: birch, willow, holly, hazel, oak, apple and alder. This sequence also holds good for the days of the week, since we can confidently assign the alder to Saturn (Bran); the apple to the Love-goddess Venus or Freia; the oak to the Thunder-god Juppiter or Thor; the willow to the Moon (Circe or Hecate); the holly to Mars, the scarlet-faced War-god; and the birch naturally begins the week as it begins the solar year.[1] The tree of Wednesday, sacred to the God of Eloquence, one would expect to be Woden's ash; but with the ancient Irish the tree of eloquence and wisdom was the hazel, not the ash, the Belgic god Odin or Woden having been a latecomer to Ireland. So these are the seven trees, with their planets, days and letters:

Sun	Sunday	Birch	B
Moon	Monday	Willow	S
Mars	Tuesday	Holly	T
Mercury	Wednesday	Hazel (or ash)	C
Juppiter	Thursday	Oak	D
Venus	Friday	Apple	Q
Saturn	Saturday	Alder	F

It is easy to reconstruct the appropriate formula in Classical Latin for the daily dedication to the Lord of the Heavens of the devotee's heart:

Benignissime, Solo Tibi Cordis Devotionem Quotidianam Facio.
('Most Gracious One to Thee alone I make a daily devotion of my heart.')

And the Greek, which had lost its Q (Koppa) and F (Digamma) must content itself with a second C (Kappa) and a Ph (Phi):

Beltiste Soi Tēn Cardiān Didōmi Cathēmeriōs Phylaxomenēn.
('Best One, every day I give my heart into Thy Keeping.')

So the poetic answer to Job's poetic question: 'Where shall wisdom be found and where is the place of understanding?' which his respect for Jehovah the All-wise prevented him from facing is: 'Under an apple-tree, by pure meditation, on a Friday evening, in the season of apples, when the moon is full.' But the finder will be Wednesday's child.

The sacred grove is perhaps referred to in *Ezekiel, XLVII* (a passage quoted in the Gnostic Epistle to *Barnabas, XI, 10*). Ezekiel in a vision sees the holy waters of a river issuing eastward from under the threshold of the House of God, full of fish, with trees on both sides of the river 'whose leaves shall not fade nor their fruit be consumed. Each shall bring forth new fruit according to their months, the fruit for meat and the leaves for medicine: and this shall be the border whereby you shall inherit the land according to the tribes of Israel, and Joseph shall have two portions.' The reference to thirteen tribes, not twelve, and to the 'months' of the

---

[1] In the North Country ballad of *The Wife of Usher's Well*, the dead sons who return in the dead of winter to visit their mother, wear birch leaves in their hats. The author remarks that the tree from which they plucked the leaves grew at the entrance of the Paradise where their souls were housed, which is what one would expect. Presumably they wore birch as a token that they were not earth-bound evil spirits but blessed souls on compassionate leave.

trees, suggests that the same calendar is being used. Moreover, the theme of roe and apple-tree occurs in the *Canticles*.

The *Canticles*, though apparently no more than a collection of village love-songs, were officially interpreted by the Pharisee sages of Jesus's day as the mystical essence of King Solomon's wisdom, and as referring to the love of Jehovah for Israel; which is why in the Anglican Bible they are interpreted as 'Christ's love for his Church'. The fact is that originally they celebrated the mysteries of an annual sacred marriage between Salmaah the King of the year and the Flower Queen, and their Hellenistic influence is patent.

The second chapter of the *Canticles* runs:

I am the rose of Sharon, the lily of the valleys.

As the lily among thorns, so is my love among the daughters.

As the apple tree among the trees of the grove, so is my beloved among the sons. I sat down under his shadow with great delight and his fruit was sweet to my taste.

He brought me to the banquet-house and his banner over me was love.

Stay me with flagons, comfort me with apples, for I am sick of love.

His left hand is under my head, his right hand doth embrace me.

I charge you, O ye daughters of Jerusalem by the roes and by the hinds of the field that ye stir not up, nor wake my love till he please.

The voice of my beloved! Behold he cometh leaping upon the mountains, skipping upon the hills.

My beloved is like a roe or a wild hart. . . .

My beloved is mine, I am his, he feedeth among the lilies.

The 'lilies' are the red anemones that sprang up from the drops of blood that fell from Adonis's side when the wild boar killed him. The apple is the Sidonian (i.e. Cretan) apple, or quince, sacred to Aphrodite the Love-goddess, and first cultivated in Europe by the Cretans. The true apple was not known in Palestine in Biblical times and it is only recently that varieties have been introduced there that yield marketable fruit. But the apple grew wild in ancient times on the Southern shores of the Black Sea, the provenience of the other trees of the series, and around Trebizond still occasionally forms small woods. It also occurred in Macedonia—the original home of the Muses—and in Euboea where Hercules received the injury that sent him to the pyre on Mount Oeta; but in both these cases may have been an early importation.

There seems to be a strong connexion between the tree-calendar and the ritual at the Feast of the Tabernacles at Jerusalem, already mentioned in connexion with the willow and alder. The worshippers carried in their right hand an *ethrog*, a sort of citron, and in their left a *lulab*, or thyrsus, consisting of the intertwined boughs of palm, willow and myrtle. The *ethrog* was not the original fruit, having been introduced from India after the Captivity, and is thought to have displaced the quince because of the quince's erotic connotations. In the reformation of religion which took place during the Exile the Jews broke as far as possible all the ties which bound them to orgiastic religion. The ritual of Tabernacles was taken over by the Hebrews with other rites in honour of the Moon-goddess, and the ordinances for its observance were fathered on Moses, as part of the great recension of the Law ascribed to King Josiah but probably made during the Exile. I have already mentioned the disparaging *Haggadah* on the willow; the meaning of the myrtle was also changed from the shadow of death to the pleasant shade of summer, on the authority of Isaiah who had praised the tree (*Isaiah, XLI, 19; LV, 13*).

The feast began on the first new moon of the year, and in the quince season. Both willow and apple have 5—the number especially sacred to the Moon-goddess—as the number of their letter-strokes in the Ogham finger-alphabet. The myrtle does not occur in the Beth-Luis-Nion, but may well be the Greek equivalent of the remaining consonant in the Beth-Luis-Nion that has 5 as its number of strokes—the elder. The myrtle was sacred to the Love-goddess Aphrodite all over the Mediterranean, partly because it grows best near the sea shore, partly because of its fragrance; nevertheless, it was the tree of death. Myrto, or Myrtea, or Myrtoessa was a title of hers and the pictures of her sitting with Adonis in the myrtle-shade were deliberately misunderstood by the Classical poets. She was not vulgarly courting him, as they pretended, but was promising him Life-in-Death; for myrtle was evergreen and was a token of the resurrection of the dead King of the year. The myrtle is connected in Greek myth with the death of kings: Myrtilus, son of Hermes (Mercury) who was charioteer to Oenomaus the King of Elis, pulled the linch-pins from the wheels of his master's chariot and so caused his death. Pelops, who then married Oenomaus's widow, ungratefully threw Myrtilus into the sea. Myrtilus cursed the House of Pelops with his dying breath and thereafter every Pelopid monarch was dogged by his ghost. The 'wheel' was the life of the King; R, the last consonant of the alphabet 'pulls out the pin' at the last month of his reign. Pelops's dynasty obtained the throne of Elis, but all his successors similarly met their end in the R month. (Myrtilus became the northern constellation *Auriga*, the charioteer.) The myrtle resembles the elder in the medicinal qualities attributed to its leaves and berries; the berries are ripe in December, the R month. Myrtle boughs were carried by Greek emigrants when they intended to found a new colony, as if to say: 'The old cycle is ended; we hope to start a new one with the favour of the Love-goddess, who rules the sea.'

Thus the thyrsus contained three trees, each representing a flight of five calendar letters, or one-third of the year; besides the palm which represented the extra day (or period of five days) on which the Sun-god was born. The number fifteen was therefore of prime importance in the Festival: the Levites sang the fifteen Songs of Ascent (attributed to King David) as they stood on the fifteen steps leading up from the Women's Court to the Court of Israel. The number also figures in the architecture of Solomon's 'house of the Forest of Lebanon' which was more than twice the size of the House of the Lord. It was built on three rows of cedar pillars, fifteen to a row, and was 50 cubits long by 30 high and wide; with an adjoining porch 30 cubits wide, 50 long, height not given—probably 10 cubits.

The Hebrew canon of the trees of the week, the seven pillars of Wisdom, is not difficult to establish. For the birch, which was not a Palestinian tree, the most likely substitute is the *retem* or wild broom, which was the tree under which the prophet Elijah rested on Mount Horeb ('the mountain of glowing heat') and seems to have been sacred to the Sun. Like the birch, it was used as a besom for the expulsion of evil spirits. Willow remains the same. For the holly, the kerm-oak, already mentioned in Chapter Ten as the tree from which the ancients obtained their royal scarlet dye. This ascription of the kerm-oak to Nergal or Mars, is confirmed by a characteristic passage in Frazer's *Golden Bough*:

> The heathen of Harran offered to the sun, moon and planets human victims who were chosen on the ground of their supposed resemblance to the heavenly bodies to which they were sacrificed; for example, the priests, clothed in red and smeared with blood, offered a red-haired, red-cheeked man to 'the red planet Mars' in a temple which was painted red and draped with red hangings.

The substitute for the hazel was the almond: this was the tree from which Aaron took his magic rod, and the *Menorah* the seven-branched candlestick in the Temple Sanctuary at Jerusalem had its sconces in the form of almonds and represented Aaron's rod when it budded. It was this branch that Jeremiah (*Jeremiah I, 11*) was shown as a visionary token that God had granted him prophetic wisdom. The sconces stood for the seven heavenly bodies of the week, and the central sconce was the fourth, namely that dedicated to Wisdom, which gives its name to all the rest; its branch formed the shaft of the candlestick. For the oak, the terebinth sacred to Abraham. For the apple, the quince. For the alder, since we know that the alder was banned in Temple worship, the pomegranate which supplies a red dye as the alder does. The pomegranate was Saul's sacred tree, and sacred to Rimmon, a name for Adonis from whose blood it is said to have sprung. Also, the Paschal victim was traditionally spitted on pomegranate wood. The pomegranate was the only fruit

allowed to be brought inside the Holy of Holies—miniature pomegranates
were sewn on the High Priest's robes when he made his yearly entry.
Since the seventh day was sacred to Jehovah and Jehovah was a form of
Bran, or Saturn, or Ninib,[1] everything points to the pomegranate as the
tree of the seventh day. So:

Sun	—Broom
Moon	—Willow
Mars	—Kerm
Mercury	—Almond
Juppiter	—Terebinth
Venus	—Quince
Saturn	—Pomegranate.

The one doubtful tree here is the broom, or its Irish counterpart, the birch.
The seven trees of the Irish grove all belong to the summer months except
B, the birch, which has taken the place of H, the hawthorn: and has apparently been chosen because it is the leading letter of the first flight of five
trees, as H is of the second. But, as will be shown in the next chapter, B
was used as the cypher equivalent of H not only in Hyginus's *Fable* 271
but in the third century A.D. Ogham inscription on the Callen Stone. So it
seems that Sunday's original letter was not B, but H, of which the Hebrew
tree, corresponding with the hawthorn, was the *Sant*, or wild acacia, the
sort with golden flowers and sharp thorns, better known to readers of the
Bible as 'shittim'-wood, i.e. from Cyprus. It was from its water-proof
timber that the arks of the Sun-hero Osiris and his counterparts Noah and
Armenian Xisuthros were built; also the Ark of the Covenant, the recorded measurements of which proved it sacred to the Sun. This is a
host-tree of the mistletoe-like loranthus, Jehovah's oracular 'burning
bush', and the source of manna.

The use of H for Sunday's letter explains Lucan's puzzling account of
the sacred grove at Marseilles which Julius Caesar felled because it inter-
fered with his fortification of the city. Marseilles was a Greek city, a centre
of Pythagoreanism, and Caesar had to use an axe himself on one of the
oaks before he could persuade anyone to begin the work of desecration.
The grove, according to Lucan, contained holly-oak, Dodonian oak, and
alder—T, D and F. He specifies none of the remaining trees except the

[1] Ninib, the Assyrian Saturn, was the god of the South, and therefore of the noon-day
Sun, and also of mid-Winter when the Sun attains its most southerly point and halts for a
day. In both these capacities he was the god of Repose, for noon is the time for rest in hot
climates. That Jehovah was openly identified with Saturn-Ninib in Bethel before the Northern Captivity is proved in *Amos, V, 26* where the image and star of 'Succoth-Chiun' are
mentioned as having been brought to the shrine; and that the same was done in Jerusalem
before the Southern Captivity is proved by the vision of *Ezekiel, VII, 3, 5* where his image,
'the image of jealousy' was set up at the north gate of the Temple, so that devotees would face
southwards while adoring him; and close by (verse *14*) women were wailing for Adonis.

cypress, which the Massiliots had brought from their parent state of Phocis where it was sacred to Artemis. One would not have expected the cypress in the grove; but elsewhere in Greece, particularly at Corinth and Messene, it was sacred to Artemis Cranaë or Carnasia; which makes it an H tree, an evergreen substitute for the hawthorn also sacred to Cranaë or Carnea. Thus as the tree of Sunday, succeeding the alder of Saturday, it symbolized resurrection in the Orphic mysteries, the escape of the Sun-hero from Calypso's alder-girt island, and became attached to the cult of Celestial Hercules. Cypress is still the prime resurrection symbol in Mediterranean church-yards.[1]

There is a clear correspondence between this canon and that of the seven days of Creation as characterized in the first chapter of *Genesis*.

Sun	— Light
Moon	— Division of Waters
Mars	— Dry Land, Pasture and Trees
Mercury	— Heavenly Bodies and the Seasons
Juppiter	— Sea-beasts and Birds
Venus	— Land-beasts, Man and Woman
Saturn	— Repose.

The apparent illogic of the creation of Light, and even of Pasture and Trees, before that of the Heavenly Bodies and Seasons—though here it has been ingeniously suggested by Mr. Ernst Schiff that the Heavenly Bodies were not visible until the fourth day because of the 'damp haze' mentioned in verse 9 of the Creation story, and therefore not created in the sense of not being manifested—is accounted for by the powers proper to the deities who rule over the planetary days of the week. The Sun-

---

[1] The cypress occurs in the riddling list of *Ecclesiasticus XXIV*, *13–17*, (I quote the text as restored by Edersheim) where Wisdom describes herself as follows:

I was exalted like a cedar in Lebanon and like a cypress-tree on Mount Hermon.

I was exalted like a palm-tree in Engedi and as a rose-tree in Jericho, as an olive in the field, and as a plane-tree.

I exhaled sweet smell like cinnamon and aromatic asphalathus, I diffused a pleasant odour like the best myrrh, like galbanum, onyx and sweet storax, and like the fumes of frankin-cense.

Like an oleander ['turpentine-tree' in A.V.] I stretched out my branches which are branches of glory and beauty.

Like a vine I budded forth beauty and my flowers ripen into glory and riches.

Ecclesiasticus has mixed alphabetic trees with aphrodisiac perfumes and trees of another cate-gory; but H for cypress and M for vine suggests that the last-mentioned, or only, trees in verses 13, 14, 16 and 17, spell out *Chokmah*, the Hebrew word for Wisdom: *Ched, Kaf, Mem, He*. (In Hebrew, vowels are not written.) If this is so, the oleander is CH; and the plane is a surro-gate for the almond, K, which as the tree of Wisdom herself cannot figure as a part of the tree-riddle of which it is the answer; in the time of Ecclesiasticus the plane had long been associated by the Greeks with the pursuit of wisdom. The four other trees, cedar, palm, rose and sweet olive, represent respectively sovereignty, motherhood, beauty and fruitfulness— Wisdom's characteristics as a quasi-goddess.

god rules over Light, the Moon over Water, Mars over Pasture and Trees, and Mercury is the God of Astronomy. Clearly the *Genesis* legend is subsequent to the fixing of the canon of planets, days and gods. The allocation of Sea-beasts and Birds to the fifth day is natural, because the god of the oak or terebinth cult is, in general, the son of a Sea-goddess to whom the Dove, the Eagle and all other birds are sacred, and himself takes the form of a sea-beast. The order to man and woman to couple and produce their kind, like the creatures over which they have dominion, is appropriate to the day of Venus. The pleasant sloth of Saturn—in whose golden day, according to the Classical poets, men ate honey and acorns in a Terrestrial Paradise and did not trouble to till the soil, or even to hunt, since the earth brought forth abundantly of her own bounty—explains the seventh day as one of repose. The Jewish apocalyptic prophecy (which Jesus took literally) of the Heavenly Kingdom of Jehovah referred to a restoration of this same golden age if only man would cease to busy himself with wars and labours; for Jehovah required rest on the seventh day. As has been already explained, the geographical situation of the former Terrestrial Paradise was variously given. The Babylonians placed it in the Delta of the Euphrates; the Greeks in Crete; the pre-Exilic Hebrews at Hebron in Southern Judaea.

It is of the highest theological importance that Jehovah announced himself to Moses as 'I am that I am' or (more literally) 'I am whoever I choose to be' from the acacia rather than from any other tree; because this constituted a definition of his godhead. Had he announced himself from the terebinth, as the earlier Jehovah had done at Hebron, this would have been to reveal himself as Bel, or Marduk, the god of Thursday and of the seventh month, the Aramaean Juppiter, the Paeonian Apollo. But from the acacia, the tree of the first day of the week, he revealed himself as the God of the Menorah, the transcendental Celestial God, the God who presently said: 'Thou shalt have none other Gods but me . . . for I the Lord thy God am a jealous God.' The acacia is, indeed, a thorny, jealous, self-sufficient tree, needs very little water and, like Odin's ash, strangles with its roots all other trees growing near it. Uath, the month dedicated to the acacia, was the one in which the annual Hebron Fair took place, and so holy that (as has been mentioned in Chapter Ten) all sexual congress and self-beautification was tabooed during it: it was the month of the annual purification of the temples in Greece, Italy and the Near East.

The not yet completed Ages of the World, quoted from Nennius by Gwion, are based on the same planetary canon:

[Sunday]   'The first Age of the World is from Adam to Noah.'
Adam's was the first human eye to see the light of the sun, or the Glory of God. Sunday is the day of light.

266

[Monday]   'The second Age is from Noah to Abraham.'
                  Noah's Age was introduced by the Deluge. Monday is
                  the day of Water.

[Tuesday]   'The third Age is from Abraham to David.'
                  Abraham was famous for his flocks and herds and for
                  having the fertile Land of Canaan promised to his de-
                  scendants. Tuesday is the day of Trees and Pasture.

[Wednesday]   'The fourth Age is from David to Daniel.'
                  The third Age should really run from Abraham to
                  Solomon and the fourth from Solomon to Daniel—the
                  change was apparently made in honour of St. David—
                  since in the introductory paragraph Nennius gives the
                  number of years, 1048, from Abraham to the building of
                  Solomon's Temple, which David was to have built if he
                  had not sinned. Solomon's wisdom was embodied in the
                  Temple. Wednesday is the day of Wisdom.

[Thursday]   'The fifth Age is from Daniel to John the Baptist.'
                  In the introductory paragraph Nennius gives the
                  number of years, 612, 'from Solomon to the rebuilding
                  of the Temple which was accomplished under Darius
                  King of the Persians.' Here Daniel has been substituted
                  for Darius (who put him in the lions' den at Babylon) as
                  being under the particular guidance of God; but in the
                  myth of Jonah the power of Babylon was symbolized by
                  the whale which swallowed and then spewed out the
                  chosen people when they cried out from its belly. Thurs-
                  day is the day of Sea-beasts and Fishes.

[Friday]   'The sixth Age is from John the Baptist to the
                  Judgement Day.'
                  Nennius gives the number of years: 548, from Darius
                  to the Ministry of Jesus Christ; so John the Baptist
                  figures here as having assisted at Jesus's Baptism. The
                  object of the Ministry was to preach the Gospel of Love;
                  to separate the sheep from the goats; to make the lion lie
                  down with the lamb; to persuade man to be born again—
                  the Second Adam redeeming the First Adam. Friday is
                  the day of Land-beasts, Man and Love.

[Saturday]   'In the seventh Age our Lord Jesus Christ will come
                  to judge the living and the dead, and the world by
                  fire.'

In the present Age, the sixth, of which 973 years had passed when Nennius wrote, man must look hopefully forward to the seventh Age for eventual repose of soul. Saturday is the day of Repose.[1]

The Rabbinical explanation of the Menorah, in terms of the creation of the world in seven days, is obviously faulty: the ascription of the central light to the Sabbath contradicts the 'Let there be Lights' text of the fourth day. The more ancient tradition preserved in the *Zohar*: 'These lamps, like the seven planets above, receive their light from the Sun', goes back to the pre-exilic Sun-cult. The Menorah was placed in the Sanctuary to face W.S.W., towards On-Heliopolis, as the original home of the Sun-god to whom Moses was priest.

Josephus (*Antiquities v. 5; 5*) writes of the three wonders of the Sanctuary, namely the table of shew-bread, and the altar of incense:

> 'Now, the seven lamps signified the seven planets, for so many there were springing out of the candlestick; the twelve loaves that were upon the table signified the circle of the Zodiac and the year; and the altar of incense by its thirteen kinds of sweet-smelling spices with which the sea replenished it, signified that God is the lord of all things in both the uninhabitable and the habitable parts of the earth, and that they are all to be dedicated to his use.'

These thirteen (rather than four) spices must belong to an early secret tradition not mentioned in the Law, coeval with the instructions in *Numbers xxix, 13* for the sacrifice of thirteen bullocks on the first day of the Feast of Tabernacles. (Incidentally, the total number of bullocks to be sacrificed from the inauguration of the critical seventh month to the end of the seven days of the Feast was the sacred seventy-two again. The sacrifice of a single bullock on the eighth day was a separate matter.) Josephus is hinting that the number thirteen refers to Rahab, the prophetic Goddess of the Sea, Guardian of Sheol ('the uninhabitable parts of the world') where God also, however, claims suzerainty.

[1] The tradition of Nennius's Seven Ages has survived in an English folk-saying which runs:

The lives of three wattles, the life of a hound;
The lives of three hounds, the life of a steed;
The lives of three steeds, the life of a man;
The lives of three men, the life of an eagle;
The lives of three eagles, the life of a yew;
The life of a yew, the length of a ridge;
Seven ridges from Creation to Doom.

A wattle (hurdle) lasts for three years: therefore a hound for 9, a horse for 27, a man for 81, an eagle for 243 and a yew for 729. 'The length of a *ridge*' is evidently a mistake, the saying being translated from the monkish Latin *aevum*, age, miscopied as *arvum*, ridge. With the length of an Age averaging 729 years, the total length of the seven Ages is 5103, which corresponds well enough with Nennius's account.

What appears to have been a jewel-sequence corresponding with Ezekiel's tree-sequence was arrayed in three rows on the golden breast-plate worn by the High Priest, called in Greek the *logion* or 'little word-giver' (*Exodus XXVIII, 15*). It was made by Egyptian craftsmen; and the King of Tyre wore a similar one in honour of Hercules Melkarth (*Ezekiel, XXVIII, 13*). The jewels, which gave oracular responses by lighting up in the dark of the Sanctuary, were probably hollow-cut with a revolving drum behind them on which was a small strip of phosphorus: when the drum was revolved the message was spelt out in ouija style as the strip of phosphorus came to rest behind different letters in turn.

The account of the breastplate given in *Exodus* mentions twelve precious stones, inscribed with the names of the Twelve Tribes, set in a gold plaque eight inches square. But there is a thirteenth stone which is given such importance elsewhere in the Bible, for example in *Isaiah, LIV, 12,* that we may assume it to have been part of the original series. This is the *kadkod,* mistranslated in the Authorised Version as 'agate', probably the red carbuncle, and we may assign it to the tribe of Gad which disappeared early in Israelite history. All the jewels are mistranslated in the Authorised Version, and a slightly different set appears, in *Revelation, XXI, 19,* as forming the foundations of the New Jerusalem. The breast-plate was still in existence in the time of Josephus, though it no longer lighted up, and probably contained all the original stones except the *kadkod.* We can build up our jewel-sequence from it, relying on J. I. Myers' solid scholarship to identify the jewels and then re-arranging them in a likely seasonal order. For we may assume that the order given in the Bible, like the order of the elements in the *Song of Amergin,* has been pur-posely confused for reasons of security.

We know that amethyst, *ahlamah,* is the wine stone—its Greek name means 'charm against drunkenness'—and can be assigned to M, the vine month. Similarly, yellow serpentine, *tarsis,* naturally belongs to G, the yellow-berried ivy month. The banded red agate, *sebo,* belongs to C, the month before the vintage, when the grapes are still red. The white carnelian, *yahalem,* and the yellow cairngorm, *lesem,* may belong to the glaring hot D and T months; the blood-red carbuncle, *kadkod,* to S, the month of the *razzia* or raiding party; and the lapis lazuli, *sappur,* to H, the first month of summer, since it typifies the dark blue sky. *Sappur* is trans-lated 'sapphire' in the Authorised Version, and Ezekiel mentions it as the colour of the Throne of God. The light green jasper, *yāsepheh,* and the dark green malachite, *soham,* suit NG and R, the winter rain-months of Palestine. *Nophek,* the bright red fire-garnet, or pyrope, is likely to be F, the month of the Spring equinox. The rusty-red Edomite sard, *odem,* comes first in the year in honour of Adam, the red man—for 'Edom', 'Adam' and 'Odem' are all variants of the same word meaning rusty-red:

odem belongs to the month B. The remaining two stones corresponding with L, the month of Hercules's golden cup, and N, the month of his sea-voyage, are *pitdan*, clear yellow chrysolite, and *bareketh*, green beryl—the name *beryl* meaning, in Greek, the sea-jewel.

We can go further: with the help of the names given to the tribes by their mothers in *Genesis XXIX* and *XXX*, and of the prophetic blessings or curses bestowed on them by Jacob in *Genesis XLVIII* and *XLIX*, we can assign a letter and month to each tribe. To Ephraim ('fruitful') and Manasseh ('forgetfulness'), the two sons of Joseph who was a 'fruitful vine' we can assign the months C and M; and B to Reuben the first-born, who had Edomite connections. To Reuben's four full-brothers, Gad ('a robber band') Levi ('set apart') Asher ('royal dainties are on his plate') and Simeon ('the bloody brother whose anger is fierce'), the months of S, H, D and T. Gad has the month of the *razzia*, when the corn is invitingly ripe; Levi has the H month because it is the month of peculiar holiness; Asher has the important royal D month because his name is connected with the Ashera, the terebinth groves of the midsummer sacrifice; Simeon has T, the murderous month when the sun is at its fiercest. To Issachar, 'the strong ass between two burdens', we can assign L, the month of rest between sowing and harvest. To Zebulon, 'among the ships', belongs the sea-voyage month of N; to Judah ('lion's whelp'), the Spring solstice month of F; to Naphtali, 'he strove', the ploughing month, R. And to 'Little Benjamin their ruler' belongs New Year's Day, the day of the Divine Child. When we have assigned to Dan, 'like a serpent', the serpentine month of G, we naturally fill the Ng month, which alone remains vacant, with the tribe of Dinah: for Dinah, the female twin of Dan, was another tribe that disappeared early (see *Genesis, XXXIV*), and since the Ng month marks the beginning of the rains and the resumption of the seasonal cycle of growth, a woman naturally belongs there.

In my *King Jesus* I have tentatively reconstructed the hymn to Hercules Melkarth on which 'Jacob's Blessing' seems to be based. It combines the words of the Blessing with the traditional meanings of the tribal names and begins with Hercules swaying to and fro in his golden cup. I take this opportunity of correcting my misplacement of the brothers Levi, Gad and Asher:

Reuben—B
SEE THE SON *on the water tossed*
In might and excellency of power,

Issachar—L
Resting at ease between two feats—
He has paid the shipman all his HIRE—

Zebulon—N
DWELLING secure in the hollow ship
Until by winds he is wafted home.

Judah—F
Hark, how he roars like a lion's whelp,
Hark, how his brothers PRAISE his name . . .

Gad—S
Though A TROOP of raiders cast him down
He will cast them down in his own good time.

Levi—H
He is SET APART from all his brothers
And held in service to the shrine.

Asher—D
HAPPY is he; his bread is fat,
Royal dainties are on his plate, etc.

Here then, for what it is worth, is a list of the jewels of the months and of the tribes. (The breastplate was made entirely of gold in honour of the Sun: but if a sequence of five metals corresponded with the five vowels A.O.U.E.I. it was probably, to judge from the traditional planetary signs still attached to them: silver, gold, copper, tin, lead.)

B	Dec. 24	Red Sard	Reuben
L	Jan. 21	Yellow Chrysolite	Issachar
N	Feb. 18	Sea-green Beryl	Zebulon
F	March 18	Fire-Garnet	Judah
S	April 15	Blood-red Carbuncle	Gad
H	May 13	Lapis Lazuli	Levi
D	June 10	White Carnelian	Asher
T	July 8	Yellow Cairngorm	Simeon
C	Aug. 5	Banded Red Agate	Ephraim
M	Sept. 2	Amethyst	Manasseh
G	Sept. 30	Yellow Serpentine	Dan
Ng	Oct. 28	Clear Green Jasper	Dinah
R	Nov. 25	Dark Green Malachite	Naphtali

For the extra day, Dec. 23rd, which belongs to Benjamin 'Son of My Right Hand', that is to say 'The Ruler of the South', (since the Sun reaches its most southerly stage in mid-winter) the jewel is amber, which Ezekiel makes the colour of the upper half of Jehovah's body; the lower half being fire. Benjamin's tree was the hyssop, or wild caper, which grows green in walls and crannies and was the prime lustral tree in Hebrew use, or the holy loranthus, which preys on desert tamarisks.

Chapter Sixteen

THE HOLY UNSPEAKABLE
NAME OF GOD

The *Ogham Craobh*, which is printed in Ledwich's *Antiquities of Ireland* and attested by an alphabetic inscription at Callen, County Clare, Ireland, ascribed to 295 A.D., runs as follows:

$$
\begin{array}{llll}
\text{B} & \text{L} & \text{N} & T & \text{S} \\
B & \text{D} & \text{T} & \text{C} & \text{Q} \\
\text{M} & \text{G} & \text{Ng} & \text{Z} & \text{R}
\end{array}
$$

This is the ordinary Ogham alphabet as given by Macalister; except that where one would expect F and H it has T and B—the very consonants which occur mysteriously in Hyginus's account of the seven original letters invented by the Three Fates. There was evidently a taboo at Callen on the F and H—T and B had to be used instead; and it looks as if just the same thing had happened in the 15-consonant Greek alphabet known to Hyginus, and that he refrained from specifying Palamedes's contribution of eleven consonants because he did not wish to call attention to the recurrence of B and T.

If so, the Palamedes alphabet can be reconstructed as follows in the Ogham order:

$$
\begin{array}{llll}
\text{B} & \text{L} & \text{N} & \text{F} & \text{S} \\
\text{H} & \text{D} & \text{T} & \text{C} \\
\text{M} & \text{G} & \text{[Ng]} & \text{R}
\end{array}
$$

There is no warrant for Ng in Greek, so I have enclosed it in square brackets, but it must be remembered that the original Pelasgians talked a non-Greek Language. This had nearly died out by the fifth century B.C. but, according to Herodotus, survived in at least one of the oracles of Apollo, that of Apollo Ptous, which was in Boeotian territory. He records that a certain Mys, sent by the son-in-law of King Darius of Persia to consult the Greek oracles, was attended by three Boeotian priests with triangular writing tablets. The priestess made her reply in a barbarous tongue which Mys, snatching a tablet from one of the priests, copied down. It proved to be in the Carian dialect, which Mys understood, being a 'European', that is to say of Cretan extraction—Europë, daughter of Agenor, having ridden to Crete from Phoenicia on the back of a bull. If Cretan was, as is probable, a Hamitic language it may well have had Ng at place 14. Ng is not part of the Greek alphabet and Dr. Macalister points out that even in Old Goidelic no word began with Ng, and that such words as NGOMAIR, and NGETAL which occur in the Ogham alphabets as the names of the Ng letter are wholly artificial forms of GOMAIR and GETAL. But in Hamitic languages the initial Ng is common, as a glance at the map of Africa will show.

The existence of this dubious Pelasgian letter Ng, which had not been borrowed by the makers of the Cadmean alphabet, may explain the uncertainty of 'twelve, or some say thirteen letters' ascribed by Diodorus Siculus to the Pelasgian alphabet; and may also explain why Ng in the middle of a word was in Greek spelt GG, as *Aggelos* for *Angelos,* G being the letter which immediately precedes Ng in the Beth-Luis-Nion. Yet from the analogy of the Beth-Luis-Nion it may be suspected that the Palamedes alphabet contained two secret letters which brought the number up to fifteen. The Latin alphabet at any rate was originally a 15-consonant one, with 5 vowels, and was probably arranged by 'Carmenta' as follows:

$$\begin{array}{ccccc} B & L & F & S & N \\ H & D & T & C & Q \\ M & G & Ng & P & R \end{array}$$

For the Romans continued to use the Ng sound at the beginning of words in Republican times—they even spelt *natus* as *gnatus,* and *navus* ('diligent') as *gnavus*—and probably pronounced it like the *gn* in the middle of such French words as *Catalogne* and *seigneur.*

It looks as if Epicharmus was the Greek who invented the early form of the Cadmean alphabet mentioned by Diodorus as consisting of sixteen consonants, namely the thirteen of the Palamedes alphabet as given above, less the Ng; plus *Zeta,* and *Pi* as a substitute for *Koppa* (Q); plus *Chi* and *Theta.* But only two letters are ascribed to Epicharmus by Hyginus; and these are given in the most reputable MSS. as *Chi* and *Theta.* So *Pi* (or *Koppa*) and *Zeta* are likely to have been concealed letters of the Palamedes alphabet, as *Quert* and *Straif* are concealed letters of the Beth-Luis-Nion; not mentioned by Hyginus because they were merely doubled C and S.

We know that Simonides then removed the H aspirate and also the F, *Digamma,* which was replaced by *Phi,* and added *Psi* and *Xi* and two vowels—long E, *Eta,* to which he assigned the character of H aspirate, and long O, *Omega;* which brought the total number of letters up to twenty-four.

All these alphabets seem to be carefully designed sacred alphabets, not selective Greek transcriptions of the commercial Phoenician alphabet of twenty-six letters as scratched on the Formello-Cervetri vases. One virtue of the Epicharmian alphabet lay in its having sixteen consonants—sixteen being the number of increase—and twenty-one letters in all, twenty-one being a number sacred to the Sun since the time of the Pharaoh Akhenaton who introduced into Egypt about the year 1415 B.C. the monotheistic cult of the sun's disc. Epicharmus, as an Asclepiad, was descended from the Sun.

It must be noted that Simonides's new consonants were artificial ones—previously *Xi* had been spelt *chi-sigma* and *Psi, pi-sigma*—and that there was no real need for them compared, for instance, with the need of new letters to distinguish long from short A, and long from short I. I suspect Simonides of having composed a secret alphabetical charm consisting of the familiar letter-names of the Greek alphabet arranged with the vowels and consonants together, in three eight-letter parts, each letter suggesting a word of the charm; for example *xi, psi* might stand for *xiphon psilon*, 'a naked sword'. Unfortunately the abbreviations of most of the Greek letter names are too short for this guess to be substantiated; it is only an occasional letter, like *lambda*, which seems to stand for *lampada* ('torches') and *sigma*, which seems to stand for *sigmos* ('a hissing for silence'), that hints at the secret.

But can we guess why Simonides removed F and H from the alphabet? And why Hyginus the Spaniard and the author of the Irish Callen inscription used B and T as cipher disguises for these same two letters? We can begin by noting that the Etruscan calendar, which the Romans adopted during the Republic, was arranged in *nundina*, or eight-day periods, in Greek called 'ogdoads' and that the Roman Goddess of Wisdom, Minerva, had 5 (written V) as her sacred numeral. We can identify Minerva with Carmenta, because she was generally credited at Rome with the invention of the arts and sciences and because flower-decorated boats, probably made of alder wood, were sailed on her festival, the *Quinquatria*. 'Quinquatria' means 'the five halls', presumably five seasons of the year, and was celebrated five days after the Spring New Year feast of the Calendar Goddess Anna Perenna; this suggests that the five days were those left over when the year had been divided into five seasons of 72 days each, the sanctity of the five and the seventy-two having been similarly established in the Beth-Luis-Nion system.

An alphabet-calendar arranged on this principle, with the vowels kept apart from the consonants, implies a 360-day year of five vowel-seasons, each of 72 days, with five days left over; each season being divided into three periods each consisting of twenty-four days. The 360-day year can also be divided, in honour of the Triple Goddess, into three 120-day seasons each containing five periods of equal length, namely twenty-four days—with the same five days over; and this is the year that was in public use in Egypt. The Egyptians said that the five days were those which the God Thoth (Hermes or Mercury) won at draughts from the Moon-goddess Isis, composed of the seventy-second parts of every day in the year; and the birthdays of Osiris, Horus, Set, Isis and Nephthys were celebrated on them in this order. The mythic sense of the legend is that a change of religion necessitated a change of calendar: that the old Moon-goddess year of 364 days with one day over was succeeded by a year of 360 days with five over, and that in the new system the first three periods of the year were allotted to Osiris, Horus and Set, and the last two to Isis and Nephthys. Though, under Assyrian influence, each of the three Egyptian seasons was divided into four periods of 30 days, not five of 24, the 72-day season occurs in the Egypto-Byblian myth that the Goddess Isis hid her child Horus, or Harpocrates, from the rage of the ass-eared Sun-god Set during the 72 hottest days of the year, namely the third of the five seasons, which was astronomically ruled by the Dog Sirius and the two Asses. (The hiding of the Child Horus seems to have been assisted by the Lapwing, a bird much used in the Etruscan science of augury which the Romans borrowed; at any rate, Pliny twice mentions in his *Natural History* that the Lapwing disappears completely between the rising of Sirius and its setting.)

But here the argument must be held up by a discussion of Set and his worship.

The Greek legend that the God Dionysus placed the Asses in the Sign of Cancer ('the Crab') suggests that the Dionysus who visited Egypt and was entertained by Proteus King of Pharos was Osiris, brother of the Hyksos god Typhon, *alias* Set. The Hyksos people, non-Semitic pastoral-ists, coming from Armenia or beyond, pressed down through Cappadocia, Syria and Palestine into Egypt about the year 1780 B.C. That they managed so easily to establish themselves in Northern Egypt with their capital at Pelusium, on the Canopic arm of the Nile Delta, can be accounted for only by an alliance with the Byblians of Phoenicia. Byblos, a protectorate of Egypt from very early times, was the 'Land of Negu' ('Trees') from which the Egyptians imported timber, and a cylinder seal of the Old Empire shows Adonis, the God of Byblos, in company with the horned Moon-goddess Isis, or Hathor, or Astarte. The Byblians who, with the Cretans, managed the Egyptian carrying-trade—the Egyptians hated the sea—had trading stations at Pelusium and elsewhere in Lower Egypt from very early times. To judge from the Homeric legend of King Proteus, the earliest Pelasgian settlers in the Delta used Pharos, the lighthouse island off what afterwards became Alexandria, as their sacred oracular island. Proteus, the oracular Old Man of the Sea, who was King of Pharos and lived in a cave—where Menelaus consulted him—had the power of changing his shape, like Merddin, Dionysus, Atabyrius, Llew Llaw, Periclymenus and all Sun-heroes of the same sort. Evidently Pharos was his Isle of Avalon. That Apuleius connects the *sistrum* of Osiris, used to frighten away the God Set, with Pharos suggests that Proteus and Osiris were there regarded as the same person. Proteus, according to Virgil, had another sacred island, Carpathus, between Crete and Rhodes; but that was the Thessalian Proteus. Another Proteus, spelt Proetus, was an Arcadian.

It would be a great mistake to think of Pharos as a secluded sacred island inhabited only by the attendants of the oracle: when Menelaus came there with his ships he was entering the largest port in the Mediterranean.[1] Gaston Jondet in his *Les ports submergés de l'ancienne Île de Pharos* (1916) has established the existence here even in pre-Hellenic times of a vast system of harbour-works, now submerged, exceeding in extent the island itself. They consisted of an inner basin covering 150 acres and an outer basin of about half that area, the massive sea-walls, jetties and quays being constructed of enormous stones, some of them weighing six tons. The work seems to have been carried out towards the end of the third millennium B.C. by Egyptian labour according to plans submitted to the local authorities by Cretan or Phoenician marine architects. The wide landing-quay at the entrance to the port consisted of rough blocks, some of them sixteen feet long, deeply grooved with a chequer-work of pentagons. Since pentagons are inconvenient figures for a chequer, compared with squares and hexagons, the number five must have had some important religious significance. Was Pharos the centre of a five-season calendar system?

The island was oddly connected with the numbers five and seventy-two at the beginning of the Christian era: the Jews of Alexandria used to visit the island for an annual (five-day?) festival, the excuse for which was that the Five Books of Moses had been miraculously translated there into Greek by seventy-two doctors of the Law ('the Septuagint') who had worked for seventy-two days on them, each apart from the rest, and agreed exactly in their renderings at the conclusion of their task. There is something behind this myth. All similar festivals in the ancient world commemorated some ancient tribal treaty or act of confederacy. What the occasion here was remains obscure, unless the Pharaoh who married

[1] Homer says that Pharos lies a full day's sail from the river of Egypt. This has been absurdly taken to mean from the Nile; it can only mean from the River of Egypt (*Joshua, XV, 4*) the southern boundary of Palestine, a stream well known to Achaean raiders of the thirteenth and twelfth centuries B.C.

The same mistake has been made by a mediaeval editor of the *Kebra Nagast*, the Ethiopian Bible. He has misrepresented the flight of the men who stole the Ark from Jerusalem as miraculous, because they covered the distance between Gaza and the River of Egypt in only one day, whereas the caravan time-table reckoned it a thirteen days' journey. The absence of pre-historic remains on the island itself suggests that all except the shore was a tree-planted sanctuary of Proteus, oracular hero and giver of winds.

Sarah, the goddess mother of the 'Abraham' tribe that visited Egypt at the close of the third millennium, was the priest-king of Pharos. If so, the festival would be a record of the sacred marriage by which the ancestors of the Hebrews joined the great confederacy of the Peoples of the Sea, whose strongest base was Pharos. Hebrews seem to have been in continuous residence in Lower Egypt for the next two millennia, and the meaning of the festival would have been forgotten by the time that the Pentateuch was translated into Greek.

In the *Odyssey*, which is a popular romance not at all to be depended on for mythical detail, Proteus's transformations are described as lion, serpent, panther, boar, water, fire and leafy tree. This is a mixed list,[1] reminding one of Gwion's deliberately muddled 'I have been's'. The boar is the symbol of the G month; lion and serpent are seasonal symbols; the panther is a mythical beast half-leopard, half-lion, sacred to Dionysus. It is a pity that Homer does not particularize the leafy tree; its association here with water and fire suggests the alder, or cornel-tree, as sacred to Proteus, a god of the Bran type—though in the story Proteus is degraded to a mere herdsman of seals in the service of the Ash-god Poseidon.

The Nile is called Ogygian by Aeschylus, and Eustathius the Byzantine grammarian says that Ogygia was the earliest name for Egypt. This suggests that the Island of Ogygia ruled over by Calypso daughter of Atlas, was really Pharos where Proteus, *alias* Atlas or 'The Sufferer', had an oracular shrine. Pharos commanded the mouth of the Nile, and Greek sailors would talk of 'sailing to Ogygia' rather than 'sailing to Egypt'; it often happens that a small island used as a trading depôt gives its name to a whole province—Bombay is a useful example. The waters of Styx are also called Ogygian by Hesiod; not (as Liddell and Scott suggest) because Ogygian meant vaguely 'primeval', but because the head-waters were at Lusi, the seat of the three oracular daughters of Proetus, who is apparently the same cult-character as Proteus.

When the Byblians first brought their Syrian Tempest-god to Egypt, the one who, disguised as a boar, yearly killed his brother Adonis, the god always born under a fir-tree, they identified him with Set, the ancient

---

[1] Compare the equally mixed list given by Nonnus of Zagreus's transformations: 'Zeus in his goat-skin coat, Cronos making rain, an inspired youth, a lion, a horse, a horned snake, a tiger, a bull'. The transformations of Thetis before her marriage with Peleus were, according to various authors from Pindar to Tzetzes, fire, water, wind, a tree, a bird, a tiger, a lion, a serpent, a cuttlefish. The transformations of Tam Lin in the Scottish ballad were snake or newt, bear, lion, red-hot iron and a coal to be quenched in running water. The zoological elements common to these four versions of an original story, namely snake, lion, some other fierce beast (bear, panther, or tiger) suggest a calendar sequence of three seasons corresponding with the Lion, Goat and Serpent of the Carian Chimaera, or the Bull, Lion and Serpent of the Babylonian *Sir-rush*; if this is so, fire and water would stand for the sun and moon which between them rule the year. It is possible, however, that the animals in Nonnus's list, bull, lion, tiger, horse and snake, form a Thraco-Libyan calendar of five, not three, seasons.

Egyptian god of the desert whose sacred beast was the wild ass, and who yearly destroyed his brother Osiris, the god of the Nile vegetation. This must be what Sanchthoniatho the Phoenician, in a fragment preserved by Philo, means when he says that the mysteries of Phoenicia were brought to Egypt. He reports that the two first inventors of the human race, Up-souranios and his brother Ousous consecrated two pillars, to fire and wind—presumably the Jachin and Boaz pillars representing Adonis, god of the waxing year and the new-born sun, and Typhon, god of the waning year and of destructive winds. The Hyksos Kings under Byblian influence, similarly converted their Tempest-god into Set, and his new brother, the Hyksos Osiris, *alias* Adonis, *alias* Dionysus, paid a courtesy call on his Pelasgian counterpart, Proteus King of Pharos.

In pre-dynastic times Set must have been the chief of all the gods of Egypt, since the sign of royalty which all the dynastic gods carried was Set's ass-eared reed sceptre. But he had declined in importance before the Hyksos revived his worship at Pelusium, and reverted to obscurity after they were thrown out of Egypt about two hundred years later by the Pharaohs of the 18th Dynasty.[1] The Egyptians identified him with the long-eared constellation Orion, 'Lord of the Chambers of the South', and 'the Breath of Set' was the South wind from the deserts which, then as now, caused a wave of criminal violence in Egypt, Libya and Southern Europe whenever it blew. The cult of ass-eared Set in Southern Judaea is proved by Apion's account of the golden ass-mask of Edomite Dora, captured by King Alexander Jannaeus and cleverly stolen back again from Jerusalem by one Zabidus. The ass occurs in many of the more obviously iconotropic anecdotes of *Genesis* and the early historical books of the Bible: Saul chosen as king when in search of Kish's lost asses; the ass that was with Abraham when he was about to sacrifice Isaac; the ass whose jawbone Samson used against the Philistines; the ass of Balaam with its human voice. Moreover, Jacob's uncle Ishmael son of Hagar with his twelve sons is described in *Genesis, XVI, 12* as a wild ass among men: this suggests a religious confederacy of thirteen goddess-worshipping tribes of the Southern desert, under the leadership of a tribe dedicated to Set. Ishmael perhaps means 'the beloved man', the Goddess's favourite.

The legend of Midas the Phrygian and the ass's ears confirms this association of Dionysus and Set, for Midas, son of the Mother Goddess, was a devotee of Dionysus. The legend is plainly an iconotropic one and Midas has been confidently identified with Mita, King of the Moschians, or Mushki, a people from Thrace—originally from Pontus—who broke the power of the Hittites about the year 1200 B.C. when they captured

---

[1] Typhon's counterpart in the Sanscrit *Rig-veda*, composed not later than 1300 B.C., is Rudra, the prototype of the Hindu Siva, a malignant demon, father of the storm-demons; he is addressed as a 'ruddy divine boar'.

Pteria the Hittite capital. Mita was a dynastic name and is said to have meant 'seed' in the Orphic language; Herodotus mentions certain rose-gardens of Midas on Mount Bermios in Macedonia, planted before the Moschian invasion of Asia Minor. It is likely that their Greek name *Moschoi*, 'calf-men', refers to their cult of the Spirit of the Year as a bull-calf: a golden calf like that which the Israelites claimed to have brought them safely out of Egypt.

That no record has survived in Egypt of a five-season year concurrent with the three-season one, is no proof that it was not in popular use among the devotees of Osiris. For that matter absolutely no official Pharaonic record has been found in Egypt of the construction, or even the existence, of the port of Pharos though it commanded the mouths of the Nile, controlled the South-Eastern terminus of the Mediterranean sea-routes, and was in active use for at least a thousand years. Osiris worship was the popular religion in the Delta from pre-dynastic times, but it had no official standing. Egyptian texts and pictorial records are notorious for their suppression or distortion of popular beliefs. Even the *Book of the Dead*, which passes for popular, seldom expresses the true beliefs of the Osirian masses: the aristocratic priests of the Established Church had begun to tamper with the popular myth as early as 2800 B.C. One of the most important elements in Osirianism, tree-worship, was not officialized until about 300 B.C., under the Macedonian Ptolemies. In the *Book of the Dead* many primitive beliefs have been iconotropically suppressed. For instance, at the close of the Twelfth Hour of Darkness, when Osiris' sun-boat approaches the last gateway of the Otherworld before its re-emergence into the light of day, the god is pictured bent backwards in the form of a hoop with his hands raised and his toes touching the back of her head. This is explained as 'Osiris whose circuit is the Otherworld': which means that by adopting this acrobatic posture he is defining the Other-world as a circular region behind the ring of mountains that surround the ordinary world, and thus making the Twelve Hours analogous with the Twelve Signs of the Zodiac. Here an ingenious priestly notion has clearly been superimposed on an earlier popular icon: Osiris captured by his rival Set and tied, like Ixion or Cuchulain, in the five-fold bond that joined wrists, neck and ankles together. 'Osiris whose circuit is the Otherworld' is also the economical way of identifying the god with the snake Ophion, coiled around the habitable earth, a symbol of universal fertility out of death.

Gwion's 'Ercwlf' (Hercules) evidently used the three-season year when he laid his 'four pillars of equal height', the Boibel-Loth, in order:

1	2	3	4	5
H	D	T	C	Q

5 N					M 1
4 S					G 2
3 F					NG 3
2 L					Z 4
1 B					R 5

A	O	U	E	I
1	2	3	4	5

The vowels represent the five extra days, the entrance to the year, and the lintel and two pillars each represent 120 days. But Q and Z have no months of their own in the Beth-Luis-Nion and their occurrence as twenty-four day periods in the second part of the Boibel-Loth year makes Tinne, not Duir as in the Beth-Luis-Nion, the central, that is the ruling, letter. Tinnus, or Tannus, becomes the chief god, as in Etruria and Druidic Gaul. From this figure the transition to the disc arrangement is simple:

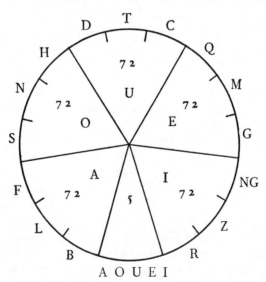

A O U E I

As 8 is the sacred numeral of Tinne's month—and in the Imperial Roman Calendar also the ruling month was the eighth, called Sebastos ('Holy') or Augustus—so the eight-day period rules the calendar. In fact, Tannus displaces his oak-twin Durus and seems to be doing him a great kindness —the same kindness that Celestial Hercules did for Atlas—in relieving him of his traditional burden. The twins were already connected with the numeral 8 because of their eight-year reign, which was fixed (as we have seen) by the approximation at every hundredth lunation of lunar and solar time. That a calendar of this sort was in use in ancient Ireland is suggested by numerous ancient Circles of the Sun, consisting of five stones surrounding a central altar; and by the ancient division of the land into five provinces—Ulster, the two Munsters, Leinster and Connaught—meeting at a central point in what is now West Meath, marked by a Stone of Divisions. (The two Munsters had already coalesced by the time of King Tuathal the Acceptable, who reigned from 130–160 A.D.; he took off a piece of all four provinces to form his central demesne of Meath.) And there is a clear reference to this calendar system in the tenth-century A.D. Irish *Saltair na Rann* where a Heavenly City is described, with fifteen ramparts, eight gates, and seventy-two different kinds of fruit in the gardens enclosed.

Now, it has been shown that the God Bran possessed an alphabetic secret before Gwydion, with Amathaon's help, stole it from him at the Battle of the Trees in the course of the first Belgic invasion of Britain; that close religious ties existed between Pelasgia and Bronze Age Britain; and that the Pelasgians used an alphabet of the same sort as the British tree-alphabet, the trees of which came from the north of Asia Minor.

As might be expected, the myth connecting Cronos, Bran's counterpart, with an alphabetic secret survives in many versions. It concerns the Dactyls (fingers), five beings created by the White Goddess Rhea, 'while Zeus was still an infant in the Dictaean Cave', as attendants on her lover Cronos. Cronos became the first king of Elis, where the Dactyls were worshipped, according to Pausanias, under the names of Heracles, Paeonius, Epimedes, Jasius and Idas, or Aces-Idas. They were also worshipped in Phrygia, Samothrace, Cyprus, Crete and at Ephesus. Diodorus quotes Cretan historians to the effect that the Dactyls made magical incantations which caused a great stir in Samothrace, and that Orpheus (who used the Pelasgian alphabet) was their disciple. They are called the fathers of the Cabeiroi of Samothrace, and their original seat is said to have been either Phrygia or Crete. They are also associated with the mysteries of smith-craft, and Diodorus identifies them with the Curetes, tutors of the infant Zeus and founders of Cnossos. Their names at Elis correspond exactly with the fingers. Heracles is the phallic thumb; Paeonius ('deliverer from evil') is the lucky fore-finger; Epimedes ('he who thinks too late') is the middle, or fool's, finger; Jasius ('healer') is the physic finger; Idas ('he of Mount Ida'—Rhea's seat) is the oracular little finger. The syllable *Aces* means that he averted ill-luck, and the Orphic willow tree, the tree belonging to the little finger-tip, grew just outside the Dictaean Cave which was, perhaps for that reason, also called the Idaean Cave.

The Alexandrian scholiast on Apollonius Rhodius gives the names of three of the Dactyls as Acmon ('anvil') Damnameneus ('hammer') and Celmis ('smelter'). These are probably names of the thumb and first two fingers, used in the Phrygian (or 'Latin') blessing: for walnuts are cracked between thumb and forefinger; and the middle finger based on U, the vowel of sexuality, still retains its ancient obscene reputation as the smelter of female passion. In mediaeval times it was called *digitus impudicus* or *obscenus* because, according to the seventeenth-century physician Isbrand de Diemerbroek, it used to be 'pointed at men in infamy or derision'—as a sign that they had failed to keep their wives' affection. Apollonius had mentioned only two Dactyls by name: Titias and Cyllenius. I have shown that Cyllen (or Cyllenius) was son of Elate, 'Artemis of the fir tree'; so the Dactyl Cyllenius must have been the thumb, which is based on the fir-letter A. And Titias was king of Mariandynë in Bithynia, from where Hereules stole the Dog, and was killed by Hercules at a funeral games. Some mythographers make Titias the father of Mariandynus, founder of the town. Since Hercules was the god of the waxing year which begins with A, the thumb, it follows that Titias was the god of the waning year, which begins with U, the fool's finger—the fool killed by Hercules at the winter-solstice. The name 'Titias' is apparently a reduplication of the letter T, which belongs to the fool's finger, and identical with the Giant Tityus whom Zeus killed and consigned to Tartarus.

Here is a neat problem in poetic logic: if the Dactyl Cyllenius is an *alias* of Hercules, and Hercules is the thumb, and Titias is the fool's finger, it should be possible to find in the myth of Hercules and Titias the name of the intervening finger, the forefinger, to complete the triad used in the Phrygian blessing. Since the numerical sequence *Heis, Duo, Treis*, 'one, two, three', corresponds in Greek, Latin and Old Goidelic with the H.D.T. letter sequence represented by the top-joints of the Dactyls used in this blessing, it is likely that the missing name begins with D and has a reference to the use or religious associations of the finger. The answer seems to be 'Dascylus'. According to Apollonius he was king of the Mariandynians, and presided at the games at which Hercules killed Titias. For the forefinger is the index-finger and Dascylus means 'the little pointer' Greek *didasco*, Latin *disco*. Presidents at athletic contests use it for solemn warnings against foul play. The root *Da-* from which Dascylus is derived is also the root of the Indo-Germanic word for thunder, appropriate to D as the letter of the oak-and-thunder god. Dascylus was both father and son of Lycus (wolf); the wolf is closely connected with the oak-cult.

The argument can be taken farther. It has been mentioned in Chapter Four that Pythagoras was a Pelasgian from Samos who developed his doctrine of the Transmigration of Souls as the result of foreign travel. According to his biographer Porphyrius he went to Crete, the seat of the purest Orphic doctrine, for initiation by the Idaean Dactyls. They ritually purified him with a thunderbolt, that is to say they made a pretence of killing him with either a meteoric stone or a neolithic axe popularly mistaken for a thunderbolt; after which he lay face-downwards on the sea shore all night covered with black lamb's wool; then spent 'three times nine hallowed days and nights in the Idaean Cave'; finally emerged for his initiation. Presumably he then drank the customary Orphic cup of goat's milk and honey at dawn (the drink of Cretan Zeus who had been born in that very cave) and was garlanded with white flowers. Porphyrius does not record exactly when all this took place except that Pythagoras saw the throne annually decorated with flowers for Zeus; which suggests that the twenty-eight days that intervened between his thunderbolt death and his revival with milk and honey were the twenty-eight-day month R, the death-month ruled by the elder or myrtle; and that Pythagoras was reborn at the winter solstice festival as an incarnation of Zeus—a sort of Orphic Pope or Aga Khan—and went through the usual mimetic transformation: bull, hawk, woman, lion, fish, serpent, etc. This would account for the divine honours subsequently paid him at Crotona, where the Orphic cult was strongly established; and also for those paid to his successor Empedocles, who claimed to have been through these ritual transformations. The Dactyls here are plainly the Curetes, the dancing priests of the Rhea and Cronos cult, tutoring the infant Zeus in the Pelasgian calendar-alphabet, the Beth-Luis-Nion; the tree-sequence of which had been brought to Greece and the Aegean islands from Paphlagonia, by way of Bithynian Mariandynë and Phrygia, and there harmonized with the alphabetic principle originated in Crete by 'Palamedes'. For climatic reasons the canon of trees taught by the Cretan Dactyls must have differed from that of Phrygia, Samothrace and Magnesia—Magnesia where the five Dactyls were remembered as a single character, and where the Pelasgian Cheiron ('the Hand') son of Cronos and Philyra (Rhea), successively tutored Hercules, Achilles, Jason the Orphic hero, with numerous other sacred kings.

It seems however that Pythagoras,[1] after mastering the Cretan Beth-Luis-Nion, found that the Boibel-Loth calendar, based on a year of 360 + 5 days, not on the Beth-Luis-Nion year of 364 + 1 days, was far better suited

---

[1] The influence of Pythagoras on the mediaeval mystics of North-Western Europe was a strong one. Bernard of Morlaix (*circa* 1140) author of the ecstatic poem *De Contemptu Mundi*, wrote: 'Listen to an experienced man. . . . Trees and stones will reach you more than you can learn from the mouth of a doctor of theology.' Bernard was born in Brittany of English parents and his verse is in the Irish poetic tradition. His ecstatic vision of the Heavenly Jerusalem is prefaced by the line:

Ad tua munera sit via dextera, Pythagoraea.

'May our way to your Pythagorean blessings be an auspicious one.'

For he was not a nature worshipper, but held that the mythical qualities of chosen trees and chosen precious stones, as studied by the Pythagoreans, explained the Christian mysteries better than Saint Athanasius had ever been able to do.

than the Beth-Luis-Nion to his deep philosophic speculations about the holy *tetractys*, the five senses and elements, the musical octave, and the Ogdoad.

But why was it necessary to alter the alphabet and calendar in order to make eight the important number, rather than seven? Simonides's alphabet, it has been seen, was expanded to 3 × 8 letters; perhaps this was to fulfil the dark prophecy current in Classical Greece that Apollo was fated to castrate his father Zeus with the same sickle with which Zeus had castrated his father Cronos and which was laid up in a temple on the sickle-shaped island of Drepane ('sickle'), now Corfu. In so far as the supreme god of the Druids was a Sun-god, the fulfilment of this prophecy was demonstrated every year at their ritual emasculation of the sacred oak by the lopping of the mistletoe, the procreative principle, with a golden sickle—gold being the metal sacred to the Sun. Seven was the sacred number of the week, governed by the Sun, the Moon and the five planets. But eight was sacred to the Sun in Babylonia, Egypt and Arabia, because 8 is the symbol of reduplication—2 × 2 × 2. Hence the widely distributed royal sun-disc with an eight-armed cross on it, like a simplified version of Britannia's shield; and hence the sacrificial barley-cakes baked in the same pattern.

Now to examine Diodorus's famous quotation from the historian Hecateus (sixth century B.C.):

Hecateus, and some others, who treat of ancient histories or traditions, give the following account: 'Opposite to the coast of Celtic Gaul there is an island in the ocean, not smaller than Sicily, lying to the North—which is inhabited by the Hyperboreans, who are so named because they dwell beyond the North Wind. This island is of a happy temperature, rich in soil and fruitful in everything, yielding its produce twice in the year. Tradition says that Latona was born there, and for that reason, the inhabitants venerate Apollo more than any other God. They are, in a manner, his priests, for they daily celebrate him with continual songs of praise and pay him abundant honours.

'In this island, there is a magnificent grove (or precinct) of Apollo, and a remarkable temple, of a round form, adorned with many consecrated gifts. There is also a city, sacred to the same God, most of the inhabitants of which are harpers, who continually play upon their harps in the temple, and sing hymns to the God, extolling his actions. The Hyperboreans use a peculiar dialect, and have a remarkable attachment to the Greeks, especially to the Athenians and the Delians, deducing their friendship from remote periods. It is related that some Greeks formerly visited the Hyperboreans, with whom they left consecrated gifts of great value, and also that in ancient times Abaris, coming from the Hyperboreans into Greece, renewed their family intercourse with the Delians.

'It is also said that in this island the moon appears very near to the earth, that certain eminences of a terrestrial form are plainly seen in it, that Apollo visits the island once in a course of nineteen years, in which period the stars complete their revolutions, and that for this reason the Greeks distinguish the cycle of nineteen years by the name of "the great year". During the season of his appearance the God plays upon the harp and dances every night, from the vernal equinox until the rising of the Pleiads, pleased with his own successes. The supreme authority in that city and the sacred precinct is vested in those who are called Boreadae, being the descendants of Boreas, and their governments have been uninterruptedly transmitted in this line.'

Hecateus apparently credited the pre-Belgic Hyperboreans with a knowledge of the 19-year cycle for equating solar and lunar time; which involves an intercalation of 7 months at the close. This cycle was not publicly adopted in Greece until about a century after Hecateus's time. As a 'golden number', reconciling solar and lunar time, 19 can be deduced from the thirteen-month Beth-Luis-Nion calendar which contains fourteen solar stations (namely the first day of each month and the extra day) and five lunar stations. Probably it was in honour of this Apollo (Beli) that the major stone circles of the Penzance area in Cornwall consisted of 19 posts, and that Cornwall was called Belerium. There is evidently some basis for the story that Abaris the Hyperborean instructed Pythagoras in philosophy. It looks as if the Bronze Age people (who imported the Egyptian beads into Salisbury Plain from Akhenaton's short-lived capital, the City of the Sun, at Tell Amarna about 1350 B.C.) had refined their astronomy on Salisbury Plain and even anticipated the invention of the telescope. Since, according to Pliny, the Celtic year began in his day in July (as the Athenian also did) the statement about the country producing two harvests, one at the beginning and one at the end of the year, is understandable. The hay harvest would fall in the old year, the corn harvest in the new.

The Lord of the Seven-day Week was 'Dis', the transcendental god of the Hyperboreans, whose secret name was betrayed to Gwydion. Have we not already stumbled on the secret? Was the Name not spelt out by the seven vowels of the threshold, cut with three times nine holy nicks and read sunwise?

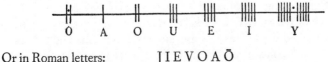

Or in Roman letters: J I E V O A Ō

If so, the link between Britain and Egypt is evident: Demetrius, the first-century B.C. Alexandrian philosopher, after discussing in his treatise *On Style* the elision of vowels and hiatus, and saying that 'with elision the effect is duller and less melodious', illustrates the advantage of hiatus with:

In Egypt the priests sing hymns to the gods by uttering the seven vowels in succession, the sound of which produces as strong a musical impression on their hearers as if flute and lyre were used. To dispense with the hiatus would be to do away altogether with the melody and harmony of language. But perhaps I had better not enlarge of this theme in the present context.

He does not say what priests they were or to what gods they addressed themselves, but it is safe to guess that they were the gods of the seven-day week, comprising a single transcendent deity, and that the hymn contained the seven vowels with which Simonides provided the Greek alphabet and was credited with a therapeutic effect.

When the Name was revealed, Amathaon and Gwydion instituted a new religious system, and a new calendar, and new names of letters, and installed the Dog, Roebuck and Lapwing as guardians not of the old Name, which he had guessed, but of the new. The secret of the new Name seems to be connected with the substitution of the sacred numeral 7 by the sacred numeral 8, and with a taboo on the letters F and H in ordinary alphabetic use. Was it that the Name was given 8 letters instead of 7? We know from Hyginus's account that Simonides added *Omega* (long O) and *Eta* (long E) to the original seven letters AOUEIFH, invented by the Fates, 'or some say, by Mercury', and that he also removed H aspirate from the alphabet by allotting its character to *Eta*. If he did this for religious reasons, the eight-fold Name of God, containing the Digamma F (V) and H aspirate—the Lofty Name which gave Gwion his sense of power and authority—was perhaps:

JEHUOVAŌ

but spelt, for security reasons, as:

JEBUOTAŌ

It certainly has an august ring, lacking to 'Iahu' and 'Jahweh', and if I have got it right, will be 'the eight-fold City of Light' in which the 'Word', which was Thoth, Hermes, Mercury and, for the Gnostics, Jesus Christ was said to dwell. But the Fates had first invented F and H; why?

JIEVOAŌ, the earlier seven-letter form, recalls the many guesses at the 'Blessed Name of the Holy One of Israel' made by scholars, priests and magicians in the old days. This was a name which only the High Priest was allowed to utter, once a year and under his breath, when he visited the

Holy of Holies, and which might not be committed to writing. Then how in the world was the Name conveyed from one High Priest to another? Obviously by a description of the alphabetical process which yielded it. Josephus claimed to know the Name, though he could never have heard it spoken or seen it written. The Heads of the Pharisaic academies also claimed to know it. Clement of Alexandria did not know it, but he guessed an original IAOOUE—which is found in Jewish-Egyptian magical papyri, 'Zeus, Thunderer, King Adonai, Lord Iaooue'—also expanded to IAOUAI and IAOOUAI. The disguised official formula, JEHOWIH, or JEHOWAH, written JHWH for short, suggests that by the time of Jesus the Jews had adopted the revised Name. The Samaritans wrote it IAHW and pronounced it IABE. Clement's guess is, of course, a very plausible one because I.A.O.OU.E is the name spelt out by the vowels of the five-season year if one begins in the early winter, the opening of the agricultural year.[1] The Name taught in the Academies is likely to have been a complicated one of either 42 or 72 letters. Both forms are discussed by Dr. Robert Eisler in the Jubilee volume for the Grand Rabbi of France in *La Revue des Études Juives*. The calendar mystery of 72 has already been discussed; that of 42 belongs to the Beth-Luis-Nion system.[2]

In Chapter Nine the first-century writer Aelian was quoted as having said that Hyperborean priests regularly visited Tempe. But if their busi-

[1] Clement is very nearly right in another sense, which derives from the suppression in the Phoenician and early Hebrew alphabets of all the vowels, except *aleph*, occurring in the Greek alphabet with which they are linked. The introduction into Hebrew script of pure vowel signs in the form of dots is ascribed to Ezra who, with Nehemiah, established the New Law about the year 430. It is likely that the vowels had been suppressed at a time when the Holy Name of the deity who presided over the year consisted of vowels only; and the proof that Ezra did not invent them but merely established an inoffensive notation for a sacred series long fixed in oral tradition lies in the order which he used, namely I.E.E.U.O.A.OU.O. This is the Palamedan I.E.U.O.A. with the addition of three extra vowels to bring the number up to eight, the mystic numeral of increase. Since the dots with which he chose to represent them were not part of the alphabet and had no validity except when attached to consonants, they could be used without offence. Nevertheless, it is remarkable that the consonants which compose the Tetragrammaton, namely *yod*, *he* and *vav* may cease to carry consonantal force when they have vowel signs attached to them; so that JHWH could be sounded IAŌOUĀ. This is a peculiarity that no other Hebrew consonant has, except *ain*, and *ain* not in all dialects of Hebrew. Clement got the last vowel wrong, E for Ā, perhaps because he knew that the letter H is known as *He* in Hebrew.

[2] 42 is the number of the children devoured by Elisha's she-bears. This is apparently an iconotropic myth derived from a sacred picture of the Libyo-Thraco-Pelasgian 'Brauronia' ritual. The two she-bears were girls dressed in yellow dresses who pretended to be bears and rushed savagely at the boys who attended the festival. The ritual was in honour of Artemis Callisto, the Moon as Bear-Goddess, and since a goat was sacrificed seems to belong to the Midsummer festivities. 42 is the number of days from the beginning of the H month, which is the preparation for the midsummer marriage and death-orgy, to Midsummer Day. 42 is also the number of infernal jurymen who judged Osiris: the days between his midsummer death and the end of the T month, when he reached Calypso's isle, though this is obscured in the priestly *Book of the Dead*. According to Clement of Alexandria there were forty-two books of Hermetic mysteries.

ness was with Apollo, why did they not go to the more important shrine of Delphi? Tempe, Apollo's earlier home, lies in the valley of the Peneus between Mounts Ossa and Olympus and seems to have become the centre of a cult of a Pythagorean god who partook of the natures of all the Olympian deities. We know something about the mysteries of the cult because Cyprian, a third-century bishop of Antioch, was initiated into them as a youth of fifteen. As he records in his *Confession,* he was taken up on to Mount Olympus for forty days and there seven mystagogues taught him the meaning of musical sounds and the causes of the birth and decay of herbs, trees and bodies. He had a vision of tree-trunks and magical herbs, saw the succession of seasons and their changing spiritual representatives, together with the retinues of various deities, and watched the dramatic performances of demons in conflict. In an Egyptian magical papyrus published by Parthey in 1866, a close connexion between this Druid-like instruction and Essene mysticism is made in the following lines:

> *Come foremost angel of great Zeus IAO [Raphael]*
> *And thou too, Michaël, who holdest Heaven [rules the planets],*
> *And Gabriel thou, the archangel from Olympus.*

Gabriel, it has been shown, was the Hebrew counterpart of Hermes, the official herald and mystagogue of Mount Olympus.

Was Stonehenge the temple of Apollo the Hyperborean? The ground plan of Stonehenge suggests a round mirror with a handle—a round earthwork, entered by an avenue, with a circular stone temple enclosed. The outer ring of stones in the temple once formed a continuous circle of thirty arches, built of enormous dressed stones: thirty posts and thirty lintels. This circle enclosed an ellipse, broken at one end so that it resembled a horseshoe, consisting of five separate dolmens, each of two posts and a lintel, built of the same enormous stones. Sandwiched between the circle and the horseshoe stood a ring of thirty much smaller posts; and within the horseshoe, again, stood another horseshoe of fifteen similar small posts, arranged in five sets of three to correspond with the five dolmens.

Perhaps 'horseshoe' is wrong: it may well have been an ass-shoe from its narrowness. If Stonehenge was Apollo's temple and if Pindar, in his *Tenth Pythian Ode,* is referring to the same Hyperboreans as Hecateus it must have been an ass-shoe; for Pindar shows that Apollo was worshipped by the Hyperboreans in the style of Osiris or Dionysus, whose triumph over his enemy Set the ass-god was celebrated by the sacrifice of a hundred asses at a time. But it is clear that by the middle of the fifth century B.C., the connexion between Greece and the Hyperboreans had long been broken, presumably by the seizure of the approaches to Britain by the Belgic tribes.

Pindar is demonstrably wrong in his *Third Olympian Ode* when he makes Hercules go to the springs of the Ister to bring back wild olive to Olympia from the servants of Apollo, the Hyperboreans. We know from other sources that he fetched back the white poplar, not the olive which had been cultivated in Greece centuries before his time and which is not native to the upper Danube; the connexion of poplar with amber, which came from the Baltic by way of the Danube and Istria, and which was sacred to Apollo, has already been noted. Pindar's mistake derives from a confusion of the Hercules who fetched the poplar from Epirus with the earlier Hercules who fetched the olive from Libya to Crete. He writes in the *Tenth Pythian Ode*:

Neither by ships nor by land can you find the wonderful road to the trysting-place of the Hyperboreans.

Yet in times past, Perseus the leader of his people partook of their banquet when he entered their homes and found them sacrificing glorious hecatombs of asses in honour of the God. In the banquets and hymns of that people Apollo chiefly rejoices and laughs as he looks upon the brute beasts in their ramping lewdness. Yet such are their ways that the Muse is not banished, but on every side the dances of the girls, the twanging of lyres and sound of flutes are continually circling, and with their hair crowned with golden bay-leaves they make merry . . . yet avoid divine jealousy by living aloof from labour and war. To that home of happy folk, then, went Danaë's son [Perseus] of old, breathing courage, with Athena as his guide. And he slew the Gorgon and returned with her head.

Pindar seems to be wrong about the Gorgon and about the bay-leaves, sacred to Apollo only in the South; and since he does not tell us at what season the sacrifice took place we cannot tell what leaves they were. If at mid-winter, they may have been elder-leaves; at any rate, asses are connected in European folk-lore, especially French, with the mid-winter Saturnalia, which took place in the elder month, and at the conclusion of which the ass-eared god, later the Christmas Fool, was killed by his rival. This explains the otherwise unaccountable connexion of asses and fools in Italy as well as in Northern Europe: for asses are more intelligent animals than horses. That there was an ass-cult in Italy in early times is suggested by the distinguished Roman clan-names Asina and Asellus, which were plebeian, not patrician; the patricians were an immigrant horse-worshipping aristocracy from the East who enslaved the plebeians. The use of holly at the Italian Saturnalia supports this theory: holly was the tree of the ass-god, as the oak was the tree of his wild-ox twin who became paramount in patrician Rome.

Plutarch in his *Isis and Osiris* writes: 'Every now and then at certain festivities they (the Egyptians) humiliate the broken power of Set, treating it despitefully, to the point of rolling men of Typhonic colouring in the mud and driving asses over a precipice.' By 'certain festivities' he must mean the celebration of the divine child Harpocrates's victory over Set, at the Egyptian Saturnalia. So Set, the red-haired ass, came to mean the bodily lusts, given full rein at the Saturnalia, which the purified initiate repudiated; indeed, the spirit as rider, and the body as ass, are now legitimate Christian concepts. The metamorphosis of Lucius Apuleius into an ass must be understood in this sense: it was his punishment for rejecting the good advice of his well-bred kinswoman Byrrhaena and deliberately meddling with the erotic witch cult of Thessaly. It was only after uttering his *de profundis* prayer to the White Goddess (quoted at the close of Chapter Four) that he was released from his shameful condition and accepted as an initiate of her pure Orphic mysteries. So also, when Charitë ('Spiritual Love') was riding home in chaste triumph on ass-back from the robbers' den, Lucius had joked at this as an extraordinary event: namely, that a girl should triumph over her physical desires, despite all dangers and assaults. The Orphic degradation of the ass explains a passage in Aristophanes's *Frogs*, which, as J. E. Harrison points out, is staged in a thoroughly Orphic Hell. Charon shouts out 'Anyone here for the Plains of Lethe? Anyone here for the Ass Clippings? For Cerberus Park? Taenarus? Crow Station?' Crow Station was evidently Set-Cronos's infernal seat to which Greeks consigned their enemies in the imprecation 'To the Crows with you!'; and the Ass Clippings was the place where criminals shaggy with sin were shorn to the quick. The horse was a pure animal for the Orphics, as the ass was impure, and the continuance of this tradition in Europe is shown most clearly in Spain where *caballero* 'horseman', means gentleman and where no gentleman's son is allowed to ride an ass, even in an emergency, lest he lose caste. The ancient reverence of unchivalrous Spaniards for the ass appears perversely in the word *carajo*, the great mainstay of their swearing, which is used indiscriminately as noun, adjective, verb or adverb; its purpose is to avert the evil eye, or ill-luck, and the more often it can be introduced into an oath, the better. Touching the phallus, or an amulet in phallus form, is an established means of averting the evil eye, and *carajo* means 'ass's phallus'; the appeal is to the baleful God Set, whose starry phallus appears in the Constellation Orion, to restrain his anger.

The great dolmens of Stonehenge, all of local stone, look as if they were erected to give importance to the smaller stones, which were placed in position shortly after they themselves were, and to the massive altar stone lying in the centre. It has been suggested that the smaller ones, which are known to have been transported all the way from the Prescelly Mountains in Pembrokeshire, were originally disposed in another order there and rearranged by the people who erected the larger ones. This is likely, and it is remarkable that these imported stones were not dressed until they were re-erected at Stonehenge itself. The altar stone has also been transported from the same region, probably from Milford Haven. Since this transportation was done over a thousand years before the Belgic invasion it is clear at least that Gwydion was not responsible for the building.

The plan of the five dolmens corresponds exactly with the disc alphabet, since there is a broad gap between the two standing nearest to the avenue (like the gap which contains the five holy days of the Egyptian, or Etruscan, year) and between the gap and the avenue stood a group of four smaller undressed stones, corresponding with the groups of three stones in the inner horseshoe, but with a gap in the middle; and far back, in the avenue itself, the huge undressed 'Heel' stone made a fifth and central one. This is not to assume that Stonehenge was built to conform with the disc-alphabet. The calendar may have anteceded the alphabet by some centuries. All that seems clear is that the Greek alphabetic formula which gives the Boibel-Loth its letter-names is at least a century or two earlier than 400 B.C. when the Battle of the Trees was fought in Britain.

The formula is plain. The Sun-god of Stonehenge was the Lord of Days, and the thirty arches of the outer circle and the thirty posts of the inner circle stood for the days of the ordinary Egyptian month; but the secret enclosed by these circles was that the solar year was divided into five seasons, each in turn divided into three twenty-four-day periods, represented by the three stones of the dolmens, and each of these again into three ogdoads, represented by the three smaller posts in front of the dolmens. For the circle was so sited that at dawn of the summer solstice the sun rose exactly at the end of the avenue in dead line with the altar and the Heel stone; while, of the surviving pair of the four undressed stones, one marks the sun's rising at the winter solstice, the other its setting at the summer solstice.

But why were the altar stone and the uprights transported all the way from South Wales? Presumably to break the religious power of the Pembrokeshire Death-goddess—the pre-Celtic Annwm, as we have seen, was in Pembroke—by removing her most sacred undressed stones and re-erecting them, dressed, on the Plain. According to Geoffrey of Monmouth, this was done by Merlin. Geoffrey, who mistakenly dates the event to the time of Hengist and Horsa, says that Merlin obtained the stones from Ireland, but the tradition perhaps refers to the Land of Erin— Erin, or Eire or Eriu, being a pre-Celtic Fate-goddess who gave her name to Ireland. 'Erin', usually explained as the dative case of Eriu's name, may be the Greek Triple Fate-goddess 'Erinnys' whom we know as the Three Furies. The amber found in the barrows near Stonehenge is for the most part red, not golden; like that found on the Phoenician coast.

Seventy-two will have been the main canonical number at Stonehenge: the seventy-two days of the midsummer season. Seventy-two was the Sun's grandest number; eight, multiplied ninefold by the fertile Moon. The Moon was Latona, Hyperborean Apollo's mother, and she determined the length of the sacred king's reign. The approximate concurrence of solar and lunar time once every nineteen years—19 revolutions of the Sun, 235 lunations of the Moon—ruled that Apollo should be newly married and crowned every nineteenth year at the Spring solstice, when he kept a seven months' holiday in the Moon's honour. The number 19 is commemorated at Stonehenge in nineteen socket-holes arranged in a semi-circle on the South-east of the arched circle.[1] The fate of the old king was perhaps the hill-top fate of Aaron and of Moses, darkly hinted at in *Exodus*, and the fate of Dionysus at Delphi: to be disrobed and dismem-

[1] The number occurs also in two royal brooches—'king's wheels'—found in 1945 in a Bronze Age 'Iberian' burial at Lluch in Majorca, the seat of a Black Virgin cult, and dated about 1500 B.C. The first is a disc of seven inches in diameter, made for pinning on a cloak and embossed with a nineteen-rayed sun. This sun is enclosed by two bands, the outer one containing thirteen separated leaves, of five different kinds, perhaps representing wild olive, alder, prickly-oak, ivy and rosemary, some turned clockwise, some counter-clockwise, and all but two of them with buds or rudimentary flowers joined to them half-way up their stalks. The inner hand contains four roundels at regular intervals, the spaces between the roundels filled up with pairs of leaves of the same sort as those in the outer ring, except that the alder is not represented. The formula is: thirteen months, a pentad of goddesses-of-the-year, a nineteen-year reign.

The other, slightly smaller, royal disc found in the same burial has a border of nineteen semi-circles, a central sun with twenty-one detached rays and, between the sun and the border, two intervening bands—the inner one containing forty-five small bosses, the outer twenty hearts. The head of the pin is shaped like a swan's; as that of the other, which has perished, may have also been. Here the formula is: a nineteen-year reign, with a fresh victim (the twenty hearts) offered at the beginning of every year, the king himself being the twentieth. The White Swan, his Mother, will carry him off to her Hyperborean paradise. Twenty-one is the number of rays on Akhenaton's sun. Forty-five is the pentad of goddesses-of-the-year, multiplied by the number nine to show that each is an aspect of the Moon-goddess.

So far as I know, the Bronze Age and early Iron Age smiths who, like the poets and physicians, came under the direct patronage of the Muse, never embellished their work with meaningless decoration. Every object they made—sword, spear-head, shield, dagger, scabbard, brooch, jug, harness-ring, tankard, bucket, mirror, or what not—had magical properties to which the shape and number of its various decorations testified. Few archaeologists lay any emphasis on magic, and this makes most museum-guides pretty dull reading. For example, in the *British Museum Guide to the Antiquities of the Early Iron Age* (1905), fig. 140 shows a beaded bronze collar from Lochar Moss, Dumfriesshire. The editorial comment is only on the melon-like shape of the beads which has, it is said, affinities with that of turquoise-coloured glass beads common on sites in Roman Britain. What needed to be pointed out was that there are thirteen of these beads in the collar, each with seven ribs, and that the design on the rigid crescent-shaped part is an interlace of nine S's: a collar replete with lunar fate. Similarly, the open-work bronze disc (fig. 122) found in the Thames at Hammersmith is interesting because the sun which forms its centre has eight rays and is pierced with a Maltese cross; but the editor's only comment is on its stylistic relation with open-work bronze horse-poitrels from a Gaulish chariot-burial at Somme Bionne (Plate III), one of which contains pierced crosses. This is irrelevant, unless attention is paid to the three swastikas in this poitrel and to the numbers nine and thirteen which characterize the horse head-stall ornaments shown in the same plate.

bered by his successor and, when the pieces were gathered together, to be secretly buried in a chest with the promise of an eventual glorious resurrection.

Stonehenge is now generally dated between 1700 and 1500 B.C. and regarded as the work of broad-skulled Bronze-Age invaders. The stones are so neatly cut and jointed that one responsible archaeologist, G. F. Kendrick of the British Museum, suggests that they were not placed in position until Belgic times; but the more probable explanation is that the architects had studied in Egypt or Syria.

If then the God of Stonehenge was cousin to Jehovah of Tabor and Zion, one would expect to find the same taboos on the eating or killing of certain animals observed in Palestine and ancient Britain, taboos being far more easily observable than dogma. This proposition is simply tested by inquiring whether the edible but tabooed beasts in *Leviticus* which are native to both countries were ever tabooed in Britain. There are only two such beasts, the pig and the hare; for the 'coney' of *Leviticus* is not the British coney, or rabbit, but the hyrax, an animal peculiar to Syria and sacred to the Triple Goddess because of its triangular teeth and its litters of three. Both hare and pig were tabooed in ancient Britain: we know of the hare-taboo from Pliny; and that the hare was a royal animal is proved by the story of the hare taken by Boadicea into battle. The Kerry peasants still abominate hare-meat: they say that to eat it is to eat one's grandmother. The hare was sacred, I suppose, because it is very swift, very prolific—even conceives, Herodotus notes, when already pregnant—and mates openly without embarrassment like the turtle-dove, the dog, the cat or the tattooed Pict. The position of the Hare constellation at the feet of Orion suggests that it was sacred in Pelasgian Greece too. The pig was also sacred in Britain, and the pig-taboo survived until recently in Wales and Scotland; but as in Egypt, and according to Isaiah among the Canaanites of Jerusalem, this taboo was broken once a year at mid-winter with a Pig-feast, the feast of the Boar's Head. The fish-taboo, partial in *Leviticus*, was total in Britain and among the Egyptian priesthood and must have been most inconvenient. It survived in parts of Scotland until recent times. The bird-taboos, already mentioned in the lapwing context as common to Britain and Canaan, are numerous. The porpoise (mistranslated 'badger') whose skins made the covering for the Ark of the Covenant has always been one of the three royal 'fish' of Britain, the others being the whale— the first living thing created by Jehovah, and 'whale' includes the narwhal —and the sturgeon, which does not occur in the Jordan but was sacred in Pelasgian Greece and Scythia. According to Aelian, fishermen who caught a sturgeon garlanded themselves and their boats; according to Macrobius it was brought to table crowned with flowers and preceded by a piper.

The Hebrews seem to have derived their Aegean culture, which they shared with the descendants of the Bronze Age invaders of Britain, partly from the Danaans of Tyre and the Sabians of Harran, but mostly (as has already been suggested in Chapter Four) from the Philistines whose vassals they were for some generations; the Philistines, or Puresati, being immigrants from Asia Minor mixed with Greek-speaking Cretans. Those of Gaza brought with them the cult of Zeus Marnas (said to mean 'virgin-born' in Cretan) which was also found at Ephesus, and used Aegean writing for some time after the Byblians had adopted Babylonian cuneiform. The Philistine city of Ascalon was said by Xanthus, an early Lydian historian, to have been founded by one Ascalos, uncle to Pelops of Enete on the Southern Black Sea Coast, whose king was Aciamus, a native of the same region. Among the Philistines mentioned in the Bible are Piram and Achish, identifiable with the Trojan and Dardanian names Priam and Anchises; the Dardanians were among the tribes under Hittite leadership that Rameses II defeated at the Battle of Kadesh in 1335 B.C. It is probable that the Levitical list of tabooed beasts and birds was taken over by the Israelites from the Philistines: and perhaps written down in the ninth century B.C., which is when the Lycian tale of Proetus, Anteia and Bellerophon was inappropriately incorporated in the story of Joseph —Anteia becoming Potiphar's wife.

Avebury undoubtedly dates from the end of the third millennium B.C. It is a circular earthwork enclosing a ring of one hundred posts and these again enclosing two separate temples, all the stones being unhewn and very massive. The temples consist of circles of posts, of which the exact numbers are not known because so many have been removed and because the irregular size of the remainder makes calculation difficult: but there seem to have been about thirty in each case. Within each of these circles was an inner circle of twelve posts: one of them containing a single altar post, the other three.

One hundred months was the number of lunations in the Pelasgian Great Year, which ended with an approximation of lunar and solar time, though a much rougher one than at the close of the nineteen-year cycle. The twin kings each reigned for fifty of these months; which may account for the two temples. If in one temple the posts of the outer circle numbered twenty-nine, and in the other thirty, this would represent months of alternately twenty-nine and thirty days, as in the Athenian calendar—a lunation lasting for 29½ days. On the analogy of the story in *Exodus, XXIV, 4* we may assume that the inner circles represented the king and his twelve clan-chieftains, though in one case the central altar has been enlarged to three, perhaps in honour of the king as three-bodied Geryon.

A serpentine avenue enters the Avebury earthwork from the south-east and south-west and encloses two barrows, one of them heaped in the shape of a phallus and the other in the shape of a scrotum. To the south, beyond these, rises Silbury Hill, the largest artificial mound in Europe, covering over five acres, with a flat top of the same diameter as that of New Grange but thirty feet higher. I take Silbury to be the original Spiral Castle of Britain, as New Grange is of Ireland; the oracular shrine of Bran, as New Grange was of The Dagda. Avebury itself was not used for burials.

An interesting subject of poetic speculation is: why the Beth-Luis-Nion order of vowels, A.O.U.E.I., which is an order phonetically expressive of the progress and retreat of the year, with U as its climax, was altered in the Cadmean and Latin alphabets to A.E.I.O.U. The clue lies perhaps in the numerical values known to have been assigned in mediaeval Irish literature to the vowels, namely A, one; E, two; I, three; O, four. The numerical value five was assigned to B, the first consonant of the alphabet, which suggests that it originally belonged to U, the remaining vowel, which had no numerical value in this system, but which is the character that expresses the Roman numeral 5. If the vowels are regarded as a seasonal sequence, with A for New Year, O for Spring, U for Summer, E for Autumn and I for Winter, the original numerical values make poetic sense. A had One, as the New Year Goddess of origin; E had Two, as the Autumn Goddess of rutting and combat; I had Three, as the Winter Goddess of Death, pictured as the Three Fates, or the Three Furies, or the three Graeae, or the three-headed Bitch; O had Four, as the Spring Goddess of increase; U had Five, as the Summer Goddess, the leafy centre of the year, the Queen of the whole Pentad. It follows speculatively that the original numerical value of the Pelasgian vowels—A, One; E, Two; I, Three; O, Four; U, Five— suggested to the makers of the Cadmean alphabet that the vowels should be logically arranged in simple arithmetical progression from One to Five.

The numerical values given by the Irish to the remaining letters of the 13-consonant Beth-Luis-Nion are as follows:

B	Beth	Five
L	Luis	Fourteen
N	Nion	Thirteen
F	Fearn	Eight
S	Saille	Sixteen
H	Uath	*No value*
D	Duir	Twelve
T	Tinne	Eleven
C	Coll	Nine
M	Min	Six
G	Gort	Ten
P	Peth	Seven
R	Ruis	Fifteen

Exactly why each of these values was assigned to its consonant may be debated at length; but obvious poetic reasons appear in several cases. For example, Nine is the number traditionally associated with Coll, the Hazel, the tree of Wisdom; Twelve is the number traditionally associated with the Oak—the Oak-king has twelve merry men; Fifteen is the number of Ruis, the last month, because it is the fifteenth consonant in the complete alphabet. The numbers Eight and Sixteen for the consonants F and S which follow on the Spring vowel O, or Four, make obvious sense in the context of increase. That H and U are denied numerical values suggests that they were kept out of the sequence for religious reasons. For U was the vowel of the Goddess of Death-in-Life, whom the Sun-god deposed; H was the consonant of Uath, the unlucky, or too holy, May month.

If this number system is of Apollonian origin and belongs to the period when the Irish had come under Greek influence, it is likely that P has been given seven, and L fourteen, and N thirteen as their values, in honour of Apollo. For the assignment of these values to the consonants of his seven-lettered Greek name turns it into a miniature calendar: P, the seven days of the week; LL, the twenty-eight days of a common-law month; N, the thirteen common-law months of the year. The vowel values complete the table: A, the single extra day; O, the four weeks of the common-law month; long O, the two halves of the year: APOLLŌN.

This sort of ingenious play with letters and numerals was characteristic of the Celtic poets. What fun they must have had in their forest colleges! And such restorations of their lore as can still be made from surviving records are more than quaint historical curiosities; they illustrate a poetic method of thought which has not yet outlasted its usefulness, however grossly abused by mystical quacks of the intervening centuries.

Consider, for instance, the Bird-ogham and Colour-ogham in the *Book of Ballymote*. The composers of these two cyphers had to bear in mind not only the initial of every word but its poetic relation to the already established letter-month. Thus no migratory bird appears in the list of winter months, and *samad* (sorrel) is not applied to the S-month, as one might have expected, because the sorrel plant goes sorrel-colour only in the late summer. The lists could have been made more nearly poetic if the initials had allowed; thus the Robin would doubtless have led in the year, had he begun with a B, not an S (*spidéog*), and there was no word for Owl that could be used for the Ng-month when owls are most vocal.

I can best make my point by glossing the cyphers in imitation of the style used in the *Book of Ballymote* itself, drawing on bardic lore in every case.

Day of the Winter Solstice—A—aidhircleóg, lapwing; *alad*, piebald.
Why is the Lapwing at the head of the vowels?

Not hard to answer. It is a reminder that the secrets of the Beth-Luis-Nion must be hidden by deception and equivocation, as the lapwing hides her eggs. And Piebald is the colour of this mid-winter season when wise men keep to their chimney-corners, which are black with soot inside and outside white with snow; and of the Goddess of Life-in-Death and Death-in-Life, whose prophetic bird is the piebald magpie.

Day of the Spring Equinox—O—*odorscrach*, cormorant; *odhar*, dun.
Why is the Cormorant next?
Not hard. This is the season of Lent when, because of the Church's ban on the eating of meat and the scarcity of other foods, men become Cormorants in their greed for fish. And Dun is the colour of the newly ploughed fields.

Day of the Summer Solstice—U—*uiseóg*, lark; *usgdha*, resin-coloured.
Why is the Lark in the central place?
Not hard. At this season the Sun is at his highest point, and the Lark flies singing up to adore him. Because of the heat the trees split and ooze resin, and Resin-coloured is the honey that the heather yields.

Day of the Autumn Equinox—E—*ela*, whistling swan; *erc*, rufous-red.
Why is the Whistling Swan in the next place?
Not hard. At this season the Swan and her young prepare for flight. And Rufous-red is the colour of the bracken, and of the Swan's neck.

Day of the Winter Solstice—I—*illait*, eaglet; *irfind*, very white.
Why is the Eaglet in the next place?
Not hard. The Eaglet's maw is insatiable, like that of Death, whose season this is. And Very White are the bones in his nest, and the snow on the cliff-ledge.

* * *

Dec. 24–Jan. 21—B—*besan*, pheasant; *bán*, white.
Why is the Pheasant at the head of the consonants?
Not hard. This is the month of which Amergin sang: 'I am the Stag of Seven Tines'; and as venison is the best flesh that runs, so Pheasant is the best that flies. And White is the colour of this Stag and of this Pheasant.

Jan. 22–Feb. 18—L—*lachu*, duck; *liath*, grey.
Why is the Duck in the next place?
Not hard. This is the month of floods, when Ducks swim over the meadows. And Grey is the colour of flood-water and of rainy skies.

Feb. 19–Mar. 18—N—*naescu*, snipe; *necht*, clear.
Why is the Snipe in the next place?
Not hard. This is the month of the mad March Wind that whirls like a Snipe. And Clear is the colour of Wind.

Mar. 19–Apr. 15—F—*faelinn*, gull; *flann*, crimson.
Why is the Gull in the next place?
Not hard. In this month Gulls congregate on the ploughed fields. And

Crimson is the colour of the *glain*, the magical egg which is found in this month, and of alder-dye, and of the Young Sun struggling through the haze.

Apr. 16–May 13—S—*seg*, hawk; *sodath*, fine-coloured.

Why is the Hawk in the next place?

Not hard. Amergin sang of this month: 'I am a Hawk on a Cliff.' And Fine-coloured are its meadows.

The same—SS—*stmolach*, thrush; *sorcha*, bright-coloured.

Why is the Thrush joined with the Hawk?

Not hard. The Thrush sings his sweetest in this month. And Bright-coloured are the new leaves.

May 14–Jun. 10—H—*hadaig*, night-crow; *huath*, terrible.

Why is the Night-crow in the next place?

Not hard. This is the month when we refrain from carnal pleasures because of terror, which in Irish is *uath*, and the Night-crow brings terror. Terrible is its colour.

Jun. 11–July 8—D—*droen*, wren; *dub*, black.

Why is the Wren in the central place?

Not hard. The Oak is the tree of Druids and the king of trees, and the Wren, *Drui-én*, is the bird of the Druids and the King of all birds. And the Wren is the soul of the Oak. Black is the colour of the Oak when the lightning blasts it, and black the faces of those who leap between the Midsummer fires.

July 9–Aug. 5—T—*truith*, starling; *temen*, dark-grey.

Why is the Starling in the next place?

Not hard. Amergin sang of this month: 'I am a Spear that roars for blood.' It is the warrior's month, and the Starlings' well-trained army will wheel swiftly and smoothly on a pivot, to the left or to the right, without a word of command or exhortation; thus battles are won, not by single feats and broken ranks. And Dark-grey is the colour of Iron, the warriors' metal.

Aug. 6–Sept. 2—C—[*corr*, crane]; *cron*, brown.

Why is the Crane in the next place?

Not hard. This is the month of wisdom, and the wisdom of Manannan Mac Lir, namely the Beth-Luis-Nion, was wrapped in Crane-skin. And Brown are the nuts of the Hazel, tree of wisdom.

The same—Q—*querc*, hen; *quiar*, mouse-coloured.

Why is the Hen joined with the Crane?

Not hard. When the harvest is carted, and the gleaners have gone, the Hen is turned into the cornfields to fatten on what she can find. And a Mouse-coloured little rival creeps around with her.

Sept. 2–Sept. 30—M—*mintan*, titmouse; *mbracht*, variegated.

Why is the Titmouse in the next place?

Not hard. Amergin sang of this month: 'I am a Hill of Poetry'; and this is the month of the poet, who is the least easily abashed of men, as the Titmouse is the least easily abashed of birds. Both band together in companies in this month, and go on circuit in search of a liberal hand; and as the Titmouse climbs spirally up a tree, so the Poet also spirals to immortality. And Variegated is the colour of the Titmouse, and of the Master-poet's dress.

Oct. 1–Oct. 29—G—*géis*, mute swan; *gorm*, blue.

Why is the Mute Swan in the next place?

Not hard. In this month he prepares to follow his companion the Whistling Swan. And Blue is the haze on the hills, Blue the smoke of the burning weed, Blue the skies before the November rain.

Oct. 29–Nov. 25—Ng—*ngéigh*, goose; *nglas*, glass-green.

Why is the Goose in the next place?

Not hard. In this month the tame goose is brought in from misty pasture to be cooped and fattened for the mid-winter feast; and the wild goose mourns for him in the misty meadows. And Glassy-green is the wave that thuds against the cliff, a warning that the year must end.

Nov. 26–Dec. 22—R—*rócnat*, rook; *ruadh*, blood-red.

Why is the Rook in the last place?

Not hard. He wears mourning for the year that dies in this month. And Blood-red are the rags of leaves on the elder-trees, a token of the slaughter.

*   *   *

The Pheasant was the best available bird for the B-month, *bran* the raven and *bunnan* the bittern being better suited to later months of the year. The author of the article on pheasants in the *Encyclopaedia Britannica* states that pheasants (sacred birds in Greece) are likely to have been indigenous to the British Isles and that the white, or 'Bohemian', variety often appears among pheasants of ordinary plumage.

It is possible that the original S-colour was *serind*, primrose, but that the primrose's erotic reputation led to its replacement by the euphemism, *sodath*.

The omission of *corr*, the Crane, for the C-month is intentional; the contents of the Crane-bag were a close secret and all reference to it was discouraged.

And what of Dec. 23rd, the extra day of the year, on which the young King, or Spirit of the Year, was crowned and given eagle's wings, and which was expressed by the semi-vowel J, written as double I? Its bird was naturally the Eagle, *iolar* in Irish, which has the right initial. The Irish poets were so chary of mentioning this day that we do not even know what its tree was; yet that they regarded the Eagle as its bird is proved by the use of the diminutive *illait*, Eaglet, for the letter I: that is to say that if the extra day, double-I, had not been secretly given the cypher-equivalent *iolar*, there would be no need to express the preceding day, that of the Winter Solstice, namely single I, by *illait*, Eaglet—for E is not expressed by Cygnet, nor A by Lapwing-chick.

These cyphers were used to mystify and deceive all ordinary people who were not in the secret. For example, if one poet asked another in public: 'When shall we two meet again?' he would expect an answer in which elements of several cypher alphabets were used, and which was further disguised by being spelt backwards or put in a foreign language, or both. He might, for instance, be answered in a sentence built up from the Colour, Bird, Tree and Fortress oghams:

> When a *brown-plumaged rook* perches on the *fir* below the Fortress of *Seolae*.

That would spell out the Latin CRAS—'tomorrow'.

Besides the one hundred and fifty regular cypher-alphabets that the candidate for the ollaveship had to learn, there were countless other tricks for putting the uninitiated off the scent; for example, the use of the letter after, or before, the desired one. Often a synonym was used for the tree-cypher word—'the chief overseer of Nimrod's Tower' for *Beth*, birch; 'activity of bees' for *Saille*, willow; 'pack of wolves' for *Straif*, blackthorn, and so on.

In one of the cypher-alphabets, *Luis* is given as elm, not rowan, because the Irish word for elm, *lemh*, begins with an L; Tinne is given as elder because the Irish word for elder, *trom*, begins with a T; similarly, *Quert* is given as *quulend*, holly. This trick may account for *Ngetal*, reed, being so frequently read as broom, the Irish of which is *n'gilcach*; but there is also a practical poetic reason for the change. The *Book of Bally-mote* gives broom the poetic name of 'Physicians' Strength', presumably because its bitter shoots, being diuretic, were prized as 'a remedy for surfeits and to all diseases arising therefrom'. (A decoction of broom-flowers was Henry VIII's favourite medicine.) A medical tree suited the month of November, when the year was dying and the cold winds kept well-to-do people indoors with little diversion but eating and drinking.

Chapter Seventeen

THE LION WITH THE STEADY HAND

Llew Llaw Gyffes ('the Lion with the Steady Hand'), a type of Dionysus or Celestial Hercules worshipped in ancient Britain, is generally identified with Lugh, the Goidelic Sun-god, who has given his name to the towns of Laon, Leyden, Lyons and Carlisle (Caer Lugubalion). The name 'Lugh' may be connected with the Latin *lux* (light) or *lucus* (a grove); it may even be derived from the Sumerian *lug* meaning 'son'. 'Llew' is a different word, connected with *leo* (lion), an appellation of Lugh's. In Ireland he was called 'Lugh the Long-handed', defeater of the Africans, the earliest settlers in Ireland; he possessed a magic spear which thirsted for blood and flashed fire or roared aloud in battle; and he was the first to use the horse in warfare. When he approached from the West, at the Battle of Moytura, Breas (Boreas?) Balor, the one-eyed King of the old Gods and later styled Lugh's grandfather, cried out: 'I wonder that the Sun has risen in the West today rather than in the East.' His druids answered: 'Would that it were no more than the Sun! It is the glowing face of Lugh the Long-handed'—which nobody could gaze upon without being dazzled. Another account of his parentage quoted by H. d'Arbois de Joubainville in his monumental *Cycle Mythologique Irlandaise* makes him the son not of Balor's daughter Ethne by one Cian, but of Clothru (who is apparently a single form of the Triple Goddess Eire, Fodhla and Banbha) by Balor's three grandsons Brian, Iuchar and Iuchurba; a row of red circles on his neck and belly marking off the parts of his body that each father had begotten. His death on the first Sunday in August—called *Lugh nasadh* ('Commemoration of Lugh'), later altered to 'Lugh-mass' or 'Lammas'—was until recently observed in Ireland with Good Friday-like mourning and kept as a feast of dead kinsfolk, the mourning procession being always led by a young man carrying a hooped wreath. Lammas was also observed as a mourning feast in most parts of England in mediaeval times; which accounts for the extraordinary popular demonstrations when William Rufus's body was brought up from the New Forest for burial. The peasants were bewailing a mythical Lugh when along came the body of their own red-headed king laid on a harvest cart. Nowadays the only English Lammas celebrated is the Lancashire Wakes Week, the dismal meaning of which has been forgotten among the holiday distractions of Blackpool.

The famous Tailltean Games of Ireland, originally funeral games in the Etruscan style, with chariot races and sword-play, take place at Lammas. The Irish tradition that they were held in memory of one Tailte, Lugh's dead foster-mother, is late and misleading. The games, which in early mediaeval times were so well-frequented that the chariots occupied six miles of road, were marked by Tailtean (or Teltown) marriages in honour of Lugh and his capricious bride. These were trial marriages and lasted 'for a year and a day', that is, for 365 days, and could be dissolved only by an act of divorce performed in the place where they had been celebrated. Then the man and woman stood back to back in the centre of the Black Rath and walked apart, one to the north, the other to the south. Lugh was incarnate in the famous Ulster hero Cuchulain: he flew in at the mouth of Cuchulain's mother Dechtire in the form of a may-fly. Cuchulain was so much of a sun-god that when he plunged into a cold bath the water hissed and began to boil. That Lugh's magical weapon was a spear suggests that he belongs to the earlier Bronze Age invaders of Ireland; the later ones were armed with swords. He may be identified with Geryon, King of the West, 'with three bodies in one', whom Hercules despoiled of his red cattle, guarded by a two-headed dog, and killed in Erytheia ('red island').

According to the mythographers, Hercules sailed to the West from Greece, with ships from Crete, and went by way of North Africa, the Straits of Gibraltar, Tartessus, and Gaul (where he fathered the Celts). This is the same course as the Milesians took, and the Tenth Labour of Hercules reads like one more account of the defeat of the New Stone Age invaders—Partholan's and Nemed's peoples—by Bronze Age men from Spain; but Erytheia is perhaps Devonshire, famous for its bright red soil and red cattle, which the Bronze Age men also conquered from New Stone Age people. It was during this Labour that Hercules borrowed the golden cup from the Sun, and became lotus-borne. Geryon appears to have been a Western version of the Vedic god Agni, the earliest Indian trinity, who had three births and three bodies. As born of water, Agni was a calf who yearly grew to 'a bull that sharpens his horns'; as born of two sticks (the fire-drill), he was a glutton with a fiery tongue; as born in the highest heaven, he was an eagle. The Vedic hymns also celebrate him as a supporter of the sky, namely the pillar of cloud that rises up when fires are lighted in his honour, and as an omniscient immortal who has taken up his abode among mortals. Thus when Hercules killed Geryon and carried off his cattle he was, in fact, gaining a victory over one of his own selves.

In some parts of Wales Lammas is still kept as a fair. Sir John Rhys records that in the 1850's the hills of Fan Fach and South Barrule in

Carmarthenshire were crowded with mourners for Llew Llaw on the first Sunday in August, their excuse being that they were 'going up to bewail Jephthah's daughter on the mountain'. This, oddly enough, was the very same excuse that the post-Exilic Jewish girls had used, after the Deuteronomic reforms, to disguise their mourning for Tammuz, Llew Llaw's Palestinian counterpart. But with the Welsh Revival the practice was denounced as pagan and discontinued.

Here is Llew Llaw's own story (translated by Lady Charlotte Guest) which forms the second part of the *Romance of Math the Son of Mathonwy*. Though not a saga in the grand style, like that of Cuchulain, and in part falsified by the intrusion of the God Woden (Gwydion) into territory not originally his, it is one of the best summaries extant of the single poetic Theme.

The first part of this romance relates to Gwydion's stealing of the sacred pigs from Pryderi the King of the Pembrokeshire Annwm, on behalf of Math the son of Mathonwy, King of North Wales. Math is pictured as a sacred King of the ancient type whose virtue was resident in the feet. Except when his kingdom was attacked and he was obliged to ride into battle, Math was bound by convention to keep his foot in the lap of a priestess. The office of royal foot-holder survived in the Welsh princely courts until early mediaeval times, but was then assigned to a man, not a woman. Math's was a matrilinear kingdom, his heirs being his sister's sons; that is to say the husbands of his sister-in-law's daughters. One of them, Gilvaethwy, attempts to usurp the throne by seducing the reigning queen, Math's foot-holder, while Math is away on campaign. Math counters with all his magical resources, eliminates his rival, and then decides to marry his niece Arianrhod. The holding of the foot was doubtless protective, the heel being the one vulnerable point of sacred kings: witness the heel of Achilles pierced by Paris's arrow; the heel of Talus pierced by Medea's pin; the heel of Diarmuid pierced by the bristle of the Benn Gulban Boar; the heel of Harpocrates stung by the scorpion; the heel of Balder (in the Danish version of the myth) pierced by the mistletoe flung by the god Holder at the instigation of Loki; the heel of Ra stung by the magic snake sent by Isis; the heel of Mopsus the Lapith stung by the black snake of Libya, the heel of Krishna in the *Mahabharata*, pierced by an arrow which his brother Jara the Hunter shot. Talus is closely related to Achilles in Apollodorus's version of the myth, where the cause of his death is given as a wound in the foot from an arrow shot by Hercules's heir, Poeas.

Since recently I had the ill-luck to tread on a Pyrenean viper—a variety stated to be eight times more lethal than the English—I can take the argument further and assert confidently that 'Silver Island' or 'White Island', or 'Revolving Island', to which the sacred king goes at his death, is prophetically seen by him when his heel is bitten by the serpent or scorpion, or pricked with the (presumably) poisoned arrow. Soon after the first pain and vomiting my eyesight began to fail. A small silver spot appeared in the centre of my field of vision, which gradually enlarged into an island with sharply defined bastions; the shores spread wider and wider, as though I were nearing it across a sea. When I started to walk home, I could not see where I was going; and then the island began slowly to revolve in a clockwise direction. I cannot say whether it would have revolved the canonical four times if the poison had been more virulent or if I had been obsessed by the sense of coming death as these kings were; the illusion had faded long before I was given an anti-toxin. I was thankful that, unlike my youngest son whom I was carrying on my shoulder at the time, I had not been born on the day of the winter solstice. My foot remained so swollen for a couple of months that I could only hobble. Finally a Catalan doctor prescribed hot fomentations of wild-olive leaves, which reduced the swelling within three days. This traditional remedy has mythological sense as well as practical value: the wild-olive was the timber of Hercules's club, and therefore a prime expulsive of lingering venom.

I should, of course, have remembered the Emperor Claudius's special edict recorded in Suetonius, 'how there is nothing better for the bite of a viper than the juice of yew'. This was the correct homoeopathic treatment; as wild-olive was the allopathic. I find that Topsell in his *Serpents* (1658), recommends the juice of the periwinkle; this is another homoeopathic remedy, the periwinkle being 'the flower of death'.

THE ROMANCE OF LLEW LLAW GYFFES

. . . Math the Son of Mathonwy said: 'Give your counsel unto me, what maiden I shall seek.' 'Lord,' said Gwydion the son of Don, 'it is easy to give thee counsel; seek Arianrod, the daughter of Don, thy niece, thy sister's daughter.'

And they brought her unto him, and the maiden came in. 'Ha, damsel,' said he, 'art thou the maiden?' 'I know not, lord, other than that I am.' Then he took up his magic wand, and bent it. 'Step over this,' said he, 'and I shall know if thou art the maiden.' Then stepped she over the magic wand, and there appeared forthwith a fine chubby yellow-haired boy. And at the crying out of the boy, she went towards the door. And thereupon some small form was seen; but before anyone could get a second glimpse of it, Gwydion had taken it, and had flung a scarf of velvet around it, and hidden it. Now the place where he hid it was the bottom of a chest at the foot of his bed.

'Verily,' said Math the son of Mathonwy, concerning the fine yellow-haired boy, 'I will cause this one to be baptized, and Dylan is the name I will give him.'

So they had the boy baptized, and as they baptized him he plunged into the sea. And immediately when he was in the sea, he took its nature, and swam as well as the best fish that was therein. And for that reason was he called Dylan, the son of the Wave. Beneath him no wave ever broke. And the blow whereby he came to his death, was struck by his uncle Govannion. The third fatal blow was it called.

As Gwydion lay one morning on his bed awake, he heard a cry in the chest at his feet; and though it was not loud, it was such that he could hear it. Then he arose in haste, and opened the chest: and when he opened it, he beheld an infant boy stretching out his arms from the folds of the scarf, and casting it aside. And he took up the boy in his arms, and carried him to a place where he knew there was a woman that could nurse him. And he agreed with the woman that she should take charge of the boy. And that year he was nursed.

And at the end of the year he seemed by his size as though he were two years old. And the second year he was a big child, and able to go to the Court by himself. And when he came to the Court, Gwydion noticed him, and the boy became familiar with him, and loved him better than anyone else. Then was the boy reared at the Court until he was four years old, when he was as big as though he had been eight.

And one day Gwydion walked forth, and the boy followed him, and he went to the Castle of Arianrod, having the boy with him; and when he came into the Court, Arianrod arose to meet him, and greeted him and bade him welcome. 'Heaven prosper thee,' said he. 'Who is the boy that followeth thee?' she asked. 'This youth, he is thy son,' he answered. 'Alas,' said she, 'what has come unto thee that thou shouldst shame me thus, wherefore dost thou seek my dishonour, and retain it so long as this?' 'Unless thou suffer dishonour greater than that of my bringing up such a boy as this, small will be thy disgrace.' 'What is the name of the boy?' said she. 'Verily,' he replied, 'he has not yet a name.' 'Well,' she said, 'I lay this destiny upon him, that he shall never have a name until he receives one from me.' 'Heaven bears me witness,' answered he, 'that thou art a wicked woman. But the boy shall have a name how displeasing soever it may be unto thee. As for thee that which afflicts thee is that thou art no longer called a damsel.' And thereupon he went forth in wrath, and returned to Caer Dathyl, and there he tarried that night.

And the next day he arose and took the boy with him, and went to walk on the sea shore between that place and Aber Menei. And there he saw some sedges and sea weed, and he turned them into a boat. And out of dry sticks and sedges he made some Cordovan leather, and a great deal thereof, and he coloured it in such a manner that no one ever saw leather more beautiful than it. Then he made a sail to the boat, and he and the boy went in it to the port of the castle of Arianrod. And he began forming shoes and stitching them, until he was observed from the castle. And when he knew that they of the castle were observing him, he disguised his aspect, and put another semblance upon himself, and upon the boy, so that they might not be known. 'What men are those in yonder boat?' said Arianrod. 'They are cordwainers,' answered they. 'Go and see what kind of leather they have, and what kind of work they can do.'

So they came unto them. And when they came he was colouring some Cordovan leather, and gilding it. And the messengers came and told her this. 'Well,' said she, 'take the measure of my foot, and desire the cord-wainer to make shoes for me.' So he made the shoes for her, yet not according to the measure, but larger. The shoes then were brought unto her, and behold they were too large. 'These are too large,' said she, 'but he shall receive their value. Let him also make some that are smaller than they.' Then he made her others that were much smaller than her foot, and sent them unto her. 'Tell him that these will not go on my feet,' said she. And they told him this. 'Verily,' said he, 'I will not make her any shoes, unless I see her foot.' And this was told unto her. 'Truly,' she answered, 'I will go unto him.'

So she went down to the boat, and when she came there, he was shaping shoes and the boy stitching them. 'Ah, lady,' said he, 'good day to thee.' 'Heaven prosper thee,' said she. 'I marvel that thou canst not manage to make shoes according to a measure.' 'I could not,' he replied, 'but now I shall be able.'

Thereupon behold a wren stood upon the deck of the boat, and the boy shot at it, and hit it in the leg between the sinew and the bone. Then she smiled. 'Verily,' said she, 'with a steady hand did the lion aim at it.' 'Heaven reward thee not, but now has he got a name. And a good enough name it is. Llew Llaw Gyffes be he called henceforth.'

Then the work disappeared in sea weed and sedges, and he went on with it no further. And for that reason was he called the third Gold-shoemaker. 'Of a truth,' said she, 'thou wilt not thrive the better for doing evil unto me.' 'I have done thee no evil yet,' said he. Then he restored the boy to his own form. 'Well,' said she, 'I will lay a destiny upon this boy, that he shall never have arms and armour until I invest him with them.' 'By Heaven,' said he, 'let thy malice be what it may, he shall have arms.'

Then they went towards Dinas Dinllev, and there he brought up Llew Llaw Gyffes, until he could manage any horse, and he was perfect in features, and strength, and stature. And then Gwydion saw that he languished through the want of horses, and arms. And he called him unto him. 'Ah, youth,' said he, 'we will go to-morrow on an errand together. Be therefore more cheerful than thou art.' 'That I will,' said the youth.

Next morning, at the dawn of day, they arose. And they took way along the sea coast, up towards Bryn Aryen. And at the top of Cevn Clydno they equipped themselves with horses, and went towards the Castle of Arianrod. And they changed their form, and pricked towards the gate in the semblance of two youths, but the aspect of Gwydion was more staid than that of the other. 'Porter,' said he, 'go thou in and say that there are here bards from Glamorgan.' And the porter went in. 'The welcome of Heaven be unto them, let them in,' said Arianrod.

With great joy were they greeted. And the hall was arranged, and they went to meat. When meat was ended, Arianrod discoursed with Gwydion of tales and stories. Now Gwydion was an excellent teller of tales. And when it was time to leave off feasting, a chamber was prepared for them, and they went to rest.

In the early twilight Gwydion arose, and he called unto him his magic and his power. And by the time that the day dawned, there resounded through the land uproar, and trumpets, and shouts. When it was now day, they heard a knocking at the door of the chamber, and therewith Arianrod asking that it might be opened. Up rose the youth and opened unto her, and she entered and a maiden with her. 'Ah, good men,' she said, 'in evil plight are we.' 'Yes, truly,' said Gwydion, 'we have heard trumpets, and shouts; what thinkest thou that they may mean?' 'Verily,' said she, 'we cannot see the colour of the ocean by reason of all the ships, side by side. And they are making for the land with all the speed they can. And what can we do?' said she. 'Lady,' said Gwydion, 'there is none other counsel than to close the castle upon us, and to defend it as best as we may.' 'Truly,' said she, 'may Heaven reward you. And do you defend it. And here may you have plenty of arms.'

And thereupon went she forth for the arms, and behold she returned, and two maidens, and suits of armour for two men, with her. 'Lady,' said he, 'do thou accoutre this stripling, and I will arm myself with the help of thy maidens. Lo, I hear the tumult of the men approaching.' 'I will do so, gladly.' So she armed him fully, and that right cheerfully. 'Hast thou finished arming the youth?' said he. 'I have finished,' she answered. 'I likewise have finished,' said Gwydion. 'Let us now take off our arms, we have no need of them.' 'Wherefore?' said she. 'Here is the army around the house.' 'Oh, lady, there is here no army.' 'Oh,' cried she, 'whence then was this tumult?' 'The tumult was but to break thy prophecy and to obtain arms for thy son. And now has he got arms without any thanks unto thee.' 'By Heaven,' said Arianrod, 'thou art a wicked man. Many a youth might have lost his life through the uproar thou hast caused in this Cantrev to-day. Now will I lay a destiny upon this youth,' she said, 'that he shall never have a wife of the race that now inhabits this earth.' 'Verily,' said he, 'thou wast ever a malicious woman, and no one ought to support thee. A wife shall he have notwithstanding.'

They went thereupon unto Math the son of Mathonwy, and complained unto him most bitterly of Arianrod. Gwydion showed him also how he had procured arms for the youth. 'Well,' said Math, 'we will seek, I and thou, by charms and illusion, to form a wife for him out of flowers. He has now come to man's stature, and he is the comeliest youth that was ever beheld.' So they took the blossoms of the oak, and the blossoms of the broom, and the blossoms of the meadow-sweet, and produced from them a maiden, the fairest and most graceful that man ever saw. And they baptized her, and gave her the name of Blodeuwedd.

After she had become his bride, and they had feasted, said Gwydion, 'It is not easy for a man to maintain himself without possessions.' 'Of a truth,' said Math, 'I will give the young man the best Cantrev to hold.' 'Lord,' said he, 'what Cantrev is that?' 'The Cantrev of Dinodig,' he answered. Now it is called at this day Eivionydd and Ardudwy. And the place in the Cantrev where he dwelt, was a palace of his in a spot called Mur-y-Castell, on the confines of Ardudwy. There dwelt he and reigned, and both he and his sway were beloved by all.

One day he went forth to Caer Dathyl, to visit Math the son of Mathonwy. And on the day that he set out for Caer Dathyl, Blodeuwedd walked in the court. And she heard the sound of a horn. And after the sound of the horn, behold a tired stag went by, with dogs and huntsmen following it. And after the dogs and the huntsmen there came a crowd of men on foot. 'Send a youth,' said she, 'to ask who yonder host may be.' So a youth went, and inquired who they were. 'Gronw Pebyr is this, the lord of Penllyn,' said they. And thus the youth told her.

Gronw Pebyr pursued the stag, and by the river Cynvael he overtook the stag and killed it. And what with flaying the stag and baiting his dogs, he was there until the night began to close in upon him. And as the day departed and the night drew near, he came to the gate of the Court. 'Verily,' said Blodeuwedd, 'the Chieftain will speak ill of us if we let him at this hour depart to another land without inviting him in.' 'Yes, truly, lady,' said they, 'it will be most fitting to invite him.'

Then went messengers to meet him and bid him in. And he accepted her bidding gladly, and came to the Court, and Blodeuwedd went to meet him and greeted him, and bade him welcome. 'Lady,' said he, 'Heaven repay thee thy kindness.'

When they had disaccoutred themselves, they went to sit down. And Blodeuwedd looked upon him, and from the moment that she looked on him she became filled with his love. And he gazed on her, and the same thought came unto him as unto her, so that he could not conceal from her that he loved her, but he declared unto her that he did so. Thereupon she was very joyful. And all their discourse that night was concerning the affection and love which they felt one for the other, and which in no longer space than one evening had arisen. And that evening passed they in each other's company.

The next day he sought to depart. But she said, 'I pray thee go not from me to-day.' And that night he tarried also. And that night they consulted by what means they might always be together. 'There is none other counsel,' said he, 'but that thou strive to learn from Llew Llaw Gyffes in what manner he will meet his death. And this must thou do under the semblance of solicitude concerning him.'

The next day Gronw sought to depart. 'Verily,' said she, 'I will counsel thee not to go from me to-day.' 'At thy instance will I not go,' said he, 'albeit, I must say, there is danger that the chief who owns the palace may return home.' 'To-morrow,' answered she, 'will I indeed permit thee to go forth.'

The next day he sought to go, and she hindered him not. 'Be mindful,' said Gronw, 'of what I have said unto thee, and converse with him fully, and that under the guise of the dalliance of love, and find out by what means he may come to his death.'

That night Llew Llaw Gyffes returned to his home. And the day they spent in discourse, and minstrelsy, and feasting. And at night they went to rest, and he spoke to Blodeuwedd once, and he spoke to her a second time. But, for all this, he could not get from her one word. 'What aileth thee,' said he, 'art thou well?' 'I was thinking,' said she, 'of that which thou didst never think of concerning me; for I was sorrowful as to thy death, lest thou shouldst go sooner than I.' 'Heaven reward thy care for me,' said he, 'but until Heaven take me I shall not easily be slain.' 'For the sake of Heaven, and for mine, show me how thou mightest be slain. My memory in guarding is better than thine.' 'I will tell thee gladly,' said he. 'Not easily can I be slain, except by a wound. And the spear wherewith I am struck must be a year in the forming. And nothing must be done towards it except during the sacrifice on Sundays.' 'Is this certain?' asked she. 'It is in truth,' he answered. 'And I cannot be slain within a house, nor without. I cannot be slain on horseback nor on foot.' 'Verily,' said she, 'in what manner then canst thou be slain?' 'I will tell thee,' said he. 'By making a bath for me by the side of a river, and by putting a roof over the cauldron, and thatching it well and tightly, and bringing a buck, and putting it beside the cauldron. Then if I place one foot on the buck's back, and the other on the edge of the cauldron, whosoever strikes me thus will cause my death.' 'Well,' said she, 'I thank Heaven that it will be easy to avoid this.'

No sooner had she held this discourse than she sent to Gronw Pebyr. Gronw toiled at making the spear, and that day twelvemonth it was ready. And that very day he caused her to be informed thereof.

'Lord,' said Blodeuwedd unto Llew, 'I have been thinking how it is possible that what thou didst tell me formerly can be true; wilt thou show me in what manner thou couldst stand at once upon the edge of a cauldron and upon a buck, if I prepare the bath for thee?' 'I will show thee,' said he.

Then she sent unto Gronw, and bade him be in ambush on the hill which is now called Bryn Kyvergyr, on the bank of the river Cynvael. She caused also to be collected all the goats that were in the Cantrev, and had them brought to the other side of the river, opposite Bryn Kyvergyr.

And the next day she spoke thus. 'Lord,' said she, 'I have caused the roof and the bath to be prepared, and lo! they are ready.' 'Well,' said Llew, 'we will go gladly to look at them.'

The day after they came and looked at the bath. 'Wilt thou go into the bath, lord?' said she. 'Willingly will I go in,' he answered. So into the bath he went, and he anointed himself. 'Lord, 'said she, 'behold the animals which thou didst speak of as being called bucks.' 'Well,' said he, 'cause one of them to be caught and brought here.' And the buck was brought. Then Llew rose out of the bath, and put on his trowsers, and he placed one foot on the edge of the bath and the other on the buck's back.

Thereupon Gronw rose up from the hill which is called Bryn Kyvergyr, and he rested on one knee, and flung the poisoned dart and struck him on the side, so that the shaft started out, but the head of the dart remained in. Then he flew up in the form of an eagle and gave a fearful scream. And thenceforth was he no more seen.

And soon as he departed Gronw and Blodeuwedd went together unto the palace that night. And the next day Gronw arose and took possession of Ardudwy. And after he had overcome the land, he ruled over it, so that Ardudwy and Penllyn were both under his sway.

Then these tidings reached Math the son of Mathonwy. And heaviness and grief came upon Math, and much more upon Gwydion than upon him. 'Lord,' said Gwydion, 'I shall never rest until I have tidings of my nephew.' 'Verily,' said Math, 'may Heaven be thy strength.' Then Gwydion set forth and began to go forward. And he went through Gwynedd and Powys to the confines. And when he had done so, he went into Arvon, and came to the house of a vassal, in Maenawr Penardd. And he alighted at the house, and stayed there that night.

The man of the house and his household came in, and last of all came there the swineherd. Said the man of the house to the swineherd, 'Well, youth, hath thy sow come in to-night?' 'She hath,' said he, 'and is this instant returned to the pigs.' 'Where doth this sow go to?' said Gwydion. 'Every day, when the sty is opened, she goeth forth and none can catch sight of her, neither is it known whither she goeth more than if she sank into the earth.' 'Wilt thou grant unto me,' said Gwydion, 'not to open the sty until I am beside the sty with thee?' 'This will I do, right gladly,' he answered.

That night they went to rest; and as soon as the swineherd saw the light of day, he awoke Gwydion. And Gwydion arose and dressed himself, and went with the swineherd, and stood beside the sty. Then the swineherd opened the sty. And as soon as he opened it, behold she leaped forth, and set off with great speed. And Gwydion followed her, and she went against the course of a river, and made for a brook, which is now called Nant y Llew. And there she halted and began feeding. And Gwydion came under the tree, and looked what it might be that the sow was feeding on. And he saw that she was eating putrid flesh and vermin. Then looked he up to the top of the tree, and as he looked he beheld on the top of the tree an eagle, and when the eagle shook itself, there fell vermin and putrid flesh from it, and these the sow devoured. And it seemed to him that the eagle was Llew. And he sang an Englyn:

> *Oak that grows between the two banks;*
> *Darkened is the sky and hill!*
> *Shall I not tell him by his wounds,*
> *That this is Llew?*

Upon this the eagle came down until he reached the centre of the tree. And Gwydion sang another Englyn:

> *Oak that grows in upland ground,*
> *Is it not wetted by the rain? Has it not been drenched*
> *By nine score tempests?*
> *It bears in its branches Llew Llaw Gyffes!*

Then the eagle came down until he was on the lowest branch of the tree, and thereupon this Englyn did Gwydion sing:

> *Oak that grows beneath the steep;*
> *Stately and majestic is its aspect!*
> *Shall I not speak of it*
> *That Llew will come to my lap?*

And the eagle came down upon Gwydion's knee. And Gwydion struck him with his magic wand, so that he returned to his own form.

No one ever saw a more piteous sight, for he was nothing but skin and bone.

Then he went unto Caer Dathyl, and there were brought unto him good physicians that were in Gwynedd, and before the end of the year he was quite healed.

'Lord,' said he unto Math the son of Mathonwy, 'it is full time now that I have retribution of him by whom I have suffered all this woe.' 'Truly,' said Math, 'he will never be able to maintain himself in the possession of that which is thy right.' 'Well,' said Llew, 'the sooner I have my right, the better shall I be pleased.'

Then they called together the whole of Gwynedd, and set forth to Ardudwy. And Gwydion went on before and proceeded to Mur-y-Castell. And when Blodeuwedd heard that he was coming, she took her maidens with her, and fled to the mountain. And they passed through the river Cynvael, and went towards a court that there was upon the mountain, and through fear they could not proceed except with their faces looking backwards, so that unawares they fell into the lake. And they were all drowned except Blodeuwedd herself, and her Gwydion overtook. And he said unto her, 'I will not slay thee, but I will do unto thee worse than that. For I will turn thee into a bird; and because of the shame thou hast done unto Llew Llaw Gyffes, thou shalt never show thy face in the light of day henceforth; and that through fear of all the other birds. For it shall be their nature to attack thee, and to chase thee from wheresoever they may find thee. And thou shalt not lose thy name, but shalt be always called Blodeuwedd.' Now Blodeuwedd is an owl in the language of this present time, and for this reason is the owl hateful unto all birds. And even now the owl is called Blodeuwedd.

Then Gronw Pebyr withdrew unto Penllyn, and he despatched thence an embassy. And the messengers he sent asked Llew Llaw Gyffes, if he would take land, or domain, or gold, or silver, for the injury he had received. 'I will not, by my confession to Heaven,' said he. 'Behold this is the least that I will accept from him; that he come to the spot where I was when he wounded me with the dart, and that I stand where he did, and that with a dart I take my aim at him. And this is the very least that I will accept.'

And this was told unto Gronw Pebyr. 'Verily,' said he, 'is it needful for me to do thus? My faithful warriors, and my household, and my foster-brothers, is there not one among you who will stand the blow in my stead?' 'There is not, verily,' answered they. And because of their refusal to suffer one stroke for their lord, they are called the third disloyal tribe even unto this day. 'Well,' said he, 'I will meet it.'

Then they two went forth to the banks of the river Cynvael, and Gronw stood in the place where Llew Llaw Gyffes was when he struck him, and Llew in the place where Gronw was. Then said Gronw Pebyr unto Llew, 'Since it was through the wiles of a woman that I did unto thee as I have done, I adjure thee by Heaven to let me place between me and the blow, the slab thou seest yonder on the river's bank.' 'Verily,' said Llew, 'I will not refuse thee this.' 'Ah,' said he, 'may Heaven reward thee.' So Gronw took the slab and placed it between him and the blow.

Then Llew flung the dart at him, and it pierced the slab and went through Gronw likewise, so that it pierced through his back. And thus was Gronw Pebyr slain. And there is still the slab on the bank of the river Cynvael, in Ardudwy, having the hole through it. And therefore is it even now called Llech Gronw.

A second time did Llew Llaw Gyffes take possession of the land, and prosperously did he govern it. And as the story relates, he was lord after this over Gwynedd.

Chapter Eighteen

THE BULL-FOOTED GOD

Poets who are concerned with the single poetic Theme, cannot afford to draw disingenuous distinction between 'sacred history' and 'profane myth' and make the usual dissociation between them, unless prepared to reject the Scriptures as wholly irrelevant to poetry. This would be a pity, and in these days of religious toleration I cannot see why they need accept so glaringly unhistorical a view of the authorship, provenience, dating and original texts of the Old Testament, that its close connexion with the Theme is severed. In the following chapter I will knit up a few more broken strands.

The myth of Llew Llaw Gyffes has kept its original outlines pretty well, though carefully edited so as to give gods all the credit for magic feats which we know, by comparison with myths of the same type, were originally performed by goddesses. For example, the Divine Child Llew Llaw is born of a virgin, but by the wizardry of Math, and Arianrhod is not only unaware that she has brought forth a child, but righteously indignant that she is accused of being an unmarried mother; whereas in the Cuchulain version of the Llew story his mother Dechtire conceives by swallowing a may-fly without magical aid. And Nana, who is the Phrygian counterpart of Arianrhod and whose son Attis has much the same later history as Llew Llaw, conceives of her own free will by the magic use of an almond or, some mythographers say, a pomegranate; again, Blodeuwedd, Llew's wife, is created by Gwydion from the blossoms of oak, broom, meadow-sweet and six other plants and trees; whereas in the older legend she is Cybele the Mother of All Living, and wholly independent of any male demiurge.

That Blodeuwedd's fingers are 'whiter than the ninth wave of the sea' proves her connexion with the Moon; nine is the prime Moon-number, the Moon draws the tides, and the ninth wave is traditionally the largest. Thus Heimdall, Llew's counterpart, porter of the Norse heaven and rival of Loki, was 'the Son of the Wave' by being born from nine waves by Odin's (Gwydion's) enchantment. After his fight with Loki, in which both of them dressed in seal-skins, Heimdall was given the apple of Life-in-death by Iduna, born of flowers, Blodeuwedd's counterpart, and rode his horse 'Golden-mane' along the Milky Way which also occurs in the Llew Llaw story. But the Norse scalds have tampered with the myth, awarding Heimdall the victory and doubly disguising Loki's seduction of Heimdall's bride, Iduna.

When Blodeuwedd has betrayed Llew, she is punished by Gwydion who transmogrifies her into an Owl. This is further patriarchal interference. She had been an Owl thousands of years before Gwydion was born —the same Owl that occurs on the coins of Athens as the symbol of Athene, the Goddess of Wisdom, the same owl that gave its name to Adam's first wife Lilith and as Annis the Blue Hag sucks the blood of children in primitive British folk-lore. There is a poem about Blodeuwedd the Owl by Davydd ap Gwilym, in which she swears by St. David that she is daughter of the Lord of Mona, equal in dignity to Meirchion himself. This is to call herself a 'Daughter of Proteus'—Meirchion could change his shape at will—and perhaps to identify herself with the old bloody Druidic religion suppressed by Paulinus in Anglesey in A.D. 68. Davydd ap Gwilym, the most admired of all Welsh poets, was distressed by the contemporary attitude to women and did his best to persuade a nun whom he loved to break out of her cloister.

In the Romance, only the carrion-eating Sow of Maenawr Penardd is independent of the male magician's rod. She is Cerridwen, the White Sow-goddess, in disguise. It will be seen that Arianrhod the Birth-goddess; and Arianrhod the Goddess of Initiation who gives a name and arms to Llew; and Blodeuwedd, the Love-goddess; and Blodeuwedd the Owl, Goddess of Wisdom; and Cerridwen, the Old Sow of Maenawr Penardd, form a pentad. They are the same goddess in her five seasonal aspects: for which *Ailm, Onn, Ura, Eadha,* and *Idho* are the corresponding vowels in the Beth-Luis-Nion calendar. Why the two Arianrhods and the two Blodeu-wedds are not distinguished here is because the pentad can also be viewed as a triad: the author of the Romance, in order to keep a more intelligible narrative sequence, is story-telling in terms of a three-season year.

Similarly, Llew Llaw changes his name with the seasons. Dylan the Fish is his New Year name—though in some accounts Dylan and Llew are twins; Llew Llaw the Lion is his Spring-Summer name; his Autumn name is withheld; in mid-Winter he is the Eagle of Nant y Llew. He is represented in the Romance as being a wonderful horseman; for so Hercules rode the wild horse Arion, and Bellerophon rode Pegasus. In Irish legend his counterpart Lugh is credited with the invention of horsemanship.

The story of his deception by Blodeuwedd recalls that of Gilgamesh's deception by Ishtar, and Samson's deception by Delilah. Samson was a Palestinian Sun-god who, becoming inappropriately included in the corpus of Jewish religious myth, was finally written down as an Israelite hero of the time of the Judges. That he belonged to an exogamic and therefore matrilinear society is proved by Delilah's remaining with her own tribe after marriage; in patriarchal society the wife goes to her husband's tribe. The name 'Samson' means 'Of the Sun' and 'Dan', his tribe, is an appellation of the Assyrian Sun-god. Samson, like Hercules, killed a lion with his bare hands, and his riddle about the bees swarming in the carcase of the lion which he had killed, if returned to iconographic form, shows Aristaeus the Pelasgian Hercules (father of Actaeon, the stag-cult king, and son of Cheiron the Centaur) killing a mountain lion on Mount Pelion, from the wound in whose flesh the first swarm of bees emerged. In the Cuchulain version of the same story, Blodeuwedd is named Blathnat and extracts from her husband King Curoi—the only man who ever gave Cuchulain a beating—the secret that his soul is hidden in an apple in the stomach of a salmon which appears once every seven years in a spring on the side of Slieve Mis (the mountain of Amergin's dolmen). This apple can be cut only with his own sword. Her lover Cuchulain waits for seven years and obtains the apple. Blathnat then prepares a bath and ties her husband's long hair to the bedposts and bedrail; takes his sword and gives it to her lover who cuts the apple in two. The husband loses his strength and cries out: 'No secret to a woman, no jewel to slaves!' Cuchulain cuts off his head. There is a reference to this story in one of Gwion's poems. A Greek version of the same story is referred to Minoan times: Nisus King of Nisa—an ancient city near Megara destroyed by the Dorians—had his 'purple' lock plucked by his daughter Scylla who wished to kill him and marry Minos of Crete. The Greeks have given this story an unlikely moral ending, that Minos drowned Scylla as a parricide from the stern of his galley; at any rate, the genealogy of the Kings of Nisa makes it plain that the throne went by matrilinear succession. Still another version occurs in the *Excidium Troiae*, a mediaeval Latin summary of the Trojan War, compiled from very early sources; here the secret of Achilles's vulnerable heel is wormed from him by his wife Polyxena 'since there is no secret that women cannot extract from men in proof of love'. It may be assumed that, in the original legend of Osiris, Isis was a willing accomplice in his yearly murder by Set; and that, in the original legend of Hercules, Deianeira was a willing accomplice in his yearly murder by Acheloüs, or by Nessus the Centaur; and that each of these heroes was killed in a bath— as in the legends of Minos's bath-murder by the priestess of Cocalus, at Daedalus's instigation, and of Agamemnon's bath-murder by Clytemnestra at Aegisthus's instigation—though in the popular version of the Osiris story it is a coffin, not a bath, into which he is decoyed. The Jackals, who were sacred in Egypt to Anubis, Guardian of the Dead, because they fed on corpse-flesh and had mysterious nocturnal habits, must have known all about the murder.

THE JACKALS' ADDRESS TO ISIS

Grant Anup's children this:
To howl with you, Queen Isis,
Over the scattered limbs of wronged Osiris.
What harder fate than to be woman?
She makes and she unmakes her man.

In Jackal-land it is no secret
Who tempted red-haired, ass-eared Set
To such bloody extreme; who most
Must therefore mourn and fret
To pacify the unquiet ghost.

And when Horus your son
Avenges this divulsion
Sceptre in fist, sandals on feet,
We shall return across the sana
From loyal Jackal-land
To gorge five nights and days on ass's meat.

A Canaanite version of the same story appears in iconotropic form in the patently unhistorical *Book of Judith*, composed in Maccabean times. The Jews seem always to have based their religious anecdotes on an existing legend, or icon, never to have written fiction in the modern sense. Return the account of Judith, Manasses, Holofernes and Achior to pictorial form, and then re-arrange the incidents in their natural order. The Queen ties her royal husband's hair to the bedpost to immobilize him, and beheads him with a sword (*XIII*, *6–8*); an attendant brings it to the lover whom she has chosen to be the new king (*XIV*, *6*); after mourning to appease the ghost of the old king, the Corn-Tammuz, who has died at the barley-harvest (*VIII*, *2–6*), she purifies herself in running water and dresses as a bride (*X*, *3–4*); presently the wedding procession forms up (*X*, *17–21*); and the marriage is celebrated with much merriment (*XII*, *15–20*), bonfires (*XIII*, *13*), religious feasting (*XVI*, *20*), dancing and waving of branches (*XV*, *12*), many gifts (*XV*, *2*), killing of victims (*XV*, *5*), and the ritual circumcision of the bridegroom (*XIV*, *10*). The Queen wears a crown of olive as an emblem of fruitfulness (*XV*, *13*). The head of the old king is put up on the wall of the city as a prophylactic charm (*XIV*, *11*); and the Goddess appears in triad, Hag, Bride and Maid (*XVI*, *23*) to bless the union.

That the Goddess Frigga ordered a general mourning for Balder incriminates her in his death. She was really Nanna, Balder's bride, seduced by his rival Holder; but like the Egyptian priests of Isis, the Norse scalds have altered the story in the interests of marital rectitude. In precisely what part of the heel or foot were Talus, Bran, Achilles, Mopsus, Cheiron, and the rest mortally wounded? The myths of Achilles and Llew Llaw give the clue. When Thetis picked up the child Achilles by the foot and plunged him into the cauldron of immortality, the part covered by her finger and thumb remained dry and therefore vulnerable. This was presumably the spot between the Achilles tendon and the ankle-bone where, as I point out in my *King Jesus*, the nail was driven in to pin the foot of the crucified man to the side of the cross, in the Roman ritual borrowed from the Canaanite Carthaginians; for the victim of crucifixion was originally the annual sacred king. The child Llew Llaw's exact aim was praised by his mother Arianrhod because as the New Year Robin, alias Belin, he transfixed his father the Wren, alias Bran to whom the wren was sacred, 'between the sinew and the bone' of his leg.

Arianrhod's giving of arms to her son is common Celtic form; that women had this prerogative is mentioned by Tacitus in his work on the Germans—the Germany of his day being Celtic Germany, not yet invaded by the patriarchal square-heads whom we call Germans nowadays.

Gronw Pebyr, who figures as the lord of Penllyn—'Lord of the Lake'—which was also the title of Tegid Voel, Cerridwen's husband, is really Llew's twin and tanist. Llew never lacks a twin; Gwydion is a surrogate for Gronw during the visit to the Castle of Arianrhod. Gronw reigns during the second half of the year, after Llew's sacrificial murder; and the weary stag whom he kills and flays outside Llew's castle stands for Llew himself (a 'stag of seven fights'). This constant shift in symbolic values makes the allegory difficult for the prose-minded reader to follow, but to the poet who remembers the fate of the pastoral Hercules the sense is clear: after despatching Llew with the dart hurled at him from Bryn Kyvergyr, Gronw flays him, cuts him to pieces and distributes the pieces among his merry-men. The clue is given in the phrase 'baiting his dogs'. Math had similarly made a stag of his rival Gilvaethwy, earlier in the story. It seems likely that Llew's mediaeval successor, Red Robin Hood, was also once worshipped as a stag. His presence at the Abbot's Bromley Horn Dance would be difficult to account for otherwise, and 'stag's horn' moss is sometimes called 'Robin Hood's Hatband'. In May, the stag puts on his red summer coat.

Llew visits the Castle of Arianrhod in a coracle of weed and sedge. The coracle is the same old harvest basket in which nearly every antique Sun-god makes his New Year voyage; and the virgin princess, his mother, is always waiting to greet him on the bank. As has already been mentioned, the Delphians worshipped Dionysus once a year as the new-born child, *Liknites*, 'the Child in the Harvest Basket', which was a shovel-shaped basket of rush and osier used as a harvest basket, a cradle, a manger, and a winnowing-fan for tossing the grain up into the air against the wind, to separate it from the chaff.

The worship of the Divine Child was established in Minoan Crete, its most famous early home in Europe. In 1903, on the site of the temple of Dictaean Zeus—the Zeus who was yearly born in Rhea's cave at Dicte near Cnossos, where Pythagoras spent 'thrice nine hallowed days' of his initiation—was found a Greek hymn which seems to preserve the original Minoan formula in which the gypsum-powdered, sword-dancing Curetes, or tutors, saluted the Child at his birthday feast. In it he is hailed as 'the Cronian one' who comes yearly to Dicte mounted on a sow and escorted by a spirit-throng, and begged for peace and plenty as a reward for their joyful leaps. The tradition preserved by Hyginus in his *Poetic Astronomy* that the constellation Capricorn[1] ('He-goat') was Zeus's foster-brother Aegipan, the Kid of the Goat Amalthea whose horn Zeus also placed among the stars, shows that Zeus was born at mid-winter when the Sun entered the house of Capricorn. The date is confirmed by the alternative version of the myth, that he was suckled by a sow—evidently the one on whose back he yearly rode into Dicte—since in Egypt swine's flesh and milk were permitted food only at the mid-winter festival. That the Sun-gods Dionysus, Apollo and Mithras were all also reputedly born at the Winter solstice is well known, and the Christian Church first fixed the Nativity feast of Jesus Christ at the same season, in the year A.D. 273. St. Chrysostom, a century later, said that the intention was that 'while the heathen were busied with their profane rites the Christians might perform their holy ones without disturbance', but justified the date as suitable for one who was 'the Sun of Righteousness'. Another confirmation of the date is that Zeus was the son of Cronos, whom we have securely identified with Fearn, or Bran, the god of the F month in the Beth-Luis-Nion. If one reckons back 280 days from the Winter Solstice, that is to say ten months of the Beth-Luis-Nion calendar, the normal period of human gestation, one comes to the first day of *Fearn*. (Similarly, reckoning 280 days forward from the Winter Solstice, one comes to the first day of the G month, *Gort*, sacred to Dionysus; Dionysus the vine and ivy-god, as opposed to the Sun-god, was son to Zeus.) Cuchulain was born as the result of his mother's swallowing a may-fly; but in Ireland may-flies often appear in late March, so his birthday was probably the same.

Llew's soul escapes in the form of an eagle, like the soul of Hercules, and perches on an oak. This apotheosis was in the ancient royal tradition. The souls of lesser men might fly off in the form of white birds or golden butterflies, but a sacred king's soul had the wings of an eagle or royal gryphon. Lion-headed eagles appear on seals in Minoan Crete. It was of the highest political importance that when the Emperor Augustus died he

[1] In the Egyptian Zodiac he is shown with a fish tail, which aligns him with the Water-carrier and the Fishes as a Sign of the three months of Flood. But the Egyptian floods come in the summer with the melting of the Abyssinian snows, so that the Zodiac must have been an importation from some other region.

should be translated to Heaven and become the prime deity of the Roman Empire; and a Roman knight who declared on oath that he had seen the Emperor's soul rising from his pyre in the form of an eagle was therefore rewarded by Livia, Augustus's widow, with a handsome present. Ganymede in the original legend was a Phrygian prince who rose to Heaven as an eagle; he was not carried off on an eagle's back to be Zeus's cup-bearer, as in the version dear to homosexuals. It is likely that, like Cretan Dionysus, son of Zeus; Icarus, son of Daedalus; Phaëthon, son of Apollo; Aesculapius, son of Apollo; Demophoön, son of Celeus; Melicertes, son of Athamas; Mermerus and Pheres, sons of Jason; Gwern, son of Matholwch; Isaac, son of Abraham, and many other unfortunate princes of the same sort, Ganymede son of Tros was invested with a single-day royalty and then burned to death.[1] As I showed in the case of Peleus, Thetis and Achilles, the Pelasgian sacred king of the Minos type could not continue in office beyond the hundred months allowed him by law, but that he could become the successor of a son who was titular king for the one day that did not form part of the year. During the day of his son's reign, to judge from the story of Athamas, the old king pretended to be dead, eating the foods reserved for the dead; immediately it ended he began a new reign by marriage to his widowed daughter-in-law, since the throne was conveyed by mother-right. When the statutory reign was lengthened to a hundred months the old king often lengthened it still further by abducting the nearest heiress, who was theoretically his own daughter, as in the case of King Cinyras of Cyprus. The stories of Sextus Tarquin and Lucretia, David and Bathsheba, Math and Arianrhod, are to be read in this sense.

The subsequent resurrection of Llew takes place in the dead of Winter, in the season of the Old Sow, the time of the annual Athenian pig-sacrifice to the Barley-goddess, her daughter Persephone and Zeus: 'nine-score tempests', that is to say 180 days, have elapsed since his murder at midsummer. The holed stone called *Llech Gronw*, 'the stone of Gronw', was perhaps one of the very common prehistoric holed stones, apparently representing the mouth of the baetylic Mother Goddess, through which spirits passed in the form of winds and entered the wombs of passing women. In other words, Gronw by interposing the stone between his body and Llew's dart assured himself of regeneration.

The death of Blodeuwedd's maidens in the lake refers, it seems, to the conquest of the priestesses of the old religion by the new Apollo priest-

---

[1] Dr. Rafael Patai suggests in his *Hebrew Installation Rites* (Cincinnati, 1947), that the attempted murder by Saul of his son Jonathan (*I Samuel, XIV*, 15) which was avoided only by the provision of a surrogate, and the burning by fire from Heaven of two sons of Aaron on the day of his coronation (*Leviticus, X*, 1–2), were both ritual sacrifices. If he is right about Aaron, the story has been telescoped: one of his 'sons' must have been burned at the close of each year of office, not both at his first installation.

hood—and so recalls the story of how Melampus cured the mad daughters of Proetus and washed away their madness in a spring at Lusi. But there is a clearer parallel than this: the death of the fifty Pallantid priestesses of Athens who leaped into the sea rather than submit to the new patriarchal religion.

The Romance ends with the killing of Gronw by the re-born Llew Llaw, who reigns again over Gwynedd. This is the natural close of the story, except that Llew Llaw should really have another name when he kills Gronw: for Gronw corresponds with the god Set who kills Osiris and tears him in pieces, also with the Greek Typhon and the Irish Finn Mac Coll, all gods of the same sort. Osiris dies, but is re-born as Harpocrates ('the Child Horus') and takes his revenge on Set just as Wali avenges Holdur's murder of Balder; thus the Egyptian Pharaohs were honoured with the name of Horus and spoken of as 'suckled by Isis'.

Llew's autumn name, omitted in the story, can be recovered by the logic of myth. That his rivalry with Gronw Lord of Penllyn for the love of Blodeuwedd is the same as that of Gwyn with Gwythyr ap Greidawl for the love of Creiddylad is proved by *Triad 14*, where Arianrhod is described as the mother of the twin heroes Gwengwyngwyn and Gwanat. Gwengwyngwyn is merely 'The Thrice-white-one', or Gwyn's name three times repeated, and Gwyn's duty, as we have seen, was to conduct souls to the Castle of Arianrhod, like Thrice-great Hermes; in fact, Gwyn, like Dylan and Llew, was Arianrhod's son. But Dafydd ap Gwilym reports that the autumnal owl, Blodeuwedd in disguise, was sacred to Gwyn; it follows that when Llew who began the year as Dylan, reached goat-haunted Bryn Kyvergyr, the midsummer turning-point— and was killed by his rival 'Victor, son of Scorcher', he disappeared from view and presently became Gwyn the leader of the autumnal Wild Chase. Like the White Goddess, alternately Arianrhod of the silver wheel, Blodeuwedd of the white flowers, and Cerridwen the spectral white sow, he also was Thrice-white: alternately Dylan the silver fish, Llew the white stag, and Gwyn the white rider on the pale horse leading his white, red-eared pack. That Gwyn's father was Nudd or Lludd, and Gwengwyn-gwyn's was one Lliaws, does not spoil the argument. Hermes's fatherhood was similarly disputed in Greece.

The chest in which Llew is laid by Gwydion is an ambivalent symbol. It is in one sense the chest of re-birth, of the sort in which dead Cretans were laid. In another it is the ark in which the Virgin and Child—Danaë and Perseus is the most familiar of several instance—are customarily set adrift by their enemies; this is the same acacia-wood ark in which Isis and her child Harpocrates sailed over the waters of the flooded Delta seeking the scattered fragments of Osiris. In this case, however, Arian-rhod is not in the chest with Llew. The author is doing his best to keep the Goddess, in her maternal aspect, out of the story; she does not even suckle Llew.

Mur-y-Castell, now called Tomen-y-Mur is a mediaeval British fort—a fair-sized artificial mound surmounted by a stockade—in the hills behind Ffestiniog in Merioneth. It has been constructed around the north gate of a Roman camp, and the considerable remains of the Roman baths, supplied by water from the river Cynfael, are still clearly visible near by. Apparently the Camp was occupied by the pagan Welsh when the Romans evacuated it in the fifth century, and then became the centre of a Llew Llaw cult—if it had not been so already, like the Roman camps of Laon, Lyons and Carlisle. The bath system lent itself to the story. The mound may be funerary, with the remains of a dead king buried in the ruins of the Roman gate around which it has been heaped.

The bath in the story of Llew's murder is, as I have said, familiar. Sacred kings often meet their end in that way: for example, Minos the Cretan Sun-god at Agrigentum in Sicily at the hands of the priestess of Cocalus and her lover Daedalus; and Agamemnon, the sacred king of Mycenae, at the hands of Clytemnestra and her lover, Aegisthus. It is a lustral bath of the sort that kings take at their coronation: for Llew Llaw anoints himself while in it. The merry-men in attendance are usually depicted as goat-legged satyrs. In the Romance of Llew Llaw, too, they are summoned as goats to assist in the sacrifice of their master.

The shoe-making business is odd, but it throws light on the mysterious twelfth-century French ballad of the Young Shoemaker.

Sur les marches du palais
L'est une tant belle femme

Elle a tant d'amouroux
Qu'elle ne sait lequel prendre.

C'est le p'tit cordonnier
Qu'a eu la preférence.

Un jour en la chaussant
Il lui fit sa demande:

'La belle si vous l'vouliez,
Nous dormirons ensemble.

'Dans un grand lit carré.
Orné de têle blanche,

'Et aux quatre coins du lit
Un bouquet de pervenches.

'Et au mitan du lit
La rivière est si grande

'Que les chevaux du Roi
Pourroient y boire ensemble

'Et là nous dormirions
Jusqu'à la fin du monde.'

The beautiful lady with the many lovers and a great square bed hung with white linen is unmistakably the Goddess, and the young shoemaker is Llew Llaw. The speaking parts have been interchanged. In stanza 2 *Elle a tant d'amouroux* should be, for the rhyme's sake *Elle a tant d'enamourés.* In stanza 4, *'En la chaussant Il lui fit sa demande'* should be *Sur la chaussée Elle lui fit sa demande. 'La belle'* should be *'Bel homme'* in stanza 5, *roi* should be *rei* in stanza 9, and in the last stanza, *'nous dormirions'* should be *'vous dormiriez'.* Those posies of periwinkles show that the 'river' (still a term for the sag furrowed in a mattress by love-making) where all the King's horses could drink together, is the river of death, and that the shoemaker will never rise again from the bridal couch. His bride will bind him to the bedpost, and summon his rival to kill him. The periwinkle was the flower of death in French, Italian and British folklore. In mediaeval times a garland of periwinkles was placed on the heads of men bound for execution. The flower has five blue petals and is therefore sacred to the Goddess, and its tough green vines will have been the bonds she used on her victim. This can be deduced from its Latin name *vincapervinca* ('bind all about'), though mediaeval grammarians connected it with *vincere*, 'to conquer', rather than *vincire*, 'to bind', and so *'pervinke'* came to mean 'the all-conquering'. But death is all-conquering; so it came to the same thing. Most likely that the custom of garlanding the criminal with periwinkle was taken over from the sacrifice ritual in honour of Llew Llaw the shoemaker. It is clear that the magical power of Arianrhod, like that of Math, rested in her feet and that once Llew had taken her foot in his hand as if to measure it for a shoe, he was able to make her do what he wished. Perhaps Perrault's story of Cinderella's slipper is a degenerate version of the same myth. Foot-fetishists are by no means rare even in modern times—the aberrants spend all their spare time buying or stealing women's high-heeled shoes for the exaltation of spirit that the possession gives them. What is more, it is possible that foot-fetishism was an ancient cult in Ardudwy, the scene of this Romance, though I do not know whether the evidence has ever been officially recorded. A few miles from Mur-y-Castell, on the hills between Harlech (where I lived as a boy) and Llanfair, there is a Goidels' Camp—a cluster of ruined round huts dating from perhaps the fourth century A.D.—and not far off, towards Llanfair, a woman's footprint is sunk an inch or so deep in a large flat stone. It is locally called 'the Virgin's footprint', and another mark near by is called the 'Devil's thumb print'. The stone is at the far left-hand corner of a field as one comes along the road from Harlech. Similar sacred footprints are still worshipped in Southern India.

Why 'Cordovan' leather? Probably because the Llew cult came to Britain from Spain, as it is known that the buskin did. At Uxama in Spain a dedication has been found to 'the Lugoves', i.e. the Lughs, by a guild of shoemakers. And why coloured and gilded shoes? Because such shoes were a symbol of royalty among the Celts. They used also to figure in the English Coronation ceremony, but dropped out after the reign of George II. Though officially styled 'sandals', they were gilded half-boots, like the purple buskins in which the Byzantine Emperors were crowned, with purple soles and wooden heels covered with scarlet leather. Scarlet was a product of the kerm-oak and doubtless the heels were oaken. In the Romance the colour of the shoes is not specified; which suggests a further connexion with Spain, where *bosʒeguis de piel colorado* does not mean 'buskins of coloured leather', but 'buskins of scarlet leather'. Similar buskins are thought to have been used in the sanctification of the kings of Rome, since they were part of the sacred dress of the Triumphant General in Republican times, and this dress was of regal origin. Sandals also occur in the legends of the solar hero Theseus, whose Goddess mother gave him a pair at the same time as she gave him his arms and sent him out to slay monsters; of Perseus, another monster-slayer; and of Mercury.

The implication of this part of the story is that Llew Llaw kept the third pair of gold shoes for his own use. He was one of the Three Crimson-stained Ones of Britain, as we learn from *Triad* 24; another of these was King Arthur. To be 'crimson-stained' is to be a sacred king: at Rome the Triumphant General had his face and hands stained red as a sign of temporary royalty. Sacred kings, it seems, were not allowed to rest their heels on the ground but walked on their toes, like the Canaanite Agag. The *cothurnus*, or high-heeled buskin, of the God Dionysus can be explained only in this sense, though the reason was disguised in Greece by the observation that buskins gave an effect of height.

In *Genesis, XXXII* Jacob wrestles all night with an angel at Peniel and is lamed by him so that the sinew in the hollow of his thigh is shrunken. Jacob sustained an injury once common to wrestlers, the inward displacement of the hip first described by Hippocrates. The result of this dislocation, which is produced by forcing the legs too widely apart, is that the injured person finds his leg flexed, abducted and externally rotated: in other words he can only walk, if at all, with a lurching or swaggering gait and on his toes. The leg affected is lengthened by the peculiar position of the head of the femur, or at least looks longer than the other. The lengthening of the leg tightens the tendons in the thigh and the muscles go into spasm, which is presumably what is meant by the shrinking of the sinew in the hollow of the thigh. Since Jacob belongs to the mother-right age, and since he won his sacred name and inheritance, both of which could only be given him by a woman, on this same occasion, the story has evidently been censored by the patriarchal editors of *Genesis*. But the Arabic lexicographers agree that the result of Jacob's injury was that he could walk only on the toes of his injured leg; and they should know.

While still in the womb Jacob supplants his twin Esau by catching at his heel, and so draining him of royal virtue. *Hosea, XII, 4* connects this supplanting with the wrestling incident, which suggests that Jacob's real name was Jah-aceb, 'the heel-god'. Jacob is translated 'the supplanter' in the Authorised Version of the Bible and what does 'supplant' mean but to put one's hand *sub plantam alicujus,* under someone's foot, and trip him up? The Greek word *pternizein,* used by the Septuagint in this context, is still more accurate: it means 'to trip up someone's heel' and is the first recorded use of the word in this sense. Jacob is the sacred king who has succeeded to office by tripping up a rival; but the penalty of his victory is that he must never again set his own sacred heel to the ground. The comment in *Genesis* on Jacob's lameness is: 'Therefore the Children of Israel eat not of the sinew which shrank, which is in the hollow of the thigh, to this day.' Jacob's grandfather, Abraham, also had a sacred thigh and in *Genesis XXIV, 2* he makes his servant put his under it when taking an oath, just as Jacob makes Joseph do in *Genesis XLVII, 29.* Mrs. Hermione Ashton writes that several tribes of Southern Arabia kiss the thigh of their Emir in homage; she has seen this done herself by the Qateibi who live about a hundred miles north of Aden—one of the four tribes of the Amiri race who boast that they are the sons of Ma'in and the oldest race in the world.

The mincing or swaggering gait of sacred kings, either due to this dislocation or assumed in imitation of it, was used by tragic actors on the Greek stage who wore the *cothurnus* in honour of Dionysus. As an off-stage affectation it was generally understood by the Greeks in an erotic sense: the letters SALM which occur in the names of several ancient kings suggest the word *saleuma,* an oscillation or waggling; with 'of the buttocks' added, or understood, this implied a deliberate flaunting of sexual charms. Greek prostitutes were called 'Salmakides'. *Isaiah, III, 16* chides the Daughters of Israel for walking in this lascivious style, rolling their eyes as they walk.

Plutarch asks in his *Greek Questions*: 'Why do the women of Elis summon Dionysus in their hymns to come among them with his bull-foot?' It is a good question, but as J. E. Harrison has pointed out, Plutarch was always better at asking questions than at answering them. Well, why with his bull-foot? Why not with his bull-horns, bull-brow, bull-shoulders, bull-tail—all of which are more symbolic of the bull's terrible power than its feet? And why foot, not feet? Plutarch does not even make a guess, but fortunately he quotes the ritual hymn used in the mystery to which he refers; from which it appears that the 'women of Elis' were dramatic representatives of the 'Charites', the Three Graces who at Elis shared an altar with Dionysus. The answer seems to be: 'Because in ancient times the sacred king of the mystery drama who appeared in response to the invocation of the Three Graces really had a bull-foot.' That is to say, the dislocation of his thigh made one of his feet resemble that of a bull, with the heel as the fetlock, and that he hurried among them with a rush and clatter of buskins. Plutarch should have remembered that in the Pelasgian island of Tenedos a sacred cow had once been 'kept for Dionysus' and when in calf had been treated like a woman during her confinement. If she bore a bull-calf it was put into buskins and despatched with a sacrificial axe, or *labris,* as if it were Zagreus, the infant Dionysus—which shows the ritual connexion of bulls' feet with buskins; but Aelian, the authority for this ceremony, does not mention that the calf was robed, crowned or otherwise adorned. It is perhaps worth noting that in the Spanish bull-fight,[1] brought from Thrace to Rome by the Emperor Claudius and thence introduced into Spain, the matador who kills his bull with outstanding heroism and grace is rewarded by the President with the *pata,* or foot.

The connexion of the buskin with sexuality is explained by Egyptian and Cypriot inscriptions. The name of the Goddess Mari of Cyprus is written with a 'buckled post' which stands for a reed-hut, meaning 'dwelling in', and a buskin; so she was resident in a buskin, like the Goddess Isis who in Egypt bore her name 'Asht' on her head, together with a buskin. In both cases some stick-like object protrudes from the mouth of the buskin, which Mr. E. M. Parr takes as a symbol of fertilization since the buskin hieroglyph is reas as *Ush,* 'the mother'. This throws new light on

[1] There may, however, have been an earlier introduction of the bullfight into Spain by the Iberian settlers of the third millennium B.C., who had cultural affinities with Thrace. Archaeological evidence from Crete suggests that the *fiesta* originated as an annual display of the bull's domination by acrobatic Moon-goddesses after he had been allowed to tire himself by chasing and killing men; and that the bull was a surrogate for the sacred king. However, in no Minoan painting or sculpture is there any picture of the final episode of the *fiesta,* in which the bull is despatched with a sword, and this may have been omitted in Crete, as in the Provençal bullfight. Even in Spain, where the bull is always killed and where the *fiesta* is a royal institution, a glorification of man's courage (supposed to be resident in his testicles) for the benefit of the ladies seated near the President's box—especially for the Queen, and Isabella II was not ashamed to accept the most famous bullfighter of her day as her lover—the tradition of the woman bullfighter persists obstinately. When Prince Charles went to Madrid in 1623 to court the Infanta he saw a woman-fighter despatch her bull with skill and grace, and there are still two or three women in the profession.

the second marriage of the Eleusinian Mysteries, after the performance of which it is known that the initiate said: 'I have fitted what was in the drum to what was in the *liknos*.' We know what was in the *liknos*—a phallus—and on the analogy of the buskins ceremonially presented to the sacred king at his marriage, it may be concluded that the drum contained a buskin into which the phallus was inserted by the initiate as a symbol of coition.

An act of invocation corresponding with the Elian ritual mentioned by Plutarch is recorded in *I Kings, XVIII, 26*, where the priests of Baal dance at the altar and cry out 'Baal, hear us!': appealing to him to light the Spring bonfires and burn up the corpse of the old year. They leaped up and down, according to the Authorised Version; but the original Hebrew word is formed from the root PSCH which means 'to dance with a limp', and from which *Pesach*, the name of the Passover Feast, is derived. The Passover appears to have been a Canaanite Spring festival which the tribe of Joseph adopted and transformed into a commemoration of their escape from Egypt under Moses. At Carmel, the dance with a limp must have been sympathetic magic to encourage the appearance of the God with a bull's foot who was armed, like Dionysus, with a torch. 'Baal' merely means 'Lord'. The annalist refrains from mentioning his real name; but since the priests of Baal were Israelites it is likely to have been 'Jah Aceb' or 'Jacob'—the Heel-god. Jah Aceb seems to have been also worshipped at Beth-Hoglah—'The Shrine of the Hobbler'—a place between Jericho and the Jordan south of Gilgal and identified by Epiphanius with the threshing floor of Atad, mentioned in *Genesis, L, 11,* as the place where Joseph mourned for Jacob. Jerome connects this place with a round dance, apparently performed in honour of Talus the Cretan Sun-hero—Hesychius says that Talus means 'Sun'—to whom the partridge was sacred. In Athenian legend Talus was thrown down by Daedalus from a height and transformed into a partridge while in the air by the Goddess Athene. The Arabic word for 'hobble' which gives its name to Beth-Hoglah is derived from the word for partridge; the deduction being that the dance was a hobbling one. The partridge is a Spring migrant, sacred to the Love-goddess because of its reputation for lasciviousness (mentioned by Aristotle and Pliny) and the dance must have mimicked the love dance of the cock-partridge which it carries out, like the wood-cock, on a regular dancing floor. It is a war dance, performed for a hen audience: the cocks flutter around in circles with a hobbling gait, one heel always held in readiness to strike at a rival's head. The hens look on, quaking with excitement. The proverb quoted by Jeremiah: 'The partridge gathers young that she has not brought forth', means that Jewish men and women were attracted to these alien orgiastic rites. So also the understanding Titian gives us a glimpse of a partridge through the window of the room in which his naked Love-goddess is lasciviously meditating fresh conquests.[1]

The connexion between the hobbling partridge and the lame king is confirmed by the mythographers Hyginus and Ovid, who identify the hero Perdix ('partridge') with Talus. Apollodorus and Diodorus Siculus make Perdix feminine, the mother of Talus, but this is as much as to say that Talus was virgin-born; because, according to Aristotle, Pliny and Aelian the hen-partridge can be impregnated by the sound of the cock-partridge's voice or by his scent blown down the wind. Pliny says 'in no other animal is there any such susceptibility in the sexual feelings', and that when the female is sitting on her eggs the cocks relieve their emotions by practising sodomy—an observation which may have inspired the organized sodomy in the temples of the Syrian Moon-goddess, though dogs and doves, also associated with her worship, are credited with the same habit. The Aegean island most famous for its partridges was Anaphe, the Argonauts' first landfall on their homeward voyage from Crete after Medea had killed Talus; where Radiant Apollo was worshipped with rites closely paralleling those of the Hebrew Tabernacles, though of an erotic cast. This Apollo was a Sun-god, not an Underworld one.

Partridges become so deeply absorbed in their dance that even if a man comes up close and kills some of the dancers the rest continue undeterred; a habit of which the ancients took full advantage. In the mating-season they used to put a decoy cock-partridge in a cage at the end of a long narrow winding brushwood tunnel and gave it corn to eat. Its lonely cry, combining the call to love with the call to food, attracted the hens along the tunnel, and when they reached the cage and it uttered its usual challenge call, other cocks would come running up, only to be knocked on the head with sticks by the waiting hunters as soon as they emerged from the tunnel. Thus in *I Samuel, XXVI*, 20 Saul is taunted for his unkingly behaviour in hunting David, who is not only as insignificant as a flea but as easily caught as a mountain partridge. The decoy partridge was one that had dislocated its leg in trying to escape from the horse-hair slip-knot in which it was snared. This lame, and therefore easily tamed, decoy was fattened in a cage like a sacred king in his palace—both honoured prisoners—and the more numerous its victims, the more gleeful its cry. In *Ecclesiasticus* (*XI, 30*) the caged partridge is an allegory of the proud man who rejoices

---

[1] The quail, sacred to Delian Apollo and Hercules Melkarth, was decoyed in the same way and had a similar erotic reputation. The moral of the flock of migrating quails that invaded the Israelites' camp in the Wilderness is carefully pointed in *Numbers* (*XI, 33, 34*). Whereas in *Exodus* (*XVI, 13*), the earlier version of the story, the Israelites apparently eat without evil consequences according to the Lord's promise, the author of *Numbers* does not let them so much as chew a morsel; but records that God smote them with a great plague and that the place was called Kibroth-Hattaavah, 'the grave of lust'. He is allegorically warning his post-Exilic audience against having anything to do with Melkarth worship.

at the disasters into which he has decoyed his neighbours. This form of sport is still practised in Mediterranean countries as far west as Majorca.

It seems, then, that in the *pesach* a bull-cult had been superimposed on a partridge cult; and that the Minotaur to whom youths and maidens (from Athens and elsewhere) were sacrificed had once represented the decoy partridge in the middle of a brushwood maze, towards which the others were lured for their death dance. He was, in fact, the centre of a ritual performance, originally honouring the Moon-goddess, the lascivious hen-partridge, who at Athens and in parts of Crete was the mother and lover of the Sun-hero Talus. But the dance of the hobbling cock-partridge was later transformed into one honouring the Moon-goddess Pasiphaë, the cow in heat, mother and lover of the Sun-hero, the bull-headed Minos. Thus the spirally-danced Troy-game (called the 'Crane Dance' in Delos because it was adapted there to the cult of the Moon-goddess as Crane) had the same origin as the *pesach*. The case is proved by Homer who wrote:

> *Daedalus in Cnossos once contrived*
> *A dancing-floor for fair-haired Ariadne*

—a verse which the scholiast explains as referring to the Labyrinth dance; and by Lucian who in his *Concerning the Dance,* a mine of mythological tradition, gives as the subjects of Cretan dances: 'the myths of Europë, Pasiphaë, the two Bulls, the Labyrinth, Ariadne, Phaedra [daughter of Pasiphaë], Androgeuos [son of Minos], Icarus, Glaucus [raised by Aesculapius from the dead], the magic of Polyidus, and of Talus the bronze man who did his sentry round in Crete.' Polyidus means 'the many-shaped' and since the Corinthian hero of that name had no connexion with Crete, the dance was probably the shape-shifting dance of Zagreus at the Cretan Lenaea.

Here some loose ends can be tied up. The maze pattern has been shown to represent 'Spiral Castle' or 'Troy Town', where the sacred Sun-king goes after death and from which, if lucky, he returns. The whole myth is plainly presented on an Etruscan wine-jar from Tragliatella, dated from the late seventh century B.C. Two mounted heroes are shown; the leader carries a shield with a partridge device, and an ape-like demon perches behind him; his companion carries a spear and a shield with a duck device. They are riding away from a maze marked 'TRUIA' ('Troy'). Apparently the sacred king, though due to die like the partridge in the brushwood maze, and be succeeded by his tanist, has escaped. How he escaped, another picture on the same vase shows: an unarmed king leads a sunwise procession, escorted by seven footmen each carrying three javelins and a huge shield with a boar device; the spear-armed tanist, whose badge this is, brings up the rear. These seven footmen evidently represent the tanist's seven winter months which fall between the apple harvest and Easter. The king is being warned of his ritual death. A Moon-priestess has come to meet him: a terrible robed figure with one arm menacingly akimbo, as she offers an apple, his passport to Paradise. The javelins threaten death. Yet a diminutive female figure, robed like the priestess, guides the king—if the hero is Theseus, we may call her Ariadne—who has helped him to escape from the maze. And he boldly displays a counter-charm—namely an Easter-egg, the egg of resurrection. Easter was the season when Troy Town dances were performed on the turf-cut mazes of Britain; and of Etruria, too, where the famous Lars Porsena of Clusium built a labyrinth for his own tomb. (Similar labyrinth tombs existed in pre-Hellenic Greece: near Nauplia, on Samos, and on Lemnos.) An Etruscan egg of polished black trachite, found at Perugia, with an arrow in relief running around it, is the same holy egg. Against the spearmen on the vase is written MAIM; against the king, EKRAUN; against the priestess, MITHES. LUEI. If, as seems probable, these words are Western Greek, they mean respectively: 'Winter', 'He reigned', and 'Having pronounced, she sets free'. The letters written against Ariadne are indecipherable.

The lame King is frequently connected with the mysteries of smithcraft. Jacob was connected with the cult of the Kenite Smith-god; Talus in one account was son, or maternal nephew, to Smith Daedalus, in another was forged in the furnace of Smith Hephaestus. Dionysus, because of his titles *pyrigenes* and *ignigena* ('engendered by fire')—a reference to the autumnal Toadstool-Dionysus engendered by lightning—may have been equated with Talus in this sense. Wieland the Scandinavian Smithgod, was lamed by a woman.

But what evidence is there for any lameness in Dionysus? Why should the buskins not have been worn merely to add to his height, rather than as surgical boots to compensate for his deformity? The best evidence is his name, Dio-nysus, usually translated as 'The Light God of Mount Nyse' but more likely to mean 'The Lame God of Light'. *Nysos* was a Syracusan word for 'lame' and therefore probably of Corinthian origin, for Syracuse was a colony of Corinth. Yet, as Mr. E. M. Parr has pointed out to me, Dionysus may really have taken his name from Nysë, Nyssa or Nysia, a name attached to various shrines in the area where the sacred lameness was cultivated. There are three Nyssas in Asia Minor, three Nysias in Thrace, a Nyza near Mosul, and a Nysia in Arabia where, according to Diodorus, the Goddess Isis was born. This suggests that Nyse was a title of Isis, and that since Dionysus was a title of the Libyo-Thracian Harpocrates, her lame son, the Corinthian Greeks read Nysus, which was really his matronymic, as meaning 'lame'. Mr. Parr writes: 'There seem to be confusing results when an established divine title is retained in a new tongue. For instance: Apollo Agieueis of Athens is described as the *leader* of colonies, but is more likely to have been the Cyprian Apollo who wore a wreath (*aga, agu*).' Dionysus, who was regarded by the Greeks of the Classical age as a Thracian God, is said to have come there from Crete, as his counterpart, King Proteus, is said to have come from Pharos. In Crete he was not lame, neither was Velchanos, a Cretan Cock-demon who became Vulcan when his worship was introduced into Italy. But in Italy Vulcan was said to be lame and to walk with the help of high-heeled gold shoes, because he was identified with Hephaestus,[1] a Pelasgian deity from Lemnos, who like Talus was hurled down from a height—the tradition of sacred lameness seems to have been Danaan, not early Cretan. And, according to Homer, Hephaestus's wife was Charis, whom he elsewhere calls Aphrodite. The Three Graces are thus explained as the Love-goddess Aphrodite in triad; and when they invoke Dionysus at Elis they are calling their lame buskined husband to perform the act of love with them.

Here we may reconsider another of Dionysus's titles, 'Merotraphes', which is usually translated 'thigh-nursling' because of a silly Olympian fable about Dionysus having been sewn up in Jove's thigh, while an infant, to hide him from the jealous anger of Hera; the simpler meaning is 'one whose thigh is taken very good care of'. And what of Mercury's winged sandals, and those of Theseus and Perseus? Mercury, or Hermes, is commonly represented as standing on tiptoe: was this because he could not put his heel to the ground? It is likely that the eagle-wings on his sandals were originally not a symbol of swiftness but a sign of the holiness of the heel, and so, paradoxically, a symbol of lameness. In the Hittite cylinder-seal reproduced as an illustration to my *King Jesus*, the king who is about to be crowned after mounting three steps of a throne has his sacred heel protected by a dog-demon. In Latin those sandals were called *talaria* from the word *talus*, meaning a heel: and dice were called *tali* because they were made from the heel-bones of the sheep or goats sacred to Hermes or Mercury, though those of the *boibalis*, the Libyan antelope, were more highly prized by the illuminated.

Mercury was not only patron of dice-players but prophesied from dice. He used five dice with four markings on each, in honour of his Mother, precisely like those given an Indian King at his coronation in honour of the Mother; and if, as I suppose, he used them for alphabetic divination he had his own alphabet of fifteen consonants and five vowels. The game of

---

[1] Hephaestus, according to Hesiod, was the parthogenous son of Hera—in other words, he belonged to the pre-Hellenic civilization—and not even Homer's authority for the view that Zeus was his father carried any weight with subsequent Greek and Latin mythographers. Servius makes this clear in his comment on *Aeneid, VIII, 454*.

hucklebones is still played in Great Britain with the traditional set of five. In the case of six-sided dice, however, three made a set in ancient times; these would provide the diviner with eighteen letters of the alphabet, as in the thirteen-consonant Beth-Luis-Nion.

But was the sacred king chosen because he had accidentally suffered this injury, or was the injury inflicted on him after he had been chosen for better reasons? The answer is to be found in the otherwise meaningless story of Llew Llaw's balancing between the rim of his sacred cauldron and the back of a buck. Llew was to become a sacred king by marriage with Blodeuwedd, the May Bride, a king of the delicately-treading golden-shoed or purple-buskined sort; but he was not properly equipped for his office until he had sustained Jacob's injury which would prevent him from ever again putting his sacred heel on the ground, even by mistake. This injury was artificially produced by an ingenious incident in the coronation ritual. His bride made him stand with one foot on the rim of the bath, the other on the haunch of a sacred beast with his hair tied to an oak-branch above his head. And then a cruel trick was played on him. Messrs. Romanis and Mitchener in their *Surgery* put it in these words: 'Such inward or anterior dislocations of the hip, produced by wide abduction of the thighs, may result when a person embarking in a boat remains undecided whether to get in or remain on land.' As with quay and boat, so with cauldron and buck. The buck moved suddenly away from the cauldron. Llew could not save himself by throwing himself forward, because his head was fixed by the hair. The result was this anterior dislocation, but when he fell, his sacred heel did not touch the ground: because his hair held him up, which is exactly what happened to Absalom ('Father Salm') when the beast moved from under him in the oak-wood of Ephraim. I postulate as a main source of the anecdotal parts of the early books of the Bible a set of icons, captured by the Israelites at Hebron, illustrating the ritual fate of the sacred king; one part of the series becomes iconotropically reinterpreted as the story of Saul, another as that of Samson, another as that of Absalom, another as that of Samuel. A restoration of the icons is attempted in the *King Adam* chapter of my *King Jesus*

It will be noticed that all these names look like corrupt forms of the same word Salma, or Salmon, a royal title among the Kenites, who were King David's ancestors, among the Phoenicians (Selim), among the Assyrians (Salman), among the Danaans of Greece and late Minoan Crete (Salmoneus). Solomon adopted the title too. His original name seems to have been Jedidiah (*2 Samuel XII, 25*); if not, he would have had a less convincing right to the throne than Adonijah. Absalom's original name is unknown, but that he was David's favourite, not his son except by courtesy, is shown in *2 Samuel XII, 11*, where he is described as David's neighbour. The discrepancy between the account of his parentage in 2 *Samuel III, 3* and 2 *Samuel XIII, 37* suggests that his real name was Talmai, son of Ammihud, King of Geshur and one of David's allies, and that he became Absalom only when he seized David's throne and married the royal harem of heiresses at Hebron. As a god, Salma is identified with Reseph the Canaanite Osiris. Among these icons there may have been one showing Absalom with his hair tied to an oak-branch —really an incident in the marriage of the King. The assassination of the king on such an occasion was easy, but sanctification, not death, was the object of the trick; and if we can accept A. M. Hocart's conclusion that the coronation ceremony throughout the ancient world typified the marriage of the Sun King to the Earth Queen, his death as a member of his former tribe and his re-birth with a new name into that of his Queen, then the ritual on which all these myths are based must have included a mock-assassination of the king in the course of the bath-ceremony; which is proved by the victims offered in the king's stead in many forms of the ritual known to us. The confused elements in the myth of Hephaestus, who was married to the Love-goddess and deceived by her, and lamed by suddenly being thrown down from Olympus by the Goddess Hera, and mocked by the whole company of Heaven, compose another variant of the same ritual. Originally the king died violently as soon as he had coupled with the queen; as the drone dies after coupling with the queen-bee. Later, emasculation and laming were substituted for death; later still, circumcision was substituted for emasculation and the wearing of buskins for laming.

Once we know that the sacred king was ritually lamed in a way that obliged him to swagger or lurch on high heels, we understand at last two or three hitherto mysterious ancient icons. Tantalus, suspended over the water with a fruit-branch above his head and the water always slipping away is evidently being lamed in Llew Llaw fashion: originally his hair is tied to the branch, one foot is on the bank, the other rests on something in the water—perhaps a large boat-shaped basin—that slips away. Tantalus is a perfect type of Dionysus: he was married to Euryanassa (another form of Eurynome) a Moon-goddess; he was thrown down from Mount Sipylus, in Pelasgian Lydia, where he was afterwards buried and had a hero shrine; he was Pelops's cannibalistic father; he helped to steal a Dog from a Cretan cave; and from his name derive three other Greek words meaning, like *saleuein*, from which *saleuma* is formed, 'to swagger or lurch in one's gait': *tantaloein, tantaleuein* and, by a metathesis, *talantoein*.

Like Ixion and Salmoneus, Tantalus belonged to the old religion super-seded by Olympianism, and the Olympian priests have deliberately mis-interpreted the icons in favour of Father Zeus by presenting him as an odious criminal. Tantalus's crime, the mythographers explain, was that, having been privileged to eat ambrosia, the food of the gods, with the

Olympians, he later invited commoners to try it. *Ambrosia* was the name of Dionysus's autumnal feast in which, I suggest, the intoxicant toadstool once inspired his votaries to a divine frenzy; and in my *What Food the Centaurs Ate*, I show that the ingredients given by Classical grammarians for ambrosia, nectar, and *kekyon* (Demeter's drink at Eleusis) represent a food-oghan—their initial letters all spell out forms of a Greek word for 'mushroom'. The story of Tantalus's crime may have been told when wine displaced toadstools at the Maenad revels, and a toadstool—perhaps not *amanita muscaria*, but the milder, more entrancing *panaeolus papilionaceus*—was eaten by adepts at the Eleusinian, Samothracian and Cretan Mysteries, who became as gods by virtue of the transcendental visions it supplied. However the dislocation may have been produced—and it is likely that still another method was practised on a hill-top not beside a river—there was a taboo in Canaan on eating the flesh around the thigh-bone, as is expressly stated in *Genesis* in the story of Jacob's wrestling at Peniel. Robertson-Smith rightly connects this taboo with the practice, common to all Mediterranean countries, of dedicating the thigh-bones of all sacrificial beasts, and the parts about them, to the gods: they were burned first and then the rest of the beast was eaten by the worshippers. But the anthropological rule 'No taboo without its relaxation' applies here. In primitive times the flesh-covered thighbone of the dead king must have been eaten by his comrades. This practice was until recently followed, as Mgr. Terhoorst, a Roman Catholic missionary records, by the younger warriors of the Central African Bantu tribe of Bagiushu among whom he worked. The flesh was eaten on the death of their Old Man, or when the chief of an enemy tribe was killed in battle. Mgr. Terhoorst states that this was done to inherit the courage of the dead man which was held to reside in the thigh, and that the rest of the body was not touched. The Bagiushu, who file their front teeth into a triangular shape, are not cannibalistic on other occasions.

In my *King Jesus* I suggest that the Hebrew tradition found in the *Talmud Babli Sanhedrin* and the *Tol' Doth Yeshu*, that Jesus was lamed while attempting to fly, refers to a secret Coronation ceremony on Mount Tabor, where he became the new Israel after being ritually lamed in a wrestling match. This tradition is supported by Gospel evidence which I adduce, and by a remark of Jerome's that Jesus was deformed. Mount Tabor was one of Jehovah's chief shrines. Tabor is named after Atabyrius, the son of Eurynome and grandson of Proteus, as the Septuagint recognized, and we know a good deal about this god, who also had a shrine built to him on Mount Atabyria in Rhodes by one 'Althaeamenes the Cretan'. Althaeamenes means 'Mindful of the Goddess Althaea' and Althaea ('she who makes grow') was another name for Atabyrius's mother Eurynome, the Moon-goddess of the Orphics. The marshmallow—in Welsh *hocys bendi-*

gaid the holy mallow—was Althaea's flower, and she loved Dionysus the Vine-god. She became the mother by him of Deianeira, the same Deianeira who played the part of Blodeuwedd to Hercules of Oeta. Atabyrius, being one of the Cretan Telchines, had the power, like Dionysus or Proteus, to transform himself into any shape; and in his Rhodian shrine brazen bulls were dedicated to him which bellowed whenever anything extraordinary was about to happen—the same sort of brazen bull that was made by Daedalus for King Minos of Crete. And we know that Atabyrius was the god, worshipped as a golden calf, whom Israel credited with having brought them out of Egypt. But the *byrius* termination occurs in the royal title of Burna-buriash, one of the Third Dynasty Kassite (Indo-European) Kings of Babylon who reigned from 1750 to 1173 B.C.; Atabyrius was clearly not a native Cretan, nor a Semite, but a Kassite god who entered Syria early in the second millennium. How and when his cult was carried to Thrace, Rhodes and Crete is not clear; but he is likely to have gone into Egypt with the Hyksos. He was also called Tesup.

This mythological rigmarole adds up to an identification of the Israelite Jehovah of Tabor, or Atabyrius, with Dionysus the Danaan White Bull-god: an identification which rests on respectable Classical authority. In Plutarch's *Convivial Questions* one of the guests claims to be able to prove that the God of the Jews is really Dionysus Sabazius, the Barley-god of Thrace and Phrygia; and Tacitus similarly records in his *History* (v. 5) that 'some maintain that the rites of the Jews were founded in honour of Dionysus'. Also, the historian Valerius Maximus records that about the year 139 B.C. the Praetor of Foreigners, C. Cornelius Hispallus, expelled from Rome certain Jews who were 'trying to corrupt Roman morals by a pretended cult of Sabazian Jove'. The inference is that the Praetor did not expel them for a legitimate worship of this god, but because they foisted novelties on the Thracian cult—probably circumcision, which was regarded by the Romans as self-mutilation and a corruption of morals—for they admitted aliens to their Sabbaths. According to Leclercq's *Manual of Christian Archaeology*, burials in the cemetery of Praetextatus at Rome confirm this cult of a Jewish Sabazius. That the Jews of the Dispersion may have used false etymology to equate 'Sabazius' with 'Sabaoth'—Jehovah was the Lord of the Sabbath, and also of Sabaoth, 'of hosts'—does not disprove the original identity of the two gods.

Sabazian Zeus and Sabazian Dionysus were different names of the same character, the Son of Rhea; which means that he was of Cretan origin. The Phrygians called him Attis and made him the son of Cybele, but this amounted to the same thing; and an inscription of Jewish origin has been found in Rome: 'To Attis the Most High God who holds the Universe together.' The serpent was sacred to Sabazius; and this recalls the Brazen Seraph Ne-esthan or Nehushtan, which Moses used as a standard and

335

which is said to have been destroyed as idolatrous by Good King Hezekiah because incense was burned to it as to a god.[1] But the Jewish sect of Ophites, centred in Phrygia, revered the Serpent in early Christian times, holding that the post-exilic Jehovah was a mere demon who had usurped the Kingdom of the Wise Serpent, the Anointed One. Sabazian Dionysus was represented with bull's horns because, as Diodorus Siculus records, he was the first to yoke oxen to the plough for agriculture: in other words to plant barley. Since Jehovah was pre-eminently a protector of barley—the Passover was a barley harvest-festival—Plutarch's convivial guest would have had little trouble in proving his contention, especially since, according to the legend, Sabazius was torn by the Titans into seven pieces. Seven was Jehovah's mystical number; so also was 42, the number of letters in his enlarged Name, and according to Cretan tradition, the number of pieces into which the Titans tore the bull-god Zagreus.

Dionysus Sabazius was the original Jehovah of the Passover; and Plutarch also identifies the Jehovah of the Feast of Tabernacles with Dionysus Liber, or Lusios ('he who frees from guilt'), the Wine-god, by suggesting that the word 'Levite' is formed from *Lusios*; and he says that the Jews abstain from swine's flesh because their Dionysus is also Adonis, who was killed by a boar. The rituals of Jehovah and Dionysus, as Plutarch pointed out, corresponded closely: mysteries of barley-sheaves and new wine, torch dances until cock-crow, libations, animal sacrifices, religious ecstasy. It also appears that the promiscuous love-making of the Canaanite rites, though severely punished at Jerusalem in post-exilic times, still survived among the peasantry who came up for the Tabernacles. The Temple priests in the time of Jesus admitted the original nature of the Feast, while declaring that its nature had changed, by announcing at the close: 'Our forefathers in this place turned their backs on the Sanctuary of God and their faces to the East, adoring the Sun; but we turn to God.' For the Sun represented the immortal part of Dionysus; the barley and the vine his mortal part.

There is even numismatic evidence for the identification of Jehovah and Dionysus: a silver coin of the fifth century B.C., (which appears in G. F. Hill's *Catalogue of the Greek Coins of Palestine*) found near Gaza with on the obverse a bearded head of Dionysus type and on the reverse a bearded figure in a winged chariot, designated in Hebrew characters JHWH—Jehovah. This is not, of course, by any means the whole story of Jehovah, whose affinity with other gods, especially Cronos (Bran), has already been mentioned. It is easiest perhaps to write about him in terms of days of the week. His first pictorial appearance is at the copper-

---

[1] J. N. Schofield in his *Historical Background to the Bible* suggests that he destroyed it for political reasons—the Serpent cult being Egyptian, and Hezekiah wishing to signalize his return to Assyrian vassalage.

workings of Ras-Shamra in Sinai in a carving of about the sixteenth century B.C. He is then Elath-Iahu a Kenite Smith-god, the God of Wednesday, presumably the lover of Baalith the local Aphrodite and Goddess of Friday. Later in his theophanies at Moreh, Hebron and Ophrah he is the terebinth-god Bel, the God of Thursday. The story of his defeat of the prophets of Carmel concerns the conquest of his Bel aspect by Cronos the God of Saturday in the person of Elijah. Bel and Cronos are always appearing in opposition, Bel being Beli and Cronos, Bran; as has been shown. 'When Israel was in Egypt', Jehovah was Set, the God of Sunday. At the Jerusalem feast of Tabernacles, on the Day of Willows, he was the God of Monday, His name El, connected with the scarlet oak, proves him to have been also the God of Tuesday. Thus the universality claimed for him by the Pharisees and typified by the Menorah, the seven-branched candlestick, rests on a solid enough mythological basis.

Further, the name Iahu is far older than the sixteenth century B.C. and of wide distribution. It occurs in Egypt during the Sixth Dynasty (middle of the third millennium B.C.) as a title of the God Set: and is recorded in Deimel's Akkadian-Sumerian Glossary as a name for Isis. It also seems to be the origin of the Greek name Iacchus, a title of the shape-shifting Dionysus Lusios in the Cretan mysteries. Thus although I.A.U. are the vowels of the three-season year of Birth, Consummation and Death— with Death put first because in the Eastern Mediterranean the agricultural year begins in the I season—they seem to be derived from a name that was in existence long before any alphabet was formed, the components of which are IA and HU. 'Ia' means 'Exalted' in Sumerian and 'Hu' means Dove'; the Egyptian hieroglyph 'Hu' is also a dove. The Moon-goddess of Asianic Palestine was worshipped with doves, like her counterparts of Egyptian Thebes, Dodona, Hierapolis, Crete and Cyprus. But she was also worshipped as a long-horned cow; Hathor, or Isis, or Ashtaroth Karnaim. Isis is an onomatopoeic Asianic word, *Ish-ish*, meaning 'She who weeps', because the Moon was held to scatter dew and because Isis, the pre-Christian original of the *Mater Dolorosa*, mourned for Osiris when Set killed him. She was said to be the white, or, according to Moschus, the golden Moon-cow Io who had settled down in Egypt after long wanderings from Argos. The *o* in Io's name is an *omega*, which is a common Greek variant of *alpha*.

Ia-Hu therefore seems to be a combination of *Ia*, 'the Exalted One', the Moon-goddess as Cow, and *Hu*, the same goddess as Dove. We know from Plutarch that at the mid-winter solstice mysteries Isis, as the golden Moon-cow, circled the coffin of Osiris seven times in commemoration of the seven months from solstice to solstice; and we know also that the climax of the orgiastic oak-cult with which the Dove-goddess was concerned came at the summer solstice. Thus Ia-Hu stands for the Moon-goddess as ruler of the whole course of the solar year. This was a proud title and Set seems to have claimed it for himself when his ass-eared sceptre became the Egyptian symbol of royalty. But the Child Horus, the reincarnation of Osiris, overcomes Set yearly and it is a commonplace that conquering kings their titles take from the foes they captive make. Thus Horus was Iahu also, and his counterparts the Cretan Dionysus and Canaanite Bel became respectively IACCHUS and (in an Egyptian record) IAHU-BEL. The Welsh god Hu Gadarn and the Guernsey god Hou, or Har Hou, are likely to be the same deity: that Hou was an Oak-god is suggested by the same formula having been used in his mediaeval rites as in those of the Basque Oak-god Janicot, who is Janus.

Iahu as a title of Jehovah similarly marks him out as a ruler of the solar year, probably a transcendental combination of Set, Osiris and Horus (alias Egli-Iahu, the Calf Iahu). But the Hu syllable of his name has come to have great importance in Christianity: for when at Jesus's lustration by John the Baptist the Coronation Psalm was chanted and a Dove descended, this must be read as the *ka*, or royal double, that descended on him in a stream of light from his father Iahu—as it descended on the Pharaohs at their coronation from their father the Sun-god Ra, in the form of a hawk.

No mention has been made so far of the religious meaning of the cedar, which figures so prominently in the Old Testament as the loftiest and grandest of all trees: 'even the cedars of Libanus which Thou hast planted.' It was used by Solomon with the 'choice fir' in the building of the three contiguous temples which he raised in honour of a Trinity consisting of Jehovah and two Goddesses. The identity of the second of these temples is disguised by Pharisee editors as 'the House of the Forest of Lebanon', meaning the temple of the Mountain-goddess, the Love and Battle goddess of Midsummer; that of the third is disguised as 'The House of Pharaoh's daughter', who is shown by the story of Moses to have been the Birth-goddess of the Winter Solstice. Since we know that the fir was sacred to the Birth-goddess and that the floor of the Temple was of fir planking, it follows that the cedar of the pillars and beams was sacred to the Love-and-Battle goddess of Mount Lebanon, Astarte or Anatha. Cedar stood, in fact, for the vowel U, of which the tree in Byblos and Western Europe was the Heather. The only other timber used in these Temples was olive, which as has been already mentioned in the context of Hercules and the Dactyls stood for the Spring Sun—Jehovah as Marduk, *alias* Paeonian Apollo.

Cedar is also coupled with hyssop (probably the wild-caper tree which grows very green in the crannies of rocks or walls, in Egypt and Palestine) in the two most primitive sacrifices of the Old Testament: the red heifer sacrifice of *Numbers, XIX, 6* and the 'sparrow' sacrifice of *Leviticus, XIV, 4,* both originally offered to a goddess not a god. The hyssop was evidently the Palestine equivalent of the mistletoe, the tree of the Day of Liberation, which it resembles by growing sometimes in the fissures of old trees where there is leaf mould to keep it alive; so that the mythological conjunction of cedar and hyssop means the whole course of the sun from its infancy at the winter solstice to its prime at the summer solstice, and back again. Thus when it is recorded in *I Kings, IV, 33*:

> And God gave Solomon wisdom and understanding exceeding much . . . and he spake of trees, from the cedar that is in Lebanon even unto the hyssop that is upon the wall,

this is as much as to say that he knew all the mystic lore of the tree-alphabet. But hyssop was the tree of the winter solstice, IA: and the cedar was the tree of the summer solstice, HU; so Solomon is credited with knowing the Divine Name of which IAHU was the permissible synonym.

JHWH's Massoretic title, supposedly the oldest, was Q're Adonai ('Lord Q're')—though some Hebrew scholars prefer to interpret the words as meaning: 'Read Adonai', i.e. 'give the consonants of JHWH the same vowels as in "Adonai".' Q're sounds Cretan. The Carians, Lydians and Mysians, who were of Cretan stock, had a common shrine of Zeus Carios at Mylassa in Caria, a god whom their cousins the Tyrrhenians took to Italy as Karu, and who is also Carys, the founder of Megara. The Quirites of Rome came from a Sabine town Qures, which apparently bore his name or that of his mother Juno Quiritis, mentioned by Plutarch; and the Curetes of Delos, Chalcis, Aetolia and Crete are perhaps also called after him, though to the Greeks, who could make nothing of the barbarous word *Q're*, 'Curetes' meant boys who had sacrificed their hair-trimmings (*Kourai*) to the god. These Curetes are identified by Pausanias with the Children of Anax, the ten-cubit-high Son of Uranus. Anax was a Carian who ruled Miletus before its conquest by the Milesians of Crete, gave it the name of Anactoria, and was the father of the ten-cubit-high Asterius. Pausanias connects Anax with the Pelasgian mysteries of Samothrace. The Children of Anax appear in the Bible as the tall people of Hebron whom Caleb expelled and who subsequently lived in Gaza and neighbouring cities. In other words, they were Asianic 'People of the Sea' who worshipped the God Q're, or (as he was called in Syria in the time of Thothmes, a Pharaoh of the Middle Kingdom) 'the Great God Ker'. His chief Carian title was Panemerios ('of the live-long day')—at least this was the Greek version of a Carian original—and he seems to have been a god of the solar year who, like Samson of Tyre or Nisus of Nisa (Megara), was annually shorn of his hair and power by the Moon-goddess; his male adorants dedicating their forelocks to him in mourning, at a festival called the Comyria. That Jehovah as *Q're* continued to have hair sacrificed to him, as to his Carian counterpart, until the reformation of his religion during the Exile is indicated by the Deuteronomic injunction 'Ye shall not make a baldness between your eyes for the dead'. The radical letters of his name—Q, apple, or quince or *ethrog*, and R, myrtle—were represented in the *lulab*, or thyrsus, used at the Feast of Tabernacles as a reminder of his annual death and translation to Elysium. This moon-festival, indeed, initiated the season of the year which runs from Q to R.

But Q're probably derived his title from his Moon mother—later, in Greece, his twin-sister—the White Goddess Artemis Caryatis ('of the nut-tree') whose most famous temple was at Caryae in Laconia. She was the goddess of healing and inspiration, served by Caryatid priestesses and is to be identified with the nymph Phyllis[1] who, in the Thesean Age, was metamorphosed into an almond tree—Phyllis may be a Greek variant of Belili. At any rate, he became for a time Nabu the Wise God of Wednesday, represented by the almond-tree stem of the seven-branched *Menorah*; and it was particularly to him that Job referred his question, 'Where shall Wisdom be found?', on the ground that it was he who measured, weighed out and enunciated the powers controlled by his six fellow-deities; such as Sin, Monday's Rain-god; Bel, Thursday's god of Thunder and Lightning; and Ninib, Saturday's god of Repose, controller of the Chthonian Winds. Artemis Caryatis may be identified with Carmenta, the Muse mother of Evander the Arcadian, who adapted the Pelasgian alphabet to the Latin. Her name, which Plutarch in his *Roman Questions* absurdly derives from *carens mente*, 'out of her mind' seems to be compounded of *Car* and *Menta*: the first syllable standing for Q're, the second presumably for *Mante* 'the revealer'. Pliny preserves the tradition that 'Car, after whom Caria takes its name, invented augury'; this Car, evidently Thothmes's Great God Ker, is mentioned by Herodotus as brother to Lydus and Mysus, the eponymous ancestors of the Lydians and Mysians. Another Car, the son of Phoroneus, and brother of Pelasgus, Europë and Agenor, is said by Pausanias to have been an early king of Megara after whom the acropolis of the city was named. Car's sex seems to have been changed in both cases: for the Carians, Mysians and Lydians were matrilinear, and the Megarean acropolis must have been called after the White Goddess who ruled all important hills and mountains. The Goddess Car seems also to have given the river Inachus its original name, Carmanor, before Inachus the father of Phoroneus, as Plutarch reports, went mad and leapt into it.

At this point we can reconsider the Myvyrian account of the *Battle of the Trees* and suggest a textual emendation which makes better sense of it:

[1] Gower derives the word 'filbert' from this Phyllis, though the orthodox explanation is that filberts are first ripe on St. Philebert's Day (August 22nd, Old Style).

There was a man in that battle who unless his name were known could not be overcome, and there was on the other side a woman called Achren ('Trees'), and unless her name were known her party could not be overcome. And Gwydion ap Don, instructed by his brother Amathaon, guessed the name *of the woman*. . . .

For it has already been shown that the Battle of the Trees was fought between the White Goddess ('the woman') for whose love the god of the waxing year and of the waning year were rivals, and 'the man', Immortal Apollo, or Beli, who challenged her power. In other words, the sacred name IEVOA, or JIEVOAO its enlargement, revealed by Amathaon to Gwydion and used as a means of routing Bran, was the name of the Fivefold Goddess Danu. This was a name in which Bran could claim to speak oracularly from her kingdom of Dis, as one who had had intimate experience of each of her five persons—by being born to her, initiated by her, becoming her lover, being lulled to sleep by her, and finally killed by her. The new name of eight letters which replaced it was Beli-Apollo's own, not shared with the White Goddess, and it was therefore conveniently forgotten by later mythographers that the original one belonged to Bran, or Q're, or Iahu, only by virtue of his birth, marriage and death under female auspices. Professor Sturtevant, expert on the Hittites, translates Q're as *Karimni* which means merely 'to the god'; but, as Mr. E. M. Parr points out, El is both the common word for 'god' in Syria and a proper name for the oak-god El. He holds that other forms of this same word are Horus, or Qouros, a god of the island of Thera—the Semitic form of Horus is Churu. The identity of Q're is confused by the Gods Nergal and Marduk having also assumed the name (Qaru): Marduk's Amorites called him Gish Qaru, 'Q're of trees and herbs', to identify him with Nergal, the God of Tuesday on which trees and herbs were first created.

Chapter Nineteen

THE NUMBER OF THE BEAST

Little Gwion forced himself on me pleasantly but importunately, as children do, at a time when I was too busy with another book to think of anything else. He refused to be shaken off, though I protested that I had not the least intention of breaking into the field of bardic myth and no scholarly equipment for doing so. Despite my present appearance of easy familiarity with Celtic literature I could not at the time have answered a single question in the *Hanes Taliesin* puzzle (which at first sight recalled the 'lovely riddle—all in poetry—all about fishes' that the White Queen asked Alice at the final banquet in Looking-Glass Land) if I had not known most of the answers beforehand by poetic intuition. Really, all that I needed to do was to verify them textually; and though I had no more than one or two of the necessary books in my very small library the rest were soon sent, unasked for, by poet friends or tumbled down into my hands from the shelves of a second-hand sea-side bookshop. I drafted this whole volume at about one-half of its present length, in six weeks, then returned to the other book; but spent six years polishing the draft.

The train of coincidences that made my task possible was of a sort familiar to poets. What after all does 'coincidence' mean? What did it mean to Euclid? It meant, for example, that if in certain circumstances you applied the triangle Alpha-Beta-Gamma to the triangle Delta-Epsilon-Zeta then Gamma and Zeta would be more or less identically situated. Similarly, since I knew in advance the answers to Gwion's riddles, this presupposed the necessary book-knowledge as extant and accessible and therefore the books subsequently coincided with my needs. Zeta and Gamma gently kissed, and I could dress up in reasonable form an arrangement of thought arrived at by unreason.

One day William Rowan Hamilton, whose portrait occurs on the centenary stamps of Eire issued in 1943, was crossing Phoenix Park in Dublin, when the foreknowledge came to him of an order of mathematics, which he called 'quaternions', so far in advance of contemporary mathematic development that the gap has only recently been bridged by a long succession of intervening mathematicians. All outstanding mathematicians have this power of making a prodigious mental leap into the dark and landing firmly on both feet. Clerk Maxwell is the best known case, and he gave away the secret of his unscientific methods of thought by being such a poor accountant: he could arrive at the correct formula but had to rely on his colleagues to justify the result by pedestrian calculation.

Most outstanding physicians diagnose the nature of a disease by the same means, though afterwards they may justify their diagnoses by a logical examination of the symptoms. In fact, it is not too much to say that all original discoveries and inventions and musical and poetical compositions are the result of proleptic thought—the anticipation, by means of a suspension of time, of a result that could not have been arrived at by inductive reasoning—and of what may be called analeptic thought, the recovery of lost events by the same suspension.

This need mean no more than that time, though a most useful convention of thought, has no greater intrinsic value than, say, money. To think in temporal terms is a very complicated and unnatural way of thinking, too; many children master foreign languages and mathematic theory long before they have developed any sense of time or accepted the easily disproved thesis that cause precedes effect.

I wrote about the Muse some years ago in a poem:

> *If strange things happen where she is*
> *So that men say that graves open*
> *And the dead walk, or that futurity*
> *Becomes a womb, and the unborn are shed—*
> *Such portents are not to be wondered at*
> *Being tourbillions in Time made*
> *By the strong pulling of her bladed mind*
> *Through that ever-reluctant element.*

Poets will be able to confirm this from their own experience. And because since I wrote this poem J. W. Dunne's *Experiment with Time* has prosaicized the notion that time is not the stable moving-staircase that prosemen have for centuries pretended it to be, but an unaccountable wibblewobble, the prose men too will easily see what I am driving at. In the poetic act, time is suspended and details of future experience often become incorporated in the poem, as they do in dreams. This explains why the first Muse of the Greek triad was named Mnemosyne, 'Memory': one can have memory of the future as well as of the past. Memory of the future is usually called instinct in animals, intuition in human beings.

An obvious difference between poems and dreams is that in poems one is (or should be) in critical control of the situation; in dreams one is a paranoiac, a mere spectator of mythographic event. But in poems as in dreams there is a suspension of temporal criteria; and when the Irish poets wrote of enchanted islands where three hundred years went by as if they were a day, and put these islands under the sovereignty of the Muse, they were defining this suspension. The sudden shock of a return to the familiar temporal mode of thought is typified in the myths by the breaking of the saddle girth when the young hero rides back home on a visit from the Island. His foot touches the ground and the charm is broken: 'then the troubles of old age and sickness fell suddenly upon him.'

A sense of the equivocal nature of time is constantly with poets, rules out hope or anxiety about the future, concentrates interest detachedly in the present. I wrote about this with proleptic detail in 1934, in a poem 'The Fallen Tower of Siloam', which began:

> Should the building totter, spring for an archway!
> We were there already ...

But an interesting feature of prolepsis and analepsis is that the coincidence of the concept and the reality is never quite exact: Gamma coincides with Zeta, but not so closely that either loses its identity. The coincidence is as close, you may say, as between the notes B natural and C flat which, for economy's sake, are given only a single string on a pianoforte: they have slightly different vibration lengths, but only a remarkably true ear can distinguish one from the other. Or, as close as between the values $\frac{22}{7}$ and *pi*: if you wish to calculate, say, how much binding you will need for the bottom of a bell-tent three yards in diameter, $\frac{22}{7}$ will be an adequate formula.

In September 1943, when I could not stop my mind from running all day and all night in chase of the Roebuck, so rapidly that my pen could not keep up with it, I tried to preserve a critical detachment. I said to myself: 'I am not particularly enjoying this jaunt. I am not greatly interested in the strange country through which my broom-stick mind is flying me, and not at all sure whether I should trouble to chart it.' Then I addressed myself schizophrenically: 'I'll tell you what, Robert. I'll propound a simple, well-known, hitherto unsolved riddle and if you can make sense of that, very well, I'll pay attention to your other discoveries.'

The riddle that I propounded was the last verse of the thirteenth chapter of the *Apocalypse*:

> Here is wisdom. Let him that hath understanding count the number of the Beast: for it is the number of a man and his number is 666.

I vaguely remembered, from my school days, the two traditional solutions of St. John's cryptogram. They are both based on the assumption that, since letters of the alphabet were used to express numerals in Greek and Hebrew alike, 666 was a sum arrived at by adding together the letters that spelt out the Beast's name. The earliest solution, that of the second-century bishop Irenaeus, is LATEINOS, meaning 'The Latin One' and so denoting the race of the Beast; the most widely accepted modern solution —I forgot whose—is NERON KESAR, namely the Emperor Nero regarded as Antichrist.[1] Neither solution is quite satisfactory. 'The Latin One' is too vague a characterization of Beast 666, and KAISAR, not KESAR, was the ordinary Greek way of writing 'Caesar'. Besides, the possible combinations of letter-values which add up to 666, and the possible anagrammatic arrangements of each of these sets of letter-values, are so numerous that the aggregate of possibility approaches as near to infinity as anyone could wish.

The *Apocalypse* was written in Greek, but my analeptic self, when thus addressed, stubbornly insisted on thinking in Latin; and I saw in a sort of vision the Roman numerals flashed across the wall of the room I was in. They made a placard:

D. C. L. X.
V. I.

When they steadied, I looked at them slantwise. Poets will know what I mean by slantwise: it is a way of looking through a difficult word or phrase to discover the meaning lurking behind the letters. I saw that the placard was a *titulus*, the Roman superscription nailed above the heads or criminals at the place of execution, explaining their crime. I found myself reading out:

DOMITIANUS CAESAR LEGATOS XTI
VILITER INTERFECIT

'Domitian Caesar basely killed the Envoys of Christ.' I.N.R.I. was the *titulus* of Christ; D.C.L.X.V.I. was the *titulus* of Antichrist.

The only word I stumbled at was VILITER; it had a blurred look.

The persecution of the Church under Nero and Domitian had never greatly interested me, and the test that I had set my mind was therefore a routine one—just as I might have tested myself with the routine formula: 'The Leith police dismisseth us,' if I had suspected myself of being drunk. No historical prejudice was involved, and my clinical observations on the case are therefore to be trusted.

In the first place I had been aware that the *Apocalypse* was referred by most Biblical scholars to the reign of Nero (A.D. 54–67), not to that of Domitian (A.D. 81–96), the whole trend of the visions being anti-Neronic. And yet my eye read '*Domitianus*'. In the second, I was aware that

[1] The solution is based on the Hebrew. *Nun* = 50; *Resh* = 200; *Vav* = 6; *Nun* = 50 = *Neron*. *Koph* = 100; *Samech* = 60; *Resh* = 200 = *Kesar*. But Nero in Latin remains Nero when written in Hebrew, and Kaisar (which meant 'a head of hair' in Latin and 'a crown' in Hebrew— perhaps both words were borrowed from a common Aegean original) should be spelt with a *Kaph* (= 20), not a *Koph*, which makes the sum add up to only 626.

viliter, in the Silver Age of Latin, means 'cheaply,' and that its derived sense of 'basely' implies worthlessness, not wickedness. And yet my eye read '*viliter*'.

It was some weeks before I began to understand this paradox. It seemed to me that the work which my analeptic self had done was sound enough: D.C.L.X.V.I. was the correct text, and the solution was correct. But my eye, under the influence of my reasonable self, had evidently been at fault: it had misread, as it frequently misreads letters and newspaper headings when I am not quite awake in the morning. The text had really been:

DOMITIUS CAESAR LEGATOS XTI
VIOLENTER INTERFECIT

But since '*Domitius Caesar*' meant nothing to my reasonable self—indeed, there was no person of that name—it had officiously corrected the mistake by reading '*Domitianus*'. Now I remembered that Domitius was Nero's original name before the Emperor Claudius adopted him into the Imperial family and changed his name to Nero Claudius Caesar Drusus Germanicus, and that he hated to be reminded of his plebeian origin. (I think it is Suetonius who mentions this sensitivity of Nero's.) Nero's criminal father, Gnaeus Domitius Ahenobarbus, when congratulated on the child's birth, replied coolly that any offspring of himself and his wife Agrippinilla could bring only ruin on the State. So 'Domitius Caesar' was a suitable taunt for the cryptogram—as anti-Hitlerians in 1933 made political capital out of 'Chancellor Schickelgruber'. St. John the Divine would naturally not have respected Nero's feelings when composing it, and the use of D.C. for N.C. would have served to protect the secret.

Violenter means something more than 'roughly' or 'impetuously': it contains the sense of sacrilegious fury and outrage. So it seemed that my amending eye had brought up the EN from VIOLENTER into the word written just above it, to form DOMITIENUS, which came near enough to 'Domitianus' to make no odds; and that the meaningless word VIOLTER which remained below was a blur which I stumblingly read as VILITER, recognizing it as a word of condemnation.

(I do not claim more for this reading than that it makes historical sense. Who can say whether the sense was put there by St. John, as it were for my benefit, or by myself, as it were for St. John's benefit? All I know is that I read the words off just about as easily and unthinkingly as, say, the censor of soldiers' mail reads the cryptogram at the close of a letter to a wife: 'X.X.X.—W.I.W.R.D.D.Y?' as 'Kiss–kiss–kiss—wish it was real, darling, don't you?')

This is not all. When I came to scrutinize the *Apocalypse* text, I found in the margin a cross-reference to *Chapter XV, verse 2*, which runs:

And I saw as it were a sea of glass mingled with fire and them that had gotten the victory over the Beast, and over his image, and over his mark, and over the number of his name, standing on the sea of glass, having the harps of God.

The 'image' is the one mentioned in the previous context: apparently the meaning is that Christians were martyred who loyally refused to worship Nero's statue. So 'them that had gotten the victory over the Beast and over his image and over his mark and over the number of his name' were the Envoys of Christ who refused to be terrorized into Emperor worship, and who when sacrilegiously slain were carried straight up into Paradise.

Now the question arose: why had my eye read 'Domitianus' when the text was 'Domitius'? That had to be answered, for my eye had been convinced that Domitian, not Nero, was meant, and had rapidly amended the text to prove its point. Perhaps my eye had been a servant of my crazy analeptic self after all. Perhaps both Domitius and Domitian *were* meant. I mean, perhaps the *Apocalypse* was originally written in the time of Nero's persecutions, but expanded and brought up-to-date in the reign of Domitian, who revived the Neronic persecutions and whose name means 'of Domitius's kind'. What about the verses:

I saw one of the Beast's heads as it were wounded to death, and his deadly wound was healed and all the world wondered at the Beast.

And they ... worshipped the Beast saying: 'Who is like unto the Beast? Who is able to make war with him?'

And there was given unto him a mouth speaking great things and blasphemies and power was given unto him to continue forty-and-two months. ...

And it was given unto him to make war with the saints, and to overcome them.

The reference is clearly to the well-known contemporary belief that Nero would come again, surviving his deadly sword-wound, and to the natural Christian supposition that he was reincarnate in Domitian.

[Excellent: I now find that this is the conclusion of Dr. T. W. Crafer in his recent work on the *Apocalypse*.]

Forty-two is the number of years (A.D. 54–96) between the accession of Nero the seventh Caesar and the death, by the sword, of Domitian the twelfth and last Caesar. In this sort of prophetic writing years are usually expressed as months, and months as days. The sentence 'and power was given unto him to continue forty-and-two months' seems to be an interpolated gloss on the original prophecy that Domitian, who blasphemously called himself Lord and God, would come to a violent end. The

Church had a comparatively peaceful time under Domitian's successor, Nerva.

That some MSS. read 616, not 666, does not spoil my argument it, merely cuts out the L for *legatos*. DCXVI means that, in St. Paul's words the Beast 'crucified the Son of God afresh'.

The result of the test satisfied me, and I hope will satisfy others, that I had not slid into certifiable paranoia.

I should add, however, that since the eleventh chapter of the *Apocalypse* predicts the preservation of the Temple, the original version of the book must have been written after the death of Nero, but before the destruction of the Temple and at a time when rumours of his reappearance in the flesh were widely current. Also that the Hebrew letters TRJVN, which add up to 666 (*Tav* = 400; *Resh* = 200; *Yod* = 10; *Vav* = 6; *Nun* = 50), form the common cypher-disguise in Talmudic literature for Nero (*trijon* means 'little beast') and that the authors of the *Talmud* are most unlikely to have borrowed from the Gentile Christians. It is possible, then, that the first version of the *Apocalypse* was a Jewish nationalist tract, written in Aramaic before A.D. 70, in which 666 was a cypher meaning 'Little Beast', which pointed to Nero; but that it was re-written in Greek and expanded for Christian readers at the close of the first century, by which time the Pauline converts, who knew no Hebrew, were at pains to prove that Jesus had rejected the Law of Moses and transferred Jehovah's blessing from the Jews to themselves. And that in this second version, with its many interpolations and uncritical retention of out-of-date material, the cypher 666 was given a new solution, and one that any intelligent person could understand without recourse to Hebrew: namely DCLXVI. If this is so, the legend was never *Domitius Caesar* etc., yet my analeptic eye was right to recognize that since the original Hebrew meaning of the cypher was TRIJON; the beastly spirit of Domitius was latent in Domitianus.

The proleptic or analeptic method of thought, though necessary to poets, physicians, historians and the rest, is so easily confused with mere guessing, or deduction from insufficient data, that few of them own to using it. However securely I buttress the argument of this book with quotations, citations and footnotes, the admission that I have made here of how it first came to me will debar it from consideration by orthodox scholars: though they cannot refute it, they dare not accept it.

Chapter Twenty

A CONVERSATION AT PAPHOS—
A.D. 43

Circling the circlings of their fish,
Nuns walk in white and pray;
For he is chaste as they....

These lines will serve as a text to demonstrate the peculiar workings of poetic thought. They came to me, from nowhere in particular, as the first three lines of a rhyming stanza, in the epigrammatic style of the Welsh *englyn*, which required two more to complete it. Their manifest meaning is that the white nuns walk in silent prayer in their convent garden, circling the fish pool and circling their rosaries in chaste prayer; the fish swims around inside. The fish, like the nuns, is proverbial for his sexual indifference, and the Mother Superior permits him as a convent pet because he cannot possibly awake any lascivious thoughts in her charges.

A neat piece of observation, but not yet a poem; the truth, but not the whole truth. To tell the whole truth, I had to consider first the phenomenon of nuns, who voluntarily forgo the pleasures of carnal love and motherhood in order to become the Vestal brides of Christ, and then the phenomenon of sacred fish of all sorts and sizes, from the great fish that swallowed Jonah to the little spotted fish in wishing wells that still grant lovers or babies to peasant women in remote parishes; not forgetting the 'mighty and stainless Fish from the Fountain whom a pure virgin grasped' in the epitaph of the late second-century bishop Aviricius of the Phrygian Pentapolis. Only when I had asked and answered some scores of teasing questions would the fourth and fifth lines be found, to complete the poem with a simple concentration of difficult meaning.

I began by noting the strange continuance in Christianity of the original pagan title of Chief Pontiff, which the Bishop of Rome, the successor of St. Peter the Fisherman, assumed two centuries after Christianity had become the Roman state religion. For the Chief Pontiff, in Republican and early Imperial times, was personally responsible to the Capitoline Trinity (Juppiter, Juno and Minerva), for the chaste behaviour of the

Vestals, as his successor now is to the Christian Trinity for that of Roman Catholic nuns. Then I threw my mind back in an analeptic trance. I found myself listening to a conversation in Latin, helped out with Greek, which I understood perfectly. Presently I began to distinguish the voices as those of Theophilus, a well-known Syrian-Greek historian and Lucius Sergius Paulus, a Roman Governor-General of Cyprus under the Emperor Claudius.

Paulus was saying rather heavily: 'My learned friend, a festal system of such complexity cannot have been conveyed from country to country among the bales of merchandize that traders carry in barter. It may have been imposed by conquest, yet had there ever been an Empire of Europe which included all the distant parts you mention—'

'I should also have included Portugal among them,' interjected Theophilus.

'—doubtless we should have heard of it. But Alexander's conquests were all in the East: he dared not challenge the power of Republican Rome.'

Theophilus said: 'What I mean is this. I postulate a constant emigration, in ancient times, of tribes inhabiting the Southern coast of the Black Sea, a process that has indeed ceased only in the last century or two. The climate was healthy, the people vigorous and well organized, but the coastal strip narrow. Every hundred years or so, as I suppose, the land grew over-populated, and one tribe or another was necessarily sent away to seek its fortune and make room for the rest. Or it may be that they were forced to move by pressure from the East, when wandering hordes from the plains of Asia broke through the Caspian Gates of the Caucasus mountains. Of these tribes, some took the route southward across Asia Minor and ventured through Syria and as far as Egypt—we have the authority of Herodotus for this; some took the route westward across the Bosphorus and Thrace and into Greece, Italy and Gaul and even, as I say, to Spain and Portugal. Some struggled south-eastward into Chaldaea across the Taurus mountains; some moved northward up the Western shore of the Black Sea and then followed the Danube to Istria, continuing their march across Europe until they reached the north-westerly tip of Gaul; whence, it is said, some crossed over into Britain, and from Britain into Ireland. They took the festal system with them.'

'Yours is a very daring theory,' said Paulus, 'but I can recall no authentic tradition that supports it.'

Theophilus smiled. 'Your Excellency is a true Roman—"no truth unless hallowed by a tradition." Well, then: tell me, from what land did your hero Aeneas come?'

'He was a King of Dardanus on the Bosphorus before he settled in Troy.

'Good: Dardanus is three-quarters of the way back from Rome to the Black Sea. And, tell me, what was the priceless possession that Aeneas brought with him from Troy? Pray forgive the dialectical method.'

'You must mean the Palladium, most learned Socrates,' answered Paulus in ironically academic tones, 'on the safety of which the fate of Troy once depended; and the fate of Rome depends now.'

'And what, honoured Alcibiades, is the Palladium?'

'A venerable statue of Pallas Athene.'

'Ah, but who is she?'

'You suggested this morning, during our visit to the wrestling-school, that she was originally a Sea-goddess like our local Cyprian deity; and mythographers record that she was born by the Lake of Triton in Libya.'

'So she was. And who or what is Triton, besides being the name of a once extensive lake which is now shrinking into salt marsh?'

'Triton is a marine deity with a fish's body who accompanies Poseidon the Sea-god and his wife Amphitrite the Sea-goddess, and blows a conch in their honour. He is said to be their son.'

'You give me the most helpful answers. But what does Pallas mean?'

'How long is this cross-examination to last? Would you send me back to school again? Pallas is one of Athene's titles. I have never accepted Plato's derivation of the word from *pallein*, to brandish; he says, you know, that she is called Pallas because she brandishes her *aegis*, or shield. Plato's etymology is always suspect. What puzzles me is that Pallas is a man's name, not a woman's.'

'I hope to be able to explain the paradox. But, first, what do you know about men called Pallas?'

'Pallas? Pallas? There have been many men of the name, from the legendary Pallas the Titan to our present egregious Secretary of State. The Emperor made the Senate snigger the other day by declaring that the Secretary was of the famous Pallas family that gave its name to the Palatine Hill.'

'I doubt whether the remark was as absurd as it must have sounded. Claudius, for all his eccentric habits, is no mean historian, and as Chief Pontiff has access to ancient religious records denied to others. Come, your Excellency, let us go together through the list of ancient Pallases. There was, as you say, Pallas the Titan, who was brother to Astraeus ("the Starlike") and Perses ("the Destroyer") and who married—whatever that means—the River Styx in Arcadia. He was the father of Zelos ("Zeal"), Cratos ("Strength"), Bia ("Force") and Nicë ("Victory"). Does that not convey his mystical nature to you?'

'I regret to admit that it does not. Pity me as a stupid, legalistic and practical Roman.'

'If your Excellency is not careful I shall begin praising your elegiac poem on the Nymph Egeria, a copy of which was lately sent me from Rome by one of our mutual friends. Well, next comes Homer's Pallas, whom he calls the father of the Moon. And next another Titan, the Pallas who was flayed by Athene; it was this Pallas from whom she is said to have taken her name.'

'I never heard that story.'

'It rests on good authority. And then comes Pallas, the founder of Pallantium in Arcadia, a Pelasgian son of the Aegeus who gave his name to the Aegean Sea; now, he is of interest to us because his grandson Evander emigrated to Rome sixty years before the Trojan war and brought your sacred alphabet with him. It was he who founded a new city of Pallantium on the Palatine Hill at Rome, long since incorporated in the City. He also introduced the worship of Nicë, Neptune, (now identified with Poseidon), Pan of Lycos, Demeter and Hercules. Evander had a son named Pallas, and two daughters, Romë ("Strength") and Dynë ("Power"). And I had almost forgotten still another Pallas, brother of Aegeus and Lycos, and therefore uncle to Evander's grandfather Pallas.'

'A fine crop of Pallases. But I am still in the dark.'

'Well, I do not blame your Excellency. And I hardly know where to shine the lantern. But I appeal to you for patience. Tell me, of what is the Palladium made?'

Paulus considered. 'I am rather rusty on mythology, my dear Theophilus, but I seem to remember that it is made of the bones of Pelops.'

Theophilus congratulated him. 'And who was Pelops? What does his name mean?'

'I was reading Apollonius Rhodius the other day. He says that Pelops came to Phrygia from Enete in Paphlagonia and that the Paphlagonians still call themselves Pelopians. Apollonius was curator of the great Alexandrian Library and his ancient history is as reliable as anyone's. As for the name "Pelops", it means dusky-faced. The body of Pelops was served up as a stew by Tantalus, his father, for the Gods; they discovered that it was forbidden food just in time. Only the shoulder had been eaten—by Demeter, was it not?—but some say Rhea, and restitution was made with an ivory shoulder. Pelops was brought back to life.'

'What do you make of this cannibalistic myth?'

'Nothing at all, except that we now seem to have traced the Dardanians back to the Black Sea, if the sacred Palladium was made of the bones of their ancestor from Enete.'

'If I suggest to you that Pelops and Pallas are different titles of Kings of the same early Greek dynasty, will that help your Excellency?'

'Not in the least. Pray, give me a hand out of this quaking bog.'

'Allow me to ask you a riddle: What is it with a dusky face and an ivory shoulder that comes rushing victoriously up a river, as if to a wedding, full of Zeal, Force and Strength, and whose hide is well worth the flaying?'

'I am good at riddles, though bad at myths. A fish of sorts. I guess the porpoise. The porpoise is not an ordinary fish, for it couples, male with female: and how royally it charges into a river-mouth from the sea! It is pale below and dark above, with a blunt, dusky muzzle. And it has a fine white shoulder-blade—broad like a paddle; and porpoise leather makes the best-wearing shoes procurable.'

'It is not a fish at all. It is a warm-blooded creature, a *cetos*, a sea-beast with lungs, not an *ichthus*, a fish with gills and cold blood. To the sea-beast family, according to Aristotle's system, belong all whales, seals, porpoises, grampuses and dolphins. Unfortunately in Greece we use the same word *delphis* indiscriminately for both the beaked dolphin and the blunt-muzzled porpoise; and though Arion's musical mount is likely to have been a true dolphin, it is uncertain whether Delphi was originally named after the dolphin or the porpoise. "Pallas" in Greek once meant a lusty young man, and I suppose that it became the royal title of Peloponnesian kings, whose sacred beast was the lusty porpoise, when the tribe of Pelops came down into Greece from the Black Sea. Do you remember Homer's much disputed epithet for Lacedaemon—*Cetoessa*, which literally means "Of the Sea-beast"?'

'I will try to think along the lines you lay out for me,' said Paulus. 'The Peloponnese is, of course, sometimes called the Land of Poseidon, who is the Achaean god of all sea-beasts and fishes. Arcadia is the centre of the Peloponnese, and Pallas the Sea-beast-god reigned there, and in Lacedaemon too. Let me work this out for myself—yes—Pallas is married to the River Styx, meaning that the porpoise comes rushing up the Crathis towards the Styx in his mating season. (At the mouth of the Crathis is Aegae—I once served in that part of Greece—which explains the connexion with Aegeus. Opposite Aegae, across the Gulf of Corinth, stands Delphi, sacred to Apollo the Dolphin-god or Porpoise-god.) Later, Evander a grandson of Pallas, and with a son of the same name, is driven out of Arcadia, about the time of the great Achaean invasion, and comes to Rome. There he forms an alliance with the people of Aeneas, claiming kinship with them in virtue of a common descent from Pelops. Is that how you read the story?'

'Exactly. And Evander was probably a Pallas too, but changed his name, after killing his father, to throw the avenging Furies off the scent.'

'Very well. He introduces the worship of the Sea-god Neptune; of Nicë, the daughter of the original Pallas; of Hercules—why Hercules?'

'His sexual lustiness commended him, and he was not only a great-grandson of Pelops but an ally of the Enetians, the original Pelopians.'

'And why Demeter?'

'To rescue her from Poseidon the god of the Achaeans who, it is said, had raped her. You remember perhaps that she retreated from him up the Crathis to the Styx and there cursed the water. Demeter was old Deo, the barley-planting Mother-goddess of the Danaan Arcadians. That some mythographers call her Rhea proves her Cretan origin. Her famous mare-headed statue at Phigalia, by the River Neda in Western Arcadia, held a porpoise in one hand and in the other a sacred black dove of the sort that is used at the oak-oracle of Dodona.'

'Why mare-headed?'

'The horse was sacred to her, and when the Pelopians intermarried with the original Arcadians, this was recorded in myth as a marriage between Pelops and Hippodameia, "the Horse-tamer", who is also called Danais by some mythographers. And among their children were Chrysippos, "Golden Horse"; Hippalcmos, "Bold Horse"; Nicippe, "Victorious Mare"—new clan-names.'

'I see. It is not so nonsensical as it sounds. Well, now I can fill out the story. The Mother-goddess was served by the so-called Daughters of Proetus or Proteus,[1] who lived in a cave at Lusi, by the headwaters of the Styx. Her priestesses had a right to the shoulder-blade of the sacred porpoise at a sacrificial feast. Porpoise beef makes very good eating, especially when it has been well hung. And Proteus, according to Homer, became herdsman to Poseidon and tended his sea-beasts. That must have been after Poseidon's conquest of the Goddess, which he celebrated by calling himself the Mare-tamer. I take Proteus to be another name for Pallas, the Sea-beast: the Achaeans, in fact, enslaved the Pelopians, who were now also styled Danaans, and Poseidon took over the prerogatives and titles of Pallas.'

'I congratulate your Excellency. You evidently agree with me in dismissing as mistaken the view that Pelops was an Achaean—unless perhaps an earlier Achaean horde had entered Greece many centuries before with the Aeolians; I suppose that the mistake arose from the knowledge that Pelops was once worshipped in the northern province of the Peloponnese now called Achaea. For the enslavement of the Pelopians by the Achaeans is confirmed in another, rather frivolous myth: Poseidon is said to have fallen in love with Pelops, as Zeus with Ganymede, and to have carried him off to be his cup-bearer. Neptune, who emigrated to Italy was, you will agree, also Pallas and must not be identified with Poseidon as the custom is. But I should guess Proteus to be a general name of the god who is the son, lover and victim of the old Mother Goddess, and assumes a variety of shapes. He is not only Pallas, the sea-beast, but Salmoneus the human oak-king, Chrysippos the golden horse, and so forth.'

'But Pan of Lycos? What had Evander to do with him?'

[1] 'Proetus' is the earlier spelling of the word, which means 'the early man', formed from the adverb *proi* or *pro*.

'His ancestor Pelops probably brought him from the River Lycos, which flows into the Black Sea not far from Enete. Another lusty god. You will recall that he danced for joy when Pelops was fitted out with his new white shoulder. By the way, do you recall the various stories of Pan's parentage?'

'The usual one makes him a son of the nymph Dryope by Hermes.'

'What does that convey to you?'

'I have never considered. "Dryope" means a woodpecker of the sort that nests in oaks and makes an extraordinary noise with its bill in the cracks of trees, and climbs spirally up the trunk. It has a barbed tongue and portends rain, as the dolphin and porpoise portend storms by their frisking. And the nymph Dryope is connected with the cult of Hylas, a Phrygian form of Hercules who dies ceremonially every year. And Hermes—he's the prime phallic god, and also the god of eloquence, and his erotic statues are usually carved from an oak.'

'The tree of shepherds, the tree of Hercules, the tree of Zeus and Juppiter. But Pan, as the son of an oak-woodpecker, is hatched from an egg.'

'Hold hard,' said Paulus. 'I remember something to the point. Our Latin god Faunus, who is identical with Pan, the god of shepherds, is said to have been a King of Latium who entertained Evander on his arrival. And Faunus was the son of Picus, which is Latin for woodpecker. Evidently another Pelopian tribe had reached Latium from the Black Sea before either Evander or Aeneas. Faunus is worshipped in sacred groves, where he gives oracles; chiefly by voices heard in sleep while the visitant lies on a sacred fleece.'

'Which establishes the mythical connexion between Pan, the oak, the woodpecker, and sheep. I have read another legend of his birth, too. He is said to have been the son of Penelope, Ulysses' wife, by Hermes who visited her in the form of a ram. A ram, not a goat. This is odd, because both Arcadian Pan and his Italian counterpart Faunus have goat legs and body. I think I see how that comes about. Pallas the Titan, the royal sea-beast, was the son of Crios (the Ram). This means that the Pelopian settlers from Enete formed an alliance with the primitive Arcadians who worshipped Hermes the Ram, and acknowledged him as the father of their sea-beast King Pallas. Likewise the Aegeans—the goat-tribe—formed an alliance with the same Arcadians and acknowledged Hermes as the father of their Goat-king, Pan, whose mother was Amalthea and who became the He-goat of the Zodiac.'

Paulus said smiling: 'Neatly argued. That disposes of the other scandalous legend that Pan was the son of Penelope by *all* her suitors in the absence of Ulysses.'

'Where did you get that version? It is extraordinarily interesting.'

'I cannot remember. From some grammarian or other. It makes little sense to me.'

'I knew that Pan was the son of Penelope, but your version is a great improvement on it. Penelope, you see, is not really Ulysses' wife except in a manner of speaking; she is a sacred bird, the *penelops* or purple-striped duck. So again, as in the Dryope version of his parentage, Pan is born from a bird—which explains the legend that he was perfectly developed from birth, as a hatched chicken is. Now to come to the suitors, by what I fear will be a longish argument. I postulate first of all that the Palladium is made from the bones of Pelops, that is to say from the ivory shoulder-blades of porpoises, a suitable and durable material, and that it is a phallic statue, not the statue of a goddess. I support my thesis by the existence, until a few years ago, of another sacred shoulder-blade of Pelops in the precinct which his great-grandson Hercules built in his honour at Olympia. Now, according to the myth, Pelops had only one sacred shoulder-blade, the right one; yet nobody has ever questioned the genuineness either of the relic at Olympia or of the Palladium. The history of the Olympian blade is this. During the siege of Troy the Greeks were told by an oracle that the only offensive counter-magic to the defensive magic of the Palladium preserved in the Citadel of Troy was the shoulder-blade of Pelops which a tribe of Pelopians had taken to Pisa in Italy. So Agamemnon sent for the thing, but the ship that was bringing it to him went down off the coast of Euboea. Generations later, a Euboean fisherman dragged it up in his net and recognized it for what it was—probably by some design carved on it. He brought it to Delphi and the Delphic Oracle awarded it to the people of Olympia, who made the fisherman its pensioned guardian. If the bone was the shoulder-blade of a sacred porpoise, not of a man, the difficulty of Pelops's having had more than one right shoulder-blade disappears. So does the difficulty of believing that when boiled and eaten by the gods he came alive again—if the fact was that a new sacred porpoise was caught and eaten every year at Lusi by the devotees of Deo. Does all this sound reasonable?'

'More reasonable, by far, than the usual fantastic story, though cannibalism in ancient Arcadia is not incredible. And that the Palladium is a phallic statue, rather than that of a goddess, may explain why such a mystery has been made of its appearance and why it is hidden out of sight in the Penus of the Temple of Vesta. Yes, though your thesis is startling and even, at first hearing, indecent, it has much to commend it.'

'Thank you. To continue: you remember that two or three of the early kings of Rome had no discoverable father?'

'Yes. I have often wondered how that happened.'

'You remember, too, that the Kingdom descended in the female line: a man was king only by virtue of marriage to a queen or of descent from a queen's daughter. The heir to the Kingdom, in fact, was not the king's son but the son of either his youngest daughter or his youngest sister—which explains the Latin word *nepos,* meaning both nephew and grandson. The focus of the community life was literally the *focus,* or hearth-fire, of the royal house, which was tended by the princesses of the royal line, namely the Vestal Virgins. To them the Palladium was delivered for safe-keeping as the *fatale pignus imperii,* the pledge granted by the Fates for the permanency of the royal line.'

'They still have it safe. But if you are right about the statue's obscene nature, the Vestal Virgins seem rather an odd choice of guardians, because they are strictly forbidden to indulge in sexual intercourse!'

Theophilus laid his forefinger along his nose and said: 'It is the commonplace paradox of religions that nothing is *nefas,* unlawful, that is not also *fas,* lawful, on particularly holy occasions. Among the Egyptians the pig is viewed with abhorrence and its very touch held to cause leprosy —indeed, the Egyptian pig as a scavenger and corpse-eater merits this abhorrence—yet the highest-born Egyptians eat its flesh with relish at their midwinter mysteries and fear no untoward consequence. The Jews, it is said, formerly did the same, if they do not do so now. Similarly, the Vestal Virgins cannot always have been debarred from the full natural privileges of their sex, for no barbarous religion enforces permanent sterility on nubile women. My view is that at midsummer during the Alban Holiday, which was a marriage feast of the Oak-queen—your Excellency's charming nymph Egeria—with the Oak-king of the year, and the occasion of promiscuous love-making, the six Vestals, her kins-women, coupled with six of the Oak-king's twelve companions—you will recall Romulus's twelve shepherds. But silently, in the darkness of a sacred cave so that nobody knew who lay with whom, nor who was the father of any child born. And did the same again with the six other companions at midwinter during the Saturnalia. Then, failing a son of the Oak-queen, the new king was chosen from a child born to a Vestal. So Penelope's son by six suitors is explained. The Lusty God—call him Hercules or Hermes or Pan or Pallas or Pales or Mamurius or Neptune or Priapus or whatever you please—inspired the young men with erotic vigour when they had first danced around a blazing bonfire presided over by his obscene statue—the Palladium itself. Thus it happened that a king was said to be born of a virgin mother, and either to have no known father, or to be the son of the god.'

'That is a still more startling notion than the other,' protested Paulus, 'and I cannot see either that you have any proof of it, or that you can explain how the Vestals ceased to be love-nymphs and became barren spinsters as now.'

'The cessation of the royal love-orgies,' said Theophilus, 'follows

357

logically on the historical course that we discussed yesterday—the extension of the kingship in ancient times from one year to four years; from four to eight; from eight to nineteen; until finally it became a life-tenure. Though popular love-orgies might continue—and at Rome continue still —to be held at midsummer and at the close of the year, they ceased to have any significance as occasions for breeding new kings. As we know, children are often born of these holiday unions and are considered lucky and cheerfully legitimized; but they have no claim to the kingship, because their mothers are no longer princesses, as formerly. It seems to have been King Tarquin the Elder who first prescribed for the Vestals what amounts to perpetual virginity, his object being to prevent them from breeding claimants to the throne. It was certainly he who introduced burying alive as a punishment for any Vestal who broke the rule; but even now the prescribed virginity is not perpetual—for after thirty years a Vestal Virgin is, I understand, entitled to unsanctify herself, if she pleases, and marry.'

'It happens very seldom; after thirty years of illustrious spinsterhood it is hard for a woman to win a husband of any worth, and she soon wearies of the world and usually dies of remorse.'

'Now, as to the proof that the Virgins were once permitted occasional erotic delights: in the first place the novice, when initiated by the Chief Pontiff on behalf of the God, is addressed as "Amata", beloved one, and given a head-dress bordered with pure purple,[1] a white woollen fillet and a white linen vestment—the royal marriage garments of the bride of the God. In the second, we know that Silvia, the mother of Romulus and Remus, was a Vestal Virgin of Alba Longa and unexpectedly became the bride of Mamurius or Mars, then a red-faced, erotic Shepherd-god; and was not buried alive as a Vestal would now be if she became pregnant— even though she claimed that a god had forced her.'

'They drowned Silvia in the River Anio, at all events.'

'Only in a manner of speaking, I think. After the birth of her twins, whom she laid in the ark of osier and sedge, which is a commonplace in nativity myths of this sort, and consigned to the mercy of the waves, she took much the same baptismal bath in renewal of her virginity as the Priestess of Aphrodite yearly takes here at Paphos[2] in the blue sea, and the nymph Dryope in her fountain at Pegae.'

'The connexion between Rome and Arcadia is, I grant, very close.

---

[1] *Purpureus* is a reduplication of *purus*, 'very, very pure.'

[2] Aphrodite persists tenaciously at Paphos. In the village of Konklia, as it is now called after the sea-shell in which she rode ashore there, a rough anaconic stone, her original neolithic image, remains on the site of the early Greek sanctuary and is still held in awe by the local people. Close by is a Frankish church, re-built about 1450 as an ordinary Greek chapel, where the saint is a golden-haired beauty called Panagia Chrisopolitissa, 'the all-holy golden woman of the town'—a perfect figure of Aphrodite with the infant Eros in her arms. Mr. Christopher Kininmonth who gives me these particulars, says that the beach is a particularly

The Shepherd-god sends a wolf, *lycos,* to alarm Silvia and then over-powers her in a cave. And when the twins are born, a wolf and a wood-pecker bring them food. By the way, can you explain how Pan comes to have a wolf in his service, if he is a god of shepherds?'

'It was probably a were-wolf. The Arcadian religious theory is that a man is sent as an envoy to the wolves. He becomes a were-wolf for eight years, and persuades the wolf-packs to leave man's flocks and children alone during that time. Lycaon the Arcadian initiated the practice, they say, and it is likely that your ancient Guild of Lupercal priests originally provided Rome with her were-wolf too. But to speak again of Silvia. The God not only ravished her in a dark cave overshadowed by a sacred grove, but took advantage of a total eclipse of the sun. He was hiding his true shape, I suppose; which was that of a sea-beast.'

'You seem to have the whole business worked out. Perhaps you can also explain why the hair of a Vestal is cut at marriage and never allowed to grow?'

'That must have been King Tarquin's prudent regulation. Women with their hair cut cannot perform magical spells. Doubtless he feared that they would revenge themselves on him for his severity towards them. Vestal Virgins were under the king's sole charge in those days. It was he, not the Chief Pontiff, who had the privilege of scourging any Vestal who let the sacred fire go out, and scourging to death any Vestal who took a private lover.'

'And can you also tell me why they use spring-water mixed with powdered and purified brine in their sacrifices?'

'Tell me first what are the medical properties of water mixed with brine?'

'It is a strong emetic and purge.'

'Suitable for preparing celebrants for the midsummer and midwinter feasts? I had not thought of that supplementary use. What I am suggesting is that when the twelve young shepherds—the leaping priests of Mamurius or Pallas—performed their orgiastic dance for hour after hour around the blazing bonfires they must have sweated terribly and come near to faint-ing.'

'I see what you mean. In the harvest-fields countrymen always refresh themselves with brine-water in preference to plain: it restores the salt that has been lost by sweating. Brine-water fetched by Vestals at the mid-summer orgy must have restored the vigour of the shepherds like a charm. Still another question, in revenge for all those that you asked me: how does Triton come to be a son of Poseidon?'

fine one and that the Romans, who substituted their massive and tasteless Temple of Venus for the earlier Greek building, did not despise the conical image but incorporated it in their shrine.

'In the same way as Proteus comes to be his herdsman. Originally Poseidon had nothing to do with the sea. The porpoise of the Crathis, the Delphic dolphin and the Phocian seal all belong to the earlier civilization. Poseidon won them as his own when he seized the Peloponnese and the opposite shores of the Gulf of Corinth and married the Sea-goddess Amphitrite. Triton must have been her son, probably by Hermes; perhaps he ruled at "Lacedaemon of the Sea-beast". At any rate, Poseidon becomes his foster-father by marrying the Sea-goddess Amphitrite—I take this to be one of Athene's original titles. (By the way, the ancient Seal-king Phoceus, who gave his name to Phocis, was the son of Ornytion, which means Son of the Chicken—and the Chicken, I suppose, is Pan again who was hatched from a woodpecker's egg or the egg of a penelope duck.) Of one thing I am sure: unless we recognize Triton and Pallas and Pelops as originally a sea-beast incarnate in a dynasty of ancient kings, we can hope to find no sense in the legends of heroes who rescued maidens from sea-beasts. The heroes are princes who challenge the sea-beast king to combat and kill him, and marry the royal heiress whom he has put under close restraint and reign in his stead by virtue of this marriage. The royal heiress is his daughter, but she is also an incarnation of the Moon; which explains why Homer's Pallas was the Moon's father. You find the same story in the marriage of Peleus to the Sea-goddess Thetis after his killing of Phocus, the Seal-king of Aegina. Peleus means "the muddy one" and may be a variant form of Pelops—as Pelias, the name of the king whose former territory Peleus annexed, certainly is. There was a sea-beast at Troy; Hercules, in company with the same Peleus, killed it and rescued the princess Hesionë and made himself master of the city. And clearly the many stories of princes who were saved by dolphins from drowning suggest sacred paintings of these princes riding on dolphin-back in proof of sovereignty. Arion and Icadius and Enalus ...'

'Theseus, of course ...'

'And Coeranus too, and Taras and Phalanthus. The common people always prefer anecdote, however improbable, to myth, however simple: they see a prince pictured astride a dolphin and take this for literal truth and feel obliged to account for his strange choice of steed.'

'But what you undertook to explain at the beginning of this conversation, and have not yet explained, is why the Goddess Athene has a male name as her principal title.'

'She has become androgynous: there are many such deities. Sin, for example, the Moon-deity of the Semites, and the Phoenician Baalith, and the Persian Mithras. The Goddess is worshipped first and is all-powerful; presently a God enters into equal power with her, and either they become twins, as happened when Artemis agreed to share Delos with Apollo of Tempe, or else they are joined in a single bi-sexual being. Thus the

Orphic hymn celebrates Zeus as both Father and Eternal Virgin. Your own Juppiter is in the same hermaphroditic tradition.'

'Our own Juppiter? You surprise me.'

'Yes, do you not know the couplet written by Quintus Valerius Soranus, whom Crassus praised as the most learned of all who wore the toga? No? It runs:

Juppiter Omnipotens, rerum regum-que repertor,
Progenitor genetrix-que Deum, Deus unus et idem.

> All kings, all things, entire
> From Jove the Almighty came—
> Of Gods both dam and sire
> Yet God the sole and same.

And Varro, his rival in learning, writing of the Capitoline Trinity, agreed that together they form a single god: Juno being Nature as matter, Juppiter being Nature as the creative impulse, and Minerva being Nature as the mind which directs the creative impulse. Minerva, as you know, often wields Juppiter's thunderbolts; therefore if Juppiter is Eternal Virgin, Minerva is equally Eternal Father. And there we are again: Minerva is universally identified with Pallas Athene, who is the Goddess of Wisdom. Athene is to Pallas as Minerva is to Juppiter: his better half.'

'I am getting confused in my mind between these various goddesses. Are they all the same person?'

'Originally. She is older than all the gods. Perhaps her most archaic form is the Goddess Libya. If you read Apollonius recently you will recall that she appeared in triad by Lake Triton to Jason, wearing goatskins.'

'A bi-sexual deity naturally remains chaste, or so I judge from Minerva's case,' Paulus commented.

'Chaste as a fish.'

'But when Juppiter began he was as unchaste as a sea-beast.'

'Minerva reformed him.'

'I daresay that is why she is called his daughter. My daughter Sergia reformed me. All daughters reform their fathers. Or try to. I was a leaping sea-beast as a young man.'

'So was Apollo before his sister Artemis reformed him: he was a lusty dolphin once. But now chaste sacred fish are kept in his temples at Myra and Hierapolis.'

'That reminds me of a question on which I am most anxious to be informed: what do you know of sea-beasts and fish in the Jewish religion? I understand that you have read their sacred books with some care.'

'Not recently. But I remember that there is a partial taboo on fish in the

Jewish Torah, or Law; which suggests Egyptian influence. But not on scaled fish, only on the unscaled, and that would point to their having once held sea-beasts, such as the porpoise and dolphin, in reverence. Moreover, their sacred Ark—now lost—was covered with sea-beast skins; that is important. The Jews were tributary once to the Philistines, whose God was a sea-beast of many changes named Dagon—the Philistines are originally immigrants of Cretan Stock, despite their Semitic language. As I remember the story, the Philistines conquered the Jews and laid up the Ark in Dagon's temple before his phallic statue, but the God enclosed in the Ark wrestled with Dagon and broke his statue into pieces. Yes, and the legendary hero who led the Jews into Judaea was called Jeshua, son of the Fish.'

'Ha! That is exactly what I wanted to know. You see, a curious thing happened the other day. A written report reached me that a Jew named Barnabas was preaching some new mystical doctrine in a Jewish synagogue at the other end of the island; it was described by my informant, a Syrian Greek from Antioch with a Jewish mother, as a doctrine endangering the peace of the island. I sent for Barnabas and the other fellow and heard what both had to say. I forget his original name, but he had become a Roman citizen and asked my permission to call himself Paulus, to which I had weakly assented. I will not go into the story in detail: suffice it to say that Barnabas was preaching a new demigod, so far as I can make out a recent reincarnation of this heroic Jeshua. I did not know until you mentioned it just now that Jeshua was son of the Fish; perhaps this explains the mystery. At all events, my Oriental Secretary, a harmless little man called Manahem, took Barnabas's part warmly, rather too warmly, and sent the other fellow about his business with a fierceness of which I should never have believed him capable.'

'I know Manahem; he came to you from the Court of Antipas of Galilee, did he not?'

'That's the man. He is now away on leave in Alexandria. Well, when the case was settled and Barnabas and the other fellow had both been sent out of the island with a warning never to return, I called Manahem to my private room and gave him a piece of my mind. I am not naturally observant, but long experience as a magistrate has taught me to use my eyes in court, and I had caught Manahem surreptitiously signalling to Barnabas to leave the case in his hands. He was making a secret sign with his foot, the outline of a fish traced on the pavement. I gave Manahem the fright of his life—threatened to put him to the torture unless he explained that fish to me. He confessed at once, and begged me to forgive him. The fish sign, it appears, is the pass-word of Barnabas's society which cultivates a sort of universal pacifism under the guidance of a demi-god named Jeshua—Jesus in Greek—who has the title of the Anointed One. The pass-word is for use among Greek-speaking Jews and stands, Manahem says, for *Jesus Christos Theos* which are, of course, the first letters of *ichthus*, fish. But there is more to it than that, I believe.'

'I have heard of the society. They celebrate a weekly love-feast with fish, wine and bread, but tend to Pythagorean asceticism. You may be sure that Jeshua the Fish is of the chaster sort. The Jeshua who founded it was executed under Tiberius; and oddly enough his mother was a Temple Virgin at Jerusalem, and there was a mystery about his birth.'

'Yes, Manahem revealed it under an oath of secrecy. You are right about this God's chastity. Erotic religion is going out of fashion everywhere; it is inconsistent with modern social stability, except of course among the peasantry. Do you know, Theophilus, a picture rises in my mind, almost a vision. I see the white-clad Vestal Virgins in their Temple grounds offering up little prayers to chaste Juppiter, Father and Virgin, whom they serve. I see them devoutly circling the fish-pool which the sacred fish also mystically circles—the cool, pale-faced fish, as chaste as they—'

Theophilus interrupted: '—*Who was dark-faced and hot in Silvia's day,*' '*And in his pool drowns each unspoken wish,*' Paulus agreed.

*   *   *

Theophilus was wrong to suggest that the hero rescues the chained virgin from a male sea-beast. The sea-beast is female—the Goddess Tiamat or Rahab— and the God Bel or Marduk, who wounds her mortally and usurps her authority, has himself chained her in female form to the rock to keep her from mischief. When the myth reaches Greece, Bellerophon and Hercules are more chivalrously represented as rescuing her from the monster. It has even been suggested that in the original icon, the Goddess's chains were really necklaces, bracelets and anklets, while the sea-beast was her emanation.

Chapter Twenty-One

THE WATERS OF STYX

In Parry's edition of Archbishop Ussher's *Letters*—Ussher was the learned Primate of Ireland in the reign of Charles I who dated the creation of Adam in the year 4004 B.C.—appears a note that Langbaine the Irish antiquarian communicated to Ussher the following bardic tradition:

> Nemninus being upbraided by a Saxon scholar as a Briton and therefore ignorant of the rudiments of learning, invented these letters by an improvisation, to clear his nation of the charge of dullness and ignorance.

ALAP	A	PARTH	P
BRAUT	B	QUITH	Q
CURI	C	RAT	R
DEXI	D	TRAUS	T
EGIN	E	SUNG	S
FICH	F	UIR	U
GUIDIR	G	JEIL	X
HUIL	H	OFR	E
JECHUIT	I	ZEIRC	Z
KAM	K	AIUN	AE
LOUBER	L	ESTIAUL	ET
MUIN	M	EGUI	EU
NIHN	N	AUR	AU
OR	O	EMC	EI
	KENC	ELAU	

This obviously was a joke at the stupid Saxon's expense, because the British bards had used an alphabet for centuries before the arrival of the Saxons. But what do these improvised letter-names mean? Since the stupid Saxon would have used the ABC Latin order of letters and was apparently unaware that any other order existed, let us try restoring the Alap-Braut-Curi to its BLFSN Ogham order. And since we can be pretty sure that Nemninus was showing off his superior learning—probably his knowledge of Greek to tease the stupid Saxon who knew only a little monkish Latin—let us try writing out the letter-names in Greek, and see whether certain familiar combinations of words do not strike the eye.

This is a difficult puzzle, because the extra words KENC, ELAU and ESTIAUL have been inserted without explanation among the letter-names and because the vowels have been mixed. (If E is OFR, OR is probably ER.) Nevertheless the DEXI-TRAUS-KAM-PARTH sequence is striking; we evidently have hit on an Egyptian Christian formula. With Clement of Alexandria's specialized vocabulary in mind we read it as:

DEXITERAN TRAUSEI PARTHENOMETRA KAMAX

'The spear will wound the Virgin Mother as she stands at his right hand.' This neatly constructed pentameter is a reminiscence of St. Luke's Gospel (II, 35). Kamax is both a spear and a vine-prop, and therefore a most appropriate word. The weapon mentioned by Luke is a sword; but the fulfilment of the prophecy, for Christian mystics, came with the spear that pierced the side of Jesus at the Crucifixion. And as I read the eight-lettered Holy Name sequence at the end, the Lintels of Heaven (OPHREA OURANEIA) are invited to raise a shout (IACHESTHAI) of 'Shiloh' (JEIL) since the love-fish (EROS ALABES) has neared (EGGIKEN) the land of On (AUNAN). Aunan, or On, known to the Greeks as Heliopolis and probably the oldest city in Egypt, was the centre of the Osiris cult and probably also of the Christ-as-Osiris cult. At 'Aun', according to Coptic tradition, the Virgin Mary washed the Infant Jesus's swaddling clouts in the spring Ain-esh-Shems, formerly sacred to the Sun-god Ra. From the drops that dripped from the strings, up sprang the sacred Balsam-tree. It is probable that this legend was originally told of the Goddess Isis and the Infant Horus. Gwion is, I think, referring to it in the line: 'I have been the strings of a child's swaddling clout' in the Câd Goddeu and in 'Whence is the sweetness of the balm?' in the Angar Cyvyndawd. The Alabes was worshipped at Aun, and was a Nilotic cat-fish.

But this is a digression, and I will leave whatever Greek scholar may be interested to work out the rest of the charm, without troubling him with my own approximate solution.

Of the various objectives proposed in Chapter Eight one has not yet been attained: it still remains to find out the meaning of the letter-names of the Beth-Luis-Nion. We may assume them originally to have stood for something else than trees, for the Irish tree-names, with the exception of Duir and Saille, are not formed from roots common to the Greek, Latin and Slavonic languages, as one might have expected.

The meaning of the vowels in the Boibel-Loth proved to be a sequence of stages in the life of the Spirit of the Year, incarnate in the sacred king, and the trees named in the vowels of the *Beth-Luis-Nion* similarly proved to form a seasonal sequence. Is it possible that the separation of the vowels from the consonants was a late development and that originally they were distributed among the consonants at regular intervals, as they are in the Greek and Latin alphabets? That A, the birth letter, rather than B, the letter of inception, really began the alphabet; and that the form 'Ailm-Beth' was even earlier than 'Beth-Luis-Nion'? Since Irish legends about the alphabet particularize Greece as the place where it was invented and there is an obstinate countryside tradition in Ireland that the Tuatha dé Danaan spoke Greek, why not put the Beth-Luis-Nion into ancient Greek and distribute the vowels in their seasonal order among the consonants, placing A at the winter solstice, O at the spring equinox, U at the summer solstice, E at the autumn equinox, I at the winter solstice again; and placing Straif at the beginning and Quert at the end of the summer flight of letters? Would they spell out another religious charm?

Thus:

Ailm, Beth, Luis, Nion, *Onn*, Fearn, Saille, Straif, Huath, *Ura*, Duir, Tinn, Coll, Quert, *Eadha*, Muin, Gort, Ngetal, Ruis, *Idho*.

Ailm Beth does not make a hopeful start until one recalls that *Ailm* (silver fir) is pronounced *Alv* or *Alph* in Irish. The root *alph* expresses both whiteness and produce: thus *alphos* is dull white leprosy (*albula* in Latin) and *alphe* is 'gain' and *alphiton* is pearl barley and *Alphito* is the White Grain-goddess or Pig-Demeter, *alias* Cerdo (which also means 'gain'), whose connexion with Cerridwen the Welsh Pig-Demeter, *alias* the Old White One, has already been pointed out. The principal river in the Peloponnese is the Alpheus. *Beth* or *Beith* is the birch month and since the birch is *betulus* in Latin, we may transliterate it into Greek and write *Baitulus*. At once the words begin to make sense as an invocation. Alphito-Baitule, a compound word like Alphito-mantis ('one who divines from pearl barley') suggests a goddess of the same sort as ASHIMA BAETYL and ANATHA BAETYL, the two Goddess-wives of the Hebrew Jehovah in his fifth-century B.C. cult at Elephantine in Egypt. The meaning of Baitulos is a sacred stone in which a deity is resident; it seems to be connected with the Semitic *Bethel* ('House of God') but whether *Baitulos* is derived from *Bethel* or vice versa is not known. The Lion-goddess Anatha Baetyl was not originally Semitic, and was worshipped as Anaitis in Armenia.

Luis, the next Beth-Luis-Nion letter, suggests *Lusios*, a divine title of many Greek deities, meaning 'One who washes away guilt'. It is particularly applied to Dionysus, the Latin equivalent being *Liber*. But Dionysus in the *Orphic Hymns* is also called Luseios and Luseus, which suggests that the adjective is formed not directly from *louein*, 'to wash', but from the city Lusi in Arcadia famous for its connexion with Dionysus. Lusi is overshadowed by the enormous mountain Aroania, now Mount Chelmos, and lies close to the valleys of the Aroanius River, which flows into the Alpheus, and of the Styx which flows into the Crathis. The Styx ('hateful') was the death-river by which the Gods were said to swear, and which Demeter, the Barley Mother, cursed when Poseidon pursued her with his unwelcome attentions, presumably during the Achaean conquest of the Crathis valley.

ALPHITO-BAITULE LUSIA

'White Barley Goddess, Deliveress from guilt'

Here is Pausanias's account of Lusi and its neighbourhood:

> As you go westward from Pheneus, the road to the left leads to the city of Clitor beside the channel which Hercules made for the river Aroanius. . . . The city is on the river Clitor which falls into the Aroanius not more than seven furlongs away. Among the fish in the Aroanius are the spotted ones which are said to sing like thrushes. I saw some that had been caught but they did not utter a sound, though I stayed by the river till sunset when they are supposed to sing their best. The most famous shrines at Clitor are those of the Barley Mother, Aesculapius and the Goddess Ilithyia whom Olen the ancient Lycian poet, in a hymn which he composed for the Delians, calls 'the deft spinner' and so clearly identifies with the Fate Goddess.
>
> The road to the right leads to Nonacris and the waters of the Styx. Nonacris ['nine heights'] was once an Arcadian city, named after the wife of Lycaon.

Lycaon the Pelasgian, son of the Bear-goddess Callisto, practised cannibalism and must have been an oak-god, since he was killed by a flash of lightning. His clan used the wolf-totem and Lycaon as wolf-king (or werewolf) reigned until the ninth year. The choice of King was settled at a cannibalistic feast. His wife Nonacris was clearly the Ninefold Goddess, and he is described as the first man to civilize Arcadia.

> Not far from the ruins of Nonacris is the highest cliff I have ever seen or heard of, and the water that trickles down from it is called the Water of Styx. . . . Homer puts a mention of the Styx into the mouth of Hera:

Witness me now, Earth and broad Heaven above
And the down-trickling Stygian stream!

This reads as if Homer had visited the place. Again he makes the Goddess Athene say:

> *Had I but known this in my wary mind*
> *When Zeus sent Hercules below to Hades*
> *To bring up Cerberus from his loathed home,*
> *Never would he have cheated Styx's water*
> *Tumbling from high.*

The water which, tumbling from this cliff at Nonacris falls first on a high rock and afterwards into the river Crathis, is deadly to man and to every other living creature. . . . It is remarkable too that a horse's hoof alone is proof against its poison, for it will hold the water without being broken by it . . . as cups of glass, crystal, stone, earthenware, horn and bone are. The water also corrodes iron, bronze, lead, tin, silver, electrum and even gold, despite Sappho's assurance that gold never corrodes. Whether or not Alexander the Great really died of the poison of this water I do not know: but the story is certainly current.

Above Nonacris are the Aroanian mountains and in them is a cave to which the Daughters of Proetus are said to have run when madness overtook them. But Melampus by secret sacrifices and purificatory rites brought them down to Lusi, a town near Clitor, of which not a vestige now remains. There he healed them of their madness in a sanctuary of the Goddess Artemis, whom the people of Clitor have ever since called 'the Soother'.

Melampus means 'black foot' and he was the son of Amythaon and the nymph Melanippe ('black mare'). The story of how he purged the daughters of Proetus with black hellebore and pig-sacrifices, and afterwards washed away their madness in a stream, probably refers to the capture of this Danaan shrine by the Achaeans, though Melampus is reckoned as an Aeolian Minyan. He also conquered Argos, the centre of the Danaan cult. The three daughters were the Triple Goddess, the Demeter of the Styx, who must have been mare-headed, else a horse's hoof would not have been proof against the poison of the water. But according to Philo of Heraclea and Aelian, the horn of a Scythian ass-unicorn was also proof against the poison; and Plutarch in his *Life of Alexander* says that an ass's hoof makes the only safe vessel. Near by, at Stymphalus, was a triple sanctuary founded by Temenus ('precinct') the Pelasgian, in honour of the Goddess Hera as 'girl, bride and widow', a remarkable survival of the original triad. She was called 'widow', the Stymphalians told Pausanias, because she quarrelled with Zeus and retired to Stymphalus; this probably refers to a later revival of the primitive cult in defiance of Olympianism.

Sir James Frazer visited Lusi in 1895, and he has given a valuable account of it which allows us to read Nonacris as a name for the succession of nine precipices of Mount Aroania which overhang the gorge of the Styx. Even in the late summer there was still snow in the clefts of what he described as the most 'awful line of precipices' he had ever seen. The Styx is formed by the melting snow and seems to run black down the cliff-side because of the dark incrustation of the rock behind, but afterwards bright blue because of the slatey rocks over which it flows in the gorge. The whole line of precipices is vertically streaked with red and black—both death colours in ancient Greece—and Frazer accounts for Hesiod's description of the 'silver pillars' of the Styx by observing that in winter immense icicles overhang the gorge. He records that a chemical analysis of Styx water shows it to contain no poisonous substance, though it is extremely cold.

The next letter of the Beth-Luis-Nion being *Nion* we can continue the dactylic invocation:

ALPHITO-BAITULE LUSIA NONACRIS
'White Barley Goddess, Deliveress from guilt, Lady of
the Nine Heights'

Frazer found that the belief in the singing spotted fish still survived at Lusi—they recall the spotted poetic fish of Connla's Well[1]—and so did the tradition of the snakes that Demeter set to guard the Styx water. He visited the cave of the Daughters of Proetus which overlooks the chasm of the Styx, and found that it had a natural door and window formed by the action of water.

The next letter is *Onn*. A and O being so easily confused in all languages, we can continue with:

ANNA

on the strength of the Pelasgian Goddess Anna, sister of Belus, whom the Italians called Anna Perenna or 'Perennial Anna'. Ovid in his *Fasti* says that this Anna was regarded by some as the Moon-goddess Minerva, by others as Themis, or Io of Argos. He also connects her with barley cakes. Her festival fell on March 15th, which is just where *Onn* occurs in the Beth-Luis-Nion calendar. Anna probably means 'queen', or 'Goddess-

---

[1] Pausanias had evidently come at the wrong time of year: for in the mayfly season trout do utter a sort of dry squeak, when they throw themselves ecstatically out of the water and feel the air on their gills. The Irish legend of 'singing trout' apparently refers to an erotic Spring dance, in the White Goddess's honour, of fish nymphs who mimicked the leaping, squeaking trout: for the Irish princess Dechtire conceived her son Cuchulain, a reincarnation of the God Lugh, as the result of swallowing a mayfly, and he was able to swim like a trout as soon as born. Cuchulain's Greek counterpart was Euphemus ('well-spoken') the famous swimmer, son of the Moon-Goddess Europë, who was born by the Cephissus river in Phocis but had a hero-shrine at Taenarus, the main Peloponnesian entrance to the Underworld. Euphemus's way of swimming was to leap out of the water like a fish and skim from wave to wave; and in Classical times Poseidon, God of Fishes, claimed to be his father.

mother'; Sappho uses *Ana* for *Anassa* (queen). She appears in Irish mythology as the Danaan goddess Ana or Anan, who had two different characters. The first was the beneficent Ana, a title of the Goddess Danu, mentioned in Cormac's *Glossary* as equivalent to Buan-ann (glossed as 'Good Mother'). She was the mother of the original three Danaan gods Brian, Iuchurba and Iuchar, and she suckled and nursed them so well that her name 'Ana' came to signify 'plenty'; she was worshipped in Munster as a Goddess of Plenty. Two mountains in Kerry, 'the Paps of Anu', are named after her. She has also been identified by E. M. Hull with Aine of Knockaine, a Munster Moon-goddess who had charge of crops and cattle and is connected in legend with the meadow-sweet to which she gave its scent, and with the midsummer fire-festival. The maleficent Ana was the leading person of the Fate Trinity, Ana, Badb and Macha, together known as the Morrigan, or Great Queen. Badb, 'boiling', evidently refers to the Cauldron, and Macha is glossed in the *Book of Lecan* as meaning 'raven'.

Ana occurs in British folklore as Black Annis of Leicester who had a bower in the Dane (Danaan?) Hills and used to devour children, whose skins she hung on an oak to dry. She was known as 'Cat Anna' but, according to E. M. Hull, Annis is a shortened form of Angness or Agnes, which would identify her with Yngona, 'Anna of the Angles', a well-known Danish goddess. Black Annis was concerned with a May-Eve hare-hunt, later transferred to Easter Monday, and must therefore have been nymph as well as hag. Yngona, certainly, was both Nanna (sharing her favours between Balder and his dark rival Holder) and Angurboda, the Hag of the Iron Wood, mother of Hel. But the chances are that the Hag had been in residence near Leicester long before the Danes occupied her part of Mercia, and that she was the Danaan Goddess Anu before she was Agnes. In Christian times she became a nun and there is a picture of her wearing nun's habit in the vestry of the Swithland Church. She is the Blue Hag celebrated in Milton's *Paradise Lost* and *Comus* as sucking children's blood by night disguised as a scritch-owl. The Irish Hag of Beare also became a nun; it was easy to Christianize a Death-goddess because her face was already veiled. In Chapter Three I mentioned that Beli was reckoned as the son of Danu; and the identity of Ana and Danu is made quite clearly in a pedigree in Jesus College Manuscript 20, supposed to be of the thirteenth century, where Beli the Great is a son of Anna, absurdly said to be a daughter of the Emperor of Rome. Elsewhere, the pedigree of Prince Owen, son of Howel the Good, is traced back to *Aballac filius Amalechi qui fuit Beli Magni filius, et Anna mater ejus.*[1]

---

[1] This is queer. If it stands for Abimelech son of Amalek the son of Baal, and of Anatha, it commemorates a tradition that the family were formerly lords of Canaanite Shechem. When the Israelite tribe of Ephraim settled in Shechem, a city which the *Song of Deborah* shows to have originally belonged to the tribe of Amalek, a treaty marriage was celebrated between the

It is added, as absurdly, *quam dicunt esse consobrinam Mariae Virginis, Matris Domini nostri Jhesu Christi.*

Ovid and Virgil knew their Goddess Anna Perenna to have been a sister of Belus, or Bel, who was a masculinization of the Sumerian Goddess Belili; so also the god Anu, of the Babylonian male trinity completed by Ea and Bel, was a masculinization of the Sumerian Goddess Anna-Nin, usually abbreviated to Nana.[1] Bel's wife was Belit, and Anu's wife was Anatu. Ea's wife, the third member of the Sumerian female trinity, was Dam-Kina; the first syllable of whose name shows her to have mothered the Danaans. Anna-Nin has further been identified by J. Przbuski in the *Revue de l'Histoire des Religions* (1933) with Ana-hita the Goddess of the Avesta, whom the Greeks called Anaitis and the Persians Ana-hid—the name that they gave to the planet Venus.

Mr. E. M. Parr writes to me that *An* is Sumerian for 'Heaven' and that in his view the Goddess Athene was another Anna, namely Ath-enna, an inversion of Anatha, *alias* Neith of Libya; also that *Ma* is a shortening of the Sumerian *Ama,* 'mother', and that Ma-ri means 'the fruitful mother' from *rim,* 'to bear a child'. Mari was the name of the goddess on whose account the Egyptians of 1000 B.C. called Cyprus 'Ay-mari', and who ruled at Mari on the Euphrates (a city sacked by Hammurabi in 1800 B.C.) and at Amari in Minoan Crete. So *Ma-ri-enna* is 'the fruitful mother of Heaven', *alias* Miriam, Marian of Mariandyne, the 'leaping Myrrhine' of Troy, and Mariamne: a word of triple power. But the basic word is *Anna,* which confers divinity on mere parturition and which also seems to form part of Arianrhod's name. *Arianrhod* in fact may not be a debasement of *Argentum* and *rota* 'silver, wheel' but *Ar-ri-an,* 'High fruitful mother' who turns the wheel of heaven; if so, Arianrhod's Cretan counterpart Ariadne would be Ar-ri-an-de, the *de* meaning barley, as in Demeter. The simple form Ana, or Anah, occurs as a Horite clan name in *Genesis, XXXVI*; though

Ephraimite Chieftain Gideon, who thereupon took the name Jerubbaal ('Let Baal strive'), and the local heiress, presumably a priestess of the Lion-Goddess Anatha. Her son succeeded to the throne by mother-right after a massacre of his rivals and took the Canaanite title of Abimelech; establishing his position with the help of his mother's kinsmen and the god Baal-berith.

[1] At the beginning of Chapter Eleven I described Attis son of Nana as the Phrygian Adonis; and at the beginning of Chapter Eighteen mentioned that Nana conceived him virginally as the result of swallowing either a ripe almond or else a pomegranate seed. The mythological distinction is important. The pomegranate was sacred to Attis as Adonis—Tammuz—Dionysus—Rimmon, and at Jerusalem, as has been shown, the pomegranate cult was assimilated to that of Jehovah. But the almond was also, it seems, sacred to Attis as Nabu—Mercury—Hermes—Thoth, whose cult was also assimilated to that of Jehovah; which explains the myth recorded by Euhemerus, the Sicilian sceptic, that Hermes so far from ordaining the courses of the stars was merely instructed in astronomy by Aphrodite—that is to say by his mother Nana who gave her name to the planet Venus. Thus Nana, as mother of Jehovah in two of his characters can be claimed as the paternal, as well as the maternal, grandmother of Jehovah's Only Begotten Son.

masculinized in two out of the three mentions of her, she is principally celebrated as the mother of Aholibamah ('tabernacle of the high place'), the heiress whom Esau married on his arrival in the Seir pastures. (Ana's alleged discovery of mules in the wilderness is due to a scribal error.) James Joyce playfully celebrates Anna's universality in his *Anna Livia Plurabelle*. And indeed if one needs a single, simple, inclusive name for the Great Goddess, Anna is the best choice. To Christian mystics she is 'God's Grandmother'.

The next letter, *Fearn*, explains Perenna as a corruption of *Fearina*, the adjective formed from *Feär* or *eär*, Spring. In Latin the word has kept its Digamma and is written *ver*. From this it follows that Bran's Greek name Phoroneus—of which we have already noted the variant forms Vront Berng and Ephron—was a variation of *Fearineus* and that he was originally the Spirit of the Year in his lusty, though foredoomed, Spring aspect. The Latin form seems to have been Veranus, which would accoun, for the plebeian family name Veranius; and for the verb *vernare*, 'to renew oneself in Spring', which is supposed to be irregularly formed from *ver*, *veris*, but may be an abbreviation of *veranare*.

ANNA FEARINA
'Queen of the Spring'

The next letter is *Saille*. We have seen that Saille is connected in the Boibel-Loth with Salmoneus, Salmaah and Salmon, and this suggests that the corresponding word in the charm is Salmone, another title of the Goddess. So:

SALMAONĀ

There were several places named after her in the Eastern Mediterranean including Cape Salmone in Crete, the city of Salmone in Elis, and Salmone, a village near Lusi. The title is apparently compounded of *Salma* and *Onë* as in Hesi-onë. Hesionë is said to mean 'Lady of Asia', and the meaning of Salma can be deduced from its occurrence in geographical names. It is an Aegean word of extraordinarily wide distribution and seems always to be connected with the notion of easterliness.[1] Salma was a tribe in Southern Judaea living east of the Minoan colony of Gaza; also a

[1] The complementary Aegean word to *Salma* seems to have been *Tar*, meaning the west, or the dying sun. Tartessus on the Atlantic was the most westerly Aegean trading station, as Salmydessus the most easterly. Tarraco was the port on the extreme west of the Mediterranean, and Tarrha the chief port of western Crete. The reduplication tar-tar, meaning 'the far, far west', has evidently given Tartara, the land of the dead, its name. For though Homer in the *Iliad* places Tártara 'as far below earth as Heaven is above it', Hesiod makes it the abode of Cronos and the Titans, whom we know to have gone west after their defeat by Zeus. Taranis was a Gaulish deity mentioned by Lucan as being served by even more terrible rites than was Scythian Diana, meaning the Taurian Artemis, who loved human sacrifice. Though the Romans identified Taranis with Jupiter he was at first probably a Death-Goddess, namely Tar-Anis, Annis of the West.

372

station in Central Arabia on the caravan route from the Mediterranean to the Persian Gulf. Salmalassus was a station in Lesser Armenia on the caravan route from Trebizond to the Far East; Salmydessus was the most easterly city of Thrace, fronting the Black Sea; Salmone was the most easterly cape of Crete; Salamis the most easterly city of Cyprus; the island of Salamis lay east of the Cretan city of Corinth, and the mountain sacred to Salamanes (in Assyrian Salmanu) lay east of the great river-plain behind Antioch. As has already been pointed out Salma became a divine name in Palestine and Solomon, Salmon and Absalom are all variants of it. Salma was the deity to whom the hill of Jerusalem was originally sacred; the place is mentioned in the Egyptian Tell Amarna letters (1370 B.C.) as Uru-Salim, and in Assyrian monuments as Ur-Salimu. In 1400 B.C. it was held by a chieftain with the Semite name of Abd-Khiba, a vassal of Egypt, who like Melchizedek of Salem—Uru-Salim?—claimed to rule neither by father-right nor mother-right, but by the will of the God. Professor Sayce translates Uru-Salim as 'City of the God Salim'. Josephus records that the first name of the city was Solyma. Salma, or Salim, was evidently the Semite god of the rising or renewed sun; Salmaone was the Aegean goddess from whom he took his titles, as did Salmoneus the Aeolian who opposed the later Achaean invaders and insisted on inducing thunder by rattling a brazen chariot—thereby infringing the prerogative of Olympian Zeus. But it is probable that Salma took his title as the demi-god of the renewed Sun from his Moon-bride Circe, or Belili, the Willow Mother, Sal-Ma, in whose honour willow-branches were waved at this season, and that the meaning of easterliness is a secondary one.

ANNA FEARINA SALMAONĀ
'Queen of Spring, Mother of the Willow'

Straif is the next letter. A main verb is called for, to begin the second flight of letters. *Strebloein*, or *strabloein*, formed from the verbal root *streph*, 'to twist', means 'to reeve with a windlass, to wrench, dislocate, put on the rack', and gives *Straif*, the blackthorn, its necessarily cruel connotation.

Next comes *Huath*. The *u* merely shows that the H is aspirated. We have no clue to the name of the person, or persons, whom the Goddess racks, presumably on *Duir*, the oak, but my guess is the Athaneatids, or Hathaneatids, members of one of the four original royal clans of Arcadia. It is likely that this word, like *athanatoi*, means 'the not-mortal ones', the Greek word *thnētos* ('mortal') being a shortened form of *thaneātos*. The clan from which the sacred king, the victim of the story that is unfolding, was chosen would naturally be called 'The Immortals', because the king alone could win immortality by his sufferings, the lesser members of the nation being doomed to become twittering ghosts in Hell.

For *Ura* is the next letter of the alphabet, the midsummer letter, the letter of Venus Urania, the most violent aspect of the Triple Goddess. As has already been pointed out, Ura means Summer; it also means the tail of a lion or bear, expressive of its fury, and the word *ouraios* ('uraeus'), the royal serpent of Egypt, is formed from the same root. 'Uranus', the father of the Titans according to Greek Classical mythology, is likely to have originally been their Mother—Ura-ana, Queen Ura. But we should not look for only one or even two meanings of the syllable *ur*; the more numerous the poetic meanings that could be concentrated in a sacred name, the greater was its power. The authors of the Irish *Hearings of the Scholars* connected the midsummer-letter *Ur* with *ur*, 'earth'; and we are reminded that this is the root found in the Latin words *area*, 'a plot of earth', *arvum*, 'a ploughed field', and *urvare*, which means 'to drive a plough ceremonially around the proposed site of a city'—a sense also found in the Homeric Greek *ouron*, 'a boundary marked by the plough'. Grammarians assume a primitive Greek word *ĕra*, 'earth' connected with this group of words; which suggests that Erana, or Arana, or Urana, was the Earth-goddess whose favour had to be asked when fields were ploughed or cities (*urves* or *urbes*) founded, and marriage with whose local representative gave a chieftain the right to rule in her lands. If this is so, the *uraeus* in the royal head-dress stood both for the great sea-serpent that girdled the Earth and for the Goddess's spotted oracular snakes. But her name could also carry three or four further meanings. It might stand for 'Mountain-goddess' (from the Homeric Greek *ouros*, a mountain) which would point her identity with *Mousa*, the Muse, a title of the same meaning; and for 'Queen of the Winds' (from the Homeric Greek *ouros*, a wind) which would explain the *uraeus* as symbolizing her power over the winds, all winds being snake-tailed and housed in a mountain-cave. Urana then is a multiple title: Mother Earth, Our Lady of Summer, Mountain Goddess, Queen of the Winds, Goddess of the Lion's Tail. It might equally mean 'Guardian Queen' (*ouros*, 'a guardian'); or, with reference to her aspect as a Moon-cow, 'Ruler of Wild Oxen' (*ourus*, Latin *urus*, 'a wild ox'), like the Irish Goddess Buana. And we must not overlook the Sanscrit word *varunas*, meaning 'the night firmament', from the root *var*, 'to cover', from which Varuna, the third member of the Aryan Trinity, took his name. When the first wave of Achaeans entered Greece and were forced under the sovereignty of the Triple-goddess Ana, or De-Ana, or Ath-Ana, or Di-Ana, or Ur-Ana, who ruled the world of day as well as the world of night, *varunas* lost its specialized sense, was changed from *varun-* to *uran-*, in her honour, and came to mean the sky in general. Hence Ana's classical title Urania, 'The Heavenly One'.

'Ura, reeve the Immortal ones to your oak tree'

The next word *Tinne*, or *Tann*, can be expanded to *Tanaous* 'stretched', in memory of Hesiod's derivation of the word *Titan* from *titainein*, 'to stretch'. He says that the Titans were so called because they stretched out their hands: but this explanation is perhaps intended to disguise the truth, that the Titans were men stretched, or racked, on the wheel, like Ixion. Frazer noted that the holly-oak, which is the tree of Tinne, grows nobly at Lusi, and that the valley of the Styx is full of the white poplar, *Eadha*, the tree sacred to Hercules.

The letter Coll completes the second flight of the alphabet. *Kolabreusthai* or *kolabrizein* is to dance a wild taunting Thracian dance, the *kolabros*, the sort that the Goddess Kali dances on the skulls of her foes:

DRUEI TANAOUS KOLABREUSOMENĀ
'Stretched out, ready to taunt them in your wild dance'

The dance was evidently concerned with pigs, since *kolabros* also meant a young pig. In ancient Irish poetry the skulls of men freshly killed were called 'the mast of the Morrigan', that is to say of the Fate Goddess Anna in the guise of a sow. As will be noted, a young pig figures in the dance of the nine moon-women in the Old Stone Age cave-painting at Cogul.

The next words are *Quert*, also spelt *Kirt*, *Eadha*, and *Muin*. My guess is:

KIRKOTOKOUS ATHROIZE TE MANI
'And gather the Children of Circe together to the Moon'

Circe, 'daughter of Hecate' was the Goddess of Aeaea ('wailing'), a sepulchral island in the Northern Adriatic. Her name means 'she-falcon', the falcon being a bird of omen, and is also connected with *circos*, a circle, from the circling of falcons and from the use of the magic circle in enchantment; the word is onomatopoeic, the cry of the falcon being 'circ—circ'. She was said to turn men into swine, lions and wolves, and the Children of Circe are probably women dressed as sows participating in a full-moon festival held in her honour and in that of Dionysus. Herodotus describes this ritual as common to Greek and Egyptian practice. At the Persian orgies of Mithras, which had a common origin with those of Demeter and in which a bull was sacrificed and eaten raw, the men celebrants were called *Leontes* (lions) and the women celebrants *Hyaenae* (sows). Possibly Lion-men also took part in this *kolabros* as Children of Circe.

The last letters are *Gort—Ngetal—Ruis—Idho*. Here we are on very insecure ground. The only clue to *Idho* is that the Hebrew form of the word is *iod*, and the Cadmean is *iota*; and that the one Greek word beginning with *gort* is Gortys, the name of the reputed founder of Gortys, a city in Southern Arcadia, which stands on a tributary of the Alpheus, the *Gortynios* (otherwise called the Lusios). Gortyna, the name of a famous town in Crete, may be the word needed, and represent some title of the Goddess. But perhaps the abbreviation *Gort* should be *Gorp*. Gorgōpa, 'fearful-faced', an epithet of the Death Goddess Athene, makes good sense. To preserve the metre the word must be spelt *Grogopa*, as *kirkos* is often spelt *krikos*.

GROGŌPA GNATHŎĬ RUSĒIS IOTĀ
'As the fearful-faced Goddess of Destiny you will make a snarling
noise with your chops'

Iotes (Aeolic *Iotās*) is a Homeric word meaning Divine Will or Behest; it may have supplied this personification of the Goddess of Destiny, like *Anagke* (Necessity) the first syllable of which is probably *Ana* or *Anan*, and like *Themis* (Law), both of which are likewise feminine in gender. Euripides calls Anagke the most powerful of all deities, and it was from Themis that Zeus derived his juridical authority: according to Homer, Themis was the mother of the Fates and convened the assemblies of the Olympians. Ovid's identification of her with Anna has just been mentioned.

So:

ALPHITŎ BAITŬLĔ LUSIĀ NONACRIS ANNĂ FEARINĂ SALMĂŎNĀ

STRABLŎĔ HATHĂNĔATIDĀS URĀ DRŬEI TĂNĂOUS KŎLĂBREUSŎMĔNĀ

KIRKŎTŎKOUS ĂTHRŎIZĔ TĔ MANĬ GRŌGŎPĂ GNATHŎĬ RUSĔIS IOTĂ

'White Barley Goddess, Deliveress from guilt, Lady of the Nine Heights, Queen of Spring, Mother of the Willow,

'Ura, reeve the Immortal Ones stretched out to your oak, taunt them in your wild dance,

'And gather the Children of Circe under the Moon; as the fearful-faced Goddess of Destiny you will make a snarling noise with your chops.'

Perhaps the Goddess appeared as the Triple-headed Bitch, Hecuba or Hecate, on this occasion, for *ruẓein* was used mostly of dogs; but since Cerridwen is usually in at the death of the Sun-hero, perhaps the noise intended was the whining grunt of the corpse-eating Old Sow of Maenawr Penardd, to whom 'skulls are mast'.

No Greek verse has survived of an early enough date to act as a check on the metre and verbal forms of this hypothetic song. But at least it built itself up logically against most of my original expectations of how it would turn out, so that I cannot regard it as of my own composition. The supersession of dactylic words (– ⌣) by anapaestic (⌣ ⌣ –) and iambic (⌣ –) in the second half of the song happened naturally without my noticing its significance. The dactylic and trochaic feet in Greece originally expressed praise and blessing; but the anapaestic and iambic were originally confined to satires and curses; as the spondaic (– –) foot was to funerary chants.[1] (The use of the iambic was extended to tragedy because this was concerned with the working out of a divine curse; and to comedy because it was satiric in intention.) This song suggests a dance by twelve persons around a circle of twelve standing stones—there are twelve beats in each half of it—with each alternate beat marked by a dancer striking the stone nearest him with the flat of his hand or perhaps a pig's bladder. In the middle of the circle the sacred king is corded to the lopped oak-tree in the five-fold bond of willow thongs, waiting for his bloody end.

According to some mythographers there were twelve Titans, male and female; and this canonical number was preserved in the number of the Olympian gods and goddesses who superseded them. Herodotus records that the Pelasgians did not worship gods and consented to the Olympian system only at the express command of the Dodona oracle—I suppose when the oracle, once the mouthpiece of the Pelopian woodland goddess

---

[1] The Anglo-Saxon grounding of English prevents the use of the Classical dactyl as the basic metrical foot. The dactylic or anapeestic poems attempted in the early and middle nineteenth century by Byron, Moore, Hood, Browning and others read over-exuberantly and even vulgarly; though school children enjoy them. What has gradually evolved as the characteristic English metre is a compromise between the iambic—borrowed from French and Italian, ultimately from the Greek—and the stress rhythm of Anglo-Saxon, based on the pull of the oar. Shakespeare's gradual modification of the ten-foot iambic line that he took over from Wyatt and the Earl of Surrey is illuminating:
The first lines of *King John* run:

> KING JOHN: *Now say, Chatillon, what would France with us?*
> CHATILLON: *Thus, after greeting, speaks the King of France,*
> *In my behaviour, to the majesty,*
> *The borrowed majesty of England here. . . .*

Fifteen years later, in the *Tempest*, after the opening scene which s almost wholly prose Miranda addresses Prospero:

> *If by your art, my dearest father, you have*
> *Put the wild waters in this roar, allay them!*
> *The sky, it seems, would pour down stinking pitch*
> *But that the sea, mounting to the welkin's cheek*
> *Dashes the fire out. O, I have suffered. . . .*

It has been suggested that Shakespeare was consciously working forward to a rhythmic prose. This seems to me a misreading of his intentions: after disruptive variations on the iambic ten-syllabled norm he always returned to it as a reminder that he was still writing verse; and could never have done otherwise. Here, for example, Miranda, after this first outburst of horror, finishes her speech with metrical sobriety.

Dionë, had been captured by the Achaeans. He is likely to be right: they worshipped only a Goddess and her semi-divine son of the king. In Arcadia, he seems to have worn antlers. A late Minoan gem in my possession—a banded white carnelian pendant—shows a roebuck crouched beside a wood, in the attitude heraldically called *regardant*. The ten tines of his antlers refer perhaps to the tenth month, M, the month of the vintage moon; a new moon rides above him. That these Titans figure in Greek myth as children of Uranus may mean no more than that they were companions to the Sacred King, who took his title from the Uranian Goddess. The other Titans, who number seven, rule the sacred Week.

If, as it has been suggested, Pythagoras was initiated into this alphabetic mystery by the Dactyls, it is possible that he derived from them his theory of the mystical connotations of number; and the possibility turns to probability when the initial letters of the charm are numbered from one to twenty:

A —	1	D —	11
B —	2	T —	12
L —	3	C —	13
N —	4	Q —	14
O —	5	E —	15
F —	6	M —	16
S —	7	G —	17
Z —	8	Gn —	18
H —	9	R —	19
U —	10	I —	20

In this table an even closer approximation to poetic truth is discovered than in the Irish bardic system of letter-numerals, given at the end of Chapter Sixteen, which is based on a different alphabetic order and denies any value either to H or U. Here, the dominant pentad of vowels hold the first and last places, as one would expect, also the fifth, the tenth (respectively 'the grove of the senses' and 'perfection' in the Pythagorean system), and the ecstatic fifteenth, the full-moon climax of the *Song of Ascents* at Jerusalem. The second, fourth, sixth and eighth places—even numbers are male in the Pythagorean system, odd are female—are held by B (inception), N (flood), F (fire), Z (angry passion), a sequence suggesting a rising tide of male lust which, after being checked by H, nine, the letter of pre-marital chastity enforced by the Nine-fold Goddess, finds its consummation at U, 10, where male and female principles unite. The intermediate letters are L, 3, the letter of torch-lit regeneration presided over by three-torched Hecate; O, 5, the letter of initiation into the mysteries of love; S, 7, the letter of female enchantment ('Athene' in the Pythagorean system). The eleventh and twelfth places are held respectively by D and T, the twin leaders of the company of twelve (in the Irish system the order is reversed); the thirteenth by C, the letter of the Goddess's sacrosanct swineherd magicians; and the nineteenth by R, the Death letter, appropriate to the close of the nineteen-year cycle. The numerical values of the remaining letters work out with equal facility. Since the charm taught by the Dactyls was an orgiastic one it appropriately contained twenty elements—as it were the fingers of the woman's hands and those of her lover's; but Pythagoras was content to speculate on the tetractys of his own ten fingers alone.

To sum up. This twenty-word Greek charm provided the letter-names of an alphabet which was used in late Minoan Arcadia until the second Achaean invasion, by descendants of the original invaders who had gone over to the worship of the White Goddess. Their cult involved the use of an artificial thirteen-month solar calendar, each month represented by a different tree, which had been invented independently of the alphabet and was in widespread use. Some of its seasonable elements can be shown to date from pre-dynastic times, and though the trees in the Irish version, the only one that survives complete, suggest a Pontine or Paphlagonian origin the calendar may have originated in the Aegean or Phoenicia or Libya with a somewhat different canon of trees. Nor is it likely that the alphabet arrived in Britain at the same time as the calendar. The calendar may have been introduced in the late third millennium B.C. by the New Stone Age people, who were in close touch with Aegean civilization, along with agriculture, apiculture, the maze-dance and other cultural benefits. The alphabet seems to have been introduced late in the second millennium B.C. by refugees from Greece.

Since there were always twelve stones in the *gilgal,* or stone-circle, used for sacrificial purposes, the next jaunt is to chase the White Roebuck speculatively around the twelve houses of the Zodiac.

When and where the Zodiac originated is not known, but it is believed to have gradually evolved in Babylonia from the twelve incidents in the life-story of the hero Gilgamesh—his killing of the Bull, his love-passage with the Virgin, his adventures with two Scorpion-men (the Scales later took the place of one of these) and the Deluge story (corresponding with the Water Carrier). Calendar tablets of the seventh century B.C. bear this out, but the Epic of Gilgamesh is not a really ancient one; Gilgamesh is thought to have been a Hyksos (Kassite) invader of Babylonia in the eighteenth century B.C. to whom the story of an earlier hero was transferred, a Tammuz of the familiar sort already connected with the Zodiac.

The original Zodiac, to judge from the out-of-date astronomical data quoted in a poem by Aratus, a Hellenistic Greek, was current in the late third millennium B.C. But it is likely to have been first fixed at a time when the Sun rose in the Twins at the Spring equinox—the Shepherds' festival; in the Virgin who was generally identified with Ishtar, the Love-goddess, at the Summer solstice; in the Archer, identified with Nergal (Mars) and later with Cheiron the Centaur, at the Autumn equinox, the traditional season of the chase; in the resurrective Fish at the Winter solstice, the time of most rain. (It will be recalled that the solar hero Llew Llaw's trasnformations begin with a Fish at the Winter solstice.)

The Zodiac signs were borrowed by the Egyptians at least as early as the sixteenth century B.C., with certain alterations—Scarab for Crab, Serpent for Scorpion, Mirror for He-goat, etc.,—but by that time the phenomenon known as the precession of the equinoxes had already spoilt the original story. About every 2000 years the Sun rises in an earlier sign; so in 3800 B.C. the Bull began to push the Twins out of the House of the Spring equinox, and initiated a period recalled by Virgil in his account of the Birth of Man:

> *The white bull with his gilded horns*
> *Opens the year ...*

At the same time the tail of the Lion entered the Virgin's place at the Summer solstice—hence apparently the Goddess's subsequent title of 'Oura', the Lion's Tail—and gradually the Lion's body followed, after which for a time she became leonine with a Virgin's head only. Similarly the Water-carrier succeeded the Fish at the Winter solstice—and provided the water to float the Spirit of the Year's cradle ark.

About 1800 B.C. the Bull was itself pushed out of the Spring House by the Ram. This may account for the refurbishing of the Zodiac myth in honour of Gilgamesh, a shepherd king of this period; he was the Ram who destroyed the Bull. The Crab similarly succeeded the Lion at the Summer solstice; so the Love-goddess became a marine deity with temples by the sea-shore. The He-goat also succeeded the Water-carrier at the Winter solstice; so the Spirit of the New Year was born of a She-goat. The Egyptian Greeks then called the Ram the 'Golden Fleece' and recast the Zodiac story as the voyage of the Argonauts.

The disadvantage of the Zodiac is, indeed, its failure to be a perpetual calendar like the Beth-Luis-Nion tree-sequence which makes no attempt to relate the equinoxes and the solstices to the twelve constellations of the Zodiac. Perhaps the original Zodiac myth was based on the Roebuck story which is associated with a tree-sequence in the *Song of Amergin*; a supposed scientific improvement on it because a thirteen-month year with the equinox and solstice stations falling at irregular intervals is less easy to handle than a twelve-month year with exactly three months between each of the four stations. At any rate, the archtype of Gilgamesh the Zodiac hero was 'Tammuz', a tree-cult hero of many changes; and the

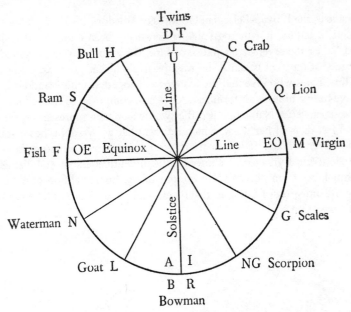

Twins
D T
U

Bull H

C Crab

Ram S

Q Lion

Line

Fish F | OE Equinox

Line EO M Virgin

Waterman N

G Scales

Solstice

Goat L A I

NG Scorpion

B R
Bowman

thirteen-month tree-calendar seems more primitive than the twelve-month one.[1] Certainly the story it tells is more coherent than those of Gilgamesh or Jason. It is pure myth uncombined with history. It so happens that the tree-alphabet, with the Twins combined in a single sign, does coincide with the Zodiac as it stands at present, with the Fishes in the House of the Spring Equinox. (See the figure above.)

But we have not yet answered the question: why are the Fates credited Hyginus with the invention of the letters F and H?

Hyginus's attribution to Palamedes of the invention of the disc is a helpful clue, if Professor O. Richter is right in suggesting that the late Cyprian female figurines which hold discs of the same proportionate size as the Phaestos disc (seven inches in diameter) anticipate Athene and her *aegis*. We know from the legend of the infant Erichthonius that the aegis was a goat-skin bag, converted into a shield by a circular stiffening. Was it a bag-cover for a sacred disc, like the crane-bag which contained the Pelasgian letters of Palamedes's Pelasgian alphabet, and with the warning Gorgon-mask similarly placed at the mouth? If so, it seems probable that the concealed disc was engraved spirally with her own Holy and Ineffable

[1] That the Osirian year originally consisted of thirteen twenty-eight day months, with one day over, is suggested by the legendary length of Osiris's reign, namely twenty-eight years—years in mythology often stand for days, and days for years—and by the number of pieces into which he was torn by Set, namely thirteen apart from his phallus which stood for the extra day. When Isis reassembled the pieces, the phallus had disappeared, eaten by a letos-fish. This accounts for the priestly fish-taboo in Egypt, relaxed only one day in the year.

Name as the Libyao-Pelasgian Goddess of Wisdom; and if this Name was spelt in letters, not hieroglyphs, it may have been either the five-letter IEUOA, or the seven-letter JIEUOAŌ, formed by doubling the first and last letters of IEUOA. Or, since she was the triple Moon-goddess, namely the Three Fates who invented the five vowels, together with F and H, it may have been a nine-letter form JIEHUOV(F)AŌ, composed to contain not only the seven-letter Name but also the two consonants, representing the first and last days of her week, which revealed her as Wisdom, hewer-out of the Seven Pillars. If it was JIEHUOVAŌ, Simonides (or more likely his predecessor Pythagoras) showed little inventiveness in stabilizing the eight-letter form JEHUOVAŌ in honour of the Immortal Sun-god Apollo, by the omission of I, the death-vowel, while retaining Y, the semi-vowel of generation.

Chapter Twenty-Two

THE TRIPLE MUSE

Why do poets invoke the Muse?

Milton in the opening lines of *Paradise Lost* briefly summarizes the Classical tradition, and states his intention, as a Christian, of transcending it:

> *Sing, heav'nly Muse, that on the secret top*
> *Of Oreb, or of Sinai, didst inspire*
> *That shepherd, who first taught the chosen seed*
> *In the beginning how the Heav'ns and Earth*
> *Rose out of Chaos: Or if Sion hill*
> *Delight thee more, and Siloa's brook that flow'd*
> *Fast by the oracle of God: I thence*
> *Invoke thy aid to my advent'rous song*
> *That with no middle flight intends to soar*
> *Above th' Aonian mount, while it pursues*
> *Things unattempted yet in prose or rhime.*

The Aonian Mount is Mount Helicon in Boeotia, a mountain a few miles to the east of Parnassus, and known in Classical times as 'the seat of the Muses'. The adjective 'Aonian' is a reminiscence of a memorable line from Virgil's *Georgics*:

> *Aonio rediens deducam vertice Musas*

which is spoken by Apollo, the God of poetry, who by Virgil's time was also recognized as the Sun-god. The line means 'On my return I shall lead the Muses down from the top of Mount Helicon'. Apollo is referring to the transplanting of the worship of the Muses from Ascra, a town on a ridge of Helicon, to Delphi, on Mount Parnassus, a place which had become sacred to himself. On Helicon rose the spring named Hippocrene, 'The Horse Well', which was horse-shoe shaped. The legend was that it had been struck by the hoof of the horse Pegasus, whose name means 'of the springs of water'. Poets were said to drink of Hippocrene for inspiration. Hence John Skelton's lines (*Against Garnesche*):

> *I gave him of the sugryd welle*
> *Of Eliconys waters crystallyne.*

But it may be supposed that Hippocrene and Aganippe were originally struck by the moon-shaped hoof of Leucippe ('White Mare'), the Mare-headed Mother herself, and that the story of how Bellerophon son of Poseidon mastered Pegasus and then destroyed the triple-shaped Chimaera is really the story of an Achaean capture of the Goddesss' shrine: Pegasus, in fact, was originally called Aganippe. *Aganos* is a Homeric adjective applied to the shafts of Artemis and Apollo, meaning 'giving a merciful death'; so Aganippe would mean: 'The Mare who destroys mercifully.' This supposition is strengthened by the Greek legend of the pursuit of Demeter, the Barley Mother, by the Achaean god Poseidon. Demeter, to escape his attentions, disguised herself as a mare and concealed herself among the horses of Oncios the Arcadian, but Poseidon became a stallion and covered her; her anger at this outrage was said to account for her statue at Onceum, called Demeter Erinnus—the Fury.

Demeter as a Mare-goddess was widely worshipped under the name of Epona, or 'the Three Eponae', among the Gallic Celts, and there is a strange account in Giraldus Cambrensis's *Topography of Ireland* which shows that relics of the same cult survived in Ireland until the twelfth century. It concerns the crowning of an Irish petty-king at Tyrconnell, a preliminary to which was his symbolic rebirth from a white mare. He crawled naked towards her on all fours as if he were her foal; she was then slaughtered, and her pieces boiled in a cauldron. He himself entered the cauldron and began sucking up the broth and eating the flesh. Afterwards he stood on an inauguration stone, was presented with a straight white wand, and turned about three times from left to right, and then three times from right to left—'in honour of the Trinity'. Originally no doubt in honour of the Triple White Goddess.

The horse, or pony, has been a sacred animal in Britain from pre-historic times, not merely since the Bronze Age introduction of the stronger Asiatic breed. The only human figure represented in what survives of British Old Stone Age art is a man wearing a horse-mask, carved in bone, found in the Derbyshire Pin-hole Cave; a remote ancestor of the hobby-horse mummers in the English 'Christmas play'. The Saxons and Danes venerated the horse as much as did their Celtic predecessors, and the taboo on eating horse-flesh survives in Britain as a strong physical repugnance, despite attempts made during World War II to popularize hippo-phagism; but among the Bronze Age British the taboo must have been lifted at an annual October horse-feast, as among the Latins. In mediaeval Denmark the ecstatic three-day horse-feast, banned by the Church, sur-vived among the heathenish serf-class; a circumstantial description is given by Johannes Jensen in his *Fall of the King*. He mentions that the priest first sprinkled bowls of the horse's blood towards the South and East—

which explains the horse as an incarnation of the Spirit of the Solar Year, son of the Mare-goddess.

In the *Romance of Pwyll, Prince of Dyfed* the Goddess appears as Rhiannon mother of Pryderi. Rhiannon is a corruption of Rigantona ('Great Queen') and Dyfed consisted of most of Carmarthen and the whole of Pembrokeshire and included St. David's; its central point was called 'The Dark Gate', an entrance to the Underworld. When Pwyll ('Prudence') first sees Rhiannon and falls in love with her, he pursues her on his fastest horse but cannot overtake her; evidently in the original story she took the form of a white mare. When at last she consents to be overtaken, and marries him twelve months later, she bears him a son afterwards called Pryderi ('Anxiety') who disappears at birth; and her maids falsely accuse her of having devoured him, smearing her face with the blood of puppies. As a penance she is ordered to stand at a horse-block outside Pwyll's palace, like a mare, ready to carry guests on her back.[1] The life of her son Pryderi is closely connected with a magical foal which has been rescued from a harpy; all the previous foals of the same mare have been snatched off on May Eve and never seen again. Pryderi, a Divine Child of the sort that is taken away from its mother—like Llew Llaw, or Zeus, or Romulus—is later, as usual, given a name and arms by her, mounts the magical horse and eventually becomes a Lord of the Dead. Rhiannon is thus seen to be a Mare-goddess, but she is also a Muse-goddess, for the sirens that appear in the *Triads,* and also in the *Romance of Branwen,* singing with wonderful sweetness are called 'The Birds of Rhiannon'. The story about the puppies recalls the Roman habit of sacrificing red puppies in the Spring to avert the baleful influence of the Dog-star on their grain; the sacrifice was really to the Barley-mother who had the Dog-star as her attendant. Rhiannon, in fact, is the Mare-Demeter, a successor of the Sow-Demeter Cerridwen. That the Mare-Demeter devoured children, like the Sow-Demeter, is proved by the myth of Leucippe ('White Mare') the Orchomenan, who with her two sisters ran wild and devoured her son Hippasus ('foal'); and by the myth recorded by Pausanias, that when Rhea gave birth to Poseidon she offered her lover Cronos a foal to eat instead of the child, whom she gave secretly into the charge of the shepherds of Arcadian Arne.

Mount Helicon was not the earliest seat of the Muse Goddesses, as their title 'The Pierians' shows; the word Muse is now generally derived from the root *mont,* meaning a mountain. Their worship had been brought there in the Heroic Age during a migration of the Boeotian people from

---

[1] This magical tradition survived in the Northern witch-cult. In 1673 Anne Armstrong the Northumbrian witch confessed at her trial to having been temporarily transformed into a mare by her mistress Ann Forster of Stockfield, who threw a bridle over her head and rode her to a meeting of five witch-covens at Riding Mill Bridge End.

Mount Pieria in Northern Thessaly. But to make the transplanted Muses feel at home on Helicon, and so to preserve the old magic, the Boeotians named the geographical features of the mountain—the springs, the peaks and grottoes—after the corresponding features of Pieria. The Muses were at this time three in number, an indivisible Trinity, as the mediaeval Catholics recognized when they built the church of their own Holy Trinity on the site of the deserted shrine of the Heliconian Muses. The appropriate names of the three Persons were Meditation, Memory and Song. The worship of the Muses on Helicon (and presumably also in Pieria) was concerned with incantatory cursing and incantatory blessing; Helicon was famous for the medicinal herbs which supplemented the incantations—especially for the nine-leaved black hellebore used by Melampus at Lusi as a cure for the Daughters of Proetus, which could either cause or cure insanity and which has a stimulative action on the heart like *digitalis* (fox-glove). It was famous also for the erotic fertility dances about a stone herm at Thespiae, a town at its foot, in which the women-votaries of the Muses took part. Spenser addresses the Muses as 'Virgins of Helicon'; he might equally have called them 'witches', for the witches of his day worshipped the same White Goddess—in *Macbeth* called Hecate—performed the same fertility dances on their Sabbaths, and were similarly gifted in incantatory magic and knowledge of herbs.

The Muse priestesses of Helicon presumably used two products of the horse to stimulate their ecstasies: the slimy vaginal issue of a mare in heat and the black membrane, or *hippomanes*, cut from the forehead of a new-born colt, which the mare (according to Aristotle) normally eats as a means of increasing her mother-love. Dido in the *Aeneid* used this *hippomanes* in her love-potion.

Skelton in his *Garland of Laurell* thus describes the Triple Goddess in her three characters as Goddess of the Sky, Earth and Underworld:

> *Diana in the leavës green,*
> *Luna that so bright doth sheen,*
> *Persephone in Hell.*

As Goddess of the Underworld she was concerned with Birth, Procreation and Death. As Goddess of the Earth she was concerned with the three seasons of Spring, Summer and Winter: she animated trees and plants and ruled all living creatures. As Goddess of the Sky she was the Moon, in her three phases of New Moon, Full Moon, and Waning Moon. This explains why from a triad she was so often enlarged to an ennead. But it must never be forgotten that the Triple Goddess, as worshipped for example at Stymphalus, was a personification of primitive woman—woman the creatress and destructress. As the New Moon or Spring she was girl; as the Full Moon or Summer she was woman; as the Old Moon or Winter she was hag.

In a Gallo-Roman '*allée couverte*' burial at Tressé near St. Malo in Brittany two pairs of girls' breasts are sculptured on one megalithic upright, two maternal pairs of breasts on another; the top of a third upright has been broken off, but V. C. C. Collum who excavated the burial suggests that it pictured a third pair—probably the shrunken breasts of the Hag. A very interesting find in this same burial, which can be dated by a bronze coin of Domitian to the end of the first century A.D., was a flint arrow-head of the usual willow-leaf shape with an incised decoration of half-moons. The willow, as we have seen, was sacred to the Moon, and in the Beth-Luis-Nion is *Saille*, the letter S. The most primitive character of the Greek letter S is C, which is borrowed from the Cretan linear script. Sir Arthur Evans in his *Palace of Minos* gives a table showing the gradual development of the Cretan characters from ideograms, and the sign C is there explained as a waning moon—the Moon-goddess as hag. The arrow-head, which in Roman Brittany was as completely out of date, except for ritual uses, as the Queen's sword of state, or the Archbishop's crozier is now, must be an offering to the third person of the female Trinity.[1] V. C. C. Collum took the trouble to have an analysis made of the charcoal found under the uprights, apparently the remains of the funerary pyre on which the dead man had been cremated. It was willow, oak and hazel charcoal, expressive of the sequence: enchantment, royalty, wisdom.

In Europe there were at first no male gods contemporary with the Goddess to challenge her prestige or power, but she had a lover who was alternatively the beneficent Serpent of Wisdom, and the beneficent Star of Life, her son. The Son was incarnate in the male demons of the various totem societies ruled by her, who assisted in the erotic dances held in her honour. The Serpent, incarnate in the sacred serpents which were the ghosts of the dead, sent the winds. The Son, who was also called Lucifer or Phosphorus ('bringer of light') because as evening-star he led in the light of the Moon, was reborn every year, grew up as the year advanced, destroyed the Serpent, and won the Goddess's love. Her love

[1] Insufficient notice has yet been taken of the shape of flint arrow-heads as having a magical rather than a utilitarian origin. The tanged arrow-head of fir-tree shape, for example, needs explanation. It must have been very difficult to knap without breaking off either one of the tangs or the projecting stem between them, and has no obvious advantage in hunting over the simple willow-leaf or elder-leaf types. For though a narrow bronze arrow-head with four tangs cannot be easily drawn out through a wound, because the flesh closes up behind, the broad two-tanged flint one would not be more difficult to draw out than an elder-leaf or willow-leaf one shot into a beast with equal force. The fir-tree shape seems therefore to be magically intended: an appeal to Artemis Elate—Diana the Huntress, Goddess of the Fir-tree—to direct the aim. The point was probably smeared with a paralysant poison—a 'merciful shaft' of the sort with which the Goddess was credited. An Irish fir-tree arrow-head in my possession, taken from an Iron Age burial, cannot have been seriously intended for archery. The chip of white flint from which it has been knapped is awkwardly curved, and it has so large a 'bulb of percussion' and so short a stem as to prevent it from being spliced to admit an arrow-shaft: it is clearly for funerary use only.

destroyed him, but from his ashes was born another Serpent which, at Easter, laid the *glain* or red egg which she ate; so that the Son was reborn to her as a child once more. Osiris was a Star-son, and though after his death he looped himself around the world like a serpent, yet when his fifty-yard long phallus was carried in procession it was topped with a golden star; this stood for himself renewed as the Child Horus, son of Isis, who had been both his bride and his layer-out and was now his mother once again. Her absolute power was proved by a yearly holocaust in her honour as 'Lady of the Wild Things', in which the totem bird or beast of each society was burned alive.

The most familiar icon of Aegean religion is therefore a Moon-woman, a Star-son and a wise spotted Serpent grouped under a fruit-tree— Artemis, Hercules and Erechtheus. Star-son and Serpent are at war; one succeeds the other in the Moon-woman's favour, as summer succeeds winter, and winter succeeds summer; as death succeeds birth and birth succeeds death. The Sun grows weaker or stronger as the year takes its course, the branches of the tree are now loaded and now bare, but the light of the Moon is invariable. She is impartial: she destroys or creates with equal passion. The conflict between the twins is given an ingenious turn in the Romance of *Kilhwych and Olwen*: Gwyn ('White') and his rival Gwythur ap Greidawl ('Victor, son of Scorcher') waged perpetual war for Creiddylad (*alias* Cordelia), daughter of Lludd (*alias* Llyr, *alias* Lear, *alias* Nudd, *alias* Nuada, *alias* Nodens), each in turn stealing her from the other, until the matter was referred to King Arthur. He gave the ironical decision that Creiddylad should be returned to her father and that the twins should 'fight for her every first of May, until the day of doom', and that whichever of them should then be conqueror should keep her.

There are as yet no fathers, for the Serpent is no more the father of the Star-son than the Star-son is of the Serpent. They are twins, and here we are returned to the single poetic Theme. The poet identifies himself with the Star-son, his hated rival is the Serpent; only if he is writing as a satirist, does he play the Serpent. The Triple Muse is woman in her divine character: the poet's enchantress, the only theme of his songs. It must not be forgotten that Apollo himself was once a yearly victim of the Serpent: for Pythagoras carved an inscription on his tomb at Delphi, recording his death in a fight with the local python—the python which he was usually supposed to have killed outright. The Star-son and the Serpent are still mere demons, and in Crete the Goddess is not even pictured with a divine child in her arms. She is the mother of all things; her sons and lovers partake of the sacred essence only by her grace.

The revolutionary institution of fatherhood, imported into Europe from the East, brought with it the institution of individual marriage. Hitherto there had been only group marriages of all female members of a particular totem society with all members of another; every child's maternity was certain, but its paternity debatable and irrelevant. Once this revolution had occurred, the social status of woman altered: man took over many of the sacred practices from which his sex had debarred him, and finally declared himself head of the household, though much property still passed from mother to daughter. This second stage, the Olympian stage, necessitated a change in mythology. It was not enough to introduce the concept of fatherhood into the ordinary myth, as in the Orphic formula quoted by Clement of Alexandria, 'The Bull that is the Serpent's father, the Serpent that is the Bull's.' A new child was needed who should supersede both the Star-son and the Serpent. He was celebrated by poets as the Thunder-child, or the Axe-child, or the Hammer-child. There are different legends as to how he removed his enemies. Either he borrowed the golden sickle of the Moon-woman, his mother, and castrated the Star-son; or he flung him down from a mountain top; or he stunned him with his axe so that he fell into perpetual sleep. The Serpent he usually killed outright. Then he became the Father-god, or Thunder-god, married his mother and begot his divine sons and daughters on her. The daughters were really limited versions of herself—herself in various young-moon and full-moon aspects. In her old-moon aspect she became her own mother, or grandmother, or sister, and the sons were limited revivals of the destroyed Star-son and Serpent. Among these sons was a God of poetry, music, the arts and the sciences: he was eventually recognized as the Sun-god and acted in many countries as active regent for his senescent father, the Thunder-god. In some cases he even displaced him. The Greeks and the Romans had reached this religious stage by the time that Christianity began.

The third stage of cultural development—the purely patriarchal, in which there are no Goddesses at all—is that of later Judaism, Judaic Christianity, Mohammedanism and Protestant Christianity. This stage was not reached in England until the Commonwealth, since in mediaeval Catholicism the Virgin and Son—who took over the rites and honours of the Moon-woman and her Star-son—were of greater religious importance than God the Father. (The Serpent had become the Devil; which was appropriate because Jesus had opposed fish to serpent in *Matthew, VII, 10,* and was himself symbolized as a fish by his followers.) The Welsh worshipped Virgin and Son for fifty years longer than the English; the Irish of Eire still do so. This stage is unfavourable to poetry. Hymns addressed to the Thunder-god, however lavishly they may gild him in Sun-god style—even Skelton's magnificent *Hymn to God the Father*—fail as poems, because to credit him with illimitable and unrestrained power denies the poet's inalienable allegiance to the Muse; and because though the Thunder-god has been a jurist, logician, declamator and prose-stylist, he has never been a poet or had the least understanding of true poems since he escaped from his Mother's tutelage.

In Greece, when the Moon-woman first became subordinated to the Thunder-god as his wife, she delegated the charge of poetry to her so-called daughter, her former self as the Triple Muse, and no poem was considered auspicious that did not begin with an appeal to the Muse for inspiration. Thus the early ballad, *The Wrath of Achilles,* which intro-duces the *Iliad* of Homer, begins: 'Sing, Goddess, of the destructive anger of Achilles, son of Peleus.' That Achilles is styled 'son of Peleus' rather than 'son of Thetis' proves that the patriarchal system was already in force, though totem society lingered on as a social convenience, Achilles being a sacred king of the Myrmidons of Thessaly, apparently an Ant clan subject to the Goddess as Wryneck; but the Goddess is clearly the Triple Muse, not merely one of the nine little Muses, mentioned in a less primitive part of the *Iliad,* whom Apollo later led down from Helicon, and up to Par-nassus when, as recorded in the *Hymn to Pythian Apollo,* he superseded the local Earth-goddess in the navel-shrine at Delphi. Apollo ('Destroyer or Averter') was at this time considered to be a male twin to the daughter-goddess Artemis; they were represented as children of the Thunder-god, born on Quail Island, off Delos, to the Goddess Latona the Hyperborean, daughter of Phoebe and Coieus ('Moonlight and Initiation').

The myths get confused here because Latona, being a newcomer to Delos, was not at first recognized by the local Triple Goddess; and because Artemis, the name of Apollo's twin, had previously been a Greek title of the Triple Goddess herself. Artemis probably means 'The Disposer of Water' from *ard-* and *themis.* Apollo, one may say, was securing his posi-tion by persuading his twin to take over the emblems and titles of her predecessor: he himself adopted the titles and emblems of a Pelasgian 'Averter' or 'Destroyer', in one aspect (as his title Smintheus proves) a Cretan Mouse-demon. Apollo and Artemis then together took over the charge of poetry from the Triple Muse (in this context their mother Latona); but Artemis soon ceased to be an equal partner of Apollo's, though she continued to be a Goddess of magical charms and eventually was credited with evil charms only. So Tatian records in his *Address to the Greeks:* 'Artemis is a poisoner, Apollo performs cures.' In Ireland, simil-arly, the Goddess Brigit became overshadowed by the God Ogma. In Cormac's *Glossary* it was necessary to explain her as: 'Brigit, daughter of The Dagda, the poetess, that is, the goddess worshipped by the poets on account of the great and illustrious protection afforded them by her.' It was in her honour that the ollave carried a golden branch with tinkling bells when he went abroad.

About the eighth century B.C. the Muse triad became enlarged under Thraco-Macedonian influence to three triads, or an ennead. Here the nine orgiastic priestesses of the Island of Sein in West Brittany, and the nine damsels in the *Preiddeu Annwm* whose breaths warmed Cerridwen's cauldron, will be recalled. A ninefold Muse was more expressive of the universality of the Goddess's rule than a threefold one; but the Apollo priesthood who ruled Greek Classical literature soon used the change as a means of weakening her power by a process of departmentalization. Hesiod writes of the Nine Daughters of Zeus, who under Apollo's patronage were given the following functions and names:

> *Epic poetry, Calliope.*
> *History, Clio.*
> *Lyric poetry, Euterpe.*
> *Tragedy, Melpomene.*
> *Choral dancing, Terpsichore.*
> *Erotic poetry and mime, Erato.*
> *Sacred Poetry, Polyhymnia.*
> *Astronomy, Urania.*
> *Comedy, Thaleia.*

Calliope ('beautiful face') was a name of the original Muse, in her full-moon aspect; so were Erato 'the beloved one'; and Urania 'the heavenly one'. The first mention of Erato in Greek myth is as the Oak-queen to whom Arcas was married; he gave his name to Arcadia and was the son of Callisto the She-bear and father of Atheneatis. The other names apparently refer to the several functions of the Muses. It will be observed that though the Muses of Helicon still had erotic tendencies, their chief function, that of healing and cursing by incantation, had been taken away from them under Olympianism. It had passed to Apollo himself and a surrogate, his physician son Aesculapius.

Apollo, though the God of Poetry and the leader of the Muses, did not yet, however, claim to *inspire* poems: the inspiration was still held to come to the poet from the Muse or Muses. He had originally been a mere Demon[1] whom his Muse mother had inspired with poetic frenzy; now he required that, as the Ninefold Muse, she should inspire individual poets in his honour—though not to the point of ecstasy. These poets, if they proved to be his faithful and industrious servants, he rewarded with a garland of laurel—in Greek, *daphne*. The connexion of poetry with laurel is not merely that laurel is an evergreen and thus an emblem of immortality: it is also an intoxicant. The female celebrants of the Triple Goddess at Tempe

---

[1] The ancients were well aware of Apollo's frequent changes of divine function. Cicero in his essay *On the Nature of the Gods* distinguishes four Apollos in descending order of antiquity: the son of Hephaestos; the son of the Cretan Corybantes; the Arcadian Apollo who gave Arcadia its laws; and lastly the son of Latona and Zeus. He might have enlarged his list to twenty or thirty.

had chewed laurel leaves to induce a poetic and erotic frenzy, as the Bacchanals chewed ivy—*daphne* may be a shortened form of *daphoine*, 'the bloody one', a title of the Goddess—and when Apollo took over the Delphic oracle the Pythian priestess who continued in charge learned to chew laurel for oracular inspiration. The laurel had become sacred to Apollo—his legendary pursuit of the nymph Daphne records his capture of the Goddess's shrine at Tempe near Mount Olympus—but he was now the God of Reason with the motto 'nothing in excess', and his male initiates wore the laurel without chewing at it; Empedocles, as Pythagoras's semi-divine successor, held laurel-chewing in as great horror as bean-eating. Poetry as a magical practice was already in decline.

The Romans conquered Greece and brought Apollo with them to Italy. They were a military nation, ashamed of their own rude poetic tradition, but some of them began to take up Greek poetry seriously as part of their education in political rhetoric, an art which they found necessary for consolidating their military conquests. They studied under the Greek sophists and understood from them that major poetry was a more musical and more philosophical form of rhetoric than could be achieved by prose and that minor poetry was the most elegant of social accomplishments. True poets will agree that poetry is spiritual illumination delivered by a poet to his equals, not an ingenious technique of swaying a popular audience or of enlivening a sottish dinner-party, and will think of Catullus as one of the very few poets who transcended the Graeco-Roman poetic tradition. The reason perhaps was that he was of Celtic birth: at any rate, he had a fearlessness, originality and emotional sensitivity entirely lacking in the general run of Latin poets. He alone showed a sincere love of women; the others were content to celebrate either comrade-loyalty or playful homosexuality. His contemporary, Virgil, is to be read for qualities that are not poetic in the sense that they invoke the presence of the Muse. The musical and rhetorical skill, the fine-sounding periphrases, and the rolling periods, are admired by classicists, but the *Aeneid* is designed to dazzle and overpower, and true poets do not find it consistent with their integrity to follow Virgil's example. They honour Catullus more, because he never seems to be calling upon them, as posterity, to applaud a demonstration of immortal genius; rather, he appeals to them as a contemporary: 'Is this not so?' For Horace as the elegant verse-writer they may feel affection, and admire his intention of avoiding extremes of feeling and the natural Roman temptation to be vulgar. But for all his wit, affability and skilful gleemanship they can hardly reckon him a poet, any more than they can reckon, say, Calverley or Austin Dobson.

To summarize the history of the Greek Muses:

The Triple Muse, or the Three Muses, or the Ninefold Muse, or Cerridwen, or whatever else one may care to call her, is originally the

Great Goddess in her poetic or incantatory character. She has a son who is also her lover and her victim, the Star-son, or Demon of the Waxing Year. He alternates in her favour with his tanist Python, the Serpent of Wisdom, the Demon of the Waning year, his darker self.

Next, she is courted by the Thunder-god (a rebellious Star-son infected by Eastern patriarchalism) and has twins by him, a male and a female—in Welsh poetry called Merddin and Olwen. She remains the Goddess of Incantation, but forfeits part of her sovereignty to the Thunder-god, particularly law-making and the witnessing of oaths.

Next, she divides the power of poetic enchantment between her twins, whose symbols are the morning star and the evening star, the female twin being herself in decline, the male a revival of the Star-son.

Next, she becomes enlarged in number, though reduced in power, to a bevy of nine little departmental goddesses of inspiration, under the tutelage of the former male twin.

Finally, the male twin, Apollo, proclaims himself the Eternal Sun, and the Nine Muses become his ladies-in-waiting. He delegates their functions to male gods who are himself in multiplication.

(The legendary origin of Japanese poetry is in an encounter between the Moon-goddess and the Sun-god as they walked around the pillar of the world in opposite directions. The Moon-goddess spoke first, saying in verse:

What joy beyond compare
To see a man so fair!

The Sun-god was angry that she had spoken out of turn in this unseemly fashion; he told her to return and come to meet him again. On this occasion he spoke first:

To see a maid so fair—
What joy beyond compare!

This was the first verse ever composed. In other words, the Sun-god took over the control of poetry from the Muse, and pretended that he had originated it—a lie that did Japanese poets no good at all.)

With that, poetry becomes academic and decays until the Muse chooses to reassert her power in what are called Romantic Revivals.

In mediaeval poetry the Virgin Mary was plainly identified with the Muse by being put in charge of the Cauldron of Cerridwen. D. W. Nash notes in his edition of the Taliesin poems:

> The Christian bards of the thirteenth and fourteenth centuries repeatedly refer to the Virgin Mary herself as the cauldron or source of inspiration—to which they were led, as it seems, partly by a play on

the word *pair*, a cauldron, and the secondary form of that word, on assuming the soft form of its initial *mair*, which also means Mary. Mary was *Mair*, the mother of Christ, the mystical receptacle of the Holy Spirit, and *Pair* was the cauldron or receptacle and fountain of Christian inspiration. Thus we have in a poem of Davydd Benfras in the thirteenth century:

> *Crist mab Mair am Pair pur vonhedd.*
> Christ, son of Mary, my cauldron of pure descent.

In mediaeval Irish poetry Mary was equally plainly identified with Brigit the Goddess of Poetry: for St. Brigit, the Virgin as Muse, was popularly known as 'Mary of the Gael'. Brigit as a Goddess had been a Triad: the Brigit of Poetry, the Brigit of Healing and the Brigit of Smith-craft. In Gaelic Scotland her symbol was the White Swan, and she was known as Bride of the Golden Hair, Bride of the White Hills, mother of the King of Glory. In the Hebrides she was the patroness of childbirth. Her Aegean prototype seems to have been Brizo of Delos, a moon-goddess to whom votive ships were offered, and whose name was derived by the Greeks from the word *brizein*, 'to enchant'. Brigit was much culti-vated in Gaul and Britain in Roman times, as numerous dedications to her attest, and in parts of Britain Saint Brigit retained her character of Muse until the Puritan Revolution, her healing powers being exercised largely through poetic incantation at sacred wells. Bridewell, the female peniten-tiary in London, was originally a nunnery of hers.[1]

A Cornish invocation to the local Brigit Triad runs:

> *Three Ladies came from the East,*
> *One with fire and two with frost.*
> *Out with thee, fire, and in with thee, frost.*

It is a charm against a scald. One dips nine bramble leaves in spring water and then applies them to the scald; the charm must be said three times to each leaf to be effective. For the bramble is sacred both to the Pentad and Triad of seasonal Goddesses, the number of leaves on a single stalk vary-ing between three and five—so that in Brittany and parts of Wales there is a strong taboo on the eating of blackberries. In this charm the Goddesses are clearly seasonal, the Goddess of Summer bringing fire, her sisters bringing frost. A fourth rhyming line is usually added, as a sop to the clergy: *In the name of the Father, Son and Holy Ghost.*

The mediaeval Brigit shared the Muse-ship with another Mary, 'Mary Gipsy' or St. Mary of Egypt, in whose honour the oath 'Marry' or 'Marry Gyp!' was sworn. This charming Virgin with the blue robe and

[1] The fourteenth-century Swedish St. Brigid, or Birgit, who founded the Order of St. Brigid was not, of course, the original saint, though some houses of the Order reverted merrily to paganism.

pearl necklace was the ancient pagan Sea-goddess Marian in transparent disguise—Marian,[1] Miriam, Mariamne ('Sea Lamb') Myrrhine, Myrtea, Myrrha,[2] Maria or Marina, patroness of poets and lovers and proud mother of the Archer of Love. Robin Hood, in the ballads, always swore by her. She was swarthy-faced, and in a mediaeval *Book of the Saints* she is recorded to have worked her passage to the Holy Land, where she was to live for years as a desert anchorite, by offering herself as a prostitute to the whole crew of the only vessel sailing there; so, once in Heaven, she showed particular indulgence to carnal sins.

A familiar disguise of this same Marian is the merry-maid, as 'mermaid' was once written. The conventional figure of the mermaid—a beautiful woman with a round mirror, a golden comb and a fish-tail—expresses 'The Love-goddess rises from the Sea'. Every initiate of the Eleusinian Mysteries, which were of Pelasgian origin, went through a love rite with her representative after taking a cauldron bath in Llew Llaw fashion. The round mirror, to match the comb, may be some bygone artist's mistaken substitute for the quince, which Marian always held in her hand as a love-gift; but the mirror did also form part of the sacred furniture of the Mysteries, and probably stood for 'know thyself'. The comb was originally a plectrum for plucking lyre-strings. The Greeks called her Aphrodite ('risen from sea-foam') and used the tunny, sturgeon, scallop and periwinkle, all sacred to her, as aphrodisiacs. Her most famous temples were built by the sea-side, so it is easy to understand her symbolic fish-tail. She can be identified with the Moon-goddess Eurynome whose statue at Phigalia in Arcadia was a mermaid carved in wood. The myrtle, murex and myrrh tree were also everywhere sacred to her; with the palm-tree (which thrives on salt), the love-faithful dove, and the colours white, green, blue and scarlet. Botticelli's *Birth of Venus* is an exact icon of her cult. Tall, golden-haired, blue-eyed, pale-faced, the Love-goddess arrives in her scallop-shell at the myrtle-grove, and Earth, in a flowery robe, hastens to wrap her in a scarlet gold-fringed mantle. In English ballad-poetry the mermaid stands for the bitter-sweetness of love and for the danger run by susceptible mariners (once spelt 'merriners') in foreign ports: her mirror and comb stand for vanity and heartlessness.

Constantine, the first Christian Emperor, officially abolished Mary-worship, but much of the ancient ritual survived within the Church: for example among the Collyridians, an Arabian sect who used to offer the same cake and liquor at her shrine as they had formerly offered to Ashtaroth. Myrrh, too, but this was more orthodox because St. Jerome had praised the Virgin as *Stilla Maris*, 'Myrrh of the Sea'. St. Jerome

---

[1] The earliest spelling of the Virgin's name in English is Marian—not Mariam which is the Greek form used in the Gospels.

[2] She was the mother of Adonis; hence the Alexandrian grammarian Lycophron calls Byblos 'The City of Myrrha'.

was punning on the name 'Mary', connecting it with Hebrew words *marah* (brine) and *mor* (myrrh) and recalling the gifts of the Three Wise Men.

When the Crusaders invaded the Holy Land, built castles and settled down, they found a number of heretical Christian sects living there under Moslem protection, who soon seduced them from orthodoxy. This was how the cult of Mary Gipsy came to England, brought through Compostella in Spain by poor pilgrims with palm-branches in their hands, copies of the Apocryphal Gospels in their wallets and Aphrodite's scallop-shells stitched in their caps—the palmers, celebrated in Ophelia's song in *Hamlet*. The lyre-plucking, red-stockinged troubadours, of whom King Richard Lion-Heart is the best remembered in Britain, ecstatically adopted the Marian cult. From their French songs derive the lyrics by 'Anon' which are the chief glory of early English poetry; as the prettiest carols derive from the Apocryphal Gospels, thanks to the palmers. The most memorable result of the Crusades was to introduce into Western Europe an idea of romantic love which, expressed in terms of the ancient Welsh minstrel tales, eventually transformed the loutish robber barons and their sluttish wives to a polished society of courtly lords and ladies. From the castle and court good manners and courtesy spread to the country folk; and this explains 'Merry England' as the country most engrossed with Mary-worship.

In the English countryside Mary Gipsy was soon identified with the Love-goddess known to the Saxons as 'The May Bride' because of her ancient association with the may-tree cult brought to Britain by the Atrebates in the first century B.C. or A.D. She paired off with Merddin, by this time Christianized as 'Robin Hood', apparently a variant of Merddin's Saxon name, *Rof Breoht Woden,* 'Bright Strength of Woden,' also known euphemistically as 'Robin Good-fellow'. In French the word *Robin,* which is regarded as a diminutive of Robert but is probably pre-Teutonic, means a ram and also a devil. A *robinet,* or water-faucet, is so called because in rustic fountains it was shaped like a ram's head. The two senses of ram and devil are combined in the illustration to a pamphlet published in London in 1639: *Robin Goodfellow, his mad pranks and merry gests.* Robin is depicted as an ithyphallic god of the witches with young ram's horns sprouting from his forehead, ram's legs, a witches' besom over his left shoulder, a lighted candle in his right hand. Behind him in a ring dance a coven of men and women witches in Puritan costume, a black dog adores him, a musician plays a trumpet, an owl flies overhead. It will be recalled that the Somersetshire witches called their god Robin, and 'Robin son of Art' was the Devil of Dame Alice Kyteler, the famous early fourteenth-century witch of Kilkenny, and used sometimes to take the form of a black dog. For the Devil as ram the classical instance is the one whom in 1303 the Bishop of Coventry honoured with a Black Mass and saluted with a posterior kiss. In Cornwall 'Robin' means phallus. 'Robin Hood' is a country name for red campion ('campion' means 'champion'), perhaps because its cloven petal suggests a ram's hoof, and because 'Red Champion' was a title of the Witch-god. It may be no more than a coincidence that 'ram' in Sanscrit is *huda*. 'Robin', meaning 'a ram', has become mythologically equated with Robin (latin: *rubens*), meaning the red-breast.

Here the story becomes complicated. The merry exploits of one Robin Hood, the famous outlaw of Sherwood Forest—whom J. W. Walker[1] has now proved to have been a historical character, born at Wakefield in Yorkshire between the years 1285 and 1295, and in the service of King Edward II in the years 1323 and 1324—became closely associated with the May Day revels. Presumably this was because the outlaw happened to have been christened Robert by his father Adam Hood the forester, and because during the twenty-two years that he spent as a bandit in the greenwood he improved on this identification of himself with Robin by renaming his wife Matilda 'Maid Marian'. To judge from the early ballad, *The Banished Man*, Matilda must have cut her hair and put on male dress in order to belong to the outlaw fraternity, as in Albania to this day young women join male hunting parties, dress as men and are so treated— Atalanta of Calydon who took part in the hunt of the Calydonian Boar was the prototype. The outlaw band then formed a coven of thirteen with Marian acting as the *pucelle*, or maiden of the coven; presumably she wore her proper clothes in the May Day orgies as Robin's bride. By his successful defiance of the ecclesiastics Robin became such a popular hero that he was later regarded as the founder of the Robin Hood religion, and its primitive forms are difficult to recover. However, 'Hood' (or Hod or Hud) meant 'log'—the log put at the back of the fire—and it was in this log, cut from the sacred oak, that Robin had once been believed to reside. Hence 'Robin Hood's steed', the wood-louse which ran out when the Yule log was burned. In the popular superstition Robin himself escaped up the chimney in the form of a Robin and, when Yule ended, went out as Belin against his rival Bran, or Saturn—who had been 'Lord of Misrule' at the Yule-tide revels. Bran hid from pursuit in the ivy-bush disguised as a Gold Crest Wren; but Robin always caught and hanged him. Hence the song:

'Who'll hunt the Wren?' cries Robin the Bobbin.

Since 'Maid Marian' had been acting as Lady of Misrule in the Yule-tide revels and deserting Robin for his rival, it is easy to see how she earned a bad name for inconstancy. Thus 'Maud Marian' was often written

for 'Maid Marian': 'Maud' is Mary Magdalene the penitent. In *Tom o'*
Bedlam's Song she is Tom's Muse—'Merry Mad Maud'.

Christmas was merry in the middle ages, but May Day was still merrier.
It was the time of beribboned Maypoles, of Collyridian cakes and ale, of
wreaths and posies, of lovers' gifts, of archery contests, of merritotters
(see-saws) and merribowks (great vats of milk-punch). But particularly of
mad-merry marriages 'under the greenwood tree', when the dancers from
the Green went off, hand in hand, into the greenwood and built themselves
little love-bowers and listened hopefully for the merry nightingale. 'Mad
Merry' is another popular spelling of 'Maid Marian', and as an adjective
became attached to the magician Merlin (the original 'Old Moore' of the
popular almanacks) whose prophetic almanacks were hawked at fairs and
merrimakes. Merlin was really Merddin, as Spenser explains in the
Faerie Queene, but Robin Hood had taken his place as the May Bride's
lover, and he had become an old bearded prophet. The 'merritotter' is
perhaps called after the scales (representing the Autumn equinox) in the
hand of the Virgin in the Zodiac, who figured in the Mad Merry Merlin
almanack: devoted readers naturally identified her with St. Mary
Gipsy, for true-lovers' fates tottered in her balance, see-sawing up and
down.

Many of these greenwood marriages, blessed by a renegade friar styled
Friar Tuck, were afterwards formally confirmed in the church-porch.
But very often 'merrybegots' were repudiated by their fathers. It is probably because each year, by old custom, the tallest and toughest village lad
was chosen to be Little John (or 'Jenkin') Robin's deputy in the Merry
Men masque, that Johnson, Jackson and Jenkinson are now among the
commonest English names—Little John's merrybegots. But Robin did
as merrily with Robson, Hobson, Dobson (all short for Robin), Robin-
son, Hodson, Hudson and Hood; Greenwood and Merriman were of
doubtful paternity. The Christmas 'merrimake' (as Sir James Frazer
mentions in *The Golden Bough*) also produced its crop of children. Who
knows how many of the Morrises and Morrisons derive their patronymics
from the amorous 'morrice-men'[1], Marian's 'merry-weathers'? Or how
many 'Princes', 'Lords' and 'Kings' from the Christmas King, or Prince,
or Lord, of Misrule?

The Christmas merry-night play was an important part of the English
Yule-tide festivities: seven or eight versions survive. The principal incidents are the beheading and restoration to life of the Christmas King,

---

[1] This same word 'morris', as the prefix to 'pike', is first written 'maris': so it is likely that
the morris-men were Mary's men, not *moriscoes* or Moorish men, as is usually supposed.
The innocent word 'merry' has deceived the editors of the *Oxford English Dictionary*.
They trace it back to an Indo-Germanic root *murgjo* meaning 'brief', arguing that when one is
merry, time flies; but without much confidence, for they are obliged to admit that *murgjo*
does not take this course in any other language.

or Christmas Fool. This is one of the clearest survivals of the pre-Christian religion, and ultimately derives from ancient Crete. Firmicus Maternus in his *On the Error of Profane Religion* tells how Cretan Dionysus (Zagreus) was killed at Zeus's orders, boiled in a cauldron and eaten by the Titans. The Cretans, he says, celebrated an annual funeral feast, in which they played out the drama of the boy's sufferings—and his shape-shifting—eating a live bull as his surrogate. Yet he did not die for, according to Epimenides, quoted by St. Paul, Minos made a panegyric over him:

> Thou diest not, but to eternity thou livest and standest.

St. Paul quoted a similar passage from the poet Aratus:

> In thee we live, move, and have our being.

At Athens, the same festival, called the Lenaea, ('Festival of the Wild Women') was held at the winter solstice, and the death and rebirth of the harvest infant Dionysus were similarly dramatized. In the original myth it was not the Titans but the wild women, the nine representatives of the Moon-goddess Hera, who tore the child in pieces and ate him. And at the Lenaea it was a yearling kid, not a bull, that was eaten; when Apollodorus says that Dionysus was transformed into a kid, Eriphos, to save him from the wrath of Hera, this means that Hera once ate him as a human child, but that when men (the Titans or tutors) were admitted to the feast a kid was substituted as victim.

The most ancient surviving record of European religious practice is an Aurignacian cave-painting at Cogul in North-Eastern Spain of the Old Stone Age Lenaea. A young Dionysus with huge genitals stands unarmed, alone and exhausted in the middle of a crescent of nine dancing women, who face him. He is naked, except for what appear to be a pair of close-fitting boots laced at the knee; they are fully clothed and wear small cone-shaped hats. These wild women, differentiated by their figures and details of their dress, grow progressively older as one looks clock-wise around the crescent. The row begins with three young girls, the first two in long skirts, on the right and ends with two thin dark elderly women on the left and an emaciated crone on the far side; the crone has a face like the old moon and is dancing widdershins. In between are three vigorous golden-haired women, one of them in a short, bright party-frock. They clearly represent the New Moon, Old Moon and Full Moon triads—the crone being Atropos, the senior member of the Old Moon triad.

In front of the senior member of the New Moon triad is an animal whose fore-quarters are concealed by her skirt—it seems to be a black pig. And in the foreground of the picture, bounding away behind the backs of the Full Moon triad, is the very creature that Oisin saw in his vision when being conveyed by Niamh of the Golden Hair to the Land of Youth: a hornless fawn. Balanced erect on the fawn's neck, and facing backwards, is a boyish-looking imp or sprite, as clearly as anything the escaping soul of the doomed Dionysus. For the wild women are closing in on him and will presently tear him in bloody morsels and devour him. Though there is nothing in the painting to indicate the season, we can be sure that it was the winter solstice.

So we get back once more to the dramatic romance of Gwion—the boy who was eaten by the wild hag Cerridwen and reborn as the miraculous child Taliesin—and to the dispute between Phylip Brydydd and the 'vulgar rhymesters' (see Chapter Five) as to who should first present a song to their prince on Christmas Day. The *Romance of Taliesin* is a sort of Christmas play, in which the sufferings of the shape-shifting child are riddlingly presented. This is the elder version, reflecting the religious theory of early European society where woman was the master of man's destiny: pursued, was not pursued; raped, was not raped—as may be read in the faded legends of Dryope and Hylas, Venus and Adonis, Diana and Endymion, Circe and Ulysses. The danger of the various islands of women was that the male who ventured there might be sexually assaulted in the same murderous way as, according to B. Malinowski in *The Sexual Life of Savages,* men of North-Western Melanesia are punished for trespasses against female privilege. At least one coven of nine wild women seems to have been active in South Wales during early mediaeval times: old St. Samson of Dol, travelling with a young companion, was unlucky enough to trespass in their precinct. A frightful shriek rang out suddenly and from a thicket darted a grey-haired, red-garmented hag with a bloody trident in her hand. St. Samson stood his ground; his companion fled, but was soon overtaken and stabbed to death. The hag refused to come to an accommodation with St. Samson when he reproached her, and informed him that she was one of the nine sisters who lived in those woods with their mother—apparently the Goddess Hecate. Perhaps if the younger sisters had reached the scene first, the young man would have been the victim of a concerted sexual assault. Nine murderous black-garbed women occur in the Icelandic saga of Thidrandi, who one night opened his door to a knock, though warned against the consequences, and saw them riding against him from the north. He resisted their attack with his sword for awhile, but fell mortally wounded.

The transformations of Gwion run in strict seasonal order: hare in the autumn coursing season, fish in the rains of winter; bird in the spring when the migrants return, finally grain of corn in the summer harvest season. The Fury rushes after him in the form first of greyhound bitch, then of bitch-otter, then of falcon, finally overtakes him in the shape of a high-crested black hen—red comb and black feathers show her to be the Death Goddess. In this account the solar year ends in the winnowing season of early autumn, which points to an Eastern Mediterranean origin of the story. In Classical times the Cretan, Cyprian and Delphic years, and those of Asia Minor and Palestine, ended in September.

However, when the victory of the patriarchal Indo-Europeans revolutionized the social system of the Eastern Mediterranean, the myth of the sexual chase was reversed. Greek and Latin mythology contains numerous anecdotes of the pursuit and rape of elusive goddesses or nymphs by gods in beast disguise: especially by the two senior gods, Zeus and Poseidon. Similarly in European folk-lore there are scores of variants on the 'Two Magicians' theme, in which the male magician, after a hot chase, outmagics the female and gains her maidenhead. In the English ballad of *The Coal Black Smith*, a convenient example of this altered form of chase, the correct seasonal order of events is broken because the original context has been forgotten. She becomes a fish, he an otter; she a hare, he a greyhound; she becomes a fly, he a spider and pulls her to his lair; finally she becomes a quilt on his bed, he a coverlet and the game is won. In a still more debased French variant, she falls sick, he becomes her doctor; she turns nun, he becomes her priest and confesses her night and day; she becomes a star, he a cloud and muffles her.

In the British witch-cult the male sorcerer was dominant—though in parts of Scotland Hecate, or the Queen of Elfin or Faerie, still ruled—and *The Coal Black Smith* is likely to have been the song sung at a dramatic performance of the chase at a witches' Sabbath; the association of smiths and horned gods is as ancient as Tubal Cain, the Kenite Goat-god. The horned Devil of the Sabbath had sexual connexion with all his witch attendants, though he seems to have used an enormous artificial member, not his own. Anne Armstrong, the Northumbrian witch already mentioned, testified in 1673 that, at a well-attended Sabbath held at Allansford, one of her companions, Ann Baites of Morpeth, successively transformed herself into cat, hare, greyhound and bee, to let the Devil—'a long black man, their protector, whom they call their God'—admire her facility in changes. At first I thought that he chased Ann Baites, who was apparently the Maiden, or female leader of the coven, around the ring of witches, and that she mimicked the gait and cry of these various creatures in turn while he pursued her, adapting his changes to hers. The formula in *The Coal Black Smith* is 'he became a greyhound dog', or 'he became an otter brown', 'and fetched her home again'. 'Home again' is used here in the technical sense of 'to her own shape', for Isobel Gowdie of Auldearne at her trial in 1662, quoted the witch formula for turning oneself into a hare:

> *I shall go into a hare*
> *With sorrow and sighing and mickle care,*
> *And I shall go in the Devil's name*
> *Aye, till I come home again.*

It is clear from her subsequent account that there was no change of outward shape, but only of behaviour, and the verse suggests a dramatic dance. I see now that Ann Baites gave a solo performance, alternately mimicking the pursued and the pursuer, and that the Devil was content merely to applaud her. Probably the sequence was seasonal—hare and greyhound, trout and otter, bee and swallow, mouse and cat—and inherited from the earlier form of chase, with the pursuer as the Cat-Demeter finally destroying the Sminthean mouse on the threshing-floor in the winnowing season. The whole song is easy to restore in its original version.[1]

An intermediate form of the 'Two Magicians' myth, quoted by Diodorus Siculus, Callimachus in his *Hymn to Artemis* and Antoninus Liberalis, the second-century A.D. mythographer, in his *Transformations*, who all refer it to different regions, is that the Goddess Artemis, *alias* Aphaea, Dictynna, Britomart or Atergatis, is unsuccessfully pursued and finally escapes in fish form. Callimachus makes Minos of Crete the erotic pursuer and Britomart the chaste pursued, and relates that the pursuit lasted for nine months from the early flood season to the winnowing season. The myth is intended to explain the fish-tail in the statues of the goddess at Ascalon, Phigalia, Crabos, Aegina, Cephallenia, Mount Dictynnaeum in Crete and elsewhere, and to justify her local devotees in remaining faithful to their pre-Hellenic rites and marital customs. Fishermen figure prominently in the story—Dictynna means a net—and fishermen are notoriously conservative in their beliefs. In the Philistine version from Ascalon, quoted by Athenaeus, the Goddess was Derketo and the pursuer was one Moxus or Mopsus: perhaps this should be Moschus the ancestor of King Midas's tribe who defeated the Hittites. Cognate with

[1] Cunning and art he did not lack
But aye her whistle would fetch him back.

O, I shall go into a hare
With sorrow and sighing and mickle care,
And I shall go in the Devil's name
Aye, till I be fetchèd hame.
    —Hare, take heed of a bitch greyhound
    Will harry thee all these fells around,
    For here come I in Our Lady's name
    All but for to fetch thee hame.
Cunning and art, etc.

Yet I shall go into a trout
With sorrow and sighing and mickle doubt,
And show thee many a merry game
Ere that I be fetchèd hame.
    —Trout, take heed of an otter lank
    Will harry thee close from bank to bank,
    For here come I in Our Lady's name
    All but for to fetch thee hame.
Cunning and art, etc.

Yet I shall go into a bee
With mickle horror and dread of thee,
And flit to hive in the Devil's name
Ere that I be fetchèd hame.
    —Bee, take heed of a swallow hen
    Will harry thee close, both butt and ben,
    For here come I in Our Lady's name
    All but for to fetch thee hame.
Cunning and art, etc.

Yet I shall go into a mouse
And haste me unto the miller's house,
There in his corn to have good game
Ere that I be fetchèd hame.
    —Mouse, take heed of a white tib-cat
    That never was baulked of mouse or rat,
    For I'll crack thy bones in Our Lady's name:
    Thus shalt thou be fetchèd hame.
Cunning and art, etc.

this myth is the fruitless attempt by Apollo on the maidenhead of the nymph Daphne.

The love-chase is, unexpectedly, the basis of the Coventry legend of Lady Godiva. The clue is provided by a miserere-seat in Coventry Cathedral, paralleled elsewhere in Early English grotesque wood-carving which shows what the guide-books call 'a figure emblematic of lechery': a long-haired woman wrapped in a net, riding sideways on a goat and preceded by a hare. Gaster in his stories from the Jewish *Targum*, collected all over Europe, tells of a woman who when given a love-test by her royal lover, namely to come to him 'neither clothed nor unclothed, neither on foot nor on horseback, neither on water nor on dry land, neither with or without a gift' arrived dressed in a net, mounted on a goat, with one foot trailing in the ditch, and releasing a hare. The same story with slight variations, was told by Saxo Grammaticus in his late twelfth-century *History of Denmark*. Aslog, the last of the Volsungs, Brynhild's daughter by Sigurd, was living on a farm at Spangerejd in Norway, disguised as a sooty-faced kitchen-maid called Krake (raven). Even so, her beauty made such an impression on the followers of the hero Ragnar Lodbrog that he thought of marrying her, and as a test of her worthiness told her to come to him neither on foot nor riding, neither dressed nor naked, neither fasting nor feasting, neither attended nor alone. She arrived on goatback, one foot trailing on the ground, clothed only in her hair and a fishing-net, holding an onion to her lips, a hound by her side.

If the two stories are combined into a picture, the 'figure emblematic of lechery' has a black face, long hair, a raven flying overhead, a hare running ahead, a hound at her side, a fruit to her lips, a net over her and a goat under her. She will now be easily recognized as the May-eve aspect of the Love-and-Death goddess Freya, *alias* Frigg, Holda, Held, Hilde, Goda, or Ostara. In neolithic or early Bronze Age times she went North from the Mediterranean, where she was known as Dictynna (from her net), Aegea (from her goat), Coronis (from her raven), also Rhea, Britomart, Artemis and so on, and brought the Maze Dance with her.

The fruit at her lips is probably the apple of immortality and the raven denotes death and prophecy—Freya's prophetic raven was borrowed from her by Odin, just as Bran borrowed Danu's and Apollo Athene's. The Goddess was established in Britain as Rhiannon, Arianrhod, Cerrid-wen, Blodeuwedd, Danu or Anna long before the Saxons, Angles and Danes brought very similar versions of her with them. Hilde was at home in the Milky Way, like Rhea in Crete and Blodeuwedd (Olwen) in Britain, both of whom were connected with goats; and in the Brocken May-eve ceremony a goat was sacrificed in her honour. As Holda she was mounted on a goat with a pack of twenty-four hounds, her daughters, running beside her—the twenty-four hours of May Eve—and was sometimes shown as piebald to represent her ambivalent character of black Earth-mother and corpse-like Death—Holda and Hel. As Ostara, the Saxon Goddess after whom Easter is named, she attended a May-eve Sabbath where a goat was sacrificed to her. The hare was her ritual animal: it still 'lays' Easter eggs. The goat spelt fertility of cattle; the hare, good hunting; the net, good fishing; the long hair, tall crops.

The May-eve goat, as is clear from the English witch ceremonies and from the Swedish May-play, 'Bükkerwise', was mated to the goddess, sacrificed and resurrected: that is to say, the Priestess had public connexion with the annual king dressed in goatskins, and either he was then killed and resurrected in the form of his successor, or else a goat was sacrificed in his stead and his reign prolonged. This fertility rite was the basis of the highly intellectualized 'Lesser Mysteries' of Eleusis, performed in February, representing the marriage of Goat-Dionysus to the Goddess Thyone, 'the raving queen', his death and resurrection.[1] At Coventry, she evidently went to the ceremony riding on his back, to denote her domination of him—as Europa rode on the Minos bull, or Hera on her lion.

The hare, as has been pointed out in Chapter Sixteen, was sacred both in Pelasgian Greece and Britain because it is swift, prolific and mates openly without embarrassment. I should have mentioned in this context that the early British tabu on hunting the hare, the penalty for a breach of which was to be struck with cowardice, was originally lifted on a single day in the year—May-eve—as the tabu on hunting the wren was lifted only on St. Stephen's Day. (Boadicea let loose the hare during her battle with the Romans in the hope, presumably, that the Romans would strike at it with their swords and so lose courage.)

The hare was ritually hunted on May-eve, and the miserere-seat 'figure of lechery'—which is a fair enough description of the Goddess on this occasion—is releasing the hare for her daughters to hunt. The folksong *If all those young men* evidently belongs to these May-eve witch frolics:

> *If all those young men were like hares on the mountain*
> *Then all those pretty maidens would get guns, go a-hunting.*

'Get guns' is eighteenth-century; one should read 'turn hounds'. There are other verses:

[1] In the corresponding ancient British mysteries there seems to have been a formula in which the Goddess teasingly promised the initiate who performed a sacred marriage with her that he would not die 'either on foot or on horseback, on water or on land, on the ground or in the air, outside a house or inside, shod or unshod, clothed or unclothed,' and then, as a demonstration of her power, manoeuvred him into a position where the promise was no longer valid—as in the legend of Llew Llaw and Blodeuwedd, where a goat figures in the murder scene. Part of the formula survives in the Masonic initiation ritual. The apprentice 'neither naked nor clothed, barefoot nor shod, deprived of all metals, hood winked, with a cable-tow about his neck is led to the door of the lodge in a halting moving posture.'

> *If all those young men were like fish in the water*
> *Then all those pretty maidens would soon follow after.*

With nets? As we know from the story of Prince Elphin and Little Gwion, May-eve was the proper day for netting a weir, and the Goddess would not bring her net to the Sabbath for nothing.

> *If all those young men were like rushes a-growing*
> *Then all those pretty maidens would get scythes go a-mowing.*

The love-chase again: the soul of the sacred king, ringed about by orgiastic women, tries to escape in the likeness of hare, or fish, or bee; but they pursue him relentlessly and in the end he is caught, torn in pieces and devoured. In one variant of the folk-song, the man is the pursuer, not the pursued:

> *Young women they run like hares on the mountain*
> *If I were but a young man I'd soon go a-hunting.*

The story of Lady Godiva, as recorded by Roger of Wendover, a St. Albans chronicler, in the thirteenth century, is that shortly before the Norman Conquest the Saxon Lady Godiva (Godgifu) asked her husband Leofric Earl of Mercia to relieve the people of Coventry from oppressive tolls. He consented on condition that she rode naked through the crowded market on a fair-day; and she did so with a knight on either side, but preserved her modesty by covering herself with her hair, so that only her 'very white legs' showed underneath. The story, which is also told of the Countess of Hereford and 'King John' in connexion with the distribution of bread and cheese at St. Briavel's in Gloucestershire, cannot be historically true, because Coventry in Lady Godiva's day was a village without either tolls or fairs. But it is certain that in 1040 she persuaded Leofric to build and endow a Benedictine monastery at Coventry, and what seems to have happened is that after the Conquest the monks disguised a local May-eve procession of the Goddess Goda, during which all pious Christians were at first required to keep indoors, with an edifying anecdote about their benefactress Lady Godiva, modelling the story on Saxo's. The fraud is given away by the 'Lady Godiva' procession of Southam (twelve miles south of Coventry and included in Leofric's earldom), where two figures were carried, one white and one black—the Goddess as Holda and Hel, Love and Death. The story of Peeping Tom the Tailor is not mentioned by Roger of Wendover, but may be a genuine early tradition. The St. Briavel's ceremony which took place, like the Southam and Coventry processions, on Corpus Christi, a date associated both at York and Coventry with mystery plays, is said to have commemorated the freeing of the people from a tax on the gathering of fire-wood in the neighbouring forest; Corpus Christi always falls on a Friday, the Goddess's own day, and corresponds roughly with May Eve; thus, it seems that the mystery-play has its origin in the May Eve festivities, Bükkerwise, in honour of Goda, the Bona Dea. If there was a prohibition against men witnessing the procession, as there was at Rome in the Bona Dea ceremonies, and as there was in Celtic Germany according to Tacitus (*Germania, chap. 40*) against any man witnessing Hertha's annual bath after her progress back to her sacred grove, and as there was in Greece in the days of Actaeon, when Diana took her woodland bath, Peeping Tom may record the memory of this.

The British are a mixed race, but the non-Teutonic goddess-worshipping strains are the strongest. This explains why the poets' poetry written in English remains obstinately pagan. The Biblical conception of the necessary supremacy of man over woman is alien to the British mind: among all Britons of sensibility the rule is 'ladies first' on all social occasions. The chivalrous man dies far more readily in the service of a queen than of a king: self-destruction is indeed the recognized proof of grand passion:

> *And for bonnie Annie Laurie*
> *I wad lay me doon and dee.*

There is an unconscious hankering in Britain after goddesses, if not for a goddess so dominant as the aboriginal Triple Goddess, at least for a female softening of the all-maleness of the Christian Trinity. The male Trinity corresponds increasingly less with the British social system, in which woman, now that she has become a property owner and a voter, has nearly regained the position of respect which she enjoyed before the Puritan revolution. True, the male Trinity antedated the Puritan revolution but it was a theological not an emotional concept: as has been shown, the Queen of Heaven with her retinue of female saints had a far greater hold in the popular imagination between the Crusades and the Civil War than either the Father or the Son. And one of the results of Henry VIII's breach with Rome was that when his daughter Queen Elizabeth became head of the Anglican Church she was popularly regarded as a sort of deity: poets not only made her their Muse but gave her titles—Phoebe, Virginia, Gloriana—which identified her with the Moon-goddess, and the extraordinary hold that she gained on the affections of her subjects was largely due to this cult.

The temporary reinstatement of the Thunder-god in effective religious sovereignty during the Commonwealth is the most remarkable event in modern British history: the cause was a mental ferment induced by the King James Bible among the mercantile classes of the great towns and in parts of Scotland and England where Celtic blood ran thinnest. The first

Civil War was fought largely between the chivalrous nobility with their retainers and the anti-chivalrous mercantile classes with their artisan supporters. The Anglo-Saxon-Danish south-east was solidly Parliamentarian and the Celtic north-west as solidly Royalist. It was therefore appropriate that at the Battle of Naseby, which decided the war, the rival battle cries were, for the Parliamentary army, 'God our Strength' and for the Royalist army 'Queen Marie'. Queen Marie was a Catholic and her name evoked the Queen of Heaven and of Love. The Thunder-god won the day, and vented his spite not only on the Virgin and her retinue of saints, but on Maid Marian and her maypole retinue, and on the other Triple Goddess cult which still survived secretly in many parts of the British Isles—the witch cult. But his triumph was short-lived because after gaining the victory he had removed the King,[1] his chief representative. He was therefore temporarily ousted at the Restoration and when he returned in 1688 with a Protestant King as his representative, his thunderous fury had been curbed. He gained a second access of strength in the enthusiastic religious revival, fostered by the merchant class, which accompanied the Industrial Revolution; but lost ground again at the beginning of the present century.

Elizabeth was the last Queen to play the Muse. Victoria, like Queen Anne, preferred the part of War-goddess in inspiring her armies, and proved an effective substitute for the Thunder-god. In the reign of her grandson the 88th Carnatics of the Indian Army were still singing:

> Cooch parwani
> *Good time coming!*
> *Queen Victoria*
> *Very good man!*
> *Rise up early*
> *In the morning.*
> *Britons never, never*
> *Shall be slave. . . .*

But Victoria expected the women of England to reverence their husbands as she had reverenced hers and displayed none of the sexual coquetry or interest in love-poetry and scholarship that serve to make a queen into a Muse for poets. Queen Anne and Queen Victoria both gave their names to well-known periods of English poetry, but the name of Queen Anne connotes passionless decorum in writing, and that of Victoria didacticism and rococo ornament.

---

[1] It is a strange paradox that Milton, though he had been the first Parliamentary author to defend the execution of Charles I and was the Thunder-god's own Laureate, fell later under the spell of 'the Northern Muse', Christina of Sweden, and in his *Second Defense of the English People* his flattery of her is not only as extravagant as anything that the Elizabethans wrote about Elizabeth, but seems wholly sincere.

The British love of Queens does not seem to be based merely on the common-place that 'Britain is never so prosperous as when a Queen is on the Throne': it reflects, rather, a stubborn conviction that this is a Mother Country not a Father Land—a peculiarity that the Classical Greeks also noted about Crete—and that the King's prime function is to be the Queen's consort. Such national apprehensions or convictions or obsessions are the ultimate source of all religion, myth and poetry, and cannot be eradicated either by conquest or education.

Chapter Twenty-Three

FABULOUS BEASTS

Indian mystics hold that to think with perfect clarity in a religious sense one must first eliminate all physical desire, even the desire to continue living; but this is not at all the case with poetic thinking, since poetry is rooted in love, and love in desire, and desire in hope of continued existence. However, to think with perfect clarity in a poetic sense one must first rid oneself of a great deal of intellectual encumbrance, including all dogmatic doctrinal prepossessions: membership of any political party or religious sect or literary school deforms the poetic sense —as it were, introduces something irrelevant and destructive into the magic circle, drawn with a rowan, hazel or willow rod, within which the poet insulates himself for the poetic act. He must achieve social and spiritual independence at whatever cost, learn to think mythically as well as rationally, and never be surprised at the weirdly azoölogical beasts which walk into the circle; they come to be questioned, not to alarm.

If the visitant is a Chimaera ('She-goat') for example, the poet will recognize her by the lion-head, goat-body and serpent-tail as a Carian Calendar-beast—another form of the winged goat, on which, according to Clement of Alexandria, Zeus flew up to Heaven. The Chimaera was a daughter of Typhon, the destructive storm god, and of Echidne, a winter Snake-goddess; the Hittites borrowed her from the Carians and carved her likeness on a temple at Carchemish on the Euphrates. Cerberus, a bitch miscalled a dog, is also likely to appear in the circle: a cognate beast, with the usual triad of heads—lioness, lynx and sow. The lynx is an autumn beast, apparently mentioned by Gwion in his *Can Y Meirch,* though he may be referring to the Palug Cat, the Anglesey Cat-Demeter: 'I have been a spotted-headed cat on a forked tree.'

The unicorn may puzzle the poet. But the unicorn of Pliny's description —which is embodied in the heraldic unicorn of the British Royal Arms, except that the horn is a straight white spiral—makes good calendar sense: it stands for the five-season solar year of the Boibel-Loth alphabet. The horn is centred in the Dog-days, and is the symbol of power: 'I will exalt your horn.' It stands for the E season, then beginning; as the head of the deer stands for the I season, in which deer were hunted; the body of the horse for the A season, at the beginning of which the October Horse was sacrificed at Rome; the feet of the elephant for the O season, in which the earth puts out her greatest strength; the tail (Ura) of the lion for the U season. The beast of the horn was originally, it seems, the rhinoceros, which is the most formidable beast in the world—'and who would cross Tom Rhinoceros does what the Panther dares not'—but owing to the difficulty of obtaining rhinoceros horn the long curved black horns of the oryx were in Pliny's time fraudulently supplied by traders as 'unicorn's horn'. Pliny, who had the usual Roman dislike and mistrust of fabulous beasts and mentioned the unicorn as a genuine zoological specimen, must have seen such a horn. In Britain, however, the narwhal horn became the accepted type, because of its white colour and superior hardness and because it is curved in the spiral of immortality, and because the variously named God of the Year always came out of the sea—as Gwion puts it in his *Angar Cyvyndawd*: 'From the Deep he came in the flesh.' The narwhal is called the 'sea-unicorn' in consequence. However, a few British mythographers, such as the early seventeenth-century Thomas Boreman, accepted Pliny's view, recording: 'His horn is as hard as iron and as rough as any file, twisted and curled like a flaming sword; very straight, sharp and everywhere black, excepting the point.' An interesting variety of the unicorn is the wild-ass unicorn, which Herodotus accepted as genuinely zoological; the wild ass is the beast of Set, whose fifth part of the year centres at midsummer and whose horn is thus exalted. But it must not be forgotten that the fifth-century B.C. historian, Ctesias, the first Greek to write about the unicorn, describes its horn, in his *Indica*, as being coloured white, red and black. These are the colours of the Triple Moon-goddess, as has been shown in the mulberry-and-calf riddle quoted from Suidas near the close of Chapter Four, to whom the God of the Year was subject.

The unicorn probably had a spatial as well as a temporal meaning, though space has always been divided by four quarters of the horizon, not by five fifths. The square cross, whether plain or converted into a swastika or cross-crosslet, has from time immemorial represented the fullest extent of sovereignty; it was a prime symbol in Minoan Crete, either alone or enclosed in a circle, and was reserved for the Goddess and her royal son, the King. In parts of India where Kali is worshipped, with rites closely resembling those of the Cretan and Pelasgian Great Goddess, as the most potent of a Pentad of deities, namely Siva, Kali, Vishnu, Surya and the elephant-god Ganesa—roughly corresponding with the Egyptian pentad, namely Osiris, Horus, Isis, Set and Nephthys—five has a definite spatial sense. In the coronation ritual of an Indian king, the officiating priest as he invests the king with a sacred mantle called 'the

Womb' in a ceremony of rebirth, gives him five dice and says: 'Thou art the master; may these five regions of thine fall to thy lot.' The five regions are the four quarters of the earth, and the zenith.

Thus the unicorn's single exalted horn represents 'the upper pole' which reaches from the king directly up to the zenith, to the hottest point attained by the sun. The unicorn's horn in Egyptian architecture is the obelisk; which has a square base tapering to a pyramidical point: it expresses dominion over the four quarters of the world and the zenith. In squatter form it is the pyramid, and the dominion originally expressed was not that of the Sun-god, who never shines from the north, but that of the Triple Goddess whose white marble triangle encloses her royal son's tomb from every side.

Kali, like her counterpart Minerva, has five as her sacred numeral. Thus her mystic, the poet Ram Prasad, addresses her as she dances madly on Siva's prostrate body:

> My heart is five lotuses. You building these five into one, dance and swell in my mind.

He is referring to the cults of the five deities, all of which are really cults of Kali. It will be recalled that both Dionysus and the sacred white cow, Io of Argos, who ultimately became the goddess Isis, are recorded to have paid visits to India.

In the Dionysian Mysteries the *hirco-cervus*, goat-stag, was the symbol of resurrection, of man's hope of immortality, and it seems that when the Hyperborean Druids visited Thessaly they recognized the goat stag, associated with apples, as their own immortal white hart or hind, which also was associated with apples. For the apple tree, *ut dicitur*, is the shelter of the white hind. It is from the goat-stag that the unicorn of heraldry and of mediaeval art derives its occasional beard; but among Christian mystics the Greek goat-unicorn of Daniel's vision has contributed bellicosity to this once pacific beast.

In Britain and France, the white hart or hind was not ousted by the unicorn; it persisted in popular tradition and figured in the mediaeval romances as an emblem of mystery. King Richard II adopted 'a white hart lodged' as his personal badge; which is how the beast found its way to the sign-boards of British inns. It sometimes wore a cross between its antlers as it had appeared to St. Hubert, patron of huntsmen, who had been chasing it through the dense forest for weeks without rest and to St. Julian the Hospitaler. Thus the Unicorn of the desert and the White Hart of the forest have the same mystical sense; but during the Hermetic vogue of the early seventeenth century were distinguished as meaning respectively the spirit and the soul. The Hermetics were neo-Platonists who patched their philosophic cloaks with shreds of half-forgotten bardic lore. In the *Book of Lambspring*, a rare Hermetic tract, an engraving shows a deer and a unicorn standing together in a forest. The text is:

> The Sages say truly that two animals are in this forest: one glorious, beautiful and swift, a great and strong deer; the other an unicorn. . . . If we apply the parable of our art, we shall call the forest the body. . . . The Unicorn will be the spirit at all times. The deer desires no other name but that of the soul. . . . He that knows how to tame and master them by art, to couple them together, and to lead them in and out of the forest, may justly be called a Master.

An anonymous beast may appear to the poet with deer's head crowned with gold, horse's body and serpent's tail. He will be out of a Gaelic poem published by Carmichael in *Carmina Gadelica*, a dialogue between Bride and her unnamed son.

> BRIDE: *Black the town yonder,*
> *Black those that are in it;*
> *I am the White Swan,*
> *Queen of them all.*
>
> SON: *I will voyage in God's name*
> *In likeness of deer, in likeness of horse,*
> *In likeness of serpent, in likeness of king.*
> *More powerful will it be with me than with all others.*

The son is evidently a god of the waning year, as the sequence of deer, horse and serpent shows.

Or a phoenix may fly into the circle. The phoenix, though literally believed in by the Romans—I suppose because its visits to On-Heliopolis were said to be so brief and far between that nobody could disprove its existence—was also a calendar beast. For the Egyptians had no leap-year: every year the fragment of a day which was left over at New Year was saved up, until finally after 1460 years, called a Sothic Year, the fragments amounted to a whole year; and the fixed festivals which had become more and more displaced as the centuries went by (with the same sort of attendant inconveniences as New Zealanders experience from their midsummer Christmas) fetched up again where they had originally stood; and a whole year could be intercalated in the annals. This was the occasion of much rejoicing, and at On-Heliopolis, the chief Sun Temple of Egypt, an eagle with painted wings was, it seems, burned alive with spices in a nest of palm branches to celebrate the event.

This eagle represented the Sun-god, and the palm was sacred to the Great Goddess his mother; the Sun had completed his great revolution and the old Sun-eagle was therefore returned to the nest for the inauguration of a new Phoenix Age. The legend was that from the ashes of the

Phoenix a little worm was born which presently turned into a real Phoenix. This worm was the six hours and the few odd minutes which were left over at the end of the Phoenix Year: in four years they would add up to a whole day, a Phoenix chick. From Herodotus's muddled account of the Phoenix it seems that there was always a sacred eagle kept at On-Heliopolis, and that when it died it was embalmed in a round egg of myrrh, which would preserve it indefinitely; then another eagle was consecrated. Presumably these eggs of myrrh were included in the final holocaust. That the Phoenix came flying from Arabia need mean no more than that, for the Egyptians, the sun rose from the Sinai desert. It is ironical that the early Christians continued to believe in a literal Phoenix, which they made a type of the resurrected Christ, long after the Phoenix had been killed. The Emperor Augustus unwittingly killed it in 30 B.C. when he stabilized the Egyptian calendar.[1]

Or a pack of tall, white Gabriel Hounds with red ears and pink noses may come streaming into view in pursuit of an unbaptised soul. Despite their spectral appearance and their sinister reputation in British myth, these animals are decently zoological. They are the ancient Egyptian hunting dogs, pictured in tomb paintings, which though extinct in Egypt are still bred in the Island of Ibiza, where they were originally brought by Carthaginian colonists. The breed may also have been introduced into Britain towards the close of the second millennium B.C. along with the blue Egyptian beads found in Salisbury Plain burials. They are larger and faster than greyhounds and hunt by smell as well as by sight; when in view of game they make the same yelping noise that migrating wild geese—especially the barnacle-goose—make when they fly far overhead at night: a sound taken in the North and West of England as an omen of approaching death. Anubis, the embalmer-god who conveyed the soul of Osiris to the Underworld, was originally a prowling jackal but came to be pictured as a noble-hearted hunting dog, only his bushy tail remaining as evidence of his jackal days.

Or the visitant may be a Cherub. The Cherub mentioned in the first chapter of *Ezekiel* is also clearly a beast of the calendar sort. It has four parts which represent the 'four New Years' of Jewish tradition: Lion for Spring; Eagle for Summer; Man for Autumn, the principal New Year; and Ox for Winter, the Judaean ploughing season. This Cherub is identified by Ezekiel with a fiery wheel, which is as plainly the wheel of the solar year as the God whom it serves is plainly the Sun of Righteousness, an emanation of the Ancient of Days. Moreover, each Cherub—there are four of them—is a wheel of this God's chariot and rolls straight forward,

[1] King Ptolemy Euergetes ('the well-doer') had sentenced the Phoenix to death in 264 B.C.; but the priests disregarded this order to reform the calendar, so Augustus has the notoriety of being its murderer.

without deflexion. Ezekiel's summary: 'And their appearance and their work was as it were a wheel in the middle of a wheel' has become proverbial for its unintelligibility. But it makes simple calendar sense. Each wheel of God's chariot is the annual cycle, or wheel, of the four seasons; and the chariot's arrival inaugurated a cycle, or wheel, of four years. Every year, in fact, wheels within a four-year wheel from the beginning to the end of time: and the Eternal Charioteer is the God of Israel. By making the Cherub-wheels themselves provide the motive power of the chariot, Ezekiel avoided having to put an angelic horse between the shafts: he remembered that horse-drawn votive chariots set up by King Manasseh in the Temple of Jerusalem had been removed as idolatrous by Good King Josiah. But Ezekiel's Eagle should really be a Ram or a Goat, and his Man a man-faced fiery Serpent; with eagle's wings for each of the four beasts. His reasons for this misrepresentation will appear in my last chapter.

The colour of these bright cloud-borne Cherubim was Apollonian amber, like that of the Man whom they served. They might well be ministers of Hyperborean Apollo the Sun-god, whose sacred jewel was amber. What is more, each golden spoke of the wheel ended in the leg of a calf; and the golden calf was the sacred beast of the god who, according to King Jeroboam, had brought Israel out of Egypt, as it also was of the God Dionysus, the changing part of the unchanging Apollo.

This apparent identification of Jehovah with Apollo seems to have alarmed the Pharisees, though they did not dare reject the vision. It is recorded that a student who recognized the meaning of *hashmal* (amber—'*hashmal*' is modern Hebrew for electricity; 'electricity' is derived from the Greek word for amber) and discussed it imprudently was blasted by lightning (*Haggada, 13.B*). For this reason, according to the Mishnah, the *Ma'aseh Merkabah* ('Work of the Chariot') might not be taught to anyone unless he were not only wise but able to deduce knowledge through wisdom ('gnosis') of his own, and no one else might be present during the teaching. And 'he who speaks of the things which are before, behind, above and below, it were better that he had never been born'. On the whole it was considered safest to leave the *Merkabah* alone, especially as it was prophesied that 'in the fullness of time Ezekiel will come again and unlock for Israel the chambers of the *Merkabah*.' (*Cant. Rabbah, I, 4*.)

Thus only a few known Rabbis taught the mystery and only to the most select of their pupils; among them Rabbi Johanan ben Zadkai, Rabbi Joshua (Vice-President of the Sanhedrin under Gamaliel), Rabbi Akiba and Rabbi Nehunia. Rabbi Zera said that even chapter headings of the *Merkabah* must not be communicated except to a person who was the head of an academy and was cautious in temperament. Rabbi Ammi said the doctrine might be entrusted only to one who possessed all the five qualities enumerated in *Isaiah, III, 3*: the captain of fifty, the honourable man, the counsellor, the skilled craftsman, the eloquent orator. The belief grew that expositions of the *Merkabah* mystery would cause Jehovah to appear. 'Rabbi Johanan ben Zadkai was riding along the road upon his ass, while his pupil Eleazar ben Arak walked behind him. Said Rabbi Eleazar: "Master, teach me about the Work of the Chariot." Rabbi Johanan declined. Rabbi Eleazar said again: "Am I permitted to repeat in your presence one thing which you have already taught me?" Rabbi Johanan assented, but dismounted from his ass, wrapped himself in his gown and seated himself upon a stone under an olive-tree. He declared that it was unseemly that he should be riding while his pupil was discoursing on so awful a mystery, and while the *Shekinah* ('the Brightness') and the *Malache ha-Shareth* ('the Angels-in-Waiting') were accompanying them. Immediately Rabbi Eleazar began his exposition, fire came down from Heaven and encircled them and the whole field. The angels assembled to listen, as the sons of man assemble to witness the festivities of a marriage; and there was a singing in the terebinth-trees: "Praise the Lord from the earth, ye dragons and all deeps, fruitful trees and all cedars, praise ye the Lord!" To which an angel answered from the fire, saying: "This is the Work of the Chariot!" When Eleazar had finished, Rabbi Johanan stood up and kissed him on the head. He said: "Praised be the God of Abraham, Isaac and Jacob, for He has given our father Abraham a wise son who knows how to discourse on the glory of our Father in Heaven." '

Rabbi Jose ha-Kohen and Rabbi Joshua had similar experiences. And once Rabbi Ben Azzai was sitting in meditation on the Scriptures when suddenly a flame encircled him. His pupils ran to Rabbi Akiba, who came up and said to Azzai: 'Art thou studying the mysteries of the *Merkabah?*'

The mystery was not monopolized by the Jews. According to Macrobius, the oracle of Colophon, one of the twelve Ionian cities of Asia Minor, gave the nature of the transcendent God Iao as fourfold. In the Winter he was Hades, or Cronos; in the Spring, Zeus; in the Summer, Helios (the Sun); in the Autumn Iao, or Dionysus. This lore must have been part of the instruction, mentioned in Chapter Fifteen, that was given to Cyprian of Antioch on Mount Olympus by his seven mystagogues. Iao in the Orphic religion was also known as the four-eyed Phanes (from *phaino*, 'I appear') first-born of the Gods. In the Orphic fragment 63, he is described as having golden wings, and the heads of ram, bull, snake and lion. Bull's heads were fastened to his side to denote his principal nature and he wore a great snake as a head-dress, which 'resembled every sort of wild beast'.

Here we can make a bold identification of the Cherub with the turning wheel that guards the Paradises of Celtic legend: for according to *Genesis, III, 24,* Cherubs were stationed at the East Gate of Eden. They were armed with 'the whirling sword of Jehovah'—the one with which (according to *Isaiah, XXVII, 1*) he killed the Dragon, as Marduk had killed Tiamat—to prevent anyone from entering. The paradise of Ezekiel's tradition (*Chapter XXXVIII, 13–16*) is a well-watered garden at the base of a hill which heroes, such as the King of Tyre, occasionally visit. It glitters with precious stones and is a place of drum and pipe. We have seen that Gwion placed it in the valley of Hebron. The Seraphs, or 'fiery serpents', associated with the Cherubs in their guardian duties, are evidently another way of expressing the sacred spirals carved as a warning on the gate of the sacred enclosure; the Cherubs, because distinguished from them, are likely to have been swastikas, or fire-wheels.

The King of Tyre in Ezekiel's account is easily recognized as the Canopic Hercules, originally an Aegean sun-hero, who became Semitized as Melkarth the chief god of Tyre. The islet off Tyre is thought to have been the chief station used by the Peoples of the Sea during the second millennium B.C. in their trade with Syria; as Pharos was in their trade with Egypt Ezekiel, cognisant of the original closeness of the cults of Jehovah and Melkarth, declares that no further religious understanding is possible between Jerusalem and Tyre, as in the time of Solomon and Hiram. King Hiram of Tyre, like Solomon whom he equalled and even surpassed in wisdom, was a priest of Melkarth, and Jehovah now admits through the mouth of Ezekiel: 'Thou sealest up the sum, full of wisdom and perfect in beauty.' However, he charges the present King of Tyre with having committed the sin of claiming to be a god, Melkarth as an Immortal, and the punishment for his presumption is death. This is an indirect warning to Ezekiel's own King, Zedekiah of Judah, a descendant of Solomon, not to be seduced by the Tyrian into similarly presuming to be Jehovah. (Zedekiah did not listen to the warning and 'the profane, wicked Prince' died blind and in chains at Riblah, the capital of his Cushite foes. He was the last King of Judah.) So Ezekiel utters a lament for Melkarth that, like Adam, he has been ousted from the Paradise by the Cherub, despite his original holiness and wisdom, and must now be burned to ashes. This was, of course, no more than Melkarth's destiny: in the Greek account he went to the apple-grove of the West—the Garden of the Hesperides—but had to obey the herald Copreus and return from its delights; and ended in ashes on Mount Oeta.

The poetic connexion of the Cherub with the burning to death of Hercules-Melkarth is that the pyre was kindled by a Cherub, that is to say, by a whirling round of the swastika-shaped fire-wheel, attached to a drill. This method of making fire by the drilling of an oak-plank survived until the eighteenth century in the Scottish highlands, but only in the kindling of the Beltane need-fire, to which miraculous virtue was ascribed. Hawthorn, the wood of chastity, was often used for the drilling. Sir James Frazer describes the need-fire ceremony at length in *The Golden*

Bough and shows that it originally culminated in the sacrifice of a man representing the Oak-god. In some Scottish parishes the victim was even called 'Baal', which was Melkarth's usual title.

So we see that Ezekiel is a master of ambivalent statement. He has made the fate of Hercules a symbol of the approaching destruction of Tyre by King Nebuchadnezzar of Babylon; in punishment for the vice of pride which since the city rose to commercial prosperity ('the multitude of thy merchandize, the iniquity of thy traffic') has corrupted its rulers.

Not all composite beasts are calendar beasts. The Sphinx, for instance, with her woman's face, lion's body and eagle's wings is Ura or Urania the goddess, with dominion over air and earth, who delegates sovereignty to her royal son, the King; and the Assyrian winged bull with his man's face is the Sphinx's patriarchal counterpart. It is likely that an iconotropic misinterpretation of the Assyrian winged bull accounts for the curious details of King Nebuchadnezzar's madness in the *Book of Daniel*:

'Father, what is that?'

'It is an old statue, my son, representing King Nebuchadnezzar who carried our ancestors away captive, more than three hundred years ago, because they had angered the Lord God. Afterwards, they say, he lost his reason for forty-nine months and wandered about like a brute beast in his beautiful palace gardens.'

'Did he really look like that?'

'No, my son. That is a symbolical statue, meaning that he partook of the nature of the creatures which compose its body and limbs.'

'Then did he eat grass like a bull and flap his arms like wings, and dig things up with his nails, and stay out in the rain all night and never have his hair cut?'

'God has even stranger ways of showing his displeasure, my son.'

The Egyptian Sphinx became masculine like the Assyrian winged bull; the Pharaonic cult being patriarchal, though also matrilinear. But the Pelasgian Sphinx remained female. 'Sphinx' means 'throttler' and in Etruscan ceramic art she is usually portrayed as seizing men, or standing on their prostrate figures, because she was fully revealed only at the close of the king's reign when she choked his breath. After her supersession as Ruler of the Year by Zeus or Apollo, this art-convention led to her being associated in Greece with disease and death and being described as a daughter of Typhon, whose breath was the unhealthy sirocco. Apollo's claim to be ruler of the year was supported by the sphinxes on his throne at Amyclae, and so was Zeus's by those on his throne at Olympia—read as a trophy of his conquest of Typhon. But Athene still wore them on her helmet, for she had once been the Sphinx herself.

A flock of bird-winged Sirens may alight in the circle. Having already ventured, in Chapter Twelve, to guess 'what name Achilles assumed when he hid himself among the women, though a puzzling question not beyond all conjecture', I feel a poetic compulsion to answer the other question that Sir Thomas Browne linked with it: 'What song the Sirens sang.' The Sirens ('Entanglers') were a Triad—perhaps originally an Ennead, since Pausanias records that they once unsuccessfully competed with the Nine Muses—living on an island in the Ionian Sea. According to Plato they were the daughters of Phorcus (i.e. Phorcis, the Sow-Demeter); according to others, of Calliope or some other of the Muses. Ovid and Hyginus connect them with the Sicilian myth of Demeter and Persephone. Their names are variously given as 'Persuader', 'Bright-face' and 'Be-witcher'; or 'Virgin-face, 'Shrill-voice' and 'The Whitened One'. Their wings were perhaps owl-wings, since Hesychius mentions a variety of owl called 'the Siren', and since owls, according to Homer, lived in Calypso's alder-girt isle of Ogygia along with the oracular sea-crows. In classical times they still had a temple dedicated to them near Surrentums

All this amounts to their having been a college of nine orgiastic moon-priestesses, attendants of an oracular island shrine. Their song, of nine stanzas, may be reconstructed without recourse to Samuel Daniel's vigorous *Ulysses and the Siren,* on the model of similar songs in ancient Irish literature: for instance 'The Sea God's Address to Bran' in *The Voyage of Bran, Son of Febal,* and 'Mider's Call to Befind' in *The Wooing of Etain.* Both poems are slightly Christianized versions of an ancient theme, the voyage of the alder-and-crow hero Bran (Cronos) to his island Elysium. In the first poem the speaker must originally have been the Island Queen, not the Sea God; in the second Befind and Mider have clearly changed parts, the original invitation being from princess to hero, not contrariwise. The Homeric story of the Danaan Odysseus and the Sirens suggests that Odysseus ('angry' according to Homer) was a title of Cronos and referred to his face artificially coloured crimson with the dye of the sacred alder. The origin of the story that Odysseus stopped his ears with wax and refused the Sirens' summons is probably that in the late thirteenth century B.C. a sacred king of Ithaca, Cronos's representative, refused to die at the end of his term of office. This would explain why he killed all the suitors for his wife Penelope's hand, after disguising himself in dirt and rags during the usual temporary abdication.

THE SIRENS' WELCOME TO CRONOS

Cronos Odysseus, steer your boat
Toward Silver Island whence we sing:
Here you shall pass your days.

Through a thick-growing alder-wood

418

We clearly see, but are not seen,
Hid in a golden haze.

Our hair the hue of barley sheaf,
Our eyes the hue of blackbird's egg,
Our cheeks like asphodel.

Here the wild apple blossoms yet,
Wrens in the silver branches play
And prophesy you well.

Here nothing ill or harsh is found.
Cronos Odysseus, steer your boat
Across these placid straits.

With each of us in turn to lie
Taking your pleasure on young grass
That for your coming waits.

No grief nor gloom, sickness nor death,
Disturbs our long tranquillity;
No treachery, no greed.

Compared with this, what are the plains
Of Elis, where you ruled as king?
A wilderness indeed.

A starry crown awaits your head,
A hero feast is spread for you:
Swineflesh, milk and mead.

The Sirens are the Birds of Rhiannon who sang at Harlech in the myth of Bran.

But if the visitant to the magic circle is the old Nightmare . . . What follows is a poem, of which I will give the prose rendering:

If the visitant is the Nightmare, the poet will recognize her by the following signs. She will appear as a small mettlesome mare, not more than thirteen hands high, of the breed familiar from the Elgin marbles: cream-coloured, clean-limbed, with a long head, bluish eye, flowing mane and tail. Her nine-fold will be nine fillies closely resembling her, except that their hooves are of ordinary shape, whereas hers are divided into five toes like those of Julius Caesar's charger. Around her neck hangs a shining poitrel of the sort known to archaeologists as *lunula*, or little moon: a thin disc of Wicklow gold cut in crescent shape with the horns expanded and turned on edge, fastened together behind her arching neck with a braid of scarlet and white linen. As Gwion says of her in a passage from his *Song of the Horses*,[1] which had been included by mistake in the *Câd Goddeu* (lines 206–209), and which is intended for the mouth of the White Goddess herself:

> *Handsome is the yellow horse,*
> *But a hundred times better*
> *Is my cream-coloured one*
> *Swift as a sea-mew . . .*

Her speed when she sets her ears back is indeed wonderful; no tall thoroughbred on earth can long keep her pace—proof of which is the pitiable condition in which hag-ridden horses used to be found at cock-crow in the stables from which they had been stolen for a midnight frolic— in a muck-sweat, panting like bellows, with bleeding sides and foam on their lips, nearly foundered.

Let the poet address her as Rhiannon, 'Great Queen', and avoid the discourtesy of Odin and St. Swithold, greeting her with as much affectionate respect as, say, Kemp Owyne showed the Laidley Worm in the ballad. She will respond with a sweet complaisance and take him the round of her nests.

One question I should myself like to ask her is a personal one: whether she ever offered herself as a human sacrifice to herself. I think her only answer would be a smiling shake of her head, meaning 'not really'; for instances of the ritual murder of women are rare in European myth and most of them apparently refer to the desecration of the Goddess's shrines by the Achaean invaders. That there were bloody massacres and rapes of priestesses is shown in the Tirynthian Hercules's battles with the Amazons, with Hera herself (he wounded her in the breast), and with the nine-headed Hydra, a beast portrayed on Greek vases as a giant squid with heads at the end of each tentacle. As often as he cut off the Hydra's heads they grew again, until he used fire to sear the stumps: in other words, Achaean attacks on the shrines, each of nine armed orgiastic priestesses, were ineffective until the sacred groves were burned down. *Hydrias* means a water-priestess with a *hydria*, or ritual water-pot; and the squid was a fish which appears in works of art dedicated to the Goddess not only in Minoan Crete but in Breton sculptures of the Bronze Age.

Tales of princesses sacrificed for religious reasons, like Iphigeneia or Jephthah's daughter, refer to the subsequent patriarchal era; and the fate supposedly intended for Andromeda, Hesionë, and all other princesses

[1] This song belongs to the account of the horse-race at the close of the *Story of Taliesin*, when Taliesin helps Elphin's jockey to beat the twenty-four race horses of King Maelgwn on the plain of Rhiannon, by charring twenty-four holly-twigs with which to strike the haunch of each horse as he overtook it, until he had passed them all. The horses represent the last twenty-four hours of the Old Year, ruled over by the Holly King, which (with the help of destructive magic) the Divine Child puts behind him one by one. It will be recalled that the main action of the *Story of Taliesin* takes place at the winter solstice.

rescued by heroes in the nick of time, is probably due to iconotropic error. The princess is not the intended victim of the sea-serpent or wild beast; she is chained naked to the sea-cliff by Bel, Marduk, Perseus or Hercules after he has overcome the monster which is her emanation. Yet the taboo on the death of a priestess may have been lifted, in theory, on certain rare occasions; for example, at the close of every *saeculum*, of 100 or 110 years, which was when the Carmenta priestess ended her life, according to Dionysius Periergetes, and the calendar was revised.

The German folk-stories of *Sleeping Beauty* and *Snow White* seem to refer to this type of death. In the first story twelve wise women are invited to the princess's birthday; eleven shower her with blessings, a thirteenth, called Held, who had not been invited because there were only twelve gold plates at the palace, curses her with death from a spindle-prick in her fifteenth year. The twelfth, however, converts this death into a century-long trance; from which the hero rescues her with a kiss after bursting through a terrible hedge of thorn, in which others have perished, the thorns turning into roses as he goes. Held is the Nordic counterpart of Hera; from whose name the word *hero* is derived, just as *held* means 'hero' in German. The thirteenth month is the death-month, ruled over by the Three Fates, or Spinners, so it must have been a yew spindle. Fifteen, as has been shown, is a number of completeness: three times five.

In the *Snow White* story a jealous stepmother, the elder aspect of the Goddess, tries to murder the young princess. First she is taken off into the woods to be killed, but the huntsman brings back the lung and liver of a young wild boar instead; and so, according to one account, a doe was substituted for Iphigeneia at Aulis. Then the stepmother, who darkens her face to show that she is the Death-goddess, uses a constrictive girdle, a poisoned comb and, finally, a poisoned apple; and Snow White is laid as if dead in a glass coffin on top of a wooded hill; but presently is rescued by the prince. The seven dwarfs, her attendants, workers in precious metals who save her from the first attempts on her life and recall the Telchins, stand perhaps for the seven sacred trees of the grove, or the seven heavenly bodies. The glass coffin is the familiar glass-castle where heroes go to be entertained by the Goddess of Life-in-Death, and the comb, glass, girdle and apple which figure in the story are her well-known properties; the owl, raven and dove, who mourn for her, are her sacred birds. These deaths are therefore mock-deaths only—for the Goddess is plainly immortal—and are staged, perhaps during the period of intercalated days or hours at the end of the sacred *saeculum*, with the sacrifice of a young pig or doe; but then the annual drama is resumed, with the amorous prince chafing, as usual, at the ascetic restrictions of theHawthorn, but free to do as he pleases in the Oak-month, the month of the hedge-rose, when his bride consents to open her half-closed eyes and smile.

Chapter Twenty-Four
THE SINGLE POETIC THEME

Poetry—meaning the aggregate of instances from which the idea of poetry is deduced by every new poet—has been increasingly enlarged for many centuries. The instances are as numerous, varied and contradictory as instances of love; but just as 'love' is a word of powerful enough magic to make the true lover forget all its baser and falser usages, so is 'poetry' for the true poet.

Originally, the poet was the leader of a totem-society of religious dancers. His verses—*versus* is a Latin word corresponding to the Greek *strophe* and means 'a turning'—were danced around an altar or in a sacred enclosure and each verse started a new turn or movement in the dance. The word 'ballad' has the same origin: it is a dance poem, from the Latin *ballare*, to dance. All the totem-societies in ancient Europe were under the dominion of the Great Goddess, the Lady of the Wild Things; dances were seasonal and fitted into an annual pattern from which gradually emerges the single grand theme of poetry: the life, death and resurrection of the Spirit of the Year, the Goddess's son and lover.

At this point it will be asked: 'Then is Christianity a suitable religion for the poet? And if not, is there any alternative?'

Europe has been officially Christian for the past sixteen hundred years, and though the three main branches of the Catholic Church are disunited all claim to derive their divine mandate from Jesus as God. This seems, on the face of it, most unfair to Jesus who made clear disavowals of deity: 'Why callest thou me good? None is good except the Father', and 'My God, my God, why hast thou forsaken me?' They have also renounced obedience to the Mosaic Law, as refined by Hillel and his fellow-Pharisees, which Jesus considered essential for salvation and, while retaining the Pharisaic ethical code, have incorporated into Christianity all the old pagan festivals commemorative of the Theme and worship Jesus as the 'Incarnate Word of God' in the pre-Christian Gnostic sense, and as the Sun of Righteousness—the crucified Man-god of prehistoric paganism.

Yet though Jesus denied the Theme by his unswerving loyalty to the only contemporary God who had cast off all association with goddesses, and by declaring war on the Female and all her works, the Christian cult can in great part be historically justified. Jesus came of royal stock, was secretly crowned King of Israel with the antique formula, preserved in the Second Psalm, that made him a titular Son of the Sun-god, and concluded that he was the destined Messiah. At the Last Supper, in the attempt to fulfil a paradoxical prophecy of Zechariah, he offered himself as a eucharistic sacrifice for his people, and ordered Judas to hasten the preparations for his death. In the event he was crucified like a harvest Tammuz, not transfixed with a sword as the Messiah was fated to be; and since Jehovah's curse on a crucified man debarred him from participation in the Hebrew after-world, there is no reason why he should not now be worshipped as a Gentile god; and indeed many poets and saints, unaware of his uncompromising Judaism, have worshipped him as if he were another Tammuz, Dionysus, Zagreus, Orpheus, Hercules or Osiris.

ACHAIFA, OSSA, OURANIA, HESUCHIA and IACHEMA—the five seasonal stations through which the Spirit of the Year passed in the cult of Canopic Hercules—could be expressed in the formula:

> *He shall be found.*
> *He shall do wonders.*
> *He shall reign.*
> *He shall rest.*
> *He shall depart.*

This saying, quoted by Clement of Alexandria from the *Gospel According to the Hebrews*, seems to be an adaptation of this formula to the needs of the Christian mystic:

> *Let him who seeks continue until he find.*
> *When he has found, he shall wonder.*
> *When he has wondered, he shall reign.*
> *When he has reigned, he shall rest.*

Since the mystic, by being made one with the solar Jesus at the Sacrament, shared his triumph over death, the fifth station was excused him; Jesus was equated with HESUCHIA (repose), the fourth station when trees cast their leaves and rest until the first stirrings of Spring. It is likely that a formula conveyed by the mystagogues to pre-Christian initiates of Hercules went something like this:

> *Seek the Lord, the beloved of the Great Goddess.*
> *When he is borne ashore, you shall find him.*
> *When he performs great feats, you shall wonder.*
> *When he reigns, you shall share his glory.*
> *When he rests, you shall have repose.*
> *When he departs, you shall go with him*
> *To the Western Isle, paradise of the blest.*

In this lost *Gospel According to the Hebrews* occurs a passage which has been preserved by Origen:

> Even now my mother the Holy Spirit took me by the hair and carried me up to the great mountain Tabor.

Tabor, as has been shown, was an ancient centre of Golden Calf worship, the Golden Calf being Atabyrius, the Spirit of the Year, son of the Goddess Io, Hathor, Isis, Althaea, Deborah, or whatever one cares to call her. Thus the connexion between Graeco-Syrian Christianity and the single poetic theme was very close in the early second century; though later the *Gospel of the Hebrews* was suppressed as heretical, apparently because it left the door open for a return to orgiastic religion.

Christianity is now the sole European faith of any consequence. Judaism is for the Jews alone, and Ludendorff's abortive revival of the primitive Teutonic religion was a matter merely of German domestic politics. Graeco-Roman paganism was dead before the end of the first millennium A.D. and the paganism of North-Western Europe, which was still vigorous in the early seventeenth century and had even taken root in New England, was destroyed by the Puritan revolution. The eventual triumph of Christianity had been assured as soon as the Emperor Constantine had made it the State religion of the Roman world. He did this grudgingly under pressure from his army, recruited among the servile masses that had responded to the Church's welcome for sinners and outcasts, and from his Civil Service which admired the energy and discipline of Church organization. The ascetic doctrine which was the main element of primitive Christianity lost power only gradually, and it was not until the eleventh century that the old Virgin Goddess Rhea—mother of Zeus and now identified with the mother of Jesus—began to be honoured with all her old titles and attributes and restored to the queenship of Heaven; the restoration was not complete until the twentieth century, though it had been anticipated by the fifth-century Emperor Zeno who re-dedicated the Temple of Rhea at Byzantium to the Virgin Mary.

The Puritan Revolution was a reaction against Virgin-worship, which in many districts of Great Britain had taken on a mad-merry orgiastic character. Though committed to the mystical doctrine of the Virgin Birth, the Puritans regarded Mary as a wholly human character, whose religious importance ended at the birth-stool; and anathematized any Church ritual or doctrine that was borrowed from paganism rather than from Judaism. The iconoclastic wantonness, the sin-laden gloom and Sabbatarian misery that Puritanism brought with it shocked the Catholics beyond expression. It was a warning to them to strengthen rather than weaken the festal side of their cult, to cling to the Blessed Virgin as the chief source of their religious happiness, and to emphasize as little as possible the orthodox Judaism of Jesus. Though the 'divided household' of Faith and Truth, that is to say the attempt to believe what one knows to be historically untrue, has been condemned by recent Popes, educated Catholics do in practice avert their eyes from the historical Jesus and Mary and fix them devoutly on the Christ and the Blessed Virgin: they are content to suppose that Jesus was speaking of himself, rather than prophesying in Jehovah's name, when he said: 'I am the Good Shepherd', or 'I am the Truth', and prophesied eternal life to whoever believed in him. Nevertheless, they have long put their house in order; though many of the mediaeval clergy not only connived at popular paganism but actively embraced it, the Queen of Heaven and her Son are now decisively quit of the orgiastic rites once performed in their honour. And though the Son is still officially believed to have harrowed Hell like Hercules, Orpheus and Theseus, and though the mystic marriage of the Lamb to a White Princess identified with the Church remains orthodox doctrine in every Christian profession, the Samson and Delilah incident is not admitted into the myth, and the Old Goat-footed Devil, his mortal enemy, is no longer represented as his twin. The old religion was dualistic: in an ivory relief of the fourteenth century B.C. found at Ras Shamra the Goddess is shown in Minoan dress, with a sheaf of three heads of barley in either hand, dividing her favours between a man-faced ram on her left, god of the waxing year, and a goat on her right, god of the waning year. The goat is bleating in protest that the Goddess's head is turned away and insists that it is now his turn to be cosseted. In Christianity the sheep are permanently favoured at the expense of the goats, and the Theme is mutilated: ecclesiastic discipline becomes anti-poetic. The cruel, capricious, incontinent White Goddess and the mild, steadfast, chaste Virgin are not to be reconciled except in the Nativity context.

The rift now separating Christianity and poetry is, indeed, the same that divided Judaism and Ashtaroth-worship after the post-Exilic religious reformation. Various attempts at bridging it by the Clementines, Collyridians, Manichees and other early Christian heretics and by the Virgin-worshipping palmers and troubadours of Crusading times have left their mark on Church ritual and doctrine, but have always been succeeded by a strong puritanical reaction. It has become impossible to combine the once identical functions of priest and poet without doing violence to one calling or the other, as may be seen in the works of Englishmen who have continued to write poetry after their ordination: John Skelton, John Donne, William Crashaw, George Herbert, Robert Herrick, Jonathan Swift, George Crabbe, Charles Kingsley, Gerard Manley Hopkins. The poet survived in easy vigour only where the priest was shown the door; as when Skelton, to signalize his independence of Church discipline, wore the Muse-name 'Calliope' embroidered on his cassock in silk and gold, or when Herrick proved his devotion to poetic myth by pouring libations of

Devonshire barley-ale from a silver cup to a pampered white pig. With Donne, Crashaw and Hopkins the war between poet and priest was fought on a high mystical level; but can Donne's *Divine Poems*, written after the death of Ann More, his only Muse, be preferred to his amorous *Songs and Sonnets?* or can the self-tortured Hopkins be commended for humbly submitting his poetic ecstasies to the confession-box?

I remarked in the first chapter that poets can be well judged by the accuracy of their portrayal of the White Goddess. Shakespeare knew and feared her. One must not be misled by the playful silliness of the love-passages in his early *Venus and Adonis*, or the extraordinary mythographic jumble in his *Midsummer-Night's Dream*, where Theseus appears as a witty Elizabethan gallant; the Three Fates—from whose name the word 'fay' derives—as the whimsical fairies, Peaseblossom, Cobweb and Mustard-seed; Hercules as a mischievous Robin Goodfellow; the Lion with the Steady Hand as Snug the Joiner; and, most monstrous of all, the Wild Ass Set-Dionysus and the star-diademed Queen of Heaven as ass-eared Bottom and tinselled Titania. He shows her with greater sincerity in *Macbeth* as the Triple Hecate presiding over the witches' cauldron, for it is her spirit that takes possession of Lady Macbeth and inspires her to murder King Duncan; and as the magnificent and wanton Cleopatra by love of whom Antony is destroyed. Her last appearance in the plays is as the 'damned witch Sycorax' in the *Tempest*.[1] Shakespeare in the person of Prospero claims to have dominated her by his magic books, broken her power and enslaved her monstrous son Caliban—though not before extracting his secrets from him under colour of kindness. Yet he cannot disguise Caliban's title to the island nor the original blueness of Sycorax's eyes, though 'blue-eyed' in Elizabethan slang also meant 'blue-rimmed with debauch'. Sycorax, whose connexion with Cerridwen has been pointed out early in Chapter Eight, came to the island with Caliban in a boat, as Danaë came to Seriphos from Argos with the infant Perseus; or as Latona came to Delos with the unborn Apollo. She was a goddess with the power to control the visible Moon—'make ebbs and flows and deal in her command'. Shakespeare says that she was banished from Argiers (was this really Argos?) for her witchcrafts. But he is poetically just to Caliban, putting the truest poetry of the play into his mouth:

[1] *The Tempest* seems to be based on a vivid dream of extremely personal content, expressed in a jumble of ill-assorted literary reminiscences: not only of the *Romance of Taliesin* but of the twenty-ninth chapter of *Isaiah*; a Spanish romance by Ortunez de Calahorra called '*A Mirror of Princely Deeds and Knighthood*'; three accounts of recent voyages to the New World; various contemporary Huguenot and anti-Spanish pamphlets; a magical book called *Steganographia* written in Latin by a monk of Spanheim; and a German play, Ayrer's *Von der schönen Sidee*. Caliban is partly Afagddu in the *Romance of Taliesin*; partly Ravaillac, the Jesuit-prompted murderer of Henry IV; partly an Adriatic devil in Calahorra's romance; partly a sea-monster, 'in shape like a man', seen off Bermuda during Admiral Sommers' stay there; partly Shakespeare's own *malus angelus*.

Be not afeared; the isle is full of noises,
Sounds and sweet airs that give delight and hurt not,
Sometimes a thousand twangling instruments
Will hum about mine ears; and sometime voices,
That if I then had wak'd after long sleep
Will make me sleep again: and then in dreaming
The clouds methought would open and show riches
Ready to drop upon me; that, when I wak'd
I cried to dream again.

It will be noticed that the illogical sequence of tenses creates a perfect suspension of time.

Donne worshipped the White Goddess blindly in the person of the woman whom he made his Muse; so far unable to recall her outward appearance that all that he could record of her was the image of his own love-possessed eye seen reflected in hers. In *A Fever* he calls her 'the world's soul', for if she leaves him the world is but her carcase. And:

Thy beauty and all parts which are thee
Are unchangeable firmament.

John Clare wrote of her: 'These dreams of a beautiful presence, a woman deity, gave the sublimest conceptions of beauty to my imagination; and being last night with the same presence, the lady divinity left such a vivid picture of her visits in my sleep, dreaming of dreams, that I could no longer doubt her existence. So I wrote them down to prolong the happiness of my faith in believing her my guardian genius.'

Keats saw the White Goddess as the *Belle Dame Sans Merci*. Her hair was long, her foot was light and her eyes were wild, but Keats characteristically transferred the lily on her brow to the brows of her victims, and made the knight set her on his steed rather than himself mount on hers, as Oisin had mounted on the steed of Niamh of the Golden Hair. So he also wrote pityingly of Lamia, the Serpent-goddess, as if she were a distressed Gretchen or Griselda.

The case of the *Belle Dame Sans Merci* calls for detailed consideration in the light of the Theme. Here is the poem as it first appeared, with a few joking comments at the end, copied out in a journal letter to Keats' brother George in America. Cancelled words are not italicized and shown in parentheses:

Wednesday Evening[1]

LA BELLE DAME SANS MERCI

O What can ail thee Knight at arms
Alone and palely loitering?

[1] Probably April 28th 1819.

The sedge is withered from the Lake
    And no birds sing!

O What can ail thee Knight at arms
    So haggard and so woe begone?
The squirrel's granary is full
    And the harvest's done.

I see (death's) a lily on thy brow
    With anguish moist and fever dew,
And on thy cheeks a fading rose
    Fast Withereth too—

I met a Lady in the (Wilds) Meads
    Full beautiful, a faery's child
Her hair was long, her foot was light
    And her eyes were wild—

I made a Garland for her head,
    And bracelets too, and fragrant Zone,
She look'd at me as she did love
    And made sweet moan—

I set her on my pacing steed
    And nothing else saw all day long,
For sidelong would she bend and sing
    A faery's song—

She found me roots of relish sweet
    And honey wild and (honey) manna dew,
And sure in language strange she said
    I love thee true—

She took me to her elfin grot
    And there she wept (and there she sighed)
        and sighed full sore,
And there I shut her wild wild eyes
    With kisses four—

And there she lulled me asleep
    And there I dream'd Ah Woe betide!
The latest dream I ever dreamt
    On the cold hill side.

I saw pale Kings, and Princes too
    Pale warriors death pale were they all

> *Who cried La belle dame sans merci*
> *Thee hath in thrall.*
>
> *I saw their starv'd lips in the gloam*
>   (All tremble)
> *With horrid warning* (wide agape) *gaped wide,*
> *And I awoke, and found me here*
>   *On the cold hill's side*
>
> *And this is why I* (wither) *sojourn here*
>   *Alone and palely loitering;*
> *Though the sedge is withered from the Lake*
>   *And no birds sing—* ...

Why four kisses—you will say—why four because I wish to restrain the headlong impetuosity of my Muse—she would fain have said 'score' without hurting the rhyme—but we must temper the Imagination as the Critics say with Judgement. I was obliged to choose a number that both eyes might have fair play, and to speak truly I think two a piece quite sufficient. Suppose I had said seven there would have been three-and-a-half a piece—a very awkward affair and well got out of on my side—

The context of the poem is discussed at length in Sir Sidney Colvin's *Life of Keats.* Keats had been reading a translation, then ascribed to Chaucer, of Alain Chartier's *La Belle Dame sans Mercy,* in which a 'gentleman finding no mercy at the hand of a gentlewoman dyeth for sorrow'. In the translation these lines occur:

> *I came into a lustie green vallay*
> *Full of floures.* .... *Riding an easy paas*
> *I fell in thought of joy full desperate*
> *With great disease and paine, so that I was*
> *Of all lovèrs the most unfortunate.*

Other literary sources of the ballad have been found. In Spenser's *Faerie Queene* (II, 6), the enchantress Phaedria is seen in a rowing-boat by the Knight Cymochiles as he wanders on the river-bank. He accepts her invitation to embark with her, and they have a pleasant time together. She sings, jests, decks her head with garlands, and puts fresh flowers about her neck, to the knight's wondrous great content. They land on an island in the 'Idle Lake', where she takes the 'wretched thrall' to a shady dale, lulls him fast asleep with his head on her lap, and there maroons him. Similarly in Malory's *Morte D'Arthur,* (IV, 1) the prophetic poet Merlin 'was assotted and doated upon' Nimue, the enchantress. She decoyed him into a grotto and there left him immured.

Amy Lowell has traced another source of the poem in the romance *Palmyrin of England* which Keats is known to have read with avidity. Palmyrin is madly in love with one Polinarda whom he fears he has offended, and ponders his grief under trees by the water-side. . . . 'And the passion therefore became so strong upon him that his strong heart failed, and such was the power of these fantastic thoughts over him that with the semblance of one dead he lay at the foot of the willow trees.' In another episode Palmyrin 'espied a damsel on a white palfrey come riding toward him, her hair spread over her shoulders and her garments seeming to be greatly misused; all the way as she rode she used many shrieks and grievous lamentations, filling the air with her cries.' She was an emissary of the sorceress Eutropa, sent to decoy him. And towards the close of the romance occurs a description of kings and princes embalmed in a mortuary temple on Perilous Isle, which seems to account for the 'pale Kings and Princes too'.

There are also reminiscences in the *Belle Dame Sans Merci* of Coleridge's *Kubla Khan* with its singing maiden and poetic honey-dew ('honey wild and manna dew' is Keats' version), of a line by Wordsworth, 'Her eyes are wild', and of another in William Browne's *Pastorals* 'Let no bird sing . . .'; but the most important source of all is the *Ballad of Thomas the Rhymer,* one version of which had recently been published by Sir Walter Scott in his *Border Minstrelsy* and another by Robert Jamieson in his *Popular Ballads.* Thomas of Erceldoune was taken up by the Queen of Elfland on her milk-white steed and carried to a garden where she fed him on bread and wine, lulled him to sleep in her lap, and gave him the gift of poetic insight; but warned him that he might be destined as a Sabbatical sacrifice to hell, going by the road that 'lies out owr yon frosty fell' (or 'cold hillside').

Keats was now twenty-four years old and at a crisis of his affairs. He had abandoned medicine for literature but was growing doubtful whether he could support himself by it; lately a 'loitering indolence' had overtaken his work. He had conceived a jealously possessive passion for the 'beautiful and elegant, graceful, silly, fashionable and strange . . . MINX' Fanny Brawne. She was evidently flattered by his addresses and willing to let him be her beau, but her frivolous ways caused him increasing pain; the more so, because he was not in any position to offer her marriage or insist on her remaining faithful to him. The 'kisses four' in the poem are likely to be autobiographical, rather than a modification, to suit the rhyme, of the ballad convention 'kisses three'. But often Fanny seems to have treated him mercilessly in resentment of his masterful ways and even, as he complains in a letter, to have made his 'heart a football by flirting with Brown', his friend. Thus the Belle Dame was, in one aspect, the elfish Fanny Brawne, whom he figuratively placed before him on the saddle of his Pegasus; and it is true that she admired his poems sufficiently to copy one or two of them out in a manuscript book of her own.

Keats, writing to his brother George who was in low water and far from home, took pains to conceal both the strength of his passion for Fanny and the serious condition of his health which complicated his other distresses. He was now in the early stages of a consumption induced, six months previously, by an exhausting walking tour in Scotland from which he had returned to find his elder brother Tom dying of the same disease. As an ex-medical student he knew that no cure had yet been found for it. He had seen the lily on Tom's brow, the hectic rose on his cheek, his starved lips a-gape in horrid warning, and had closed his wild wild eyes with coins, not kisses.

In the letter which contains the *Belle Dame Sans Merci* Keats mentions having just met Coleridge walking by Highgate Ponds with Green, a former medical instructor of his own. Coleridge's account of the meeting has been preserved. Keats asked leave to press his hand, wishing to carry away the memory of meeting him, and when he had gone Coleridge told Green: 'There is death in that hand.' He characterized it as 'a heat and a dampness', but 'fever dew' is Keats' own description. Thus the Belle Dame Sans Merci was, in another aspect, Consumption: whose victims warned him that he was now of their number. Although it was not for nearly another year that he received his 'death-warrant' in the form of violent arterial bleeding in the lungs, Keats must have already realized that even if it were financially possible to support Fanny he could not now honourably ask her to marry him; especially since the consumption was aggravated by venereal disease which he had caught two years before this at Oxford while visiting his friend Bailey the Divinity student. Thus the features of the Belle Dame were beautiful in a strange pale, thin way as Fanny's were, but sinister and mocking: they represented both the life he loved—in his letters to Fanny he identified her with both Life and Love— and the death he feared.

There is a third constituent of this nightmare figure: the spirit of Poetry. Keats' chief comfort in his troubles, his ruling passion, and the main weapon with which he hoped to clear his way to Fanny's love was poetic ambition. Now Poetry was proving an unkind mistress. In the disturbed state of his heart and mind he could not settle down to writing the romantic epics on which, in emulation of Milton, he hoped to build his fame. Recently he had stopped work on *Hyperion* after writing two and a half books, and confided to his friend Woodhouse that he was so greatly dissatisfied with it that he could not continue.

That the Belle Dame represented Love, Death by Consumption (the modern leprosy) and Poetry all at once can be confirmed by a study of the romances from which Keats developed the poem. He seems to have felt intuitively, rather than known historically, that they were all based on the same antique myth. The Queen of Elfland in *Thomas the Rhymer* was the mediaeval successor of the pre-Celtic White Goddess who carried off the sacred King at the end of his seven years' reign to her island Elysium, where he became an oracular hero. The story of the prophet Merlin and the enchantress Nimue has the same origin; so has that of Palmyrin and the enchantress on the white horse; and that of Cymochiles and the enchantress Phaedria. She was Death, but she granted poetic immortality to the victims whom she had seduced by her love-charms.

The case of Thomas the Rhymer, alias Thomas of Erceldoune, is a remarkable one. He was an early thirteenth-century poet who claimed to have been given poetic insight by the Queen of Elfland, or Elphame, who appeared suddenly to him as he lay on Huntlie Bank and chose him as her lover; and it was for this reason that his vaticinations were so highly prized by the Scots. (They were said by Thomas Chambers, in 1870, to be 'still widely current among the peasantry'.) Although it looks at first sight as though Thomas had merely borrowed the Gaelic myth of Oisin and Niamh of the Golden Hair, of which the Arthurian variant is the romance of Ogier the Dane[1] and Morgan le Faye, and applied it fancifully to himself, this is unlikely to be the case. What seems to have happened is that he was accosted on Huntlie Bank not by a phantom but by a living woman, the titular 'Queen of Elphame', the contemporary incarnation of Hecate, goddess of witches. She made him renounce Christianity and initiated him into the witch cult under the new baptismal name of 'True Thomas'.

As we know from the Scottish witch trials, the same adventure happened to other likely young Scotsmen, three or four centuries later. At Aberdeen in 1597, for instance, Andro Man confessed to carnal dealings with the then Queen of Elphame, who had 'a grip of all the craft' and who had attended that year's Harvest meeting at the Binhill and Binlocht riding on a white hackney. 'She is very pleasant and will be old and young when she pleases. She makes any King whom she pleases and lies with any she pleases.' (Old and young, naturally, because she represented the Moon-Goddess in her successive phases.) William Barton of Kirkliston similarly became the beloved of a later Queen, as he confessed at his trial in 1655,

---

[1] The late mediaeval legend of Ogier the Dane proves that Avalon was understood as an island of the dead by the Arthurian romance-writers. For Ogier is there said to have spent two hundred years in the 'Castle of Avalon', after early exploits in the East; then to have returned to France, in the days of King Philip I, with a firebrand in his hand on which his life depended—like that of Meleager the Argonaut. But King Philip reigned two hundred years after Charlemagne, Ogier's liege-lord in the Carolingian cycle; in other words, the second Ogier was the reincarnation of the first. It was nothing new for Ogier le Danois to live in Avalon. The name is merely a debased form of 'Ogyr Vran' which, as has been suggested in Chapter Five, means 'Bran the Malign' or 'Bran, God of the Dead'. His Norse counterpart Ogir ('the Terrible') was God of the Sea and of Death, and played the harp on an island where he lived with his nine daughters.

renounced Christianity, was renamed John Baptist and received the Devil's mark. But already by the thirteenth century the sacrifice of the king in the seventh, or Sabbatical, year seems to have been no longer insisted on, or only symbolically performed: for in the garden to which the Queen took Thomas of Erceldoune he was warned on pain of death not to pluck the apples growing there, the traditional food of the oracular dead. If Thomas had eaten them he would not have lived to tell his tale and keep his 'green velvet shoes and coat of even cloth' that had been his livery as the Queen's gudeman. The account of his mystical experiences corresponds with what is known of the initiation ceremonies of the witch cult. Like Ogier the Dane, he had first mistaken her for the Virgin, a pardonable mistake since (according to the confession of the witch Marion Grant of Aberdeen, an associate of Andro Man) she was addressed as 'Our Lady' by the witches and appeared like a fine lady clad in a 'white walicot'.

Keats in his letters to Fanny makes it clear that to become her lover in as complete a sense as Thomas of Erceldoune became the Queen of Elphame's, he would gladly have received the Mark and signed the blood compact which thereafter delivered his soul to hell. He was not a Christian. 'My religion is Love and you are its only tenet,' he wrote to her. But Fanny was not well cast for the part he forced upon her. Though at first, like the Queen whom William Barton met on the way to the Queen's Ferry, she pretended to be 'angry and very nyce' when he offered her gallantries, and later took pity on his distresses and humoured him to some degree, it is clear that she never 'suffered him to do that which Christian ears ought not to hear of'.

Coleridge, at his best, had a stricter poetic conscience than Keats. Though the second part of *Christabel* belies the moon-magic of the first, his description in the *Ancient Mariner* of the woman dicing with Death in the phantom ship is as faithful a record of the White Goddess as exists:

> *Her lips were red, her looks were free,*
> *Her locks were yellow as gold,*
> *Her skin was white as leprosy.*
> *The Nightmare Life-in-Death was she,*
> *Who thicks man's blood with cold.*

Anonymous English balladists constantly celebrate the Goddess's beauty and terrible power. *Tom o' Bedlam's Song* is directly inspired by her:

> *The Moon's my constant mistress*
> *And the lonely owl my marrow,*
> *The flaming drake*
> *And the night-crow make*
> *Me music to my sorrow.*

So is the *Holy Land of Walsinghame*:

> *Such a one did I meet, good sir,*
> *Such an angelic face*
> *Who like a nymph, like a queen, did appear*
> *In her gait, in her grace.*
>
> *She hath left me here alone,*
> *All alone, as unknown,*
> *That sometime did me lead with herself*
> *And me loved as her own.*

The *Holy Land of Walsinghame* recalls the tender description of the Goddess in the ancient Irish *Sickbed of Cuchulain*, spoken by Laegh after visiting the rath of the Sidhe:

> *There is a maiden in the noble house*
> *Surpassing all women of Ireland.*
> *She steps forward, with yellow hair,*
> *Beautiful and many-gifted.*
>
> *Her discourse with each man in turn*
> *Is beautiful, is marvellous,*
> *The heart of each one breaks*
> *With longing and love for her.*

For though she loves only to destroy, the Goddess destroys only to quicken.

Coleridge's mention of leprosy is strangely exact. The whiteness of the Goddess has always been an ambivalent concept. In one sense it is the pleasant whiteness of pearl-barley, or a woman's body, or milk, or unsmutched snow; in another it is the horrifying whiteness of a corpse, or a spectre, or leprosy. Thus in *Leviticus XIV, 10*, the leper's thank-offering after his cure, originally paid to the Goddess Mother, was a measure of barley flour. Alphito, it has been shown, combined these senses: for *alphos* is white leprosy, the vitiliginous sort which attacks the face, and *alphiton* is barley, and Alphito lived on the cliff tops of Nonacris in perpetual snow. Pausanias connects leprosy, the meaning of which is 'scaliness', a characteristic of true leprosy, with the town of Lepreus, which lay close to the river Alpheus in the district of Triphylia ('trefoil'), which was a leper-colony founded by a goddess called Leprea: it afterwards came under the protection of 'Zeus of the White Poplar', for another name for leprosy is *leuce*, which also means 'the white poplar'. This ties together several loose ends of argument. The white trefoils which spring up wherever the Love-goddess Olwen treads can be described as 'white as leprosy'. And we may assume that the leaves of the white poplar (the autumn tree of the Beth-Luis-Nion), which still grows in the Styx valley, were prophylactic against all forms of leprosy: for *albus* and *albulus* in Latin have all the connotations of the Greek *alphos*. When Evander came to Italy from Arcadia he brought the name of the River Alpheus with him: *Albula* was the old name for the Tiber, though its yellow waters would have earned it the name 'Xanthos', or 'Flavus', if the White Goddess had not sponsored the migration.

The priestesses of the White Goddess in ancient times are likely to have chalked their faces in imitation of the Moon's white disc. It is possible that the island of Samothrace, famous for its Mysteries of the White Goddess, takes its name from scaly leprosy; for it is known that *Samo* means white and that the Old Goidelic word for this sort of leprosy was *Samothrusc*. Strabo gives a warrant for this suggestion in his *Georgics*: he quotes Artemidorus as writing that 'there is an island near Britain where the same rites are performed in honour of Ceres and Persephone as in Samothrace.'

In the *Ancient Mariner*, when the Nightmare Life-in-Death has won her game of dice:

> *'The game is done, I've won, I've won,'*
> *Quoth she and whistles thrice.*

She whistles for the magical breeze that is presently to save the Mariner's life. Here again Coleridge is beautifully exact. The White Goddess Cardea, as has been mentioned, was in charge of the four cardinal winds; mythologically the most important was the North Wind at the back of which she had her starry castle, close to the polar hinge of the Universe. This was the same wind that blew in answer to Gwion's final riddle in the Romance and helped to liberate Elphin, and the wind which, according to Hecataeus, gave its name to the Hyperborean priesthood of Apollo. Whistling three times in honour of the White Goddess is the traditional witch way of raising the wind; hence the proverbial unluckiness of 'a crowing hen and a whistling maid'. 'I'll give thee a wind.' 'And I another.'—as the witches say in *Macbeth*. .... 'All the quarters that they know, I' the Shipman's card.' The close connexion of winds with the Goddess is also shown in the widespread popular belief that only pigs and goats (both anciently sacred to her) can see the wind, and in the belief that mares can conceive merely by turning their hindquarters to the wind.

The earliest Classical reference to this belief about mares is found in the *Iliad*, where Boreas grows amorous of the three thousand mares of Erichthonius the Dardanian; he finds them grazing on the plains about Troy, and impregnates twelve of them. Classical scholars have been content to read this merely as an allegory of the swiftness of the twelve sacred horses born to Boreas; but the myth is far more complex than that. Boreas lived with his three brothers, the other cardinal winds, in a sacred cave on Mount Haemus in Thrace, which lies due north of Troy, but was also worshipped at Athens. The Athenians gave him the honourable title of 'brother-in-law' and their ancient respect for him was heightened by his sudden descent from Haemus during the Persian invasion of Greece, when he sank most of Xerxes's fleet off Cape Sepias. Boreas was represented on the famous carved Chest of Cypselus as half man, half serpent— a reminder that winds were under the charge of the Death-goddess and came out of oracular caves or holes in the ground. He was shown in the act of carrying off the nymph Oreithuia, daughter of another Erichthonius,[1] the first King of Athens (who introduced four-horse chariots there) to his mountain home in Thrace.

This gives a clue to the provenience of the North Wind cult. The mares of Erichthonius were really the mares of Boreas himself, for Erichthonius was also half man, half serpent. Erichthonius, styled an autochthon, that

[1] This Erichthonius, alias Erechtheus, figures in the complex and nonsensical myth of Procne, Philomela and the Thracian King Tereus of Daulis, which seems to have been invented by the Phocian Greeks to explain a set of Thraco-Pelasgian religious pictures which they found in a temple at Daulis and could not understand. The story is that Tereus married Procne daughter of King Pandion of Attica, begot a son, Itys, on her, then concealed her in the country in order to be able to marry her sister Philomela. He told her that Procne was dead, and when she learned the truth cut out her tongue so that she should not be able to tell anyone. But she embroidered some letters on a peplum, which enabled Procne to be found in time. Procne returned and in revenge for her ill-treatment killed her son Itys, whom she laid on a dish before Tereus. Tereus had meanwhile attended an oracle which told him that Itys would be murdered, and suspecting that his brother Dryas was the destined murderer, had killed him. The sisters then fled, Tereus caught up an axe, and the gods changed them all into birds: Procne became a swallow, Philomela a nightingale, Tereus a hoopoe. Procne and Philomela were survived by twin brothers, Erechthonius and Butes.

This iconotropic myth, when returned to pictorial form, makes a series of instructional scenes, each depicting a different method of taking oracles.

The scene of the cutting out of Philomela's tongue shows a priestess who has induced a prophetic trance by chewing laurel leaves; her face is contorted with ecstasy, not pain, and the tongue that has been cut out is really a laurel leaf that an attendant is handing her to chew.

The scene of the letters sewn into the peplum shows a priestess who has cast a handful of oracular sticks on a white cloth, in Celtic fashion as described by Tacitus; they fall in the shape of letters, which she interprets.

The scene of the eating of Itys by Tereus shows a priest taking omens from the entrails of a sacrificed child.

The scene of Tereus and the oracle probably shows him sleeping on a sheep-skin in a temple and having a revelation in dream; the Greeks would not have mistaken this scene.

The scene of the killing of Dryas shows an oak-tree and priests taking omens under it, in Druidic fashion, from the way that a man falls when he dies.

The scene of Procne transformed into a swallow shows a priestess in swallow-disguise taking auguries from the flight of a swallow.

The scenes of Philomela transformed into a nightingale, and of Tereus transformed into a hoopoe have a similar sense.

Two further scenes show an oracular hero, depicted with snake's tail for legs, being consulted with blood-sacrifices; and a young man consulting a bee-oracle. These are respectively Erechthonius, and Butes (the most famous bee-keeper of antiquity), the brothers of Procne and Philomela. Their mother was Zeuxippe ('she who yokes horses'), evidently a mare-headed Demeter.

is to say 'one who springs from the earth', was first said to be the son of Athene by Hephaestus the demiurge, but later, when Athene's unblemished maidenhood was insisted upon by the Athenians as a matter of civic pride, he was made the son of Hephaestus and Ge, the Earth-goddess. The name of Oreithuia, the nymph whom he carried off, means 'She who rages upon the mountain'—evidently the Love-goddess of the divine triad in which Athene was the Death-goddess; which explains Boreas as her brother-in-law, and so the brother-in-law of all Athenians: whose ancient friendship with the Boreas priesthood of the Hyperboreans is mentioned by Hecataeus. But since North Winds cannot blow backwards, the story of Boreas's rape of Oreithuia to Thrace must refer to the spread to Thrace of the Athenian orgiastic cult of the Triple Goat-goddess and her lover Erichthonius, *alias* Ophion, and its adaptation there, as at nearby Troy, to an orgiastic cult of the Triple Mare-goddess; the twelve sacred horses of Boreas provided her with three four-horse chariots. Since Erichthonius shortly after birth took refuge from his persecutors in the *aegis* of Athene—the bag made from the hide of the goat Amalthaea—he must have come from Libya with her. In Libya he would have been more beloved than in Greece; northerly breezes freshen the early morning along the whole Libyan coast throughout the summer—thus Hesiod calls Boreas the son of Astraeus ('the starry one') and Eos ('dawn'). That Portuguese mares were fertilized by the zephyr—according to Varro, Pliny and Columella—is an obvious error derived from the extreme westerly position of Portugal. The philosopher Ptolemy rightly attributes only to the planet Zeus (Juppiter), which ruled the north, 'winds that fertilize', and Boraeus was one of Zeus's titles.[1] Lactantius, the late third-century Christian Father, makes this fertilization of the mares an analogy of the mysterious impregnation of the Virgin Mary by the Holy Spirit (literally 'breath'): a comment which was not at the time regarded as in bad taste.

According to the *Odyssey*, the home of the winds, that is to say the centre of the cult of Boreas and his brothers, was not on Mount Haemus but in an Aeolian island; perhaps this was the Aegean island of Tenos which lies immediately north of Delos, where a megalithic logan-stone was shown as the memorial raised by Hercules to Calaïs and Zetes, the heroic sons of Boreas and Oreithuia. But the cult of Boreas spread west as well as north from Athens—the Thurians of Italy are known to have worshipped him—and is likely to have reached Spain with other Greek colonists. In late Classical times Homer's 'Aeolian Isle' was believed to be

[1] Traces of a Palestinian North Wind cult are found in *Isaiah, XIV, 13, Ezekiel, I, 4, Psalms, XLVIII, 2* and *Job, XXXVII, 29.* God's mountain is placed in the far north and windy manifestations of his glory proceed from there. In the earliest assignment of parts of the heaven to deities, Bel had the north pole and Ea the south. Bel was Zeus-Juppiter, Thursday's god, often identified with Jehovah; but had taken over the rule of the North from his mother Belili, the White Goddess.

Lipari which had been colonized by Aeolians; Lipari bears due north from Sicily where the belief probably originated.

A slightly Christianized pagan Irish poem, printed in Vol. II of the *Ossianic Society's Publications*, 1855, gives the natal characteristics of the four cardinal winds. It not only shows the connexion of winds with Fate but presents the child who is born when the north wind blows as a type of Hercules.

Winds of Fate

The boy who is born when the wind is from the west,
He shall obtain clothing, food he shall obtain;
He shall obtain from his lord, I say,
No more than food and clothing.

The boy who is born when the wind is from the north,
He shall win victory, but shall endure defeat.
He shall be wounded, another shall he wound,
Before he ascends to an angelic Heaven.

The boy who is born when the wind is from the south,
He shall get honey, fruit he shall get,
In his house shall entertain
Bishops and fine musicians.

Laden with gold is the wind from the east,
The best wind of all the four that blow;
The boy who is born when that wind blows
Want he shall never taste in all his life.

Whenever the wind does not blow
Over the grass of the plain or mountain heather,
Whosoever is then born,
Whether boy or girl, a fool shall be.

At this point we can clear up one or two outstanding puzzles. If the Athenians worshipped the North Wind in very primitive times and had brought the cult with them from Libya, then the original Hyperboreans, the 'back-of-the-North-wind people', a priesthood concerned with a Northern other-world, were Libyans. This would explain Pindar's mistaken notion that Hercules fetched the wild olive from the distant north: he really fetched it from the south, perhaps from as far south as Egyptian Thebes where it still grew with oaks and persea-trees in the time of Pliny —just as the 'Gorgon' whom Perseus killed during his visit to the ass-sacrificing Hyperboreans was the southern Goddess Neith of Libya. This was not Hercules the oak-hero, but the other Hercules, the phallic thumb, leader of the five Dactyls, who according to the tradition that Pausanias found at Elis brought such an abundance of wild-olive from Hyperboraea that, after he had crowned the victor of the foot-race run by his brothers, they all slept on heaps of its fresh leaves. Pausanias, though he names the competitors, does not say who won; but it was obviously Paeonius the forefinger, which always comes in first when you run your fingers on the table and make them race, for the *paean* or *paeon* was the song of victory. Moreover, Pausanias says that Zeus wrestled with Cronos on this occasion, and beat him; Zeus is the god of the forefinger, and Cronos the god of the middle, or fool's finger. The Dactyl who came in second in the race was evidently Epimedes, 'he who thinks too late', the fool; for Pausanias gives the names in this order: Hercules, Paeonius, Epimedes, Jasius and Idas.

The wild olive, then, was the crown of Paeonius the forefinger: which means that the vowel of the forefinger, namely O, which is expressed by the gorse *Onn* in the Beth-Luis-Nion, was expressed by the wild olive in the Greek tree alphabet. This explains the use of olive at the Spring festival in the ancient world, which continues in Spain at the 'Ramos' (boughs) festival; and Hercules's olive-wood club—the Sun first arms himself at the Spring equinox; and the olive-leaf in the bill of Noah's dove which symbolizes the drying up of the winter floods by the Spring Sun. It also explains Paeonius as a title of Apollo Helios the god of the young Sun, which however he seems to have derived from the Goddess Athene Paeonia who first brought the olive to Athens; and the name of the peony, *paeonia*, a Mediterranean wild flower which blooms only at the Spring solstice and quickly sheds its petals.

Spenser's White Goddess is the Arthurian 'Lady of the Lake', also called 'the White Serpent', 'Nimue', and 'Vivien', whom Professor Rhys in his *Arthurian Legend* identifies with Rhiannon. She is mistress of Merlin (Merddin) and treacherously entombs him in his magic cave when, as Llew Llaw to Blodeuwedd, or Samson to Delilah, or Curoi to Blathnat, he has revealed some of his secrets to her. However, in the earliest Welsh account, the *Dialogue of Gwenddydd and Merddin*, she tells him to arise from his prison and 'open the Books of Inspiration without fear'. In this dialogue she calls him 'twin-brother' which reveals her as Olwen, and she is also styled *Gwenddydd wen adlam Cerddeu*, 'White Lady of Day, refuge of poems', which proves her to be the Muse, Cardea-Cerridwen, who inspires *cerddeu*, 'poems', in Greek, *cerdeia*.

'What is inspiration?' is a question that is continually asked. The derivation of the word supplies two related answers. 'Inspiration' may be the breathing-in by the poet of intoxicating fumes from an intoxicating cauldron, the *Awen* of the cauldron of Cerridwen, containing probably a mash of barley, acorns, honey, bull's blood and such sacred herbs as ivy, hellebore[1] and laurel, or mephitic fumes from an underground vent as at Delphi, or the fumes that rise to the nostrils when toadstools are chewed. These fumes induce the paranoiac trance in which time is suspended, though the mind remains active and can relate its proleptic or analeptic apprehensions in verse. But 'inspiration' may also refer to the inducement of the same poetic condition by the act of listening to the wind, the messenger of the Goddess Cardea, in a sacred grove. At Dodona poetic oracles were listened for in the oak-grove, and the prophetic trance was perhaps induced in the black-dove priestesses who first controlled the oracle by the chewing of acorns; at any rate, a scholiast on Lucan notes that this method was used among the Gallic Druids. In Canaan the prime oracular tree was the acacia—the 'burning bush' discussed in Chapter Fifteen—and there is a reference to this sort of inspiration in *1 Chronicles, XIV, 15*:

> When thou hearest the sound of marching in the tops of the mulberry trees, then bestir thyself.

Here, 'mulberry trees' should be 'acacias'. Jehovah himself was in the wind, and the context—David's assault on the Philistines from Gibeon to Gaza —shows that it blew from the North. This story dates from a time when Jehovah was not yet a transcendental God but lived, like Boreas, in a mountain to the far north; he was, in fact, the white bull-god Baal Zephon ('Lord of the North') who had borrowed his title from his Goddess Mother Baaltis Zapuna, a name attested in an inscription from Goshen where the tribe of Joseph was once settled. The Canaanites worshipped him as King of the Northern Otherworld and the Philistines of Ekron had taken over the cult; he was a god of prophecy and fertility. Another of his titles was Baal-Zebul, 'the Lord of the Mansion [of the North]' which named the tribe of Zebulon: they worshipped him on Mount Tabor. When King Ahaziah of Israel consulted his oracle at Ekron (*2 Kings, I, 1–4*) he earned Elijah's reproach for not consulting the native Israelite oracle, presumably on Tabor. I suspect that Baal Zabul was an autumnal Dionysus, whose devotees intoxicated themselves on *amanita muscaria*, which still grows there; the Biblical name for these toadstools being either 'ermrods' or 'little foxes'. By the time of Jesus, who was accused of traffic with Beelzebub, the Kingdoms of Israel and Philistia had long been suppressed and the shrines of Ekron and Tabor destroyed; and Baal-Zebul's functions having been taken over by the archangel Gabriel, he had declined to a mere devil mockingly called Baal-Zebub, 'Lord of Flies'.

[1] This perhaps means *Helle-bora*, 'the food of the Goddess Helle'. Helle was the Pelasgian goddess who gave her name to the Hellespont.

Yet the Levite butchers continued the old ritual of turning the victim's head to the north when they sacrificed.

The acacia is still a sacred tree in Arabia Deserta and anyone who even breaks off a twig is expected to die within the year. The common Classical icon of the Muse whispering in a poet's ear refers to tree-top inspiration: the Muse is the *dryad* (oak-fairy), or *mĕlia* (ash-fairy), or *mēlia* (quince-fairy), or *caryatid* (nut-fairy), or *hamadryad* (wood-fairy in general), or *heliconian* (fairy of Mount Helicon, which took its name as much from *helicē*, the willow-tree sacred to poets, as from the stream which spiralled round it).

Nowadays poets seldom use these artificial aids to inspiration, though the sound of wind in the willows or in a plantation of forest-trees still exercises a strangely potent influence on their minds; and 'inspiration' is therefore applied to any means whatsoever by which the poetic trance is induced. But a good many of the charlatans or weaklings resort to automatic writing and spiritism. The ancient Hebrew distinction between legitimate and illegitimate prophecy—'prophecy' meaning inspired poetry, in which future events are not necessarily, but usually, foretold—has much to recommend it. If a prophet went into a trance and was afterwards unconscious of what he had been babbling, that was illegitimate; but if he remained in possession of his critical faculties throughout the trance and afterwards, that was legitimate. His powers were heightened by the 'spirit of prophecy', so that his words crystallized immense experience into a single poetic jewel; but he was, by the grace of God, the sturdy author and regulator of this achievement. The spiritistic medium, on the other hand, whose soul momentarily absented itself so that demonic principalities and powers might occupy his body and speak pipingly through his mouth was no prophet and was 'cut off from the congregation' if it was found that he had deliberately induced the trance. The ban was presumably extended to automatic writing.

Chapter Twenty-Five
WAR IN HEAVEN

Must poetry necessarily be original? According to the Apollonian, or Classical, theory it need not be, since the test of a good poet is his ability to express time-proved sentiments in time-honoured forms with greater fluency, charm, sonorousness and learning than his rivals; these, at least, are the qualities that win a man a bardic Chair. Apollonian poetry is essentially court-poetry, written to uphold the authority delegated to poets by the King (regarded as a *Roi Soleil*, Apollo's vice-regent) on the understanding that they celebrate and perpetuate his magnificence and terror. They therefore use old-fashioned diction, formal ornament, and regular, sober, well-polished metre, as a means of upholding the dignity of their office; and make frequent eulogistic references to ancestral events and institutions. There is an extraordinary sameness in their eulogies: the Aztecs flattered their patriarchal Inca as 'a well-fed hawk, always ready for war' which was a phrase worked to death by the early mediaeval Welsh bards.

A Classical technique such as was perfected by these bards, or by the French poets of the Louis XIV period, or by the English poets of the early eighteenth-century Augustan Age is a sure sign of political stability based on force of arms; and to be original in such an age is to be either a disloyal subject or a vagrant.

The Augustan Age was so called because the poets were celebrating the same renewal of firm central government after the troubles leading to the execution of one king and the banishment of another, as the Latin poets (under orders from Maecenas, Minister of Propaganda and the Arts) had celebrated after Augustus's triumph at the close of the Roman Civil Wars. The new poetic technique was based partly on contemporary French practice—the 'Golden Age' of French literature had just begun—partly on that of the 'Golden Age' of Latin. The fashionable ten-or-twelve-syllabled iambic couplet, well-balanced and heavily packed with anti-thetical wit, was French. The use of 'poetical periphrasis' as a formal ornament was Latin: the poet was expected to refer, for instance, to the sea as the 'briny deep' or 'the fishy kingdom' and to fire as the 'devouring element'. The original reason for this convention was forgotten; it had grown out of the old religious taboo against direct mention of dangerous, powerful or unlucky things. (This taboo survived until recently in the Cornish tin-mines, where fear of the pixies made the miner refrain from speaking of 'owls, foxes, hares, cats or rats save in Tinner's language,' and in Scotland and North-Eastern England among fishermen who had a similar fear of annoying the pixies by un-periphrastic mention of pigs, cats or priests.) Because the Latin poets also had a poetic diction, with vocabulary and syntax forbidden to prose-writers, which they found useful in helping them to accommodate Latin to the Greek convention of hexameter and elegiac couplet, the English Augustans gradually developed a similar diction which they found useful in resolving awkward metrical problems.

The fanciful use of periphrasis was extended in the period of mid-Victorian Classicism. Lewis Carroll aptly parodied the poets of his time in *Poeta Fit, Non Nascitur* (1860–63).

> *'Next, when you are describing*
> *A shape, or sound, or tint*
> *Don't state the matter plainly*
> *But put it in a hint;*
> *And learn to look at all things*
> *With a sort of mental squint.'*

> *'For instance, if I wished, Sir,*
> *Of mutton-pies to tell*
> *Should I say "dreams of fleecy flocks*
> *Pent in a wheaten cell"?'*
> *"Why, yes," the old man said: "that phrase*
> *Would answer very well."'*

And the Romantic Revival had brought a highly archaic diction into fashion. It was considered improper to write:

> *But where the west winds blow,*
> *You care not, sweet, to know.*

The correct language was:

> *Yet whitherward the zephyrs fare*
> *To ken thou listest not, O maid most rare.*

and if 'wind' was used it had to rhyme with 'mind' not with 'sinned'. But Victorian Classicism was tainted with the ideal of progress. The dull, secure Augustan 'rocking-horse' alexandrine and heroic couplet had been abandoned since Keats's attack on them and a poet was encouraged to experiment in a variety of metres and to take his themes from anywhere he pleased. The change marked the instability of the social system: Chartism threatened, the monarchy was unpopular, and the preserves of the old landed nobility were being daily encroached upon by the captains of industry and the East India Company Nabobs. Originality came to be prized as a virtue: to be original in the mid-Victorian sense implied the 'mental squint' which enlarged the field of poetry by weaving poetic spells over such useful but vulgar things as steam-boats, mutton-pies, trade exhibitions and gas lamps. It also implied borrowing themes from Persian, Arabic or Indian literature, and acclimatizing the sapphic, alcaic, rondel and triolet as English metrical forms.

The true poet must always be original, but in a simpler sense: he must address only the Muse—not the King or Chief Bard or the people in general—and tell her the truth about himself and her in his own passionate and peculiar words. The Muse is a deity, but she is also a woman, and if her celebrant makes love to her with the second-hand phrases and ingenious verbal tricks that he uses to flatter her son Apollo she rejects him more decisively even than she rejects the tongue-tied or cowardly bungler. Not that the Muse is ever completely satisfied. Laura Riding has spoken on her behalf in three memorable lines:

> *Forgive me, giver, if I destroy the gift:*
> *It is so nearly what would please me*
> *I cannot but perfect it.*

A poet cannot continue to be a poet if he feels that he has made a permanent conquest of the Muse, that she is always his for the asking.

The Irish and Welsh distinguished carefully between poets and satirists: the poet's task was creative or curative, that of the satirist was destructive or noxious. An Irish poet could compose an *aer*, or satire, which would blight crops, dry up milk, raise blotches on his victim's face and ruin his character for ever. According to *The Hearings of the Scholars*, one synonym for satire was '*Brimón smetrach*', that is, word-feat-ear-tweaking:

> A brotherly trick used to be played by poets when they recited satire, namely to tweak the ear-lobe of their victim who, since there is no bone there, could claim no compensation for loss of honour—

—as he would have been able to do if the poet had tweaked his nose. Nor might he forcibly resist, since the poet was sacrosanct; however, if he was satirized undeservedly, the blotches would rise on the poet's own face and kill him at once, as happened to the poets who lampooned the blameless Luan and Cacir. Edmund Spenser in his *View of the Present State of Ireland* writes of the Irish poets of his own day:

> None dare displease them for feare to runne into reproach thorough their offence, and to be made infamous in the mouthes of men.

444

And Shakespeare mentions their power of 'rhyming rats to death', having somewhere heard of the seventh-century Seanchan Torpest, the master-ollave of Ireland who, one day finding that rats had eaten his dinner, uttered the vindictive *aer:*

> *Rats have sharp snouts*
> *Yet are poor fighters ...*

which killed ten of them on the spot.

In Greece the metres allotted to the satirist were the poetic metres in reverse. Satire can be called left-handed poetry. The Moon travels from left to right, the same way as the Sun, but as she grows older and weaker rises every night a little farther to the left; then, since the rate of plant growth under a waxing moon is greater than under a waning moon, the right hand has always been associated with growth and strength but the left with weakness and decay. Thus the word 'left' itself means, in Old Germanic, 'weak, old, palsied'. Lucky dances by devotees of the Moon were therefore made right-handed or clockwise, to induce prosperity; unlucky ones to cause damage or death were made left-handed, or 'widdershins'. Similarly, the right-handed fire-wheel, or swastika, was lucky; the left-handed (adopted by the Nazis) unlucky. There are two sides to the worship of the Indian Goddess Kali: her right side as benefactress and universal mother, her left side as fury and ogress. The word 'sinister' has come to mean more than left-handed because in Classical augury birds seen on the left hand portended ill-luck.

The word 'curse' derives from the Latin *cursus*, 'a running'—especially circular running as in a chariot race—and is short for *cursus contra solem.* Thus Margaret Balfour, accused as a witch in sixteenth-century Scotland, was charged with dancing widdershins nine times around men's houses, stark naked; and my friend A. K. Smith (late of the I.C.S.) once accidentally saw a naked Indian witch do the very same thing in Southern India as a ceremony of cursing. The Muse-priestesses of Helicon and Pieria, in a sinister mood, must have danced nine times about the object of their curse, or an emblem of it.

Most English poets have occasionally indulged in left-handed satire, Skelton, Donne, Shakespeare, Coleridge, Blake among them; those who have built up their reputation principally on satire, or parody—such as Samuel Butler, Pope, Swift, Calverley—are only grudgingly allowed the title of poet. But there is nothing in the language to match the Irish poets in vindictiveness, except what has been written by the Anglo-Irish. The technique of parody is the same as that employed by Russian witches: they walk quietly behind their victim, exactly mimicking his gait; then when in perfect sympathy with him suddenly stumble and fall, taking care to fall soft while he falls hard. Skilful parody of a poem upsets its dignity, sometimes permanently as in the case of the school-anthology poems parodied by Lewis Carroll in *Alice in Wonderland.*

The purpose of satire is to destroy whatever is overblown, faded and dull, and clear the soil for a new sowing. So the Cypriots understood the mystery of the God of the Year by describing him as *amphidexios*, which includes the sense of 'ambidextrous', 'ambiguous', and 'ambivalent', and putting a weapon in each of his hands. He is himself and his other self at the same time, king and supplanter, victim and murderer, poet and satirist—and his right hand does not know what his left hand does. In Mesopotamia, as Nergal, he was both the Sower who brought wealth to the fields and the Reaper, the God of the Dead; but elsewhere, in order to simplify the myth, he was represented as twins. This simplification has led, through dualistic theology, to the theory that death, evil, decay and destruction are erroneous concepts which God, the Good, the Right Hand, will one day disprove. Ascetic theologians try to paralyze or lop off the left hand in honour of the right; but poets are aware that each twin must conquer in turn, in an agelong and chivalrous war fought for the favours of the White Goddess, as the heroes Gwyn and Greidawl fought for the favours of Creiddylad, or the heroes Mot and Aleyn for those of Anatha of Ugarit. The war between Good and Evil has been waged in so indecent and painful a way during the past two millennia because the theologians, not being poets, have forbidden the Goddess to umpire it, and made God impose on the Devil impossible terms of unconditional surrender.

That woman must not be excluded from the company of poets was one of the wise rules at the Devil Tavern in Fleet Street, just before the Puritan Revolution, when Ben Jonson laid down the laws of poetry for his young contemporaries. He knew the risk run by Apollonians who try to be wholly independent of women: they fall into sentimental homosexuality. Once poetic fashions begin to be set by the homosexual, and 'Platonic love'—homosexual idealism—is introduced, the Goddess takes vengeance. Socrates, remember, would have banished poets from his dreary Republic. The alternative evasion of woman-love is monastic asceticism, the results of which are tragic rather than comic. However, woman is not a poet: she is either a Muse or she is nothing.[1] This is not to

---

[1] There are only a few recorded references in English Literature to a male Muse, and most of these occur in poems written by homosexuals and belong to morbid pathology. However, George Sandys in *A Relation of a Journey Begun* (1615), calls James I a 'Crowned Muse' perhaps because James behaved more like a Queen than a King towards his favourites at Court and because he published an elementary treatise on versification. And Milton writes in *Lycidas*:

> So may some gentle Muse
> With lucky words favour my destin'd urn
> And, as he passes, turn,
> And bid fair peace be to my sable shroud.

say that a woman should refrain from writing poems; only, that she should write as a woman, not as if she were an honorary man. The poet was originally the *mystes*, or ecstatic devotee of the Muse; the women who took part in her rites were her representatives, like the nine dancers in the Cogul cave-painting, or the nine women who warmed the cauldron of Cerridwen with their breaths in Gwion's *Preiddeu Annwm*. Poetry in its archaic setting, in fact, was either the moral and religious law laid down for man by the nine-fold Muse, or the ecstatic utterance of man in further-ance of this law and in glorification of the Muse. It is the imitation of male poetry that causes the false ring in the work of almost all women poets. A woman who concerns herself with poetry should, I believe, either be a silent Muse and inspire the poets by her womanly presence, as Queen Elizabeth and the Countess of Derby did, or she should be the Muse in a complete sense: she should be in turn Arianrhod, Blodeuwedd and the Old Sow of Maenawr Penardd who eats her farrow, and should write in each of these capacities with antique authority. She should be the visible moon: impartial, loving, severe, wise.

Sappho undertook this responsibility: one should not believe the malevolent lies of the Attic comedians who caricature her as an insatiable Lesbian. The quality of her poems proves her to have been a true Cerrid-wen. I once asked my so-called Moral Tutor at Oxford, a Classical scholar and Apollonian: 'Tell me, sir, do you think that Sappho was a good poet?' He looked up and down the street, as if to see whether anyone was listening and then confided to me: 'Yes, Graves, that's the trouble, she was very, *very* good!' I gathered that he considered it fortunate that so little of her work had survived. The sixteenth-century Welsh woman-poet, Gwerfyl Mechain, also seems to have played the part of Cerridwen: 'I am the hostess of the irreproachable Ferry Tavern, a white-gowned moon welcoming any man who comes to me with silver.'

The main theme of poetry is, properly, the relations of man and woman, rather than those of man and man, as the Apollonian Classicists would have it. The true poet who goes to the tavern and pays the silver tribute to Blodeuwedd goes over the river to his death. As in the story of Llew Llaw: 'All their discourse that night was concerning the affection and love that they felt one for the other and which in no longer space than one evening had arisen.' This paradise lasts only from May Day to St. John's Eve. Then the plot is hatched and the poisoned dart flies; and the poet knows that it must be so. For him there is no other woman but Cerridwen and he desires one thing above all else in the world: her love. As Blodeuwedd, she will gladly give him her love, but at only one price: his life. She will exact

However. this is a mere conceit. 'Muse' stands for 'poet possessed by a Muse': Milton had just traditionally addressed the female Muse with:

Begin, then, Sisters of the sacred well ...

payment punctually and bloodily. Other women, other goddesses, are kinder-seeming. They sell their love at a reasonable rate—sometimes a man may even have it for the asking. But not Cerridwen: for with her love goes wisdom. And however bitterly and grossly the poet may rail against her in the hour of his humiliation—Catullus is the most familiar instance—he has been party to his own betrayal and has no just cause for complaint.

Cerridwen abides. Poetry began in the matriarchal age, and derives its magic from the moon, not from the sun. No poet can hope to understand the nature of poetry unless he has had a vision of the Naked King crucified to the lopped oak, and watched the dancers, red-eyed from the acrid smoke of the sacrificial fires, stamping out the measure of the dance, their bodies bent uncouthly forward, with a monotonous chant of: 'Kill! kill! kill!' and 'Blood! blood! blood!'

Constant illiterate use of the phrase 'to woo the Muse' has obscured its poetic sense: the poet's inner communion with the White Goddess, regarded as the source of truth. Truth has been represented by poets as a naked woman: a woman divested of all garments or ornaments that will commit her to any particular position in time and space. The Syrian Moon-goddess was also represented so, with a snake head-dress to remind the devotee that she was Death in disguise, and a lion crouched watchfully at her feet. The poet is in love with the White Goddess, with Truth: his heart breaks with longing and love for her. She is the Flower-goddess Olwen or Blodeuwedd; but she is also Blodeuwedd the Owl, lamp-eyed, hooting dismally, with her foul nest in the hollow of a dead tree, or Circe the pitiless falcon, or Lamia with her flickering tongue, or the snarling-chopped Sow-goddess, or the mare-headed Rhiannon who feeds on raw flesh. *Odi atque amo:* 'to be in love with' is also to hate. Determined to escape from the dilemma, the Apollonian teaches himself to despise woman, and teaches woman to despise herself.

Solomon's wit is bitterly succinct: 'The horse-leech's two daughters: *Give* and *Give*.' The horse-leech is a small fresh-water animal akin to the medicinal leech, with thirty teeth in its jaws. When a beast goes down to a stream to drink, the leech swims into its mouth and fastens on the soft flesh at the back of its throat. It then sucks blood until completely distended, driving the beast frantic, and as a type of relentless greed gives its name to the Alukah, who is the Canaanite Lamia, or Succuba, or Vampire. The two daughters of Alukah are insatiable, like Alukah herself: and their names are Sheol and the Womb, or Death and Life. Solomon says, in other words: 'Women are greedy of children; they suck the vigour of their men-folk, like the Vampire; they are sexually insatiable; they resemble the horse-leech of the pond which plagues horses. And to what purpose are men born of women? Only in the end to die. The grave and woman are equally insatiable.' But Solomon of the *Proverbs* was a sour philosopher, not a romantic poet like the Galilean 'Solomon' of the *Canticles* who is really Salmaah, the Kenite Dionysus, making love in Hellenistic style to his twin-sister, the May bride of Shulem.

The reason why so remarkably few young poets continue nowadays to publish poetry after their early twenties is not necessarily—as I used to think—the decay of patronage and the impossibility of earning a decent living by the profession of poetry. There are several ways of supporting life which are consonant with the writing of poems; and publication of poems is not difficult. The reason is that something dies in the poet. Perhaps he has compromised his poetic integrity by valuing some range of experience or other—literary, religious, philosophical, dramatic, political or social—above the poetic. But perhaps also he has lost his sense of the White Goddess: the woman whom he took to be a Muse, or who was a Muse, turns into a domestic woman and would have him turn similarly into a domesticated man. Loyalty prevents him from parting company with her, especially if she is the mother of his children and is proud to be reckoned a good housewife; and as the Muse fades out, so does the poet. The English poets of the early nineteenth century, when the poetry-reading public was very large, were uncomfortably aware of this problem and many of them, such as Southey and Patmore, tried to lyricize domesticity, though none of them with poetic success. The White Goddess is anti-domestic; she is the perpetual 'other woman', and her part is difficult indeed for a woman of sensibility to play for more than a few years, because the temptation to commit suicide in simple domesticity lurks in every maenad's and muse's heart.

An unhappy solution to this difficult problem was attempted in Connaught in the seventh century A.D. by Liadan of Corkaguiney, a noblewoman and also an ollave-poet. She went with her train of twenty-four poet-pupils, as the immemorial custom was, on a poetic *cuairt*, or circuit of visits where, among others, the poet Curithir made an ale-feast for her and she fell in love with him. He felt an answering love and asked her: 'Why should we not marry? A son born to us would be famous.' She answered: 'Not now, it would spoil my round of poetic visits. Come to me later at Corkaguiney and I will go with you.' Then she began to brood on his words, and the more she brooded the less she liked them: he had spoken not of their love but only of their fame and of a famous son who might one day be born to them. Why a son? Why not a daughter? Was he rating his gifts above hers? And why irrelevantly contemplate the birth of future poets? Why was Curithir not content to be a poet himself and live in her poetic company? To bear children to such a man would be a sin against herself; yet she loved him with all her heart and had solemnly promised to go with him.

So when Liadan had finished her circuit of visits to the kings' and chieftains' houses of Connaught, exchanging poetic lore with the poets she found there, and receiving gifts from her hosts, she took a religious vow of chastity which it would be death to break; and did this not for any religious motive, but because she was a poet and realized that to marry Curithir would destroy the poetic bond between them. He came to fetch her presently and, true to her promise, she went with him; but, true to her vow, she would not sleep with him. Overwhelmed with grief he took a similar vow. The two then placed themselves under the direction of the severe and suspicious St. Cummine, who gave Curithir the choice of seeing Liadan without speaking to her, or speaking to her without seeing her. As a poet he chose speech. Alternately each would wander around the other's wattled cell in Cummine's monastic settlement, never being allowed to meet. When Curithir finally persuaded Cummine to relax the severity of this rule, he at once accused them of unchastity and banished Curithir from the settlement. Curithir renounced love, became a pilgrim, and Liadan died of remorse for the barren victory that she had won over him.

The Irish have been aware of the poet's love-problem since pre-Christian times. In the *Sickbed of Cuchulain*, Cuchulain, who is a poet as well as a hero, has deserted his wife Emer and fallen under the spell of Fand, a Queen of the Sidhe. Emer herself was originally his Muse and at their first meeting they had exchanged poetic conversation so abstruse that nobody present understood a word; but marriage had estranged them. Emer comes angrily to Fand's rath to reclaim Cuchulain, and Fand renounces her possession of him, admitting that he does not really love her and that he had better return to Emer:

> *Emer, noble wife, this man is yours.*
> *He has broken away from me,*
> *But still I am fated to desire*
> *What my hand cannot hold and keep.*

Cuchulain goes back, but Emer's victory is as barren as Liadan of Corkaguiney's. An ancient Irish *Triad* is justified: 'It is death to mock a poet, to love a poet, to be a poet.'

Let us consider Suibne Geilt, the poet-King of Dal Araidhe, about whom an anonymous ninth-century Irishman composed a prose tale, *The Madness of Suibne*, incorporating a sequence of dramatic poems based on certain seventh-century originals which were attributed to Suibne himself. In the tale, as it has come down to us, Suibne was driven mad because he had twice insulted St. Ronan: first, by interrupting the Saint as he marked out the site of a new church without royal permission, and tossing his psalter into a stream; and next, by flinging a spear at him as he tried to make peace between the High King of Ireland and Suibne's overlord, just before the Battle of Magh Rath. The spear hit St. Ronan's massbell, but glanced off harmlessly. St. Ronan thereupon cursed Suibne with the flying madness. Evidence found in three early chronicles, however, suggests that Suibne's second insult was directed not at St. Ronan but at an ollave, or sacrosanct poet, who was trying to make peace on the eve of Magh Rath between the rival army-commanders, namely King Domnal the Scot, and Domnal High King of Ireland. In the seventh century, such peacemaking was an ollave's function, not a priest's. Perhaps Suibne's spear struck the branch of golden bells which were the ollave's emblem of office; and the ollave vengefully threw in his face a so-called 'madman's wisp' (a magical handful of straw), which sent him fleeing crazily from the battlefield. At any rate, Suibne's wife Éorann had tried to restrain him from this act of folly, and was therefore spared the curse. The flying madness is described as making his body so light that he could perch in the tops of trees, and leap desperate leaps of a hundred feet or more without injury. (Mediaeval Latin philosophers described the condition as *spiritualizatio, agilitas* and *subtilitas,* and applied it to cases of levitation by ecstatic saints.) Feathers then sprouted on Suibne's body, and he lived like the wild things: feeding on sloes, hollyberries, watercress, brooklime, acorns; sleeping in yew-trees and rocky clefts of ivy-clad cliffs, and even in hawthorn and bramble bushes. The slightest noise would startle him into flight, and he was cursed with a perpetual distrust of all men.

Suibne had a friend, Loingseachan, who constantly went in pursuit, trying to catch and cure him. Loingseachan succeeded in this on three occasions, but Suibne always relapsed: a fury known as 'the Hag of the Mill', would soon tempt him to renew his frantic leaps. During a lucid interval after seven years of madness, Suibne visited Éorann, who was being forced to marry his successor the new king—and one most moving dramatic poem records their conversation:

SUIBNE: *'At ease you are, bright Éorann,*
                Bound bedward to your lover;
                It is not so with Suibne here—
                Long has he wandered footloose.

                'Lightly once, great Éorann,
                You whispered words that pleased me.
                "I could not live," you said, "were I
                Parted one day from Suibne."

                'Now it is clear and daylight clear,
                How small your care for Suibne;

You lie warm on a good down bed,
He starves for cold till sunrise.'

ÉORANN: 'Welcome, my guileless madman,
Dearest of humankind!
Though soft I lie, my body wastes
Since the day of your downfall.'

SUIBNE: 'More welcome than I, that prince
Who escorts you to the banquet.
He is your chosen gallant;
Your old love you neglect.'

ÉORANN: 'Though a prince may now escort me
To the carefree banquet-hall,
I had liefer sleep in a tree's cramped bole
With you, Suibne, my husband.

'Could I choose from all the warriors
Of Ireland and of Scotland,
I had liefer live, blameless, with you
On watercress and water.'

SUIBNE: 'No path for his belovéd
Is Suibne's track of care;
Cold he lies at Ard Abhla,
His lodgings cold are many.

'Far better to feel affection
For the prince whose bride you are,
Than for this madman all uncouth,
Famished and stark-naked.'

ÉORANN: 'I grieve for you, toiling madman,
So filthy and downcast;
I grieve that your skin is weather worn.
Torn by spines and brambles . . .

'O that we were together,
And my body feathered too;
In light and darkness would I wander
With you, for evermore!'

SUIBNE: 'One night I spent in cheerful Mourne,
One night in Bann's sweet estuary.
I have roved this land from end to end. . . .'

The tale continues:

'Hardly had Suibne spoken these words when the army came marching into the camp from all directions. He sped away in wild flight, as he had often done before; and presently, when he had perched on a high, ivy-clad branch, the Hag of the Mill settled close beside him. Suibne then made this poem, describing the trees and herbs of Ireland:

Bushy oak, leafy oak,
You tower above all trees.
O hazel, little branching one,
Coffer for sweet nuts!

You are not cruel, O alder.
Delightfully you gleam,
You neither rend nor prickle
In the gap you occupy.

Blackthorn, little thorny one,
Dark provider of sloes.
Watercress, little green-topped one,
From the stream where blackbirds drink.

O apple-tree, true to your kind,
You are much shaken by men;
O rowan, cluster-berried one,
Beautiful is your blossom!

O briar, arching over,
You never play me fair;
Ever again you tear me,
Drinking your fill of blood.

Yew-tree, yew-tree, true to your kind,
In churchyards you are found;
O ivy, growing ivy-like,
You are found in the dark wood.

O holly, tree of shelter,
Bulwark against the winds;
O ash-tree, very baleful one,
Haft for the warrior's spear.

O birch-tree, smooth and blessed,
Melodious and proud,

Delightful every tangled branch
At the top of your crown. . . .

Yet misery piled upon misery, until one day, when Suibne was about to pluck watercress from a stream at Ros Cornain, the wife of the monastery bailiff chased him away and plucked it all for herself, which sent him into utter despair:

Gloomy is this life,
In lack of a soft bed,
To know the numbing frost,
And rough wind-driven snow.

Cold wind, icy wind,
Faint shadow of a feeble sun,
Shelter of a single tree
On the top of a flat hill.

Enduring the rain-storm,
Stepping along deer-paths,
Slouching through greensward
On a day of grey frost.

A belling of stags
That echoes through the wood,
A climb to the deer-pass,
The roar of spumy seas. . . .

Stretched on a watery bed
By the banks of Loch Erne,
I consider early rising
When the day shall dawn.

Then Suibne thought again of Éorann. The story goes:
'Thereafter Suibne went to the place where Éorann was, and stood at the outer door of the house wherein were the queen and her women-folk, and said again: "At ease you are, Éorann, though ease is not for me."
' "True," said Éorann, "yet come in," said she.
' "Indeed I will not," said Suibne, "lest the army pen me into the house."
' "Methinks," said she, "your reason does not improve with time, and since you will not stay with us," said she, "go away and do not

visit us at all, for we are ashamed that you should be seen in this guise by those who have seen you in your true guise."

' "Wretched indeed is that," said Suibne. "Woe to him who trusts a woman. . . ." '

Suibne resumed his fruitless wanderings, until befriended by a cowman's wife, who would secretly pour a little milk for him into a hole she had stamped with her heel in the stable cow-dung. He lapped the milk gratefully, but one day the cowman mistook him for her lover, flung a spear, and mortally wounded him. Then Suibne regained his reason and died in peace. He lies buried beneath a fine headstone which the generous-hearted St. Moling raised to him. . . .

This impossible tale conceals a true one; that of the poet obsessed by the Hag of the Mill, another name for the White Goddess. He calls her 'the woman white with flour' just as the Greeks called her 'Alphito, Goddess of the Barley Flour'. This poet quarrels with both the Church and the bards of the Academic Establishment, and is outlawed by them. He loses touch with his more practical wife, once his Muse; and though, pitying such misery, she admits to a still unextinguished love for him, he can no longer reach her. He trusts nobody, not even his best friend, and enjoys no companionship but that of the blackbirds, the stags, the larks, the badgers, the little foxes, and the wild trees. Towards the end of his tale Suibne has lost even the Hag of the Mill, who snaps her neck-bone in leaping along with him; which means, I suppose, that he breaks down as a poet under the strain of loneliness. In his extremity Suibne returns to Éorann; but her heart has gone dead by now, and she sends him coldly away.

The tale seems to be devised as an illustration of the *Triad* that it is 'death to mock a poet, death to love a poet, death to be a poet'. Suibne found it death to mock a poet; and death to be a poet; Éorann found it death to love a poet. Only after he had died in misery did Suibne's fame flourish again.

This must be the most ruthless and bitter description in all European literature of an obsessed poet's predicament. The woman-poet's predicament is described in an almost equally poignant tale: *The Loves of Liadan and Curithir*, discussed above, is as sorrowful as Suibne's.

But let us not wallow in these griefs and flying-madnesses. A poet writes, as a rule, while he is young, and has the spell of the White Goddess on him.

> *My love is of a birth as rare*
> *As 'tis by nature strange and high:*
> *It was begotten by despair*
> *Upon impossibility.*

In the result, he either loses the girl altogether, as he rightly feared; or else he marries her and loses her in part. Well, why not? If she makes him a good wife, why should he cherish the poetic obsession to his own ruin? Again, if a woman-poet can get a healthy child in exchange for the gift of poetry, why not? The sovereign White Goddess dismisses both deserters with a faintly scornful smile, and inflicts no punishment, so far as I know; but then neither did she praise and cosset and confer Orders on them while they served her. There is no disgrace in being an ex-poet; if only one makes a clean break with poetry, like Rimbaud, or (more recently) Laura Riding.

Yet, is the alternative between service to the White Goddess, on the one hand, and respectable citizenship, on the other, quite so sharp as the Irish poets presented it? Suibne in his tale has an over-riding obsession about poetry; so has Liadan in hers. But was either of them gifted with a sense of humour? Doubtless not, or they would never have punished themselves so cruelly. Humour is one gift that helps men and women to survive the stress of city life. If he keeps his sense of humour, too, a poet can go mad gracefully, swallow his disappointments in love gracefully, reject the Establishment gracefully, die gracefully, and cause no upheaval in society. Nor need he indulge in self-pity, or cause distress to those who love him; and that goes for a woman-poet also.

Humour is surely reconcilable with devotion to the White Goddess; as it is, for example, with perfect sanctity in a Catholic priest, whose goings and comings are far more strictly circumscribed than a poet's, and whose Bible contains not one smile from *Genesis* to the *Apocalypse*. Andro Man said of the Queen of Elphame in 1597: 'She can be young or old, as it pleases her'; and indeed, the Goddess reserves a delightfully girlish giggle for those who are not daunted by her customary adult marble glare. She may even allow her poet an eventual happy marriage, if he has taken his early tumbles in good part. For though she is, by definition, non-human, neither is she altogether inhuman. Suibne complains about a snowstorm that caught him without clothes in the fork of a tree:

> *I am in great distress tonight,*
> *Pure wind my body pierces;*
> *My feet are wounded, my cheek pale,*
> *Great God, I have cause for grief!*

Yet his sufferings were by no means the whole story. He enjoyed life to the full in better weather: his meals of wild strawberries or blueberries, the swift flight that enabled him to overtake the wood-pigeon, his rides on the antlers of a stag or on the back of a slender-shinned fawn. He could even say: 'I take no pleasure in the amorous talk of man with woman; far more lovely, to my ear, is the song of the blackbird.' Nobody can blame Éorann for asking Suibne politely to begone, when he had reached that stage. What preserved her, and what he lacked, was surely a sense of humour? Éorann's earlier wish for a feathered body which would let her fly around with him, suggests that she too began as a poet, but sensibly resigned when the time for poetry had gone by.

Can the matter be left at this point? And should it be left there? In our chase of the Roebuck:

We'm powler't up and down a bit and had a rattling day

like the Three Jovial Huntsmen. But is it enough to have described something of the peculiar way in which poets have always thought, and to have recorded at the same time the survival of various antique themes and concepts, or even to have suggested a new intellectual approach to myths and sacred literature? What comes next? Should a practical poetic creed be drafted, which poets might debate, point by point, until it satisfied them as relevant to their immediate writing needs and in proper form for unanimous subscription? But who would presume to summon these poets to a synod or preside over their sessions? Who can make any claim to be a chief poet and wear the embroidered mantle of office which the ancient Irish called the *tugen*? Who can even claim to be an ollave? The ollave in ancient Ireland had to be master of one hundred and fifty Oghams, or verbal ciphers, which allowed him to converse with his fellow-poets over the heads of unlearned bystanders; to be able to repeat at a moment's notice any one of three hundred and fifty long traditional histories and romances, together with the incidental poems they contained, with appropriate harp accompaniment; to have memorized an immense number of other poems of different sorts; to be learned in philosophy; to be a doctor of civil law; to understand the history of modern, middle and ancient Irish with the derivations and changes of meaning of every word; to be skilled in music, augury, divination, medicine, mathematics, geography, universal history, astronomy, rhetoric and foreign languages; and to be able to extemporize poetry in fifty or more complicated metres. That anyone at all should have been able to qualify as an ollave is surprising; yet families of ollaves tended to intermarry; and among the Maoris of New Zealand where a curiously similar system prevailed, the capacity of the ollave to memorize, comprehend, elucidate and extemporize staggered Governor Grey and other early British observers.

Again, if this hypothetic synod were reserved for poets whose mother tongue is English, how many poets with the necessary patience and integrity to produce any authoritative document would respond to a summons? And even if the synod could be summoned, would not a cleavage be immediately apparent between the devotees of Apollo and those of the White Goddess? This is an Apollonian civilization. It is true that in English-speaking countries the social position of women has improved enormously in the last fifty years and is likely to improve still more now that so large a part of the national wealth is in the control of women—in the United States more than a half; but the age of religious revelation seems to be over, and social security is so intricately bound up with marriage and the family—even where registry marriages predominate—that the White Goddess in her orgiastic character seems to have no chance of staging a come-back, until women themselves grow weary of decadent patriarchalism, and turn Bassarids again. This is unlikely as yet, though the archives of morbid pathology are full of Bassarid case-histories. An English or American woman in a nervous breakdown of sexual origin will often instinctively reproduce in faithful and disgusting detail much of the ancient Dionysiac ritual. I have witnessed it myself in helpless terror.

The ascetic Thunder-god who inspired the Protestant Revolution has again yielded pride of place to Celestial Hercules, the original patron of the English monarchy. All the popular feasts in the Christian calendar are concerned either with the Son or the Mother, not with the Father, though prayers for rain, victory and the King's or President's health are still half-heartedly addressed to him. It is only the pure allegiance of Jesus, recorded in the Gospels, that has kept the Father from going 'the way of all flesh'—the way of his predecessors Saturn, The Dagda and Kai[1]—to end as chief cook and buffoon in the mid-winter masquerade. That may yet be the Father's end in Britain, if popular religious forces continue to work in their traditional fashion. An ominous sign is the conversion of St. Nicholas, the patron saint of sailors and children whose feast properly falls on the sixth of December, into white-bearded Father Christmas, the buffoonish patron of the holiday. For in the early morning of Christmas Day, clad in an old red cotton dressing-gown, Father Christmas fills the children's stockings with nuts, raisins, sugar biscuits and oranges; and, while the family are at church singing hymns in honour of the new-born king, presides in the kitchen over the turkey, roast beef, plum pudding, brandy butter and mince pies; and finally when the lighted candles of the Christmas tree have guttered down, goes out into the snow—or rain—with an empty sack and senile groans of farewell.

This is a cockney civilization and the commonest references to natural phenomena in traditional poetry, which was written by countrymen for countrymen, are becoming unintelligible. Not one English poet in fifty

[1] Vulcan is another example of a god who 'went the way of all flesh' before his final extinction. The last addition to the Vulcan legend was made by Apuleius in *The Golden Ass* where Vulcan cooks the wedding breakfast for Cupid and Psyche.

could identify the common trees of the Beth-Luis-Nion, and distinguish roebuck from fallow deer, aconite from corn-cockle, or wryneck from woodpecker. Bow and spear are antiquated weapons; ships have ceased to be the playthings of wind and wave; fear of ghosts and bogeys is confined to children and a few old peasants; and the cranes no longer 'make letters as they fly'—the last crane to breed in this country was shot in Anglesey in the year 1908.

The myths too are wearing thin. When the English language was first formed, all educated people were thinking within the framework of the Christian myth cycle, which was Judaeo-Greek with numerous paganistic accretions disguised as lives of the Saints. The Protestant revolution expelled all but a few saints, and the growth of rationalism since the Darwinian controversy has so weakened the Churches that Biblical myths no longer serve as a secure base of poetic reference; how many people to-day could identify the quotations of a mid-Victorian sermon? Moreover, the Greek and Latin myths which have always been as important to the poets (professionally at least) as the Christian, are also losing their validity. Only a severe Classical education can impress them on a child's mind strongly enough to give them emotional relevance, and the Classics no longer dominate the school curriculum either in Britain or the United States. There is not even an official canon of two or three hundred books which every educated person may be assumed to have read with care, and the unofficial canon contains many famous books which very few people indeed have really read—for example, Langland's *Piers Plowman*, Sir Thomas More's *Utopia* and Lyly's *Euphues*.

The only two English poets who had the necessary learning, poetic talent, humanity, dignity and independence of mind to be Chief Poets were John Skelton and Ben Jonson; both worthy of the laurel that they wore. Skelton, on terms of easy familiarity with Henry VIII, his former pupil, reckoned himself the spiritual superior, both as scholar and poet, of his ecclesiastical superior Cardinal Wolsey, a half-educated upstart, against whom at the risk of death he published the sharpest satires; and consequently spent the last years of his life in sanctuary at Westminster Abbey, refusing to recant. Jonson went on poetic circuits like an Irish ollave, sometimes with pupils 'sealed of the tribe of Ben', and spoke with acknowledged authority on all professional questions. As one of his hosts, the second Lord Falkland, wrote of him:

> *He had an infant's innocence and truth,*
> *The judgement of gray hairs, the wit of youth,*
> *Not a young rashness, not an ag'd despair,*
> *The courage of the one, the other's care;*
> *And both of them might wonder to discern*
> *His ableness to teach, his skill to learn.*

These lines are memorable as a summary of the ideal poetic temperament. Since Jonson there have been no Chief Poets worthy of the name, either official or unofficial ones.

The only poet, as far as I know, who ever seriously tried to institute bardism in England was William Blake: he intended his Prophetic Books as a complete corpus of poetic reference, but for want of intelligent colleagues was obliged to become a whole Bardic college in himself, without even an initiate to carry on the tradition after his death. Not wishing to cramp himself by using blank verse or the heroic couplet, he modelled his style on James Macpherson's free-verse renderings of the Gaelic legends of Oisin, and on the Hebrew prophets as sonorously translated in the Authorised Version of the Bible. Some of his mythological characters, such as the Giant Albion, Job, Erin and the Angel Uriel, are stock figures of mediaeval bardism; others are anagrams of key words found in a polyglot Bible—for example, Los for Sol, the Sun-god. He kept strictly to his system and it is only occasionally that figures occur in his prophecies that seem to belong to his private story rather than to the world of literature. Yet as a leading English literary columnist says of Blake's readers who admire the gleemanship of *Songs of Innocence*: 'Few will ever do more than dive into the prophetic poems and swim a stroke or two through the seas of shifting symbols and fables.' He quotes these lines from *Jerusalem*:

Albion cold lays on his Rock: storms and snows beat round him
Beneath the Furnaces and the starry Wheels and the Immortal Tomb:

* * * * *

The weeds of Death inwrap his hands and feet, blown incessant
And wash'd incessant by the for-ever restless sea-waves foaming abroad
Upon the White Rock. England, a Female Shadow, as deadly damps
Of the Mines of Cornwall and Derbyshire, lays upon his bosom heavy,
Moved by the wind in volumes of thick cloud, returning, folding round
His loins and bosom, unremovable by swelling storms and loud rending
Of enraged thunders. Around them the Starry Wheels of their Giant Sons
Revolve, and over them the Furnaces of Los, and the Immortal Tomb around,
Erin sitting in the Tomb to watch them unceasing night and day:
And the body of Albion was closed apart from all Nations.
Over them the famish'd Eagle screams on boney wings, and around
Them howls the Wolf of famine; deep heaves the Ocean black, thundering. . .

He comments: 'Blake's feelings and habits were those of the artisan, the handicraft worker. His point of view was that of the class whose peace and welfare were disastrously undermined by the introduction of machinery, and who were enslaved by the capitalization of industry. Recall how the imagery of wheels, forges, furnaces, smoke. "Satanic mills", is associated in the Prophetic Books with misery and torment. Remember that the years of Blake's life were also years of incessant wars. It is obvious that the imagery of this passage, as of many others, is an upsurging from Blake's subliminal consciousness of political passions. Albion as a mythical figure may typify Heaven knows what else besides, but that is neither here nor there. Note the imagery of war and mechanism ...'

It is the function of English popular critics to judge all poetry by gleeman standards. So the clear traditional imagery used by Blake is characteristically dismissed as 'neither here nor there' and he is charged with not knowing what he is writing about. The White Goddess's Starry Wheel here multiplied into the twelve wheeling signs of the Zodiac, and the intellectual Furnaces of Los (Apollo), and the Tomb of Albion—alias Llew Llaw Gyffes, who also appears as the famished Eagle with his boney wings—are misread as dark, mechanistic images of capitalistic oppression. And the perfectly clear distinction between archaic Albion and modern England is disregarded. Blake had read contemporary treatises on Druidism.

The bond that united the poets of the British Isles in pre-Christian days was the oath of secrecy, sworn by all members of the endowed poetic colleges, to hele, conceal and never reveal the college secrets. But once the Dog, Roebuck and Lapwing began to relax their vigilance and in the name of universal enlightenment permitted the secrets of the alphabet, the calendar and the abacus to be freely published, a learned age ended. Presently a sword like Alexander's severed the Gordian master-knot,[1] the colleges were dissolved, ecclesiasts claimed the sole right to declare and interpret religious myth, gleeman literature began to supersede the

---

[1] Gordium was in Eastern Phrygia, and according to local tradition whoever untied the knot would become master of Asia. Alexander, who had not the learning, patience or ingenuity to perform the task decently, used his sword. It was a raw-hide knot on the ox-yoke which had belonged to a Phrygian peasant named Gordius, and Gordius had been divinely marked out for royalty when an eagle settled on the yoke; by marriage with the priestess of Telmissus he became a petty king and presently extended his dominion over all Phrygia. When he built the fortress of Gordium he dedicated the yoke to King Zeus, it is said, and laid it up in the citadel. Gordium commanded the main trade route across Asia Minor from the Bosphorus to Antioch, so that the manifest meaning of the prophecy was that nobody could rule Asia Minor who did not hold Gordium; and it was from Gordium that Alexander began his second Eastern campaign which culminated in the defeat of Darius at Issus. Now, Gordius was the father of Midas, who has already been mentioned as a devotee of the Orphic Dionysus, so the yoke must originally have been dedicated to King Dionysus, not to Father Zeus. And the secret of the knot must have been a religious one, for another widespread early means of recording messages, besides notching sticks and scratching letters on clay, was to tie knots in string or strips of raw-hide. The Gordian knot, in fact, should have been 'untied' by reading the message it contained, which was perhaps a divine name of Dionysus, the one contained in the vowels of the Beth-Luis-Nion. By cutting the knot Alexander ended an ancient religious dispensation, and since his act seemed to go unpunished—for he afterwards conquered the whole East as far as the Indus valley—it became a precedent for rating military power above religion or learning; just as the sword of Brennus the Gaul, thrown into the scales that measured out the agreed tribute of Roman gold, provided a precedent for rating military power above justice or honour.

literature of learning, and poets who thereafter refused to become Court lackeys or Church lackeys or lackeys of the mob were forced out into the wilderness. There, with rare intermissions, they have resided ever since, and though sometimes when they die pilgrimages are made to their oracular tombs, there they are likely to remain for as long as who cares?

In the wilderness the temptation to monomaniac raving, paranoia and eccentric behaviour has been too much for many of the exiles. They have no Chief Poet or visiting ollave now to warn them sternly that the good name of poetry is dishonoured by their mopping and mowing. They rave on like Elizabethan Abraham-men, until raving becomes a professional affectation; until the bulk of modern poetry ceases to make poetic, prosaic, or even pathological sense. A strange reversal of function: in ancient times the painters were supplied with their themes by the poets, though at liberty to indulge in as much decorative play as was decent within the limits of a given theme; later, the failure of the poets to keep their position at the head of affairs forced painters to paint whatever their patrons commissioned, or whatever came to hand, and finally to experiment in pure decoration; now affectations of madness in poets are condoned by false analogy with pictorial experiments in unrepresentational form and colour. So Sacheverell Sitwell wrote in *Vogue* (August, 1945):

> Once again we are leading Europe in the Arts . . .

He lists the fashionable painters and sculptors and adds:

> The accompanying works of the poets are not hard to find. . . Dylan Thomas, whose texture is as abstract as that of any modern painter . . . There is even no necessity for him to explain his imagery, for it is only intended to be half understood.

It is not as though the so-called surrealists, impressionists, expressionists and neo-romantics were concealing a grand secret by pretended folly, in the style of Gwion; they are concealing their unhappy lack of a secret.

For there are no poetic secrets now, except of course the sort which the common people are debarred by their lack of poetic perception from understanding, and by their anti-poetic education (unless perhaps in wild Wales) from respecting. Such secrets, even the Work of the Chariot, may be safely revealed in any crowded restaurant or café without fear of the avenging lightning-stroke: the noise of the orchestra, the clatter of plates and the buzz of a hundred unrelated conversations will effectively drown the words—and, in any case, nobody will be listening.

*　　*　　*

If this were an ordinary book it would end here on a dying close, and having no wish to be tedious I tried at first to end it here; but the Devil was in it and would not give me peace until I had given him his due, as he put it. Among the poetic questions I had not answered was Donne's 'Who cleft the Devil's foot?' And the Devil, who knows his Scriptures well, taunted me with having skated too lightly over some of the elements in Ezekiel's vision of the Chariot, and with having avoided any discussion of the only Mystery that is still regarded in the Western World with a certain awe. So back I had to go again, weary as I was, to the Chariot and its historical bearing on the Battle of the Trees and the poetic problems stated at the beginning of this book. It is a matter of poetic principle never to fob the Devil off with a half-answer or a lie.

Ezekiel's vision was of an Enthroned Man surrounded by a rainbow, its seven colours corresponding with the seven heavenly bodies that ruled the week. Four of these bodies were symbolized by the four spokes of the chariot-wheels: Ninib (Saturn) by the mid-winter spoke, Marduk (Juppiter) by the Spring equinox spoke, Nergal (Mars) by the mid-summer spoke, Nabu (Mercury) by the Autumn equinox spoke. But what of the three other heavenly bodies—the Sun, the Moon and the planet Ishtar (Venus)—corresponding with the Capitoline Trinity and with the Trinity worshipped at Elephantine and at Hierapolis? It will be recalled that the metaphysical explanation of this type of Trinity, brought to Rome by the Orphics, was that Juno was physical nature (Ishtar), Juppiter was the impregnating or animating principle (the Sun) and Minerva was the directing wisdom behind the Universe (the Moon). This concept did not appeal to Ezekiel, because it limited Jehovah's function to blind paternity; so though the Sun figures in his vision as the Eagle's wings, neither the Moon nor Ishtar is present.

The Devil was right. The vision cannot be fully explained without revealing the mystery of the Holy Trinity. It must be remembered that in ancient religions every 'mystery' implied a mystagogue who orally explained its logic to initiates: he may often have given a false or iconotropic explanation but it was at least a full one. As I read Origen's second-century *In Celsum*, the early Church had certain mysteries explained only to a small circle of elders—Origen says in effect 'Why should we not keep our mysteries to ourselves? You heathen do—and the logical explanation of the Trinity, whose seeming illogic ordinary members of the Church had to swallow by an act of faith, must have been the mystagogue's most responsible task. The mystery itself is no secret—it is stated very precisely in the Athanasian Creed; nor is the mystery which derives from it, the redemption of the world by the incarnation of the Word as Jesus Christ. But unless the College of Cardinals has been remarkably discreet throughout all the intervening centuries, the original explanation of the mysteries, which makes the *Credo quia absurdum* needless, has long been lost. Yet, I believe, not irrecoverably lost, since we may be sure that the doctrine developed from Judaeo-Greek mythology which is ultimately based on the single poetic Theme.

The religious concept of free choice between good and evil, which is common to Pythagorean philosophy and prophetic Judaism, developed from a manipulation of the tree-alphabet. In the primitive cult of the Universal Goddess, to which the tree-alphabet is the guide, there was no room for choice: her devotees accepted the events, pleasurable and painful in turn, which she imposed on them as their destiny in the natural order of things. The change resulted from the Goddess's displacement by the Universal God, and is historically related to the forcible removal of the consonants H and F from the Greek alphabet and their incorporation in the secret eight-letter name of this God: it seems clear that the Pythagorean mystics who instigated the change had adopted the Jewish Creation myth and regarded these two letters as peculiarly holy since uncontaminated with the errors of the material universe. For, though in the old mythology H and F had figured as the months sacred respectively to the harsh Hawthorn-goddess Cranaea and her doomed partner Cronos, in the new they represented the first and the last trees of the Sacred Grove, the first and the last days of Creation. On the first day nothing had been created except disembodied Light, and on the last nothing at all had been created. Thus the three consonants of the Logos, or 'eightfold city of light', were J, the letter of new life and sovereignty; H, the letter of the first Day of Creation, 'Let there be Light'; and F, the letter of the last day of Creation, 'Let there be Rest', which appears as W in the JHWH Tetragrammaton. It is remarkable that these are the month-letters allotted to the three tribes of the Southern kingdom, Benjamin, Judah and Levi; and that the three jewels respectively assigned to them in the jewel-sequence—Amber, Fire-Garnet ('the terrible crystal'), and Sapphire—are the three connected by Ezekiel with the radiance of God, and with his throne. The Enthroned Man is not God, as might be supposed: God lets nobody see his face and live. It is God's likeness reflected in spiritual man. Thus, though Ezekiel retains the traditional imagery of the unchanging Sun-God who rules from the apex of a cone of light over the four regions of the round universe—the eagle poised above the four beasts—and of the ever-changing bull-calf, Celestial Hercules, he has withdrawn Jehovah from the old Trinity of Q're (Sun), Ashima (Moon) and Anatha (Ishtar) and re-defined him as the God who demands national perfection, whose similitude is a holy Being, half Judah, half Benjamin, seated on Levi's throne. This explains Israel as a 'peculiar people'—the *Deuteronomy* text is of about the same date as Ezekiel's vision—dedicated to a peculiarly holy god with a new name, derived from a new poetic formula which spells out Life, Light and Peace.

I am suggesting, in fact, that the religious revolution which brought about the alphabetic changes in Greece and Britain was a Jewish one, initiated by Ezekiel (622–570 B.C.) which was taken up by the Greek-speaking Jews of Egypt and borrowed from them by the Pythagoreans. Pythagoras, who first came into prominence at Crotona in 529 B.C., is credited by his biographers with having studied among the Jews as well as the Egyptians, and may have been the Greek who first internationalized the eight-letter Name. The Name must have come to Britain by way of Southern Gaul where the Pythagoreans were established early.

The result of envisaging this god of pure meditation, the Universal Mind still premised by the most reputable modern philosophers, and enthroning him above Nature as essential Truth and Goodness was not an altogether happy one. Many of the Pythagoreans suffered, like the Jews, from a constant sense of guilt and the ancient poetic Theme reasserted itself perversely. The new God claimed to be dominant as Alpha and Omega, the Beginning and the End, pure Holiness, pure Good, pure Logic, able to exist without the aid of woman; but it was natural to identify him with one of the original rivals of the Theme and to ally the woman and the other rival permanently against him. The outcome was philosophical dualism with all the tragi-comic woes attendant on spiritual dichotomy. If the True God, the God of the Logos, was pure thought, pure good, whence came evil and error? Two separate creations had to be assumed: the true spiritual Creation and the false material Creation. In terms of the heavenly bodies, Sun and Saturn were now jointly opposed to Moon, Mars, Mercury, Juppiter and Venus. The five heavenly bodies in opposition made a strong partnership, with a woman at the beginning and a woman at the end. Juppiter and the Moon Goddess paired together as the rulers of the material World, the lovers Mars and Venus paired together as the lustful Flesh, and between the pairs stood Mercury who was the Devil, the Cosmocrator or author of the false creation. It was these five who composed the Pythagorean *hyle*, or grove, of the five material senses; and spiritually minded men, coming to regard them as sources of error, tried to rise superior to them by pure meditation. This policy was carried to extreme lengths by the God-fearing Essenes, who formed their monkish communities, within compounds topped by acacia hedges, from which all women were excluded; lived ascetically, cultivated a morbid disgust for their own natural functions and turned their eyes away from World, Flesh and Devil. Though they retained the Bull-calf myth, handed down from Solomon's days, as emblematic of the spiritual life of mortal man and linked it to the seven-letter name of immortal God, it is clear that initiates of the highest Order cultivated the eight-letter name, or the enlarged name of seventy-two letters, and devoted themselves wholly to the meditative life: ruled by acacia and pomegranate, Sunday and Saturday, Illumination and Repose.

War had now been declared in Heaven, Michael and the archangels fighting against the Devil, namley the Cosmocrator. For in the new dispensation, God could not afford to surrender the whole working week to the Devil, so he appointed archangels as his deputies, with a day for each, which were the archangels cultivated by the Essenes. Michael was given charge over Wednesday; so it fell to him not only to collect the dust for the true creation of Adam but to offer battle to the Devil who disputed that day with him. The Devil was Nabu, pictured as a winged Goat of Midsummer; so that the answer to Donne's poetic question about the Devil's foot is: 'The prophet Ezekiel'. Michael's victory must be read as a prophecy rather than as a record: a prophecy which Jesus tried to implement by preaching perfect obedience to God and continuous resistance to the World, Flesh and Devil. He reproached the Samaritan woman at Sychar, in a riddling talk which she may or may not have understood, for having had five husbands, the five material senses, and for having as present husband one who was not really her husband, namely the Cosmocrator, or Devil. He told her that salvation came, not from the Calf-god whom her fathers had idolatrously worshipped on near-by Ebal and Gerizim, but from the all-holy God of the Jews—the God, that is to say, of Judah, Benjamin and Levi. His faith was that if the whole nation repented of their erroneous devotion to the material universe, and refrained from all sexual and quasi-sexual acts, they would conquer death and live for a thousand years, at the end of which they would become one with the true God.

The Jews were not yet ready to take this step, though many of them approved of it in theory; and a conservative minority, the Ophites, continued to reject the new faith, holding that the true God was the God of Wednesday, whom they pictured as a benign Serpent, not a goat, and that the God of the Logos was an impostor. Their case rested on the Menorah, a pre-Exilic instrument of worship, the seven branches of which issued from the central almond stem, typifying Wednesday; and indeed the revised view recorded in the Talmud, that the stem represented the Sabbath, made neither poetic nor historical sense. This Serpent had originally been Ophion with whom, according to the Orphic creation myth, the White Goddess had coupled in the form of a female serpent, and Mercury the Cosmocrator therefore used a wand of coupling serpents as his badge of office. It is now clear why Ezekiel disguised two of the four planetary beasts of his vision: recording eagle instead of eagle-winged goat and man instead of man-faced serpent. He was intent on keeping the Cosmocrator out of the picture, whether he came as Goat or Serpent. It may well have been Ezekiel who appended the iconotropic anecdote of the Serpent's seduction of Adam and Eve to the *Genesis* Creation myth, and once it was approved as canonical, in the fourth century B.C., the Ophite view became a heresy. It must be emphasized that the *Genesis* Seven Days of Creation narrative is based on the symbolism of the Menorah, a relic of the Egyptian sun-cult, not derived from the Babylonian Creation Epic, in which the Creator is the Thunder-god Marduk who defeats Tiamat the Sea-Monster and cuts her in half. Marduk—Bel in the earlier version of the story—was the God of Thursday, not Nabu the God of Wednesday nor Samas the God of Sunday. The resemblances between the two myths are superficial, though the Deluge incident in *Genesis* has been taken directly from the Epic, and Ezekiel may have edited it.[1]

In Rabbinical tradition the Tree of the Knowledge of Good and Evil, whose fruit the Serpent in the *Genesis* allegory gave Adam and Eve to eat, was a composite one. This means that though they were originally innocent and holy he introduced them to the pleasures of the material senses. Monday's willow and Tuesday's kerm-oak (or holly) do not supply human food, but they must have eaten Wednesday's almonds (or hazel-nuts), Thursday's pistachios (or edible acorns), and Friday's quinces (or wild apples). So God expelled them from the tree-paradise for fear that they might meddle with the Tree of Life—presumably Sunday's acacia grafted with Saturday's pomegranate—and thus immortalize their follies. This reading of the myth is supported by the ancient Irish legend, first published in *Eriu IV*, Part 2, of Trefuilngid Tre-eochair ('the triple bearer of the triple key'—apparently an Irish form of Hermes Trismegistos) a giant who appeared in Ireland early in the first century A.D. with immense splendour at a meeting of the great manor-council of Tara. He bore in his right hand a branch of wood from the Lebanon with three fruits on it—hazel-nuts, apples and edible acorns—which perpetually sustained him in food and drink. He told them that on enquiring what ailed the Sun that day in the East, he had found that it had not shone there because a man of great importance (Jesus) had been crucified. As the giant went off, some of the fruit dropped in Eastern Ireland and up sprang five trees—the five trees of the senses—which would fall only when Christianity triumphed. These trees have already been mentioned in the discussion of the tree-alphabet. The Great Tree of Mugna bred true to its parent branch with successive crops of apples, nuts and edible acorns. The others

---

[1] In the Babylonian Epic is was Ishtar, not any male God, who caused the Deluge. Gilgamesh (Noah) stocked an ark with beasts of every kind and gave a New Year's feast to the builders with great outpouring of new wine; the New Year's Feast being an autumnal one. The myth seems to be iconotropic, for the account of the great wine-drinking, which appears in the *Genesis* version as a moral story of Noah's drunkenness and the bad behaviour of his son Canaan (Ham), recalls the myth of the wine-god Dionysus. When captured by Tyrrhenian pirates, Dionysus changed the masts of their ship into serpents, himself into a lion and the sailors into dolphins, and wreathed everything with ivy. The original Asianic icon from which both myths are presumably derived must have shown the god in a moon-ship at the Vintage Feast, going through his habitual New Year changes—bull, lion, snake and so on—which gave rise to the Babylonian story of the cargo of animals. The pirates' ship is probably described as Tyrrhenian because it had a figure-head in the shape of a Telchin, or dog with fins for feet, an attendant of the Moon-goddess.

seem to be allegorical glosses, by some later poet. The Tree of Tortu and the Branching Tree of Dathi were ashes, presumably representing the false magic of the Brythonic and Danish ash-cults. The Tree of Ross was a Yew, representing death and destruction. I cannot find what the Ancient Tree of Usnech was: it is likely to have been a blackthorn, representing strife.

The Holy Trinity doctrine was pre-Christian, founded on Ezekiel's vision, the Trinity consisting of the three main elements of the Tetragrammaton. The First person was the true Creator, the All-Father, 'Let there be Light', represented by the letter H, the acacia, the tree of Sunday, the tree of Levi, the lapis lazuli symbolizing the blue sky as yet untenanted by the heavenly bodies; he was identified by the Jewish apocalyptics with the 'Ancient of Days' in the Vision of Daniel, a later and inferior prophecy which dates from the Seleucid epoch. The Second Person was comprised in Ezekiel's Enthroned Man—spiritual man as God's image, man who abstained in perfect peace from the dangerous pleasures of the false creation and was destined to reign on earth everlastingly; he was represented by F, the fire-garnet, the pomegranate, the tree of the Sabbath and of Judah. The apocalyptics identified him with the Son of Man in Daniels' vision. But only the lower half of the Man's body was fire-garnet: the male part. The upper half was amber: the royal part, linking him with the Third Person. For the Third Person comprised the remaining six letters of the name, six being the Number of Life in the Pythagorean philosophy. These letters were the original White-goddess vowels, A O U E I, representing the spirit that moved on the face of the waters in the *Genesis* narrative: but with the death vowel I replaced by the royal consonant J, amber, Benjamin's letter, the letter of the Divine Child born on the Day of Liberation; and with the 'birth of birth' vowel *omega* supplementing the birth vowel *alpha*. The Third Person was thus androgynous: 'virgin with child', a concept which apparently accounts for the reduplication of the letter H in the J H W H Tetragrammaton. The second H is the Shekinah, the Brightness of God, the mystic female emanation of H, the male First Person; with no existence apart from him, but identified with Wisdom, the brightness of his meditation, who has 'hewn out her Seven Pillars' of the true Creation and from which the 'Peace that passeth understanding' derives when Light is linked with Life. The sense of this mystery is conveyed in the Blessing of Aaron (*Numbers, VI, 22-27*), which only priests were authorized to utter:

The Lord bless you and keep you.
The Lord make his face to shine upon you and be gracious unto you,
The Lord lift up the light of his countenance upon you,
And give you peace.

This fourfold blessing, which was certainly not composed earlier than the time of Ezekiel, is explained in the last verse of the chapter as a formula embodying the Tetragrammaton:

And they [Aaron and his sons] shall put my Name upon the Children of Israel, and I shall bless them.

The first two blessings are really one, together representing the Third Person, Life and the Brightness, J H; the third blessing represents the First person, Light, H; the fourth blessing represents the Second Person, Peace, W. This Trinity is one indivisible God, because if a single letter is omitted the Name loses its power, and because the three concepts are interdependent. The Second Person is 'begotten by the Father before all the world' in the sense that 'the World' is a false Creation which he preceded. This interpretation of J H W H as 'Light and the Glory, Life and Peace' further explains why the priests sometimes enlarged it to 42 letters. In the Pythagorean system, 7, written as H aspirate, was the numeral of Light and 6, written as Digamma F (W in Hebrew), was that of Life. But 6 also stood for the Glory, and 7 for Peace as the seventh day of the week; so six times seven, namely 42, expressed Light, the Glory and Peace multiplied by Life. Though the Jews used the Phoenician notation of numeral letters for public purposes, it is likely that they used the early Greek in their mysteries, just as they used the Greek 'Boibalos' calendar-alphabet.

The *Menorah* symbolized the fullness of Jehovah's Creation, yet it did not contain the first of the four letters of the Tetragrammaton; and its lights recalled his seven-letter Name, but not the eight-letter one. However, at the Feast of Illumination, or 'The Feast of Lights', (mentioned in *John X*, 22 and Josephus's *Antiquities*, *XII*, 7.7), the ancient Hebrew Winter Solstice Feast, an eight-branched candlestick was used, as it still is in Jewish synagogues, known as the Chanukah candlestick. The rabbinical account is that this eight-day festival which begins on the twenty-fifth day of the month Kislev, was instituted by Judas Maccabeus and that it celebrates a miracle: at the Maccabean consecration of the Temple a small cruse of sacred oil was found, hidden by a former High Priest, which lasted for eight days. By this legend the authors of the *Talmud* hoped to conceal the antiquity of the feast, which was originally Jehovah's birthday as the Sun-god and had been celebrated at least as early as the time of Nehemiah (*Maccabees*, *I*, 18). Antiochus Epiphanes had sacrificed to Olympian Zeus, three years before Judas's re-institution of the festival, at the same place and on the same day: Zeus's birthday fell at the winter solstice too—as did that of Mithras the Persian Sun-god whose cult had greatly impressed the Jews in the time of their protector Cyrus. According to rabbinical custom one light of the candlestick was kindled each day of the festival until all eight were alight; the earlier tradition had been to begin with eight lights and extinguish one each day until all were out.

In the Chanukah candlestick which, among the Moroccan Jews (whose tradition is the oldest and purest) is surmounted by a small pomegranate, the eight lights are set in a row, each on a separate branch, as in the Menorah; and an arm projects from the pedestal with a separate light in its socket from which all the rest are kindled. The eighth light in the row must stand for the extra day of the year, the day of the letter J, which is intercalated at the winter solstice: for the pomegranate, the emblem not only of the seventh day of the week but of the planet Ninib, ruler of the winter solstice, shows that this candlestick is a Menorah enlarged to contain all the letters of the Tetragrammaton, that it is, in fact, the 'Eightfold City of Light' in which the Word dwelt. The number Eight, the Sun-god's number of increase, recalled Jehovah's creative order to increase and multiply; and the eight lights could further be understood (it will be shown) as symbolizing the eight essential Commandments.

The Chanukah candlestick was the only one ritually used in the synagogues of the Dispersion, because of the Sanhedrin law forbidding the reproduction of the Menorah or of any other object housed in the Holy of Holies. This law was designed to prevent the foundation of a rival Temple to that of Jerusalem, but aimed also, it seems, at the Ophites, who justified their heretical religious views by the centrality of the fourth light (that of the Wise Serpent Nabu) in the seven-branched candlestick; they would find no central light in this one. The separate light probably stood for the oneness of Jehovah as contrasted with the diversity of his works and brought the total number of lights up to nine, symbolizing the thrice-holy Trinity. The meaning of the pomegranate at the top has been forgotten by the Moroccan Jews, who regard it as a mere decoration though agreeing that it is of high antiquity; Central European Jews have substituted for it a knob surmounted by a Star of David. Among the Moroccan Jews a pomegranate is also placed on the sticks around which the sacred scroll of the Torah is wound, the sticks being called *Es Chajim*, 'the tree of life'; Central European Jews have reduced this pomegranate to the crown formed by its withered calyx. The common-sense Rabbinical explanation of the sanctity of the pomegranate is that it is the only fruit which worms do not corrupt.

The Ten Commandments, which are among the latest additions to the Pentateuch, are designed as glosses on the same mystery. The oddness of their choice seems to have struck Jesus when he quoted the 'Love thy God' and 'Love thy neighbour' commandments, from elsewhere in the Pentateuch, as transcending them in spiritual value. But it is a more carefully considered choice than appears at first sight. The Commandments, which are really eight, not ten, to match the numbers of letters in the Name, fall into two groups: one of three 'Thou shalts' concerned with the True Creation, and the other of five 'Thou shalt nots' concerned with the False Creation: each group is prefaced by a warning. The order is purposely 'pied', as one would expect.

The first group corresponds with the letters of the Tetragrammaton, and the warning preface is therefore III: 'Thou shalt not take God's name in vain.'

> V: 'Honour thy father and thy mother.'
> i.e. J H: Life and the Brightness.

> IV: 'Observe the Sabbath Day.
> i.e. W: Peace.

> I: 'Thou shalt worship me alone.'
> i.e. H: Light.

The second group corresponds with the powers of the five planets excluded from the Name and the warning preface is therefore II: 'Thou shalt not make nor adore the simulacrum of any star, creature, or marine monster.'

> X: 'Thou shalt not bewitch.'
> (The Moon, as the Goddess of Enchantment.)

> VI: 'Thou shalt not kill.'
> (Mars as the God of War.)

> VIII: 'Thou shalt not steal.'
> (Mercury, as the God of Thieves, who had
> stolen man from God.)

> IX: 'Thou shalt not bear false witness.'
> (Juppiter as the false god before whom oaths
> were sworn.)

> VII: 'Thou shalt not commit adultery.'
> (Venus as the Goddess of profane love.)

The eight Commandments are enlarged to a decalogue apparently because the series which it superseded, and which is to be found in *Exodus, XXXIV, 14–26,* was a decalogue too.

In Talmudic tradition this new Decalogue was carved on two tables of *sappur* (lapis lazuli); and in *Isaiah, LIV, 12,* the gates of the ideal Jerusalem were of 'fire-stones' (pyropes or fire-garnets). So the poetic formula is:

> *Light was my first day of Creation,*
> *Peace after labour is my seventh day,*

Life and the Glory are my day of days.
I carved my Law on tables of sapphirus,
Jerusalem shines with my pyrope gates,
Four Cherubs fetch me amber from the north.
Acacia yields her timber for my ark,
Pomegranate sanctifies my priestly hem,
My hyssop sprinkles blood at every door.
Holy, Holy, Holy is my name.

This mystical god differed not only from the Babylonian Bel or Marduk but from Ormazd, the Supreme God of the Persian Zoroastrians, with whom some Jewish syncretists identified him, in having separated himself from the erroneous material universe to live securely cloistered in his abstract city of light. Ormazd was a sort of three-bodied Geryon, the usual Aryan male trinity that first married the Triple Goddess, then dispossessed her and went about clothed in her three colours—white, red and dark blue, like the heifer calf in Suidas's riddle, performing her ancient functions. Thus Ormazd appeared in priestly white to create (or recreate) the world; in warrior red to combat evil; in husbandman's dark blue to 'bring forth fecundity'.

The pre-Christian Jewish apocalyptics, probably influenced by religious theory brought from India, along with the *ethrog*, by Jewish merchants, expected the birth of a divine child: the Child, prophesied by the Sibyl, who would free the world from sin. This implied that Michael and the archangels to whom the new Idealistic God had delegated the immediate care of mankind had proved no match for the World, Flesh and Devil—the grosser powers which he had repudiated. The only solution was for the Prince of Peace, namely the Second Person, the Son of Man, who had hitherto had no independent existence,[1] to become incarnate as perfect man—the human Messiah born of Judah, Benjamin and Levi. By exposing the vanity of the material Creation he would bring all Israel to repentance and thus initiate the deathless millennary kingdom of God on earth, to which the Gentile nations would ultimately be admitted. This was the faith of Jesus, who was of Judah, Benjamin and Levi and had been ritually rebegotten by God at his Coronation: he expected the actual historical appearance of the Son of Man on the Mount of Olives to follow his own prophesied death by the sword, and assured his disciples that many then living would never die but enter directly into the kingdom of God. The prophecy was not fulfilled because it was founded on a confusion between poetic myth and historical event, and everyone's hopes of the millennium were dashed.

[1] This was denounced as the Beryllian heresy at Bostia in A.D. 244.

The Grecians then claimed that those hopes had not after all been premature, that Jesus had indeed been the Second Person of the Trinity, and that the Kingdom of God was at hand, the dreadful signs which would portend its coming, the so-called Pangs of the Messiah, being apparent to everyone. But when the Gentile Church had wholly separated itself from the Judaistic Church and Jesus as King of Israel was an embarrassing concept to Christians who wished to escape all suspicion of being Jewish nationalists, it was decided that he had been born as the Second Person not at his coronation but at his physical birth; though spiritually begotten before all the world. This made Mary the Mother of Jesus into the immaculate human receptacle of the Life and Brightness of God, the Third Person of the Trinity; so that it had to be presumed that she was herself immaculately conceived by her mother St. Ann. Here was a fine breeding-ground for all sorts of heresy, and soon we return in our argument to the point where the Theme reasserted itself popularly with the Virgin as the White Goddess, Jesus as the Waxing Sun, the Devil as the Waning Sun. There was no room here for the Father God, except as a mystical adjunct of Jesus ('I and the Father are One').

Chapter Twenty-Six

RETURN OF THE GODDESS

What, then, is to be the future of religion in the West?

Sir James Frazer attributed the defects of European civilization to 'the selfish and immoral doctrine of Oriental religions which inculcated the communion of the soul with God, and its eternal salvation, as the only objects worth living for'. This, he argued, undermined the unselfish ideal of Greek and Roman society which subordinated the individual to the welfare of the State. Adolf Hitler said later, more succinctly: 'The Jews are to blame for all our troubles.' Both statements, however, were historically untrue.

Frazer, an authority on Greek religion, must have known that the salvationist obsession of the Greek Orphics was Thraco-Libyan, not Oriental, and that long before the Jews of the Dispersal had introduced to the Greek world their Pharisaic doctrine of oneness with God, city-state idealism had been destroyed from within. Once speculative philosophy had made sceptics of all educated Greeks who were not Orphics or members of some other mystical fraternity, public as well as private faith was undermined and, despite the prodigious conquests of Alexander, Greece was easily defeated by the semi-barbarous Romans, who combined religious conservatism with national *esprit de corps*. The Roman nobles then put themselves to school under the Greeks, and caught the philosophical infection; their own idealism crumbled and only the regimental *esprit de corps* of the untutored legions, combined with Emperor-worship on the Oriental model, staved off political collapse. Finally, in the fourth century A.D., they found the pressure of the barbarians against their frontiers so strong that it was only by recourse to the still vigorous faith of Christianity that they could save what remained of the Empire.

Hitler's remark, which was not original, referred to the alleged economic oppression of Europe by the Jews. He was being unfair: under Christianity the Jews had for centuries been forbidden to hold land or become members of ordinary craft-guilds, and obliged to live on their wits. They became jewellers, physicians, money-lenders and bankers, and started such new, highly skilled industries as the manufacture of optical glass and drugs; England's sudden commercial expansion in the seventeenth century was caused by Cromwell's welcome to the Dutch Jews, who brought their modern banking-system to London. If Europeans dislike the results of unlimited capitalism and industrial progress, they have only themselves to blame: the Jews originally invoked the power of money as a bulwark against Gentile oppression. They were forbidden by the Mosaic Law either to lend money at interest among themselves or to let loans run on indefinitely—every seventh year the debtor had to be released from his bond—and it is not their fault that money, ceasing to be a practical means of exchanging goods and services, has achieved irresponsible divinity in the Gentile world.

Yet neither Frazer nor Hitler were far from the truth, which was that the early Gentile Christian borrowed from the Hebrew prophets the two religious concepts, hitherto unknown in the West, which have become the prime causes of our unrest: that of a patriarchal God, who refuses to have any truck with Goddesses and claims to be self-sufficient and all-wise; and that of a theocratic society, disdainful of the pomps and glories of the world, in which everyone who rightly performs his civic duties is a 'son of God' and entitled to salvation, whatever his rank or fortune, by virtue of direct communion with the Father.

Both these concepts have since been vigorously contested within the Church itself. However deeply Westerners may admire Jesus's single-minded devotion to the remote, all-holy, Universal God of the Hebrew prophets, few of them have ever accepted whole-heartedly the antagonism between flesh and spirit implied in his cult. And though the new God-head seemed philosophically incontrovertible, once the warlike and petulant Zeus-Juppiter, with his indiscreet amours and quarrelsome Olympian family, had ceased to command the respect of intelligent people, the early Church Fathers soon found that man was not yet ready for ideal anarchy: the All-Father, a purely meditative patriarch who did not intervene personally in mundane affairs, had to resume his thunderbolt in order to command respect. Even the communistic principle, for a breach of which Ananias and Sapphira had been struck dead, was abandoned as unpractical. As soon as the Papal power was acknowledged superior to that of kings, the Popes assumed magnificent temporal pomp, took part in power-politics, waged wars, rewarded the rich and well-born with indulgences for sin in this world and promises of preferential treatment in the next, and anathematized the equalitarian principles of their simple predecessors. And not only has Hebrew monotheism been modified at Rome by the gradual introduction of Virgin-worship, but the ordinary Catholic layman has long been cut off from direct communication with God: he must confess his sins and acquaint himself with the meaning of God's word, only through the mediation of a priest.

Protestantism was a vigorous reassertion of the two rejected concepts, which the Jews themselves had never abandoned, and to which the Mohammedans had been almost equally faithful. The Civil Wars in England were won by the fighting qualities of the Virgin-hating Puritan Independents, who envisaged an ideal theocratic society in which all priestly and episcopal pomp should be abolished, and every man should be entitled to read and interpret the Scriptures as he pleased, with direct access to God the Father. Puritanism took root and flourished in America, and the doctrine of religious equalitarianism, which carried with it the right to independent thinking, turned into social equalitarianism, or democracy, a theory which has since dominated Western civilization. We are now at the stage where the common people of Christendom, spurred on by their demagogues, have grown so proud that they are no longer content to be the hands and feet and trunk of the body politic, but demand to be the intellect as well—or, as much intellect as is needed to satisfy their simple appetites. As a result, all but a very few have discarded their religious idealism, Roman Catholics as well as Protestants, and come to the private conclusion that money, though the root of all evil, is the sole practical means of expressing value or of determining social precedence; that science is the only accurate means of describing phenomena; and that a morality of common honesty is not relevant either to love, war, business or politics. Yet they feel guilty about their backsliding, send their children to Sunday School, maintain the Churches, and look with alarm towards the East, where a younger and more fanatic faith threatens.

What ails Christianity today is that it is not a religion squarely based on a single myth; it is a complex of juridical decisions made under political pressure in an ancient law-suit about religious rights between adherents of the Mother-goddess who was once supreme in the West, and those of the usurping Father-god. Different ecclesiastical courts have given different decisions, and there is no longer a supreme judicature. Now that even the Jews have been seduced into evading the Mosaic Law and whoring after false gods, the Christians have drifted farther away than ever from the ascetic holiness to which Ezekiel, his Essene successors, and Jesus, the last of the Hebrew prophets, hoped to draw the world. Though the West is still nominally Christian, we have come to be governed, in practice, by the unholy triumdivate of Pluto god of wealth, Apollo god of science, and Mercury god of thieves. To make matters worse, dissension and jealousy rage openly between these three, with Mercury and Pluto blackguarding each other, while Apollo wields the atomic bomb as if it were a thunderbolt; for since the Age of Reason was heralded by his eighteenth-century philosophers, he has seated himself on the vacant throne of Zeus (temporarily indisposed) as Triumdival Regent.

The propaganda services of the West perpetually announce that the only way out of our present troubles is a return to religion, but assume that religion ought not to be defined in any precise sense: that no good can come from publicizing either the contradictions between the main revealed religions and their mutually hostile sects, or the factual mis-statements contained in their doctrines, or the shameful actions which they have all, at one time or another, been used to cloak. What is really being urged is an improvement in national and international ethics, not everyone's sudden return to the beliefs of his childhood—which, if undertaken with true religious enthusiasm, would obviously lead to a renewal of religious wars: only since belief weakened all round have the priests of rival religions consented to adopt a good-neighbourly policy. Then why not say ethics, since it is apparent that the writers and speakers, with few exceptions, have no strong religious convictions themselves? Because ethics are held to derive from revealed religion, notably the Ten Commandments, and therefore the seemingly unethical behaviour of communists is attributed to their total repudiation of religion; and because the co-existence of contradictory confessions within a State is held by non-communists to be a proof of political health; and because a crusade against Communism can be launched only in the name of religion.

Communism is a faith, not a religion: a pseudo-scientific theory adopted as a cause. It is simple, social equalitarianism, generous and un-nationalistic in original intention, the exponents of which, however, have been forced, as the early Christians were, to postpone their hopes of an immediate millennium and adopt a pragmatic policy that will at least guarantee their own survival in a hostile world. The repository of the Communistic faith is the Kremlin and, the Slavs being what their pitiless climate has made them, the Party has slid easily enough into authoritarianism, militarism and political chicanery, which have brought with them distortion of history and interference with art, literature and even science; though all these, they assert, are temporary defensive measures only.

Well, then: since the Communistic faith, however fanatically held, is not a religion, and since all contemporary religions contradict one another, however politely, in their articles of faith, can any definition of the word *religion* be made that is practically relevant to a solution of the present political problems?

The dictionaries give its etymology as 'doubtful'. Cicero connected it with *relegere*, 'to read duly'—hence 'to pore upon, or study' divine lore. Some four-and-a-half centuries later, Saint Augustine derived it from *religare*, 'to bind back' and supposed that it implied a pious obligation to obey divine law; and this is the sense in which religion has been understood ever since. Augustine's guess, like Cicero's (though Cicero came nearer the truth), did not take into account the length of the first syllable of *religio* in Lucretius's early *De Rerum Natura*, or the alternative spelling *relligio. Relligio* can be formed only from the phrase *rem legere*, 'to choose, or pick, the right thing', and religion for the primitive Greeks and Romans was not obedience to laws but a means of protecting the tribe against evil by active counter-measures of good. It was in the hands of a magically-minded priesthood, whose duty was to suggest what action would please the gods on peculiarly auspicious or inauspicious occasions. When, for example, a bottomless chasm suddenly opened in the Roman Forum, they read it as a sign that the gods demanded a sacrifice of Rome's best; one Mettus Curtius felt called upon to save the situation by choosing the right thing, and leaped into the chasm on horseback, fully armed. On another occasion a woodpecker appeared in the Forum where the City Praetor, Aelius Tubero, was dispensing justice, perched on his head and allowed him to take it in his hand. Since the woodpecker was sacred to Mars, its unnatural tameness alarmed the augurs, who pronounced that, if it were released, disaster would overcome Rome; if killed, the Praetor would die for his act of sacrilege. Aelius Tubero patriotically wrung its neck, and afterwards came to a violent end. These unhistorical anecdotes seem to have been invented by the College of Augurs as examples of how signs should be read and how Romans should act in response to them.

The case of Aelius Tubero is a useful illustration not only of *relligio* but of the difference between taboo and law. The theory of taboo is that certain things are prophetically announced by a priest or priestess to be harmful to certain people at certain times—though not necessarily to other people at the same time, or to the same people at other times; and the primitive punishment for the breach of a taboo is ordained not by the judges of the tribe but by the transgressor himself, who realizes his error and either dies of shame and grief or flees to another tribe and changes his identity. It was understood at Rome that a woodpecker, as the bird of Mars, might not be killed by anybody except the King, or his ritual successor under the Republic, and only on a single occasion in the year, as an expiatory sacrifice to the Goddess. In a less primitive society Tubero would have been publicly tried, under such-and-such a law, for killing a protected sacred bird, and either executed, fined or imprisoned; as it was, his breach of taboo was left to his own sense of divine vengeance.

Primitive religion at Rome was bound up with the sacred monarchy: the King was restrained by a great number of taboos designed to please the various-titled Goddess of Wisdom whom he served, and the members of her divine family. It seems that the duty of his twelve priestly companions, one for every month of the year, called the *lictores*, or 'choosers', was to protect him against ill-luck or profanation and pay careful attention to his needs. Among their tasks must have been the *relictio*, or 'careful reading', of signs, omens, prodigies and auguries; and the *selectio* of his weapons, his clothes, his food and the grasses and leaves of his *lectum* or bed.[1] On the extinction of the monarchy, the purely religious functions of the King were invested in the Priest of Jove, and the executive functions passed to the Consuls: the lictors became their guard of honour. The word *lictor* then became popularly connected with the word *religare*, 'to bind', because it was a lictorial function to bind those who rebelled against the power of the Consuls. Originally there had been no Twelve Tables, nor any other Roman code of laws; there had only been oral tradition, based on instinctive good principles and particular magical announcements. Mettus Curtius and Aelius Tubero are not represented as having been under any legal obligation to do what they did; they made an individual choice for *moral* reasons.

It must be explained that the word *lex*, 'law', began with the sense of a 'chosen word', or magical pronouncement, and that, like *lictor*, it was later given a false derivation from *ligare*. Law in Rome grew out of religion: occasional pronouncements developed proverbial force and became legal principles. But as soon as religion in its primitive sense is interpreted as social obligation and defined by tabulated laws—as soon as Apollo the Organizer, God of Science, usurps the power of his Mother the Goddess of inspired truth, wisdom and poetry, and tries to bind her devotees by laws—inspired magic goes, and what remains is theology, ecclesiastical ritual, and negatively ethical behaviour.

If, therefore, it is wished to avoid disharmony, dullness and oppression in all social (and all literary) contexts, each problem must be regarded as unique, to be settled by right choice based on instinctive good principle, not by reference to a code or summary of precedents; and, granted that the only way out of our political troubles is a return to religion, this must somehow be freed of its theological accretions. Positive right choosing based on moral principle must supersede negative respect for the Law which, though backed by force, has grown so hopelessly inflated and complex that not even a trained lawyer can hope to be conversant with more than a single branch of it. Willingness to do right can be inculcated in most people if they are caught early enough, but so few have the capacity to make a proper moral choice between circumstances or actions which at first sight are equally valid, that the main religious problem of the Western world, is briefly, how to exchange demagogracy, disguised as democracy, for a non-hereditary aristocracy whose leaders will be inspired to choose rightly on every occasion, instead of blindly following authoritarian procedure. The Russian Communist Party has confused the issue by presenting itself as such an aristocracy and claiming to be inspired in its choice of policy; but its decisions bear little relation to truth,

---

[1] The English word *litter*, derived from *lectum*, has the double sense of bed and bedding; and the Lord of the Manor of Oterarsee in Angevin times held his fief 'by the service of finding litter for the King's bed: in summer grass and herbs, and in winter straw'.

wisdom or virtue—they are wholly authoritarian and merely concern the eventual fulfilment of Karl Marx's economic prophecies.

* * *

There are two distinct and complementary languages: the ancient, intuitive language of poetry, rejected under Communism, merely misspoken elsewhere, and the more modern, rational language or prose, universally current. Myth and religion are clothed in poetic language; science, ethics, philosophy and statistics in prose. A stage in history has now been reached when it is generally conceded that the two languages should not be combined into a single formula, though Dr. Barnes, the liberal Bishop of Birmingham, complains[1] that a majority of reactionary bishops would like to insist on a literal belief even in the stories of Noah's Ark and Jonah's Whale. The Bishop is right to deplore the way in which these venerable religious symbols have been misinterpreted for didactic reasons; and to deplore still more the Church's perpetuation of fables as literal truth. The story of the Ark is probably derived from an Asianic icon in which the Spirit of the Solar Year is shown in a moon-ship, going through his habitual New Year changes—bull, lion, snake and so on; and the story of the Whale from a similar icon showing the same Spirit being swallowed at the end of the year by the Moon-and-Sea-goddess, represented as a sea-monster, to be presently re-born as a New Year fish, or finned goat. The she-monster Tiamat who, in early Babylonian mythology, swallowed the Sun-god Marduk (but whom he later claimed to have killed with his sword) was used by the author of the *Book of Jonah* to symbolize the power of the wicked city, mother of harlots, that swallowed and then spewed up the Jews. The icon, a familiar one on the Eastern Mediterranean, survived in Orphic art, where it represented a ritual ceremony of initiation: the initiate was swallowed by the Universal Mother, the sea-monster, and re-born as an incarnation of the Sun-god. (On one Greek vase the Jonah-like figure is named Jason, because the history of his voyage in the *Argo* had by that time been attached to the signs of the Zodiac around which the Sun makes its annual voyage.) The Hebrew prophets knew Tiamat as the Moon-and-Sea-goddess Rahab, but rejected her as the mistress of all fleshly corruptions; which is why in the ascetic *Apocalypse* the faithful are promised 'No more sea'.

Dr. Barnes was quoting the stories of the Whale and Ark as obvious absurdities, but at the same time warning his fellow-bishops that few educated persons believe literally even in Jesus's miracles. The merely agnostic attitude, 'He may have risen to Heaven; we have no evidence for or against this claim', has now given place in the back-rooms to the positively hostile: 'Scientifically, it does not add up.' A New Zealand

[1] February, 1949.

atomic scientist assured me the other day that Christianity had received its heaviest blow in 1945: a fundamental tenet of the Church, namely that Jesus's material body was immaterialized at the Ascension had, he said, been spectacularly disproved at Hiroshima and Nagasaki—anyone with the least scientific perception must realize that any such break-down of matter would have caused an explosion large enough to wreck the entire Middle East.

Now that scientists are talking in this strain, Christianity has little chance of maintaining its hold on the governing classes unless the historical part of ecclesiastical doctrine can be separated from the mythical: that is to say, unless a distinction can be drawn between the historical concept 'Jesus of Nazareth, King of the Jews', and the equally valid mythical concepts 'Christ' and 'Son of Man' in terms of which alone the Virgin Birth, the Ascension and the miracles make unchallengeable sense. If this were to happen, Christianity would develop into a pure mystery-cult, with a Christ, divorced from his temporal history, paying the Virgin-Queen of Heaven a filial obedience that Jesus of Nazareth reserved for his Incomprehensible Father. Scientists would perhaps welcome the change as meeting the psychological needs of the masses, involving no anti-scientific absurdities, and having a settling effect on civilization; one of the reasons for the restlessness of Christendom has always been that the Gospel postulates an immediate end of time and therefore denies mankind a sense of spiritual security. Confusing the languages of prose and myth, its authors claimed that a final revelation had at last been delivered: everyone must repent, despise the world, and humble himself before God in expectation of the imminent Universal Judgement. A mystical Virgin-born Christ, detached from Jewish eschatology and unlocalized in first-century Palestine, might restore religion to contemporary self-respect.

However, such a religious change is impossible under present conditions: any neo-Arian attempt to degrade Jesus from God to man would be opposed as lessening the authority of his ethical message of love and peace. Also, the Mother-and-Son myth is so closely linked with the natural year and its cycle of ever-recurring observed events in the vegetable and animal queendoms that it makes little emotional appeal to the confirmed townsman, who is informed of the passage of the seasons only by the fluctuations of his gas and electricity bills or by the weight of his underclothes. He is chivalrous to women but thinks only in prose; the one variety of religion acceptable to him is a logical, ethical, highly abstract sort which appeals to his intellectual pride and sense of detachment from wild nature. The Goddess is no townswoman: she is the Lady of the Wild Things, haunting the wooded hill-tops—Venus Cluacina, 'she who purifies with myrtle', not Venus Cloacina, 'Patroness of the Sewage System', as she first became at Rome; and though the townsman has now begun to

481

insist that built-up areas should have a limit, and to discuss decentralization (the decanting of the big towns into small, independent communities, well spaced out), his intention is only to urbanize the country, not to ruralize the town. Agricultural life is rapidly becoming industrialized and in England, the world's soberest social laboratory, the last vestiges of the ancient pagan celebrations of the Mother and Son are being obliterated, despite a loving insistence on Green Belts and parks and private gardens. It is only in backward parts of Southern and Western Europe that a lively sense still survives in the countryside of their continued worship.

No: there seems no escape from our difficulties until the industrial system breaks down for some reason or other, as it nearly did in Europe during the Second World War, and nature reasserts herself with grass and trees among the ruins.

The Protestant Churches are divided between liberal theology and fundamentalism, but the Vatican authorities have made up their minds how to face the problems of the day. They encourage two antinomous trends of thought to co-exist within the Church: the authoritarian, or paternal, or logical, as a means of securing the priest's hold on his congregation and keeping them from free-thinking; the mythical, or maternal, or supra-logical, as a concession to the Goddess, without whom the Protestant religion has lost its romantic glow. They recognize her as a lively, various, immemorial obsession, deeply fixed in the racial memory of the European countryman and impossible to exorcize; but are equally aware that this is an essentially urban civilization, therefore authoritarian, and therefore patriarchal. It is true that woman has of late become virtual head of the household in most parts of the Western world, and holds the purse-strings, and can take up almost any career or position she pleases; but she is unlikely to repudiate the present system, despite its patriarchal framework. With all its disadvantages, she enjoys greater liberty of action under it than man has retained for himself; and though she may know, intuitively, that the system is due for a revolutionary change, she does not care to hasten or anticipate this. It is easier for her to play man's game a little while longer, until the situation grows too absurd and uncomfortable for complaisance. The Vatican waits watchfully.

Meanwhile, Science itself is in difficulties. Scientific research has become so complicated and demands such enormous apparatus that only the State or immensely rich patrons can pay for it, which in practice means that a disinterested search for knowledge is cramped by the demand for results that will justify the expense: the scientist must turn showman. Also, a huge body of technical administrators is needed to implement his ideas, and these too rank as scientists; yet, as Professor Lancelot Hogben points out,[1] (and he is exceptional in being an F.R.S. with sufficient knowledge

[1] *The New Authoritarianism*, Conway Memorial Lecture, 1949.

of history and the humanities to be able to view science objectively) they are no more than 'fellow-travellers'—careerists, opportunists, and civil-service-minded authoritarians. A non-commercial benevolent institution like the Nuffield Foundation, he says, is as high-handed in its treatment of scientists as a Treasury-controlled Government department. In consequence, pure mathematics is almost the only free field of science left. Moreover, the corpus of scientific knowledge, like that of law, has grown so unwieldy that not only are most scientists ignorant of even the rudiments of more than one specialized study, but they cannot keep up with the publications in their own field, and are forced to take on trust findings which they should properly test by personal experiment. Apollo the Organizer, in fact, seated on Zeus's throne, is beginning to find his ministers obstructive, his courtiers boring, his regalia tawdry, his quasi-royal responsibilities irksome, and the system of government breaking down from over-organization: he regrets having enlarged the realm to such absurd proportions and given his uncle Pluto and his half-brother Mercury a share in the Regency, yet dares not quarrel with these unreliable wretches for fear of worse to come, or even attempt to re-write the constitution with their help. The Goddess smiles grimly at his predicament.

This is the 'brave new world' satirized by Aldous Huxley, an ex-poet turned philosopher. What has he to offer in its place? In his *Perennial Philosophy* he recommends a saintly mysticism of not-being in which woman figures only as an emblem of the soul's surrender to the creative lust of God. The West, he says in effect, has failed because its religious feelings have been too long linked with political idealism or the pursuit of pleasure; it must now look to India for guidance in the rigorous discipline of asceticism. Little or nothing is, of course, known to the Indian mystics that was unknown to Honi the Circle-drawer and the other Essene therapeutics with whom Jesus had so close an affinity, or to the Mohammedan mystics; but talk of political reconciliation between Far East and Far West is in fashion and Mr. Huxley therefore prefers to style himself a devotee of Ramakrishna, the most famous Indian mystic of modern times.

Ramakrishna's case is an interesting one. He lived all his life in the grounds of the White Goddess Kali's temple at Dakshineswar on the Ganges, and in 1842, at the age of six, had fallen in a faint at the beauty of a flock of cranes, her birds, flying across a background of storm clouds. At first he devoted himself to Kali-worship with true poetic ecstacy like his predecessor Ramprasad Sen (1718–1775); but, when he grew to manhood, allowed himself to be seduced: he was unexpectedly acclaimed by Hindu pundits as a re-incarnation of Krishna and Buddha, and persuaded by them into orthodox techniques of devotion. He became an ascetic saint of the familiar type with devoted disciples and a Gospel of ethics posthumously published, and was fortunate enough to marry a woman of the same mystic capacities as himself who, by agreeing to forgo physical consummation, helped him to illustrate the possibility of a purely spiritual union of the sexes. Though he did not need to declare war on the Female, as Jesus had done, he set himself painfully to 'dissolve his vision of the Goddess' in order to achieve the ultimate bliss of *samadhi*, or communion with the Absolute; holding that the Goddess, who was both the entangler and the liberator of physical man, has no place in that remote esoteric Heaven. In later life he claimed to have proved by experiment that Christians and Mohammedans could also achieve the same bliss as himself; first, by turning Christian and devoting himself to the Catholic liturgy until he achieved a vision of Jesus Christ, and then Moslem, until he achieved a vision of Mohammed—after each experience resuming *samadhi*.

What, then, is *samadhi*? It is a psychopathic condition, a spiritual orgasm, indistinguishable from the ineffably beautiful moment, described by Dostoievsky, which precedes an epileptic fit. Indian mystics induce it at will by fasting and meditation, as the Essenes and early Christian and Mohammedan saints also did. Ramakrishna had, in fact, ceased to be a poet and become a morbid-psychologist and religious politician addicted to the most refined form of solitary vice imaginable. Ramprasad had never allowed himself to be thus tempted from his devotion to the Goddess by spiritual ambition. He had even rejected the orthodox hope of 'not-being', through mystic absorption in the Absolute, as irreconcilable with his sense of individual uniqueness as the Goddess's child and lover.

> *Sugar I like, yet I have no desire*
> *To become sugar,*

and faced the prospect of death with poetic pride:

> *How can you shrink from death,*
> *Child of the Mother of All Living?*
> *A snake, and you fear frogs?*

One Kalipuja Day he followed Kali's image into the Ganges until the waters closed over his head.

The story of Ramprasad's devotion to Kali reads familiarly to the Western romantic; *samadhi*, the unchivalrous rejection of the Goddess, will not appeal even to the Western townsman. Nor are any other revivals of Father-god worship, whether ascetic or epicurean, autocratic or communist, liberal or fundamentalist, likely to solve our troubles; I foresee no change for the better until everything gets far worse. Only after a period of complete political and religious disorganization can the suppressed desire of the Western races, which is for some practical form of Goddess-worship, with her love not limited to maternal benevolence and her after-world not deprived of a sea, find satisfaction at last.

How should she then be worshipped? Donne anticipated the problem in his early poem *The Primrose*. He knew that the primrose is sacred to the Muse and that the 'mysterious number' of its petals stands for women. Should he adore a six-petalled or a four-petalled freak, a Goddess that is either more, or less, than true woman? He chose five petals and proved by the science of numbers that woman, if she pleases, has complete domination of man. But it was said of the lotus-crowned Goddess in the Corinthian Mysteries, long before the phrase was applied to the ideally benign Father-god, 'Her service is perfect freedom';[1] and, indeed, her habit has never been to coerce, but always to grant or withhold her favours according as her sons and lovers came to her with exactly the right gifts in their hands—gifts of their own choosing, not her dictation. She must be worshipped in her ancient quintuple person, whether by counting the petals of lotus or primrose: as Birth, Initiation, Consummation, Repose and Death.

There are frequent denials of her power, for example Allan Ramsay's *Goddess of the Slothful* (from *The Gentle Shepherd*, 1725):

> *O Goddess of the Slothful, blind and vain,*
> *Who with foul hearts, Rites, foolish and profane,*
> *Altars and Temples hallowst to thy name!*

> *Temples? or Sanctuaries vile, said I?*
> *To protect Lewdness and Impiety,*
> *Under the Robe of the Divinity?*

> *And thou, Base Goddess! that thy wickedness,*
> *When others do as bad, may seem the less,*
> *Givest them the reins to all lasciviousness.*

> *Rotter of soul and body, enemy*
> *Of reason, plotter of sweet thievery,*
> *The little and great world's calamity.*

> *Reputed worthily the Ocean's daughter:*
> *That treacherous monster, which with even water*
> *First soothes, but ruffles into storms soon after.*

> *Such winds of sighs, such Cataracts of tears,*
> *Such breaking waves of hopes, such gulfs of fears,*
> *Thou makest of men, such rocks of cold despairs.*

[1] Borrowed by St. Augustine from Lucius's address to Isis in Apuleius's *Golden Ass*, and now part of the Protestant liturgy.

Tides of desire so headstrong, as would move
The world to change thy name, when thou shalt prove
Mother of Rage and Tempests, not of Love.

Behold what sorrow now and discontent
On a poor pair of Lovers thou hast sent!
Go thou, that vaunt'st thyself Omnipotent.

But the longer her hour is postponed, and therefore the more exhausted by man's irreligious improvidence the natural resources of the soil and sea become, the less merciful will her five-fold mask be, and the narrower the scope of action that she grants to whichever demi-god she chooses to take as her temporary consort in godhead. Let us placate her in advance by assuming the cannibalistic worst:

> *Under your Milky Way*
> *And slow-revolving Bear,*
> *Frogs from the alder-thicket pray*
> *In terror of the judgement day,*
> *Loud with repentance there.*

> *The log they crowned as king*
> *Grew sodden, lurched and sank.*
> *Dark waters bubble from the spring,*
> *An owl floats by on silent wing,*
> *They invoke you from each bank.*

> *At dawn you shall appear,*
> *A gaunt, red-wattled crane,*
> *She whom they know too well for fear,*
> *Lunging your beak down like a spear*
> *To fetch them home again.*

And we owe her a satire on the memory of the man who first tilted European civilization off balance, by enthroning the restless and arbitrary male will under the name of Zeus and dethroning the female sense of orderliness, Themis. The Greeks knew him as Pterseus the Destroyer, the Gorgon-slaying warrior-prince from Asia, remote ancestor of the destroyers Alexander, Pompey and Napoleon.

> *Swordsman of the narrow lips,*
> *Narrow hips and murderous mind*
> *Fenced with chariots and ships,*
> *By your joculators hailed*
> *The mailed wonder of mankind,*
> *Far to westward you have sailed.*

You it was dared seize the throne
Of a blown and amorous prince
Destined to the Moon alone,
A lame, golden-heeled decoy,
Joy of hens that gape and wince
Inarticulately coy.

You who, capped with lunar gold
Like an old and savage dunce,
Let the central hearth go cold,
Grinned, and left us here your sword
Warden of sick fields that once
Sprouted of their own accord.

Gusts of laughter the Moon stir
That her Bassarids now bed
With the unnoble usurer,
While an ignorant pale priest
Rides the beast with a man's head
To her long-omitted feast.

Chapter Twenty-Seven
POSTSCRIPT 1960

People often ask me how I came to write *The White Goddess*. Here is the story.

Though a poet by calling, I make my livelihood by prose—biographies, novels, translations from various languages, and so forth. My home has been in Majorca since 1929. Temporarily exiled because of the Spanish Civil War, I wandered around Europe and the United States; and the Second World War caught me in England, where I stayed until it ended and I could return to Majorca.

In 1944, at the Devonshire village of Galmpton, I was working against time on a historical novel about the Argonauts, when a sudden overwhelming obsession interrupted me. It took the form of an unsolicited enlightenment on a subject which had meant little enough to me. I stopped marking across my big Admiralty chart of the Black Sea the course taken (the mythographers said) by the *Argo* from the Bosphorus to Baku and back. Instead, I began speculating on a mysterious 'Battle of the Trees', fought in pre-historic Britain, and my mind ran at such a furious rate all night, as well as all the next day, that it was difficult for my pen to keep pace with it. Three weeks later, I had written a seventy-thousand-word book, called *The Roebuck in the Thicket*.

I am no mystic: I avoid participation in witchcraft, spiritualism, yoga, fortune-telling, automatic writing, and the like. I live a simple, normal, rustic life with my family and a wide circle of sane and intelligent friends. I belong to no religious cult, no secret society, no philosophical sect; nor do I trust my historical intuition any further than it can be factually checked.

While engaged on my Argonaut book, I found the White Goddess of Pelion growing daily more important to the narrative. Now, I had in my work-room several small West African brass objects—bought from a London dealer—gold-dust weights, mostly in the shape of animals, among them a humpback playing a flute. I also had a small brass-box, with a lid, intended (so the dealer told me) to contain gold dust. I kept the humpback seated on the box. In fact, he is still seated there; but I knew nothing about him, or about the design on the box-lid, until ten years had gone by. Then I learned that the humpback was a herald in the service of the Queen-mother of some Akan State; and that every Akan Queen-mother (there are a few reigning even today) claims to be an incarnation of the Triple Moon-goddess Ngame. The design on the box-lid, a spiral, connected by a single stroke to the rectangular frame enclosing it—the frame having nine teeth on either side—means: 'None greater in the universe than the Triple Goddess Ngame!' These gold weights and the box were made before the British seizure of the Gold Coast, by craftsmen subservient to the Goddess, and regarded as highly magical.

Very well: put it down to coincidence. Deny any connexion between the hump-backed herald on the box (proclaiming the sovereignty of the Akan Triple Moon-goddess, and set in a ring of brass animals representing Akan clan totems) and myself, who suddenly became obsessed by the European White Goddess, wrote about her clan totems in the Argonaut context, and now had thrust upon me ancient secrets of her cult in Wales, Ireland and elsewhere. I was altogether unaware that the box celebrated the Goddess Ngame, that the Helladic Greeks, including the primitive Athenians, were racially linked with Ngame's people—Libyan Berbers, known as the Garamantians, who moved south from the Sahara to the Niger in the eleventh century A.D., and there intermarried with negroes. Or that Ngame herself was a Moon-goddess, and that the White Goddess of Greece and Western Europe shared her attributes. I knew only that Herodotus recognized the Libyan Neith as Athene.

On returning to Majorca soon after the War, I worked again at *The Roebuck in the Thicket*, now called *The White Goddess*, and wrote more particularly about the Sacred King as the Moon-goddess's divine victim; holding that every Muse-poet must, in a sense, die for the Goddess whom he adores, just as the King died. Old Georg Schwarz, a German-Jewish collector, had bequeathed me five or six more Akan gold-weights, among them a mummy-like figurine with one large eye. It has since been identified by experts on West African art as the Akan King's *okrafo* priest. I had suggested in my book that, in early Mediterranean society, the King fell a sacrifice at the end of his term. But later (to judge from Greek and Latin myths) he won executive power as the Queen's chief minister and the privilege of sacrificing a surrogate. The same governmental change, I have since learned, took place after the matriarchal Akan arrived at the Gold Coast. In Bono, Asante, and other near-by states, the King's surrogate victim was called the '*okrafo* priest'. Kjersmeier, the famous Danish expert on African art, who has handled ten thousand of these gold-weights, tells me that he never saw another like mine. Dismiss it as a coincidence, if you please, that the *okrafo* figurine lay beside the herald on the gold box, while I wrote about the Goddess's victims.

After *The White Goddess* had been published, a Barcelona antiquary read my *Claudius* novels and invited me to choose myself a stone for a seal-ring from a collection of Roman gems recently bought. Among them was a stranger, a banded carnelian seal of the Argonaut period, engraved with a royal stag galloping towards a thicket, and a crescent moon on its flank! Dismiss that as a coincidence, too, if you please.

Chains of more-than-coincidence occur so often in my life that, if I am forbidden to call them supernatural hauntings, let me call them a habit. Not that I like the word 'supernatural'; I find these happenings natural enough, though superlatively unscientific.

In scientific terms, no god at all can be proved to exist, but only beliefs in gods, and the effects of such beliefs on worshippers. The concept of a creative goddess was banned by Christian theologians almost two thousand years ago, and by Jewish theologians long before that. Most scientists, for social convenience, are God-worshippers; though I cannot make out why a belief in a Father-god's authorship of the universe, and its laws, seems any less unscientific than a belief in a Mother-goddess's inspiration of this artificial system. Granted the first metaphor, the second follows logically—if these *are* no better than metaphors. . . .

True poetic practice implies a mind so miraculously attuned and illuminated that it can form words, by a chain of more-than-coincidences, into a living entity—a poem that goes about on its own (for centuries after the author's death, perhaps) affecting readers with its stored magic. Since the source of poetry's creative power is not scientific intelligence, but inspiration—however this may be explained by scientists—one may surely attribute inspiration to the Lunar Muse, the oldest and most convenient European term for this source? By ancient tradition, the White Goddess becomes one with her human representative—a priestess, a prophetess, a queen-mother. No Muse-poet grows conscious of the Muse except by experience of a woman in whom the Goddess is to some degree resident; just as no Apollonian poet can perform his proper function unless he lives under a monarchy or a quasi-monarchy. A Muse-poet falls in love, absolutely, and his true love is for him the embodiment of the Muse. As a rule, the power of absolutely falling in love soon vanishes; and, as a rule, because the woman feels embarrassed by the spell she exercises over her poet-lover and repudiates it; he, in disillusion, turns to Apollo who, at least, can provide him with a livelihood and intelligent entertainment, and reneges before his middle 'twenties. But the real, perpetually obsessed Muse-poet distinguishes between the Goddess as manifest in the supreme power, glory, wisdom and love of woman, and the individual woman whom the Goddess may make her instrument for a month, a year, seven years, or even more. The Goddess abides; and perhaps he will again have knowledge of her through his experience of another woman.

Being in love does not, and should not, blind the poet to the cruel side of woman's nature—and many Muse-poems are written in helpless attestation of this by men whose love is no longer returned:

> '*As ye came from the holy land*
> *Of Walsinghame,*
> *Met you not with my true love*
> *By the way as ye came?*'

> '*How should I know your true love,*
> *That have met many a one*
> *As I came from the holy land,*
> *That have come, that have gone?*'

> '*She is neither white nor brown,*
> *But as the heavens fair;*
> *There is none hath her divine form*
> *In the earth, in the air.*'

> '*Such a one did I meet, good sir,*
> *Such an angelic face,*
> *Who like a nymph, like a queen, did appear*
> *In her gait, in her grace.*'

> '*She hath left me here alone,*
> *All alone, as unknown,*
> *Who sometimes did me lead with herself,*
> *And me loved as her own.*'

> '*What's the cause that she leaves you alone*
> *And a new way doth take,*
> *That sometime did you love as her own,*
> *And her joy did you make?*'

> '*I have loved her all my youth,*
> *But now am old, as you see:*
> *Love likes not the falling fruit,*
> *Nor the withered tree.*'

It will be noticed that the poet who made this pilgrimage to Mary the Egyptian, at Walsinghame, the mediaeval patron saint of lovers, has adored one woman all his life, and is now old. Why is she not old, too? Because he is describing the Goddess, rather than the individual woman. Or take Wyatt's:

> *They flee from me who sometime did me seek*
> *With naked foot stalking within my chamber* . . .

He writes: 'They flee from me', rather than 'She flees from me': namely, the women who were in turn illumined for Wyatt by the lunar ray that commanded his love—such as Anne Boleyn, later Henry VIII's unfortunate queen.

A prophet like Moses, or John the Baptist, or Mohammed, speaks in the name of a male deity, saying: 'Thus saith the Lord!' I am no prophet of the White Goddess, and would never presume to say: 'Thus saith the Goddess!' A simple loving declaration: 'None greater in the universe than the Triple Goddess!' has been made implicitly or explicitly by all true Muse-poets since poetry began.

INDEX

Aaron, 83, 263, 292, 320
  Blessing of, 469
Abaris the Hyperborean, 284, 285
Abd-Khiba (chieftan), 373
Abel, 127, 152, 162
Abimelech, 370
Abraham, 144, 162, 190, 267, 277, 325
Absalom, 87, 90, 119, 332, 333
Acab, or Achab, King, 117, 118, 120
Acacia, 121, 264, 266, 321, 440, 465, 467, 472
Acca, or Acco (goddess), 138
Achaeans, 62, 145, 176, 354
Acherusia, or Heracli, 53
Achilles, 128, 129, 213, 239, 283, 303, 316,
  317, 320, 389, 418
Achren, 49, 341
Aconite (plant), 53, 99
Acorns, 125, 266, 440, 467
Acrisius, King, 240
Actaeon, 12, 217, 316, 406
Adam, 151, 153, 155, 161, 164, 253, 257, 266,
  268, 466
Adam and Eve, Book of, 147
Adamos, 163
Adonijah, 332
Adonis, or Tammuz, (god), 102, 118, 127,
  210, 262, 264, 275, 277, 303, 336, 423
Advent, 157, 163
Aeaea (island), 66, 107, 375
Aega (goddess), 218
Aegea (goddess), 403
Aegeus, 352
Aegipan (god), *see* Goat Pan
aegis, 218, 381
Aegisthus, 316
Aegyptus, 129, 237, 238
Aelius Tubero, 478, 479
Aeneas, 105, 350, 353
Aeolians, 63, 176, 187
Aeolus, 187
Aesculapius, or Asclepius, 52, 73, 128, 132,
  225, 227, 249, 320, 391
Aeson, King, 132
Afagddu, 27, 29, 93, 123, 221, 426
Agabus (prophet), 118
Agag, King, 126, 325
Agamemnon, King, 322
Aganippe (spring), 384
Agate (jewel), 271
Agenor, or Chnas, King, 65, 238, 273
Agnes (goddess), 370
Agni (god), 302

Ailell, King, 220
Aholibamah, 372
Aine (goddess), 370
Akaiwasha (tribe), 64
Akhenaton, Pharaoh, 274, 285, 292
Alabes (cat-fish), 365
Alba Longa (city), 68, 178
Alban Holiday, 357
Albany (North Britain), 51
Albina (goddess), 67, 68
Albula (River Tiber), 435
Alcyone, 187, 188
Alder, 36, 43, 49, 51, 56, 58, 59, 75, 126, 165,
  168, 171, 191, 198, 199, 202-204, 208,
  244, 252, 254, 260, 261, 274, 418, 486
Alexander Severus, Emperor, 144, 145
Alexander the Great, 12, 81, 82, 84, 89, 119,
  144, 368, 461
Aleyn (hero), 257, 446
Allah, 176
Allansford Pursuit (poem), 402
All Hallow E'en, 103, 168
Almond, 263, 264, 314, 340, 371, 467
Alpha, 119, 153, 159
Alphabets:
  Alap-Braut-Curi, 364
  Beth-Luis-Nion, 38, 101, 116, 124, 165,
    189, 202, 225, 228, 235, 242, 243, 245,
    273, 283, 295, 332, 365, 366,
  Boibel-Loth, 116, 117, 120, 136, 141, 243,
    246, 283, 291
  Cadmean, 225, 234, 273, 295
  Cypher, 101, 296, 300
  Disc, 280, 291
  Dorian, 228
  Essene Sacred, 150
  Formello-Cervetri, 115, 116, 123, 124,
    242, 243, 274
  Goidelic, 236
  Greek, Classical, 204, 234
  Hebrew, 235
  Latin (Italian), 227, 273, 295
  Ogham, 113, 114, 200, 206, 248, 264, 272,
    296
  Ogham Craobh, 272
  O'Sullivan's Ogham, 200, 245
  Palaio-Sinaitic, 235
  Pelasgian, 141, 225, 273, 281, 283
  Phoenician, 235, 273
  Ras Shamra, 235
  Runic, 168
Alpheus, River, 366, 367, 376

493

495

502

Prospero 123
Pryderi, King, 56, 95, 107, 109
Prydwen (ship), 108, 109
Pseudo-Matthew, Gospel of, 39
Psilocybe, 45
Pteria (city), 279
Ptolemy Euergetes, King, 413
Pucelle, 397
Pulesati, or Puresati, *see* Philistines
Puppets, 175
Purple, 58, 358
Pwyll, Prince of Dyfed (romance), 107, 109, 216, 385
Pylos, 132, 229
Python, 393
Pyramid, 189, 411
Pyrrha, 226, 240
Pythagoras, Pythagoreans, 69, 71, 101, 149, 189, 251, 282, 285; 378, 379, 388, 464

Quail, 133, 328
Queen of Elfin, Elfland, Elphame, or Faerie, 401, 430, 432, 433, 450
Queen of Heaven, 426, 481
Quick-beam, or Quicken, *see* Rowan
Quince, 59, 158, 258, 261-263, 294, 467
Quincunx, 189
Quinquatria (festival), 274
Quirites, 339
Q're, 339, 340, 464

Ra (god), *see* Amen-Ra
Rachel, 161
Ragnar Lodbrog, 403
Rahab (goddess), 161, 268, 363, 480
Ram, 177, 355, 396
Ramakrishna, 483, 484
Ram Prasad, (poet), 411, 483, 484
Rameses II, 294
Raphael (angel), 153, 156, 288
Raspberry, 39, 40
Ras Shamra, 425
Rat, 445
Raven, 54, 87, 93, 143, 186, 370, 403
Ravenna (city), 170
Rebeccah, 219
Red Book of Hergest, 27, 74
Red Campion, 397
Red Dye, 171, 172
  Food, 167
  Heifer, 338
  Ochre, 167
Reed, 40, 184, 197, 208, 211, 252, 278, 300
Religion, 477-480
Remus (hero), 127, 358
Reseph (god), 333
Reuben (tribe), 270, 271
Rhadamanthus, King, 109
Rhamnusia (goddess), 73
Rhea (goddess), 86, 120, 163, 170, 179, 283, 319, 335, 385, 403, 424
Rhiannon, 95, 109, 385, 403, 419, 420, 439, 448
Rhinoceros, 410
Rhun ap Maelgwn (prince), 74

Rhys Ieuanc (prince), 20, 78, 80
Rialto, 170
Rig, *alias* Heimdall, 178, 314, 315
Rimbaud, 456
Rimmon (god), 263, 371
Robin (bird), 97, 296, 318
  (name), 199, 396, 397
  Robin Goodfellow (book), 396
Robin Hood, 96, 318, 395-398
Robin Hood's Hatband, 318
Robin Hood's Steed, 397
Roe, 261
Roebuck, 30, 52, 54, 136, 183, 211, 251, 286
Roland, Childe (hero), 107, 201
Romantic Revival, 443
Rome, Roma (city), 81, 120
Romë, 352
Romulus (hero), 85, 126, 127, 158, 162, 173, 358
Rook, 299
Rose, 261, 421
Round-barrow Burial, 55
Rowan-tree, or Quicken, Quick-beam, Mountain-ash, 36, 42, 43, 156, 165, 167, 185, 198, 202, 204, 207, 252, 300
Rudra, (god), 278
Rufus, William, 185, 301
Ruptures, 168
Rye, 153

Sabaoth, 151, 335
Sabazius (god), 197, 335
Sabians (tribe), 259, 294
Sacrament, Christian, 363
Saecular Games, 229
Sadb (goddess), 216
St. Adamnain, 147
St. Ann, 473
St. Briavel, 405
St. Brigit, 143, 168, 394
St. Brigid, or Birgit, 394
St. Ciaran, 241
St. Columcille, 143
St. Cummine, 450
St. Dasius, 163
St. David's, See of, 77, 87, 142, 145, 176, 267
St. Hubert, 411
St. Joseph, or Jose, 86, 117, 120
St. Julian, 411
St. Monica's Day, 175
St. Patrick, 147, 198
St. Paul, 362, 399
St. Peter Chrysologos, 255
St. Ronan, 450
St. Samson, 400
St. Swithold, 25, 420
Salamon, 120
Salem, 161
Salma, or Salmon, Salmaah, Salman, Salmoneus, 261, 332, 333, 354, 372, 373, 449
Salma (tribe), 372
Salmakides, 325
Salmalassus, 373
Salmaone (goddess), 373

507